P9-CRA-802

The Piano in Chamber Ensemble

DORDT COLLEGE LIBRARY
Sioux Center, Iowa 51250

MAURICE HINSON

The Piano in Chamber Ensemble

An Annotated Guide

INDIANA UNIVERSITY PRESS

Bloomington and London

3204913

Copyright © 1978 by Maurice Hinson

All rights reserved

No part of this book may be reproduced or utilized in any form or by any means, electronic or mechanical, including photocopying and recording, or by any information storage and retrieval system, without permission in writing from the publisher. The Association of American University Presses' Resolution on Permissions constitutes the only exception to this prohibition.

Manufactured in the United States of America

Library of Congress Cataloging in Publication Data

Hinson, Maurice.
The piano in chamber ensemble.
Bibliography
Includes indexes.
1. Piano with instrumental ensemble—Bibliography.
2. Chamber music—Bibliography.   I. Title.
ML128.C4H5   016.7857   77-9862
ISBN 0-253-34493-X   1 2 3 4 5 82 81 80 79 78

To Peggy

CONTENTS

Music for Four Instruments

Music for Five Instruments

Music for Six Instruments

Music for Seven Instruments

Music for Eight Instruments

Preface

The true spirit of chamber music, "the music of friends," has never been more eloquently expressed than by Henry Peacham, who stated it this way in 1622, in his book *The Compleat Gentleman:*

> Infinite is the sweete varietie that the Theorique of Musicke exerciseth the mind withal, as the contemplation of proportions, of Concords and Discords, diversitie of Moods and Tones, infiniteness of Invention, etc. But I dare affirme, there is no one Science in the world, that so affecteth the free and generous spirit, with a more delightfull and in-offensive recreation, or better disposeth the minde to what is commendable and vertuous.

Some of the most glorious literature written for the piano is found in the chamber music repertoire. Throughout the centuries composers have used chamber music to express their most intensely personal ideas. Surely Haydn, Mozart, and Beethoven gave Western culture some of their most sublime thoughts clothed in this medium, and contemporary composers are also using it for many of their most exciting expressions and avant-garde experiments.

In an attempt to make this vast literature more available to performers, teachers, librarians, music dealers, and all those interested in this rich area involving the piano, *The Piano in Chamber Ensemble* is here presented. As in *Guide to the Pianist's Repertoire* (Indiana University Press, 1973), which describes solo piano literature, answers will be found to the key questions: What is there? What is it like? Where can I get it?

Selection. Since the chamber music field is enormous, certain criteria had to be followed to make this volume manageable: 1. The listing includes compositions requiring no more than eight instruments (including piano). Larger ensembles would probably require a conductor, and this consideration suggested a logical and reasonable limitation. 2. The time span covered is mainly from 1700 to the present, but a few works dating from before 1700 are included because of their special musical interest. The listing contains some music composed before the invention of the piano, especially in the area of the trio sonata, for much of that literature is effective when performed on the piano. 3. In selecting composers an attempt was made to cover all standard composers thoroughly and to introduce contemporary composers of merit, especially those of the United States. 4. The guide includes only works that involve the piano on an equal basis. Even among trio sonatas, only those with well-developed keyboard realizations in good taste were chosen. 5. Transcriptions of music originally written for other instruments, as a rule, have been excluded, unless the arrangement has been made by the composer, or, in the view of the author, is highly effective. 6. Information on works listed but not described has been obtained from publishers' catalogues.

Special effort has been made to examine as many contemporary works as possible, both published and unpublished. Recent avant-garde pieces are difficult to judge since most of them have not met the test of time, although many avant-garde techniques of the 1950s and 60s are becoming more refined and accepted into the compositional style of the 1970s. A number of contemporary composers use the piano strictly as a sonorous sound source in a chamber group, rather than identify the instrument with its past history. In any event, the piano is still being included in ensembles by almost all of our prominent and many of our less well-known composers.

A certain amount of subjectivity is unavoidable in a book of this nature, but I have attempted to be as fair and objective as possible. Composers who wish to submit compositions for possible inclusion in future editions are encouraged to do so.

Because of constant change in the publishing world it is impossible to list only music currently in print. Some works known to be out of print were listed because of their merit, and many of them can be located at second-hand music stores, in the larger university or municipal libraries, or, more especially, in the Library of Congress.

Acknowledgments. Many people in many places have generously given me their help. I gratefully acknowledge the assistance of Martha Powell, Music Librarian of the Southern Baptist Theological Seminary; Rodney Mill of the Library of Congress; David Fenske, Librarian of the Indiana University School of Music; Marion Korda, Music Librarian of the University of Louisville; Fernando Laires of the piano faculty of Peabody Conservatory of Music; Lee Luvisi, Professor of Piano at the University of Louisville; David Appleby, Professor of Music at Eastern Illinois University; my graduate assistant, Robert C. Smith; and the Southern Baptist Theological Seminary for making possible the typing of the manuscript and the aid of graduate assistants through the years. The American Composers Alliance Library and the Canadian Music Centre have been most helpful, as have the many composers who have graciously supplied me with scores and tapes.

Without the generous assistance of numerous publishers this volume would not be possible. Special appreciation goes to John Bice of Boosey and Hawkes, Inc.; Norman Auerbach of Theodore Presser Co.; Don Malin of Edward B. Marks Music Corp. and Belwin-Mills Publishing Corp.; Gertrud Mathys of C. F. Peters Corp.; Susan Brailove of Oxford University Press; Ronald Freed of Peer International Corp.; Ernst Herttrich of G. Henle Verlag; Barry O'Neal of G. Schirmer, Inc.; John Wiser of Joseph Boonin, Inc.; Robert Mabley of Galaxy Music Corp.; W. Ray Stephens of Frederick Harris

Music Co., Ltd.; Mike Warren of Alphonse Leduc; Judy Carnoske and Almarie Dieckow of Magnamusic-Baton, Inc.; Angelina Marx of McGinnis & Marx; Henson Markham and Michael Barnard of Éditions Salabert; Arthur Ephross of Southern Music Co.; Howard Waterman of Western International Music, Inc.; Franz König of Tonos Verlag; B. J. Harrod of Alexander Broude, Inc.; Henri Elkan; and John Woodmason of Novello & Co., Ltd.

I also wish to express appreciation to my children, Jane and Susan, for living with the inconvenience necessarily caused by the preparation of this book.

As this volume has drawn to a close, I have been reminded of Dr. Samuel Johnson's request in the preface to his great Dictionary: "In this work, when it shall be found that much has been omitted, let it not be forgotten that much likewise is performed."

Louisville, Kentucky   MAURICE HINSON
February 1977

Using the Guide

Arrangement of entries. Instrumentation is indicated by categories, e.g., "Music for Two Instruments: Duos for Piano and Double Bass." (Tape is not considered a separate instrument, i.e., a work for piano, flute, violin, and tape is catalogued as a trio.) Within each category the composers are listed alphabetically. Under each composer's name, individual compositions are given by opus number or by title or by musical form, or by a combination of the three.

In the scores of the baroque composers, *basso continuo* refers to the bass part that is to be performed by the keyboard, together with a viola da gamba or a cello. Sometimes only a figured bass is given, but frequently an editor has realized the part by writing in the required chords, passing tones, etc. *Continuo* literally means "continuing throughout the piece." The trio sonata, the most important type of baroque chamber music, is written in three parts but is usually performed on four instruments—two violins (or other treble instruments), a cello (viola da gamba) for the bass part, and a keyboard instrument for the bass part together with the realization of the keyboard accompaniment. Trio sonatas are listed in the Guide under "Music for Three Instruments."

Descriptions. Descriptions have been limited to general style characteristics, form, particular and unusual qualities, interpretative suggestions, and pianistic problems inherent in the music. Editorial procedures found in a particular edition are mentioned. The term "large span" is used when a span larger than an octave is required in a piece, and that occurs in many contemporary chamber works. "Octotonic" refers to lines moving in the same direction one or more octaves apart. "Shifting meters" indicates that varied time signatures are used within the space mentioned (a few bars, a movement, the entire work). "Proportional rhythmic relationships," e.g., ⌐— 5"4 —⌐, indicates 5 notes are to be played in the time space for 4. "3 with 2" means 3 notes in one voice are played with (against) 2 notes in another voice. "Chance music" (aleatory, aleatoric) is described or mentioned, not analyzed, since it has no definitely ordered sequence of events. "Synthetic scale(s)" are made up by the composer whose work is being discussed; the range may be less than one octave. "Stochastic techniques" refers to "a probabilistic compositional method, introduced by Iannis Xenakis, in which the overall contours of sound are specified but the inner details are left to random or chance selection" (DCM, p.708). The term "multiphonics" concerns the wind-instrument technique in which one instrument plays two or even three pitches simultaneously.

Grading. An effort has been made to grade the piano part in representative works of each composer. Four broad categories of grading are used: Easy, for the first years of study; Intermediate (Int.), for the above-average high school pianist; Moderately Difficult (M-D), for the above-average college pianist; Difficult (D), for advanced performers only. These categories must not be taken too strictly but are only listed for general indications of technical and interpretative difficulties.

Details of entries. When known, the date of composition is given after the title of the work. Then, in parentheses, are as many of the following as apply to the particular work: the editor, the publisher, the publisher's number, and the copyright date. When more than one edition is available, the editions are listed in order of preference, the most desirable first. The number of pages and parts and the performance time are frequently listed. The spellings of the composers' names and of the titles of the compositions appear as they do on the music being described. Details of the percussion parts are given only if the percussion ensemble is extensive. Specifically related books, dissertations or theses, and periodical articles are listed following individual compositions or at the conclusion of the discussion of a composer's work (a more extended bibliography appears at the end of the book).

Sample Entries and Explanation.

Music for Two Instruments: Duos for Piano and Cello

Johann Christoph Friedrich Bach. *Sonata* A 1770 (August Wenzinger—Br 3970 1961) 15pp., parts. Larghetto; Allegro; Tempo di Minuetto.

A indicates the key of A major; 1770 is the date of composition; Wenzinger is the editor, Bärenreiter the publisher; 3970 is the edition number; 1961 is the copyright date. The work is 15 pages long and has separate parts available. Larghetto, Allegro, and Tempi di Minuetto are the titles of the three movements.

Music for Six Instruments: Sextets for Piano(s) and Miscellaneous Instruments

Morton Feldman. *The Viola in My Life* (I) 1970 (UE 15395) 10pp., parts. $9\frac{1}{2}$ min. For flute, violin, viola (solo), cello, piano, and percussion. M-D.

(I) means that this work is the first of four pieces by Feldman with the same title; 1970 is the date of composition; UE is the abbreviation for Universal Edition; 15395 is the edition number. The work is 10 pages long and contains separate parts; the piece lasts $9\frac{1}{2}$ minutes. The complete instrumentation is for flute, violin, viola (used in a solo capacity), cello, piano, and percussion; M-D means moderately difficult.

Other assistance. See "Abbreviations" (pp. xvii–xix) for terms, publishers, books, and periodicals referred to in the text; and the directories, "American

Agents or Parent Companies of Music Publishers'' and ''Addresses of Music Publishers'' (pp. xxi–xxxiii), to locate publishers. The two special indexes—''Works for Two or More Pianos and Other Instruments'' and ''Works for Piano, Tape, and Other Instruments''—direct the user to entries in the text for music in these categories, and the comprehensive index of composers represented in this volume gives birth and death dates, when known.

Abbreviations

AA	Authors Agency of the Polish Music Publishers	CCSCM	*Cobbett's Cyclopedic Survey of Chamber Music*
ABRSM	Associated Board of the Royal Schools of Music	CeBeDeM	CeBeDeM Foundation
		CF	Carl Fischer
ACA	American Composers Alliance	CFE	Composers Facsimile Edition
ACA-CFE	American Composers Alliance—Composers Facsimile Edition	CFP	C. F. Peters
		CMC	Canadian Music Centre
		CMP	Consolidated Music Publishers
AL	Abr. Lundquist AB Stockholm	CPE	Composer/Performer Edition
AM	*Acta Musicologia*		
AMC	American Music Center	D	Difficult
AME	American Music Editions	DCM	*Dictionary of Contemporary Music*, ed. John Vinton (New York: E.P. Dutton, 1974).
AMP	Associated Music Publishers		
AMS	American Musicological Society	DDT	Denkmäler deutscher Tonkunst
AMT	*American Music Teacher*		
ASUC	American Society of University Composers	Der	Derry Music Co.
		DM	Diletto Musicale (Dob)
		Dob	Doblinger
B&VP	Broekmans & Van Poppel	DSS	Drustva Slovenskih Skladateljev
BB	Broude Brothers		
BMC	Boston Music Co.	DTB	Denkmäler der Tonkunst in Bayern
BMI	Broadcast Music, Inc.		
Bo&Bo	Bote & Bock	DTOe	Denkmäler der Tonkunst in Oesterreich
Bo&H	Boosey & Hawkes		
Br	Bärenreiter	DVFM	Deutscher Verlag für Musik
Br&H	Breitkopf & Härtel		
		EAM	Editorial Argentina de Música
ca.	circa		
CAP	Composers' Autograph Publications	EB	Editions J. Buyst

EBM	Edward B. Marks	IMC	International Music Co.
EC	Edizioni Curci	IMI	Israel Music Institute
ECIC	Editorial Cooperativa Interamericana de Compositores	Int.	Intermediate difficulty
		IU	Indiana University School of Music Library
ECo	Edition Cotta'sche		
ECS	E. C. Schirmer	JAMS	*Journal of the American Musicological Society*
EFM	Editions Françaises de Musique/Technisonor	JF	J. Fischer
EGZ	Editore Gugliemo Zanibon	JWC	J. W. Chester
EHM	Edwin H. Morris		
ELK	Elkan & Schildknecht	K	Kalmus
EM	Edition Musicus	K&S	Kistner and Siegel
EMB	Editio Musica Budapest	Ku	Kultura
EMH	Editions Musikk-Huset		
EMM	Ediciones Mexicanas de Música	L	Longo, Alessandro
		LAMC	Latin American Music Center, Indiana University
EMT	Editions Musicales Transatlantiques		
EPS	Eulenburg Pocket Scores	LC	Library of Congress
ESC	Max Eschig	L'OL	L'Oiseau-Lyre
EV	Elkan-Vogel		
		M&M	*Music and Musicians*
FSV	Feedback Studio Verlag	MAB	Musica Antiqua Bohemica (Artia)
Gen	General Music Publishing Co.	MCA	MCA Music (Music Corporation of America)
GM	Gehrmans Musikförlag	M-D	Moderately Difficult
GS	G. Schirmer	Mer	Mercury Music Corp.
GWM	General Words and Music Co.	MJ	*Music Journal*
		MJQ	MJQ Music
GZ	Gugliemo Zanibon	MK	Musikaliska Konstföreningen
HAM	*Historical Anthology of Music*	ML	*Music and Letters*
		MM	*Modern Music*
Hin	Hinrichsen	MMR	*Monthly Musical Record*
HM	Hortus Musicus (Bärenreiter)	MO	*Musical Opinion*
		MQ	*Musical Quarterly*
HV	Heinrichshofens Verlag	MR	*Music Review*
HWG	H. W. Gray	M-S	*Music-Survey*
		MS, MSS	manuscript(s)
IEM	Instituto de Extension Musicale	MT	*Musical Times*
		MVH	Musica Viva Historica (Artia)
	Calle Compañia		
	Universidad de Chile		
	Compañia 1264	Nag	Nagel's Musik-Archive
	Santiago, Chile	NME	New Music Edition

NMO	Norsk Musikförlag		Andar, Rio de Janeiro,
NMS	Nordiska Musikförlaget		Brazil
Nov	Novello	SHV	Státní hudbení vy-
NV	Noetzel Verlag		davatelství
		SM	Skandinavisk Musikförlag
OBV	Oesterreichischer Bundes-	SP	Shawnee Press
	verlag	SPAM	Society for the Preservation
OD	Oliver Ditson		of American Music
OUP	Oxford University Press	SSB	*Sonata Since Beethoven*, by
			W.S. Newman (Chapel
PAU	Pan American Union		Hill: University of North
PIC	Peer International Corpora-		Carolina Press, 1969; 2d
	tion		ed., New York: W.W.
PMP	Polish Music Publications		Norton, 1972).
PNM	*Perspectives of New Music*	ST	Southern Music, San An-
PQ	*Piano Quarterly*		tonio, TX
PWM	Polskie Wydawnictwo	St&B	Stainer & Bell
	Muzyczne	SZ	Suvini Zerboni
R&E	Ries & Erler	TP	Theodore Presser Co.
Ric	Ricordi	TWV	*Telemann Werke Ver-*
Ric Amer	Ricordi Americana S.A.		*zeichnis*
SA	Sonata-Allegro	UE	Universal Edition
Sal	Salabert	UME	Unión Musical Española
SB	Summy-Birchard	UMKR	Unbekannte Meister der
SBE	*Sonata in the Baroque Era*,		Klassik und Romantik
	by W.S.Newman		(Boonin)
	(Chapel Hill: University	UMP	United Music Publishers
	of North Carolina Press,	USSR	Mezhdunarodnaya Kniga
	1959; rev. ed. 1966; 3d		(Music Publishers of the
	ed., New York: W. W.		USSR)
	Norton, 1972).		
SCE	*Sonata in the Classic Era*,	VKDR	*Violin and Keyboard: The*
	by W.S. Newman		*Duo Repertoire*, 2 vols.,
	(Chapel Hill: University		by Abram Loft (New
	of North Carolina Press,		York: Grossman Pub-
	1963; 2d ed., New York:		lishers, 1973).
	W.W. Norton, 1972).	VU	Vienna Urtext Edition (UE)
SCL	Southeastern Composers'		
	League	WH	Wilhelm Hansen
SDM	Servico de Documentacão	WIM	Western International
	Musical da Ordem dos		Music
	Músicos do Brazil, Av,		
	Almte. Barroso, 72-7°	ZV	Zenemükiadó Vállalat

American Agents or Parent Companies of Music Publishers

1. Associated Music Publishers, Inc., 866 Third Avenue, New York, NY 10022.
2. Belwin-Mills Publishing Corp., 25 Deshon Drive, Melville, NY 11746.
3. Big 3 Music Corp., 729 Seventh Avenue, New York, NY 10019.
4. Joseph Boonin, Inc., P. O. Box 2124, South Hackensack, NJ 07606.
5. Boosey & Hawkes, Inc., P. O. Box 130, Oceanside, NY 11572.
6. Brodt Music Co., P. O. Box 1207, Charlotte, NC 28231.
7. Alexander Broude, Inc., 225 West 57th Street, New York, NY 10019.
8. Broude Bros., Ltd., 56 West 45th Street, New York, NY 10036.
9. Chappell & Co., Inc., 810 Seventh Avenue, New York, NY 10019.
10. Concordia Publishing House, 3558 South Jefferson Avenue, St. Louis, MO 63118.
11. Henri Elkan Music Publisher, 1316 Walnut Street, Philadelphia, PA 19107.
12. Elkan-Vogel Inc., (see Theodore Presser), Presser Place, Bryn Mawr, PA 19010.
13. Carl Fischer, Inc., 56–62 Cooper Square, New York, NY 10003.
14. Mark Foster Music Co., P. O. Box 4012, Champaign, IL 61820.
15. Sam Fox Publishing Co., P.O. Box 850, Valley Forge, PA 19482.
16. Frank Music Corp., 119 West 57th Street, New York, NY 10019.
17. Galaxy Music Corp., 2121 Broadway, New York, NY 10023.
18. Hansen Publications, Inc., 1842 West Avenue, Miami Beach, FL 33139.
19. MCA Music, 25 Deshon Drive, Melville, NY 11746.
20. Magnamusic-Baton, 10370 Page Industrial Boulevard, St. Louis, MO 63132.
21. Edward B. Marks Music Corp., 1790 Broadway, New York, NY 10019.
22. Music Distribution Center, 265 Secaucus Road, Secaucus, NJ 07094.
23. Music Sales Corp., 33 W. 60th Street, New York, NY 10023.
24. Oxford University Press, Inc., 200 Madison Avenue, New York, NY 10016.
25. C. F. Peters Corp., 373 Park Avenue South, New York, NY 10016.
26. Theodore Presser Co., Presser Place, Bryn Mawr, PA 19010.
27. E. C. Schirmer Music Co., 600 Washington Street, Boston, MA 02100.
28. G. Schirmer, Inc., 4 East 49th Street, New York, NY 10022.
29. Shawnee Press, Inc., Delaware Water Gap, PA 18327.
30. Southern Music Co., P.O. Box 329, 1100 Broadway, San Antonio, TX 78206.
31. Southern Music Publishing Co., 1740 Broadway, New York, NY 10019.
32. Summy-Birchard Co., 1834 Ridge Avenue, Evanston, IL 60204.
33. Warner Bros., Seven Arts Music, 75 Rockefeller Plaza, New York, NY 10019.
34. Location or American agent unverified.

Addresses of Music Publishers

A number following the name of a publisher corresponds to that of its American agent or parent company (see previous directory).

Ahn & Simrock, Meinekestrasse 10,
  1 Berlin 15, West Germany
Aibl   34
Alfred Music Co., 75 Channel Drive,
  Port Washington, NY 11050
Alpeg Editions (USA)   25
Editorial Alpuerto, Madrid, Spain
Alsbach   25
  Amsterdam, Netherlands
Amadeus-Paüler   25
  Adliswil, Germany
Casa Amarilla, San Diego 128, Santiago, Chile
American Composers Alliance—
  Composers Facsimile Edition, 170
  West 74th St., New York, NY
  10023
American Music Center, 145 West
  58th St., New York, NY 10019
American Music Editions   13
  263 East 7th St., New York, NY
  10009
American Society of University Composers   4
Gli Amici della Musica da Camera,
  Via Bocca di Leone 25, Rome,
  Italy
Amphion Editions Musicales (see E.
  C. Kerby, Ltd.)
Amsco Music Publishing Co.   23
Andre   34

Anglo-French Music Co.   24
Anglo-Soviet Press   28
APR Publishers, P.O. Box 5075,
  Fresno, CA 93755
A-R Editions, 315 West Gorham St.,
  Madison, WI 53703
Arcadia Music Publishing Co., Ltd.,
  10 Sherlock Mews, Baker St.,
  London, W. 1, England
Archambault, 500 Est, rue Ste-
  Catherine, Montreal, Quebec,
  Canada
Collecion Arion   31
Arno Press, 330 Madison Ave., New
  York, NY 10017
Arno Volk Verlag   19
  Cologne, Germany
Arrow Press   5
Ars Nova   26
Ars Viva Verlag, Mainz, Germany
Ars Polona (see Polskie Wydaw-
  nictwo Muzyczne)
Artia   5
  Smečkách 30, Prague I, Czecho-
  slovakia
Ascherberg, Hopwood & Crew, Ltd.
  (England)   6, 15
Edwin Ashdown, Ltd.   5, 6
Associated Board of the Royal School
  of Music (England)   2
Augener   17

Music for Two Instruments

Duos for Piano and Violin

Evaristo Felice Dall'Abaco. *Six Sonatas* Op.1 (Kolneder—Schott 1956). Gamba or cello ad lib. Op.1/2, 4, 5, 6, 7, 11.
_____ *Six Sonatas* Op.4 (Br&H). Cello ad lib.
_____ *Sonatas* Op.1 and Op.4 are contained in DTB, Vol.I.
_____ *Two Sonatas* (USSR).
_____ *Sonata* a (Salmon—Ric R748).
_____ *Sonata* F (Salmon—Ric R354).
See: VKDR, I: pp.84–86.

Carl Friedrich Abel. *Sonatas* (Bacher, Woehl—Br). Vol. I: Sonatas e, D, G. Vol II: Sonatas C, A, A. For viola da gamba (violin or flute) and basso continuo.
_____ *Sonata* G (Broe—CFP B.330).
_____ *Two Sonatinas* (Raphael—Hin) Op.5/4 C and 5/5 A. Cello ad lib.
_____ *Sonata* Op. 13/A (F. Piersig—Br&H 4165 1928) 11 pp., parts. Editorial additions identified. Un poco moderato; Andante; Un poco vivace. Keyboard has a prominent part. Active melodic line in piano. M-D.
_____ *Soñata* G (F. Brüggen—Br&VP 1960). For violin or flute.
_____ *Sonata* B♭ (Fritz Piersig—Br&H 4104 1928) 9 pp., parts. Editorial additions identified. Allegro moderato: large movement; piano part more important than violin; broken-chord figuration; trills; triplets; *p* closing. Tempo di Menuetto: tastefully edited. M-D.

Walter Abendroth. *Sonata* Op.26 (Simrock 1961) 20pp., parts. Moderato opening with piano providing punctuated rhythmic chords. Leads to Andante section, more free and rhapsodic. Attacca moves to Energico (Allegretto) with more rhythmic propulsion, triplets, and syncopated usage. Centers around g or G with chromatically altered harmony. M-D.

Jean Absil. *Sonata* Op.146 1970 (CeBeDeM) 28 pp., parts. 18 min. Allegro Moderato; Andantino; Vivo leggiero; Lento mysterioso; Allegretto. Displays a novel language with subtle rhythms of Rumanian folklore and varied artistry throughout. D.

Joseph Achron. *Suite* II Op.22 1906 (UE 7692 1925) 28pp., parts. En Passant; Menuet & Trio; Moulin; Intermezzo; Marionettes. Piano part very important. Colorful, post-Romantic writing. M-D.

———— *Sonata* Op.29 d 1910 (Belaieff 1914) 51pp., parts. Bewegt und ausgeregt; Hirtenliebe (Traümend); Interludium; Keck und sehr freudig. Highly chromatic, thick textures, first-rate pianism required. D.

———— *Deuxieme Sonate* Op.45 A 1918 (UE 7561 1924) 72pp., parts. Giocondo; Misterioso e fantastico; Burla; Focoso. In Regerian harmonic style, virtuoso writing for both instruments. D.

Samuel Adler. *Sonata* II (OUP 1968) 23pp., parts. 14½ min. For piano or harpsichord. Allegro moderato; Lento espressivo; Allegro molto, ma non troppo. Neoclassic style. Numerous dynamic effects would not be possible on a harpsichord. M-D.

———— *Sonata* III 1965 (Bo&H 1974) 28pp., parts. In six episodes to be performed without interruption. Fast and intense: serial, atonal, dissonant. Very slowly: sustained, chordal, with sudden interruptions of fast short sections. Very lively: linear, staccato left hand chords, octotonic, rhythmic melodies. Very slowly: requires large span, expressive. Like a waltz, gracefully: flowing lines, contains a few *ff* figuration surprises. Fast and intense: similar to opening episode, sparse textures. D.

Hans Ahlgrimm. *Sonata* g (Lienau 1938) 20pp., parts. 14 min. For violin or alto flute. Includes a separate part for alto flute. Moderato; Allegro non troppo. Chromatic, opening three bars in first movement contain thematic material for movement. Much alternating writing between hands in last movement. D.

Tomaso Albinoni. *Six Sonatas* Op.4 (Walter Kolneder—Eulenburg 1973-4). Cello part optional. Melodies have a fine sweep about them. Good realization of the figured bass.

———— *Two Chamber Sonatas* Op.6/1 C, 2 A (Walter Upmeyer—Nag 9).

———— *Three Sonatas* Op.6/4 d, 5 F, 7 D (Reinhart—Hug). Cello part optional. No. 4 is perhaps the finest in the set. M-D.

———— *Sonata* g Op.6/2 (F.F. Polnauer—Schott 1967).

———— *Sonata* a Op.6/6 (B. Paumgartner—Hug 1951).

See: VKDR, I: p. 83.

———— *Sonata* a (Schäffler—Nag). Cello part optional.

———— *Sonata* b (Scheck, Ruf—Symphonia SY502). Cello part optional.

Amalie, Princess of Prussia. *Sonata* F (Gustav Lenzewski—Vieweg 108 1975) 8pp., parts for flute or violin. See detailed entry under duos for piano and flute.

Rene Amengual. *Sonata* 1943-4 (IU) 26pp., parts. Moderato: SA, 7/4, freely tonal, flowing, imitation, centers around B♭; harmonic ninths require large span. Recitado, libremente: declamatory opening; leads to Andante espressivo; flowing; hemiola; returns to dramatic opening mood to close out; centers freely around F. Presto: rondo, built on opening idea in piano, contrasting episodes. The whole work has an attractive gentle flowing quality about it. M-D.

William Ames. *Dust of Snow* (CF 1946) 5pp., parts for violin and/or cello. Chordal with left-hand figuration. Descriptive. M-D.
———— *Sonata* (CFE).

David Amram. *Sonata* 1960 (CFP 6686) 25pp., parts. 18 min. Allegro moderato; Andante espressivo; Theme and (8) Variations. Thoroughly contemporary style, much dissonance, expert handling of both instruments, eclectic. Effective alternation of contrasting moods. D.

George Antheil. *Sonata* I 1923 (MS at Library of Congress) 70pp., parts. One movement. Relentless ostinatos, much repetition of rhythmic cells. Antheil throws overboard most traditions of Western music in this jarring Stravinsky/Bartók influenced work. D.
———— *Sonata* II 1923 (MS at Library of Congress) 45pp., parts. One movement. Music-hall dance rhythms permeate everything. Instruments exchange glissandi. Slow fox-trot, habañera, and Charleston are given to the melodic violin while the piano pounds out an ostinato. Stringent polytonality infuses some of the popular elements with sarcastic jolts. Percussion is brought in only at the end (à la Ives?) in an Oriental duet with the violin. Musical humor at its best. Part for percussion is indicated with violin cues in score. D.
———— *Sonata* III 1924 (MS at Library of Congress) 42pp., parts. 12 min. One movement. There is little development in this work, thematic and rhythmic material are frequently repeated, sometimes in polytonal layers. Generally more subdued and longer than the first two sonatas. Copy at the Library of Congress is in ink with several pages plus additions and corrections in the composer's hand. Stravinskyisms are lightly sprinkled everywhere. D.
———— *Sonatina* 1945 (MS at Library of Congress) 21pp., parts. Three movements. Shostakovich influence shows in the opening march, which

returns at the conclusion of the last movement, as well as the "wrong" notes in opening theme. Contrapuntal dissonance, neoclassic sophistication. M-D.

Pietro Degli Antonii. *Three Sonatas* Op.5/1, 4, 6 (Bernhard Paumgartner—Hug GH9339 1947) 31pp., parts. Preface in German, French, and English. 1. Con affetto; Vivace; Aria grave; Adagio; Allegro. 4. Grave; Aria-Vivace; Posato; Adagio; Vivace. 6. Adagio; Allegro; Grave; Vivace. These works have a personal physiognomy and an original style that date from the high Bolognese baroque. They have a warm, pulsating, and dignified character about them and represent the finest type of chamber music from this period. Excellent edition. M-D.

Theodor Antoniou. *Scherzo* Op.3 1958 (MS available from composer, c/o Philadelphia Musical Academy, 313 Broad St., Philadelphia, PA 19107) 12pp., parts. Multiple meters 3+2+3/8, strong rhythms, alternating hands, freely tonal, large span required, three-part counterpoint between hands and violin, thin textures, Presto coda. M-D.
_____ *Sonatina* Op.6 1958 (MS available from composer) 18pp., parts. 12 min. Allegro: freely tonal, short patterns, broken octaves, repeated major sevenths, surprise ending. Pastorale: imitation, "limping" rhythmic treatment. Allegro: shifting meters, exciting rhythms, open fourths and fifths alternate between hands, sudden dynamic changes. Effective, has much audience appeal. M-D.
_____ *Lyrics* 1967 (Br 6103) 18 pp., parts. These seven short varied pieces present a free musical approach to forms of ancient lyric poetry. The verses are by the Greek poet Tassos Roussos and are based on ideas of the composer. If the verses are not recited during the performance, they should be printed in the program. Threnos; Epigram; Elegy; Nomos; Hymn; Ode; Skolion. Serial, some pointillistic treatment, harmonics, plucked strings, glissandi on strings, repetition as desired. A book is to be placed on strings covering specific pitches. Meaningful and expressive writing. M-D.

Attilio Ariosti. *Two Sonatas* (S. Renzo—DeSantis 982) 1 E♭, 2A. From *Six Sonatas* for viola d'amore contained in "Six Lessons for Viola d'amore."
_____ *Sonata* II transposed to D (Saint-George—Augener).
_____ *Sonata* e (Salmon—Ric R346).
_____ *Sonata* G (Salmon—Ric R347).

Thomas A. Arne. *Sonata* B♭ (Craxton—OUP 20.007 1931) 5pp., parts. 4 min. Transcribed for violin or cello. Poco largo: serves as introduction, with short cadenza to Gavotta: much eighth-note figuration for piano. Charming, with purity of style. M-D.

Richard Arnell. *Sonata* II Op.55 (Schott 10214 1950) 23pp., parts. 14½ min. Vivace: chromatic alternation of hands; opening motif is main idea and is thoroughly worked over. Andante: same chromatic idea is transformed; piano gets some lyric melodic interest; repeated octaves; wide skips; *ppp* ending. Allegro vivace: bitonal cover conceals chromatic motif but is present in a rocking 6/8; Presto coda, movement ends abruptly. M-D.

Malcolm Arnold. *Sonata* I 1947 (Lengnick) 31pp., parts. Allegretto; Andante tranquillo; Allegro vivace. A large dramatic work. Third movement scampers lightly to provide contrast with the other weighty movements. Thorough pianistic equipment required. D.
_____ *Sonata* II Op.43 (Paterson's 1953) 9pp., parts. 9 min. In one movement: Allegretto–Vivace–Andantino quasi allegretto–Adagio molto. Tonal, chromatic coloring, sweeping scales for piano in Allegretto. Somber, peaceful closing on G. M-D.

Claude Arrieu. *Sonate* 1949 (Leduc) 29pp., parts. 20 min. Risoluto maestoso: mildly dissonant chords, violin cadenza, *a tempo* sections contrasted with slower sections, big chordal C closing. Andante non troppo: chromatic inner voices of seconds and thirds provide unusual sonorities. Allegro vivo: very rhythmic, sweeping arpeggi, Più lento section concludes with opening figuration from first movement in stringendo fashion. Brilliant writing. D.

Tony Aubin. *Concertinetto* (Leduc 1962) 9pp., parts. 6 min. Driving rhythmic opening. Adagietto mid-section, some changing meters. Finale, Allegro, bounces along to a short violin cadenza. Scherzando character returns with both instruments contributing color and verve. A ritard appears just before the unexpected closing *a tempo*. M-D.

Georges Auric. *Sonata* G 1936 (Chant du Monde 1937) 32pp., parts. Assez lent et librement: varied tempi, textures, ideas. Vif: scherzo-like with clear figurations. Lent: chordal until Très calme et expressif, haunting melody. Vif: clear and light through most of movement, brilliant closing. D.

Menahem Avidom. *Concertino* (Israeli Music Publications 1951) 19pp., parts. Moderato; Andante quasi Allegro; Finale. Clear textures, lively color, and an Oriental atmosphere. The piano is treated equally and not as an orchestral substitute. M-D.

Thomas Avinger. *Sonata* 1968 (MS available from composer, 7622 Grape St., Houston, TX 77036) 28pp., parts. 12 min. Moderato; Adagio; Presto. Rhythmic vitality, melodic treatment notable, colorful and clever counterpoint, thick textures, effective work for both instruments. D.

Emil Axman. *Sonata* (Hudební Matice 1924) 33pp., parts. Poetical, serious emotional quality, rustic strength. D.

_____ *Capriccio* (Hudební Matice 1947).

Arno Babadjanian. *Sonata* b♭–B♭ (USSR 1970) 44pp., parts. Grave: frequent tempo changes, sweeping lines. Andante sostenuto: Presto midsection, much interplay of ideas. Allegro risoluto: much alternation of 6/8 and 4/8 meters, driving, motoric, slows down to a brief Largo before an Andante sostenuto leads to the concluding Maestoso. Powerful writing. D.

Milton Babbitt. *Sextets* 1966 (CFP 66409 1975) 65pp., parts. 13 min. Total serialization, pointillistic, bristling with complicated intricacies, enormous dynamic range with more dynamic marks than notes, proportional rhythmic relationships. Great clarity with a certain amount of sterility, little or no emotional qualities present. Only for the most dedicated and experienced ensemble performers. D.

William Babell. *Sonata* g (Michael Tilmouth—OUP 1963) 5pp., parts also for oboe or flute. See detailed entry under duos for piano and flute.

Grazyna Bacewicz. *Partita* (PWM 1957) 26pp., parts. Preludium: 6/8 alternating octaves and major sevenths between hands in Grave tempo. Toccata: large skips, highly rhythmic, glissandi. Intermezzo: widely spaced sonorities, hypnotic. Rondo: dancelike. D.

_____ *Sonata da Camera* I (PWM 1945) 11 min.

_____ *Sonata* III 1947 (PWM) 33pp., parts, 18 min. Allegro moderato: much chromatic figuration, melodic and harmonic. Adagio: builds to climax in middle of movement, subsides. Scherzo: sprightly, colorful, dance rhythms, bitonal arpeggi at closing. Finale: a sustained Andante with a long crescendo; opening idea hammered out at conclusion. D.

_____ *Sonata* IV 1951 (PWM) 31pp., parts. 20 min. A large work with clear textures. Piano part is expressive and contrasts with the violin. Pliability, unity, and homogeneity are all characteristic of the work. D.

_____ *Sonata* V 1955 (PWM) 28 pp., parts. 28 min. Moderato: sweeping chromatic lines. Nokturn: based on material from opening two bars. Finale: uneasy and constantly boiling. D.

_____ Other small pieces, all published by PWM.

Carl Philipp Emanuel Bach. *Sonata* D 1731 W.71 (Ric SY570 1954) 14 pp., parts. Adagio ma non molto; Allegro; Adagio: highly elaborate; Menuetto I and II. M-D.

_____ *Sonata* d 1731 W.72 (Ruf—Ric SY571 1954) 14pp., parts. Editorial additions identified. Adagio ma non troppo: turn is prominently featured in melodic line; Allegro (Gigue); Allegro. M-D.

—— *Sonata* b 1763 (Hans Sitt—CFP 3619A) 22pp., parts. Allegro moderato; Poco andante; Allegretto siciliano. D.

—— *Sonata* c 1763 (Hans Sitt—CFP 3619b) 23pp., parts. Allegro moderato; Adagio ma non troppo; Presto. M-D.

Keyboard part is highly prominent in both sonatas.

—— *Sonata* C (Ruf—Ric SY572).

—— *Sonata* B♭ (Ruf—Ric SY576).

—— *Sonata* C (Klengel—Br&H). Originally for gamba.

—— *Sonata* D (Klengel—Br&H). Originally for gamba.

—— *Phantasy-Sonata* f♯ 1787 W.67 (Arnold Schering—Kahnt 1938) 16pp., parts. 13 min. Sehr traurig und ganz langsam: numerous tempi and mood changes. Allegro: heavily ornamented. D.

—— *Six Sonatas* (Kultura).

—— *Sonata* b (Ruf—Schott 1965).

—— *Sonata* B♭ (Scheck, Ruf—Symphonia SY503). Cello optional.

—— *Sonata* D (Scheck, Ruf—Symphonia SY505).

Johann Christian Bach. *Five Sonatas* (Landschoff—Hin). Vol.I: Op.10/1, 2, 3. Vol.II: Op.10/4, 5.

—— *Sonata* Op.10/4 A (Fritz Piersig—Br&H 1928) 9pp., parts. Allegretto; Rondeau—Allegro moderato. Some tricky spots in last movement. M-D.

—— *Six Sonatas* Op.16 1779 (Heinrichshofen) 37pp., parts. Reprint of an early (first?) edition. Sonatas in D, G, C, A, D, F.

—— *Sonata* Op.16/1 A (Fritz Piersig—Br&H 4167 1928) 11pp., parts. Allegro assai; Andante grazioso. Charming and graceful. M-D.

—— *Two Sonatas* Op.16/1 D, 2 G 1779 (Albert Küster—Nag 1 1927) 19pp., parts. Two movements each, ornamentation discussed in preface. M-D.

—— *Sonata* Op.16/4 A (Küster—Nag 104 1933) 9pp., parts. For violin or flute. Allegretto; Pastorale. Charming and facile writing. Int.to M-D.

—— *Sonata* I d (Ruf—Schott).

—— *Sonata* E♭ (Zirnbauer—Schott 1951) 19pp., parts. Four movements. M-D.

Johann Christoph Friedrich Bach. *Sonata* F (Hinnenthal—Br&H).

Johann Sebastian Bach. *Sechs Sonaten* (Hans Epstein—Henle 1971) 126pp., parts. Fingering added by Hans-Martin Theopold. Vol. I: S.1014 b, S.1015 A, S.1016 E. Vol. II: S.1017 c, S.1018 F, S.1019 G. Independent keyboard part so these are true sonatas for two instruments. Two earlier versions of movements from No.6 are included in the appendix. Editorial additions are printed in brackets. Contains comments on the individual works. D.

———— *Sechs Sonaten* (R. Gerber—Br 1967) 2 vols. S.1014–1019. *Neue Ausgabe sämtlicher Werke.*

———— *Six Sonatas* (Stock, Müller—VU 1973) 2 vols. Keyboard part is frequently written out in full instead of using a figured bass. Critical commentaries and detailed performance directions. Also available from Jacobsen—CFP 232-3C; Naumann—Br&H; Debussy—Durand; David, Carse—Augener; Lea; David—IMC; De Guarnieri—Ric. Available separately: S.1014 b (Dyke—J. Williams; Kortschak, Hughes—GS). S.1015 A (Dyke—J. Williams; Kortschak, Hughes—GS; M. Reger—Simrock). S.1016 E (Dyke—J. Williams; Kortschak, Hughes—GS). S.1017 c (Kortschak, Hughes—GS). S.1018 f (Kortschak, Hughes—GS). S.1019 G (Kortschak, Hughes—GS).

———— *Two Sonatas* (Gunter Kehr—VU 1973) S.1021 G, S.1023 E. Figured bass has been realized by Kurt-Heinz Stolze. Both works are in four movements. S.1023, with its toccata-like first movement, is especially interesting. S.1021 was discovered only in 1928 and includes two highly ornamented slow movements. Reliable edition.

———— *Sonata* S.1021 G (F. Blume, A. Busch—Br&H 1929; Hausswald—Br).

———— *Sonata* S.1023 e (Hausswald—Br; Ferguson—Schott; W. Davisson—Br&H).

———— *Sonata* F (CFP 4464). Bach's arrangement of his *Trio* G.

———— *Toccata* S.1024 c (Herrmann—ESC). *Sonata* S.1024 c (David, Hermann—CFP).

See: VKDR, I: pp.109–31.

Wilhelm Friedemann Bach. *Sonata* (Beer, Walbrun—Leuckart).

Henk Badings. *Sonata* I (Schott 1933) 22pp., parts. 15 min. Dark, chromatic harmony, Germanic. M-D to D.

———— *Sonata* II (Schott 1940) 19pp., parts. 15 min. Allegro ma non troppo; Andante; Allegro. Neoclassic. Moderately thick textures. Thematic material mutually dispersed between instruments. M-D.

———— *Sonata* III 1952 (Donemus) 42pp., parts. 20 min. Hindemith-inspired. Allegro: dark. Adagio: foreboding. Rondo giocoso: delightful, but suffers somewhat from overuse of same melodic ideas. D.

Leonardo Balada. *Sonata* I 1969 (Gen 1971) 35pp., parts. Moderato: short, freely chromatic, changing meters, varied figurations, moves directly to

Lento Molto: leisured pacing, mid-section Molto espressivo e dramatico provides contrast and extends to a short Largo coda that calms and lets the violin finish by itself. Allegro scherzando: fragmented chromatic thematic treatment, piano part moves over entire keyboard, attacca. Moderato energico: sweeping gestures in both instruments. Lento coda begins with solo violin and leads to Allegretto giocoso and "As fast as possible" conclusion. Requires experienced and first-rate players. Well written, imaginative, reveals a major developing talent. D.

Simon Balicourt. *Sonata* II 1750 (Les Editions Ouvrières 1967) 11pp., parts. For flute or violin and basso continuo. See detailed entry under duos for piano and flute.

Claude Ballif. *Sonate* Op.17 (Bo&Bo 1961) 26pp., parts. Three movements, uses tempo markings in lieu of terms. Expressionistic, pointillistic. Carefully marked pedal indications. D.

Don Banks. *Sonata* (Schott 1954) 24pp., parts. 13 min. Allegro moderato, risoluto leads to Marcato e ritmato and pulls back to a more sustained Molto moderato section. The Maestoso section is broad and is quickly followed by a 9/8 Scorrevole for four pages. The Càlmo section features a prominent left-hand punctuated figuration. Marcato e ritmato returns with chromatic unison passages two octaves apart in the piano that swell to a dramatic climax. Other contrasted tempo and character markings add to the turbulence and excitement before the final stringendo closes out breathlessly. D.

Granville Bantock. *Sonata* I G (OUP 1929) 44pp., parts. Allegro con moto; Andante sostenuto; Allegro vivo non tanto.

———— *Sonata* II D (Goodwin & Todd, through Belwin-Mills 1940) 43pp., parts. 31 min. Lentamente non troppo; A piacere, quasi recitativo; Andante con moto rubato.

George Barati. *Sonata* 1956 (Zimmermann) 28pp., parts. 16 min. Andantino tranquillo: 2 with 3, chromatic, close intervals preferred. Molto risoluto non troppo allegro: misterioso, flowing lines build to con fuoco before subsiding. A long crescendo leads to an imposing close with cascading octaves in the piano. Freely tonal, much chromatic usage throughout the entire composition, both instruments thoroughly exploited. Although this sonata appears to be in only two movements, the considerable tempi and character changes in both movements suggest the idea of more movements. Piano part is pianistic at all times although difficult. This work has much to commend it. D.

———— *Two Dances* (PIC 1948) 17pp., parts. Slow Dance: Andantino e poco rubato. Centers around a, chromatic coloring. Calmando sixteenth-note figuration effectively used to close the piece. Fast Dance: Allegro vivo, Feroce opening. Piano propels rhythm. One bar of a quick crescendo rushes to the conclusion. M-D.

Emanuele Barbella. *Sonata* I A (F.F. Polnauer—Hug GH10723 1966) 14pp., parts. Allegretto; Andantino e gustoso; Allegro ma non poco. Editorial dynamic marks are placed in parentheses. Delightful and effective period writing. M-D.

Ramón Barce. *Sonata* II 1972 "Sonata Kupelwieser" (Alpuerto 1973) 15pp., parts.

Henry Barraud. *Sonatine* (Amphion 102 1943) 28pp., parts. 14 min. Moderato; Aria; Allegro. Piano is handled in a craftsmanlike manner throughout. Piece unfolds logically and efficiently in a mildly contemporary style for both instruments. M-D.

Lubor Bárta. *Sonata* II 1959 (Artia 1962) 39pp., parts. 17 min. Allegro, con larghezza: figurative, contrapuntal section; rich harmonies with some dissonance. Vivace: triplets exploited in various dynamic levels. Adagio: use of pedal provides overtones reinforcement for violin; sweeping gestures. Allegro vivo: metric accents between the hands do not coincide. Driving rhythms. D.

Béla Bartók. *Sonata* 1903 (Dille—Hungarian Academy of Sciences 1964) in a collection entitled *Documenta Bartókiana*. Dille was the curator at the Bartók Archives in Budapest. This volume available through Harrassowitz.
———— *Sonata* I (Bo&H 1921; UE) 35 min. Three movements. Extreme tonal and formal freedom. The two instruments are completely independent yet they are forced together by a unique expressive quality. Rough "edges" of the piece must be kept intact. Aggressively dissonant. Freely in C♯. D.
———— *Sonata* II (Bo&H 1922; UE) 20 min. Two parts. More concentrated and economical than *Sonata* I. Fantasy element permeates this work; individualistic in form. Rhythmic element is vital to this masterpiece. Freely in C. Both sonatas (I and II) show Bartók at his closest to Schönbergian atonality and with leanings towards the twelve-tone technique. D.
———— *Rhapsody* I (Bo&H 1928) 10 min. Two movements, slow–fast. Rumanian folkmusic permeates this work and shows Bartók's use of this material in one of his least astringent moods. Also arranged for cello. M-D.
———— *Rhapsody* II (Bo&H 1928, rev. 1944) 12 min. Two movements, slow–fast. Florid, gypsy-like. M-D.

Jan Zdeněk Bartoš. *Duo* II (Artia).

Leslie Bassett. *Sonata* 1959 (CFE) 33pp., parts. Allegro risoluto; Adagio, molto espressivo; Allegro brillante. Freely tonal, dissonant counterpoint, clear textures, deeply felt Adagio movement, superb craft, logical development. D.

———— *Sounds Remembered* (CFP 1975) 28pp., parts. 15 min. This is an homage to Roberto Gerhard (1896–1970), who was a friend of the composer. Bassett recalls sounds from several of Gerhard's works—"a chord, a quickly-ascending line, an insistent high note, a characteristic manner of working a line. They are Gerhard-like in spirit, not exact quotations, and they serve as the generative basis for the four movements. The work is an unfolding of these key sounds, which become transformed, then return periodically to reassert themselves, as in memory" (from the program notes). The pianist must stop notes by pressing the finger on the string. Clusters are used. Sections have no meter signature, and the pace remains essentially the same, but with slight freedom. Harmonics, bell-like sonorities, half pedaling, chromatic dramatic gestures. Since a preference for the upper register is noted, the piano should have this register bright and clear. Mature musicianship and pianism required. D.

Stanley Bate. *Sonata* I Op.47 (Lengnick 1951) 35pp., parts. Allegro; Lento; Tempo di marcia; Presto. Neoclassic, highly pianistic. Requires a large span. M-D.

Marion Bauer. *Fantasia quasi una Sonata* Op.18 (GS 1928) 35pp., parts. $16\frac{1}{2}$ min. Moderato romantico; Ben ritmico e vivace; Lento espressivo–Allegro con moto e marcato. Strong post-Romantic writing with many dramatic moments. Always pianistic. D.

John Bavicchi. *Sonata* IV "Fantasy-Sonata on Lithuanian Folk Melodies" (OUP 1974) 15pp., parts. 10 min. Nine Lithuanian folksongs are woven into the three movements of this work. The first lines of each are given, along with the English translation. Moderato; Andante; Allegretto. Folk material is treated in a highly dissonant and individual yet effective style. Colorful Bartók-like idiom. D.

Arnold Bax. *Ballade* (Chappell) $8\frac{1}{2}$ min.

———— *Legend* (Augener) 9 min.

———— *Mediterranean* (Heifitz—CF B2298).

———— *Sonata* I E 1915 (Chappell 1921, rev. 1945) 52pp., parts. $32\frac{1}{2}$ min. Moderate tempo–Idyllic and Serene; Allegro vivace; Moderate tempo–Smooth and Serene. D.

———— *Sonata* II D (Chappell 1923) 34pp., parts. 31 min. Fantasy—Slow and Gloomy; The Grey Dancer in the Twilight—Fast Valse measure; Very broad and Concentrated, but extremely expressive; Allegro feroce. D.

———— *Sonata* III g (Chappell 1929–43) 38pp., parts. 20 min. Moderato; Allegro moderato. D.

Mrs. H. H. A. Beach. *Sonata* Op.34 (Schmidt 1899) 35pp., parts. Copies at Library of Congress and IU. Allegro moderato; Scherzo—Molto vivace; Allegro con fuoco. Strong writing for both instruments. This work is more than worthy of being revived. D.

James Beale. *Sonata* Op.22 1956 (CFE) 36pp., parts. 23 min. Allegro: "Each bracketed grouping (in the violin) should be slightly hurried in the middle, and held back at the beginning and end, so as to coincide with the piano which remains in tempo" (from the score). Requires large span. Vivace: brusque rhythms and syncopations, octotonic, chromatic, tonal closing in D. Cantabile–Allegretto: added-note technique, free counterpoint, hand crossings, dance characteristics in the Allegretto, neoclassic. M-D to D.

Arthur Conrad Beck. *Sonatine* (Schott 1928) 23pp., parts. Allegretto; Andantino; Allegro energico. Strongly chromatic. M-D.

———— *Sonatine* II (Heugel 1948) 15pp., parts. Lively rhythmic style, neoclassic, preference for lush harmonies. M-D.

John J. Becker. *Soundpiece III, Sonata* 1936 (CFE) 10 min.

Alfred von Beckerath. *Weisen-Sonate* (Moeck 1104).

Jack Beeson. *Sonata* (TP).

Ludwig van Beethoven. *Sonaten* Vol.I: Op.12, 23, 24. Vol.II: Op.30, 47, 96 (Sieghard Brandenburg, Hans-Martin Theopold, Max Rostal—Henle 1975). From the new edition of Beethoven's Complete Works. Preface in German, English, and French describes sources consulted and editorial procedure. Includes valuable footnotes. Separate parts in this urtext but also practical edition.

———— *Duos mit Klavier* (Henle 1974) Band 2. viii+184pp., facsimile. Urtext and practical edition.

———— *Ten Sonatas* (Francescatti—IMC; Auer, Ganz—CF L789; Brodsky, Vogrich—GS L232; Fischer, Kulenkampff—Ric ER2295-6). 2 vols: (Joachim—IMC; Joachim—CFP 3031; Kreisler—Augener 8670;

Kreisler—IMC; Weiner—Kultura; Lea; Woytowicz—PWM 1973; Oborin, Oistrakh—CFP 1971; Oistrakh—IMC).
Available separately: *Sonata* Op.12/1 D (Kreisler—Augener). *Sonata* Op.12/2 A (Kreisler—Augener). *Sonata* Op.12/3 E♭ (Kreisler—Augener). *Sonata* Op.23 d (Kreisler—Augener). *Sonata* Op.24 F "Spring"(Lampe, Schäffer—Henle 162; Auer, Ganz—CF 03385; Brodsky, Vogrich—GS L468; Kreisler—Augener; Kreisler—Schott; Principe, Vitali—Ric ER1475; CFP 4066; Carisch). *Sonata* Op.30/1 A (Kreisler—Augener). *Sonata* Op.30/2 c (Brodsky, Vogrich—GS L467; Kreisler—Augener). *Sonata* Op.30/3 G (Kreisler—Augener). *Sonata* Op.47 A "Kreutzer" (Auer, Ganz—CF 03758; Fischer, Kulenkampff—Ric ER 2506; Brodsky, Vogrich—GS L74; Kreisler—Augener; Kreisler—Schott). *Sonata* Op.96 G (Kreisler—Augener).
———— *Six German Dances* (Br&H).
———— *Variations* Woo 40 F on "Se vuol ballare" from Mozart's *Marriage of Figaro* (Br&H).
———— *Rondo* Woo 41 G (Br&H).
———— *Variations* Op.105 (VU;Br&H). For violin or flute.
———— *10 Variierte Themen* Op.107 (Br&H).
———— *Serenade* Op.41 D for flute or violin and piano (Rampal—IMC). Also arranged by composer from Op.25 for violin and piano (CFP 4663).
See: Richard A. Kramer, "The Sketches for Beethoven's Violin Sonata, Op.30: History, Transcription, Analysis," Ph.D. diss., Princeton University, 1974, 659pp. Frederick Niecks, "Beethoven's Sonatas for Pianoforte and Violin," MMR 20 (1890): 145–47, 169–71, 193–97. Joseph Szigeti, *The Ten Beethoven Sonatas for Piano and Violin*, edited by Paul Rolland (Urbana, Ill.: American String Teachers Association, 1965).

Filippo Carlo Belisi. *Sonata* C (A. Briner—Hug GH10425 1961) 3pp., parts. Preface in German and English. Poco Adagio; Allegro; Tempo di menuetto. This work excels in melodic spontaneity and in a strong sense of form. Fine keyboard realization by the editor. M-D.

Enzo de Bellis. *Sonata* (Zanibon 1948) 40pp., parts. Animato: splashing gestures, changing meters. Calmo, con tristezza: free, lyric, arpeggi coloration. Allegro giojoso: driving, enormous conclusion. D.

Vikter Belyi. *Sonata* 1953 (USSR) 19pp., parts. Allegro moderato; Andante cantabile; Allegro maestoso. Freely tonal but centers around d–D. More contemporary sounding than other comparable works from the USSR. D.

Peter Benary. *Sonata* (Möseler 1975) Hausmusik 127.

Franz Benda. *Four Sonatas* (Štĕdroň—Artia 1962) MAB57. Benda's sonatas represent a transition from baroque to classical style and provide a fine documentation of the musical culture from which the great Viennese sonata style emerged. M-D.

_____ *Sonata* VIII a (Jensen—Augener 7433).

_____ *Sonata* XXVI (Chaumont—Senart 5396).

_____ *Sonata* XXXI (Chaumont—Senart 5402 1925) 11pp., parts. Three movements, fast–slow–fast.

_____ *Sonata* G (Ric R747).

_____ *Sonata* F. (CFP 3226 1909). See Arnold Schering, ed. *Alte Meister des Violinspiels*.

_____ Adagio un poco Andante from *Sonata* A, in simple notation and two embellished versions of the violin part provided by the composer, in Ferand, *Improvisation*, a volume in the Anthology of Music series. For complete sonata in facsimile with unrealized figured bass, see Hans-Peter Schmitz, *Kunst der Verzierung im 18. Jahrhundert: Instrumentale und vokale Musizierpraxis in Beispielen*, 2nd ed. (Kassel: Bärenreiter, 1965). For the complete sonata with realization see the last of the *Four Sonatas* in MAB 57, listed above.

Georg Benda. *Sonata* G. See detailed entry under duos for piano and flute.

Arthur Benjamin. *Five Negro Spirituals* (Primrose—Bo&H).

_____ *Sonatina* b (OUP). A three-movement work rising to considerable heights of technique and expression. Final movement, a rondo, is compact and well knit with lively rhythms and melodic charm. Highly representative of the composer. M-D.

Robert Russell Bennett. *A Song Sonata* (Chappell 1958) 43pp., parts. Quiet and Philosophic; Same tempo, but belligerent; Slow and lovely; Madly Dancing; Gracefully strolling. Movement titles give clue to moods. Mildly contemporary with more emphasis on the melodic side. M-D.

Pascal Bentoiu. *Sonata* Op.14 (Editura Muzicala a Uniunii Compozitorilor din R.P.R. 1964) 21pp., parts. Lento, un poco rubato; Animato. Second movement uses white- and black-key clusters, flexible meters, glissandi, and displays a preference for harmonic sevenths and ninths. M-D to D.

Arthur Berger. *Duo* I (ACA 1948) 13 min. One movement in five sections. Neoclassic in Stravinsky style, pandiatonic with chromatic elements. Main thematic material consists of a declamatory line and a scherzo-like series that bounces around frantically. The sonorous relation of the two instruments is carefully matched. Irregular-length ostinatos unfold during a tight development. A large piece for both instruments. D.

———— *Duo* II (ACA 1950) 12 min. Syncopated rhythms, disjunct melodic lines, and atonal harmonies in a sophisticated synthesis. A fine sense of taste and intellect comes through. Fluent and lyrical in Stravinsky's neo-classicism. D.

Wilhelm Georg Berger. *Sonata* (Editura Muzicala 1963) 50pp., parts. Agitato: g, SA, freely tonal, ninteenth-century pianistic idioms in a more contemporary harmonic language. Broad sweeping gestures, frequent modulation. Larghetto: C pedal point, piano sustains but has some of its own melodic line against violin arpeggi. Allegro giocoso: B♭, strong rhythmic dance feeling, bitonal, big dramatic closing. D.

Rudolph Bergh. *Sonata* Op.20 (Birnbach 1905) 37pp., parts. Poco adagio-allegro risoluto; Allegretto desi deroso e mesto, molto moderato; Molto appassionato, come cercando invano. In Brahms idiom. D.

Lennox Berkeley. *Sonatina* Op.17 A (JWC 1945) 17pp., parts. 14 min. Limpid writing with effective thematic treatment. Moderato; Lento; Allegretto (theme and five variations plus coda). M-D.

———— *Elegy* Op.32/2 A (JWC) 3½ min.

———— *Toccata* Op.33/3 e (JWC) 2 min.

———— *Sonata* II D (JWC 1934) 25pp., parts. 15½ min. Allegro risoluto; Andante; Rondo—Allegro moderato. D.

Herman Berlinski. *Sonata* d (CFE 1949) 16 min. First movement is one of tempestuous expression and great rhythmic drive. The scherzo is a poignantly melodic trio. D.

Robert Bernard. *Sonata* D (Durand 1927) 45pp., parts. Allegro moderato: fourteen-bar piano introduction, Ravel influence. Largo: fifteen-bar piano interlude. Très animé: dancelike, twenty-bar piano interlude. More like a piano sonata. Clear textures and some delightful and charming writing. D, especially for piano.

Wallace Berry. *Duo* (CF 04447) 19pp., parts.

Gérard Bertouille. *Sonata* I 1936 (CeBeDeM 1958) 37pp., parts. 18 min. Maestoso; Poco adagio; Allegro con fuoco. Chromatic, varied pianistic figurations.

———— *Sonata* III (CeBeDeM 1962) 11pp., parts. 13 min.

———— *Sonata* IV (CeBeDeM 1954).

Franz Berwald. *Duo* (GM 1946) Rev. by Sven Kjellström. 35pp., parts. Transparent form with clearly marked sections, some national traits, contrapuntal writing between parts, ingenious rhythms: Romantic harmonic tendencies including some surprising and bizarre effects. M-D to D.

Thomas Beversdorf. *Sonata* 1965 (ST 1967) 32pp., parts. Andantino ma non tanto: SA, freely tonal, black-key glissandi, large span required, interval of minor ninth plays important role. Attacca subito Andante: G pedal point, flowing, chromatic, broken octaves, sustained closing. Allegro con brio: syncopated idea; after hesitation finally gets going; repeated sixteenth notes in alternation of hands; sweeping scales; long trills; left-hand glissandi on white keys, right-hand on black keys. Sizzling conclusion punctuated by widely spread chords. D.

Philip Bezanson. *Sonata* II (CFE) 31pp., parts. Maestoso–Allegro molto: chordal introduction, chromatic, many sixteenth-notes, octotonic, fast harmonic rhythm, very "busy." Intermezzo: octotonic and chromatic, thinner textures in outer parts. Vivace: 7/8, toccata-like. Similarity of mood in all movements. D.

Günter Bialas. *Sonata Piccola* (Br 3471 1959) 23pp., parts. 13 min. Allegro vivo; Romanza; Kleiner Walzer; Nachtstück; Rondo. Thin textures, freely tonal, neoclassic. 4/8 alternates with 5/8 in Allegro vivo, imitation in the Kleiner Walzer and Rondo. M-D.

Heinrich Ignaz Fran von Biber. *Fifteen Mysteries* (Rietz—UE 7283-84, 2 vols.; G. Lenzewski—Wilhelmiana 1954, 3 vols.). These are the *Mystery* or *Rosary* Sonatas intended to honor fifteen sacred mysteries of the life of Christ and Mary. Each sonata has a small engraving at the beginning depicting a New Testament scene. 1.The Annunciation of the Birth of Christ, 2.Mary visits Elizabeth, 3.The Adoration of the Shepherds, 4. The Presentation of Christ in the Temple, 5.The Twelve-year old Jesus in the Temple, 6.Christ on the Mount of Olives, 7.The Flagellation of Christ, 8.The Crowning with Thorns, 9.The Climbing of Calvary, 10.The Crucifixion, 11.The Resurrection of Christ, 12.The Ascent of Christ to Heaven, 13.The Coming of the Holy Ghost, 14.The Ascent of Mary to Heaven, 15.The Crowning of Mary, 16.An apocryphal scene, depicting the child Jesus, hand in hand with an angel, and represented by an extended Passacaglia for solo violin. Sonatas 14, 15, and 16 are the longest works. Each sonata is made up of several short movements separated by short breaks. No.16 is one continuous movement. See VKDR, I: pp.26–38 for a discussion of the scordatura tunings Biber requested.
_____ *Acht Violinsonaten* (Guido Adler—DTOe Jahrgang V/2, Band 11).

———— *Surrexit Christus hodie* from *Mysterien* Sonata No.11 in translated (nonscordatura) version, in HAM II, No.238.

———— *Sonata* c (CFP 4344). From *Acht (8) Violinsonaten*.

John Biggs. *Dialogue and Fugue* (Consort Press 1963) 18pp., parts. 8 min. Chromatic motifs contrast with open fifths. A more sustained mid-section exploits lower register of the piano. Motif returns but subject is inverted, augmented, and brought to an exhilarating conclusion. Dialogue idea carefully worked out. M-D.

Christlieb Siegmund Binder. *Sonata* G (C. Hausswald—HM 62) 18pp., parts. Allegro; Adagio; Tempo di minuetto. Continuous flowing and expressive lines, keyboard part of equal interest. M-D.

Gordon Binkerd. *Sonata* 1974 (Bo&H). A conservative idiom, fine craftsmanship, strong ideas. Very effective first movement and a lively scherzo. Large-scale retrogradation is found in the first and third movements. Binkerd has something to say and he says it eloquently in this work. D.

Johann Adam Birkenstock. *Sonata* Op.1/2 B♭ (Woehl—Nag). Cello optional.

———— *Sonata* Op.1/3 (M. Ettinger—CFP 4225) 4pp., parts. The Allegro movement only. A sunny SA movement. M-D.

———— *Sonata* Op.1/4 E (Polnauer—Schott). Cello optional.

———— *Sonata* e (Ruf—Schott). Cello optional.

———— *Sonata* e (J. Salmon—Ric 1918) 14pp., parts. Adagio; Courante; Largo; Gigue. A good deal of filling-in by the editor. M-D.

Marcel Bitsch. *Sonate* (Leduc 1959) 9pp., parts. One movement, contrasting tempi, sections, and moods. Mildly contemporary. M-D.

Boris Blacher. *Sonate* Op.18, 1941 (Bo&Bo 1947) 15pp., parts. Neoclassic, clear textures and form, terse and straightforward writing. M-D.

Easley Blackwood. *Sonata* Op.7 1960 (GS) 36pp., parts. Allegro rigoroso; Adagio; Allegro molto. Expansive writing, rich sonorities. D.

———— *Sonata* II (Library of Congress 1975). Three movements. Freely tonal; fairly straightforward, rhythmically speaking; and convincing. Opening movement strongest and most coherent of the three. D.

Ernest Bloch. *Sonata* I 1920 (GS) 63pp., parts. 32 min. Agitato; Molto quieto; Moderato. More tightly constructed than *Sonata* II, all three movements interwoven thematically. When the material appears to be exhausted the work closes quietly. Proportions are similar to Bloch's *Piano Quintet*. D.

_____ *Poème Mystique* (*Sonata* II) (Leuckart 1925) 31pp., parts. 22 min. Poetic style, freely rhapsodic, pedal points, open fkfths, modal melodies, bitonal spots but always euphonious. D.

Waldemar Bloch. *Sonatina* C (Dob 1957) 6pp., parts.

Luigi Boccherini. *Six Sonatas* Op.5 (E. Polo—Societă Anonima Notari 1919). B♭, c, B♭, D, g, E♭. Vol.4, I Classical Musicali Italiana.

_____ *Sonata* Op.5/3 B♭ (Borholz—CFP).

_____ *Sonata* c (Carisch).

_____ *Sonata* G.570 E♭ (E. Bonelli—Zanibon 3555 1944) 14pp., parts. Allegro; Adagio; Allegro assai. Rather freely arranged, editorially heavy-handed. M-D.

Anatoliĭ Vasilevich Bogatyrev. *Sonata* I Op.16 (USSR 1955) 62pp., parts. Allegro con fuoco; Largo; Allegretto. Effective writing in a late ninteenth-century idiom. Brahmsian, dark, foreboding in spots. D.

René de Boisdeffre. *Sonata* I Op.12 f♯ (Hamelle) 45pp., parts. Allegro; Allegretto scherzando; Andante con moto; Final—Allegro vivace.

_____ *Sonata* II Op. 50 e (Hamelle) 45pp., parts. Allegro ma non troppo; Allegro grazioso; Lento e espressivo; Allegro con brio.

_____ *Sonata* III Op. 67 G (Hamelle) 43pp., parts. Allegro ma non troppo; Scherzando; Andante; Finale—Allegro vivace.

Written in late Romantic style, with broad and expansive gestures and long, unwinding themes. Full resources of the piano are realized. All three sonatas D.

Jacques Bondon. *Sonatine d'Été* (EMT 1958) 15pp., parts. Promenade; Ronde Champêtre. Highly chromatic, flowing. Last movement has a special sprightly bounce made even more effective by some sudden dynamic changes. M-D.

Francesco Antonio Bonporti. *Ten Inventions* Op.10 "La Pace" (Giegling—Br HM 44, 45, 77) 3 vols. Cello optional. Vol.I: Inventions A, b, F. Vol.II: Inventions g, B♭, c. Vol.III: Inventions D, e, A, E.

_____ *Four Inventions* (Grueters—CFP 2957). Cello optional.

_____ *Sonata* Op.10/8 e (Barbian—Carisch).

Modesta Bor. *Sonata* 1963 (Universidad Central de Venezuela 1967) 44pp., parts. Allegro moderato; Andantino; Rondo—Allegro deciso. Mildly contemporary, extensive first movement, some South American rhythms slightly suggested, freely tonal at times. M-D.

Luigi Borghi. *Sonata* a (Carisch).
———— *Sonata* A (Bonelli—Zanibon).
————*Sonata* A (C. Barison—Carisch 1965) 16pp., parts. Allegro moderato; Adagio; Allegro. Pleasant and attractive. Int. to M-D.
———— *Sonata* E (Carisch).
———— *Sonata* IV Op.4 g (Jensen—Augener 7414).
———— *Sonata* f♯ (J. Salmon—Ric R740) 13pp., parts. Allegro brillante; Adagio; Allegretto grazioso. Piano part is effective but of secondary importance. M-D.

Pavel Bořkovec. *Sonata* 1934 (Panton 1973) 42pp., parts.
———— *Sonata* II 1956 (Artia 1959) 47pp., parts. 21 min. Poco allegro; Adagio; Allegro giusto; Grave—Agitato assai. Freely tonal; some changing meters; dance element present, especially in first and third movements. Broad range of pianistic devices used. Tonal D conclusion. D.

Siegfried Borris. *Sonate* II Op.30/2 (Sirius).
———— *Sonate* III Op.30/3 (Sirius).
———— *Sonatine* Op.65/2 (Sirius).

Sergei Bortkiewicz. *Sonata* Op.26 g (Simrock 1924) 39pp., parts. Sostenuto–Allegro dramatico; Andante; Allegro vivace e con brio. Big post-Romantic sounds and gestures but still rather effective with performers who readily identify with this idiom. D.

Roger Boutry. *Sonate* (Sal 1966) 35pp., parts. 20 min. Difficult ensemble and technical problems. Allegro con fuoco: opening marcato theme treated by both instruments, flexible meters, large span required. Adagio: treated in variation form with theme at opening and closing of the movement. Allegro vivace: spread out over entire keyboard, rhythmic motif developed, freely tonal with numerous bitonal implications, Prestissimo coda. D.

York Bowen. *Sonata* Op.112 e (JWC 1946) 37pp., parts. 22 min. Maestoso con fuoco: SA, dramatic chordal opening interspersed with chromatic scalar passages, leads directly to Allegro commodo, with syncopated left-hand subject accompanied with right-hand tremolo, broken chordal figures in alternating hands, octotonic. Romantic second idea, 3 with 2, animated coda. Lento: recitative-like, double trills, arpeggi figuration, chromatic chords. Finale: quick skips, alternating contrary and parallel chords, hemiola, strong rhythms, arpeggi, concludes with a flourish. Very pianistic. M-D.

Johannes Brahms. Brahms's three sonatas for piano and violin (notice priority given to piano by listing it first) have not yet been exceeded for ingenuity in combining the two instruments. *Sonata* I Op.78 G exhibits masterly and effective workmanship. A highly successful coherence is obtained by the thematic relationship between the first and last movements. *Sonata* II Op.100 A displays a more reflective mood. The piano is used effectively to suggest fragments of a theme after the theme has been exposed by the violin. *Sonata* III Op.108 d contains unusual rhythmic features and forceful use of pedal point. The slow movement is outstanding for its directness of expression.

———*Sonaten* (Hans O. Hiekel, H. M. Theopold, K. Röhrig— Henle 1967) rev. ed. Performance directions and notes. Excellent critical and practical edition. This edition also includes *Scherzo* c.

———*Sonatas* (G. Kehr, J. Demus—VU). Contains a preface, performance directions, and critical notes. Available separately.

———*Sonatas* (IMC).
Available separately: Sonata Op.78 (Flesch, Schnabel—CF 03715; Auer, Ganz—CF 03772; Corti—Ric ER1444; Br&H; Schnirlin—Schott; Kneisel, Bauer—GS L1310; Jacobsen—Augener 4761). Sonata Op.100 (same as listed for Op.78). Sonata Op.108 (same as listed for Op.78).

——— *F.A.E. (Frei aber einsam) Sonata* (Henle; CFP 6083; Br&H; Heinrichshofen). This work, in honor of Joseph Joachim, was written by three composers: Allegro a by Albert Dietrich; Intermezzo F by Robert Schumann; Allegro (scherzo) c by Brahms; Finale a by Robert Schumann. FAE (*Frei aber einsam*—"Free, yet lonely) is the basic thematic material of the sonata except for the third movement. Brahms did not use the FAE idea.

Helmut Bräutigam. *Sonate* Op.23 (Br&H 1951) 31pp., parts. Mit schwung: SA, freely tonal but centers around D. Langsam: ostinato-like treatment. Gemächlich: based on hunting song "O du wunderschöner Waldmann," alternating 4/4, 3/4, 2/4 adds much bounce and freedom. D.

Jan Bresser. *Sonata* g (Donemus 426 1966) 51pp., parts. Allegro molto vivace ed appassionato; Allegretto ma non troppo (7 variations); Interludium; Allegro molto Vivace e energico. Post-Romantic style, requires large span, Honegger influence, varied pianistic idioms and techniques. D.

Jean-Baptiste Bréval. *Sonata* G (Salmon—Ric R808).

Frank Bridge. *Sonata* 1932 (Augener) 45pp., parts. 23½ min. One large movement. D.

Benjamin Britten. *Suite* Op.6 (Bo&H 1935). Cheerful, full of much virtuosity and invention. March; Moto perpetuo; Lullaby; Waltz. Brief introduction precedes March and is alluded to in Waltz. M-D to D.
———— *Gemini Variations* Op.73 (Faber Fo14 1965). Quartet for two or four players for violin, flute, and piano four-hands. If two players are used, it is performed by flute and piano or by violin and piano. Twelve variations and fugue on epigram of Kodály. M-D.

František Brož. *Sonata* (Artia 1956) 48pp., parts. 20 min. Allegro moderato; Scherzo—Presto; Tema con (6) variazioni. Basically tonal around d–D, exploits resources of the piano in late nineteenth-century idioms. D.

Max Bruch. *Scottish Fantasy* Op.46 (Galamian—IMC 2534).

Adolf Brunner. *Sonate* (Br 2691 1952) 32pp., parts. Neoclassic style. Allegro: numerous tempo changes. Adagio: much interplay between instruments. Allegro assai: "pressing on" feeling, wide chordal skips, fugal. D.

Michel Brusselmans. *Sonate* (Senart 1920) 34pp., parts. Modéré–Allegro non troppo; Lent; Vif. Romantic harmonies and melodies. Pianistic figuration explores most of keyboard. D.

Willy Burkhard. *Sonatine* Op.45 (Schott 1937) 11pp., parts. Allegro moderato: Poco adagio; Rondo—Allegretto. Outer movements are flowing and dancelike while the Poco adagio is in recitative style and more free in construction. M-D.
———— *Sonata* Op.78 (Br 1949) 36pp., parts. Neoclassic style. Moderato, poco sostenuto; Lento; Intermezzo; Finale—Allegretto grazioso. Good octave technique required in Intermezzo. 5/8 meter and hemiola in Finale are especially effective. D.

Cecil Burleigh. *Sonata* Op.29 "From the Life of St. Paul" (CF 1926) 29pp., parts. With power and determination; With repose; Impetuously—threateningly. Colorful if somewhat dated. Programmatic concepts are self-evident. D.

Geoffrey Bush. *Sonata* (Augener 1959) 42pp., parts. One large movement with tempo and mood contrasts. Colorful writing with varied and extended ninteenth-century pianistic idioms and techniques. D.

Ferruccio Busoni. *Sonata* Op.29 e (Br&H; Rahter 1891) 39pp., parts. 25 min. Allegro deciso; Molto sostenuto; Allegro molto e deciso. This is a fine orthodox work with an intelligent design, but it is not a masterpiece. It fulfils all academic standards and is strongly influenced by Beethoven and Brahms. All elements appear to be exact, ordered, and precise. D.

―――― *Sonata* Op.36a e 1898 (Br&H) 51pp., parts. 28 min. In one large movement with four contrasting sections. Written in a late Romantic harmony, neoclassic style, an embrace-everything type of piece. Reminiscent of Brahms in thematic materials, and concludes with nine variations in mixed classical style on the Bach chorale "Wie wohl ist mir." Boldly dramatic, often impassioned writing. D.

Thomas Byström. *Trois Sonates* Op.1 (Anja Ignatius―Fazer 1970). Editorial additions in parentheses. Preface in Finnish, German, and English. Bright and melodious, more like sonatinas, classic fluent style. Treatment of harmony and rhythm is often surprisingly original and stimulating. M-D. *Sonata* I Bb 19pp., parts. Allegro; Adagio; Allegro vivace. *Sonata* II g 21 pp., parts. Adagio–Allegro; Menuetto; Allegro. *Sonata* III Eb 26pp., parts. Allegro; Adagio; Rondo.

Charles Wakefield Cadman. *Sonata* G (JF 1932) 36pp., parts. Allegretto con spirito (quasi recitativo); Andante grazioso; Allegro animato. Sweeping nineteenth-century-like gestures and pianistic techniques. Opening idea of first movement returns at conclusion of last movement. Mainly lyric but small influences of contemporary harmony creep in from time to time. D.

John Cage. *Nocturne* (CFP 1947) Shows Cage can write real music! According to Nicholas Slonimsky (*High Fidelity,* November 1975, p.134) Cage says the purpose of this piece is "to dissolve the difference between string and piano sounds." Coloristic music before it was in fashion! M-D.

Hector Campos-Parsi. *Sonatina* II 1953 (PIC 1964) 27pp., parts. Vivo; Adagio; Comodo e grazioso. Freely tonal, centers around D. Adagio is more contrapuntally oriented. Wide skips, glissandi in last movement, clear textures throughout. Piano is handled as a co-equal. M-D.

Lucien Capet. *Sonate* Op.7 (Mathot 1908).

John Alden Carpenter. *Sonata* G (GS 1913) 35pp., parts. Larghetto: widely spread figuration, sonorous arpeggi chords, chromatic inner voices; mood of repose is broken twice by greater intensity. Allegro: marcato driving theme; poco meno mosso section Db, lyric and dolce; tempo I and mood return, sonorous rolled chords, vivo ending; a happy contrast to the Larghetto. Largo mistico: contrasting mid-section, poco più mosso E♭; influence of Grieg and Franck present. Presto giocoso: harmonic fourths are important for piano part; tempo, key, and mood changes are numerous: con molto brio, largo, quasi ad lib, come cadenza, molto adagio, lento, molto più mosso, moderato; Appassionato conclusion dies away to *p* closing. Solid piece for both instruments. M-D to D.

Adam Carse. *Sonata* c (Augener 1921) 31pp., parts. Allegro appassionata; Andante; Allegro molto. Craftsmanlike writing for both instruments. Nineteenth-century idioms. M-D.

———— *Sonatina* A (Augener 11308).

———— *Sonatina* D (Augener 11306).

———— *Sonatina* g (Augener 11307).

Elliott Carter. *Duo* 1974 (AMP) 50pp., parts. "The composition draws its basic character primarily from the contrast between the sounds made by stroking the violin with a bow, that can be sensitively controlled during their duration and the sounds made by striking the piano that, once produced, die away and can only be controlled by being cut short. Deriving its various moods and its dramatic interplay from this contrast of stroking and striking—of variously inflected sounds as opposed to those that invariably fade away—the work starts with the violin's rugged recitative projected against an impassive background of slow piano sonorities. It continues with a series of episodes each emerging from previously stated material— variations of the opening which present the violin as constantly changing in character while the piano follows its own path more systematically and regularly. This contrast between the two instruments is maintained throughout, while many different moods are expressed, some in quick succession, others in a more leisurely way" (note from the score). The piano opens the work with long notes, while the violin has much activity. The roles alternate with aggression and withdrawal. Complete virtuosity required of both performers. Pointillistic, harmonics, unusual pedal effects, requires a large span, highly organized, uncompromisingly hewn timbres. D.

Robert Casadesus. *Sonata* II Op.34 (Durand 1950) 40pp., parts. Dedicated to Zino Francescatti. Allegro vivo; Allegretto a capriccio; Adagio; Allegro molto. Piano part is beautifully laid out. Mildly contemporary, easy to read, spread out on page. Excellent pianism required. Ensemble problems take care of themselves. A neoclassic, peppery, and somewhat eclectic work. D.

Gaspar Cassado. *Sonata* 1926 (UE 8567) 24pp., parts. Fantaisie; Pastorale; Finale (dans le style populaire)—Allegro risoluto. Chromatic idiom, post-Romantic style. Cassado was a virtuoso cellist. D.

Dario Castello. *Two Sonatas* (F. Cerha—Dob 1965) 16pp., parts. No.37 in DM. Castello was concertmaster at St. Marks in Venice around 1629. He wrote two books of "Sonate Concertate in stilo moderno" printed in 1621 and 1629. These two sonatas are from the second book and display a soloistic and virtuoso spirit. The slow expressive sections look far into the future. Fast and slow tempi alternate in sections. Int. to M-D.

Mario Castelnuovo-Tedesco. *Concerto Italiano* g (Ric 119998).
_____ *Humoresque on the Name of Tossy Spivakovsky* Op.70/81 1954 (Gen 1975) 11pp., parts. Clever handling of the letters assigned to specific pitches; freely tonal in a Romantic harmonic vocabulary. Name motto tossed between both instruments, quartal harmony, long lines in piano, large span required, parallel chords, glissando and pizzicato finish. M-D.
_____ *Sonata—quasi una Fantasia* 1929 (Ric 1930) 36pp., parts. Prologo; Intermezzo—vivace e danzante; Epilogo. Colorful, even picturesque writing. Most of keyboard utilized. A vivid imagination displayed here. D.

René de Castéra. *Sonate* Op.13 e 1910 (Rouart, Lerolle) 48pp., parts. Modéré; Assez lent; Modéré. A large work with a short introduction to the opening movement. Second movement is a Lied in five sections based on a Basque folksong. The finale is a sonata–rondo using elastic and varied rhythms. Post-Romantic techniques used throughout. Piano is given much prominence and displays a broad spectrum of pianistic styles. D.

Jacques Castérède. *Sonata* (Leduc 1956) 33pp., parts. Con moto; Intermezzo—scherzando; Adagio; Allegro energico. Highly chromatic and complex writing, many changing meters, glissandi, metrical groupings of five sixteenths to a pulse, rolled chords in contrary motion. Numerous ensemble problems for both performers; first-rate pianism required. D.

Alexis de Castillon. *Sonate* Op.6 1871-2 (Heugel) 61pp., parts. Allegro moderato–Allegro scherzando; Andante; Allegro molto. Written in Franck idiom, symphonic proportions. D.
See: CCSCM: I, pp.233–34 for a discussion of this work.

José María Castro. *Sonata Poética* 1957 (Library of Congress) 29pp., parts. 19 min. Allegro moderato: freely tonal around D; large span required; second theme has much rhythmic activity, flexible meters, Lento—Aria: E, chordal, sustained. chromatic. Allegro: b; toccata figuration given to violin and piano takes melody; chordal chromatic mid-section alternates with motoric activity. M-D.

Georgii L. Catoire. *Poem—Second Sonata* Op.20 1909 (USSR 1966) 51pp., parts. One expansive movement, in Rachmaninoff style; sometimes four bars take a complete page. Enormous technique necessary to bring off a successful performance. Piano part by far the more important. D.

Norman Cazden. *Suite* Op.43 1943 (ACA) 14½ min. Prelude: long lines, two contrasting ideas developed by both instruments. Gavotte: contemporary treatment similar to Ravel's and Prokofieff's approach to this genre. Sarabande: inventive. Reel: not merely background music for a square dance but balances out the "classic" suite idea in an up-to-date setting. D.

Alfredo Cece. *Sonata* D (Zanibon 3827).

Giacomo Cervetto. *Sonata* C (Salmon—Ric R70 1914) 16pp., parts. Adagio; Allegro; Cantabile; Allegro.
———— *Sonata* G (Salmon—Ric R352) 14pp., parts. Siciliano; Allegro; Andante espressivo; Allegro. Both sonatas seem more like suites. The editor has added freely to the piano part. Int. to M-D.

Luciano Chailly. *Sonata Tritematica* No.8 Op.219 1955 (Forlivesi 1960) 22pp., parts. 16 min. One large movement with tempo changes generally delineating major sections. Subdivisions of the meter (8/8 = 3 + 2 + 3, etc.) are prominent. Stylistic mixture provides mainly mildly contemporary sonorities. D.
———— *Sonatina Tritematica* No. 12 (EC).

August Chapuis. *Sonate* g (Durand 1921). Strong Franckian influence. M-D.

Carlos Chavez. *Sonatina* 1924 (Belwin-Mills 1928) 11pp., parts. A one-movement work elemental in its primitivism, relentless rhythms, and harsh sonorities. Contrary glissandi, mechanistic, anti-Romantic, contrasted sections.
———— *Variations* (GS).

Charles Chaynes. *Sonate* (Leduc 1953) 27pp., parts. Risoluto; Lento—Molto sostenuto; Allegro giocoso. Thoroughly contemporary writing. Some metrical subdivisions (8/4 = 5 + 3) among changing meters. Textural clarity in performance must match compositional textural clarity. D.

Camille Chevillard. *Sonata* Op.8 g (Durand 1894). Opening violin idea is basic for much of this work. The slow movement presents an expansive recitative on the subjects of the first movement. Franckian influence. D.

Raymond Chevreuille. *Sonata* Op.57 1953 (CeBeDeM) 16 min.

Barney Childs. *Sonata* II (CFE).

Mircea Chiriac. *Sonatina* (Editura Muzicala 1964) 23pp., parts. Allegro giocoso; Lento; Allegretto. Flexible meters, modal quality, preference for fourths and fifths in Lento, highly pianistic. M-D.

Osvald Chlubna. *Sonata* Op.66 1948 (Artia 1958) 59pp., parts. 25 min. Allegro energico; Molto lento consolante; Allegro burlescamento; Allegro risoluto. Sweeping lines, dissonantal treatment, well constructed, nineteenth-century pianistic treatment of twentieth-century harmonic vocabulary. D.

Henning Christiansen. *Sonate* Op.13 1962 (Samfundet til Udgivelse Al Dansk Music 1965) 22pp., parts. Centrum; Elementer og varianter; Flader (Ritornel I) Episode I; Ritornel II; Episode II; Ritornel III; Episode III; Ritornel IV; Episode IV; Ritornel V; Oplösning. Aleatoric, numerous directions (in English and Danish) for the performers, clusters. Most precise pedal indications. D.

Giovanni Paolo Cima. *Three Sonatas* (Grebe—Sikorski 472). 1 g, 2 d, 3 a. Sonatas 2 and 3 are for violin or oboe and keyboard.

Muzio Clementi. *Three Sonatas* Op.15 1786 (LC) 36pp. First edition. For the piano forte, with an accompaniment obbligato for violin. M-D.
_____ *Three Sonatas for the Piano or Harpsichord with the Accompaniment of a Flute or Violin* Op.2 (Hin 1971). See detailed entry under duos for piano and flute.

Louis-Nicolas Clérambault. *Sonate l'Impromptu* (B. Wahl—Ouvrières 1968) 11pp., parts. Largo; Allegro; Aria—gracioso; Maestoso. Attractive writing with keyboard part realized in excellent taste. M-D.

Halfdan Cleve. *Sonata* Op.21 e (Musikk-Huset).

Ulric Cole. *Sonata* (SPAM 1930) 42pp., parts. Moderato; Scherzo; Intermezzo; Finale—Moderato. Big dramatic work with a few examples of twentieth-century writing. Piece deserves looking into. D.

Samuel Coleridge-Taylor. *Sonata* Op.28 d (Albert Sammons—Hawkes 1917) 27pp., parts. Allegro ma non tanto; Larghetto; Allegro vivo con fuoco. Big, strong, colorful nineteenth-century pianistic idioms and harmonies. Dvořák influence; more like a suite than a sonata. M-D to D.

Dan Constantinescu. *Sonata* 1962 (Editura Muzicala 1965) 28pp., parts. 18 min. Adagio; Allegro. Unusual printing format—when either piano or violin does not play the staff for that part is deleted—gives the appearance of many "empty" spaces in the score. Chromatic germ is inspiration for first movement. The Allegro is a scherzando with flexible meters and some unusual sonorities. D.

Paul Constantinescu. *Sonatina* (Editura Muzicala 1964) 15pp., parts. Allegro moderato; Andante; Allegro assai. Freely tonal, outer movements have dancelike qualities. Traditional pianistic techniques, mildly contemporary. M-D.

Arnold Cooke. *Sonata* I G 1939 (OUP) 32pp., parts. 15 min. Allegro moderato; Lento ma non troppo; Rondo—Allegro ma non troppo. Mildly contemporary. M-D.
————— *Sonata* II A 1951 (Nov 1961) 50pp., parts. 23 min. Allegro con brio; Andante con moto; Allegro vivace. Slightly more contemporary sounding than No.I. More expansive, formal structure handled more logically than in No.I. D.

Paul Cooper. *Soliloquies* (JWC 1971) 6pp., parts. 9 min. Six short pieces, essentially a lyric set that requires no percussive effects from either player. The work concentrates on more traditional pitch and technical demands in the violin and softer effects in the piano. Instructions on the meanings of new signs are included. Rhythmic approximation through the spacing of signs rather than by their individual detail of appearance is probably the most conspicuous new technique used. Clusters, dampening of strings with left hand inside piano, harmonics, preparation with a 1/8" bolt, and some improvisation are required. D.
See: Edith Borroff, "A New Notation: *Soliloquies* for Violin and Piano (1971) by Paul Cooper," in *Notations and Editions* (Dubuque, Iowa: Wm. C. Brown, 1974), pp.191–204. Also includes the score in MS and printed version.
————— *Variations* (JWC 1967) 19pp., parts. 12 min. Twelve-tone idiom makes these variations within variations. Pianist has to read alto clef and pluck a few strings inside the instrument. A few errors in the score. D.

Aaron Copland. *Sonata* 1942-3 (Bo&H) 33pp., parts. 19 min. A miniature lyric and noble drama with excellent writing for both instruments. More robust and taut than Copland's *Piano Sonata*. Andante semplice: austere but pensive elegy with subjects evolving from motivic hinting; strong harmonic tension. Lento: modal; sensitive; pedal points support cantabile line; slow-paced but effective evolution of theme. Allegretto giusto: dancelike; biting melodic leaps; greatly contrasted rhythms and dynamics; opening idea of first movement returns to round off the work. D.

Roque Cordero. *Sonatina* 1946 (PIC 1962) 20pp., parts. Adagio–Allegro con spirito; Largo e recitativo–Andante, quasi adagio; Allegro moderato e burlesco. Serially organized, terse atonal writing. D.

Archangelo Corelli. *Twelve Sonatas* Op.5 (Paumgartner, Kehr—Schott; Abbado—Ric ER2660; Dolmetsch—Nov; G. Jenson—GS), 2 vols; (Gal), 4 vols. This opus is a summary of Corelli's style, taste, and technique. The first six sonatas are the more learned sonata da chiesa, while the last six are the sonata da camera type with their variety of dance movements.
Also available: *Six Sonatas* from Op.5 (Klengel—CFP) Vol.I: 1,4,8. Vol. II: 3,5,9. *Three Sonatas* from Op.5 (Jenson—Augener 7406) Nos.8, 9, 11. *Sonata* Op.5/5 g (Augener 11355; Salmon—Ric R721). *Sonata* Op.5/8 (Moffat—Simrock; PWM; Augener 11358). *Sonata* Op.5/9 A in Schering *Alte Meister,* pp.4ff. Complete and showing suggested additional ornamentation (PWM). *Sonata* Op.5/12 d "La Follia" (David, Auer—CF 03719; David, Petri—Br&H; Kreisler—Foley 1127; Leonard—CF B3288 with cadenza; Meyer—Schott; Salmon—Ric R720; Carish; Augener 7419). This sonata is the famous set of variations on "La Follia." It is a bowing textbook.

John Corigliano. *Sonata* 1964 (GS 1967) 47pp., parts. 22 min. Allegro: highly concentrated. Andantino: melodic peak of the work. Lento (quasi recitativo): brooding and moody. Allegro: not as focused as the other movements. Virtuoso neoclassic writing of the highest order. Cadenza for the piano. Thoroughly contemporary yet tonally based in the broadest sense of the term. D.

Michel Corrette. *Sonata* A (Lemoine 1924).
———— *Sonata* C (Ruf—Ric 1955).
———— *Sonate* D (Ruf—Schott 1968).
———— *Sonata* II 1735 (F. Petit—Ouvrières 1965) 6pp., parts. For violin or flute and keyboard. Allemanda–Aria; Minuetto 1 & 2. Charming period writing, tasteful realization. M-D.

Ramiro Cortés. *Elegy* (EV 1960) 5pp., parts. Serial, long lines. expressive, arpeggi gestures, repeated chords, atonal. M-D.

DORDT COLLEGE LIBRARY
Sioux Center, Iowa 51250

Jean Coulthard. *Duo Sonata* (BMI-Canada 1952) 36pp., parts. 18 min. Cyclic work developing from the opening theme given out by the violin. The three movements are connected by links. M-D.

François Couperin. The *Concerts Royaux* are ''French'' suites of dances with much Italian influence, especially in their aria-like melodies. No instruments are specified except keyboard and whatever instruments are available. They come off well using violin and harpsichord or piano.
Concerts Royaux, Troisième Concert (F. Polnauer—Schott 1970). Nos.1, 2, and 4 available separately from Schott. Some movements are scored for keyboard and violin, others are in trio settings. *Les Goûts Réunis, Quatorzième Concert* (Boulay—EMT). *Concert* 5 F (Dukas—Durand); *Concert 6 Bb (Dukas—Durand); Concert* 7 g (Dukas—Durand); *Concert* 9 E (Dukas—Durand).

Henry Cowell. *Homage to Iran* (CFP 6114 1959) 23pp., parts. 13 min. Andante rubato; Interlude; Andante rubato; Con spirito. Not based on actual ethnic material from Iran but written in the style and spirit of Persian music. ''In the first and third movements, the piano strings may be muted by pressing the strings of the indicated notes near the bridge, while playing the keys. The resulting sound is somewhat similar to the sound of an Iranian drum'' (from the score). M-D.
———— *Suite* (AMP 1926) 17pp., parts. Largo; Allegretto; Andante tranquillo; Allegro marcato; Andante calmato; Presto. Many clusters in piano part, tonal, six short contrasted movements. M-D.
———— *Sonata* I 1945 (AMP 1947) 24pp., parts. 17 min. Hymn; In Fuguing Style; Ballad; Jig; Finale. A few muted strings in Finale for the pianist are the clue to Cowell in this otherwise traditionally written but fresh sounding work. M-D.

Paul Creston. *Suite* Op.18 (GS 1939) 9½ min. Prelude; Air; Rondo. Rhapsodic excitement, energetic rhythmic treatment, natural flowing melodic charm. M-D.

George Crumb. *Four Nocturnes. Night Music* II 1964 (CFP 1971) 9 min. Explores colorful sonorities, such as pianist rapping on metal frame of piano, sweeping strings with wire brush, scraping fingernail rapidly over metal winding of string. Numerous performance instructions. Extremes in dynamic range explored. Piano harmonics are exploited in this ethereal dialogue between instruments. D.

Ivo Cruz. *Sonata* (Sassetti 1956) 27pp., parts. Moderato; Lento; Con moto. Large, dramatic work in post-Brahms and Impressionist idiom. Much planing is used throughout. Well written for both parts, thoroughly integrated. D.

César Cui. *Sonate* Op.84 D 1911 (Jurgenson 1916) 26pp., parts. Allegro; Andante non troppo; Allegro. Not one of Cui's best works. M-D.

Luigi Dallapiccola. *Due Studi* 1947 (SZ 1950) 15pp., parts. 11 min. Very communicative serial writing. Sarabanda: ABA, based on a twelve-tone series. Fanfare e Fuga: close and serious fugal treatment. Based on the same series as the B section of the Sarabanda; moves over keyboard. M-D to D.

———— *Tartiniana Seconda* 1956 (SZ) 12 min. A divertimento in four movements. Pastorale; Tempo di Boureo; Presto; Variazioni. Material by Tartini is freely adapted (as is the Paganini material in Dallapiccola's piano work *Sonatina Canonica*). Dissonant contrapuntal and accompaniment elements permeate the writing. M-D.

Gyula Dávid. *Sonata* 1968 (EMB 1969) 27pp., parts. Allegro molto; Andante, molto tranquillo; Allegro. Sparse textures, rhythmic vitality, fine lyric lines, outstanding sense of color, strong Bartók influence. M-D.

Claude Debussy. *Sonata* g 1917 (Durand) 33pp., parts. 12 min. Allegro vivo; Intermède (fantasque è léger); Finale. Refined workmanship and meticulous taste are characteristic of this last fully completed work. It is full of animated, melodious, and even vehement writing. Harmonic ambiguity is firmly put away with a brilliant G conclusion. D.
See: VKDR, II: pp.216–23.

Frederick Delius. *Sonata* B 1892. Unpublished, in preparation, 1976 (Bo&H). A passionately lyrical work.
———— *Sonata* I 1905–15 (Forsyth) 21pp., parts. This is the most extended of the violin sonatas. Dreamy, rhapsodic, based on five descending notes. One expansive movement. In all three sonatas the piano is used more for a harmonic background than for asserting its own independence. D.
———— *Sonata* II (Bo&H 1912) 12pp., parts. Lush and declamatory in style, somewhat Straussian but not knit together very strongly. An impassioned lyricism flows through this entire sonata. M-D.
———— *Sonata* III (Bo&H 1931) 12pp., parts. Eloquently musical with most interest for the violin. Slow; Andante scherzando; Lento. Melancholy mood, most classical in structure of the three sonatas. A certain longing beauty is characteristic of passages marked "slow and mysterious." M-D to D.

Norman Dello Joio. *Colloquies* (EBM 1966) 20pp., parts. 3 movements. 9 min.

———— *Fantasia on a Gregorian Theme* (CF 1949) 9pp., parts. Simple and mature style with plenty of distinctive and expressive power. M-D.

———— *Variations and Capriccio* (CF 1949) 19pp., parts. Imaginative, lucid, and poetic writing that makes musical sense. M-D.

Albert Delvaux. *Sonatine* 1956 (CeBeDeM) 8½ min.

———— *Sonate* 1962 (CeBeDeM) 41pp., parts. 17 min. Allegro con anima; Andante; Allegro vivo. Tonal but with much chromatic usage. Lines have a tendency to be short and corky. Much activity at all times. D.

David Diamond. *Sonata* 1943–6 (GS 1950) 48pp., parts. 22 min. Allegro moderato; Allegretto con moto; Adagio sospirando; Allegro con energia. Full battery of pianistic expertise required. Exciting transparent writing in a classical manner. Strong tonalities for each movement. D.

———— *Chaconne* 1948 (PIC 1951) 24pp., parts. 11½ min. Introduction, theme, 22 variations, and coda. Resources of both instruments exploited. D.

Emma Lou Diemer. *Sonata* 1949 (Seesaw) 25pp., parts. 10 min. Scherzo; Pastorale; Finale. Free dissonant counterpoint; octotonic; inner voice motives take on added significance; large span required; subtle syncopation in Pastorale; driving rhythms; detached chords in Finale; intervals of seconds and thirds exploited; impressive conclusion. D.

Albert Dietrich. *F. A. E. Sonata.* See entry under Brahms, this section.

Charles Dieupart. *Suite* IV e (J-C. Veilhan, D. Salzer—Leduc 1974) 9pp., parts for flute or violin and basso continuo.

Karl Ditters von Dittersdorf. *Sonata* B♭ (Mlynarczky—Hofmeister 1929) 11pp., parts. Allegro; Adagio; Variationes—Tempo di Minuetto. M-D.

———— *Sonata* G (Mlynarczky—Hofmeister 1929) 14pp., parts. Adagio; Allegro molto; Tema con variazioni. M-D.
Clean editions with ornaments written out. Both sonatas have final movements consisting of four variations and a coda.

Ernst Dohnányi. *Sonata* Op.21 c♯ (Simrock 1913) 30pp., parts. 18 min. Quiet first movement. Second movement (variation–scherzo) follows without a break and incorporates the second subject of the first movement in a variation and trio treatment. The finale opens with the motto figure (c♯–d♯–e) of the first movement, but in chords and develops into a free scherzo with a reflective trio in A. A long pedal point prepares for the return of the opening tempo of the first movement; finale concludes with much Romantic pathos. Requires thorough musicianship and pianistic expertise. D.

Samuel Dolin. *Sonata* (BMI-Canada 1968) 28pp., parts. 16½ min. Adagio; Allegro non troppo; Andante; Vivo. The second movement is marchlike and rhythmic. M-D.

Gaetano Donizetti. *Sonate* f (B. Paüler—Amadeus Verlag 1972) 12pp., parts. Short, graceful, more like a large-scale aria. A maestoso introduction leads to a SA section entitled Allegro, where both instruments toss off operatic themes in solo-tutti style. M-D.

David Dorward. *Triad* (OUP 1975) 16pp., parts.

Jaroslav Doubrava. *Sonata* 1941 (Orbis 1949) 19pp., parts. Allegro moderato; Presto tenebroso; Adagio. Preference for bitonal sonorities with resolutions at cadence points. Second movement is toccata-like. Adagio is atmospheric. Folk sources are part of the style but never quoted directly. M-D.
———*Sonata* II 1959 (Panton 1963) 43pp., parts. Turbulent, monothematic. Allegro: dramatic agitation evolves from folk ballades; SA design with secondary subject supplementing the main theme; a motive of diatonic seconds first heard at bar 22 becomes very important. Molto moderato: restless piano part in style of a cymbalom supports violin melody; ABA; balladic mood. Presto: turbulent idea of opening returns but is permeated by a lively and dancing rhythm; theme is varied and links up in mosaic fashion with first and second movements; ABA. Convincing and expressive work. D.

Pierre Max Dubois. *Sonata* Op.91 (Leduc 1963) 36pp., parts. Allegro inquieto—ma non troppo vivo; Prestissimo comico; Andante cantabile; Impetuoso. Varied figurations, chordal, chromatic, textural clarity. Final movement with driving percussive chords is reminiscent of Bartók's style. D.

Vernon Duke. *Sonata* D (Ric 1960) 32pp., parts. Poco maestoso; Allegretto non troppo; Brilliante e tumultuoso. Mildly contemporary, well crafted. The final movement is written in a 6/8 3/4 meter and is delightfully lilting. M-D.

Petar Dumičić. *Sonata* Op.16 1939 (Udruženje Kompozitora Hrvatske 1966) 47pp., parts. Andante–Allegro moderato; Scherzo—Allegro molto; Andante tranquillo; Allegro. Freely tonal, individual style based on nineteenth-century compositional practices and pianistic concepts. M-D.

Marcel Dupré. *Sonate* Op.5 g (Leduc 1920) 36pp., parts. Allegro; Andantino; Presto. Tonal, Impressionistic techniques, pianistic, requires large span. Toccata-like finale in 9/16. D.

Jan Ladislav Dussek. *Sonatas* Op.69/1 B♭, 2 G (Štědroň—Artia 1959) MAB 41. 72pp., parts. *Sonata* G is the more interesting of the two. Colorful harmony coupled with youthful spirit makes it a favorite with audiences. Biographical and analytical notes in Czech, German, and English. M-D.

François Duval. *Two Sonatas* (Ruf—Schott 1953) 1 D, 2 G. From *Amusemens pour la Chambre,* Livre VI. Cello or viola da gamba optional.

Jiří Dvořáček. *Sonata Capriccioso* 1956 (Artia 1969) 44pp., parts. Con moto–Rubato–Allegretto; Rubato–Lento; Feroce; Allegro con fuoco. A capricious exuberant optimism pervades this work. Even the songful slow movement has a youthful spirit about it. D.

Antonin Dvořák. *Sonata* Op.57 F 1912 (Artia; Simrock) 30pp., parts. 22 min. Allegro, ma non troppo; Poco sostenuto; Allegro molto. Idyllic, introspective, delicate, simple throughout. Outer movements are most original, while the Poco sostenuto shows the influence of Brahms. Has an irresistible zest about it. M-D.
————*Sonatina* Op.100 G (D. Vorholz—Litolff 32pp., parts; CFP; Kehr, Lechner—Schott; CF 03214; Stoessel—BMC; Lengnick). Allegro risoluto; Larghetto; Scherzo—molto vivace; Finale—Allegro. Stems from the composer's American visit and shows American Indian and Negro influences, which permeated his writing at that time. M-D.

Petr Eben. *Sonatina* (Artia 1957) 27pp., parts. 12 min. For violin or flute and piano. Separate part written when too low for flute. Allegro giusto: sprightly, broken octaves, chromatic. Moderato e cantabile: lyric and expressive. Vivace e accentato: freer tonal relationships, corky rhythms. M-D.

Helmut Eder. *Sonatine* Op.34/1 (Dob 1963) 12pp., parts. 5½ min. Lento espressivo–Allegro; Andante; Allegro mobile. Small only in length. Expressionistic, changing meters, intense. D.

Klaus Egge. *Sonata* I Op.3 1932 (Musikk-Huset 1946) 27pp., parts. 22 min.

Moderato; Romanza—Adagio; Finale—Rondo, vivace. Slätter intervals, polyphonic textures, freely tonal. D.

Gottfried von Einem. *Sonata* Op.11, 1949 (UE) 16pp., parts. 12 min. Allegro moderato: in 7/8, sustained, ingenious, much variety. Larghetto; Allegro. Neoclassic style, tonally free, large span required, tight construction, clear textures, lively rhythms. M-D.

Edward Elgar. *Sonata* Op.82 e (Nov 1919) 37pp., parts. 23 min. Allegro: rugged thematic material, freely treated, much vitality and fire. Romance: ABA design with an element of mysticism in the A section; tender romanticism; the broad B section provides a fine contrast; A section is recapped with theme played con sordino. Allegro non troppo: tranquil opening to bar 40, where a new idea ushers in a wistful theme; large development of these ideas leads to the recap, where a reference to the Romance, now in 3/2 meter, appears; short, strenuous coda rounds out the movement. D.

George Enesco. *Sonata* I Op.2 D (Enoch 1898; Editions d'Etat 1956 47pp., parts; Ashdown).
———— *Sonata* II Op.6 f (Enoch 1901 47pp., parts; Editions d'Etat 1956; Ashdown).
———— *Sonata* III Op.25 a (Enoch 1933 43pp., parts; Editions d'Etat 1956; Ashdown). Moderato malinconico; Andante sostenuto e misterioso; Allegro con brio, ma non troppo mosso.

Manuel Enríque. *Sonata* 1964 (IU) 16pp. Three atonal movements with only the first being entitled Tranquillo. Serial, violin opens by itself with piano joining at Deciso. Pointillistic, constantly moving over keyboard, dynamic extremes, expressionistic, cascading gestures. Piano used percussively; certain sonorities are maintained by timed seconds, a few avant-garde techniques, complex, abstract use, and abstract writing. Only for the most venturesome duo. D.

Ivan Eröd. *Sonata* I 1969–70 (Dob) 36pp., parts. Allegro moderato: SA, freely tonal, clear textures, strong rhythms. Thema and (3) Variations: effectively contrasted variations, harmonics. Presto: triplets in tenths, arpeggi figuration, neoclassic. M-D.

Andrej Eschpaj. *Sonate* (Sikorski 1966 38pp., parts, composer's MS but easy to read; USSR 1967 27pp., parts). Broad expansive movement that effectively utilizes octaves, fourths, and chromatics; varied tempi and moods. D.

Carlo Esposito. *Sonata* II (Edizioni Musicali Mercurio 1962) 30pp., parts. Tempo—Allegro Moderato; Tempo—Lentamente e accorato; Tempo—Rondo brillante. Fond of expanding intervals; chromatic; bitonal; long scalar passages for the pianist; pesante writing in coda. D.

Robert Evett. *Sonata* 1960 (ACA) 16pp., parts. 12 min. Andante–Allegretto: two basic tempi; changing meters; freely tonal around C; clear textures; quasi recitativo section for violin; subtle lilting character permeates this movement. Allegro con brio: strong octave opening, dancelike, quartal harmony, short and brilliant coda; requires large span. Neoclassic. M-D.

Joseph Leopold Eybler. *Drei Sonaten* Op.9 (A. Weinmann—Amadeus/Päuler 1973) 46pp., parts.

Blair Fairchild. *Sonate* Op.43 (Durand 1919) 32pp., parts. Moderato; Allegretto vivo; Quasi adagio; Molto allegro. Impressionistic. M-D.

Gabriel Fauré. *Sonata* Op.13 A 1876 (Br&H; Francescatti, Casadesus—IMC; Loeffler—BMC) 44pp., parts. 27 min. Allegro molto: SA, piano opening followed by a dialogue that leads to the second tonal area; traditional development but beautiful working out of ideas. Andante: pure line juxtaposed with charming rocking 9/8 theme in the piano. Allegro vivo: a light scherzo of darting passages, contrasted middle melodic section. Allegro quasi presto: declamatory, robust writing and formal experimentation; agitated, restless, Schumannesque. D.
_____ *Sonata* Op.108 e 1916 (Durand) 44pp., parts. 25 min. Allegro non troppo; Andante; Final. Strange, austere melody, sustained by unconventional modal harmony (mainly Lydian). Metrical patterns avoid symmetry and squareness—typical of Fauré's late style. A work of great elegance, sympathetically written for both instruments, that deserves more frequent performances. D.

Howard Ferguson. *Sonata* 1931 (Bo&H) 28pp., parts. 16 min. Molto moderato; Allegro furioso; Quasi Fantasia. Preference for octaves and figuration noted. Final movement surges and recedes. 3/4 6/8 meter in the second movement adds intensity. D.

Giorgio Ferrari. *Sonata* I (Zanibon 1974) 29pp., parts, photostat.
_____ *Sonata* II (Zanibon 1974) 30pp., parts, photostat.

Pierre Octave Ferroud. *Sonate* (Durand 1929) 33pp., parts. Allegro vivo e scherzando; Andante; Rondo vivace. Impressionist influences are felt but a virile style is also present. Pianistic techniques are a continuation and expansion of nineteenth-century practice. D.

Willem de Fesch. *Sechs Sonaten* (W. Woehl—HM 127, 128) 2 vols. For violin, flute, oboe or viola, and keyboard. Six sonatas from the set of twelve, Op.8. Vol.I: D, c, e. Vol.II: G, A, b. Excellent preface and performance notes. Short movements; appealing melodies. Provides excellent duo training; would be successful on recital programs. M-D.

Michael Christian Festing. *Two Sonatas* Op.4/2 c, 3 E 1736 (G. Beechey—OUP 1975) Musica da Camera 24. 16pp., parts. 8 min. Figured bass tastefully realized. Includes parts for bass instrument. Preface in English and German. Varied harmonies, imitation, attractive melodies. M-D.
———— *Sonata* Op.8/5 D 1744 (W. Bergmann-Schott 1955) 10pp., parts. Largo–Spiritoso; Largo–Poco allegro, gratioso; Allegro spiritoso; Andante amoroso–Più lento e dolce–Amoroso. Short attractive movements. A delightful sonata. Editorial marks indicated in brackets. M-D.

Zdenko Fibich. *Sonata* D (J. Zich—Orbis 1950; Artia).
———— *Sonatina* Op.27 d 1869 (Artia; Urbánek; BMC) 11pp., parts. Allegro moderato; Andante; Allegro molto. Colorful, folk elements present. M-D.

Jacobo Ficher. *Primera Sonata* Op.15 1929, rev., 1960 (IU) 38pp., parts. Allegro: SA; chromatic linear lines; syncopated chords; contrapuntal; two main ideas are synthesized and thoroughly worked out with a brilliant concluding coda. Lento: ABA; chromatic; chordal; violin has some lyric lines. Presto: syncopated chordal opening; arpeggi patterns divided between hands; contrasts with more tuneful meno mosso section; both main ideas return and a coda combines elements of both for an exciting closing. Very difficult writing for both instruments. D.
———— *Sonata* II Op.56 1945–6 (IU) 48pp., parts. Allegro moderato: SA; undulating tonal (D) opening; second idea is dancelike; requires good octave technique. Lento: mistico octotonic subject; linear and chordal juxtaposed sections; effective ending in B. Allegro moderato: scalar passages serve as counterpoint to subject; imitation; thin and thick textures juxtaposed. Dramatic writing for both instruments. D.
———— *Tercera Sonata* Op.93 1959 (IU) 42pp., parts. Allegro Agitato; Lento; Allegro molto. Many of the same techniques used in the first two sonatas are used here. D.
Ficher is a colorist; his love of complex chromatic scalar passages and his unique manner of handling chordal textures shine through in all three works. All three require advanced pianism.

Irving Fine. *Sonata* (Warner Brothers 1948) 32pp., parts. In Stravinsky's neoclassic style. Moderato; Lento con moto; Vivo. Thorny, chromatic. Large span required. Last movement has thinner textures and bouncing rhythms and seems to be the most successful. Strong tonal centers. D.

Izrail Borisovich Finkelshtein. *Sonata* (USSR 1968) 88pp., parts. Allegro moderato; Scherzo—Allegro; Aria—Lento assai in modo improvisato; Finale—Allegro risoluto. Expansive work, short lines, some contrapuntal usage, mildly contemporary, long *pp* closing. Requires fortitude and plenty of reserve power. D.

Ross Lee Finney. *Sonata* II (AME 1954) 21pp., parts. Tranquilly; Capriciously; Tenderly, but with passion; Vigorously in march tempo; Tranquilly. Neoclassic tendencies, much interplay of ideas between instruments. M-D.

———— *Sonata* III 1955 (Valley Music Press 1957) 29pp., parts. Allegro caminando; Allegro scherzando; Adagio sostenuto con variazioni (9 variations). Beautiful balance between the two instruments. Serial with tonal implications. The set of variations is a "tour de force" in variation technique. D.

Giovanni Battista Fontana. *Sechs Sonaten* (Friedrich Cerha—Dob) Nos.13, 14, and 15 in DM series. 3 vols., two sonatas in each. Multimovement works. Valuable foreword. M-D.

Wolfgang Fortner. *Sonate* 1945 (Schott) 23pp., parts. Allegro; Adagio; Rondo—Vivace; Thema con Variazioni (5 variations and coda). Neoclassic, freely tonal, changing meters in Rondo, thin textures, M-D.

Jean Françaix. *Sonatine* 1934 (Schott) 15pp., parts. 11 min. Vivace; Andante; Théme Varié (5 variations). Plenty of Gallic wit and humor are displayed. Chromatic, sprightly rhythms, light, neoclassic style. M-D.

César Franck. *Sonata* A 1886 (M. Steegman—Henle 1975; Hamelle; Busch—Br&H; Francescatti, Casadesus—IMC; Lehmann—CF L766; Lichtenberg, Adler—GS L1235; Polo—Ric ER 2068; Sauret—Schott; Durand; M. Jacobsen—CFP 3742) 45pp., parts. The Henle edition has a most informative preface. One of the finest and most moving works in its form since Brahms. Graceful and tranquil first movement followed by the most important second movement, one of a troubled and searching nature. In place of an expected adagio or andante, the third movement is a Recitativo–Fantasia, with great sweep and freedom. The final movement, a rondo, displays the recurring theme in canonic fashion. Chromaticism and cyclic form add tautness and coherence to the entire unified work. D.

A cello version of this sonata is also available. The violin part appears to have been merely transposed in part by Jules Delsart. See the Henle preface for more information concerning this edition.

François Francoeur. *Sonate* 6, Ier Livre E (Petit—Ouvrières 1968) 16pp., parts. Adagio; Allemande; Sarabande; Gavotte I, II; Gigue. Elements of both sonata and suite are present in this attractive work. Keyboard realization by the editor is in good taste. M-D.

Peter Racine Fricker. *Sonata* Op.12 (Schott 1950) 30pp., parts. Three movements of highly concentrated and engaging writing which becomes progressively slower. Allegro: SA; rich and full of material; extended development; melody varied in the recapitulation. Allegretto: begins muted "comme un valse distante"; formally it might be called a fantasy–rondo, with the mid-section of the opening idea serving as the refrain. The Adagio finale is in three sections, each followed by a brief decorative cadenza to a complex chord—a different resolution evolves each time, the last one to a C triad. D.

Géza Frid. *Sonate* Op.50 1955 (Donemus) Photostat of MS. 26pp., parts. $14\frac{1}{2}$ min. Quasi improvisando–Allegro marcato; Andante cantabile; Presto leggero. Sweeping lines opening the work are interrupted by a ruvido section. These alternate during the first movement. The lyric second movement erupts in maestoso chromatic chords before it signs itself out. The finale carries on a question–answer style until a meno mosso section becomes more intense. An *a tempo* moves quickly to the end. D.

Pierre Froidebise. *Sonate* 1938 (CeBeDeM 1956) 15pp., parts. 9 min. A one-movement work with contrasting sections. Highly Impressionistic and pleasant. D.

Gunnar de Frumerie. *Sonata* I Op.27 (Nordiska Musikförlaget 1934, rev. 1962) Photostat of MS. 34pp., parts. Andante; Allegro molto rigoroso e energico; Siciliano; Andante espressivo–Molto vivo. D.

_____ *Sonata* II 1944 (Nordiska Musikförlaget 1950) 46pp., parts. Allegro amabile; Andante espressivo; Scherzo, molto allegro misterioso; Allegretto grazioso. D.

Both sonatas are conceived in a neoclassic style and show a fine craft, with polished writing along lines of established tradition. A mildly contemporary flavor is present.

Sandro Fuga. *Sonata* 1938–9 (Ric) 34pp., parts. 25 min. Molto tranquillo; Molto allegro; Sostenuto espressivo. Sonorous use of piano, broad pianistic gestures. Large span required. D.
———— *Sonata* II (EC 1972) 38pp., parts.

Arthur Furer. *Sonate* Op.18 1954 (Krompholz) 32pp., parts. Allegro moderato; Molto tranquillo; Allegro con brio. Drive, color, and excitement, respectively, describe the three movements. Plenty of pianistic interest. Mildly contemporary. D.

Wilhelm Furtwängler. *Sonate* I d (Br&H 1938) 96pp., parts. Ruhig beginnen; Sehr langsam, still; Moderato; Finale—Etwas breit. A work of enormous proportions. Reger–Strauss tradition underlined by Brahms. Virtuoso technique and plenty of reserve stamina required. D.
———— *Sonate* II D (G. Kulenhampff—Bo&Bo 1940).

Niels W. Gade. *Sonata* II Op.21 d 1850 (Br&H) 27pp., parts. Adagio–Allegro di molto; Larghetto; Adagio–Allegro moderato; Allegro molto vivace. Owes much to Mendelssohn, with Romantic charm on every page. Sounds somewhat old-fashioned today but still has musicality to recommend it. M-D.
———— *Fantasias* Op.43 (JWC). See detailed entry under duos for piano and clarinet.

Blas Galindo. *Sonata* 1945 (EMM 1950) 45pp., parts. Allegro; Largo; Molto allegro. Freely tonal, flexible meters, folk influence, some driving rhythms, pandiatonic. D.

Keith Gates. *Sonata* (Galaxy 1976) 26pp., parts.

Francesco Geminiani. *Twelve Sonatas* Op.1(a) (W. Kolneder—Schott) 4 vols. Cello part optional. Originally published in London in 1716. Indications of the revised edition of 1739 have been used for the articulation of the violin part in Kolneder's edition. Vol.I: Sonatas A, d, e. Vol.II: Sonatas D, g, g. Vol.III: Sonatas c, b, F. Vol.IV. Sonatas E, a, d. M-D.
Available separately: *Sonata* Op.1/1 A (Ruf—HM 173; Betti—GS) 11pp., parts. *Sonata* Op.1/4 D (Ruf—HM 174) 11pp., parts. *Sonata* Op.1/12 d "Impetuosa" (Moffat—Simrock 1929) 9 min. A "new concert version."
———— *Six Sonatas* Op.5 (W. Kolneder—CFP 9042). Cello part optional. Originally published in London in 1747 for cello and continuo but reappeared in this form almost immediately. The keyboard realization is somewhat thick but usable. Slow, fast, slow, fast movement order. Fast-moving

harmonies, irregular phrase groups, unusual patterns, opportunities for many cadenza passages. Int. to M-D.

_____ *12 Compositioni* (T. Orszagh, L. Böhm—EMB 1959) 2 vols. Thesaurus Musicus 7 & 8. Twelve movements included by the composer in his *The Art of Playing the Violin,* 1751. This treatise is available in a facsimile of the first edition (David Boyden—OUP).

Harald Genzmer. *Sonata* I 1943 (Schott 3663) 15pp., parts. Mässig bewegt; Mit grosser ruhe; Sehr schwungvoll und lebendig vorzutragen.

_____ *Sonata* II 1949 (Schott 4022) 27pp., parts. Langsam: Breit strömend; Andante amabile; Finale: Sehr lebhaft.

_____ *Sonatine* 1953 (Schott 4482) 16pp., parts. Allegro; Adagio; Presto; Allegro.

_____ *Sonata* III 1954 (Schott 5870) 12 min.

Roberto Gerhard. *Gemini: Duo Concertante* (OUP 1966) 12 min. The composer's note from the score states: "The work consists of a series of contrasting episodes, whose sequence is more like a braiding of diverse strands than a straight linear development. Except for the concluding episodes, nearly every one recurs more than once, generally in a different context. These recurrences are not like refrains, and do not fulfill anything remotely like the function of the classical refrain. Rather might they be compared to thought persistently on some main topic." The piano part uses clusters, widely spaced intervals, long trills, and other devices that help create sustained resonance. Strings damped by the hands; glissandi strummed on the strings with plectrum or nail file. An exciting experiment in duo sonority. D.

Felice Giardini. *Sonate* Op.3 (E. Polo—Fondazioni Eugenio Bravi 1941) *I Classici Musicali Italiani,* vol.3. For violin or flute and keyboard. 1 G, 2 C, 3 F, 4 A, 5 G, 6 D. "Elegant, balanced, and at many points of a delicate and original inspiration" (from the preface by Polo). Two instruments are treated equally.

Joseph Gibbs. *Sonata* I d (Salter—Augener).

_____ *Sonata* III G (David Stone—Schott 1974) 12pp., parts. Continuo realization by Colin Tilney. Preface in English and German.

_____ *Sonata* IV E (David Stone—Schott 1974) 12pp., parts. Continuo realization by Colin Tilney. Preface in English and German.

_____ *Sonata* V d (Moffat—Nov).

Walter Gieseking. *Variationen über ein Thema von Edvard Grieg* (Fürstner

A8375 8358F 1938) 23pp., parts. For flute or violin and piano. See detailed entry under duos for flute and piano.

Richard Franko Goldman. *Sonata* (Mercury 1964) 19pp., parts. Allegro moderato; Molto adagio; Molto allegro. Neoclassic. M-D.

Eugene Goossens. *Sonata* I Op.21 e 1918 (JWC 321) 55pp., parts. Allegro con anima: contrary broken chordal figuration; inner and outer voice trills; freely tonal; syncopated chords; changing key signatures; arpeggi; parallelism; large span required. Molto adagio: seventh and ninth chords; chromatic; poetic; cantabile and expressive; broad arpeggi lines; two subjects are heard together with suggestions of a third. Con brio: dramatic gestures, glissando, light rocking motion, punctuated chords, 5 with 6 and 6 with 7 in arpeggi style, chords in contrary motion. Highly Romantic writing with a few mildly contemporary sonorities. Second movement is probably the best of the two sonatas. D.

———— *Sonata* II 1930 (JWC 370) 67pp., parts. Moderato con anima; Intermezzo—A la Sicilienne; Finale. Contains many of the devices found in *Sonata* I. Some of the French influences are retained, but there is also a German influence, especially that of Richard Strauss. Extreme chromaticism, large forms, textures with three individual layers, but firmly grounded in the Romantic tradition. D.

Johann Gottlieb Graun. *Six Sonatas* (G. Müller—Sikorski 1957) published separately. Exciting and imaginative writing in most of the movements. Graun tried to incorporate all current trends and fashions in these pieces. See the Adagio of No.3 for highly unusual harmonic usage. There is plenty to keep both performers busy in these multi-movement works. 1 D, 2 E, 3 A, 4 F, 5 g, 6 G. M-D.

Christoph Graupner. *Two Sonatas* (A. Hoffmann—HM 121) 19pp., parts. 1 g, 2 g. Treble line of keyboard part is written out, and the figured bass is abandoned. The two instruments are treated as equals, with the violin and the keyboard treble projected as the duetting solo lines. The editor points out in the preface that these pieces are ''an enrichment of our domestic player's estate.'' Excellent preparation for J. S. Bach's *Six Sonatas* with obbligato keyboard. M-D.

Edvard Grieg. *Sonata* I Op.8 F 1866 (C. Herrmann—CFP 1340 26pp., parts; Lichtenberg—GS L980; Spiering, Ganz—CF L271) 17 min. Opening graceful movement flows in Mendelssohn–Schumann style. Second movement shows charming Norwegian folk music influence. Third movement is fresh and scintillating. M-D.

_____ *Sonata* II Op.13 G 1869 (CFP 2279 31pp., parts; Br&H; GS L525; Auer, Ganz—CF 03699) 20 min. Called the dance sonata; rhapsodic in form. Full of youthful enthusiasm and vigor. Pleasing and refined with well-sustained interest throughout the relatively large form. M-D.

_____ *Sonata* III Op.45 c 1887 (CFP 2414 45pp., parts; Spiering, Ganz—CF L786; GS L981) 24 min. Dramatic, classical form, simple lines, the most fiery and important of the three sonatas. The second movement a romanza, is one of Grieg's most beautiful works. Of these three sonatas, this one is closer to the level of other major Romantic violin sonatas (such as those by Brahms, Fauré, and Franck). D.

Camargo Guarnieri. *Sonata* Op.1/2 D 1930 (Ric BA 1957).

_____ *Sonata* III 1950 (MS available from composer: Rua Pamplona, 825 apt. 83-01-405 São Paulo, São Paulo, Brazil) 28pp., parts. 15 min. For Henryk Szering. Moderato espressivo; Terno; Decidido. Subtle nationalistic influences are present and are coupled with a complete command of the general technical resources of composition. Elastic counterpoint is resourcefully utilized. Expert craftsmanship. D.

_____ *Sonata* IV 1956 (Ric BA11508) 36pp., parts. Energico ma espressivo; Intimo; Allegro appassionato. Flexible meters, freely tonal, much rhythmic drive in final movement along with splashing chords. D.

_____ *Sonata* V 1961 (MS available from composer) 41pp., parts. Comodo: modal, well-developed thematic material. Terno: melodic writing of a high order. Gingando: syncopated; piano part has as much thematic interest as the violin part. D.

Elizabeth Jacquet de la Guerre. *Sonata* D (Borroff—University of Pittsburgh Press).

Gabriel Guillemain. *Sonata* Op.11/2 A (F. Polnauer—Sikorski 773 1972) 23pp., parts. Cello part optional. Allegro; Aria Gratioso; Presto. "The sonatas of Guillemain belong to the late epoch of the thoroughbass period and represent the galant style of the rococo" (from the preface). M-D.

George Frederick Handel. *Seven Sonatas* Op.1 (Stanley Sadie—Henle 1971). Based on the most reliable sources available. Clean edition, practical as well as scholarly. Also includes *Sonata* Op.1/6 g for oboe, marked for "Violino Solo" in Handel's autograph, which was left out of the Handel Halle edition (Br 1955). The keyboard part is simply realized, and the editor invites the more accomplished continuo player to feel free to elaborate. Editorial additions are shown in brackets. Textual commentary on each work is included. Also includes Op.1/10 g, 12 F, 13 D, 14 A, 15 E. Also available: *Six Sonatas* Op.1 (L. Bus, U. Haverkampf—Br&H 1974)

35pp., parts. Vol.I: Op.1/3 A, 10 g, 12 D. Vol.II: Op.1/13 D, 14 A, 15 E. *Sechs Sonaten* (J.P. Hinnenthal—Br 1955) Hallischer Händel-Ausgabe, Serie IV, Instrumentalmusik, Band 4. *Six Sonatas* from Op.1 (Sikorski, Wysocka-Ochiewska, Felinski—PWM) 2 vols. *Six Sonatas* from Op.1 (Auer, Friedberg—CF L846; Betti—GS L1545; Davisson, Ramin—CFP 4157A,B 2 vols.; Jacobsen—CFP 2475C,D 2 vols.; Doflein—Schott 2 vols.; Francescatti, Fuessl—IMC 2 vols.; Gevaert, Busch—Br&H 2 vols.; Maglioni—Ric ER2449; Augener 8668 2 vols.; Novello) includes Op.1/3 A, 10 g, 12 F, 13 D, 14 A, 15 E. *Four Sonatas* Op.1 (Hillemann—Schott). Available separately: Op.1/3 A (Auer, Friedberg—CF B3280; Hermann—Augener 7336; CFP). Op.1/10 g (Jensen—Augener 7426; Seiffert—Br&H; Wessely—J. Williams). Op.1/12F (Riemann—Augener 7502; Wessely—J. Williams; Br&H). Op.1/13 D (Auer, Friedberg—CF B2703; Jensen—Augener 7427; Wessely—J. Williams; Br&H). Op.1/14 A (Seiffert—Br&H; Wessely—J. Williams). Op.1/15 E (Br&H; Auer, Friedberg—CF B3325; Gibson—Augener 7377; Wessely—J. Williams).

———— *Sonata* d (Roy Howat—OUP 1975) 15pp., parts. 8 min. Musica da Camera 25. A fresh and exciting work with a fine sense of proportion between the four movements. Impeccable edition. M-D.

Algot Haquinius. *Svit* (GM 1943) 7pp., parts. Andante moderato; Andante espressivo; Allegro moderato. Post-Romantic, tonal, Sibelius-like in style. Requires large span. M-D.

Roy Harris. *Sonata in Four Movements.* 1942 (Belwin-Mills 1953) 41pp., parts. Rev. ed. 1974. Fantasy; Dance of Spring; Melody; Toccata. One of Harris's most impressive chamber works. The four large movements are freely tonal, with strong unities and bold contrasts. The movements are linked subjectively rather than thematically. The Toccata sizzles in excitement. D.

Charles Haubiel. *Sonata* d (Composers Press) 17 min. D.

Franz Joseph Haydn. The eight or nine sonatas for violin and piano of this great composer are either transcriptions or arrangements. *Eight Sonatas* (CFP 190). *Sonata* 1 G is an arrangement of piano *Trio* H. (Hoboken) XV 32. 11 min. *Sonata* 2 D is an arrangement of piano *Sonata* H.XVI 24. 10 min. *Sonata* 3 E♭ is an arrangement of piano *Sonata* H.XVI 25. *Sonata* 4 A is an arrangement of piano *Sonata* H.XVI 26. 8 min. *Sonata* 5 G is an arrangement of piano *Sonata* A♭, H.XVI 43. 10 min. *Sonata* 6 C is an arrangement of piano *Sonata* H.XVI 15. *Sonata* 7 F is an arrangement of string *Quartet* H.III 82. 19 min. *Sonata* 8 G (for violin or flute) is an arrangement of string *Quartet* H.III 81.

_____ *Nine Sonatas* (Betti—GS L1541). Includes an extra *Sonata* D.
_____ *Eight Sonatas* (David—Augener 8672).

Bernhard Heiden. *Sonata* 1954 (AMP 1961) 27pp., parts. Molto tranquillo, rubato; Molto vivace; Andante; Allegro deciso. Graceful and grateful in form and material, clear textures. Moves with ease in a neoclassic style. M-D.

Paavo Heininen. *Sonata* Op.25 1970 (Finnish Music Information Center) 25 min. One movement. Moves from Tranquillo through a Tempo giusto (Allegro moderato) section before returning to a Tranquillo, misterioso and Tranquillo al fine to conclusion. Twelve-tone. Trill is exploited in both instruments. Large span required. Expressionistic, pointillistic. D.

Everett Helm. *Sonata* (Schott 4047 1950) 28pp., parts. 19 min. Allegro; Lento ma non troppo; Presto. Contrasting movements, mildly contemporary, impressive melodic treatment. The Presto is treated contrapuntally with interspersed chorale-like episodes. Large span required. D.

Fini Henriques. *Sonata* Op.10 g (WH). A large four-movement post-Romantic work with some interest, although dated. M-D to D.

Hans Werner Henze. *Sonata* 1946 (Schott 3859) 25pp., parts. 15 min. Prélude; Nocturne; Intermezzo; Finale. Neo-Romantic style, somewhat surprising for Henze. Finale uses fast chords in alternating hands. Large span required. D.

Kurt Hessenburg. *Sonate* Op.25 F 1942 (Schott 3787) 21 min.

Lejaren A. Hiller. *Sonata* III (TP 1971) 40pp., parts. Furioso: clusters; serial; changing meters; pointillistic; spread out over entire keyboard; dynamic extremes; pianist has to play some clusters with the chin; outer notes in some chords must be played with elbows. Largo: long pedal effects with damper and sostenuto pedals; many repeated chords in low register; many strings of the bottom octave have to be hit inside piano with a large, soft tam-tam beater. Prestissimo: sweeping gestures in both instruments; sprawling layout; ends with a cluster chord; large span required. Requires virtuoso pianism throughout most of the work. D.

Paul Hindemith. *Sonata* Op.11/1 1918 (Schott) 9 min. A short two-movement work, one fast (Frisch), the other a slow dance (Im Zeitmass eines langsamer, feierlichen Tanzes) with much chromatic harmony. Extensive melodic development with harmonic barbs thrown in from time to time. M-D.

_____ *Sonata* Op.11/2 1918 (Schott) 27pp., parts. 18 min. Lebhaft; Ruhig und gemessen; Im Zeitmasse und Charakter eines geschwinden Tanzes. Brahms and Reger influence. Linear development much more important than in Op.11/1. Third section is a fast dance-movement. Lacks a uniformity of terse style but foreshadows later developments in the composer's career. D.

_____ *Sonata* E (Schott 2455 1935) 15pp., parts. 9 min. Lusty strength and clear textures in these two short movements. Not nearly as difficult as the first two sonatas. Ruhig bewegt: 9/8, SA, subjects recapitulated in reverse. Langsam: slow–very lively–slow–again lively; 6/8 seems to evolve from the 9/8 of the first movement; a lively dance contrasts with the slow sections. Connective principle binds the work formally. M-D.

_____ *Sonata* C 1939 (Schott) 12 min. More elaborate and involved than *Sonata* E. Lebhaft: short, monothematic, prelude-like, athletic, cohesive stability. Langsam: deliberately paced ABA with the mid-section a rhythmically delightful scherzo in 5/8. Fugue: rondo form, complex triple fugue, combination of subjects especially difficult for the pianist, dynamic writing; C termination is most satisfying. D.

See: VKDR, II; pp. 267–77.

Alun Hoddinott. *Sonata* II (OUP). Not truly a sonata, more a work for two to play. Cluster-like chords, cadenza, thin-textured moto perpetuo. Opening movement material returns in concluding Episodi e Coda. Plenty of technical problems for both instruments. D.

_____ *Sonata* III Op.78/1 (OUP 1973) 24pp., parts. Intense organization, serial, homogenous density, uncomprisingly dissonant at certain places, strong lyric writing. Works to a strong climax through the first movement and then unwinds palindromically. D.

Franz Anton Hoffmeister. *Sonata* Op.13 C 1795–1805 (Hans-Peter Schmitz—Nag 236 1973) 40pp., parts., 20 min. with repeats. For flute or violin and piano. See entry under duos for piano and flute.

Karl Höller. *Sonata* Op.4 (Litolff 1929, new ed. 1968) 26pp., parts.

_____ *Vierte Sonate* Op.37 F♯ (CFP 5975 1965) 36pp., parts. Allegro appassionato: SA; chromatic; arpeggi figuration; develops logically. Andante sostenuto: more diatonic and linear; long, contoured lines, chordal midsection. Agitato, tema con variazioni e fuga: quartal harmony; large arpeggiated chords; chromatic octaves and chords; theme and six contrasting variations lead to a highly chromatic fugue. Extension of Brahms–Reger tradition. D.

Arthur Honegger. *Sonate* I 1916–18 (Sal) 28pp., parts. 18 min. Andante
sostenuto; Presto; Adagio–Allegro assai. Added-note technique, crossed
hands, chromatic, glissandi, octotonic, subito dynamic changes. Multiple
meters in finale—10/4 (4+2+4) in piano with 3+3+4 in violin. Ostinati,
impressionistic, strong formal construction. Requires large span. D.

———— *Sonate* II 1919 (Sal) 11½ min. Opening movement is sensuous and
swinging in triple- and quadruple-pulse patterns. In place of a development
a fugato section is substituted. A monothematic slow movement is constructed with figuration that twines around the main theme. The finale
introduces two main ideas in the low register of the piano. D.

Alan Hovhaness. *Oror* Op.1 (CFP 1964) 6pp., parts. 3 min. A tonal, colorful
lullaby. Int.

———— *Varak* Op.47 (CFP 1971) 9pp., parts. 5 min. Andante, noble and
majestic: interplay between parts. Allegro: piano has many sixteenth-note
figurations and much pattern repetition. Contrasted movements. M-D.

———— *Khirgiz Suite* Op.73 (CFP 1968) 9pp., parts. 4 min. Variations; A
Khirgiz Tala; Allegro molto. Cumulative hypnotic effect. Each movement
revolves around a few notes. Neither dissonant nor consonant. M-D.

———— *Three Visions of Saint Mesrob* Op.198 (CPF 1963) 7pp., parts. Celestial Mountain: broken and solid chords, cluster-like. Celestial Bird: freely
measured; violin may begin at any time; piano part represents twittering of
celestial birds; pandiatonic throughout. Celestial Alphabet: harmonic
sevenths for piano. M-D.

———— *Saris* (CFP 1947) 16pp., parts. 8 min. Saris was the ancient Urarduan
love goddess. Violin opening is followed by three pages of highly repetitious writing in the style of a Saz, a long-necked, plucked string instrument
of the Near East with a small, round, convex belly. Violin and piano merge
with the two figurations heard first separately. Pedal is held for long sections. Written in the composer's international style. M-D.

Mary Howe. *Sonata* D (CFP 1962) 28pp., parts. The style is neo-Romantic,
with the piano treated in a Brahmsian manner. Effective writing, if dated
for the period. Allegro ma non troppo: SA. Lento recitativo: allegro scherzando mid-section; opening idea returns before a final allegro vivo boldly
ends the movement. Allegro non troppo: two basic ideas developed; *pp*
coda, *ppp* closing. M-D.

Herbert Howells. *Sonata* I Op.18 E 1918 (Bo&H) 16 min. One movement
with four designated sections. Fantasy-like with a kind of rhapsodic element, broad sweeping lines, contemplative, remote, shifting rhythms.
M-D.

———— *Sonata* III Op.38 e 1923 (OUP) 20 min. Poco allegro, semplice; Allegro moderato, assai ritmico; Vivace, assai ritmico. Explores new (for Howells) tonal treatment and has more dissonance than *Sonata* I. D.

Johann Nepomuk Hummel. *Sonata* Op.5/1 B♭ 1798 (Franz Samohyl—Dob 1963) 36pp., parts. DM 100. Allegro moderato; Andante con variazioni; Rondo. Piano is most important but much interplay takes place between the instruments. Delightful and grateful part writing; fun but difficult, especially for the pianist. Does not stand up too well with repeated hearings. A thorough stylistic understanding of the period is necessary to realize this work properly. M-D.

Karel Husa. *Sonata* 1972–3 (AMP) 20 min. A super-virtuoso show-piece full of spiccatos, double stops, scales, arpeggi. Contemporary sounding throughout. Difficult to follow thematic ideas in performance, but the work has much to recommend it. D.

Vincent d'Indy. *Sonata* Op.59 C (Durand 1905). A strong and original work even though the opening and the rhythmic patterns owe much to Franck. The airy and rather strange Scherzo movement is more chromatic than Franck's style and leads to a tonally ambiguous feeling. D.

John Ireland. *Sonata* I d 1909 (Galliard) 28 min. Strong lyricism. Allegro leggiardo: SA, second tonal area in the relative major, three subsidiary themes. Romance: long melodic lines, chordal episode. Rondo: Grieg influence, least satisfactory movement. M-D.
———— *Sonata* II a 1915–17 (Bo&H) 49pp., parts. 27 min. This is Ireland's masterpiece from this period. Exhibits fine craftsmanship throughout. Allegro: dramatic, rugged, craggy. Poco lento quasi adagio: lyric, elegaic, suave theme. In tempo moderato: lively popular-type melodies, releases tensions built up in first two movements. D.

Miloslav Istvan. *Sonata* 1955–6 (Panton 1971) 28pp., parts.

Charles E. Ives. *Sonata* I 1903–8 (PIC 1953) 30pp., parts. 26 min. Andante–Allegro vivace; Largo cantabile; Allegro. Abstract writing. The finely organized slow movement is extended, free, and noble, and filled with rich melodic invention and contrapuntal texture. The hymn "Watchman, Tell us of the Night!" is used with dissonant accompanied treatment in the final movement. D.
———— *Sonata* II 1902–10 (GS 1951) 26pp., parts. Portraits are offered of: Autumn: thickest of the movements. In the Barn: a square dance, in effect

the scherzo; much snap and fun here with the improvising of a country-dance fiddler; the tone-cluster "drum music" adds to the fantastic effect of the closing pages. The Revival: recalls the mounting intensity of a camp meeting and works over thoroughly the hymn tune "Nettleton" in variation technique; the closing is touchingly beautiful. D.

———— *Sonata* III 1902–14 (Sol Babitz, Ingolf Dahl—NME 1951) 26 min. Adagio (verse 1)–Andante con moto (verse 2)–Allegretto (verse 3)–Adagio (last verse); Allegro; Adagio. Abstract writing, grandly conceived, intense expression. All three movements evolve from the hymn tune "I Need Thee Every Hour," although the derivations are very obscure. The first movement is in reality variations with improvisatory excursions. Verse 3 is a fast, tricky, syncopated dance tune with ragtime elements extravagantly thrown in. The Adagio is very beautiful with the hymn tune finally heard in its original form. D.

———— *Sonata* IV 1912–15, "Children's Day at the Camp Meeting" (AMP 1942) 20pp., parts. 10 min. Allegro; Largo; Allegro. This work, based on hymn tunes, has a special American flavor. The final movement quotes from the hymn "Shall We Gather at the River," with the piano providing a strong dissonant chordal setting. The weaker registers of the violin are pitted against a full piano part.

See: Laurence Perkins, "The Sonatas for Violin and Piano by Charles Ives," Ph.D. diss., University of Rochester, Eastman School of Music, 1961.

Leoš Janáček. *Ballada* (Philharmusica 1974) 8pp., parts. For violin, flute, or oboe and piano. Undulating passage work (32nd notes) interspersed with two chromatic chordal episodes. M-D.

———— *Dumka* 1880 (Hudební Matice 1947). More ballade-like than a true "dumka." Long lines. Not the best of this composer. M-D.

———— *Sonata* 1913, rev. during World War I, completed in 1921 (Artia 1966). Written in Janáček's nationalist and rugged style. Uses difficult keys (c♯, d♭, e♭, g♯) and broad deliberate tempos. Con moto: SA; mainly monothematic, second subject being an extension of the first (new theme in coda); tremolo in piano part accounts for atmospheric sonorities; abrupt tempo changes. Ballada: more tuneful; ABA design; exploits a folk-like theme in B section with fluid chromatic runs in both instruments used to great effect. Adagio: almost mosaic-like in small sections; brings back some of the unusual figurations from the first movement. Fascinating rhythmic procedure, unusual texture and highly original writing, especially for the piano. Strong mood and texture continuity maintained in each movement. D.

Ivan Jirko. *Sonata* 1959 (Artia) 61pp., parts. Con moto tranquillo; Allegro moderato; Andante–Allegro non troppo. Freely tonal, octotonic, broken chords in alternating hands, tertial harmonies. Second movement is toccata-like and contains arpeggi figuration. Strong rhythmic drive in the finale. MC, some nationalistic coloring. Large span required. M-D to D.

Lockrem Johnson. *Sonata Breve* Op.26 1948, rev. 1949, 1953 (Dow) 6 min. Lyrical, intensely expressive, rich in constructive melodic devices that give it an organic coherence and vitality. Unusual and well-calculated form. M-D.

Charles Jones. *Sonatina* 1942 (CFP 6019) 16pp., parts. 7 min. Allegro; Larghetto; Allegro deciso. Positive influence of Darius Milhaud felt. Full of lyricism, sound structure, rhythmic vigor and brilliance. Imaginative and unique unconventional compositional language. Requires a firm rhythmic control. D.

Richard Jones. *Four Suites* (G. Beechey—OUP 1974) 1 A, 2 g, 3 D, 4 B♭. Each suite has five movements: a Preludio, usually serious in character, followed by four dance movements. Fluently written, attractive entertainment music. The continuo player may realize his own bass part, for the continuo part contains only the bass line and the original figures. Int. to M-D.

Mihail Jora. *Sonata* Op.46 (Editura Muzicala 1964) 36pp., parts. Allegro brillante: SA, 5/8, chromatic changing meters. Andante cantabile: ABA; long lines; chromatic; constant tonal insecurity; large span required. Allegro assai: duple with some triple interrupting from time to time; triplets; dancelike section has shifting rhythms; dramatic run from top to bottom of keyboard; thankfully ends on a D chord! A big "splashing" kind of work, colorful if a little contrived at spots. D.

Pal Kadosa. *Suite* Op.6 (Bo&H) Five movements, no fingerings, piano part more effective than violin. M-D.
——— *Sonata* II Op.58 (EMB 1962). Preambule: rhapsodic. Scherzo: trio is most successful part. Finale: sustained sections contrasted with dancelike sections. M-D.

Heinrich Kaminski. *Hauskonzert* 1941 (Br 2050 1973) 28pp., parts. Praeludium; Opfertanz; Frühlingstanz; Finale. Neobaroque style with a few complex polyphonic entanglements set in a freely tonal framework. M-D.

Armin Kaufmann. *Sonatina* Op.53/1 (Dob 1974) 36pp., parts. Perky rhythms, tunes seem to be inspired by Bartók and Hindemith, mildly contemporary sounding. M-D.

Ulysses Kay. *Partita* A 1950 (ACA) 15 min.

———— *Sonatina* 1943 (ACA) 9 min. Easy flowing, warm sentiments. M-D.

Donald Keats. *Polarities* 1970 (MS available from composer: % Lamont School of Music, University of Denver, Denver, CO 80210) 15pp., parts. Andante: serially influenced; intense; builds to dramatic climax; quiet ending; free cadenza for violin; piano part requires large span. Allegro: alternation of free and strict tempi, changing meters, fiery conclusion. Requires a first-rate pianist and experienced ensemble players. Can be stunning with the proper performers. D.

Robert Kelly. *Sonata* Op.22 1952 (ACA) 25pp., parts. 14 min. Vigorous; Slow; Moderate. Freely tonal around e, fluent rhythms, clear textures, traditional forms, spontaneous quality, forceful and distinctive style. M-D.

Harrison Kerr. *Sonata* (Berben 1973) 28pp., parts. Large one-movement work. Dramatic gestures in the short Tempo liberamente introduction lead to a chromatic, secco, staccato Allegretto, in which there is much sixteenth-note motion. Changing tempi provide contrast for rest of work. Highly chromatic, but tonal. Requires first-rate pianistic equipment. D.

Willem Kersters. *Partita* Op.9 1956 (CeBeDeM) 24pp., parts. 9½ min. Intrada; Allemande; Courante; Sarabande; Gigue. Neoclassic structures, chromatic language. Relies heavily on octotonic technique. D.

Karen Khachaturian. *Sonata* Op.1 1957 (USSR) 44pp., parts. Allegro; Andante; Presto. This work has a difficult time achieving its goal. Each movement has some interesting colorful material but a tendency to wander prevents much direction. Large span required. M-D to D.

Leon Kirchner. *Duo* (Mercury 1947) 12 min. Aaron Copland wrote of this rhapsodic work: "Kirchner's best pages prove that he reacts strongly (to today's unsettled world); they are charged with an emotional impact and explosive power that is almost frightening in intensity. Whatever else may be said, this is music that is most certainly 'felt.' No wonder his listeners have been convinced." *Notes,* VII (1950): 434.

———— *Sonata Concertante* (Mercury 1952) 28pp., parts. 22 min. In one continuous intense and gloomy yet lyrical movement with "attacca" separating the Adagio molto from the Grazioso. Many metronome markings (30!). Varied musical texture, chromatic idiom, dissonant, driving rhythms. Many accelerations and ritardandos shift mood, texture, and rhythms; these are vital to successful performance. Separate cadenzas for both violin and piano provide a unique blending of the instruments. A complex, involved work requiring the best from experienced and highly sensitive performers. D.

Kenneth B. Klaus. *Diferencias for Violin, Piano, and Plastic Knitting Needle with Fisherman's Cork* 1972 (MS from composer: School of Music, Louisiana State University, Baton Rouge, LA 70803) 24pp., parts. Clusters, needle used as plectrum and plays glissandi on strings, cork used on needle-head in the manner of a drumstick, freely tonal, ad lib repetitions, harmonics, independent tempi between instruments, sudden dynamic extremes, octotonic. Mixture of traditional and avant-garde. Requires large span. D.

Giselher Klebe. *Sonata* Op.14 (Schott 1953) 8½ min. Short, three-movement work in Webernesque style, twelve-tone. The piece is full-textured but delicate sounding, colorful and not contrived. Major and minor seconds are in abundance both vertically and linearly. D.

_____ *Sonate* Op.66 (Br 1973) 33pp., parts. Three movements. Written for Boris Blacher's seventieth birthday and based on the letters B_ _ _ _ (E)s B_ _ ACHE_ from his name. Written in a lyric, neo-Impressionistic, dodecaphonic-like texture. M-D.

Erland von Koch. *Rytmiska Bagateller* 1957–75 (GM 1976) 24pp., parts. Ten short pieces using fresh and unusual rhythms and meters. Originally written for solo piano. Violin part may also be played by a flute, oboe, recorder, clarinet, or other instrument. A fine introduction to contemporary techniques. M-D.

Joonas Kokkonen. *Duo* 1955 (Finnish Music Information Center) 50pp., parts. 17½ min. Allegro moderato; Allegretto grazioso; Un poco adagio– Allegro. Neoclassic; much unison writing two octaves apart; serial overtones provide much chromatic usage; clear and consistent stylistic idiom. The two instruments are thoroughly integrated in an exciting manner. D.

Egon Kornauth. *Sonatine* Op.46a (Dob 1959) 16pp., parts. 11 min. Available for flute (violin) and piano as well as for viola and piano. Rondino; Intermezzo; Siciliano. Centers around e–E, chromatic, quartal harmony, thin textures, flowing, appealing neoclassic writing. M-D.

György Kósa. *Gaba Szonáta* (Zenmükiado Vállalat 1964) 8pp., parts. Allegretto; Sostenuto tragico; Vivace. More like a short Hungarian dance suite. Mildly contemporary, attractive. Int.

Hans Kox. *Sonata* IV 1966 (Donemus).

Ernst Křenek. *Sonata* 1944–45 (UE 11839) 24pp., parts. 14 min. Andante con moto; Adagio; Allegro assai, vivace. Twelve-tone technique similar to serial method used in Křenek's Seventh Quartet, atonal. "The large figures in the staves refer to the rhythmic units (half-notes in the first and second, quarter-notes in the third movement). All trills end with the upper (auxiliary) note" (note in score). D.

Rodolphe Kreutzer. *Sonate* I C (J. Hardy—Sal 5243) 15pp., parts. Moderato; Andantino; Rondo. Comfortable if not the most idiomatic writing. M-D.

Gail Kubik. *Sonatina* 1941 (SPAM) 18pp., parts. Moderately fast, unhurried: contrary thirds, flowing melody, triple meter divided in half, flexible meters, dance rhythms. Fairly slow, but with movement: long flowing lines, moving thirds, impressionistic. In the manner of a Toccata—fast, briskly, with rough force: driving rhythms; subito dynamic changes; conclusion is to be played "savagely." M-D.

Meyer Kupferman. *Fiddle Energizer* 1971 (Gen 1973) 10pp., parts. Repeated harmonic seconds, varied textures, freely tonal, contemporary "Alberti bass" treatment, broad chords at conclusion. Mildly contemporary. M-D.
_____ *Fantasy Sonata* (Gen 1972) Commissioned by the Library of Congress. 29pp., parts. Rhapsodic, large gestures, repeated patterns and ostinati, grateful writing. Requires a few effects inside the piano. M-D.

Ladislav Kupkovic. *Souvenir* 1971 (UE) 16pp., parts. Explanations in German, French, and English. "'Souvenir' is the third part of the musical non-stop-revue 'K-Rhapsodie.'"

Paul Kurzbach. *Sonatine* 1962 (Litolff 5366) 18pp., parts. 12 min. Allegro moderato; Aria; Finale. Tonal, mildly contemporary. Aria is Impressionistic. M-D.

Toivo Kuula. *Sonata* e 1907 (Fazer) 42pp., parts. Allegro agitato; Adagio; Allegro molto. Overworked thematic treatment by use of imitation and sequences, lengthy, much decorative figuration, long phrases and climaxes well-sustained, clear formal structure, Romantic harmonies. D.

Ezra Laderman. *Duo* (OUP 92.601 1971) 30pp., parts. 15 min. Three movements. Interval of minor second is exploited. Dissonant, semi-serial. D.

———— *Sonata* 1958–9 (OUP 92.302) 22pp., parts. 15 min. Three movements, large gestures for both instruments. D.

Edouard Lalo. *Sonata* Op.12 D (Durand) 29pp., parts. Allegro moderato; Variations; Rondo. Classical influence is present in this striking and beautifully written work, from the Beethovenesque opening of the first movement to the Mendelssohnian second movement theme and variations. Even Brahms is present to assist when Lalo leans on more Romantic techniques, as in the finale rondo, a moto-perpetuo with quasi-rhapsodic characteristics. D.

Philibert de Lavigne. *Six Sonatas* Op.2 ca.1740 (Willi Hillemann—Noetzel). Published separately. Each work also includes a cello part ad lib. See detailed listing under duos for piano and flute.

Henri Lazarof. *Rhapsody* 1966 (AMP 1972) 13pp., parts. Written in a full-blooded and highly intense international style. A few harmonics, long pedals, quasi-cadenza passages, clusters. The rest uses traditional notation. Dynamic extremes, flexible tempi, pointillistic inspiration. Exciting, aggravating, and violent effects. D.

Lojze Lebic. *Atelier* 1973 (Društva Slovenskih Skladateljev) 10pp. Two copies necessary for performance. Explanations in Croatian and English.

Jean Marie Leclair. *Zwölf Sonaten für Violine und Generalbass nebst einem Trio für Violine Violoncell und Generalbass Op.2, 2. Buch der Sonaten* Paris ca.1732 (R. Eitner—Br&H 1903) Vol. XXVII, Publikation aelterer praktischer und theoretischer Musikwerke. Reprint BB 1966). In spite of the title, there are twelve pieces in all; the trio is No.8 of the dozen.

———— *Sonatas* Op.5, Op.9, and Op.15 (R.E. Preston—A-R Editions) Recent Researches in the Music of the Baroque Era: Vol. IV: Op.5, Sonatas I–V 1968; Vol.V: Op.5, Sonatas VI–XII 1969; Vol.X; Op.9, Sonatas I–VI 1970; Vol.XI: Op.9, Sonatas VII–XII, Op.15, Posthumous Sonata 1971.

———— *Six Sonatas* (M. Pincherle, L. Boulay—l'OL 1952). Published separately: *Sonata* Op.1/8; *Sonatas* Op.2/1, 12; *Sonatas* Op.5/1, 4; *Sonata* Op.9/4.

———— *Sonata* Op.2/3 C (H. Ruf—Ric SY500) 10pp., parts.

———— *Sonata* Op.2/11 (H. Ruf—Ric SY501) 7pp., parts.

———— *Sonata* Op.5/6 c "Le Tombeau" (F. David—IMC 1945) 11pp., parts. Grave; Allegro ma non troppo; Gavotte; Allegro. M-D.

———— *Sonata* Op.5/5 (H. Ruf—Br 3414) 8pp., parts.

———— *Sonata* Op.5/7 a (H. Ruf—Br 3415) 12pp., parts. Largo; Allegro;

Adagio; Tempo di Gavotta. Leclair's "personal style unites the best qualities of the Italian style, the nobility and pathos of the Corelli school, with
the lively spirit of French composition" (from the Preface). M-D.

_____ *Sonata* Op.9/2 e (F. Polnauer—JWC 1970) 20pp., parts. Continuo
Series No.3. For violin or flute and keyboard. Andante; Allemanda—
Allegro ma non troppo; Sarabanda—Adagio; Menuetto—Allegro non
troppo; fifth movement "Not for Flute" but for violin only. The dance
movements in particular show the influence of Leclair's earlier profession
as a dance master. M-D.

_____ *Sonata* Op.9/1 (Polnauer—CF B3347).

_____ *Sonata* Op.9/4 A (Polnauer—CF B3348).

_____ *Sonata* Op.9/5 (Polnauer—Schott 1969).

_____ *Sonata* Op.9/6 D (Polnauer—CF B3349).

Jacques Leduc. *Sonate* Op.27 1967 (CeBeDeM) 33pp., parts. 18 min.
Moderato; Tempo Scherzando; Sostenuto; leads directly to Ritmico, ma
non troppo, Vivo. Written in a colorful style that has characteristics of both
Poulenc and Prokofiev. D.

Simon Le Duc. *Four Sonatas* (Doflein—Schott 1964) 2 vols. Op.4/1, 6;
Op.1/1, Op.4/4. Beautifully written, elegant and cultivated taste. Grateful
to play. M-D.

Noël Lee. *Dialogues* (TP 1958) 12pp., parts. Opens with an Adagio,
recitative-like, chromatic, octotonic section. Moves to a Moderato syncopated section interspersed with linear lines. A sustained chordal section
follows with thick but quiet sonorities. A fugue-like short section is followed by the sustained, chordal section but *ff*. These basic ideas are varied
in further treatment with a coda that resembles the opening section.
Chromatic style. D.

Benjamin Lees. *Sonata* I (Bo&H 1953) 20 min. Neoclassic style with
Romantic influences. D.

_____ *Sonata* II 1972–3 (Bo&H) 43pp., parts. Moderato; Adagio; Allegro.
Interval of the seventh operates in various ways throughout this work.
Treatment of thematic material suggests serial procedures but closer inspec-
tion reveals this is not the case. Although no key signature is used the aura
of tonality is present. Plenty of sequence is employed. The piano introduces
the second movement with alternating bitonal harmonies; this movement is
a series of crescendos and diminuendos with a bitonal conclusion. The final
Allegro is toccata-like and moves to a brilliant assertive ending with the
final chord built of major sevenths. A work of fine craft and confidence. D.

René Leibowitz. *Rhapsody Concertante* Op.36 1955 (Boelke-Bomart) 7 min.
———— *Sonata* Op.12 1944 (Boelke-Bomart) 6 min.

Kenneth Leighton. *Sonata* I a (Lengnick 1951) 35pp., parts. Allegro molto appassionata: arpeggi figuration; chords; ostinato-like right-hand treatment; freely centered around a. Attacca second movement—Lento e liberamente: Romantic chordal sonorities; builds to *fff* climax; returns to opening idea and diminishes to *ppp* closing. Attacca third movement—Presto energico: 6/8; highly rhythmic; piano has second idea in G; cantabile; closes with reference from main idea of second movement; a rollicking good movement. M-D.
———— *Sonata* II Op.20 (Lengnick 1956) 41pp., parts. 18½ min. Fluent, neo-Romantic, large-scale work, eclectic idiom, some twelve-tone themes and popular modernistic harmonic usage. D.
Technical craftsmanship with a tendency toward contrapuntal complexity permeates both sonatas.

Guillaume Leku. *Sonata* G (Lerolle; IMC) 55pp., parts. 32 min. Reminiscent of Franck, with its restless chromaticism and bold sweeps. Beautiful if somewhat rambling music, especially the passionate finale. Piano part is highly challenging. Exemplifies many felicitous devices in expressing similar ideas with both instruments. D.

Alfonso Letelier. *Sonatina* 1953 (IU) 18pp., parts. Adagio; Allegro moderato. Contemporary treatment of harmonies and melodies; interval of diminished octave plays an important part in opening movement. Neoclassic influence mixed with a personal style. M-D.

Peter T. Lewis. *Of Bells . . . and Time, a Dialogue for Violin and Piano* (Merion 1975) 11pp., 2 copies needed for performance.

Douglas Lilburn. *Sonata* 1950 (Price Milburn) 10 min. One continuous movement, diatonic with chromatic inflections. Well written for both instruments. M-D.

Bo Linde. *Sonata* Op.10 (Busch 1972) 30pp., parts.

Malcolm Lipkin. *Sonata* (JWC 1957) 24pp., parts. 15½ min. Allegro; Adagio; Presto. Mildly contemporary writing. Contains some especially dramatic gestures in the Presto. D.

Franz Liszt. *Duo Sonata* 1832–5 (Tibor Serly—PIC 1957) 52pp., parts. Four movements of broad sweeping lines, all based on Chopin's *Mazurka* c♯ Op.6/2, in cyclic form. The mazurka is subjected to a full range of sophisticated thematic metamorphoses. One theme, a folksong from Liszt's piano pieces "Glanes de Woronince" appears in "Paganini harmonics." Chopin's and Paganini's influences are reflected throughout the complete work. Moderato: freely treated SA; brief introduction by piano; violin enters with mazurka theme; a clever fugue closes exposition; development contains varied treatment of the thematic segments; many pianistic passages point to Debussy and Impressionism fifty years later; movement ends attacca. Tema con Variazioni: theme is divided into four thematic sections; Paganini's influence clearly seen in piano part; bars 299–300 allude to Chopin's *Etude* E Op.10/3. Allegretto: a miniature concerto with syncopated jazzlike rhythms, strange-sounding chord sequences and modulations. Allegro con brio: a lively rondo, ends with a brilliant coda. D.

See: Alan Walker, "Liszt's Duo Sonata," *MT* 1589 (July 1975): 620–21.

_____ *Grand Duo über die Romance 'Le Marin' von Philippe Lafont* and *Epithalam* (Hochzeitmusik) (Z. Gardonyi—EMB and Br).

_____ *La Notte* (Night) 1864–6 (R. C. Lee. Score available from the editor: 4915 Wallingford North, Seattle, WA 98103). This work, in a Lento molto funebre mood, is prefaced by a few verses by Michelagniolo Buonarroti. The main body of the work is in ABA design. A four-bar introduction in e is followed by a funeral march mood in c♯, which leads directly into a soaring angelico theme in A. This theme gains in intensity and finally returns, in a dramatic way, to the opening funebre theme. The piano part has more interest than the violin part. Dotted rhythms with sustained chords make up much of the piano part. An effective character piece showing many characteristics of Liszt's later style. M-D.

Pietro Locatelli. *Sei Sonate da Camera per Violino e Basso dall' Op.6* (G. Benvenuti, E. Polo, M. Abbado—Fondazione Eugenio Bravi 1956) *I Classici Musicali Italiani,* Vol.14. Includes sonatas 1–6 of the twelve sonatas in this opus. *Sonata Op.6/12* (M. Abbado—Ric 1970).

_____ *Sonata* D (Lemoine).

_____ *Sonata* E (C. Barison—Casisch 1965). Overly realized.

_____ *Sonata* f "Le Tombeau" (CFP Sch27).

_____ *Sonata* G (Moffat, Mlynarczyk—Simrock).

_____ *Sonata* g (Carisch).

Nikolai Lopatnikoff. *Fantasia Concertante* (MCA).

_____ *Sonata* II Op.32 1948 (MCA). Neoclassical with much dissonance, but strongly tonal. M-D.

István Lorand. *Sonata* (EMB 1967). Appassionata: rhapsodic. Scherzando.

Semplice, moderato: theme with five variations. Mildly contemporary. Excellent choice for the professional duo. D.

Otto Luening. *Sonata* 1917 (Highgate; also published in Vol.II of the American Society of University Composers Journal of Musical Scores, through J. Boonin) 19pp., parts. Luening considers this to be his first professional composition. One movement with two contiguous sections: Allegro marcato; Allegro fugato. Freely tonal, tempo changes within large sections, dramatic gestures in strong disjunct octaves, rhythmic imitation. Presto coda. Effective. D.

———— *Sonata* II (Galaxy) 30pp., parts. Maestoso–Allegro vivace e con brio: chromatic runs in one hand; chords in the other; broken chordal figuration; sectional tempo contrasts; requires large span. Andante con moto: octotonic; piano has fine share of thematic material; varied tempi; strong pianistic figuration. D.

———— *Sonata* III 1950 (Galaxy) 24pp., parts. Andante tranquillo: flowing line with sixteenth-note broken figuration in piano; contrapuntal; freely tonal; works to expressive and broad closing; requires large span. Variations: neoclassic sixteen-bar theme; variation treatment ranges from scherzo-like to Allegro, alla marcia; intense conclusion. A beautiful and effective work. M-D to D.

Robert McBride. *Depression Sonata* (ACA) 15 min.

Charles McLean. *Sonata* Op. 1/2 g (D. Johnson—OUP 1975) 6pp., parts. Musica da Camera 23. Preface in English and German. Adagio; Allegro; Adagio; Allegro. These movements show a slight influence of Corelli and Handel. In accordance with the practice of the time, the use of a cello or bassoon to reinforce the keyboard bass is desirable but not essential. Serviceable edition. Int. to M-D.

Ernst Mahle. *Sonatina* 1955 (Ric 1972) 5pp., parts. Allegro moderato: SA, one basic thematic idea cleverly worked over. M-D.

———— *Sonata* 1968 (Tonos 1973) 24pp., parts. 12½ min. Allegro moderato: SA, serially organized. Andante: piano provides subtle chordal background for violin. Vivace: linear writing between the two instruments; some changing meters; chromatic; pianist must tap on wooden part of piano. D.

Arthur Malawski. *Sonate sur des thèmes de Janiewicz* 1951 (PWM).

Riccardo Malipiero. *Sonata* 1956 (SZ) 23 min. Attractive, eclectic, fairly conservative idiom. M-D.

Francisco Manalt. *Sonatas* I–II (P. José A. de Donostia—Instituto Español de Musicologia 1955) 27pp. I E: Larghetto; Allegro; Tempo di Minuetto. II F: Largo; Vivace grazioso. Both sonatas are written in a classic Spanish style, somewhat similar to Soler's. M-D.

Frank Martin. *Sonata* Op.1 g (Hug 1914) 43pp., parts. Quasi recitative-Allegro maestoso; Scherzo; Andantino piacevole; Allegro con fuoco. Written in a style that owes something to Franck, Richard Strauss, and Mahler. Reveals talent but not much originality. D.
_____ *Sonata* E 1931–2 (UE 12874) 28pp., parts. 15 min. Trés vif; Chaconne (Adagio); Finale (ben moderate). Dense and complex textures, extended. Each movement is written in a continuous nonsymmetrical form. The Chaconne embraces the baroque style. D.

Jean Martinon. *Second Sonatine* Op.19/2 (Billaudot). One movement. Opens with an Adagio that briefly returns later. Main part of the work is fast and concludes with an extended Presto and Coda. M-D.
_____ *Duo: Musique en Forme de Sonate* Op.47 (Schott 1959). Four large movements. Opening and closing movements are in SA design. Second movement, Molto vivace, is a scherzo with trio. The third, Lento, treats the instruments differently: the piano has more disjointed lines and rough rhythmic treatment while the violin has more cantabile phrases. This work is for the concert ensemble and both this work and the *Sonatine* treat the instruments equally. D.

Bohuslav Martinů. *Sonata* C 1919 (Panton 1973) 71pp., parts.
_____ *Sonata* d 1926 (Panton 1966) Allegro moderato; Andante moderato; Allegro.
_____ *Sonata* I 1929 (Leduc) 19 min. Allegro: opens with long solo violin passage and has a longer violin solo before conclusion of movement; the duo sections are a fox-trot. Andante: more violin solos, slower dance rhythms. Allegretto–Allegro con brio: piano gets the solos here—that is the most interesting aspect of this movement. Plenty of lively rhythmic wit. M-D.
_____ *Sonata* II 1931 (Sal) 11½ min. Allegro moderato: a bright tune in D opens the movement; much interplay between the instruments with the two main ideas. Larghetto: diffuse wanderings eventually arrive at a climax and wither away. Poco allegretto: flexible meters that seem to have no reason and weaken the perpetual-motion rhythmic drive. M-D.
_____ *Sonatina* 1937 (V. Nopp—Gen 1970) 15pp., parts. 9 min. Moderato: folk-like melodic ideas. Andante: much repetition of ideas, octotonic. Poco allegretto: lively dance rhythms make this the most successful movement. M-D.

———— *Five Madrigal Stanzas* 1943 (AMP) 10½ min. Dedicated to Albert Einstein. Strong rhythmic orientation. D.

———— *Sonata* III 1944 (AMP 1950) 21 min. Poco allegro; Adagio; Scherzo; Lento–Poco allegro.

———— *Rapsodie Tchèque* 1945 (ESC 1962) 17pp., parts. Lento opening is followed by other contrasting sections. Basically diatonic but contains a broad harmonic range encompassing simple progressions juxtaposed with more complex ones. Czech dance rhythms are present. M-D.

See: John Clapham, "Martinů's Instrumental Style," *MR*, XXIV (1963): 158. Richart Kent, "The Violin and Piano Sonatas of Bohuslav Martinů," Ph.D. diss., University of Illinois, 1973, 126pp. (University Microfilm, 73-17, 621).

William Mathias. *Sonata* Op.15 (OUP 1963) 24pp., parts. 14 min. Molto vivace: thin textures are juxtaposed against thicker ones; flexible meters; freely chromatic; bitonal implications; sweeping scales before coda; *pp* conclusion. Lento, ma con moto: long lines for the piano; sustaining quality of piano very important; rondo form; attacca senza pausa. Lento–Allegro ritmico: four-bar flowing arpeggio introduction leads directly into Allegro ritmico section characterized by martial quality with subject in the violin soon tossed back and forth between the instruments. Second section keeps martial idea in violin while piano has leggiero sixteenth-note figuration. These two figurations lock in battle and eventually unwind with a final chord socked by the pianist. M-D.

Nikolai Medtner. *Sonata* Op.21 b 1910 (USSR Complete Works, Vol. 7; Edition Russe de Musique) 30pp., parts. 20 min. A serious if somewhat dry work of restrained contemplation, except in the final movement, where the clang of bells and jubilant sounds make this movement one of the most vivid and imaginative in the duo repertoire. D.

———— *Sonata* Op.44 G (Zimmermann 1924; USSR) 59pp., parts. Three movements. The first movement opens with a mood of concentrated and austere emotion and continues with a sustained academic artistry. The second movement is a grandiose set of variations. The whole work displays profound seriousness and requires enormous stamina from both performers (as well as the audience!). D.

———— *Sonata Epica* Op.57 e (Novello 1936; USSR) 84pp., parts. Four movements. Suffers from numerous motives that are not melodically distinctive and do not lend themselves to developmental technique. The problem of "heavenly length" is also present. D.

All three sonatas are admirably laid out for both instruments.

Nelly Mele Lara. *Sonata* (PIC 1971) 62pp., parts. Neoclassic orientation.

Allegro moderato: 4/4, b, SA, serious opening, second idea more dance-like. Allegretto grazio: 2/2, e–g, clear lines, chromatic, imitation; mid-section 4/4, e♭, more chordal; opening section returns. Allegro con brio: 4/4, b, rondo with contrasting episodes; piano provides driving figuration punctuated with widespread chords; brilliant coda concludes work. D.

Alfred Mendelssohn. *Sonata Brevis* (Editura Muzicala 1964) 36pp., parts. Allegretto, affettuoso; Vivo, con fuoco; Lento, rubato–quasi recitative; Presto. Colorful mildly contemporary writing with a middle-European flavor that adds interest. M-D.

Felix Mendelssohn. *Sonata* Op.4 f 1823 (F. Hermann—CFP No. 1732; Rietz—Br&H; Rauch—Litolff) 18 min. Three movements. Opening violin recitatives in first and third movements recall Beethoven's piano sonata Op.31/2. Bold harmonies add interest. The simple melody of the slow movement has a bit more originality to it with hints of Weber present. Problems of balance occur but this impassioned, almost rhapsodic piece should not be overlooked by the aspiring young student and/or amateur. M-D.

_____ *Sonata* F 1838 (Y. Menuhin—CFP 6075) 38pp., parts. 19 min. Contains a facsimile from the autograph and a preface by Menuhin. This recently published sonata contains similarities between the *String Quartet* Op.44/1 and the cello *Sonata* Op.45, all composed during the same year. Allegro vivace: excitement builds; suavity and refinement always present. Adagio: a simple, lovely, and elegaic movement full of the sentimental characteristics frequently associated with Mendelssohn; the performers can control some of this. Assai vivace: an elfin flight that constantly intertwines both piano and violin parts. The whole piece is a fine work and worthy of more performances.
See: VKDR, II; pp.91–97 for more discussion.

Peter Mennin. *Sonata Concertante* 1956 (CF 04113). Solidly crafted with clear and rugged melodic lines, transparent harmonic fabric, and insistent, propulsive rhythms. Vigorously energetic but logically developed and neatly structured. A dramatic tour de force for both players. D.

Olivier Messiaen. *Thème et Variations* (Leduc 1932) 14pp., parts. 8 min. A 28-bar melody constructed in AABA[1] design of 7, 7, 6, and 8 bars, respec-tively. Adheres somewhat closely to the shape of the theme in the five variations. A highly accomplished and effective work. M-D.

Paul Baudouin Michel. *Sonate* 1960 (CeBeDeM) 18 min.
_____ *Serenade Concertante* 1962 (J. Maurer) 11½ min.
_____ *Ballade—jeu* (CeBeDeM 1976) 12pp., parts. 5 min.

Darius Milhaud. *Sonata* I 1911 (Durand) 35pp., parts. Lent et robuste: centers around d♯, chordal, arpeggiation, tremolo. Joyeux: trés décidé et trés large section before final two bars of Lent closes the movement. Trés lent: 6/8 rocking feeling, four sharps but feels more like B; mid-section in C, 5/4, with piano taking much chordal figuration; B closing in rocking character. Trés rhythmé, joyeux: C♯, arpeggiation in piano while violin supplies most melodic emphasis; contrasting section in Moins vite, trés rhythmé; rhythmic activity is most important element in this movement. M-D.

——— *Sonata* II 1917 (Durand) 25pp., parts. Straightforward handling of polytonality, canonic writing, many "wrong-note" sounds. M-D.

Charles Mills. *Sonata* I (ACA) 17 min.

——— *Sonata* II 1941 (ACA) 20 min. Intense, aristocratic, reticent, strong melodies, exquisitely idiomatic writing. D.

——— *Sonata* III (ACA) 30 min.

——— *Sonatine* (ACA) 8 min.

Jean-Joseph Mondonville. *Pièces de Clavecin en Sonates avec Accompagnement de Violon* Op.3 ca.1734 (M. Pincherle, Publications de la Société française de Musicologie, Première Série, Tome IX, 1969— Heugel). Sonatas 1 g, 2 F, 3 B♭, 4 C, 5 G, 6 A.
Available separately:*Sonata* 4 C (C. Saint-Saëns—Durand).*Sonata* 2 F (W. Höckner—Heinrichshofen 1963). Keyboard instrument is the dominant part; violin has supporting role but is never dispensible. Keyboard part is realized. "All sonatas in Op.3, except No.1, have 3 movements each, typically in the order of a fugal or imitative allegro, an 'Aria' of moderate tempo in binary design with repeated 'halves,' and a similarly binary 'Giga' in compound or 'Allegro' in alla breve meter" (SCE, p. 619). Left hand mainly provides support. Sonata No.2 is an excellent example of the "accompanied sonata," which displays an equality between the violin and the keyboard. The violin seemingly has the bass line with numerous leaps. As Louis-Claude Daquin wrote in 1752, Mondonville "has so ably married the clavecin to his favorite instrument" (Lionel de la Laurencie, *L'École française de violon de Lully à Viotti*, 3 vols., Paris: Delagrave, 1922–24).

——— *Sonata* Op.4/2 C ca.1735 (F. Polnauer—Heinrichshofen 1970) 19pp., parts. Andantino; Allegro; Aria; Giga. One of the earliest sonatas to introduce harmonics. M-D.

Lawrence Moss. *Sonata* (Seesaw).

Wolfgang A. Mozart. *Jugendsonaten I: Four Sonatas for Keyboard and Violin* K.6–9 (E. Reeser—Br 1967) 55pp., parts. Rev. separate edition, based on W. A. Mozart New Complete Edition. K.6 C, K.7 D, K.8 B♭,

K.9 G. These sonatas are for keyboard with optional violin accompaniment. Each has three movements and concludes with a double minuet. Keyboard part has more interest, and the violin part stays out of the way. Int. to M-D.

Available separately: K.6, 7, 8, 9 (Zeitlin, Levy—Markert).

_____ *Jugendsonaten II: Six Sonatas for Keyboard and Violin* K.10–15 (W. Plath, W. Rehm—Br 1969) K.10 B♭, K.11 G, K.12 A, K.13 F, K.14 C, K.15 B♭. These sonatas date from 1764 and mark the historical point at which the piano trio and the accompanied piano sonata..began to diverge as musical forms. They are the first step in the transition from the keyboard sonata accompanied ad lib. to the later classical piano trio. Valuable preface. Int. to M-D.

_____ *Jugendsonaten III: Six Sonatas for Keyboard and Violin* K.26–31 (E. Reeser—Br 1964). K.26 E♭, K.27 G, K.28 C, K.29 D, K.30 F, K.31 B♭. The title of this set, Op.4, indicates "with the accompaniment of the violin," so the violin is not ad lib. even though the keyboard is still the dominant partner.

_____ *Sonatas for the Youth* (Szelényi—EMB) 2 vols.

_____ *Sonaten für Klavier und Violine* K.196–570 (E. F. Schmid, W. Lampe, K. Röhrig—Henle 1969) 2 vols. Vol.I: K.301 G, K.302 E♭, K.303 C, K.304 e, K.305 A, K.306 D, K.376 F, K.296 C, K.377 F, K.378 B♭, K.379 G, K.380 E♭. Vol.II: K.402 A, K.454 B♭, K.481 E♭, K.526 A, K.547 F, K.359 *Variations* G "La Bergère Célimène," K.360 *Variations* g "Hélas, j'ai perdu mon amant," K.403 C, K.570 B♭. Practical and scholarly edition. Excellent preface includes a discussion of the chronology, background of each work, and sources consulted. Mozart brought the violin sonata to a successful birth and gave the equal partnership its first masterpieces. Note placement of the word *piano* before *violin* in these mature sonatas.

Available separately: *Sonata* K.296 C (GS 8). *Sonata* K.301 G (PWM). *Sonata* K.304 e (Kehr, Schröter—Schott; GS 4). *Sonata* K.305 A (Kehr, Schröter—Schott). *Sonata* K.454 B♭ (Kehr, Schröter—Schott). *Variations* K.359, K.360 (Schmid, Lampe, Röhrig—Henle 181).

For a discussion of these works see: VKDR, I: pp.228–303.

_____ *20 Sonatas* (Br&H) 2 vols.

_____ *19 Sonatas* (CFP 3315; Flesch, Schnabel—IMC; Nachrez—Augener 8669a, b) 2 vols.

_____ *18 Sonatas* (Schradieck—GS L836; Principe, Vitali—Ric ER59-60) 2 vols.

_____ *6 Sonatas* K.55–60 "Romantic" (Gärtner—Br&H; CFP 3329). Authenticity doubtful.

Thea Musgrave. *Colloquy* 1960 (JWC) 16pp., parts. 11 min. A study in four untitled movements in the style of Webern. Short motifs, fragmented meters, irregular patterns with quick upbeat figurations. Eclectic writing with ideas appearing in various guises. Harmonics, some figures repeated ad lib. D.

Taro Nakamura. *Ballade* III (Mumyo) 1969 (Japan Federation of Composers 1973) 21pp., parts. Mumyo, a Buddhist term, means to be harassed by worldly and sinful desires. Moderato: opening section free and unbarred; seventh chords; moves into a steady 4/4 with piano syncopation, contemporary Alberti bass treatment, arpeggi figuration. Allegretto: interval of second frequently used in left hand, syncopated melody in right hand; solo cadenza for violin leads to another Allegretto–Allegro: broken-chord figuration; Adagio free section uses tremolo in right hand over short figures in left hand lower register; Allegretto returns and leads to più mosso coda, with much activity for both instruments. Mildly contemporary. M-D.

Carl Nielsen. *Sonata* Op.9 A 1895 (Telmányi—WH 3311) 22 min. Allegro glorioso: 4/4; SA with snappy opening; second subject appears twice, in C and E in 3/4, and in 4/4 in the recapitulation. Andante: steady, cumulative effect; piano part is mainly chordal. Allegro piacevole e giovanile: strong writing, unusual harmonic resolutions. D.

_____ *Sonata* II Op.35 1912 (WH 1982) 20 min. Allegro con tiepidezza: "tepidity" marking seems out of place in this heated and powerful movement; strong themes push forward in their intrinsic growth; brief interruptions provide contrast but there is plenty of upheaval and excitement held tightly together by clear and concise control. Molto adagio: broad, rhapsodic writing of the highest order. Allegro piacevole: great rhythmic originality; final section stops on C when suddenly the piano gives forth with a series of thunderous B flats, and both instruments quickly agree on C in the final diminishing bars of this weighty chamber music work. Difficult but worth the effort. D.

Jon Nordal. *Sonata* (Iceland Music Information Centre 1956) 16 pp., parts.

Jan Novák. *Pocket Sonata* 1974 (Zanibon) 14 pp., parts.

Syodai Okada. *Sonata* 1968–9 (Japan Federation of Composers).

Harold Oliver. *Sonata* (CF 1970) 8 min. Two movements. D.

Leo Ornstein. *Sonata* Op.26 (Br&H 1917).
_____ *Two Russian Barcarolles* (Br&H).

Juan Orrego-Salas. *Sonata* Op.9 (PIC).

Ignace Jan Paderewski. *Sonata* Op.13 1885 (Bo&Bo 1975) 39pp., parts. Allegro con fantasia; Intermezzo; Finale. Epilogue in Polish, English, and German. Fresh in its melodic appeal. Displays expert formal craftsmanship. The piano part, rich and effective, makes the most of the instrument's possibilities. The violin part, with a clear texture, affords the performer the opportunity of displaying graceful playing and good taste. The entire work encourages easy, natural playing from both performers. D.

Jean Papineau-Couture. *Dialogues* (PIC 1967) 29pp., parts. 15 min. Lourd; Très lent; Enjoué; Solennel. Serial organization, much use of staccato touch, kind of a stencilled style. M-D.
——— *Sonate en Sol* (CMC 1944) 24pp., parts. 11 min. Allegro: opening theme soft but energetic and characterized by great flexibility of meter; second theme in waltz rhythm; first theme returns after development, forte. Variations: opens with a lyrical theme followed by three variations in progressively faster tempo. Second movement linked to the third, a Rondo in the character of a scherzo in which some virtuosity is displayed, more in the violin than the piano. M-D.
——— *Trois Caprices* (CMC 1962) 11 min. Allegro; Adagio; Scherzando. Written to give the performers an opportunity to show their ability in a modern idiom. After this work was completed the composer noticed a definite relation between the character of the three movements and the personalities of his three children and gave the children's names as subtitles: Nadia, Ghilaine, and François. D.

Charmine Pepe. *Sonata* 1965 (IU) 27pp., parts. Vivace; Dirge; Con spirito. Strong serial writing. Piano has full chords as well as being pointillistically spread over the keyboard. Ensemble problems in sheer rhythmic complexities. Last movement has long lines. D.

Giovanni B. Pergolesi. *Sonata* G (P. Oboussier—Schott 10504 1956) 12pp., parts. Largo; Allegro; Largo; Spiritoso. The only known sonata for violin and figured bass by Pergolesi. Unencumbered realization. M-D.

Goffredo Petrassi. *Introduzione e Allegro* 1933 (Rico 1968) 13pp., parts. Originally for violin and eleven instruments. Has serial overtones but is strongly tonal. Chordal, rich sonorities, *pp* ending. M-D.

Hans Pfitzner. *Sonata* Op.27 e (CFP 3620 1922) 44pp., parts. Bewegt, mit empfindung; Sehr breit und ausdruckvoll; Ausserst schwungvoll und feurig. Expansive lyricism, chromatic richness, traditional cadences. Some dissonant counterpoint and involved rhythms all add up to a moving and expressive work. D.

Anne Danican Philidor. *Premier livre de pièces pour la flûte traversière ou la flûte a bec alto ou le violon et basse continue* (clavecin ou piano). Restitution de Maurice-Pierre Gourrier, realisation de Colette Teniere (Ouvrières 1972) 10pp., parts. See detailed entry under duos for piano and flute.

Burrill Phillips. *Sonata* C (GS). Dramatic gestures, clear harmonic content, incisive rhythms, and clear lines are found throughout this work. M-D.

Willem Pijper. *Sonata* I 1919 (JWC) 20pp., parts. 15 min. Mainly tonal but polytonal and polyrhythmic influences are felt. Commodo: sostenuto pedal usage, left hand figuration based on broken fifths, 3 with 4, quartal harmony, triplets. Tempo di menuetto tranquillo: seventh parallel chords, arpeggi and scalar figures, trills, cross rhythms. Quasi scherzando: light fast broken-fourth figuration, mixture of chords and arpeggi, Impressionistic *ppp* ending. M-D.

———— *Sonata* II (Donemus 1922) 14 min. Short motifs provide the source or "germ-cell" from which the whole work develops. No elaborate themes but much musical vitality is found here in spite of the pedestrian melodic writing. D.

Filipe Pires. *Sonatina* (EC 1975) 8pp., parts. Allegramente: rhythmic, syncopated, preference for major sevenths and minor ninths noted. Andante con malinconia: 5/8, equal and legatissimo, flowing lines, chromatic; large span required. Moto perpetuo: freely tonal, punctuated chords, many repeated notes in violin; piano provides chromatic chords as sub-structure. M-D.

Walter Piston. *Sonata* (AMP 1939) 30pp., parts. 18 min. Austere, economical style with many devices of retrograde, passacaglia, and fugato. Moderato: 6/8, mildly contemporary and slightly dissonant; clear SA form in F-f. Andantino quasi Adagio: 5/4, long lyric flowing lines, impressive episode, darkly expressive, in b. Allegro: clearly structured rondo, rhythmic patterns overworked, much activity, contrapuntal ingenuity in an episodic fugue. Piano is mostly treated linearly throughout the entire work. D.

See: Ross Lee Finney, "Piston's Violin Sonata," MM, 17/4 (May–June 1940): 210-13.

———— *Sonatina* (Bo&H) for violin and harpsichord or piano. Contains one of Piston's most moving and profound slow movements. M-D.

Ildebrando Pizzetti. *Sonata* A 1919 (JWC) 54pp., parts. 31 min. Inspired by the First World War. Tempestoso: in four parts, the last being a short coda;

incisive and quick main theme in triple meter; violin has a melancholy subject in duple meter; both subjects develop independently and with one another; other ideas are heard in this dramatic movement; long flowing lines, large chords, hemiola effects, tremolo; though in the key of a, this movement has the signature of one flat. Preghiera per gl'innocenti ("Prayer for the Innocents"): strongly emotional; piano theme is chantlike; violin enters with a passionate idea; three separate episodes plus connecting material make up the movement; chordal, triplets, reiterated figures. Vivo e fresco: rondo; folksong-like lively theme intertwines with other melodies; tremolo; freely tonal figuration; parallel chords; all diverse elements pulled together to form a brilliant conclusion. D.

Robert Pollock. *First Duo* 1969 (Boelke-Bomart) 9 min.
––––––– *Second Duo* 1970 (Boelke-Bomart) 11 min.
––––––– *Third Duo* 1973 (Boelke-Bomart) 8 min.

Quincy Porter. *Sonata* II 1933 (SPAM 32) 28pp., parts. 15 min. A work of consummate skill and ingenuity. Problems of formal balance and motivic unity are thoroughly solved; writing of amplitude and intensity. D.
See: Robert Eugene Frank, "Quincy Porter: A Survey of the Mature Style and a Study of the Second Sonata for Violin and Piano," Ph.D., diss., Cornell University, 1973, 128pp.

Francis Poulenc. *Sonata* (ESC 1942–3) 11pp., parts. Rev. ed. 1949. 19 min. Romantic harmonic and melodic writing full of "tragic" passion. Allegro con fuoco: much activity, Franckian sequences. Intermezzo—La guitare fait pleurer les songes (a quotation from Federico García Lorca [1899–1936] to whose memory the sonata was written). Presto tragico: an overabundance of material in lyric style that seems to betray the title of this movement. All movements are free in form. A large-sized work with a smaller-sized impact. D.

John Powell. *Sonata Virginianesque* Op.7 (GS 1919) 38 pp., parts. In the Quarters; In the Woods; At the Big House—Virginia Reel. A thoroughly charming and attractive work full of folksong inspiration. Requires mature pianism. Powell was an outstanding pianist, and his type of big technique is what is necessary here. D.

Sergei Prokofieff. *Sonata* I Op.80 f 1946 (D. Oistrakh—CFP 4718; Szigeti—MCA; D. Oistrakh—IMC) 38pp., parts. 28 min. "In mood it is more serious than the Second [Sonata]. The first movement, Andante assai, is severe in character and is a kind of extended introduction to the second movement, a sonata allegro, which is vigorous and turbulent, but has a broad second theme. The third movement is slow, gentle, and tender. The finale is fast and written in complicated rhythm" (from an article by the composer, "What I am Working On," in I. V. Nestyev, *Prokofiev*, trans. Florence Jonas. Stanford: Stanford University Press, 1960, p.385). There is wonderful dialogue between the two instruments throughout the sonata. Nestyev says concerning the second movement, Allegro brusco, that its "march-like phrases, with their rigid, clipped cadences and strident harmonies, create an image of brutal military power. This has much in common with the music of the Teutonic invasion in *Alexander Nevsky*. . . . But later these coarse, mechanical images give way to a rich, soaring theme (marked 'eroico') sung out by the violin, which sounds particularly appealing after the harmonic and tonal harshness of the opening phrases" (Nestyev, *Prokofiev*, p.387). A serious foreboding quality permeates this entire work. D.

———— *Sonata* II Op. 94 a (D. Oistrakh—IMC 36pp., parts; Szigeti—MCA 48pp., parts) 25 min. This lighter work was originally written for flute and piano, but David Oistrakh, to whom it is dedicated, inspired Prokofieff to arrange and rework it into its present form for violin and piano. The Szigeti edition gives both flute and violin versions, so quick comparison is a must! This sonata differs greatly from *Sonata* Op.80 for violin and piano. Its main feature is a graceful melodic treatment, somewhat similar to the composer's *Classical Symphony*. The Moderato is transparent and serene. The Scherzo is elegance personified, and is one of Prokofieff's most outstanding achievements in this style of writing. The Andante, with its emotional coolness and measured rhythm, and the lively and vivacious finale are both "classically" fashioned. The flute and the violin versions are scored differently for the respective instruments and present an insight into Prokofieff's amazing instrumental scoring ability; such facility is sendom seen in his or other composer's works. D.

Both sonatas are very difficult and only the most skilled duo will do justice to them.

Bronislaw K. Przybylski. *Variazioni sopra un tema di Paganini* (PWM 1975) 22pp., parts. 7 min.

Héctor Quintanar. *Sonata* I (IU) 9pp. Commissioned by the Sociedad de Autores y Compositores de Música S. de A. Plucked and stopped strings, glissandi on strings, harmonics, serial, pointillistic, *pp* alternating clusters on white and black keys, long pedals, mainly soft. Interesting sonorities, avant-garde. D.

Einojuhani Rautavaara. *Dithyrambos* Op.55 (Fazer 1970) 7pp., parts. Toccata-like, using chords and sixteenth-note figuration; freely tonal. Contrasting mid-section allows for violin acrobatics. Brilliant closing in upper register. M-D.

Maurice Ravel. *Sonate Posthume* 1897 (Sal 1975) 17pp., parts. The autograph of this one-movement work is dated April 1897. "The piece was probably performed at the Conservatoire by Georges Enesco and the composer who were classmates; for whatever reason, it was never heard of again. Consisting of an exposition, development and recapitulation, this sonata points out the spiritual influence of Fauré's lyricism as well as that of Franck's harmonic language. The theme adumbrates the beginning of Ravel's *Trio,* and on occasion the themes are treated similarly (Cf., bar 13 of the *Sonata* with bar 52 of the *Trio*). Thus, if the opening of the *Trio* is 'Basque in colour,' as the composer asserted, the same observation may be applied to the beginning of the *Sonata.* It turns out that this youthful composition is not a forerunner of the composer's well-known *Sonata* for violin and piano (listed below), but is rather an independent work, whose main theme foreshadows the opening of the *Trio*" (from the introduction by Arbie Orenstein). M-D.

———— *Sonata* G 1923–7 (Durand 32pp., parts; USSR 1975 40pp., parts) 18 min. Allegretto; Blues; Perpetuum mobile. Clear textures; cool, colorful, and objective writing. Same material shared by both instruments but they contrast it rather than cooperate with it. The Blues and finale lend themselves to virtuoso performances. M-D to D.
See: VKDR, II: pp. 223–30.

Alan Rawsthorne. *Sonata* 1958 (OUP) 28pp., parts. 16 min. Adagio; Allegretto; Toccata (allegro di bravura); Epilogue (Adagio rapsodico). Cyclic, concise, and flexible formal treatment. Triads of D and e♭ form the basis for motivating tonalities. The Toccata is by far the most difficult movement. D.

Gardner Read. *Sonata Brevis* (Seesaw).
———— *Sonoric Fantasia* II Op.123 1966 (TP 1974) 16pp., parts. 10½ min. Originally for violin and orchestra; piano reduction by the composer. Rhapsodic, broad gestures, some astringent dissonances, imitation, subtle dynamics, long pedals, effective trills in low register, pointillistic in spots, very slow and deliberate *ppp* closing. Large span required. D.

Max Reger. *Sonata* Op.1 d (Schott 1911) 18 min.
———— *Sonata* Op.3 D (Schott 1911) 22 min.
———— *Sonata* Op. 41 A (UE 1208 1900) 43pp., parts. 23 min. Allegro con moto; Intermezzo—Prestissimo assai; Largo con gran espressione; Allegro. Chromatic, exploits resources of both instruments. Intermezzo is highly effective. D.

_____ *Sonata* Op.72 C (T. Prusse—Bo&Bo 1967) 51pp., parts. 32 min. Allegro con spirito; Prestissimo; Largo con gran espressione; Allegro con brio. In spite of some effective writing and colorful harmonies, the rhythmic procedure is repetitious. D.

_____ *Sonata* Op.84 f♯ (T. Prusse—Bo&Bo 1965; UE No. 1968) 51 pp., parts. 22 min. Allegro moderato, ma agitato; Allegretto; Andante sostenuto con variazioni. The finale, a large set of variations, is the most interesting movement. D.

_____ *Suite im Alten Stil* Op.93 (CFP 1973) 27pp., parts. The Allegro commodo opens in the style of a Brandenburg concerto. The middle movement, Largo, has often been performed separately. Its expressive long lines are very beautiful. The closing Allegro con spirito is a fugue that opens quietly and builds to a brilliant contrapuntal movement. D.

_____ *Suite* Op.103a (Bo&Bo) 28pp., parts. Präludium; Gavotte; Aria; Burleske; Menuet; Gigue. D.

Reger's study of Bach is seen in both these suites. The ideas are more concentrated and clarified, while the thematic treatment is more plastic.

_____ *Kleine Sonate* Op.103b/1 (Bo&Bo 1937) 17 min. Three movements. Easier than 103b/2. Concludes with appealing variations. M-D.

_____ *Kleine Sonate* Op.103b/2 (Bo&Bo 1965) 19 min. Four smaller movements than usual. M-D.

These two shorter sonatas are well suited to today's audiences.

_____ *Sonate* Op.122 e (Bo&Bo 1971; UE 3429) 50pp., parts. 37 min. Moderato; Vivace; Adagio; Allegretto espressivo. D.

_____ *Sonate* Op.139 c (CFP 1915) 51pp., parts. 36 min. Con passione; Largo; Vivace; Andantino con variazioni. There is great beauty in this work, especially in the soaring and passionate opening movement. Heavily chromatic with harmonic elaboration stretched almost to the breaking point. D.

Albert Reiter. *Sonatina in Einem Satz* (Dob 1973) 8pp., parts. Neoclassic, mildly contemporary. M-D.

Franz Reizenstein. *Sonata* g♯ 1945 (Lengnick) 52pp., parts. Tranquillo: undulating sixths, flowing, chromatic, alternating octaves between hands, tremolo. Allegro ma non troppo: effective scherzo. Finale—Misterioso: sinewy chromatic figuration in thirds with both hands, long lines, emphatic octaves. D.

Ottorino Respighi. *Sonata* b 1917 (Ric 117619) 33pp., parts. 18 min. Moderato; Andante espressivo; Passacaglia. Teutonic Romantic writing with some Impressionist influences. D.

Hermann Reutter. *Sonate* Op.20 (Schott 1932).

——— *Rhapsodie* Op.51 (Schott 3690 1939) 24pp., parts. Contrasting sections use varied pianistic figuration with colorful rhythmic treatment. Freely tonal with opening and closing around f♯–F♯. D.

Phillip Rhodes. *Duo* 1965–6 (CFE 1968) 27pp., parts. 13 min. This work is to be played in its entirety without pause, but it is divided into three movements and two cadenzas as follows: Recitative: violin plays the leading role while the piano serves to comment and punctuate; a dialogue develops but is broken off by the violin. Cadenza: sums up preceding material. Aria: essentially monothematic and consists of varied repetition of the single theme in different tempi, registers, overlappings, etc., and leads to the piano Cadenza: ideas are worked through over the entire range of the keyboard. Ripresa: most of the musical material of the first two movements and the cadenzas reappears here. The names represent in general the character of the movements. Highly organized abstract writing, pointillistic. Complex ensemble problems but well worth the effort. A major work. D.

Wallingford Riegger. *Sonatina* Op.39 (EBM 1948) 15pp., parts. 7 min. Moderato; Allegro. Firm, clear structure, direct dialogue between the two instruments, lyric. Sounds like Brahms with wrong notes. Allegro has some effective toccata-like passages. Dolce *pp* ending. M-D.

Ferdinand Ries. *Introduzione e Gavotta* Op.26 (GM) 7pp., parts. Chordal and some interchange of ideas. M-D.

——— *Drei Sonatinen* Op.30 C, a, F (R&E 1969) 30pp., parts. Light and brilliant and not too difficult. Fine for the student duo. Each sonatina has three movements, with the outside movements larger. Int. to M-D.

——— *Grande Sonate* Op.83 D (R&E 1969) 24pp., parts. Allegro con brio; Andantino con moto; Rondo—Allegro vivace. Provides a good introduction and preparation for the middle Mozart sonatas and the early Beethoven. Early Romantic traits are found here. M-D.

Vittorio Rieti. *Sonata Breve* 1967 (Gen) 20pp., parts. Allegretto mosso; Adagio cantabile; Allegro. Freely tonal but strong sense of key in this trim and attractive neoclassic piece. M-D.

Knudåge Riisager. *Sonate* (WH 2456 1923) 27pp., parts. Fresco con ritmo; Jocoso e risoluto. Virtuoso academic writing in neoclassic style mixed with French influence. Large span required. D.

Bernard Rogers. *Sonata* 1962 (TP) 29pp., parts. Lento spirituale; Vivacissimo; Largo austero; Allegro. Colorful writing, strong craft, expert handling of both instruments. The Vivacissimo is built on *soave* sprightly arpeggi figures that are particularly effective. Keen and subtle sonorities are present in the Largo austero. A fine work that deserves more performances. M-D to D.

Ned Rorem. *Day Music* 1971 (Bo&H) 33pp., parts. Eight short sections with titles—i.e., "Wedge and Doubles," "A Game of Chess 4 Centuries Ago"—and comments by the composer. Dissonant and harsh sounds get some relief in the "Pearls" section with flowing polytonal layers of sonorities. Striking rhythmic and coloristic effects. D.

_____ *Night Music* 1972 (Bo&H) 31pp., parts. 20 min. A sequel to *Day Music*. Eight short sections with titles—i.e., "Answers," "Mosquitos and Earthworms," "Gnats," "The Lighthouse," "Saying Goodby Driving Off"—and comments by the composer. Similar idiom to *Day Music*. Colorful writing throughout. Requires first-rate performers on both instruments. D.

_____ *Sonata* (CFP 6211) 19 min.

Hilding Rosenberg. *Sonata* I (NMS 1926).

_____ *Sonata* II C (NMS 1941) 16 min.

Albert Roussel. *Sonata* I Op.11 d 1903, rev. 1931 (Sal 1931) 60pp., parts. 32 min. Three long movements in cyclic form. Lent–Très animé; Assez animé; Très animé. The first movement is in SA design with a slow introduction that contains the cyclic theme. In the middle movement, a scherzo, a slow movement, Très lent, is inserted where the trio is usually placed. The lively finale is in sonata–rondo form. D.

_____ *Sonata* II Op.28 A 1925 (Durand) 16½ min. More effective than No.I. Allegro con moto: SA, three themes carefully worked out. Andante: ABA with a violent B section. Presto: 6/8 alternated with 4/8, scherzo-like opening and closing, a dramatic and introspective mid-section. M-D.

Miklós Rózsa. *Variations on a Hungarian Peasant Song* Op.4 1929 (Br&H) 12 min.

_____ *North Hungarian Peasant Songs and Dances* Op.5 (Br&H).

_____ *Duo* Op.7 1931 (Br&H) 18 min. A theme in the second and fourth movements resembles the one used in the variation set listed above. Enormous rhythmic vitality and frequent climaxes are prevalent in both works. All three works have a strong Hungarian flavor. They are colorful pieces that require energetic and polished performances. All are M-D.

Edmund Rubbra. *Sonata* II 1932 (OUP 23.410) 38 pp., parts. 17 min. Allegretto liberamente e scorrevole; Lament; Allegro vivo e feroce (strident and very rhythmic). Displays Rubbra's early personal harmonic style infused with some counterpoint. Finale is toccata-like. Large span required. D.

———— *Sonata* III Op.133 (Lengnick 1968) 24pp., parts. Allegro: hemiola, broadly conceived themes, neo-Romantic. Andante poco Lento e mesto: expressive; parallel chords; chromatic climax; requires a large span. Tema con Variazioni: rhythmic theme, eight contrasting variations, coda (molto scherzando e leggiero) built on theme. Traditional writing in twentieth-century clothes. D.

Marcel Rubin. *Sonata* (Dob 1976) 40pp., parts. 25 min.

Anton Rubinstein. *Sonata* I Op.13 G (CFP; Hamelle) 39pp., parts. Moderato con moto; Theme and (2) Variations; Scherzo; Finale.

———— *Sonata* II Op.19 a (Hamelle).

———— *Sonata* III Op.98 b (Hamelle).

The three violin and piano sonatas are perhaps Rubinstein's best chamber works. An eclectic–Romantic style is fed into classic forms. All three sonatas contain imaginative writing but the piano part is treated in a more virtuoso manner in *Sonata* III.

Anton Ruppert. *Vorübergehen. 7 Stationen* (Orlando 1973) 12pp. Photostat. Two copies necessary for performance. Explanations in German only.

Antoni Rutkowski. *Sonata* Op.5 c (PWM 1975) 47pp., parts. Prepared for publication by Tadeusz Przybylski. Preface in Polish and English.

Joseph Ryelandt. *Sonata* IV Op.63 (CeBeDeM 1976) 25pp., parts.

Pedro A. Saenz. *Sonata* D (Ric Amer) 28pp., parts. Allegro con brio; Romanza; Allegro assai. Post-Romantic orientation with a few mildly contemporary sonorities. D.

Joseph B. Chevalier de Saint-Georges. *Sonata* I 1781 (IU) 15pp., parts. Allegro; Tempo di menuetto. Delightful, simple, and straightforward classic style. Int. to M-D.

Camille Saint-Saëns. *Sonata* I Op.75 d 1885 (Durand) 39pp., parts. 23½ min. Allegro agitato–Adagio: two main subjects; flowing and lyric; closing Allegro prepares for the Adagio, whose melody is contemplative. Allegretto moderato–Allegro molto: light, graceful interaction between the two parts. Finale: rich sonorities announced, dancelike and brilliant, strong accentuation. Difficult ensemble problems. D.

—————— *Sonata* II Op.102 E♭ 1896 (Durand). Allegretto: dreamy, poetical. Andante: aria style, somber pacing in piano. Allegretto scherzando: delicate, subtle, whimsical. Allegro: conceived in a classic vein, pastorale. More accessible than *Sonata* I, shows great skill. M-D.

Erkki Salmenhaara. *Trois Scènes de Nuit* 1970 (Finnish Music Information Center) 14pp., parts. 18 min. Oiseaux de nuit: twelve-tone; row is frequently spread in arpeggio figuration; tonal implications; pictorial. Clair de lune: piano provides chromatic chordal accompaniment while the violin sings in a freely tonal decorative idiom. Chaconne: ten-note row is announced in bass of the piano; chordal; chromatic; atonal; tonal ending. Colorful and interesting writing in all three pieces. M-D.

Curt Sanke. *Concertino* (Hofmeister 1972) 11pp., parts.

Claudio Santoro. *Sonata* IV 1951 (Cembra 1956) 26pp., parts. Allegro: unison opening; piano provides syncopated accompaniment for first subject; violin has melody; leads to Meno ancora, where both instruments play syncopated thematic material; Meno e resuluto (Quasi recitativo) leads to recapitulation; short, quiet closing; centers around a–A. Lento: ABA, centers around g, melodic. Allegro: rondo form—ABCDABCD coda; highly rhythmical with a great deal of syncopation in both instruments; contains some slower sections (Meno; Lento); centers around C. M-D.

Giuseppe Sarti. *Sonata* Op.3/3 B♭ (W. Plath—Nag 243 1975) 38pp., parts.

Erik Satie. *Choses vues à Droite et à Gauche* (Sans Lunettes) (Rouart-Lerolle 1916) 8pp., parts. Choral hypocrite, Grave: chordal. Fuge à tâtons, pas vite: linear, salon style mid-section, *ff* closing. Fantaisie musculaire, un peu vif: much staccato in piano part, short violin cadenza, kind of a spoof. M-D.

Angel Sauce. *Sonata* (Radio Caracas 1944) 22pp., parts. Moderato: G. Andante: c. Rondó-Allegro: G. Classical style with a few neoclassic characteristics. M-D.

A. Adnan Saygun. *Sonata* Op.20 1941 (PIC 1961) 38pp., parts. Andante: freely tonal, changing meters, arpeggi, intense; requires large span. Molto vivo: 7/16, repeated chords à la toccata style, quartal harmony, brilliant. Largo: parallel chords, full but quiet sonorities. Allegro: chordal punctuation combined with independent lines, contrasting sections, expressive E conclusion. D.

—————— *Suite* Op.33 (PIC 1964) 27pp., parts. Lento: repeated octaves in syncopated triplets, ornamental Oriental melodic fioraturas. Horon: 7/8, fast and exciting dance. Zeybek: slow, recitative-like, chordal. M-D.

Domenico Scarlatti. *Sonatas* (L. Salter—Augener 1950). Published separately. L.217 c, L.168 d, L.75 F, L.271 e, L.36 g, L.211 d, L.106 d, L.176 G.
Of Scarlatti's 550-odd sonatas, these eight are the only ones for violin with figured bass; the rest are for solo keyboard. The violin sonatas generally have good basso continuo realizations. They differ from the keyboard sonatas in that the former have several movements and the latter usually have only one. In place of the active left-hand work normally found in the keyboard sonatas there is substituted in the violin sonatas what E. J. Dent has aptly termed a "table-leg bass," while the inner harmony is almost completely missing. M-D.
See: Lionel Salter, "Scarlatti's Violin Sonatas," *Listener,* 38 (1947):116.

Johann Heinrich Schmelzer. *6 Sonatae Unarum Fidium* 1664 (F. Cerha— UE 1960) 2 vols. 1 C, 2 F, 3 g, 4 D, 5 c, 6 A.

Florent Schmitt. *Chant du Soir* (Rouart-Lerolle 1931) 7pp., parts. Has parts for violin or English horn and piano. Impressionistic opening and closing. Builds to chordal climax in mid-section. Subtle rhythmic flexibility, expressive closing. M-D.

Artur Schnabel. *Sonata* (Bo&H 1961) 57pp., parts. Allegro ma non troppo (quasi moderato) e sempre semplice; Allegretto poco vivace; Adagio; Vivace. Extremely chromatic, complex expressionistic style, almost completely polyphonic. Idiom suggests Schönberg and Sessions. Serious, meditative content. Roman numerals used to indicate length of the musical phase. D.

Alfred Schnitke. *Sonata* I 1963 (USSR). "Adheres to neoclassic forms but uses serial structures as the source of thematic material" (DCM, p. 698).
———— *Quasi una Sonata* 1968 (UE 15826) 32pp., parts. Traditional and nontraditional chords, solid and tremolo clusters, graphic and proportional rhythmic notation, pointillistic, changing meters, quasi cadenza passages for both instruments, sectional, dynamic extremes, same repeated chords over long period of time. Avant-garde. Large span required. D.

Johann Schobert. *Ausgewählte Werke* (H. Riemann, rev. H. J. Moser— DDT, series 1, Vol.39). Contains sonatas Op.2/1 B♭, Op.14/2 B♭, Op.14/3 c, Op.14/1 D, Op.14/5 A. Also contains trios and quartets.
———— *Sonata* A (W. Kramolisch—Nag 199 1962).

Othmar Schoeck. *Sonata* Op.16 D (Hug 1909) 17½ min. Neoclassic, melodious style, much spontaneity. M-D.

_____ *Sonate* Op.46 1931 (Hug 1934).

Arnold Schönberg. *Phantasy* Op.47 1949 (CFP 1952) 8 min. A compact piece that contains the elements for several movements. The opening declamatory subject is followed by a contrasting lyrical second idea, which is developed with a lilting character. A three-part scherzo follows, moving to an altered and condensed recapitulation. A highly effective work in twelve-tone writing. Difficult and challenging but technically very playable. The piano part is frequently treated chordally and very complementary to the violin. D.

See: Allen Forte, *Contemporary Tone Structures*. New York: Da Capo Press, 1973.

Richard S. Hill, "Arnold Schönberg: Phantasy, Op.47," *Notes*, 9/4 (September 1952).

Franz Schubert. *Sonatas* (Sonatinas) D.384 D, D.385 a, D.408 g (Op.137), D.574 a (M. Holl, D. Oistrakh, H. Kann—VU 1973) 83pp., parts. Notes 28pp. The three sonatinas of Op.137 appear here under Schubert's original title of *Sonatas for Piano and Violin*. This carefully researched version includes comparisons with the autographs and the earliest editions, but the violin part is printed in the piano score and it is very difficult to distinguish original from editorial phrasings. Oistrakh provides helpful fingerings and bowings for the violin, while Hans Kann's fingerings for the piano are carefully thought out. M-D.

_____ *Sonatinen* (G. Henle, K. Röhrig—Henle 1963) rev. ed. 48pp., parts. Contains the same works as listed above. Based on original Schubert MS; only fingering and signs for down-bow and up-bow have been added. Other editions are: Hermann—CFP 1561; Br&H; Kehr, Schröter—Schott; David—GS L921; Pessina—Ric BA11060; Augener 7571. Available separately from CFP.

For a discussion of these pieces see VKDR, II: pp.67–77.

_____ *Duos* (Ernst Herttrich—Henle 1976) 87pp., parts. Fingering by M. Rostal, H.-M. Theopold. Contains *Sonata* D.574, Op. post. 162 A; *Rondo* D.895, Op.70 b; *Fantasie* D.934, Op. post. 159 C. Sources are identified and the most important variants between the sources are listed. Signs obviously missing in the sources are noted in parentheses. Outstanding urtext-performing edition, superlative printing, informed editorial comment.

_____ *Duos* (Carl Hermann—CFP 156B 1934). Includes the *Duos* listed above plus the *Introduction* and (7) *Variations* Op.160. The *Rondo* D.895 is magnificent salon music. The *Fantasie* D.934, in seven connected sections has Hungarian touches as well as brooding drama implicit in the development episodes. The song "Sei mir gegrüsst" is the basis for the slow section. A rousing march concludes the work. The *Duo* D.574 is gentle and charming.

Robert Schumann. *Two Sonatas* Op.105, Op.121 (F. Hermann—CFP; Z. Francescatti—IMC). Op.105 (Br&H; Bauer—GS L1696; Hamelle). 19 min. Op.121 (Bauer—GS L1699) 39pp., parts. 28 min.

———— *Sonata* III a (O. W. Neighbour—Schott 1956) 30pp., parts. Ziemlich langsam; Lebhaft; Intermezzo; Finale. Valuable preface, editorial notes. M-D.

———— *F.A.E. Sonata* 1853. See entry under Brahms, this section.

Joseph Schuster. *Sei Divertimenti da Camera* (W. Plath—Nag 1973 Vols.229, 232, 233). Vol.I: F, G. Vol.II: F, C. Vol.III: D, G. 6 separate volumes, score, and parts. Preface by editor. Date from around 1777 in Munich. No. V in D is the most important of the series. Delightful writing with keyboard part almost as important as the violin. M-D.

Elliott Schwartz. *The Decline and Fall of the Sonata (A Fable)* 1972 (CF) facsimile. 14pp., parts. 11 min. Notation is generally proportional, each system (with a very few exceptions) being equal to 15 seconds. Also, many traditionally notated passages, aleatoric. Contains other performing instructions: pianist must play muted strings, pluck strings, make percussive sounds with palms or knuckles on wooden part of piano or metal crossribs inside, slap palms on strings, and needs a large wooden mallet. Two brief sections can use an optional tape, which heightens and intensifies theatrical tendencies. Tape directions are included for pianist to make tape. Pointillistic, serial influence, long pedals, arm clusters, extensive directions in score; theatrical tendencies should be played up as much as possible. Avant-garde. D.

Mátyas Seiber. *Sonata* (Schott 1963). First movement has complex percussive harmonic usage in the piano. Second movement is a kind of intermezzo, measured and dancelike. Finale is a lyrical slow movement, where the conflict between the instruments in the first movement is settled. M-D.

Jean Baptiste Senaillié. *Sonata* c (Lemoine).

———— *Sonata* d (J. A. Parkinson—OUP 1963).

———— *Sonata* E (Lemoine).

———— *Sonata* e (G. Beechey—OUP) 12pp., parts. A four-movement work, typical of late eighteenth-century elegant style. This is No.5 of ten sonatas published in Paris in 1721. Last movement presents most challenge to the keyboard player. Figured bass is well realized. Excellent introductory note. M-D.

———— *Sonata* Op.5 G (Jensen—Augener 7405).
———— *Sonata* G (Moffat—Simrock).
———— *Sonata* G (Salmon—Ric).

Roger Sessions. *Duo* (EBM 1942) 42pp., parts. A strong and valuable work for the combination. Very difficult.

Harold Shapero. *Sonata* 1942 (PIC 1954) 32pp., parts. Moderato: incisive repeated chords, widely spread broken-chord figuration, independent lines, freely tonal; large span required. Adagio: short motivic ideas, chromatic, serious. Allegro preciso: marcato and secco contrasted with semi-legato style, repeated harmonic fourths, a few long lines interspersed, brilliant and pesante conclusion. D.

Ralph Shapey. *Duo* 1957 (MS available from composer: % Music Department, University of Chicago, Chicago, IL 60637) 17pp., Shapey is fond of multiple meters, i.e., 2/4 + 3/16, 2/4 + 1/8, 1/4 + 1/16 + 2/4, etc. Andante con Espressivo; Quasi cadenza (segues to) Leggiero (segues to) opening Andante con Espressivo. Complex expressionistic writing of the highest order. Ensemble problems will present themselves to even the most experienced players but the piece is most deserving and warrants being heard. D.

Arthur Shepherd. *Sonate* (Senart 1927). Rich and plangent sonorities, long lines, chromatic, secondary seventh chords strung together, brief modal effects juxtaposed with disjunct intervals. All these elements are used for expressive purposes and lend an individual color to the work. M-D.

Seymour Shifrin. *Duo* (CFP 1968–9) 19pp., parts. 12 min. One movement of atonal writing, complex rhythmic problems, fragmentary melodic ideas equally shared by the two instruments. M-D.

Dmitri Shostakovich. *Sonata* Op.134 1968 (USSR 1970; Sikorski) 93pp., parts. A milestone of twentieth-century chamber music. Opening theme in the piano is built around the twelve notes of the chromatic scale but is not a true tone-row. This terse work moves closer to atonality than any previous works by Shostakovich. The entire compelling piece is built on a dependence–independence relationship between the two instruments that results in a continual musical tension, especially noticeable in the rhythmic and melodic elements. A gloomy Nachtmusik passage appears in the opening movement and returns cyclically to close the final movement—a tidy and effective unifying device. D.

Jean Sibelius. *Sonatine* Op.80 (J. A. Burt—WH 1921, reprint 1949).

_____ *4 Stücke* Op.115 (Br&H) Published separately. Auf der Heide; Ballade; Humoreske; Die Glocken.

_____ *3 Stücke* Op.116 (Br&H 1930) Published separately. Scène de danse; Danse caractéristique; Rondeau romantique.

Elie Siegmeister. *Sonata* I 1951–9 (CF) 54pp., parts. 22 min. Allegro con fuoco; Allegro ritmico; Adagio non troppo; Vivo, con spirito. Intense virtuoso writing of the highest order. Large span required. D.

_____ *Sonata* II 1965–70 (CFP 1976) 38pp., parts. Lyric, long lines, poise, serene and elegant themes, conservative contemporary idiom. D.

_____ *Sonata* III 1965 (CFP) 15 min. Two seething movements. Long lyric lines, panchromatic, soaring expression. "Bartók pizzicati" used as an effective device, sinewy texture, astringent harmonies. D.

_____ *Sonata* IV 1971 (CF) 36pp., parts. 18 min. Andante con moto; Andante; Allegro con spirito. A broad sweeping work. Many colorful ideas and dramatic moments. Large span required. D.

_____ *Sonata* V 1972 (CF) 36pp., parts. 20 min. Andante: freely tonal and chromatic; varied tempi; harmonic seconds are prevalent; subtle syncopation; texture thins at conclusion; requires large span. Andante: imitation, colorful and contrasting figuration. Allegro giocoso, molto ritmico: broken ninth figures in alternating hands, changing meters, strong rhythms and advanced eclectic style, firm control of the medium, bristling dissonance. D.

Otto Simek. *Concertino* 1959 (Panton 1972) 13pp., parts.

Christian Sinding. *Sonata* Op.12 C 1892 (WH 5) 41pp., parts. Allegro moderato; Andante; Finale. Nationalistic Norwegian melodic style coupled with Wagnerian technique. D.

_____ *Sonata* Op.27 E (CFP 2826). Brilliant opening movement, Romantic second movement, lively finale with a delightful and flowing development. D.

Emil Sjögren. *Sonata* Op.19 g 1885 (CFP 2215) 27pp., parts. Allegro vivace; Andante; Finale. Exudes a youthful passion. Warm and some delicate melodies; strong Romantic and rich harmonies. Very fresh sounding when written. M-D.

_____ *Sonata* II Op.24 e 1888 (NMS 807) 35pp., parts. Allegro moderato; Allegretto scherzando; Andante sostenuto; Con fuoco. The most famous of Sjögren's piano and violin sonatas. Form and construction are clearer than in first sonata. M-D.

_____ *Sonata* IV Op.47 1906 (Br&H) 31pp., parts.

_____ *Five Sonatas* (GM 1956) 169pp., parts. Contains Sonatas Op.19,

Op.24, Op.32 g (1900), Op.47, Op.61 a (1914). Reprints of the original editions.

Roger Smalley. *Capriccio* I 1966 (Faber) 14 min. Fantasia; Scherzo; Nocturne; Coda.

Hale Smith. *Duo* Op.9 1953 (CFP) 33pp., parts. Energetic; Slow; Aggressively (Cadenza). Abstruse and dramatic writing, some neoclassic characteristics, highly individual style. Rhythmic problems for pianist; large span required. D.

Miloš Sokola. *Sonata* 1968 (Panton 1973) 42pp., parts.

Alojz Srebotnjak. *Sonatina* II (GS 1971) 32pp., parts. Andante, rapsodico: flexible meters; works to climax; subsides. Vivace: 3 + 2 + 3/8, thin textures, rhythmic propulsion, *pp* ending. Larghetto: serious dramatic gestures; leads to Andantino, pastorale then returns to Larghetto mood. Allegro molto: a fast dance, Bartók-like, glissandi, straightforward writing. Effective. M-D.

Johann V. Stamitz. *Sonata* Op.6a G (F. Brož—Artia 1956) MAB 28. 9pp., parts. Adagio; Allegro; Minuetto. More like a sonata da camera or a suite. Musical expression and melodic lines show some characteristics of the Mannheim instrumental concertante style. Playful, folklike melodies with frequent embellishments. M-D.

John Stanley. *Six Solos for Flute, Violin or Oboe and Keyboard Instrument* (Concordia).
——— *Six Solos for a German Flute or Violin and Continuo* Op.4 (George Pratt—JWC 1975) 44pp., parts for flute or violin and viola da gamba or cello. See detailed entry under duos for piano and flute.

Erich Walter Sternberg. *Sonata* 1955, rev. 1965 (IMI 1968) 39pp., parts. 17 min. Allegro sostenuto: SA, "full of vitality, giving expression to the exuberance of the adolescent rushing out into life to conquer it" (from the score). Variations on J. S. Bach's "Come Sweet Death": this movement "expresses an old man's feelings" (from the score); written in different canonic forms, one being a canon cancrizans; in Variation 5 the theme of the first movement appears in counterpoint to the Bach chorale. M-D.

Edward Steuermann. *Improvisation and Allegro* 1955 (New Valley Music Press 1971) 26pp., parts. 12 min. "The violin piece is not a row composition, although it is 12-tone. The first 'statement' of the violin comprises six tones, the answer of the piano the other six tones. Then an inversion in the violin, which curiously, gives the same tones with this difference, that D appears instead of E. In this way each instrument has a reservoir of seven tones, and only these are used in the Improvisation. The form I see as a kind of sonata exposition (until bar 46). At bar 55 begins a kind of recapitulation, but as each instrument speaks in a different language, this is all, of course, only hinted (one feels it, however, very exactly in the form). Bar 74 begins the 'coda' of the Improvisation. The Allegro is a Rondo (it was first planned as a true 12-tone composition, but that would have sounded like milk after wine). The instruments simply exchange their 'keys.' The violin plays B for the first time in bar 99. Towards the end the instruments exchange more and more frequently; there are also small 'modulations.' The ending should have the effect of A minor in the violin and C minor in the piano" (from a letter by Edward Steuermann to Erwin Ratz, January 23, 1962). D.

Halsey Stevens. *Sonata* I (CFE 1947) 17 min. Allegro; Molto adagio; Allegretto ben accentato; Allegro. Expertly constructed; dissonance used dramatically yet warm and lyric writing permeates this fluent work. M-D.

———— *Sonatina Piacevole* 1956 (PIC 1968) 12pp., parts. 4½ min. For alto recorder or flute or violin, and piano or harpsichord. See detailed entry under duos for piano and flute.

———— *Sonatina* III 1959 (Helios) 15pp., parts. 8 min. Allegro: theme treated imitatively between instruments; dancelike; quartal and quintal harmony; freely centered around d. Adagio: expressive, overlapping sonorities, sustained, e tonal implications. Allegro: rhythmic drive, octotonic, imitation and diminution, two sustained episodes, repeated notes and octaves; the whole movement has much snap to it. Highly effective. M-D.

Karlheinz Stockhausen. *Sonatine* 1951 (UE 15170) 18pp., parts. 10 min. Schönberg influence noted even though this is a "school work" written while Stockhausen was a student at the State Conservatory in Cologne. Lento espressivo: thin textures, trills are important. Molto moderato e cantabile: ostinato-like bass of broken octaves, chordal sonorities gradually added. Allegro scherzando: octotonic; repeated bitonal chords; three staves required to notate some parts; vigorous rhythms; large span required. M-D.

Richard Strauss. *Sonata* Op.18 E♭ 1888 (UE 1047) 51pp., parts. 27 min. This scintillating work is indebted to Brahms and Schumann. Makes considerable technical demands on both players. Allegro ma non troppo: strongly rhythmic; beautifully contrasted second theme; brilliant piano writing but violin is not overpowered. Improvisation—Andante cantabile:

nocturne-like, passionate mid-section. Finale—Andante–Allegro: piano
has short solo introduction; main idea appears in the Allegro and is rhythmically unusual; expressive theme in the violin follows while the piano
rustles through various arpeggi figurations; dancelike idea substitutes for a
scherzo, and a climactic coda in 6/8 brilliantly ends the work. D.

Igor Stravinsky. *Duo Concertante* 1931–2 (Bo&H 1947) 18 min. A kind of
sonata for piano and violin in five movements: Cantilène; Eglogues I & II;
Gigue; Dithyrambe. Stravinsky said of this work in his autobiography,
"The spirit and form of my 'Duo Concertante' were determined by my love
of the pastorale poets of antiquity and their scholarly art and technique. The
theme which I had chosen developed through all the five movements of the
piece which forms an integral whole, and, as it were, offers a musical
parallel to the old pastoral poetry." This writer can find no theme that is
common to all five movements. There seems to be only a wonderful consistency of style exemplified by the avoidance of pure consonance and the use
of two juxtaposed diatonic chords in one way or another. For a more
thorough analysis of this work see VKDR, II: pp.257–61.

Endre Szervanszky. *Sonata* I 1945 (EMB 1972) 32pp., parts.

Karol Szymanowski. *Sonata* Op.9 d (UE 1904) 21 min.
———— *Mythes* Op.30 (UE 1915) 3 Poems. Available separately: "La Fon-
taine d'Arethuse" 14pp., parts. 6 min. "Narcissus" 12pp., parts. 7 min.
"Dryads et Pan" 16pp., parts. 7 min. These pieces show a strong instrumental style with programmatic tendencies. They describe ancient legends
using a refined harmonic hypersensitiveness that yields to a tendency to
over-elaboration. The piano part is luminous and very independent of the
violin, with a profusion of notes everywhere. D.
———— *La Berceuse D Aitacho Enia* Op.52 (UE 1925; PWM 1953) 5pp.,
parts. Mainly lyric, trill effectively used, tonal yet freely chromatic. M-D.

Germaine Tailleferre. *Sonate* I c♯ 1921 (Durand) 39pp., parts. 17 min.
Modéré sans lenteur: SA, polytonal, delightful and piquant writing.
Scherzo: 5/8, dainty, swaying rhythms in trio, spontaneous sounding.
Assez lent: emotional, intense; builds to dramatic climax and leads directly
to the Final: varied rhythmic and polytonal effects, effervescent closing in
G. Beautifully balanced dialogue between the instruments. D.
———— *Sonate* II B♭ 1951 (Durand) 30pp., parts. Allegro non troppo: chord-
al, flowing second section, parallel chords; varied key signatures but ends
in B♭. Adagietto: d, strongly Impressionistic. Final: F, repeated notes and
chords evolve into a toccata-like closing. M-D.

———— *Sonatina* 1973 (S. Weiner—Billaudot) 13pp., parts. Moderato; Andantino; Allegro-gaiement. In a Poulencian style with a little more dissonance. Pianistic. M-D.

Toru Takemitsu. *Hika* (Sal 1973) 6pp., parts. Serial, flexible meters, pointillistic, expressionistic, generally uses quiet dynamics, complex. Three staves required to notate most of the piece. Large span required. D.

Joseph Tal. *Sonata* (Israeli Music Publications 1952) 16pp., parts. 12 min. Moderato; Andantino; Moderato. Presents a three-movement sonata in the scheme of a classical first movement, with the opening Moderato representing the first subject and exposition, the Andantino corresponding to an expressive development, and the final movement serving as the recapitulation and coda. Forceful and expressive writing. M-D.

Alexander Tansman. *Sonata quasi una Fantasia* (Senart).
———— *Sonata* II (ESC).

Simón Tapia Colman. *Sonata* "El Afilador" (EMM 1958) 28pp., parts. Poco recitativo–senza rigore–Andante mosso; Largo; Vivo. Many sevenths and seconds add dissonance, parallel fourths, chromatic, rhythmic push even in the espressivo cantabile section, spread-out quick figures. Arpeggi and chordal gestures in the Vivo, shifting rhythms, some strongly tonal sections. Short violin cadenza leads to a Presto coda. D.

Béla Tardos. *Sonate* 1965 (EMB Z.6157) 30pp., parts. Allegro con fuoco; Lento; Presto con bravura. Octotonic, 2 with 3, glissandi, full chords, chromatic arpeggi figuration, strong rhythms in finale, parallel chords, folkdance influence. Large span required. M-D to D.

Giuseppe Tartini. *Sonatas* Op.1 (E. Farina—Carisch) 2 vols., 12 sonatas. Each sonata has three or four movements; the second (slow) movement is often very short, only a few bars. Mature Tartini style even though Op.1. Careful editing, excellent introductory note. Cello part optional. M-D.
———— *Two Sonatas* from Op.1, e and G (Lichtenberg—GS L725).
———— *Six Sonatas* (Polo—Ric ER177). Includes Op.1/1 A, 2 C, 4 G, 5 e.
———— *Sonata* Op.1/5 (Lengnick).
———— *Sonata* Op.1/10 "Devil's Trill" (CFP 1099b; Auer—CF B2695; Abbado—Ric; Joachim—Simrock; Nachez—Schott; Bo&H; Barison—Carisch; PWM; Kreisler—IMC; Jensen—Augener).
———— *Sonata* Op.2/12 G (Schott; Polo—Ric).
———— *Six Sonatas* Op.5 (Bonelli—Zanibon 1951) 1 a, 2 B♭, 3 A, 4 G, 5 F, 6 B♭.

_____ *Seven Sonatas* (CFP 1099A,B,C) 3 vols. Vol.I: 2 F, 4 G, 5 e. Vol.II: 10 g, Devil's Trill g. Vol.III: 6 D, Sonata C.

_____ *Three Sonatas* (F. Hermann—CFP 1099C) F, G, e.

_____ *Three Sonatas* (Artia).

_____ *Sonata* g "Didone Abondonata" (H. Marteau—Steingräber 1961) 7pp., parts. Adagio; Presto non troppo; Allegro commodo. M-D.

_____ *Sonata* 11 F (Nadaud, Kaiser—Senart 5264).

_____ *Sonata* 13 B♭ (Nadaud, Kaiser—Senart 5265).

_____ *Sonata* 18 A (Nadaud, Kaiser—Senart 5266).

_____ *Sonata* 21 b (Nadaud, Kaiser—Senart 5267).

_____ *Sonata* 23 A (Nadaud, Kaiser—Senart 5267).

_____ *Sonata* 25 D (Nadaud, Kaiser—Senart 5269).

_____ *Sonata* E (Nadaud, Kaiser—Senart 5208).

_____ *Sonata* G (Corti—Carisch).

_____ *Sonata* g (Auer—CF B2665).

_____ *Sonata* g (Ric R429).

Alexander Tcherepnin. *Sonata* Op.14 F 1921 (Durand) 12 min. This youthful three-movement cyclic work shows a strong Tschaikowsky-Rachmaninoff influence plus polychords and harmonic shifts à la Prokofieff. The outer movements (Allegro moderato; Vivace) have a motoric moto perpetuo rhythmic drive that also reminds one of Prokofieff. A limpid fugue makes up the middle movement (Larghetto). M-D.

Georg Philipp Telemann. *Sechs Sonaten* (W. Friedrich—Schott 4221 1954). Published by Telemann in Frankfurt in 1715.

_____ *Zwölf Methodische Sonaten 1–6 für Violine oder Querflöte und Basso continuo, 7–12 für Querflöte oder Violine und Basso continuo,* Hamburg 1728 und 1732 (M. Seiffert—Br 2951 1955).

_____ *Three Sonatas* for violin or flute and continuo (H. Kölbel—Heinrichshafen). The first three of a set of twelve sonatas written in 1734. Continuo realizations are by Ernst Meyerolbersleben in a somewhat flamboyant but tasteful style. The other nine sonatas are available in three volumes from the same publisher.

_____ *Six Sonatas* (TP).

_____ *Six Sonatinas* (Kauffman—Br&H).

_____ *Six Sonatinas* (Schweickert, Lenzewski—Schott). Cello part optional.

_____ *Sechs Sonatinen* (W. Maertens, W. H. Bernstein—CFP 9096 1967).

_____ *Sonata* F (H. Ruf—Schott 5477 1965). This sonata is Solo No.1 from the *Essercizii Musici.*

_____ *Sonata* A (H. Ruf—Schott 5478 1965). This sonata is Solo No.7 from the *Essercizii Musici.*

_____ *Sonata* IV C (G. Frotscher—CFP 5644 1951).

———— *Sonata* IV C (Mitteldeutscher). Cello part optional.

———— *Sonata* C, from *Getreuer Musikmeister* (CFP 4550). Cello part optional.

———— *Sonata* c (Hinnenthal—Br&H 4176 1938).

———— *Sonata* I D (Mitteldeutscher). Cello part optional.

———— *Sonata* d (Broe—CFP B557). Cello part optional.

———— *Sonata* F (Broe—CFP B560). Cello part optional.

———— *Sonata* II G (Mitteldeutscher). Cello part optional.

———— *Sonata* G (Schott).

———— *Sonata* III g (Mitteldeutscher). Cello part optional.

———— *Tafelmusik* II: Solo A-dur für Violine und Basso continuo (J. P. Hinnenthal—Br 3542 1966). Separate edition for practical use from *Georg Philipp Telemann, Musikalische Werke,* Vol. XIII (Gesellschaft für Musikforschung).

———— *Six Partitas* B♭, G, c, g, e, E♭ (W. Woehl—HM 47). For flute (violin or oboe) and continuo.

———— *Sonatas and Pieces* (D. Degen—HM 7). From *Der Getreue Musikmeister.* For flute (violin or oboe) and continuo. Sonata a, Sonata g, L'hiver, Air Trompette, Niaise, Napolitana. M-D.

———— *Six Concerti* (Br 2961). See detailed entry under duos for piano and flute.

Virgil Thomson. *Sonata* I 1930 (Arrow 1941) 17pp., parts. 18 min. Allegro: diatonic, clear textures, free counterpoint, meticulous craft. Andante nobile: flowing lyric lines, parallel harmonies. Tempo di Valzer: Poulencian charm. Andante–Doppio movimento: linear introduction, arpeggi and chordal figuration, subtle charm; only strong chordal and tremolo conclusion seems out of character. Neo-Romantic. M-D.

Ernst Toch. *Sonate* II Op.44 (Schott 1928) 12 min.

Roy Travis. *Duo Concertante* 1967 (University of California Press 1970) 53pp., parts. Gakpa; Adagio; Allegro marcato; Adagio espressivo e rubato; Asafo. The rhythms of the first and last movements have been adapted from two Ewe dances (contained on pp.52–53). Complex, expressionistic, chromatic. Great sense of freedom must permeate fourth movement. Full resources of piano exploited. D.

Karl Ottomar Treibmann. *Sonata* 1967, rev. 1971 (DVFM 8114) 39pp., parts. Allegro; Adagio; Vivace. Octotonic treatment, flexible meters, toccata-like figuration spread between alternating hands, pointillistic, figures repeated ad lib., glissandi, mixture of avant-garde and traditional notation. Piano part uses clusters. Large span required. D.

Joaquin Turina. *Sonata* I Op.51 d (Rouart-Lerolle 1930) 20pp., parts. 12 min. Lento; Aria—Lento; Rondeau—Allegretto. Tempo changes in outer movements add contrast. Colorful writing frequently employing Impressionistic techniques. M-D.

———— *Sonata* II Op.82 "Sonata Espagñola" (Rouart-Lerolle 1934) 24pp., parts. Freely in C. Mainly Hispanic atmosphere with an abundance of charming themes. Violin sings in the opening movement with the piano providing harmonic and rhythmic contribution. Plucked sounds and a hushed ending to the variations movement provide some of the most colorful writing in the piece. The middle movement alternates scherzando with slower sections. Idiomatic writing. A sense of frustration at never arriving "anywhere." D.

Charles Turner. *Serenade for Icarus* (GS 1961) 16pp., parts. $10\frac{1}{2}$ min. Freely tonal, varied sections, tempi and moods, somewhat Impressionistic, effective. M-D.

Fartein Valen. *Sonata* Op.3 (Norsk 1916). Regerian style; chromatic with interlaced themes that produce a dissonant polyphony. Freely tonal. D.

Ralph Vaughan Williams. *Sonata* a 1954 (OUP 23.100) 40pp., parts. 25 min. A substantial work that uses thick and heavy piano writing. Although a late work in the composer's career it still has a fresh viewpoint. Fantasia: bithematic; unwinds its counterpoint dramatically. Scherzo: 4/4 mixed with irregular accents. Variations: theme wanders into some interesting surroundings in the six variations. M-D.

Francesco Maria Veracini. *Twelve Sonatas* Op.1 (W. Kolneder—CFP 4937a–d 1958) 4 vols. No.1 g, No.2 a, No.3 b, No.4 c, No.5 d, No.6 e, No.7 A, No.8 B♭, No.9 C, No.10 D, No.11 E, No.12 F.
Available separately: No.1 (Jacobsen, Klengel—CFP 1060). No.2 (Salmon—Ric 1131), transposed to g. No.3, Largo and Rondo (Bonelli—Zanibon 2906). No.5, Giga all'antico (Elman—Schott). No.7 (Wotquenne, Cornelis—Schott 2788). *Three Sonatas* Op.1/1, 4, 8 (Albert Lazan—AMP), superb music but poorly edited.

———— *Sonate accademiche* Op.2 (W. Kolneder—CFP 9011-a-m 1961–71). Each Sonata accademica, Nos. 1–12, appears in its own volume in this edition. Originally published in 1744.
Available separately: No.1 D (Br 316). Cello part optional. No.2 B♭ (Br 317). Cello part optional. No.3 C (Br 318). Cello part optional. No.8 e (W. Kolneder—CFP). *Sonata* No.8, a sonata–concerto hybrid, serves as a good example of the set. All three movements have passages where the keyboard player is required to play only the written bass line. The absence of chords

gives the impression of a solo–tutti effect. Continuo realization is in good taste. No.12 d (CFP 9011M). Cello part optional. Int. to M-D.

———— *Sonata* Op.3 a (Jensen—Augener 7416).

———— *Twelve Sonatas after Arcangelo Corelli* Op.5 (W. Kolneder—Schott 1961). 4 vols. (Nos. 5157, 5158, 5170, 5171). These pieces are a reworking of the twelve sonatas of Corelli's epochal Op.5 and will provide much interest for players already familiar with the Corelli sonatas. They bear the same relationship to the original sonatas as J. S. Bach's transcriptions do to the works of Vivaldi.

———— *Sonata* a (Salmon—Ric R726).

———— *Sonata* d (Moffat, Winn—CF B2726).

———— *Sonata* VI d (Respighi—Ric ER278).

———— *Sonata* d (Salmon—Ric R724).

———— *Sonata* e (David—IMC).

———— *Sonata* e (Salmon—Ric R727).

———— *Sonata* e (Carisch).

———— *Concert Sonata* e (CFP 4345).

———— *Sonata* g (Salmon—Ric R725).

———— *Sonata* VIII (Respighi—Ric ER279).

———— *Sonata* b (Jahnke—PWM with cadenza by R. Padlewski).

———— *Sonata* d (Br 349).

———— *Sonata* F (Br 347).

———— *Sonata* G (Br 348).

There is much fine music in these works. It is time Veracini's contributions were reassessed.

Sándor Veress. *Sonatina* 1932 (SZ). Neoclassic, contrapuntal and dissonant, melodically attractive. M-D.

———— *Sonata* II 1939 (SZ 1943) 15 min. Nationalistic flavor. Written while Veress was assistant to Bartók in the folk-music department at the Academy of Sciences, Budapest. D.

Heitor Villa-Lobos. *Sonata–Fantaisie* I "Désespérance" 1912 (ESC) 12pp., parts. 10 min. Four movements. Chromatic chordal figuration, 3 with 4. All movements lead into others; freely tonal. M-D.

———— *Sonata–Fantaisie* II 1914 (ESC 1953) 44pp., parts. 22 min. Allegro non troppo; Largo; Rondo Allegro Final. Bravura writing, colorful, chromatic, tremolos, octotonic, requires finesse and endurance. D.

———— *Sonata* III (ESC 1920) 40pp., parts. 22 min. Adagio non troppo; Allegro vivace scherzando; Molto animato e final. Final is two pages long and serves as coda. Pianistic figurations spread over keyboard; large span required. D.

———— *Sonata* IV (ESC 1923) 20 min. Four movements.

Imre Vincze. *Sonata* (EMB 1956).

Giovanni Battista Viotti. *Six Sonates a violon seul et basse, 2ᵉ Livre.* Paris: Nadermann, ca.1800. This edition is in the Music Division of the New York Public Library. This same collection also contains Viotti's *Six Sonates pour violon et basse . . .Oeuvre 4, 1ᵉʳ Livre de Sonates.* Paris: Boyer, 17_ _ ?

———— *Artifici Musicali* Op.XIII 1689 (L. Rood, G. P. Smith—Smith College Music Archives, XII). Contains "Canons of various kinds, double counterpoints, curious inventions, capricii and sonatas." There are two sonatas at the end of this collection. The first is in five movements, slow, fast, slow, fast, slow, the second in four, slow, fast, slow, fast. The second sonata is thematically related. Excellent material for the less experienced duo but also would work well in the recital program, placed in the proper context. M-D.

Tommaso Antonio Vitali. Son of Giovanni Battista Vitali. *Concerto di Sonate* Op.4 (D. Silbert, G. P. Smith, L. Rood—Smith College Music Archives, XII). Cello part optional. Twelve pieces in the set; the last is an ostinato work on the "folia" theme. Nos. 8 C, 9 G, and 11 b are especially attractive and would be fine choices for the student duo.

———— *Sonate* Op.4/2 (J. P. Hinnenthal—Br 1959) HM 38. A delightful work with contrasting movements and some surprising harmonic procedure. Int. (except for the improvised ornamentation).

Antonio Vivaldi. *12 Sonatas* Op.2 1709 (W. Hillemann—Schott 1953) 2 vols. (4212, 4213). (S. A. Luciani—Instituto di Alta Cultura). This edition is a miniature score with the figured bass line unrealized. These works are fine and deserve playing even though they are closely related to Corelli's works. A preview of later things to come.
Available separately: No.1 g (Moffat—Simrock). No.2 A (Pierre—Ouvrières; Jensen—Augener 7423). No.3 d (IMC). No.7 c (Mompellio—Zanibon 3751).

———— *4 Sonatas* Op.5 1716 (W. Upmeyer—Nag 162 1954). No.1 F, No.2 A, No.3 B♭, No.4 b. There is a good deal of rhythmic monotony in these sonatas; No.4 is the finest of the group. This set also contains two trio sonatas. M-D.

———— *4 Sonatas for Maestro Pisendel* 1716–7 (H. Grüss, W. H. Bernstein—DVFM 8101 1965). These works are some of Vivaldi's best efforts.
Available separately (Vivaldi left thirty sonatas for violin and basso continuo): The F. number refers to the classification system devised by Antonio Fanna and used by the Instituto Italiano Antonio Vivaldi, under whose sponsor-

ship the complete works of Vivaldi are being brought out. *Sonata* F.XIII/5 g (Malipiero—Ric PR1006; Br&H). *Sonata* F.XIII/6 D (Respighi—Ric 128437; Malipiero—Ric 1014). *Sonata* F.XIII/7 d (Malipiero—Ric PR1015). *Sonata* F.XIII/8 C (Malipiero—Ric PR1016). *Sonata* F.XIII/9 d (Malipiero—Ric PR1017). *Sonata* F.XIII/10 c (Malipiero—Ric PT1018). *Sonata* F.XIII/11 C (Malipiero—Ric PR1019). *Sonata* F.XIII/12 A (Malipiero—Ric PR1020). *Sonata* F.XIII/13 G (Malipiero—Ric PR1021). *Sonata* F.XIII/14 (Malipiero—Ric PR1022). *Sonata* F.XIII/15 g (Malipiero—Ric PR1023). *Sonata* F.XIII/16 B♭ (Malipiero—Ric PR1024). *Sonata* F.XIII/29 g (Malipiero—Ric PR1069). *Sonata* F.XIII/30 A (Malipiero—Ric PR1070). *Sonata* F.XIII/31 (Malipiero—Ric PR1071). *Sonata* F.XIII/32 F (Malipiero—Ric PR1072). *Sonata* F.XIII/33 b (Malipiero—Ric PR1073). *Sonata* F.XIII/34 C (Malipiero—Ric PR1074). *Sonata* F.XIII/35 c (Malipiero—Ric PR1075). *Sonata* F.XIII/36 (Ric). *Sonata* F.XIII/37 e (Ric). *Sonata* F.XIII/38 f (Ric). *Sonata* F.XIII/39 D (Ric). *Sonata* F.XIII/40 a (Ric). *Sonata* F.XIII/41 F (Ric PR1105). *Sonata* F.XIII/42 A (Ric PR1106). *Sonata* F.XIII/43 B♭ (Ric PR1105). *Sonata* F.XIII/44 b (Ric PR1108).

Václav Vodička. *Sei (6) Sonate* (C. Schoenbaum—Artia 1962) MAB 30. This set, Op.1, was published in Paris in 1739 and in London in 1745. The pieces have no great musical depths but are fresh and energetic throughout. No.1 B♭, No.2 C, No.3 d, No.4 G, No.5 A, No.6 F. No.6 is probably the best in the set. The opening Siciliana is followed by a virtuoso Allegro. A concluding Menuetto with variations gives very full chords to the keyboard part, adding a massive effect to the end of the set. Int. to M-D.

Alexander Voormolen. *Sonate* (Rouart-Lerolle).

Jan Hugo Voříšek. *Sonata* Op.5 G (J. Štědroň, B. Štědroň—Artia 1956) MAB 30. 49pp., parts. Introduzione—Allegro moderato: poetic beginning; opening and closing sections of the movement are emphasized; the Allegro moderato (SA) consists of the main subject, which is progressively repeated with rising dramatic intensity. Scherzo: ranks among the most magnificant of Voříšek's writings; written in a scintillating, buoyant, and brilliant piano style; large ABA form in which B has an independent Trio; short coda. Andante sostenuto: violin pours out an ardent song supported by a basso ostinato in the piano; profoundly emotional writing; leads directly to Finale: SA; exciting; briskly flowing triplets alternate with lyrical song idea; short coda. A marvelous Romantic-type sonata on a par with the Romantic sonatas of the greatest masters. Has much audience appeal. D.

George Walker. *Sonata in One Movement* 1958 (AMP 1097). 20pp., parts.

10 min. Lento–Allegro–Moderato–Meno mosso–Andante (senza mesura)–Molto Adagio. Key signatures of two flats and three sharps are encountered. Centers around Phrygian mode on D. A short introduction is followed by a fugue, a scherzo-like meno mosso (g♯), a recitative, and the final Molto Adagio reworks the opening introductory material. Pianistic. M-D.

Johann Jakob Walther. *Scherzi da Violino solo con il Basso Continuo* 1676 (Nag 1953). Unaltered reprint of *Das Erbe deutscher Musik,* Vol. 17 (1941).

———— *Sonate* (E. Bethan—Nag 89 1931). This is *Sonata* No. 4 of the *Scherzi* set. 9pp., parts.

———— *Sonate mit Suite* für Violine und Generalbass, Hortulus Chelicus 1688 No.2 (M. Seiffert—K&S 1930) No.28 Organum, Dritte Reihe.

William Walton. *Sonata* (OUP 1950) 42pp., parts. 26 min. Violin part edited by Yehudi Menuhin, for whom the piece was written. In two movements that are mainly lyric and with enough formal structure to produce clear designs. Allegro tranquillo: freely tonal and biting harmonies with rhythmic quirks add much interest. Variazioni: seven variations with enough thematic variety so that square sectionalism is nicely avoided; the theme presents two statements of a twelve-note series, which takes on more importance as the movement progresses but is never treated strictly. D.
See: H. Murrill, "Walton's Violin Sonata," M&L, 31/3 (July 1950): 208–15.

Robert Ward. *Sonata* I 1950 (PIC) 20pp., parts. Andante amabile: opens in a slow tempo with a sensitive lyric melody; fast part of this movement has much rhythmic vitality, changes in meter, quiet and relaxed closing. Allegro barbaro: much rhythmic activity, a cheerful second subject and an interesting fughetta add color. Demanding writing for both instruments, especially some of the complex rhythms. Requires a large span. D.

R. Bedford Watkins. *Four Burlesques* (CF 1962). 6 min. Facsimile edition. D.

Ben Weber. *Sonata* I Op.5 1939 (CFE) 10pp., parts. 8 min. One movement of bold gestures, bouncy rhythms, varied tempi, exhilarating, atonal, witty. Requires large span. D.

———— *Sonata* II Op.16 1940–2, rev. 1943 (CFE) 19pp., parts. 8 min. Poco andantino; Allegro moderato. Strong tonal implications in this twelve-tone ornate work, coloristic and brilliantly effective, well constructed. D.

———— *Sonata da Camera* Op.30 (Bo&H 1954) 20pp., parts. 9 min. Lento, con gran eleganza; Moderato; Allegro con spirito. Atonal melodic lines that produce mildly dissonant counterpoint. Light textures with successive movements that are noble, declamatory, graceful, meditative, and animated. Piano part is brilliant and difficult, but effective. D.

Carl Maria von Weber. *Six Sonatas* Op.10B 1810 (E. Zimmermann, H.-M. Theopold, K. Röhrig—Henle 1971 48pp., parts; David—CFP). Written for amateurs, with each sonata supposedly more difficult, but the idea is scarcely evident. In the Henle edition editorial marks are printed in brackets, and some performance suggestions are included in the preface. The piano part is much more interesting. *Sonata* 1 F (8 min.); *Sonata* 2 G "Carattere Espagnuolo" (8 min.); *Sonata* 3 d "Air russe" (4½ min.); *Sonata* 4 E♭, Variations. "Thema aus 'Silvana'"; *Sonata* 5 A; *Sonata* 6 C (8½ min.). M-D.
Available separately: Larghetto (Romance) from *Sonata* 1 (Kreisler—Schott).
See: VKDR, II: pp.65–66.

Anton Webern. *Vier Stücke* Op.7 (UE 1922) 5½ min. 1. Sehr langsam; 2. Rasch; 3. Sehr langsam; 4. Bewegt. In his catalogue of Webern's works, Friedrich Wildgans says of Op.7: "These highly concentrated pieces . . . already demonstrate the composer's conscious attempts to express every musical thought in the briefest possible form. They are, so to speak, the basis, as well as the point of departure, for those works of the middle period—without being built on the concept of a 12-note structure—that finally break with the old tonal connections; they also finally do away with traditional thematic form. In their place motivic working appears, with extremely brief motifs of only a few notes, sometimes only highly expressive, isolated single notes acting as motifs." *Anton Webern,* trans. Edith T. Roberts and Humphrey Searle (London: Calder and Boyars, 1966), "Critical Catalogue of Works," p.24. Ethereal and strange music that requires the most careful attention to dynamic polarity. D.

Leo Weiner. *Sonata* Op.9 D (Rózsavölgyi 1911) 24 min.
_____ *Sonata* II Op.11 f♯ (EMB 1918).

Stanley Weiner. *Sonata* IV Op.33 (Billaudot 1973) 56pp., parts. Andante misterioso: freely tonal around d, octotonic, 3 with 2, large rolled chords, arpeggi figuration in left hand under varied melodic line in right hand, passages in thirds. Allegro feroce: percussive chords in low register, bitonal scales, extreme ranges exploited together, brilliant conclusion with glissando. Un poco lento: octotonic, shifting meters, chromatic, involved syncopated rhythmic passages, parallel chromatic chords. Allegro vivo: 3/8 3/8

2/8, octaves, repeated chords in alternating hands, toccata-like, virtuoso writing à la Prokofieff. D.

Adolph Weiss. *Sonata* 1941 (ACA) 16 min. A dynamic fabric of contrapuntal movement with cumulative activity produced through a structure of constant vitality. D.
_____ *Five Fantasies Based on Gagaku* 1956 (CFE) 4–6 min. each.

Eberhard Werdin. *Vier Fantasien* (Möseler 1974) Hausmusik 110. 11pp., parts.

Thomas Wilson. *Sonata* (Chappell).

Ermanno Wolf-Ferrari. *Sonata* Op.10 a (Rahter 1902) Elite Edition 202. This is the second of two sonatas for violin and piano, the other is Op.1. Two movements. Fast, intricate interweaving of both instruments in chromatic lines full of Romantic harmonies. Very difficult for both performers. D.

Christian Wolff. *Duo* (CFP 6494).

Stefan Wolpe. *Sonata* 1949 (McGinnis & Marx 1955) 71pp., parts. Un poco allegro; Andante appassionato; Lento; Allegretto deciso. Extreme dissonance, atonal melodic lines, complex rhythms. Special signs are used to indicate phrase units and focal points. Bar lines in piano and violin parts frequently do not coincide. Variation technique at work throughout. D.
_____ *Sonata* (CFE). Uses electronic sounds.

Charles Wuorinen. *Duo* 1966–7 (CFP 66376) 39pp., parts. 15 min. Serial, pointillistic, frequently changing meters, proportional rhythmic relationships, harmonics. Stretches the sonic limits of both instruments with some incredible effects. Large gestures and form, extraordinary virtuoso vehicle for both pianist and violinist, strong avant-garde writing. Requires large span. D.
_____ *Fantasia* (CFP) 15 min.

Yehudi Wyner. *Concert Duo* 1955–7 (AMP 1968) 38pp., parts. 20 min. I. Chromatic, atonal, serial influence, changing meters and tempi, tremolo, ferocious, optional number of repeated figures, expressionistic. II. Broad, slow, voicing problems, subtle bop style, discreetly irregular, many character and performance directions, maximum power required of piano, sudden dynamic changes, pointillistic, virtuoso writing for both instruments. D.
_____ *Three Informal Pieces* 1961, rev. 1969 (MS available from composer:

% School of Music, Yale University, New Haven, CT 06520). 1. Chromatic, dynamic extremes, pointillistic; parts sometimes play independently of each other. 2. Alternating hands, triplets spread over keyboard, tremolo, varied tempi, enormous climax; rhythmic notation is approximate at one place. 3. Subtle, sempre dolcissimo, highly expressive. All three pieces fit both instruments uniquely and make a most effective grouping. M-D.

Julien-Francois Zbinden. *Sonata* Op.15 (SZ 5278 1956). Four movements; the first two are the most engaging. The opening Preludio shows off both instruments in dialogue, reaches numerous climaxes, then ends calmly. The lively Scherzo uses flexible meters and driving rhythms. A short Romanza precedes a sparkling finale, which features a brilliant display in the piano part. Thematic material from the opening movement returns to conclude the work. D.

Efrem Zimbalist. *Sonata* g (GS).

Bernd Alois Zimmermann. *Sonata* 1950 (Schott 4485) 24pp., parts. 15 min. Sonata; Fantasia; Rondo. Freely tonal and dissonant; effective and thoroughly contemporary writing throughout. D.

Duos for Piano and Viola

Carl Friedrich Abel. *Six Sonatas* 1759 (HM 39&40) 2 vols. For viola da gamba, continuo, and cello ad lib. Vol. I: (Joseph Bacher, W. Woehl) *Sonatas* e, D, G. Vol.II: (Waldemar Woehl) *Sonatas* C, A, A. Excellent continuo realizations. M-D.

Charles-Valentine Alkan. *Sonate de Concert* Op.47 1857 (Hugh Mac-Donald—Br 19122 1975) for cello (or viola) and piano. See duos for piano and cello for more detailed entry.

William Ames. *Sonata* (CFE 1953) 51pp., parts. Moderately fast: chromatic, triplet chordal figuration, thick sonorities in middle keyboard range. Slow: extensive introduction in piano with melodic octaves, freely chromatic, span of ninth required. Fast: syncopation, piano introduction, similar chordal treatment as in first movement, fugal treatment; coda uses both instruments in a broad melodic presentation of main ideas. Requires stamina. D.

David Amram. *The Wind and the Rain* 1963 (CFP) 9pp., parts. 7 min. Based on the second movement of the "Shakespearean Concerto for Small Orchestra." A gentle opening featuring open fifths builds to an intense and chromatic climax before subsiding. An effective and colorful character piece. M-D.

Hendrik Andriessen. *Sonata* 1967 (Donemus).

Jorges Antunes. *Microformóbiles I* 1971 (SZ) 4pp. two scores required for performance. This work is formed by four Microformóbiles, A, B, C, and D. The violist arranges the four choosing one of the 24 possibilities listed. After choosing the combination, the performers play continuously without interruption. Diagrammatic notation in part, clusters, aleatoric, pointillistic, avant-garde. D.

Edward Applebaum. *Foci* (JWC 1973) 6pp., parts. 7½ min. Harmonics for both players, some spatial handling in piano part. A "tour de force" for viola. Serially oriented. D.

Michael J. Appleton. *Sonata* g 1967 (Thames 1973) 8pp., parts. The piano part is for left hand alone. M-D.

Attilio Ariosti. *Sonatas* 1, 2 (Sabatini Renzo—DeSantis 981). From *Six Sonatas for Viola d'Amore* 1724.

———— *Stockholm Sonatas* (Günther Weiss—HM 221) 19pp., parts. Continuo realized by Theodor Klein. Part I: *Sonatas* F, a, G. These sonatas were among fifteen recently discovered by the editor in a copy made by the Swedish composer Johann Helmich Roman (1694–1758), probably while Roman was studying with Ariosti in London. Attractive writing in the traditional style of the period, but the phrases are short and some of the cadence treatment is not too exciting. *Sonatas* F and a are in four movements; *Sonata* G is in three. Idiomatic continuo realization. M-D.

See: David D. Boyden, "Ariosti's Lessons for Viola d'Amore," MQ, 32 (1946): 545–63.

Günther Weiss, "57 Unbekannte Instrumentalstücke (15 Sonaten) von Attilio Ariosti in einer Abschrift von Johan Helmich Roman," *Die Musikforschung,* 33 (1970):127–38.

Malcolm Arnold. *Sonata* Op.17 (Lengnick 1948) 20pp., parts. 13 min. Andante; Allegretto grazioso; Presto feroce. Tempo changes are integral parts of the outside movements. Effective tremolo writing for the piano. Span of ninth required in middle movement. Mildly contemporary. M-D.

Jacob Avshalomoff. *Sonatine* (Music Press 1947) 28pp., parts. Allegro appassionato: d; open fifth chords alternate between hands; arpeggio figuration coupled with melody at points; freely tonal. Lento: f♯; slow legato chords in outer sections; more movement in mid-section. Allegro con brio: d; driving rhythmic octaves in right hand over punctuated left-hand moving octaves; meno mosso, grazioso section flows freely before opening rhythmic idea returns. Neoclassically oriented. M-D.

Milton Babbitt. *Composition for Viola and Piano* 1950 (CFP 1972) 26pp., parts. 10 min. Opening and closing sections use the viola muted and the piano una corda. The basic row series of the work is most easily heard in these sections. Fluid rhythmic treatment throughout this compelling and forceful work. D.

Carl Philipp Emanuel Bach. *Sonata* g (Primrose—IMC).

Wilhelm Friedemann Bach. *Sonata* c (Yella Pessl—OUP 1945) 32pp., parts. 15 min. Adagio e mesto; Allegro non troppo; Allegro scherzando. Realization of the figured bass is set in small print. It follows good eighteenth-century style in bringing out the melodic possibilities of the keyboard, but it is only a suggestion. A charming and delightful work. M-D.

Henk Badings. *Sonata* 1951 (Donemus) 26pp., parts. Allegro: driving rhythms in viola, full pesante chords in piano, cluster-like sonorities, free dissonant counterpoint, many major sevenths, triplet and quadruplet figuration. Largo: repeated full chords, arpeggi figures. Vivace: many chords chromatically colored, long melodic lines broadly contoured, large span required. Milhaud and Hindemith influence noted. D.

Granville Bantock. *Sonata* F 1919 (JWC). Allegro: strong, stimulating writing; agitated syncopation. Slow movement: 5/4, nocturne-like, emotional and melancholy, forceful climax before serene and wistful ending. Vivace: lilting like a Scottish jig, careful working-out of ideas and development, two episodes, long coda constructed on opening theme. M-D.

George Barati. *Cantabile e Ritmico* 1947 (PIC 1954). Cantabile: broad lines with interesting contour and harmonic experiments; requires large span. Ritmico: more contrived but effective in its own way. M-D.

David Barlow. *Siciliano* 1958 (Nov) 6pp., parts. Freely tonal, flowing, mildly contemporary, chromatic figuration. M-D.

Leslie Bassett. *Sonata* (CFE).

David S. Bates. *Sueña—Gestures and Interludes One* (APR).

Marion Bauer. *Sonata* (SPAM 1951) 32pp., parts.

Arnold Bax. *Sonata* 1921–2 (Chappell). Heroic opening movement. "Satanic" scherzo with a cataclysmic climax is followed by a wistful closing section. Finale ends with opening theme from the first movement, although the work is not cyclic in form. M-D to D.

Gustavo Becerra-Schmidt. *Sonata* (IU) 41pp., parts. Allegro giusto; Andante; Allegro con brio. Movements complement one another. Mildly contemporary. Rhythmic treatment in final movement is especially well handled. Large span required. M-D.

Jack Beeson. *Sonata* 1953 (TP 1973) 28pp., parts. Cantando: large span required, changing meters; longer lines in piano part; freely tonal; viola has to play some pitches a quarter-tone sharp or flat; grace notes used to facilitate large intervals; large span required. Presto giocoso: light arpeggi figures, sprightly and bouncy, "clattering" at one spot near end. Andante moderato: chorale-like; more intense and involved un poco più largamente section; chorale-like opening returns to close movement in a Sereno and warmly rich mood. Written within today's mainstream tradition with formal and structural problems beautifully solved. M-D.

Arthur Benjamin. *Le Tombeau de Ravel* (Bo&H). A suite of "Valse-Caprices."
———— *Sonata* (Bo&H). Elegy; Waltz; Toccata. Brilliant, entertaining, slight material. Idiomatic writing for the piano. M-D.

William Bergsma. *Fantastic Variations on a Theme from Wagner's Opera Tristan und Isolde* 1961 (Galaxy). Neoclassical, strong tonal leanings, florid melody, dissonant. M-D.

Lennox Berkeley. *Sonata* d (JWC 1947) 28pp., parts. 17 min. Allegro ma non troppo; Adagio; Allegro. Neoclassic, expansive, lyric. Clear writing. M-D.

Christlieb Siegmund Binder. *Sonata* A (Ruf—Schott). Cello part ad lib.

Easley Blackwood. *Sonata* 1953 (EV 1959) 35pp., parts. 13 min. Adagio quasi senza misura ma non troppo rubato: freely chromatic; flexible meters; six-note chords give cluster impression; lies in low or middle registers until closing, then moves up. Allegro molto: shifting rhythms in a brief introduction that leads to a Theme—Andante moderato e cantabile and six contrasting variations. Andante tranquillo: picks up mood and figuration of first movement opening for a short time, then moves to an Allegro molto e meccanico that drives to a brilliant conclusion. Neoclassic and expressionistic tendencies. D.

Arthur Bliss. *Sonata* 1933 (OUP 22.405) 60pp., parts. 28 min. Moderato: tonal, chromatic, arpeggi figuration, tremolo; requires large span. Andante: rich harmonies, buoyant melodies, ostinato-like, individual lines. Furiant: dancelike, brilliant, chordal punctuation, long trills. Coda: returns ideas from previous movements; cadenza for both instruments. Brilliant writing in the tradition of Liszt and Rachmaninoff. D.

Ernest Bloch. *Meditation and Processional* (GS 1954) 7pp., parts. Meditation: d, chromatic, serious, climax near end, *p* closing, long phrases, warm and impassioned with occasional Hebraic touches. Processional: modal, stately, well-pronounced bass line necessary, *p* closing. Colorful and imaginative writing using strong contrapuntal lines. Grateful to play. M-D.

Siegfried Borris. *Sonata* Op.51 (Sirius).

Mauro Bortolotti. *Combinazioni Libere* 1965 (Ric) 10pp., parts. "Improvvisazione per viola e pianoforte." Harmonics, plucked strings, clusters, pointillistic, mildly avant-garde. M-D.

Will Gay Bottje. *Fantasy Sonata* (CFE).

Carlos Botto. *Fantasia* Op.15 1962 (IU) 9pp. two copies necessary for performance. Opening Andante exploits interval of major seventh; mormoranto e rubato. Followed by an Adagio ma non troppo that works up more excitement with short motives and leads to a cadenza for the viola. Tempo I Adagio follows and moves directly into a highly rhythmic Allegro ma non troppo. Piano gets arpeggi figures before unwinding in a ben ritmato finish. Well written for both instruments. M-D.

York Bowen. *Sonata* I c 1909 (Tertis—Schott). Virtuoso treatment of viola. Reflective opening movement, graceful and charming slow movement, strong introduction to finale that contains much dramatic writing. M-D.

Andries de Braal. *Introduzione ed Allegro Capriccio* 1969 (Donemus) 21pp., parts. Introduzione is free, recitative-like with dramatic gestures for both instruments, cadenza passages, tremolo. Leads directly to the Allegro Capriccio: driving rhythmic first part is juxtaposed with a meno allegro free and alla cadenza section. Allegro driving rhythmic section returns and these two basic contrasts return again before the work seemingly evaporates. Mildly contemporary. An effective "show piece" for both performers. M-D.

Johannes Brahms. *Sonatas* Op.120/1,2 (Monica Steegmann—Henle; Hans-Christian Müller—VU; Br&H; Jonas—Simrock; Katims—IMC; Augener). These sonatas were first published in 1895 together with an arrangement of the clarinet part for viola. Critical notes are given in the Henle and the VU editions. They also contain very good page turns in the piano part. These works show a fusion of melodic material and development procedures unrivaled in Brahms. D.

Benjamin Britten. *Lachrymae* "Reflections on a Song by John Dowland"

Op.48 1950 (Bo&H 17817) 16pp., parts. Ten contrasting variations and a coda. Freely tonal. A catalogue of Britten's eclectic techniques. The incorporation of another composer's music in his own style is an important characteristic of Britten. The writing uses some plain simple harmonies and falls under the fingers ingeniously. M-D.

Revol S. Bunin. *Sonata* (USSR).

Eldin Burton. *Sonata* 1957 (CF 1960) 40pp., parts. 21 min. Moderato; Molto vivace; Lento drammatico; Allegro agitato. A well-crafted work with thoroughly contemporary techniques and idioms. Piano writing is efficient and fits idiomatically with the viola. M-D.

Claudio Carneyro. *Khroma* 1954 (Sociedade Portuguesa de Autores) 9pp., parts. This is the first piece by a Portuguese composer using twelve-tone technique. It is written in an atonal chromatic style in which the sporadic use of a twelve-tone series does not fulfill the task ɓa structural base. ABA design with A the exposition and expansion of the main theme, B a viola cadenza, and A¹ a re-exposition of the initial theme by contrary motion with a concluding development. M-D.

Elliott Carter. *Pastorale* 1940 (TP) 15pp., parts. 12 min. Allegretto (Tempo I) serves as a unifying factor—tempi gradually increase until they return to Tempo I. Tricky rhythmic problems, quick octave grace notes in left hand. Piano part is very active and has some interesting sonorities. Experiments with texture and tone color. M-D.
——— *Elegy* 1943, rev. 1961 (PIC 1964) 4pp., parts. 5 min. Adagio sostenuto: chromatic; low register preferred; harmonics; exquisite legato required. M-D.

Alexandre Cellier. *Sonate* G♭ (Senart 1923) 25pp., parts. Lento con molto fantasia; Allegro non troppo; Lamento; Allegretto simplice. Idiom of post-Franck, Dukas. Pianistic; all formal limitations are correct. D.

Josef Ceremuga. *Sonata Elegica* (Panton).

Jacques Chailley. *Sonate* (Leduc 1950) 32pp., parts. 26 min. Semplice: SA; first and second themes are developed concurrently; first theme is in the nature of a folksong. Grave: meditative; sombre; two themes alternate between the instruments. Scherzo: vigorous; contrasts with the supple songlike trio; somewhat reminiscent of the first idea in the Semplice. Final: various ideas treated in rondo fashion; brilliant conclusion. Freely tonal in a mildly contemporary style, attractive. D.

Rebecca Clarke. *Sonata* (JWC 1921). Three imaginative rhapsodical movements, Impressionistic. Impetuoso first movement in SA design. Fascinating scherzo of thin textures. A short introduction opens the finale, which has a pentatonic main theme combined with the introductory thematic material. Freely tonal. Instruments maintain equality throughout. M-D.

Dinos Constantinides. *Sonata* 1971 (MS available from composer: % School of Music, Louisiana State University, Baton Rouge, LA 70803) 24pp., parts. 24 min. For viola and/or cello and piano. Moderato: freely moving lines, flexible rhythms, freely tonal. Adagio: widely spread sonorities, dramatic gestures, sostenuto pedal effectively used. Allegro moderato: thin-textured opening section moves to a complex perpetual motion part that completely involves both performers. Distinctly modern in flavor. D.

Arnold Cooke. *Sonata* F 1937 (OUP 1040). Emotional reserve. Shows influence of Hindemith (Cooke's teacher).

Paul Cooper. *Variants II* (JWC 1975) 8pp., parts. 7 min. One bolt is required for piano preparation, and a few strings must be damped; strumming on strings. Six sections freely repeated, with some given number of seconds to repeat: Dramatic; Serene; Joyous; Calm; Resolute; Tranquil. Thoroughly contemporary writing, somewhat avant-garde, but all put to the best musical use. Sensitive sonorities, clear indications. M-D.

Roque Cordero. *Tres Mensajes Breves* 1966 (LAMC). Allegro comodo: rhythmic orientation. Lento: viola has introduction; piano begins *pp,* works to a *ff* climax and recedes; expressionistic sonorities. Molto allegro: dramatic gestures over keyboard. Effective set. M-D.

Michel Corrette. *Sonata* (Schott VAB38). Viola part has most bowings and some fingerings marked. Realized figured bass has an additional part for cello, which is to be used when a harpsichord is used, not with piano. M-D.

Henry Cowell. *Hymn and Fuguing Tune VIK* (PIC 1953) 14pp., parts. Hymn: Larghetto, thin textures, imitation, diatonic. Fuguing Tune: con moto, corky rhythms, imitation; longer lines developed; left-hand octaves provide a "standing bass." M-D.

Paul Creston. *Suite* Op.13 1937 (SP) 12 min.

Arthur Custer. *Parabolas* 1970 (Gen 1972) 22pp., parts. I. Ah: serial; clusters; free sections synchronized only at bar lines, sustained notes are held for duration indicated, others are played at discretion of performers;

tempo and dynamics ad lib.; both performers are to sing "Ah" and play where indicated; octotonic. II. Block That Kick: opening similar to "Ah"; both performers sing "Block That Kick" in a dirgelike manner; if there is a page turner, he should rise and conduct this section; free sections; wide dynamic range. Mixture of avant-garde and traditional. Can be a fun piece. D.

Karl Ditters von Dittersdorf. *Sonata* E♭ (Hans Mlynarczyk, Ludwig Lürmann—Hofmeister 7280) 14pp., parts. Allegro moderato; Menuetto I; Adagio; Menuetto II; Tema con (8) variazioni. The viola part has been provided with bowings and fingerings. Ornaments are written out in full. The realized piano part follows the original bass. F. J. Haydn influence noted in this charming work. M-D.
———— *Sonata* E♭ (Schroeder—Br&H). Cello ad lib.
———— *Sonata* E♭ (Vieland—IMC).

Zsolt Durkó. *Varianti* 1974 (EMB) 16pp., parts.

Henry Eccles. *Sonata* g (Klengel—CFP 4326).
———— *Sonata* g (Katims—IMC).

Helmut Eder. *Sonatina* Op.34/2 (Dob 1963) 12pp., parts., 5 min. Allegretto leggiero; Adagio molto, quasi recitativo; Allegro con spirito. Neoclassic orientation with expressionistic characteristics; dramatic gestures in finale. M-D.

Christopher Edmunds. *Sonata* D (Nov 1957) 21pp., parts. Andante comodo; Lento espressivo; Allegro moderato. Three pleasantly contrasted movements in a mildly contemporary, flowing style. M-D.

Manuel Enrique. *Cuatro Piezas* 1962 (IU) 11pp., parts. Serial. Lento: dramatic opening and closing, expressionistic. Con fuoco: impulsive, dynamic extremes, pointillistic. Allegretto: misterioso introduction leads to Allegro, other tempo changes; mainly quiet; all over keyboard. Moderato ritmico: a thorny maze. Requires experienced and fine performers. M-D to D.

Robert Evett. *Sonata* 1958 (CFE) 14 min. Based on intricate and ingenious thematic material yet it is almost singable. The opening Allegro movement is one of concentrated power and spirit with humorous splashes here and there. The finale consists of an introduction and a minuet derived from the minuet in Mozart's *Don Giovanni,* but by moving harmonic devices and in other subtle ways Evett turns out an intriguing movement. M-D.

Johann Friedrich Fasch. *Sonata* (Doktor—McGinnis & Marx).

Morton Feldman. *The Viola in My Life* 1970 (UE 15402) 3pp., parts. 6 min.
"There are four pieces by Morton Feldman with the title 'The Viola in My
Life.' They are separate and independent pieces, not single movements.
Feldman is not a violist, but a worshipper or admirer of Walter Trampler
and Karen Phillips, who are violists—very good ones" (from a letter to the
author from John D. Wiser, Vice-President, Joseph Boonin, Inc., May 18,
1976). This writer has seen only the first three of these scores. The one
listed here is metrically notated. The piano part consists of isolated six- to
eight-part chords. Tranquil, simple gestures, agreeable sounds. M-D.

Jacobo Ficher. *Sonata* Op.80 1953 (IU) 34pp., parts. Allegro moderato: C,
SA, quixotic opening motive, longer idea for second tonal area. Lento: C,
many seventh chords, chromatic. Allegro: rhythmic vitality, propulsive, C
conclusion. M-D.

Fidelio Fritz Finke. *Sonata* (Br&H).

Ross Lee Finney. *Sonata* a (Robert Courte—Henmar 66254 1971) 27pp.,
parts. 13½ min. Allegro moderato con moto: octotonic, chromatic, free
dissonant counterpoint, thin textures. Largo sostenuto: imitation, moving
harmonic thirds, more rhythmic Tranquillo section. Allegretto con spirito:
vigorous rhythms contrasted with broad and sustained chords; strong traditional forms throughout. M-D.

———— *Second Sonata* (Robert Courte—Henmar 1971) 35pp., parts. 15 min.
Andante, teneramente; Permutations; Largo, teneramente; Allegro con
moto. Clear textures, freely tonal, natural development of ideas. M-D.

William Flackton. *Sonata* C Op.2/4 (Bergmann—Schott; Renzo
Sabatini—Dob DM62 1960, cello ad lib.) 7pp., parts. Four short, contrasting movements: Largo grazioso; Allegro; Siciliano; Minuet I & II. Good
simple, clean editing. M-D.

———— *Sonata* D Op.2/5 (Sabatini—Dob). Cello ad lib.

———— *Sonata* G Op.2/6 (Sabatini—Dob, cello ad lib.; Schott).

———— *Sonata* c 1776 (Antony Cullen—Lengnick 1955) 8pp., parts. Adagio;
Allegro moderato; Siciliana; Minuetto (with one variation). Tasteful continuo realization. M-D.

Flackton's *Sonatas* Op.2 were the first original sonatas for viola composed in
England.

François Francoeur. *Sonata* IV E (Alard, Dessauer—IMC).

Robert Fuchs. *Sonata* Op.86 d 1909 (UMKR No.5) 23pp., parts. Allegro moderato, ma passionata; Andante grazioso; Allegro vivace. Written in a Brahmsian idiom with expert craftsmanship. M-D.

Sandro Fuga. *Sonata* (EC 1975) 52pp., parts.

Norman Fulton. *Sonata da Camera* 1945 (JWC 1952) 24pp., parts. 13½ min. Lento e appassionata; Poco lento, ma sempre ritmico; Poco Allegretto, con amore. Eclectic style, freely tonal, mildly contemporary, interesting rhythmic treatment. M-D.

Paul Walter Fürst. *Sonatina* Op.13 (Dob 1966) 24pp., parts. Allegro, spielerisch; Scherzando, nicht zu schnell; Langsam, mit grossern Ausdruck; Bewegt, Übermütig. Freely tonal, octotonic, repeated notes in alternating hands, flowing quality, neoclassic. M-D.
———— *Sonata* Op.33 (Dob).

Hans Gál. *Sonata* Op.101 (Simrock Elite Ed. 3150 1973) 25pp., parts. Adagio; Quasi menuetto, tranquillo; Allegro risoluto e vivace. Tonal, chromatic, Brahms influence noted, nineteenth-century pianistic idioms in a mildly contemporary guise. M-D.
———— *Suite* Op.102a (Simrock Elite Ed. 3151 1973) 29pp., parts. Cantabile: large rolled chords support melody in viola; requires large span. Furioso: chordal, syncopated, octaves, contrasted tranquillo section, octotonic. Con grazia: chromatic, counterpoint between the two instruments. Burla: dancelike, chromatic, expressive inner voices, chromatic octaves, viola cadenza. M-D.

Fritz Geissler. *Sonatina* (Br&H 5818 1954) 11pp., parts. Kleiner Marsch; Elegie; Lebhaft bewegt. In style of Hindemith. Very expressive Elegie. M-D.

Harald Genzmer. *Sonata* D 1940 (R&E) 23pp., parts. 15 min. Fantasie; Thema mit (5) variationen. Chromatic, large arpeggiated chords, secco and sustained styles contrasted, linear, strong traditional forms, neoclassic. M-D.
———— *Sonate* II 1955 (Br 3223) 38pp., parts. Allegro; Adagio; Presto; Tranquillo–Vivace. Has many characteristics of solid neoclassical style. Thorough musicianship required of both performers. Superb ensemble writing. M-D to D.
———— *Sonatine* (Litolff 1973) 15pp., parts. Short, three movements in a dissonant but mainly diatonic style. Effective finale alternates bars of 3/4 with 7/8. Int. to M-D.

Ottmar Gerster. *Sonate* (Hofmeister 7178 1956) 20pp., parts. 11½ min. Allegro; Andante (based on a Russian folksong); Finale. Tonal with chromatic coloring, traditional forms, post-Brahms style with fast harmonic rhythm in the finale. Large span required. M-D.

Diamandi Gheciu. *Cintec* (Editura Muzicală a Uniunii Compozitorilor).

Miriam Gideon. *Sonata* (CFE).

Mikhail Glinka. *Sonata* d (Musica Rara 1961) 26pp., parts. Allegro moderato; Larghetto ma non troppo. This work was written between 1825 and 1828, but remained unfinished; in the present edition it has been completed by V. Borisovsky, who also edited the viola part. Those sections realized by the editor have been printed in small type. Glinka wrote several chamber works during his visit to Italy in the early 1830s. "As Glinka himself realized, the Viola Sonata is the most successful of his pre-Italian compositions; although intended primarily for domestic music-making, it contains, to use his own expression, 'some quite clever counterpoint.' Free from the Italianate mannerisms which mar some of his larger chamber works, it has a directness and charm which make it an important addition to the viola-piano repertoire" (from the score). M-D.

Johann Gottlieb Graun. *Sonata* I B♭ (Hellmut Wolff—Br&H 1937) 12pp., parts. Cello ad lib. Adagio (suggested cadenza included); Allegretto; Allegro non troppo. Creditable editing. M-D.
———*Sonata* II F (Hellmut Wolff—Br&H 1937) 21pp., parts. Cello ad lib. Adagio non molto (suggested cadenza included); Allegro; Allegro ma non tanto. M-D.
Both sonatas contain some lovely, if traditional, writing.

Giovanni Battista Grazioli. *Sonata* F (Marchet—Augener 5569).

Camargo Guarnieri. *Sonata* 1950 (IU) 30pp., parts. Tranquillo; Scherzomolo; Con intusiasmo. This work has all of Guarnieri's characteristics: linear conception, dramatic writing for both instruments, plenty of rhythmic drive, well-developed ideas, a gift for knowing what works well at any given moment. D.

Erich Hamann. *Sonata* Op.33 (Dob 1952) 16pp., parts. Allegro ma non tanto; Thema und (8) Variationen; Allegro molto. Chromatic, mixture of chordal and linear style, minor theme with contrasting variations, octotonic, pedal points, Presto closing. Mildly contemporary. M-D.

Iain Hamilton. *Sonata* Op.9 1950 (Schott) 18 min. Three movements of aggressive writing, similar to the fierceness and intensity of early Bartók. Complex harmonies, propulsive rhythms, extremes of registers permeated with dissonance. The Alla marcia funèbre introduced in the last 30 bars of the finale has its counterpart in the stark Lento potente heard at the opening of the work. D.

Xaver Hammer. *Sonata* D (Edition Musicus).

George Frederick Handel. *Sonata* A (David, Hermann—IMC).
_____ *Sonata* Op.1/15 A (Forbes, Richardson—OUP 22.007) 13pp., parts. Originally *Sonata* E for violin and figured bass. Adagio; Allegro; Largo; Allegretto. Generally a fine transcription with the exception of a few spots where the piano texture is too thick. M-D.
_____ *Sonata* C (Folkmar Längin—Br 1953 HM 112) 13pp., parts. Larghetto; Allegro; Adagio; Allegro. Beautifully contrasted movements. Outer movements are motoric. M-D.
_____ *Sonata* e (Courte—H. Elkan).
_____ *Sonata* 10 G (Alard, Meyer—IMC).
_____ *Sonata* g (Katims—IMC).

Julius Harrison. *Sonata* c 1945 (Lengnick 3474) 41pp., parts. 23 min. Allegro energico; Andante e cantabile sempre; Scherzo—Finale. Broadly planned, neo-Romantic style, traditional pianistic techniques and idioms. Requires large span. D.

Tibor Harsanyi. *Sonata* 1953–4 (Heugel 1958) 26pp., parts. 16 min. Harsanyi's last completed work. Allegro cantabile: SA, 5/8, freely tonal around e–E, many sequences, lovely tranquillo coda. Adagio: ABA, 3/4; chromatic, angular theme, long lines in piano part, almost atonal. Allegro giocoso con vivo: SA, vigorous rhythms, octotonic, highly chromatic, attractive but difficult and fluent writing with marked individuality, large span required. D.

Walter Hartley. *Sonata* (Interlochen Press).

Bernhard Heiden. *Sonata* 1959 (AMP 1968) 44pp., parts. Allegro moderato: flowing, linear conception. Andante sostenuto: unfolds naturally to an Adagio *ppp* closing. Vivace, ma non troppo: flexible meters, clear lines; a mistake is noted 6 bars after C in left hand of piano part—Cb should be C♯. Lento: attention-getting, leads into Allegro molto: opening two-note motif ingeniously develops throughout rest of movement; Lento idea returns (now extended) before an Allegro vivace brings this jaunty movement to a climactic conclusion. M-D.

Oscar van Hemel. *Sonata* (Heuwekemgijer).

Swan Hennessy. *Sonata Celtique* Op.62 E♭ (ESC 1924) 15pp., parts. More a fantasy than a sonata. Allegro con brio: SA design, with popular tune "St. Patrick's Day in the Morning" used with counterpoint in the development section. Andante sostenuto: a simple and charming folktune, treated chordally. Allegro: two contrasting themes are the basis for the finale, one (Celtic) syncopated in 2/4, the other in 6/8. Tuneful writing with a strong Irish idiom. M-D.

Heinrich Freiherr von Herzogenberg. *Legends* Op.62 1890 (Musica Rara 1975 27pp., parts, preface in English by Harold Truscott; UWKR 34 1974 29pp., parts, preface in German and English by W. Sawodny). Andantino: a slow minuet. Moderato: a dark ballade with a radiant tune. Andante: a set of variations on a simple folk-like tune of the composer's invention. Brahms influence. These three well-contrasted pieces exhibit considerable formal and technical skill and are similar to Schumann's pieces as examples of the small form. M-D.

Paul Hindemith. *Sonata* Op.11/4 F (Schott 1919) 26pp., parts. 18 min. Fantasie (Ruhig); Theme mit Variationen; Finale (mit Variationen). Opening movement quiet; shows some French influence in the whole-tone usage but is mainly a large Brahmsian melodic idea contrasted with more delicate moments. In spite of the second and third movements both being sets of variations, the variation techniques are different enough to provide contrast and still hold the work together. Forceful and vital writing in Hindemith's most Romantic vein. D.

———— *Sonata* C 1939 (Schott) 48pp., parts. 23 min. Breit, mit Kraft–Ruhig–Lebhaft: aggressive and angular. Sehr lebhaft: shows some ragtime influence, ferocious climax. Phantasie: mysterious dialogue between the instruments. Finale (mit 2 Variationen): opens in quixotic spirit and grows to weighty proportions with fugal overtones. Formidable and inexhaustible pianism required. D.

Arthur Honegger. *Sonata* (ESC 1921) 27pp., parts. Andante: sustained introduction leads into a Vivace section; these two ideas and contrasting moods are juxtaposed throughout this movement three times. Allegretto moderato: flowing sixteenths in piano move into a Poco più allegretto with a grazioso marking; this movement is very "French" sounding. Allegro non troppo: basically sectional; diatonic material contrasts with chromatic ideas; bold melodic line in viola; pianist's left hand must span a tenth. M-D.

Zoltán Horusitzky. *Sonata* (EMB 1974) 28pp., parts. Con passione; Andante; Presto con fuoco. Freely tonal, neoclassic principles at work, parallel chords, strong and syncopated rhythms in finale, Hindemithian flavor. M-D.

Alexandru Hrisanide. *Sonata* 1965 (Gerig 1975) 15pp., parts. 8 min. Explanations in German and English.

Jaromír Hruška. *Sonata* (Artia).

Bertold Hummel. *Sonatina* (Simrock). Interesting rhythmic study. Int. to M-D.

Johann Nepomuk Hummel. *Sonata* Op.5/3 E♭ 1798 (Doktor—Dob 1960, 27pp., parts, preface by editor; Louise Rood—McGinnis & Marx 1957, 36pp., parts, preface by editor). Allegro moderato; Adagio cantabile; Rondo con moto. This impressive work is written in a lyric and polished style that shows Mozartian elements logically infused with clear Romantic characteristics. Equal demands on both performers. M-D.

Karel Husa. *Poem* 1960 (Schott 1963) 19pp., parts. 13 min. Originally written for viola and orchestra; piano arrangement by the composer. Husa's style shows a fascinating combination of influences from his background and from his study with Arthur Honegger and Nadia Boulanger. Improvvisando; Misterioso; Dolce. Chromatic, harmonics, much rhythmic freedom, tremolo, individual style with lyric and dramatic elements. M-D.

John Ireland. *Sonata* (Lionel Tertis—Augener 1924) 24 min. See description under cello and piano section. Cello part arranged for viola and edited by Tertis.

Jean Eichelberger Ivey. *Music* (CF 1976) 2 scores, 11pp. each. Facsimile edition. 10 min. The pianist requires a grand piano with lid removed, and the following percussion accessories: metal beater, untuned finger cymbals, and soft timpani sticks. Partly avant-garde, effective. D.

Gordon Jacob. *Sonatina* (Nov 1949) 22pp., parts. 12 min. For viola or clarinet (in A) and piano. Allegro giusto; Andante espressivo; Allegro con brio. Octotonic, neo-Romantic with freely tonal tendencies, careful balancing of instruments throughout. Traditional forms. M-D.

Wolfgang Jacobi. *Sonata* (Sikorski 387 1956) 31pp., parts. Allegro molto; Lento; Prestissimo, impetuoso–Allegro. Octotonic, varied textures but mainly thin, chromatic, low-register trills. Opening returns in the Prestissimo, impetuoso section. Final Allegro is fugal, brilliant ending. Large span required. D.

Joseph Joachim. *Variations* Op.10 E (Musica Rara 1975; Br&H 1855) 23pp., parts. Ten variations, with extended coda, on a theme by the composer. "The variations grow with a power similar to that found in later sets by Brahms, so that they form a single structure, not a collection of separate pieces" (from the score). Joachim's contrapuntal mastery is well in evidence in these variations. The whole set is crowned by the final variation and coda. "The music moves finally to a quiet restatement of the theme and a further part variation. Altogether the work is masterly and, in my opinion, is one of the two finest works ever written for viola and piano, the other being the Sonata by Arnold Bax" (from notes in the score by Harold Truscott). M-D to D.

John Joubert. *Sonata* Op.6 (Nov 1954) 14 min. Although strongly influenced by William Walton, this is nevertheless a work of distinction showing first-rate craftsmanship and an appreciation of the need for "light and air" in a musical work. Transparent texture, tonal. All three movements are based on a single, three-note melodic germ heard at the opening. Cyclic construction. Piano writing suggests the influence of César Franck. The exuberant Prestissimo finale tends to overwork the unifying device. M-D.

Paul Juon. *Sonata* Op.15 D (Lienau; Katims—IMC) 25pp., parts. Moderato; Adagio assai e molto cantabile; Allegro moderato. Strong Brahms influence mixed with Slavic themes and rhythms. D.

Sigfrid Karg-Elert. *Sonata* II Op.139B (Zimmermann) rev. ed. 1965, 27pp., parts. Ziemlich bewegt; Sehr rasch, mit Übermut. Constant chromatic sound full of technical difficulties; intense; great contrasts in mood, tempi, and dynamics. Requires large span. D.

Robert Keldorfer. *Sonata* 1964 (Dob 1966) 20pp., parts. Allegro moderato; Andante sostenuto; (7) Variationen über "Da Steht ein Kloster in Österreich." Tonal, chromatic, sections in free counterpoint contrasted with more chordal sections, passacaglia-like treatment in middle movement.

Variation movement is based on a tune from the *Antwerpner Liederbuch 1514*. M-D.

Homer Keller. *Sonata* (CFE).

Robert Kelly. *Sonata* (CFE) 13 min.

Rudolf Kelterborn. *9 Momente* (Bo&Bo 1973) 9 leaves (partly folded), two copies necessary for performance. 12½ min. Explanations in German. Contrasting, proportional notation, glissandi, clusters, pointillistic, serial influence, expressionistic, unusual pedal effects, dynamic extremes, avantgarde. D.

Friedrich Kiel. *Sonate* Op.67 g 1871 (Amadeus Verlag 1972, 39pp., rarts; UWKR 22 1972, 30pp., parts). Polished and tasteful writing. Allegro: broad theme, lyrical second group, full and rich harmonies. Scherzo: syncopated theme (Schumannesque), lively second subject. Andante con moto: colorful arpeggi; could be performed separately. Allegro molto: horn-fifths beginning; increased activity; interrupted by impassioned recitative; concludes quietly. Instruments equally balanced throughout. Thematic relationships between the movements. M-D.
———— *Three Romances* Op.69 ca.1870 (Harold Truscott—Musica Rara 1972) 15pp., parts. Andante con moto (B♭); Allegretto semplice (G); Allegro con passione (e). Movements well contrasted; react on one another to form one work, not three separate pieces. Beautiful balance in style and texture between the large slow movement, which is the first piece, with its broad but restrained main melody and more impassioned minor middle part; the lighter mood of the second piece, the shortest of the three; and the "appassionato" of the final one. Superb writing for both instruments. M-D.

Julius Klaas. *Sonata* Op.40 c (Heinrichshofen 1965) 40pp., parts. Bewegt; Langsam; Sehr geschwind; Mässig bewegt, aber energisch. Written in Brahms tradition. D.

Charles Koechlin. *Sonate* Op.53 (Senart) 30½ min. Dramatic first movement. Adagio is mainly an introduction that presents material and establishes mood for the rest of the work. Elfin but ominous Scherzo. Sombre but restless opening section of the finale is followed by a restful episode that continues this mood to the end of the work. D.

Egon Kornauth. *Sonata* Op.3 c♯ (Dob 1913) 33pp., parts. 24 min. Allegro deciso; Andante, molto espressivo; Allegro feroce ed impetuoso. Highly chromatic, post-Brahms idiom. D.

———— *Sonatine* Op.46a (Dob 1959) 16pp., parts. 11 min. Available for flute (violin) and piano as well as for viola and piano. Rondino; Intermezzo; Siciliano. Centers around e–E, chromatic, much thinner textures than the Sonata. M-D.

Miroslav Krejči. *Sonata* Op.57 c♯ (Hudební 1944).

Ernst Křenek. *Sonata* 1948 (Belwin-Mills) 15pp., parts. Andante; Allegro vivace; Andantino. Partial twelve-tone technique; much academic, emotionally cold note-spinning. M-D.

Kenneth Leighton. *Fantasia on the name BACH* (Nov 1957) 14 min. Neo-Romantic with some mildly contemporary techniques. M-D to D.

Frank Levy. *Sonata Ricercare* (Seesaw 1972) 15 min. M-D.

Alfonso Letelier Llona. *Sonata* 1951 (IU) 35pp. Allegro: Bien en ritmo opening moves to a short Lento section before returning to Allegro; frenetic closing. Lentamente: repeated chords in piano, freely tonal, large span required. Vivace: elaborate movement well worked out; broad gestures moving over keyboard bring this piece to a stunning conclusion. D.

Pietro Locatelli. *Sonata* g (David, Hermann—IMC).
———— *Sonata* Op.6/2 (Doktor—IMC).

Jean-Baptiste Loeillet (of Lyons). *Sonata* B♭ (IMC).
———— *Sonata* f♯ (IMC).

Edwin London. *Sonatina* 1962 (New Valley Press) 30pp., parts. Allegro ma non troppo; Molto adagio; Allegro dondolamento. Serial, free rhythmic independence between parts (in piano), bold gestures, arpeggi figures, glissando, expressionistic, shifting meters in finale, thoroughly contemporary idiom. Requires large span. D.

Otto Luening. *Suite* (Galaxy 1972) 23pp., parts. For cello or viola and piano. See detailed entry under duos for piano and cello.

Marin Marais. *Five Old French Dances* (JWC) 13pp., parts. L'Agréable; La Provençale; La Musette; La Matelotte; Le Basque. Short, contrasted, traditional treatment of piano part. Int.

_____ *Suite* I d (George Hunter—GS) for viola da gamba and basso continuo. No separate gamba part. From Book IV of *Pièces de Viole* 1717. Makes strong demands on the string player. Seven short movements, all in d. Imaginative realization of the continuo part. Several inaccuracies in notes and clefs. Facsimile included. M-D.

Benedetto Marcello. *Sonata* Op.2/2 e (Augener; Marchet—IMC) 7pp., parts. Adagio; Allegro; Largo; Allegretto. Augener edition is over-edited in dynamic and accent marks. M-D.
_____ *Sonata* F (Sosin—USSR 4935).
_____ *Two Sonatas* F, g (Katims—IMC).
_____ *Two Sonatas* G, C (Vieland—IMC).
_____ *Sonata* Op.2/6 G (Gibson—Schott).
_____ *Sonata* Op.2/4 g (Piatti, d'Ambrosio—Ric 125328).

Carlo Marino. *Sonata* D (Karl Stierhof—Dob 1973) DM 361. 11pp., parts. Grave; Allegro; Largo; Adagio; Allegro. A stylistically appropriate continuo realization has been added by F. A. Hueber. Originally for viola da gamba. Marino is considered the true founder of the Bergamo violin school.

Jean Martinon. *Rapsodie* 72 (Billaudot 1972) 15pp., parts. Sectional, numerous tempi changes, expressionistic, intense, based on opening broken-chord idea, freely dissonant, serial influence. Thorough musicianship required. D.

Bohuslav Martinů. *Sonata* I 1955 (Fuchs—AMP 1958) 32pp., parts. 17 min. Poco andante: changing meters; freely tonal around F; pedal points; full chords in introductory section; dance qualities present; varied textures and figurations; coda based on materials in introductory section; large span required. Allegro non troppo: free dissonant counterpoint; sixteenth-note patterns; octotonic; 3 with 4; broken-chord triplet figuration; varied tempi; syncopation; Allegro busy closing leads to final section that slows, thins textures, and ends on a restful C. D.

Jiří Matys. *Sonata* Op.16 (Artia).

Wilfrid Mellers. *Sonata* C 1946 (Lengnick 1949) 27pp., parts. 17 min. Lento; Rondo—Allegro agitato; Molto adagio. Mildly contemporary; piano part has much activity; preference for tritone noted in the Lento. Large span required. M-D.

Jacques de Ménasce. *Sonate en un mouvement* 1955 (Durand) 17pp., parts.

Adagio–Allegro–Fugato–Allegro–Adagio. Chromatic; verges on atonal writing; changing meters; chordal in Adagio sections; dance qualities in Allegro sections; logical thematic development; many rhythmic sequences. M-D.

Felix Mendelssohn. *Sonata* c 1823–4 (DVFM 1966) 36pp., parts. Adagio–Allegro: Introduction, SA, arpeggiated first subject, more diatonic second subject, extensive development; coda uses material from both subjects. Menuetto: Allegro molto, skilful writing, fleeting, contrasting chorale-like Trio. Andante con variazioni: theme is similar to theme in the *Variations Sérieuse* Op.54; eight extensive variations; recitativo section, Allegro molto, provides soaring conclusion. M-D.

Arthur Meulemans. *Sonata* 1953 (CeBeDeM) 16 min.

Paul Baudouin Michel. *Mystère—jeu* (CeBeDeM 1976) 8pp., parts. $4\frac{1}{2}$ min.

Marcel Mihalovici. *Sonata* Op.47 E♭ 1942 (Heugel 1948) 58pp., parts. 25 min. Allegro serioso: SA, freely tonal around E♭, staccato rhythms, octotonic, wide dynamic range; requires large span. Agitato e vehemente: ABA, vigorous rhythmic drive, flowing chromatic mid-section, percussive. Andante espressivo: ostinato-like figures, misterioso section based on left-hand arpeggi figures and right-hand rolled semi-clusters, numerous tempi changes, expressionistic. Allegro tranquillo: low octaves, ostinato-like, full syncopated chords, 3 with 2, octotonic, appassionato closing. Neoclassic with influence of Enesco, Bartók, and Les Six. D.
———— *Textes* Op.104 1974 (Heugel) 20pp., parts. Notes in French.

Darius Milhaud. *Sonata* I 1944 (Heugel) 23pp., parts. 12 min. Based on eighteenth-century themes. Entrée; Française; Air; Final. Light and transparent writing. M-D.
———— *Sonata* II 1944 (Heugel) 18pp., parts. 12 min. Champêtre: pastoral. Dramatique: funeral march. Rude: vigorous. M-D.

Philipp Mohler. *Concertante Sonate* Op.31 (Schott) 22 min. Introduction; Vivace assai; Intermezzo a la recitativo; Allegro con brio.

Wolfgang Amadeus Mozart. *Sonata* E♭ (University Music Press).
———— *Sonatina* E♭ (Courte—H. Elkan).
———— *Sonatina* F (Courte—H. Elkan).
———— *Sonata* G (Courte—H. Elkan).

Pietro Nardini. *Sonata* I B♭ (Alard, Dessauer—IMC).

_____ *Sonata* D (Katims—IMC).

_____ *Sonata* f (Zellner—IMC; Cranz) 9½ min.

Karl Ernst Naumann. *Sonata* Op.1 g (Amadeus 1975) 23pp., parts.

Willi Niggeling. *Sonata* G (Mitteldeutscher Verlag 1057) 25pp., parts. Moderato; Adagio; Allegretto. Neoclassic in Hindemith tradition but slightly more tonally oriented. M-D.

Georges Onslow. *Sonata* Op.16/2 c (Uwe Wegner—Br 1972) 41pp., parts. For viola or cello and piano. Parts for viola and cello. Dates from before 1820. Allegro espressivo; Minuetto; Adagio cantabile; Finale—Allegretto. Written in classical style (Beethoven); interesting if not innovative. M-D.

_____ *Sonata* Op.16/3 A (Höckner—Simrock).

Robin Orr. *Sonata* (Forbes—OUP 1949) 16 min.

Juan Orrego-Salas. *Mobili* Op.63 1968 (IU) 21pp., parts. Flessibile: dramatic gestures. Discontinuo: syncopation; extreme ranges of keyboard used. Ricorrente: steady chordal movement; viola has cadenza-like section. Perpetuo: changing meters; large span required. Written in a contemporary international style; well crafted. M-D.

Léon Orthel. *Sonata* Op.52 (Donemus 357 1965) 24pp., parts. 16 min. Lento non troppo; Allegro vivo; Lento non troppo–Allegro moderato. Strong emotional intensity, highly pianistic, mildly contemporary in a Stravinskyesque, neoclassic vein. D.

Hall Overton. *Sonata* 1960 (CFE) 58pp., parts. 18 min. One extensive movement. Serial influence, changing meters, syncopated chords, sonorous qualities, octotonic, percussive effects, fast chords in alternating hands; varied moods, tempi, textures, and idioms. Virtuoso writing for both instruments. Rich timbres and strongly emotional, flexible compositional technique; smoldering intensity. Large span required. D.

Robert Palmer. *Sonata* 1951 (PIC 1962) 24pp., parts. Andante con moto e sempre cantabile: octaves, freely tonal, independent lines, syncopated triplets, emphatic chords at cadence points, intense. Allegro risoluto: short pungent motives, complex layers of rhythms, vigorous and rhythmic, octotonic, important inner voices, serious brilliant conclusion; large span required. D.

Robert Parris. *Sonata* 1957 (CFE) 16pp., parts. 10 min. Andantino: flowing chromatic contrapuntal texture; octotonic; large span required; coda leads directly to Canzona: dissonant linearity, gradual increase in tempo and intensity, dramatic Allargando closing. Unique impersonal and austere style. M-D.

Alan Paul. *Sonata* F (Bosworth 1948) 16 min.

Ahmad Pejman. *Sonatine* (Dob 1975) 28pp., parts.

Elena Petrova. *Sonata* (Panton 1974) 23pp., parts.

Hans Poser. *Sonatine* Op.54/3 (Sikorski 1973) 16pp., parts.

Henry Purcell. *Suite* (Joseph Vieland—IMC 1973).

Fernand Quinet. *Sonate* (Senart).

Priaulx Rainer. *Sonata* (Schott 1945) 15pp., parts. 12 min. Thin harmonies and textures. Melodic material extended and developed. First movement treats ricercar form freely. Slow movement uses linear writing. Last movement alternates 3/8 and 5/8 rhythms. Whole work looks towards the past for its inspiration. M-D.

Günther Raphael. *Sonata* Op.13 E♭ (Br&H).
———— *Sonata* II Op.80 (Br&H 1954) 16 min.

Alan Rawsthorne. *Sonata* (OUP 1937, rev. 1954) 16 min. Sonata-form individually approached with parts omitted and recapitulations compressed. Heavy and thick piano writing. First movement consists of a slow introduction followed by a toccata-like Allegro. A condensed form of the introduction and a fast coda round off the movement. Second movement consists of a scherzo and two trios. The serious and expressive slow movement is a short set of variations that leads directly to the finale, a delightful and vivacious rondo. M-D.

Carl Reinecke. *Phantasiestücke* Op.43 (UWKR 32 1974) 25pp., parts. Romanze; Allegro molto agitato; Humoreske. Three pieces that are Schumannesque in character. Melodious; make much use of arpeggi figuration and short motivic material. M-D.

Albert Reiter. *Sonata* (Dob 1962) 24pp., parts. Ruhig bewegt; Rasch; Langsam; Lebhaft. Harmonic fourths, left-hand octaves, free counterpoint, freely tonal, octotonic, traditional forms, diatonic lines, neoclassic. Large span required. M-D.

Hermann Reutter. *Musik* (Schott 4338). Sarabande; Pastorale mit Cantus Firmus; Variationen über "Es ist ein Ros entsprungen"; Fuge.

Antal Ribári. *Sonata* (Lukacs—Kultura).

Alan Richardson. *Sonata* Op.21 (Forbes—Augener 1955) 20 min. Four movements, pentatonic usage, well crafted, many sequences and clichés. M-D.

Roger Roche and Pierre Doury. *Concertinetto* I (Chappell 1973) 3pp., parts.

Anton Rubinstein. *Sonata* Op.49 f 1857 (Br&H 35pp., parts; USSR 1960). Moderato; Andante; Moderato con moto; Allegro assai. Rapturous melodies are seemingly present everywhere. Piano part inundates viola at times, especially in arpeggi sections. Effective piano writing. M-D to D.

Witold Rudzinski. *Sonata* (PWM 1946) 14 min. Masovienne; Aria; Gigue.

Erkii Salmenhaara. *Sonata* (Fazer).

Helmut Schiff. *Sonata* (Dob 1960) 28pp., parts. Allegro agitato; Andante; Vivace assai. Thin textures, freely tonal à la Hindemith, octotonic, long lines especially in the Andante, straightforward rhythms, neoclassic. M-D.

William Schmidt. *Sonata* 1959 (WIM 1968) 30pp., parts. 11 min. In a lyrically expressive manner: spread-out broken chords, chromatic, varied tempi, independent lines; large span required. Slowly—unagitated: expressive disjunct lines, faster and lighter section, dancelike, opening tempo and mood return to close work. M-D.

Anton Schoendlinger. *Sonata* (Br&H 5819 1955) 20pp., parts. Allegro, ma non troppo; Adagio; Allegro. Freely tonal, chromatic, thin textures, quartal and quintal harmony, toccata-like finale, neoclassic. M-D.

Robert Schollum. *Sonata* Op.42/2 1950 (Dob 1963) 20pp., parts. 10 min. Ruhige, breite; Sehr rasch. Twelve-tone; timbres are related to styles of Debussy and Milhaud; austere writing. D.

Robert Schumann. Märchenbilder ("Fairytale Pictures") Op.13 (Br&H;

Litolff 19pp., parts) Nicht schnell: requires a cantabile style. Lebhaft: rhythmic, exuberant, joyful. Rasch: restless and agitated. Langsam mit melancholischen Ausdruck: tender, wistful, and cantabile. M-D.

Jean Baptiste Senaille. *Sonata* IX Op.5 (Morgan—Augener 7405a) 10 min.

Albert Sendrey. *Sonata* (EV 1947) 30pp., parts. With Spirit; Slow Alla Breve; With Humor, fast. Mildly contemporary with Impressionistic and a few jazz influences. All directions are given in English; some very unusual but helpful. Requires well-developed technique and ensemble experience. M-D.

Ralph Shapey. *Duo* (CFE 1957) 17pp., parts. The Andante con expressivo section has many combined meters (2/4 + 3/16, 1/8 + 1/4 (3/8), 2/4 + 3/16, etc.), is highly expressionistic, with complex harmonies and rhythms and a quasi cadenza for viola with piano participating. The segues to Leggiero section is pointillistic, while the segues to Andante con espressivo section accelerates to a Maestoso conclusion. Only for the most adventurous and highly qualified performers. D.

Dmitri Shostakovich. *Viola Sonata* Op.147 (Bo&H; GS 1975) 44pp., parts. The composer's last completed composition. Sparse textures; piano frequently treated percussively; viola splurges with plenty of Russian "cantabile." M-D.

Otto Siegl. *Sonata* I Op.41 (Dob 1925) 20pp., parts. Molto vivace; Adagio espressivo; Allegro vivace. Bitonal, chromatic, traditional pianistic idioms, serious and intense. Requires large span. M-D to D.
_____ *Sonata* II Op.103 E♭ (Dob).

Fritz Skorzeny. *Sonate* (Dob).

Leland Smith. *Sonata* 1954 (CFE) 16pp., parts. For heckelphone or viola and piano. Three untitled movements. Chromatic, cluster-like sonorities, harmonics. Second movement to be played "as a waltz"; fast harmonic rhythm. Final movement is energetic, intense, expressionistic. Requires large span. D.

Jozsef Soproni. *Sonatina* 1964 (Zenemükiado Vállalat) 24pp., parts. Allegretto spirituoso; Aria—Lento ma non troppo; Burletta—Animato, molto agitato. This writing, of fairly thin textures, contains an attractive amount of Hungarian flavor. The chromatic triplet in the slow movement creates a strangely haunting effect. M-D.

Vladimír Soukup. *Sonata* 1961 (Český Hudební Fond Praha 1969) 28pp., parts. Adagio: quasi recitativo opening for viola; gradually works in piano and rises to a Pesante *fff* before a subito Adagio, *ppp* closing. Allegro con brio: brilliant gestures for piano including tremolo chords between hands; martial, repeated, driving chords lead to an Allegro feroce, Pesante *fff* ending; an exciting movement. Mildly contemporary with ample dissonance. M-D.

Norbert Sprongl. *Sonata* Op.115 (Dob 1958) 32pp., parts. Andante sostenuto; Lento; Vivace. Chromatic, neoclassic, excellent craft. M-D to D.

Karl Stamitz. *Sonata* B♭ (Gustav Lenzewski—Vieweg V1678, 23pp., parts; Primrose—IMC) 14½ min. Allegro; Andante moderato; Rondo. Similar to Mozart's music but lighter in style. Contains some interesting dialogue between the instruments. M-D.
_____ *Sonata* e (Borissovsky—IMC).

Halsey Stevens. *Serenade* 1944 (Helios 1971) 4pp., parts. For viola or clarinet and piano. Piano provides rocking figure while viola soars melodically, then piano gets its own melody and, with the viola, produces a flowing duet. Sensitive chordal sonorities are used and the work centers freely around e. Large span required. M-D.
_____ *Suite* 1945, rev. 1953 (CFP 1959) 16pp., parts for clarinet and viola. 9½ min. See detailed entry under duos for piano and clarinet.
_____ *Sonata* 1950 (CFE) 23 min. Mainly diatonic with chromatic surprises and easily identifiable ideas. Chords in fourths and sometimes double thirds are suggested by the flow of melodic lines. Concentrated organic structure. Spontaneous and flowing. First movement: main idea (a three-note motive) in the slow introduction returns many times in various disguises and is developed in an urgent and vigorous movement. Second movement: slow, a leisurely siciliano; darkly colored melody floats over rich sonorities in the piano. Third movement: exciting writing with a rhythmically complex subject; main idea from first movement is brought back and treated in different ways and acts as a unifying device. M-D.
_____ *Suite* 1959 (PIC 1969) 24pp., parts. 12 min. Poco andante: flowing lines, freely centered around C, large span required. Allegro moderato: cross rhythms, mildly dissonant, hemiola, vigorous rhythmic thrust. Allegretto: octotonic, short brittle figures contrasted with octave punctuation, imitation. Allegro moderato: main theme treated percussively (quasi campane), canon, effective voice-leading, thin sonorities as in most of entire suite. Neoclassic. M-D.

Robert Still. *Sonata* II (JWC 1956) 24pp., parts. 13½ min. One continuous movement with sectional markings such as: Moderato, Lentamente, Un poco posato (with an element of the sedate), Ghiribizzoso, fuga libera. Thin textures, tonal, neoclassic, mildly contemporary. M-D.

Morton Subotnick. *Sonata* (McGinnis & Marx).

Giuseppe Tartini. *Sonata* Op.10/1 c (Forbes, Richardson—OUP 22.808) 8 min.
———— *Sonata* D (Hermann—IMC).
———— *Sonata* II F (Alard, Dessauer—IMC).

Georg Philipp Telemann. *Sonata* a (Walter Schulz, Joseph Vieland—IMC 1957) 9pp., parts. Tasteful realization is by Diethard Hellmann. Largo; Allegro; Soave (a flowing Siciliano); Allegro. M-D.
———— *Sonata* B♭ (Ruf—Schott). Cello ad lib.
———— *Sonata* D 1734 (Hans Leerink—B&VP 1948) 5 min. Vivace; Adagio; Allegro. M-D.
———— *Sonata* D (IMC).

Heuwell Tircuit. *Sonata (Homage to Mahler)* 1961 (AMP 1975) 22pp., parts. Material for this work is loosely drawn from the viola introduction to Mahler's *Tenth Symphony*. Allegro legato: chromatic, scalar, plucked strings, dynamic extremes, glissandi, pointillistic, *ppp* fist clusters; large span required. Five Canons in Rondo: thin textures; keyboard lid (shut) must be tapped; both hands are used flat on strings. Avant-garde mixed with traditional techniques. D.

Francesco Trevani. Trevani was possibly a product of the school of Alessandro Rolla (1757–1841), whose compositions for viola were exceedingly numerous and instructive. *Three Sonatas* (Karl Stierhof—Dob 1967). Published separately. 1. E♭: 16pp., parts (DM 176). Andante; Allegro spiritoso. 2. c–C: 35pp., parts (DM 177). Allegro agitato; Allegretto (moves into an Adagio followed by a Tempo di waltz). 3. B♭: 39pp., parts (DM 178). Allegro; Adagio; Rondo; Allegretto. These works sound similar to middle-period Beethoven. Much greater demands on the pianist than on the violist. All are M-D and require solid pianistic equipment.

Lester Trimble. *Duo* (CFP 66076 1968) 24pp., parts. 12 min. Adagio; Allegro. "Mr. Trimble's *Duo for Viola and Piano* is cool in its lyrical aspects (they are none the less surely there) while its harmonic, contrapuntal and textural workmanship are refined, elegant and crystal clear. Its

allegro movement is jet-propelled . . . the work is professionality itself"
(William Flanagan, *New York Herald-Tribune,* [n.d.], listed on inside
cover of work).

Giuseppe Valentini. *Sonata* 10 E (Rakowski—PWM). Cadenza by Z.
Jahnke.

Johann B. Vanhal. *Sonata* Eb after 1787 (Alexander Weinmann—Dob
1970) DM 544. 31pp., parts. Foreword in German and English. Allegro
vivace; Poco adagio; Rondo—Allegro. Haydn-like (Vanhal moved among
the Haydn circle) but interesting enough to stand on its own merits. The
slow movement is especially poignant and is more involved than it appears.
M-D.

Nancy van de Vate. *Sonata* 1965 (Tritone) 19pp., parts. 14½ min. Moderately slow; Brightly; Slowly. Reproduction of composer's MS. Well
crafted, mildly contemporary, octotonic, free dissonant counterpoint, thin
textures predominate, traditional forms, movements complement each
other. M-D to D.

Aurelia de la Vega. *Soliloquio* 1950 (IU) 13pp., parts. 7 min. Andante: viola
alone. Sostenuto (Andantino tranquillo): 7/8, *pp,* dolce, syncopated chords
over punctuated left-hand octaves; builds to appassionato climax, then subsides. Poco piu mosso: cantabile. Animato (Allegro): two eighth-note seconds in right hand with triplet in left hand. Subito appassionato: full chords
over scalar and arpeggi left-hand figuration. Poco meno mosso: chordal,
long–short rhythm. Sostenuto (Andantino tranquillo): fuller treatment than
similar opening Sostenuto. Andante: viola alone. Poco piu mosso: espressivo. Tempo I (Sostenuto): chromatic ostinato in left hand, chromatic
chords in right hand. Well written for both instruments in a mildly contemporary style. M-D to D.

Francesco Maria Veracini. *Sonata* e (IMC).

John Verrall. *Sonata* I 1942 (Dow 1956) 21pp., parts. Eclectic writing
infused with dissonant angular counterpoint. Much use of major sevenths
and minor ninths, expressionistic, energetic Magyar rhythms in finale.
Tight structure, emphatic sonorities. M-D.
———— *Sonata* II 1964 (CFP 6587) 18pp., parts. Allegro: freely tonal, much
subtle syncopation, thin textures. Andante quasi adagio: free dissonant
counterpoint, octotonic. Allegro: rocking figures, chromatic. M-D.

Henri Vieuxtemps. *Elegie* Op.30 (Amadeus 1976) 9pp., parts.

_____ *Sonata* Op.36 B♭ 1863 (F. Beyer—Eulenburg GM181 1974) 25pp., parts. Maestoso; Barcarolla; Allegretto tranquillo–Animato; Finale scherzando. Thorough instrumental treatment but thematic material is uninteresting, and lack of contrapuntal usage adds to dullness. M-D.

Antonio Vivaldi. *Sonata* A (David, Hermann—IMC).

_____ *Sonata* III a (Primrose—IMC).

_____ *Sonata* B♭ (Primrose—IMC).

_____ *Sonata* g (Katims—IMC).

Andrei M. Volkonskii. *Sonata* (Belaieff 1976) 24pp., parts.

Alexander Voormolen. *Sonata* 1953 (Donemus 87) 21pp., parts. Andante mosso–Allegro moderato; Elegia; Allegro. Impressionistic influences mixed with Dutch humor and seriousness. Chromatic. The final Allegro alternates tempi (Allegro and Andante) effectively. Large span required. M-D.

František Vrana. *Sonatina* 1940 (Panton 1971) 31pp., parts.

Richard Henry Walthew. *Sonata* D (St&B).

Leopold Matthias Walzel. *Sonata Arioso* Op.30 1960 (Dob 1962) 22pp., parts. Allegro moderato: octotonic and chordal; tranquillo section requires four staves to notate; chromatic. Andante arioso: chromatic, disjunct melody, expressionistic. Allegretto scherzando: imitation, syncopated chords, parallel octaves, dance rhythms. D.

Leo Weiner. *Sonata* (Kultura).

Henri Wieniawski. *Rêverie* (PWM 1973) 7pp., parts. Wieniawski's only known work for viola. Completed by H. Wieckmann, to whom Wieniawski dedicated the work, and first published by Rahter, Leipzig in 1885.

Frank Wigglesworth. *Sonata* 1959 (ACA) 16 min.

_____ *Sound Piece* 1948 (ACA) 12 min.

George Wilson. *Sonate* 1952 (Jobert 1969) 28pp., parts. 13 min. Lento Sostenuto–Allegro, con moto; Adagio ma non troppo; Prestissimo. Serial, atonal, thin textures, freely dissonant counterpoint. All movements end quietly. D.

Joseph Wood. *Sonata* 1940 (CFE) 32pp., parts. Allegro; Adagio; Finale—Allegro. Chromatic; bitonal; augmented fourth is prevalent; surplus of ideas, some very good but not well developed. M-D.

Eric Zeisl. *Sonata* a (Reher—Dob).

Duos for Piano and Cello

Evaristo Felice dall' Abaco. *Sonata* C "La Sampogna" (Moffat, Whitehouse—Simrock).

Jean Absil. *Suite* Op.51 (CeBeDeM 1955) 27pp., parts. Introduction and Danse; Barcarolle; Intermezzo; Final. Dramatic gestures, chromatic, fluent pianistic treatment. D.
———— *2e Suite* Op.141 1968 (CeBeDeM) 20pp., parts. 17 min. Andante moderato; Allegretto poco scherzando; Andante; Vivo. Thinner textures than in Op.51; similar harmonic language and approach to the keyboard. D.

Gaetano Agazzi. *Sonata* Op.1/4 (Zanibon 4654).

Charles-Valentine Alkan. *Sonate de Concert* Op.47 1857 (Hugh Mac-Donald—Br 19122 1975) 77pp., parts. For cello (or viola) and piano. Cello and viola parts transcribed by Casimir Ney. "The bewildering variety of accents has been somewhat tempered, and fingerings in both parts and Alkan's tenuto markings (indicating exactitude, not prolongation) have been omitted. The pedal and metronome markings, on which Alkan was always insistent, are Alkan's own" (from the preface). Allegro; Allegrettino; Adagio; Finale alla Saltarella. Highly effective Romantic virtuoso writing. The Adagio carries the following verse at the beginning: ". . . as dew from the Lord, as showers upon the grass; that tarrieth not for man. . ." (Micah 5:7). The finale was also published as a piano duet. D.

Hendrick Andriessen. *Sonate* (Senart).

Edward Applebaum. *Shantih* (JWC 1969) 10pp. 7½ min. Two scores necessary for performance. Serial-like, harmonics for both instruments, tempo changes, much rubato, abstract. D.

José Ardévol. *Sonatina* 1950 (Ric BA10927) 16pp., parts. 10½ min. Andan-

tino; Lento–Vivo; Allegretto. Neoclassic orientation with Spanish syncopations. M-D.

Attilio Ariosti. *Six Sonatas* (Carisch).
_____ *Sonata* I E♭ (Schott).
_____ *Sonata* II A (Piatti, Such—Schott).
_____ *Sonata* III e (Salmon—Ric; Piatti—Schott).
_____ *Sonata* IV F (Piatti—Schott).

Richard Arnell. *Four Serious Pieces* Op.16 (Hin 1958). Prelude; Toccata;
Intermezzo; Recitative and Scherzo.

Bonifazio Asioli. *Sonata* C (Grützmacher—Simrock).

Tony Aubin. *Cantilène Variée* (Leduc 1946) 20pp., parts. Undulating theme
is varied five times, extensive coda. Colorful and complex writing using
numerous contemporary techniques. Requires seasoned ensemble performers. D.

Georges Auric. *Imaginées* 1969 (Sal) 15pp., parts. One movement with
varied tempi and moods. Percussive piano treatment is contrasted with soft
Webernesque sonorities. Tremolo in inner and outer voices, syncopation,
chromatic octaves, sonorities are allowed to sound for a long time. Dedicated to Mstislav Rostropovitch. D.

Victor Babin. *Sonata–Fantasia* G (Augener).
_____ *Twelve Variations on a Theme of Purcell* (AMP).

Carl Philipp Emanuel Bach. *Sonata* W.136 D 1746 (P. Klengel—Br&H
4169) 13pp., parts. Andante; Allegro moderato; Allegretto. Originally for
gamba. Not as fussy as some of C.P.E. Bach's works. Slightly heavy
editing. M-D.
_____ *Sonata* W.137 (Klengel—Br&H; R. van Leyden—CFP; 13pp.,
parts). Originally for gamba.
_____ *Six Sonatas* (Balassa—Artia).

Johann Christoph Friedrich Bach. *Sonata* A 1770 (August Wenzinger—Br
3970 1961) 15pp., parts. Larghetto; Allegro; Tempo di Minuetto. "The
nobility of the melodic line in the first movement and the freshness and
grace of the quick movements mark it as one of the most charming pieces of
the literature for cello between the periods of the baroque and classic"
(from the preface).

———— *Sonata* G (Hugo Ruf—Br 3745 1959) 12pp., parts. Allegretto; Rondeaux.

———— *Sonata* D (J. Smith—Litolff).

Johann Sebastian Bach. *Sonata* S.1017 G (Schroeder—Augener 5501).

———— *Three Sonatas* 1717–23 (Rolf van Leyden—CFP 4286 Preface in French, German, and English; Naumann—Br&H; Grützmacher—CFP 239; Klengel—Br&H; Forbes—CFP; Klengel—Br&H; Naumann—IMC). S.1027 G: Adagio; Allegro, ma non tanto; Andante; Allegro moderato. S.1028 D: Adagio; Allegro; Andante; Allegro. S.1029 g: Vivace; Adagio; Allegro.

These three sonatas are included in *Seven Sonatas* (Lea 10) for flute and clavier.

Henk Badings. *Four Concert Pieces* (Donemus 1947) 25pp., parts. Serenade; Scherzo pizzicato; Air triste; Rondo giocoso. Piece can stand alone, or together as a fine recital group. M-D.

———— *Sonata* II C (Alsbach 1935) 19pp., score. Allegro molto; Adagio; Allegro vivace. Freely tonal, dynamic extremes (*ppp* to *ffff*), sweeping gestures in last movement. M-D.

Filippo Banner. *Sonata* g (Walter Upmeyer—Nag 160 1941) 7pp., parts. Grave; Allegro; Largo; Allegro. Tasteful realizations. M-D.

Granville Bantock. *Sonata* b (JWC 1941) 55pp., parts. Moderato assai; Largamente; Allegretto scherzando rubato; Allegro moderato non tanto. Post-Romantic pianistic writing. M-D to D.

Samuel Barber. *Sonata* Op.6 1932 (GS 1936) 27pp., parts. 18 min. Allegro ma non troppo; Adagio; Allegro appassionato. Sonorous, lyric melodic writing, expansive and Romantic in conception, freely tonal. D.

Jean Barrière. *Twelve Sonatas* (Marguerite Chaigneau, Walter Morse Rummel—Senart 5246, 5394) 2 vols. Vol.I: Sonatas 1–6 (39pp., parts). Vol.II: Sonatas 7–12 (52pp., parts). There is much variety in these works. All require a certain maturity, both technically and interpretatively. *Sonata* 2 has a violin part in addition to cello and keyboard. *Sonata* 10 is for two solo celli. M-D.

Lubor Barta. *Sonata* 1971 (Panton 1973) 24pp., parts. Rev. Josef Chuchro.

———— *Balada a Burleska* (Artia).

Béla Bartók. *Rhapsody* I 1928 (UE). Bartók's own alternate setting of the *Rhapsody* I for violin and orchestra. See description under violin and piano.

Robert Basart. *Variations* (Sal 1973) 21pp., parts. 14½ min. Part I: pointillistic; accidentals apply to single notes only; complex rhythms; fast-moving groups of notes; sudden dynamic shifts. Part II: linear, very few chords, dynamic mark on almost every note, serially influenced, long note groupings, nontonal throughout, tonal A final chord. D.

Leslie Bassett. *Music for Violoncello and Piano* (CFP 1971) 15pp., parts. Origin; Invention; Variation; Conclusion. Serial elements; widely spaced gestures; stopped and plucked strings in piano; harmonic ninths in full chord require large span; tightly organized. D.
_____ *Sonata* (CFE).

Jürg Baur. *Dialoge* 1962 (Br&H 6399) 22pp., parts. 16 min. Sostenuto rubato: low register exploited; shifting meters; clusters; large span required. Allegro con moto: toccata-like rhythms; glissandi; alternates with Grazioso section. Andante rubato: quasi recitativo, contrary glissandi, tremolo. Presto: pointillistic, arpeggi figures, varied tempi, astringent dissonance, expressionistic, serial influence. D.

Arnold Bax. *Legend-Sonata* (Chappell 1944) 25 min.
_____ *Sonata* E♭ (Murdoch 1925) 33 min. Much sensuous beauty. D.
_____ *Sonatina* (Chappell 1934) 14 min.

Paul Bazelaire. *Deux Images Lointaines* Op.113 (Leduc 1930). 1. Yamilé. 2. Danse nonchalante: in 7/4, lazy, indolent. M-D.
_____ *Suite Française* Op.114 (Schott Frères 1934) 8½ min. Five movements.
_____ *Funérailles* Op.120 (Durand).
_____ *Variations sur une chanson naive* Op.125 (Schott Frères).
_____ *Concertino* I Op.126 1957 (Durand) 8pp., parts. 5 min. Tonal, repeated chords, free counterpoint, witty, ends alla tarantella. M-D.
_____ *Concertino* II Op.127 (Durand).
_____ *Suite Italienne* (Consortium Musicale).

Irwin Bazelon. *Five Pieces* (Weintraub).

Gustavo Becerra Schmidt. *3ᵃ Sonata* 1957 (Sobre temas y a la memoria de Rene Amengual) (IU) 22pp., parts. Moderato; Allegro energico; Lento; Final—Allegro molto. Neoclassic, thin textures, freely tonal, rather tame rhythmically. M-D.

Conrad A. Beck. *Sonata* II (Schott 5062 1959) 23pp., parts. Allegro moderato; Intermezzo; Andante sostenuto; Allegro vivo. Linear, severe neoclassic style, concise and highly taut fabric. Each movement freely centers around a tonality. No virtuoso display for either instrument, but D.

Ludwig van Beethoven. *Sonatas* Op.5/1 F, Op.5/2 g, Op.69 A, Op.102/1 C, Op.102/2 D (Bernard van der Linde—Henle 1971) 143pp., parts. Fingering and bowing added by André Navarra and Hans-Martin Theopold. Practical urtext edition, same text as in the New Beethoven Collected Edition. Sources discussed in preface. Fingering in italics comes from the sources. Other editions: (Tovey, Such—Augener 7660; CFP 748; Schulz—GS L810; Crepax, Lorenzoni—Ric ER2026; Lea, 2 vols.).
Available separately: *Sonata* Op.5/1 (Tovey, Such—Augener). *Sonata* Op.5/2 (Tovey, Such—Augener; Rose—IMC). Beethoven wrote the Op.5 sonatas to feature himself at the keyboard. He was one of the most brilliant pianists of the day. The final movement of Op.5/1 is a catalogue of outstanding examples of effective ways to combine the cello and piano. *Sonata* Op.69 (Tovey, Such—Augener; Rose—IMC). An excellent example of effective treatment of the cello in the bass range. *Sonata* Op.102/1 (Tovey, Such—Augener). Combines the two instruments with consummate artistry.
_____ *Variations* (Hans Münch-Holland, Günter Henle—Henle; Stutschewsky—CFP 748B) 12 variations on a theme of Handel; 12 variations on a theme of Mozart; 7 variations on a theme of Mozart from *The Magic Flute*.
Available separately: *12 Variations on a Theme from Judas Maccabaeus* by Handel WoO 45 G (Such—Augener). *12 Variations on the Theme "Ein Mädchen oder Weibchen"* from *The Magic Flute* by Mozart Op.66 (Such—Augener; IMC). *7 Variations on "Bei Männern, welche Liebe fühlen"* from *The Magic Flute* WoO 46 EB (Stutschewsky—CFP 7048; Such—Augener; IMC).
_____ *Sonatina* G (Belwin-Mills).

Domenico Dalla Bella. *Sonata* C (Walter Upmeyer—Nag 83) 6pp., parts. First printing of this work. Andante; Giga–Largo; Allegro. M-D.

Arthur Benjamin. *Five Negro Spirituals* (Bo&H).
_____ *Sonatina* (Bo&H 1939) 11½ min. Preamble; Minuet; March.

Heinz Benker. *Two Part Inventions* (Br&H 1965) First Part (6478a). Second Part (6478b). Four short pieces, mainly linear, with No.4 more chordal. Imitation is prevalent, Hindemithian style, well-conceived instrumental writing. M-D.

William Sterndale Bennett. *Sonata–Duo* (G. Bush—St&B 1972). Included in "Musica Britannica," *Piano and Chamber Music,* Vol.37. The Duo is in three movements, of which the first is by far the best and should be played separately as a fine display piece for the cello. Expansive and lyrical writing. M-D.

Niels Viggo Bentzon. *Sonata* Op.43 C (Dansk 97 1947).

Arthur Berger. *Duo* 1951 (ACA) 12 min. Like a heart-to-heart talk between two friends. The cello sounds off and the piano responds with kindly and shrewd remarks. M-D.

Lennox Berkeley. *Andantino* (JWC 1955) 5pp., parts. 2½ min. A lovely, lyric character piece. In E but is freely tonal. Broken thirds provide thematic germ. M-D.
_____ *Duo* (JWC 1955) 14pp., parts. 9 min. One movement, Allegro moderato. Short, thin textures; opening turning figure is mainly used for development. D.

Herman Berlinski. *Suite* II (CFE).

Emile Bernard. *Sonate* Op.46 G (Durand).

Robert Bernard. *Sonate* C (Durand).

Franz Berwald. *Duo* Op.7 (GM 1946) 29pp., parts. Rev. Sven Kjellström. One large movement with varied sections, tempi, and textures. Written in a classic style with numerous Romantic characteristics, mainly in harmony and pianistic idioms. M-D to D.

Bruno Bettinelli. *Sonata* (Drago) 12 min. Allegretto; Calmo pensoso; Allegro ritmico.

Thomas Beversdorf. *Sonata* 1967–9 (Indiana Music Center 1974) 17pp., parts. Andante con moto; Adagio con moto; Allegro Moderato. Expressionistic; extremes of range exploited; sudden dynamic changes; stopped svrings (for pianist); wide span required. D.

Philip Bezanson. *Duo* (CFE).

Gordon Binkerd. *Sonata* 1952 (Bo&H 1971) 56pp., parts. 25 min. Grave e con rubato; Andante; Allegro. Binkerd's only thoroughly dodecaphonic piece. Piano writing is concertante throughout. Relentless repetition of

motivic germs, simultaneous statement of a line against its inversion, and tritone polarities are stylistic features found throughout the work. D.
See: Rudy Shackelford, "The Music of Gordon Binkerd," *Tempo,* 114 (September 1975): 1–13, for a more thorough discussion of this work.

Johann Adam Birkenstock. *Sonata* e (Moffat—Simrock; J. Salmon—Ric R384) 14pp., parts. Adagio; Courante; Largo; Gigue. The Salmon edition is over-edited and freely arranged but is somewhat effective. M-D.

Easley Blackwood. *Fantasy* Op.8 1960 (GS) 19pp., parts. 9 min. Expansive, Romantic, proclamatory, rich in sonorities. Octotonic, vigorous expressivity, austere dissonant idiom, strong thematic material. Large span required. D.

Charles-Henri Blainville. *Sonate ancienne* (Feuillard—Delrieu).

Herbert Blendinger. *Drei Stücke* (Orlando 1973) 13pp., parts.

Ernest Bloch. *Méditation Hébraïque* (CF B1968 1925) 7pp., parts. 7 min. Modal, cello has to play some tones a quarter tone above or below pitch. Allegro deciso mid-section adds contrast to the Moderato outer parts. Long C pedal point in piano closes work with cello moving freely above. M-D.

Waldemar Bloch. *Sonate* 1970 (Dob 1975) 36pp., parts. Vivace e con brio; Molto adagio; Presto. Freely tonal and well conceived for the medium. Writing is especially attractive in the warmly Romantic slow movement. Presto uses a French folktune. Neoclassic orientation. M-D.

Luigi Boccherini. *Six Sonatas* (Analee Bacon—GS L1874; Piatti, Crepax—Ric ER2461). 1 B♭, 2 E♭, 3 c, 4 G, 5 E♭, 6 C (GS numbering). Available separately: 1 A (Piatti—Ric). 2 C (Piatti—IMC). 3 G (Piatti—Ric; Schroeder—Augener; Schroeder, Rapp—Schott). 6 A (Piatti—Ric; Piatti, Forino—IMC; Schroeder—Augener; Schroeder, Rapp—Schott). Schroeder and Piatti editions are over-edited.
———— *Sonata* VII (Spiegl, Bergmann, Duckson—Schott).
———— *Sonata* A (Moffat—Schott).
———— *Sonata* A (Stutschewsky—CFP 4283).
———— *Sonata* C (Crepax, Zanon—Ric).
———— *Sonata* A (Ticciati—Lengnick).
———— *Sonata* B♭ (Ewerhard, Storck—Schott).
———— *Sonata* C (Feuillard—Delrieu).
———— *Sonata* c (Ewerhard, Storck—Schott).

León Boëllmann. *Sonate* Op.40 a (Durand 1897) 45pp., parts. Maestoso; Andante; Allegro molto. Modal influence; sombre Maestoso; Andante shows strong Franck influence; spirited finale. M-D.

Joseph Bodin de Boismortier. *Sonata* Op.26/4 e (Hugo Ruf—Schott).
_____ *Sonata* Op.26/5 g (Hugo Ruf—Schott).
_____ *Sonata* Op.50/3 D (Hugo Ruf—Br 3963) 13pp., parts. Moderato; Corrente; Aria; Minuetto con Variazioni. Editorial additions have been limited to a minimum and are indicated by small print in brackets. Fine realizations. M-D.
_____ *Sonata* G (Delrieu).
_____ *Sonata* (Boulay—EMT).

Giovanni Battista Bononcini. *Aria* (CFP 4213).
_____ *Sonata* a (Hugo Ruf—Schott CB101) 11pp., parts. Andante; Allegro; Grazioso (Minuett I & II). Attractive writing that shows why Bononcini, after 1720, was regarded in England, where he lived, as the leading composer next to Alessandro Scarlatti. M-D.
_____ *Sonata* A (Schroeder—Augener 5509). With *Andante Cantabile* by Stiasni.
_____ *Sonata* a (Salmon—Ric R386).

Siegfried Borris. *Kleine Suite* (Sirius).
_____ *Sonate* Op.53 (Sirius).

Will Gay Bottje. *Sonata* (CFE).

Joseph Boulnois. *Sonata* (Senart).

York Bowen. *Sonata* Op.64 (Schott 1923) 25 min. Traditional form, rhapsodic in character, strong thematic material, full sonorities. D.

Johannes Brahms. *Sonate* Op.38 e (Hans Münch-Holland—Henle; Müller, Kraus, Boettcher—VU; Br&H; Becker, Friedberg—Simrock; Klengel—CFP 3897A; Rose—IMC; Van Vliet, Hughes—GS L1411; Crepaz, Lorenzoni—Ric ER2101). This work is an "homage to J. S. Bach." Brahms based the main theme of the finale on contrapunctus 13 of the *Art of Fugue*. The piano has been placed first by Brahms in the title; it should be a partner and should never assume a purely accompanying role. Sombre and heavily saturated with mysticism. D.
_____ *Sonata* Op.99 F (Hans Münch-Holland—Henle; Müller, Boettcher—VU; Klengel—CFP; Rose—IMC; Becker, Friedberg—Simrock; Crepax, Lorenzoni—Ric ER2102). Stern dignity, display studiously avoided, no sentimentality. D.

Darker tone qualities of the cello exploited in both sonatas without overloading the lower register of the piano.

_____ *Two Sonatas* with *Two Sonatas* for clarinet and piano (Lea 7).

Henry Brant. *Sonata* 1937–62 (ACA) 28 min.

Cesar Bresgen. *Zweite Sonata* (Litolff 5812 1962) 27pp., parts. Three untitled contrasting movements. Linear, freely tonal with much chromaticism. Requires large span as well as a fine left-hand octave technique. Neoclassic. M-D.

Jean-Baptiste Bréval. *Sonata* C (Schroeder—Augener 5502; Schroeder, Rose—IMC).
_____ *Sonata* C (Stutschevsky—Schott).
_____ *Sonata* G (Ernst Cahnbley—Schott 1918) 15pp., parts. Over-edited.
_____ *Sonata* G (Cassado—IMC).
_____ *Sonata* V G (Edwin Koch, Bernhard Weigart—Schott CB67) 19pp., parts. Brillante; Adagio; Rondo. Pleasant and fluent. M-D.
_____ *Sonata* G (Salmon—Ric R809).
_____ *Sonata* (Ric R498).

Frank Bridge. *Sonata* (Bo&H 1918) 23 min. Melody pours over everything; sings and builds to impassioned climaxes. Piano part is mainly improvisational and decorative in nature. D.

Benjamin Britten. *Sonata* Op.65 C (Bo&H 1961) 35pp., parts. 21½ min. Sonata and suite principles combined although a monothematic basis controls most of the freely tonal five movements. Dialogo: SA, adjacent major and minor seconds are important in thematic elements; three contrasting themes derive from opening material and are carefully worked over in the development. Scherzo—Pizzicato: Bartók influence seen in the plucked timbre, especially in the trio, where polymodality and minor inversions converge in stretto. Elegia: also uses minor inversion. Marcia: dry humorous march with a Trio; return of march is cleverly disguised. Finale, Moto Perpetuo: monothematic with all material arising from opening idea. D. See: Peter Evans, "Britten's Cello Sonata," *Tempo,* 58 (Summer 1961). Hugh Wood, "Britten's Latest Scores" (refers to cello sonata), *MT,* 103, No.1429 (March 1962).

Earle Brown. *Music for Cello and Piano* 1955 (AMP 1961) 15pp. Two copies needed for performance. Uses "time-notation" to represent sound-relationships, independent of a strict pulse or metric system. "The durations are extended visibly through their complete space-time of sounding and are precise relative to the space-time of the score. It is expected that the performer will observe as closely as possible the 'apparent' relationships of sound and silence but act without hesitation on the basis of his perceptions. . . . The vertical correspondences between instruments are composed relative to a concept of event-time flexibility. In performance it is best that each performer execute his own part as faithfully as possible relative to the notated time but not relative to the other part, and the correspondences will occur as intended'' (from the prefatory note). Contains other performance directions. Piano techniques include plucking and damping strings, use of mallet to strike strings, as well as normal techniques. Avant-garde. D.

Willy Burkhard. *Sonate* Op.87 (Br 2685 1954) 24pp., parts. Introduzione; Scherzo Notturno; Finale. Octotonic, chromatic figures and scales, broken octaves, cello cadenza near conclusion of Introduzione. Second movement alternates moods and tempi; tremolo; neoclassic; large span required. M-D to D.

Ferruccio Busoni. *Kleine Suite* Op.23 1886 (Br&H; Kahnt) 16½ min. Charming, combines graceful rococo spirit with mildly contemporary harmonies.
––––––– *Kultaselle. Variations on a Finnish Song* (Br&H).

Dietrich Buxtehude. *Sonata* D (Folkmar Längin—Schott CB83) 7pp., parts. The only existing work by Buxtehude for a single stringed instrument with basso continuo. "Stylistically and formally this sonata is unparalleled in 17th century viola da gamba music" (from Postscript in score). The original manuscript contains no phrasing or tempo indications except "Allegro" (second movement, bar 44) and "Adagio" (bar 51). Written in a fast–slow–fast design. M-D.

William Byrd. *Lachrymae Pavane* (St&B).

Louis de Caix d'Hervelois. *Pièces de Viole avec Clavecin* (Auguste Chapuis—Durand) 2 vols. Has a part for cello and for viola. Vol.I: La Milanaise; Sarabande; Gavotte en Rondeau; L'Inconstant; La Gracieuse; Menuet I & II; Gavotte I & II. Vol. II: Les Petits Doigts; Sarabande; Menuet; La Napolitaine; Gavotte; Gigue; La Venitienne. Delightful character pieces, musical realizations. M-D.
––––––– *Sonata* a (Moffat—Simrock; Salmon—Ric R398).
––––––– *Suite* I A (Schroeder, Rapp—Schott).
––––––– *Suite* II (Feuillard—Delrieu).
––––––– *Suite* d (Kozalupova—USSR).
––––––– *Suite* (Béon—Costallat). For gamba or cello and keyboard.
––––––– *Trois Pièces* (Hamelle).

Antonio Caldara. *Sonata* (Polnauer—MCA).

Andrea Caporale. *Sonata* d (J. Salmon—Ric R387) 12pp., parts. Largo amoroso; Allegro; Adagio molto espressivo; Allegro spiritoso. Over-edited. M-D.
_____ *Sonata* d (Schott).

Elliott Carter. *Sonata* 1948 (SPAM 1953) 48pp., parts. 20 min. Corrected edition 1966. Moderato; Vivace, molto leggiero; Adagio; Allegro. Unusual time signatures such as 21/32. This is Carter's first work to make extensive use of metrical modulation, an extremely flexible and subtle structuring of the time element. A neoclassic formal framework is still present but the rhythmic emphasis opens new directions. A strong work with ringing sonorities and possibly one of the most important compositions in the cello and piano repertoire. D.
See: W. Glock, "A Note on Elliott Carter" (refers to the cello *Sonata* and *String Quartet* I), *The Score*, 12 (June 1955).

Robert Casadesus. *Sonate* Op.22 1935-6 (Sal 1947). Lyrical, passionate, well crafted in line, form, and texture. French neo-Romantic style. Brilliant virtuoso writing for the piano, great diversity of feeling. Cello is used melodically with the piano never overpowering. Allegro moderato: Dorian mode on c, diatonic Chopinesque figuration in piano, Aeolian on g for second subject. Scherzo: two subjects with one exclusively for the piano, gentle Trio, free paraphrase in recapitulation. Molto adagio: not a complete movement, fugal entries, ostinato figures; fades away on an inconclusive inverted dominant 11th and leads directly to the Allegro non troppo: C, a hybrid of SA and rondo; mysterious and exciting figuration in piano varied six times; bitonal hints; inverted 11th and 13th chords; closes brilliantly. M-D to D.

Alfredo Casella. *Sonata* C (UE 1927) Four movements in two, each consisting of a slow section followed by a fast section. Preludio; Bourrée; Largo; Rondo quasi giga. Neoclassic style, clear tonal centers but with frequent diatonic harmonies overlapped. M-D.

Gaspar Cassadó. *Sonata nello stile antico spagnuolo* (UE 7931).
_____ *Sonate* (Mathot) 23½ min. Rapsodia; Arogonesa; Saeta; Paso-doble.

Mario Castelnuovo-Tedesco. *I Nottambuli* 1927 (UE 8992) Variazioni Fantastiche. 28pp., parts. Preambolo and five long and contrasted complex variations. Colorful sonorities requiring advanced players for both parts. D.
_____ *Sonata* E♭ (Forlivesi 1929).

Alexandre Cellier. *Sonate* (Senart).

Giacomo Cervetto. *Two Sonatas* (Schroeder, Rapp—Schott).
_____ *Sonata* C (Salmon—Ric R95).
_____ *Sonata* G (Salmon—Ric 388).

Luciano Chailly. *Sonata Tritematica* V (Forlivesi).

Carlos Chavez. *Sonatina* 1924 (Belwin-Mills).

Camille Chevillard. *Sonate* Op.15 B♭ (Durand 1897).

Raymond Chevreuille. *Sonata* Op.42 (CeBeDeM).

Frédéric Chopin. *Grand Duo Concertant on Themes from Meyerbeer's Robert le Diable* composed with Auguste Franchomme (PWM, *Complete Works,* Vol.XVI; Mikuli—K&S).
_____ *Introduction et Polonaise Brillante* Op.3 (PWM, *Complete Works,* Vol.XVI; Feuermann, Rose—IMC; Gendron—Schott; Graudan—GS L1803; Franchomme—Augener 7669; CFP, published with *Sonata* Op.65; Mikuli—K&S). 8½ min.
_____ *Sonata* Op.65 g (PWM, *Complete Works,* Vol.XVI; Pierre Fournier—IMC: Schulz—GS L64; Balakirew—CFP, published with *Polonaise Brillante* Op.3; Mikuli—K&S). 25 min. For experts only. D.

Francesco Ciléa. *Sonata* Op.38 D (EC).
_____ *3 Pezzi* (Ric 127934).

Dinos Constantinides. *Sonata.* See fuller description under duos for piano and viola.

Frederick Shepherd Converse. *Sonata* 1922 (New England Conservatory Music Store; IU) 42pp., parts. Adagio. Allegro giojoso: numerous changes of tempi and mood in this movement. Post-Romantic writing with ideas that are well developed but a little old-fashioned sounding today. M-D.

Arnold Cooke. *Sonata* 1941 (Nov 1960) 59pp., parts. 26½ min. Andante poco sostenuto–Allegro; Lento; Scherzo; Rondo. Accessible writing that displays an unfailing craft throughout. Mildly contemporary approach to tonality, clear lines, good sense of thematic symmetry and balance. M-D.

Roque Cordero. *Sonata* (PIC).

Henry Cowell. *Four Declamations with Return* (CFE).
_____ *Hymn and Fuguing Tune* IX 1970 (AMP 1960) 11pp., parts. 6 min.

Chordal Hymn, contrapuntal Fuguing Tune, freely tonal. Thin textures in Fuguing Tune to the coda, which becomes chordal. M-D.

Paul Creston. *Homage* Op.41 1947 (GS) 3 min.
———— *Suite* Op.66 1956 (GS) 16 min.

Arthur Custer. *Rhapsody and Allegro* (CFE).

Noel Da Costa. *Five Verses with Vamps* (King's Crown 1976) set of two performance scores, 8pp. each.

Ingolf Dahl. *Duo* 1946 (J. Boonin) 25pp., parts. 17 min. Fantasia in Modo d'un Recitativo: complex rhythms, chromatic and freely tonal, varied tempi; concludes in C; requires large span. Capriccio: vigorous rhythms; free, dissonant counterpoint; two key signatures alternate. Corale: syncopated chords; cello line embellishes piano chorale; harmonized in unusual sonorities; *ppp* conclusion. D.
———— *Notturno* 1946 (J. Boonin) 9pp., parts. Originally the second movement of the *Duo* listed above. Short cello introduction leads immediately to vigorous but quiet repeated chords in 3/8 2/8; chords become more chromatic and intense. Other sections have individual moods and tempi, including a highly embellished part. Uncompromising writing in a convincing but dissonant and polyphonic style. Requires large span. D.

Franz Danzi. *Sonata* Op.62 F (Kurt Janetzky—Hofmeister 7336) 60pp., parts. For bassett horn or cello. Larghetto–Allegretto; Larghetto sostenuto; Allegretto. Flowing melodies, fluent instrumental writing, more Classical than Romantic characteristics, traditional pianistic idioms. M-D.

Thomas Christian David. *Sonata* (Dob 1970) 40pp., parts. Energetic first movement (Beethoven inspired). Serious and somewhat tedious Andante. Finale alternates an Andante with a whimsical Vivace. An Allegro di molto coda concludes. Errors noted in clef changes and accidentals. Neoclassic. Athleticism required of both performers. D.

Claude Debussy. *Intermezzo* c (Piatigorsky—EV 1944). An early work in a broadly melancholy ABA form. Not Impressionistic but well constructed and full of rich and opulent sonorities. M-D.
———— *Sonata* d (Durand 1915) 15pp., parts. 11 min. Prologue—Lent: centers around d; piano opens with straightforward statement; leads to a Poco animando section that is more sustained and uses parallel chords; gradually tempo and mood intensify and arrive at a climax before receding to a *ppp* D major close. Sérénade: light; has a seamless sense of unity about

it; staccato with tempo changes; leads directly to the Finale—Animé: profuse triplet figuration; changes in tempo and mood. Even though this piece does not hold together well, it is tersely crafted and the sonorities are fascinating. It is as though Debussy is searching for a partially new style. Demanding writing. D.

Frederick Delius. *Sonata* (Bo&H 1919) 12½ min. One movement organized in a three-part structure. Seems to be a more perfect piece than the violin sonatas. Short, rhapsodic, melodious, and yearning. Geared more to a cantabile style rather than to pyrotechnics. The two instruments are completely integrated. M-D.
See: Julian Lloyd Webber, "Delius and the Cello," M&M 24 June 1976, 22–23.

Norman Dello Joio. *Duo Concertato* (GS 1949). Slow introduction and epilogue with a fast main section. Lyric, well-written for both instruments, clear textures, light harmonies. M-D.

Edisson Vasil'evich Denisov. *Sonata* 1971 (CFP 5746 1973) 16pp., parts. Recitativo: pointillistic; proportional rhythmic relationships; upper register exploited; grace-note chords; requires large span. Toccata: chromatic sixteenth-note figures, chordal punctuation, changing meters, bold gestures, freely dissonant. D.

David Diamond. *Sonata* 1938 (TP) 36pp., parts. Tempo giusto e maestoso: develops emphatically; soaring melody; piano provides florid counterpoint. Lento assai: a chant evolves into a decorative cantillation and is then followed by a complex rhythmic section. Andante con grand espressione: a lyric interlude. Epilogo—Allegretto: a rhythmic jig. D.

Hilda Dianda. *Estructuras* 1960 (PAU 1965) 18pp., 2 scores necessary. 12½ min. I. Andante, II. Andante, III. Untitled. Numerous directions for both performers, e.g., strike the strings with the edge and/or palm of the hand, pluck strings with fingernails, harmonics, clusters. Avant-garde, pointillistic, meter change on almost every measure. D.

Josef Dichler. *Variationen über einen Song von Stephen Foster* 1964 (Dob) 27pp., parts. Four variations and finale based on the tune "Swanee River." References to the *New World Symphony* appear from time to time. A fun piece. M-D.

Charles Dodge. *Sonata in Five Parts* (CFE).

Martin Doernberg. *Variations* (Vieweg 6137 1974) 11pp., parts. No separation between variations, serial influence, pointillistic, expressionistic, sparse textures, Webernesque. D.

Ernö Dohnányi. *Sonata* Op.8 B♭ (Schott; IMC) 25 min.

Josef Friedrich Doppelbauer. *Sonata* I 1952 (Dob 1964) 23pp., parts. Fantasie: low octaves, large chords, dramatic, more chromatic second tonal area, restful closing. Rondo: rhythmic drive, octotonic, choralelike episode, freely tonal around g. Fuga: restful and lyric; unfolds logically; coda is similar to opening of Fantasie; *pp* and relaxed closing. M-D.

Sem Dresden. *Sonate* (Senart 1924).

Johannes Driessler. *Fantasie* Op.24/2 (Br 2696 1953) 10pp., parts. Chordal opening; moves to chords in alternating hands; ostinato-like figuration; freely tonal; meter changes at formal sections. Requires large span. M-D.
———— *Sonate* Op.41/2 1959 (Br 3968) 22pp., parts. Sostenuto ma con brio; Adagio maestoso; Allegro vivace. Freely tonal, sudden dynamic changes, free dissonant counterpoint, octotonic, neoclassic. Facile octave technique needed in finale. Requires large span. M-D to D.

Petr Eben. *Suita Balladica* (Artia 1957) 25 min. Introduzione e danza; Quazi mazurka; Elegia; Toccata.

Horst Ebenhöh. *Sonatina* Op.17/1 (Dob 1973) 13pp., parts. Molto vivace; Andante moderato; Allegro. Thin textures, rhythmic treatment varied, melodic poverty, freely tonal. M-D.
———— *Stücke* Op.17/2 (Dob 1973) 8pp., parts. Avant-garde extensions of technique. D.

Maurice Emmanuel. *Sonate* (Senart).

Georges Enesco. *Sonate* II (Sal).

Lehman Engel. *Sonata* (SPAM 1948) 33pp., parts. Allegro ma non troppo; Andante misterioso; Allegro giocoso; Vivace. Dramatic gestures (fast running scale passages followed by sudden stops, repeated syncopated full chords in low register, etc.), clear ideas and textures. Deserves more performances. M-D.

Rudolf Escher. *Sonata* (Symphonia ST371).
———— *Sonate Concertante* Op.7 1943 (Alsbach 1947) 23 min.

Ferenc Farkas. *Sonatina Based on a Hungarian Folk Song* 1955 (Artia) 11pp., parts for double bass, bassoon, or cello. Allegro moderato; Andante espressivo; Allegro. Sparkling, attractive tunes cleverly worked out. A delight for performers and audience. M-D.

Johann Friedrich Fasch. *Sonata* C (J. Wojciechowski—CFP 5893) 12pp., parts. For bassoon (cello) and basso continuo; second cello part ad lib. See detailed entry under duos for piano and bassoon.

Gabriel Fauré. *Sonata* I Op.109 d 1918 (Durand) 19½ min. Shifting, irresolute harmonies; overlapping and uneven phrases; unpredictable rhythms. Piano and cello constantly echo and contrast with each other. M-D.
_____ *Sonata* II Op.117 g 1921 (Durand) 18 min. Allegro: Fauré fuses the development and recapitulation in an unusual manner; this movement contains some ingenious melodic writing coupled with filigree harmonies. Adagio: an elegy; presents one theme after another with no transition; sustained lyricism. Allegro vivace: a persistent three-bar rhythm, which in reality makes a 3/4, gives a rich and warm effect; imitation, complex figuration, and syncopation build to triumphant conclusion. D.
Both sonatas are a mixture of nostalgia and beauty.

Jindrich Feld. *Due Composizioni* (Panton).
_____ *Sonate* (Schott 1972) 36pp., parts. Strongly contrasted materials. Plenty of technical difficulties for both players. Allegro agitato: lyric theme in dotted rhythms contrasts with an agitated theme; each is manipulated but not truly developed. Lento: ternary design; middle section recalls second subject from first movement. Allegro con brio: a moto perpetuo with a lyric theme appearing as a second subject. D.

Willem de Fesch. *Six Sonatas* Op.8 (Walter Schultz—CFP 4989) Second cello ad lib. 31pp., parts. I D, II B♭, III d, IV C, V g, VI G. Excellent keyboard realizations by Eberhard Wenzel. Short colorful multi-movements that display clarity in harmonic and contrapuntal writing. Contains some Galant style characteristics. M-D.
Available separately: III d (Ruf—Müller); IV C (Koch, Weigart—Schott); VI G (Koch, Weigart—Schott).
_____ *Sonata* Op.13/1 D (Koch, Weigart—Schott).
_____ *Sonata* Op.13/3 A (Koch, Weigart—Schott).
_____ *Sonata* Op.13/4 d (Koch, Weigart—Schott).
_____ *Sonata* Op.13/5 (Koch, Weigart—Schott).
_____ *Sonata* Op.13/6 a (Koch, Weigart—Schott).
_____ *Sonata* d (Moffat—Schott).

_____ *Sonata* F (Moffat—Simrock).

_____ *Sonata* G (Salmon—Ric).

John Field. *Sonata* (Schott CB 121).

Ross Lee Finney. *Chromatic Fantasy* E (CFP).

_____ *Sonata* II C (Valley Music Press 1953) 23pp., parts.

William Flackton. *Three Sonatas* from Op.2 (Renzo Sabatini—Dob 1962)
Available separately: I C, 8pp., parts; II B♭; III F 8pp., parts. Three other
sonatas in Op.2 are for tenor violin and keyboard. Flackton points out in his
preface that he composed the "Solos" with the intention of activating the
tenor violin. All are M-D.

Josef Boruslav Foerster. *Sonata* Op.45 f (Urbánek).

Wolfgang Fortner. *Sonata* (Schott 1949) 21pp., parts. 17 min. Formally
experimental. The first movement is a strange two-part design with a
complete sonata followed by a scherzo-like episode; further development of
the sonata mid-section is finally concluded with a restatement of the opening idea. The second movement is an ABA scherzo. First two movements
make great use of ostinato-like progressions. The third movement, a Ballata: Variations on a theme of Guillaume de Machaut, makes harmonic
references to the first two movements. M-D to D.

_____ *Zyklus* 1964 (Schott) 21pp., parts. Mouvements; Variations; Etude;
Prelude–Contrepoint–Epilogue. Serial, highly pointillistic, expressionistic.
This work hops around all over the keyboard, almost constantly. D.

John Herbert Foulds. *Sonata* Op.6 1905 (Senart 1928). A startlingly impressive piece with virtuoso writing for both instruments. Expansive, late
romantic idiom with rich figuration, Rachmaninoff-like melodic treatment,
and daring harmonies that owe something to Debussy, Richard Strauss,
and Mahler. Diatonic dissonance and huge pile-up of thirds resemble Britten a little. D.

César Franck. *Sonata* A 1886 (Hamelle). See detailed description under
duos for violin and piano.

Benjamin Frankel. *Sonata* Op.13 (Augener) 17 min. Sombre, distinctive
harmonic style. D.

_____ *Inventions in Major-Minor Modes* Op.31 (JWC 951 1960) 40pp., parts. 1. Moderato, 2. Allegro Fugato, 3. Andantino, 4. Appassionato, 5. Allegretto, 6. Improvisato, 7. Allegro Moderato, 8. Andante. Eight contrasting pieces that combine serial technique with Romantic expressiveness. Atonal chordal and broken octave figures. Major or minor *per se* are never felt except perhaps in a passing moment or at final cadences. Large span required. M-D.

Peter Racine Fricker. *Sonata* Op.28 (Schott 1957) 16 min. Four movements of well-wrought serious writing. Strong Schönberg influence apparent. D.

Robert Fuchs. *Sonata* II Op.83 e♭ 1908 (UWKR 21 1973) 25pp., parts. Preface in German by Alfons Ott. Allegro moderato assai; Adagio con sentimento; Allegro vivace. Written in a Brahmsian style. Secure craft, fresh melodies. M-D.

Sandro Fuga. *Sonata* II (EC 1974) 54pp., parts.

Blas Galindo. *Sonata* (EMM 1962) 34pp., parts. Allegro; Lento; Allegro. Neoclassic, clear lines and phrases, lean textures, some hemiola treatment. M-D.

Johann Ernst Galliard. *Six Sonatas* 1726 (J. Marx, Weiss, Mann— McGinnis & Marx 1946) 2 vols. 1 a, 2 G, 3 F, 4 e, 5 d, 6 C.
———— *Sonata* a (Moffat, Whitehouse—Simrock).
———— *Sonata* e (Salmon—Ric R393).
———— *Sonata* IV e (Moffat—Schott 1911) 7pp., parts. Adagio; Allegro; Allemanda; Sarabanda; Corrente. Over-edited. M-D.
———— *Sonata* III F (Moffat—Simrock).
———— *Sonata* G (Ruf—Br 3964).
———— *Sonata* G (Salmon—Ric R392).

Francesco Geminiani. *Six Sonatas* Op.5 1739 (CFP 9033) Second cello ad lib.
Available separately: Sonata Op.5/2 d (Merrick, James—Schott); Sonata Op.5/6 a (Merrick, James—Schott).
———— *Sonata* C (Salmon—Ric R705).
———— *Sonata* G (Salmon—Ric R705).

Harald Genzmer. *Sonata* I 1953 (Schott 4603). M-D.
———— *Sonatine* 1967 (CFP 5943) 19pp., parts. 11 min. Allegro: SA, octotonic, freely tonal around D. Adagio: thicker textures, dotted rhythms, chromatic. Rondo: secco style, seventh chords, bitonal, changing meters, moves over keyboard; neoclassic. M-D.

Roberto Gerhard. *Sonata* (OUP 1972) 30pp., parts. Three movements. Spanish rhythms and turns of phrases are evident. Much interplay between the instruments. Energetic opening movement. Slow movement displays versatile melodic writing, including exciting melismas. Finale evokes guitar and castanet sounds in an exuberant dance. D.

Miriam Gideon. *Fantasy on a Javanese Motive* (CFE).
_____ *Sonata* (CFE).

Walter Gieseking. *Konzert Sonatine* (Oertel J08428 1948) 19pp., parts. Moderato; Presto. Freely tonal but centers around C. Prestissimo concluding coda. Effective pianistic writing. M-D.

Alberto Ginastera. *Pampeanas* II "Rhapsody for Violincello and Piano" (Barry 1951) 12pp., parts. Three large sections, each displaying its own mood. Quartal harmonies predominate; full and complex texture; thematic ideas well unified. First two sections (Ricercare and Toccata) are somewhat fantasy-like, with cadenza passages, while the final section is more like a rondo with strong contrasting sections. Some frantic rhythms add color. The conclusion, full of heavy textures with added-note chords, is similar to the composer's *Piano Sonata*. D.

Radámes Gnattali. *Sonata* 1935 (IU) 32pp., parts. Movido; Lentamente; Alegremente. Post-Romantic writing with most interest residing in the free and flexible rhythmic treatment afforded various sections. M-D.

Carl Goldmark. *Sonata* Op.39 F (Schott).

Giovanni Battista Grazioli. *Sonata* A (Ticciati—Lengnick).
_____ *Sonata* F (Schroeder—Schott; Schroeder—Augener 5512 with *Sonata* e by Marcello) 8pp., parts. Allegro moderato; Adagio; Tempo di Minuetto. Heavily edited. M-D.
_____ *Sonata* G (Salmon—Ric R395) 11pp., parts. Allegro moderato; Menuet. Over-edited. M-D.

Alexander T. Gretchaninov. *Sonata* Op.113 (Schott 1549) 31pp., parts. Mesto: chordal, melody woven into texture, chromatic, arpeggi figuration; large span required. Menuetto tragico: varied tempi and moods, Furiosamente mid-section. Finale: cello cadenza introduction, chromatic octaves, much activity, rhythmic. D.

Edvard Grieg. *Sonata* Op.36 a (CFP 2157; Leonard Rose—IMC 1955) 45pp., parts. 28 min. Allegro agitato; Andante molto tranquillo; Allegro.

Norwegian folk material used in this graceful and charming work. Piano is given much prominence, while cello provides much rhythmic incisiveness. D.

Cornelis Wilhelmus de Groot. *Invocation* (Donemus 1974) 6pp., parts, photostat.
—— *Solitude* 1968 (Donemus 1974) 5pp., parts, photostat.

Alexi Haieff. *Sonata* 1963 (Gen) 30pp., parts. Allegro, e con sentimento aperto; Andante; Vivo. Freely tonal; centers around e. Chords in alternating hands, octotonic, traditional forms. Vivo is mainly toccata-like with *p* ending, neoclassic. Wide span required. M-D.

Mihály Hajdu. *Hungarian Children's Songs* (Bo&H 1974) 23pp., parts. Charming settings of 15 tunes contained in *Corpus Musicae Popularis Hungaricae* ("Collection of Hungarian Folk Music"), Vol.I: *Children's Games* (Bartók, Kodály—Zenemükiado 1951). Int.
—— *Variations and Rondo* (Artia).

Rudolfo Halffter. *Sonata* Op.26 (EMM 1962) 36pp., parts. Allegro deciso; Tempo di Siciliana; Rondo—Allegro. Large, dramatic work. Strong opposition between major and minor thirds is in part responsible for the tension felt throughout the entire first movement. Requires large span plus solid pianistic equipment and ensemble know-how. M-D.

Erich Hamann. *Sonata* Op.22 (Dob).
—— *Suite* Op.32 (Dob 1952) 12pp., parts. Andante; Allegro; Adagio ma non tanto; Presto; Andante. Tonal, mildly contemporary, bitonal spots, octotonic. Outer movements are similar. Requires large span. M-D.

Iain Hamilton. *Sonata* 1958 (Schott) 17 min. Serial technique, unusual form. Four cadenzas marked, respectively, bizarre, fantastic, passionate, and tempestuous, are separated by three "movements" of decreasing speed (allegro, con moto, placido). No thematic relationships between the seven parts are obvious. Scoring includes unusual effects, thick and complex harmonies, with a post-Webernesque twelve-tone texture. D.

George Frederick Handel. *Sonata* C (CFP 4903; Hoffmann—Schott; Jensen—IMC). Originally for gamba and cembalo.

Roy Harris. *Duo* 1964 (AMP).

Tibor Harsányi. *Sonata* (ESC).

Thomas de Hartmann. *Sonata* Op.63 (Belaieff 1948).

Charles Haubiel. *Sonata* C (CP) 22 min.

Bernhard Heiden. *Siena* (A. Broude).
_____ *Sonata* (A. Broude).
_____ *Sonata* 1958 (AMP) 25pp., parts. For Janos Starker. Allegro; Andante poco sostenuto; Allegretto vivace. Neoclassic, clear lines and textures. In Hindemithian idiom but a solid work that can stand on its own merits; well crafted; contains attractive ideas that flow naturally. M-D.

Harald Heilmann. *Katharsis* (Heinrichshofen/Sirius 1974) 15pp., parts.

Hans Henkemans. *Sonata* 1949 (Donemus 227) 26pp., parts. Allegro commodo: chordal, repeated thematic germ cells, chromatic; requires large span. Adagio: more sustained outer sections, chromatic sixteenths in midsection. Presto: marked and rhythmic, free dissonant counterpoint, many chords. Allegro ma non troppo: toccata-like, chordal punctuation, nervous emotionalism, all clothed in basically a post-Romantic pianistic idiom. M-D to D.

Kurt Hessenberg. *Sonata* Op.23 1941 (Schott) 20 min.

Julius Hijman. *Sonate* 1934 (IU) 34pp., parts. Allegretto; Adagio; Allegro con spirito, quasi presto. Fairly thick textures except for the final movement, which seems to scamper with many triplets. Neoclassic leanings. M-D.

Paul Hindemith. *Three Light Pieces* (Br&H 1917) 8pp., parts. Mässig schnell, munter; Langsam; Lebhaft. Contrasting, accessible. M-D.
_____ *Three Pieces* Op.8 (Schott 1938). Published separately. Capriccio A; Phantasiestücke B; Scherzo c. Sizable works, each complete in itself. M-D.
_____ *Sonata* Op.11/3 a 1919 (Schott 1922) 26pp., parts. 22½ min. In four sections that make two movements: Mässig schnell, Viertel–Lebhaft; Langsam–sehr lebhaft. Twelve-note scale is used for thematic development but is independent of harmonic background. The third section serves as the slow movement. A central marchlike diatonic theme provides contrast to the outer sections. The interval of the augmented fourth dominates the finale and provides a special character to the movement. Linear atonal polyphony permeates much of this striking and inventive work. D.
_____ *Sonata* (Schott 1948) 38pp., parts. 22½ min. Three movements. Opens with a dramatic "Pastoral" with exposition and condensed recapitulation of three themes. Marchlike scherzo (moderately fast–slow) serves as

the middle movement with a slow mid-section. A huge Passacaglia concludes the work. Weighty harmony full of strong dissonance recalls some of Hindemith's early daring works. D.

_____ *Variations on an Old English Nursery Song "A Frog He Went A-Courting"* (Schott 1951) 5½ min. Thirteen charming variations based on the verses of the nursery song. Clever, attractive, not easy. M-D.

Alun Hoddinott. *Sonata* Op.73/2 (OUP 1972) 16pp., parts. The first movement is improvisatory in style. The second movement plays with metric subdivisions and fluctuating harmonies. D.

York Höller. *Sonata* 1968 (Gerig 1976) 11 leaves.

Arthur Honegger. *Sonata* 1920 (ESC 1922) 31pp., parts. 13½ min. Allegro non troppo; Andante sostenuto; Presto. Clever contrapuntalism coupled with varied rhythmic ideas and tonal independence are characteristic of this whole work. The first movement has two main ideas in duple meter; one drops and the other rocks. The slow movement is a large three-part design with a fugal section in the middle. The Presto is whimsical in a kind of Stravinskian manner with a happy-go-lucky theme in E. D.

_____ *Sonatine* A 1921–2 (Rouart Lerolle). A clarinet may be substituted for the cello. Three compressed but relaxed movements. A lazy kind of theme opens the work, followed by a short fugato and a recapitulation. The Lent et soutenu is in ABA form. Concluding movement is only 37 bars long and includes jazz effects. M-D. See further description in clarinet and piano section.

John Horton. *Five Northumbrian Tunes* (Schott 1974) 11pp., parts.

Joseph Horvath. *Sonata* Op.14 1951 (Belwin-Mills) 10 min. Common chords used in not-so-common progressions. Some original twists in a dry, witty, neoclassic style. Pleasantly written and diversified with fluent invention apparent everywhere. M-D.

Alan Hovhaness. *Suite* Op.193 (CFP 6324 1962) 6pp., parts. 5 min. Andante: linear opening, chords in alternating hands, parallel and contrary motion chords. Largo: full bass chords, tremolo figures with moving chords, bitonal; requires large span. Moderato: moving inner lines, parallel chords, quartal harmonies. M-D.

_____ *Sonata* Op.255 (PIC 1975) 18pp., parts.

Alexandru Hrisanide. *Volumes—Inventions* 1963 (Editura Muzicală 1967) 18pp., parts. Three large sections, A, B, and C, can be arranged at the performer's discretion. Numerous directions for the pianist. Involves clusters, slamming piano lid closed *ffff*, plucking strings, scratching strings with the nails, stopping strings, knitting needles placed on strings. Complex ensemble problems. Playing of last note must continue for 25 seconds for volume C and 30 seconds for volume A. Avant-garde. D.

Johann N. Hummel. *Sonate* Op.104 A 1827 (UWKR 19 1971) 29pp., parts. Allegro amabile e grazioso: SA, interesting modulatory material. Romanza: expressive, melodic theme; parallel minor mid-section has much rhythmic and melodic appeal. Rondo: flowing, Maggiore and Minore sections, facile figuration. Piano is particularly favored. M-D.

Andrew Imbrie. *Sonata* 1966 (Malcolm 1970) 56pp., parts. Allegro; Andante con affetto; Andante–Allegro. Serial, thorny, well-developed rows. Textures are kept thin. Only for the finest players. D.

Herbert Inch. *Sonata* (CF 03052).

Vincent d'Indy. *Sonate* Op.84 D 1924-5 (Rouart Lerolle) 27pp., parts. Modéré; Gavotte et Rondeau; Air; Gigue. Warm Romantic writing that keeps the pianist constantly on the move. Chromatic usage sweeps into everything and opens brief tonal exercises into many keys. D.

Yannis Ioannidis. *Fragment* I 1972 (Gerig 1974) 10pp., parts.

John Ireland. *Sonata* g 1923 (Augener) 36pp., parts. 21 min. The metronome marks were revised by the composer in 1948. Moderato e sostenuto; Poco largamente; Con moto e marcato. Concise forms, close connection between movements accomplished by common thematic material (see first six bars of opening movement). Rhapsodic first movement in spirit of SA design if not in exact form. Lyric and elegaic slow movement. Strong finale. Freely tonal. Requires mature musicianship on the part of both performers. D.

Gordon Jacob. *Sonata* d (J. Williams 1957) 24pp., parts. 21min. Allegro; Allegro vivace; Adagio; Allegro molto. Freely tonal, conservative writing. Chromatic side-slips in first movement add to much activity. M-D.
————— *Sonatina* (J. Williams).

Leoš Janáček. *Pohádka* ("A Tale") 1910 (F. Smetana—Supraphon) 28pp., parts.

Karel Janeček. *Sonata* Op.33 G (Artia 1958).

Pál Járdányi. *Sonatina* (EMB) A diatonic two-movement work with an especially attractive dancelike second movement. Int. to M-D.

Ivan Jirko. *Sonata* (Artia 1954) 17min.

Otto Joachim. *Sonata* (BMI Canada) 8 min. Serial technique. D.

Lockrem Johnson. *Sonata* I Op.33 1949 (Dow) 12 min.
_____ *Sonata* II Op.42 1953 (ACA) 17 min. Vigorous, full of complex linear writing contrasted with very transparent lyric, modal passages. M-D.

André Jorrand. *IIe Sonate* (Rideau Rouge 1970) 19pp., parts. 8½ min. Modéré; Calme; Enjoué. Vigorous and compelling writing in a freely tonal, animated style. Calme uses rich harmonic palette and is somewhat impressionistic. Enjoué is livened by a meter of 4/4 + 1/8. A sure hand at work here. M-D.

Werner Josten. *Sonata* (AMP 1938) 16pp., parts. One movement, various tempi, neoclassic characteristic, cello cadenza at end, freely tonal, centers around g, ends in D. A profusion of ideas. M-D.

John Joubert. *Kontakion* Op.69 (Nov 1974) 18pp., parts. Free fantasia, dramatic and expressive. Piano part as important as cello. Based on a fragment of a Russian traditional chant for the dead. M-D.

Dmitri Kabalevsky. *Sonata* Op.22 (USSR).
_____ *Sonata* Op.71 B♭ 1962 (Rostropovich—IMC; USSR) 58pp., parts. Dedicated to Mstislav Rostropovich. Andante molto sostenuto; Allegretto; Allegro molto. The first movement is built on the contrast between the dramatic monologue in the cello and the lyrical secondary subject. Both the development section and the recapitulation are dramatically characterized. The second movement is a typical Russian waltz full of inner agitation. The waltz is repeatedly interrupted by melodic elements that are foreign to it, creating a feeling of incompleteness, of suspense and uneasiness. The finale presents a psychological conflict: The imperative toccata-like main subject is the most important element, but dramatic motifs intrude and create tension and agitation. The main subject from the first movement is brought in during the coda, reestablishing the atmosphere of that movement. All of Kabalevsky's stylistic characteristics are present. Large span required. D.

Donald Keats. *Diptych* 1974 (MS available from composer: Lamont School of Music, University of Denver, Denver, CO 80210) 23pp., parts. Allegro moderato: dissonant counterpoint, chromatic, well-developed ideas; large span required. Allegro: octotonic, dancelike, strong syncopation, proportional rhythmic relationships, thin textures. D.

Robert Kelly. *Sonata* (CFE) 13 min.

Ivor Keys. *Sonata* (Nov).

Yriö Kilpinen. *Sonata* Op.90 F (Br&H 1939).

Morris Knight. *Sonata* (Tritone) MS reproduction.

Zoltán Kodály. *Sonata* Op.4 1910 (UE 7130 1922) 23pp., parts. 17 min. Fantasia: SA, much tension created by agitated manipulating of themes from the exposition in the development section as well as emotional warmth and Hungarian character throughout. Allegro con spirito: SA, sweeps along with dance mobility using gutsy folk rhythms; concludes with a condensed return of the opening section of the first movement, which serves as a coda. Piano part is very important and requires plenty of "gusto." Debussyian harmony, classical thematic outlines. D.

Charles Koechlin. *Sonate* Op.66 (Senart 1933).

Peter Jona Korn. *Sonata* Op.6 1948–9 (Simrock Elite Edition 3336 1969) 55pp., parts. Allegro tranquillo; Introduzione (solo piano)—(15) Variationen über ein Deutsches Volkslied. Octotonic, freely tonal, some Romantic sonorities, trills in lower register, shifting rhythms. Contrasted variations treated fluently. Solid octave technique necessary; large span required. Virtuoso writing for both instruments. D.

Egon Kornauth. *Sonata* Op.28 (CFP 3771).

Gyorgy Kosa. *Sonata* 1965 (EMB).

Georg Kröll. *Erste Sonate* (Moeck 1967) 12 min.
———— *Zweite Sonate* (Moeck 1971) 15pp., 10 min.
———— *Sonata* (Moeck 5164 1975) 11pp., parts. 12 min. Explanations in German and English.

Robert Kurka. *Sonatina* Op.21 (Weintraub 1964) 16pp., parts. Fast; Slow, but flowing; Fast. Freely tonal with key signatures, parallel chords, syncopation, octotonic, à la Schostakovich, especially the last movement. M-D.

Paul Ladmirault. *Sonata* d (Ouvrières 1946).

László Lajtha. *Sonate* Op.17 (Leduc 1933) 31pp., parts. Aria; Capriccio; Fantasia. The three movements can be played as separate pieces. Mildly contemporary, freely tonal, parallel chords, octotonic; fine octave technique necessary. The Fantasia opens with a Lento introduction before moving on to an Allegro that provides the main body of the movement. M-D.

Edouard Lalo. *Sonata* (Heugel). Unusual modulations, recapitulation treated originally in first movement (Allegro moderato). Great thematic beauty. D.

John La Montaine. *Sonata* Op.8 (EV 1966) 31pp., parts. 17 min. Allegro amabile: freely tonal around D, dancelike, parallel chords, vibrant figuration, octotonic. Scherzo: 5/8, shifting meters, chordal punctuation, thicker textures in Trio. Soliloquy: for cello alone. Finale: graceful, cantabile section, elegant neoclassic style; requires large span. M-D.

Lars Erik Larsson. *Sonatin* Op.60 1969 (GM).

Armando Lavalle. *Sonata* (EMM 1973) 15pp., parts. Allegro, a piacere; Jarabe; Canto; Fuga. Serial; interesting writing, especially the animated Jarabe movement. Each movement provides fine contrast. Large span required. D.

Henri Lazorof. *Duo—1973* (TP) 12pp., parts. 12½ min.

René Leibowitz. *Duo* Op.23   1951 (Boelke-Bomart) 10 min.

Guillaume Lekeu. *Sonate* F 1888 (Rouart Lerolle 1910).

John Lessard. *Sonata* 1956 (ACA). Neoclassic style, bright and crisp sonorities, marked textural contrasts. M-D.

Nikolai Lopatnikoff. *Sonata* Op.11 (MCA).

Otto Luening. *Sonata* (CFE).
———— *Suite* (Galaxy 1972) 23pp., parts. For cello or viola and piano. Part also for viola. Recitative–Moderato: chordal opening, moves along freely; Moderato takes on many repeated notes in one hand with a subject in the other; broken octaves; short chromatic figures; large span required; mood of Recitative returns and Moderato material concludes movement. Scherzo: shifting meters, thin textures, one meter throughout for mid-section. Elegy:

chordal, sustained, lyrical. Dance: octotonic, free dissonant counterpoint, much rhythmic vigor, bitonal ending. M-D.

———— *Variations on Bach's Chorale Prelude "Liebster Jesu Wir Sind Hier"* (Galaxy) 17pp., parts. Piano alone plays chorale in A. Var.I: cello has chorale, piano counterpoints against it. Var.II: melody is in sixteenth-note figuration while cello has slow counterpoint. Var.III: piano has melody with slightly changed harmonies; cello moves along with its own separate melody. Var.IV: B♭, Alberti bass in piano with melody in octaves; cello has active counterpoint. Var.V: syncopated chordal treatment. Var.VI: varied melody in piano with counterpoint in cello similar to Var.IV. Var.VII: A, strong counter-melody in cello against chorale in piano. M-D.

Elizabeth Lutyens. *Nine Bagatelles* Op.10 (Lengnick 1947) 8 min.

Elizabeth Maconchy. *Divertimento* (Lengnick 1954) 22pp., parts. Serenade; Golubchik; The Clock; Vigil; Masquerade. Pastiche of technique and moods. A colorful suite that employs the piano admirably. Freely tonal, least interesting in the metrical treatment. M-D.

Ernst Mahle. *Sonatina* 1956 (Ric Brazil 1968) 8pp., parts. Allegro moderato: harmonic staccatissimo fourths and fifths are prevalent in the piano part. Much rhythmic drive. M-D.

Enrico Mainardo. *Sonata* (Schott 1955).
———— *Sonata quasi Fantasia* (Schott 1962).
———— *Sonatina* (Schott).

Gian Francesco Malipiero. *Sonatina* (SZ).

Marin Marais. *Suite* I d 1717 (George Hunter—AMP 1974). From *Pièces de Viole,* IV. Seven contrasting movements that cover a wide range of emotions, including a Prelude and a group of dances as well as two character pieces, "La Mignone" and "Caprice." Facile continuo realization. M-D.

Benedetto Marcello. *Six Sonatas* for cello or double bass and piano (GS 1973) 38pp., parts. Keyboard realization and cello part edited by Analee Bacon. Double bass part edited by Lucas Drew. M-D.
———— *Six Sonatas* Op.2 1712 (Bonelli, Mazzacurati—Zanibon).
———— *Six Sonatas* (CFP 4647) F, e, a, g, C, G. Second cello ad lib.
———— *Two Sonatas* C, G (Moffat—IMC; Moffat, Whitehouse—Schott).
———— *Two Sonatas* G, C (Schroeder—Augener 5511).
———— *Two Sonatas* F, g (Piatti—IMC; Schroeder—Augener 5503).

_____ *Sonata* A (Pollain—Senart 5370).
_____ *Sonata* Op.2/1 F (Zanibon 4381).
_____ *Sonata* Op.2/2 e (Zanibon 4382; Ric SY 644).
_____ *Sonata* Op.2/3 (Zanibon 4383).
_____ *Sonata* Op.2/4 g (Zanibon 4384).
_____ *Sonata* Op.2/5 (Zanibon 4385).
_____ *Sonata* Op.2/6 G (Zanibon 4386).
_____ *Sonata* F (Zanibon 4167).
_____ *Sonata* C (Ticciati—Lengnick).
_____ *Sonata* D (Moffat, Whitehouse—Schott; Salmon—Ric R98).
_____ *Sonata* e (Moffat, Whitehouse, Rapp—Schott; Salmon—Ric R403; Schroeder—IMC; Schroeder—Schott).

Tomás Marco. *Maya* (Moeck 1972) 16pp., parts (same as score but in loose leaves) 10 min.

Frank Martin. *Chaconne* 1931 (UE 12862) 10pp., parts. 6 min. Atonal bass line (row) plays against a tonal melody. Highly organized writing that presents an idea (statement) then treats it canonically. Martin "discovered" Schönberg in 1930, and this work is partly an outgrowth of that discovery. Active *dux* and *comes,* beautifully crafted variation technique (6 variations and coda). M-D.

Bohuslav Martinů. *Sonata* I 1939 (Heugel 1949) 19 min. Poco allegro; Lento; Allegro.
_____ *Sonata* II 1941 (AMP 1944) 46pp., parts. 18 min. Allegro; Largo; Allegro commodo. Many-faceted compositional style, thick and thin textures, Impressionistic mixed with Expressionistic characteristics. Freely tonal, chordal much of the time. D.
_____ *Variations on a Theme of Rossini* 1942 (Bo&H 1949) 14pp., parts. Theme, four variations, and a brilliant coda. Eclectic style employed effectively. Spontaneous and cogent writing. D.
_____ *Sonata* III 1952 (Artia 1957) 21 min. Poco andante–Moderato; Andante–Moderato–Allegro; Allegro, ma non presto.
_____ *Variations on a Slovakian Theme* 1959 (Br; Novello) 15pp., parts. Theme and five contrasting and highly colorful variations. M-D.

Eduardo Mata. *Sonata* (PIC).

Jost Meier. *Suite Concertante* (Henn 1975) 20pp., parts.

Felix Mendelssohn. *Variations Concertante* Op.17 (Cahnbley—CFP; Br&H) 11pp., parts. Theme and eight contrasting variations. Was extremely popular at one time. Piano is highly prominent in some of the variations. M-D.

———— *Sonata* I Op.45 B♭ (Such—Augener; Cahnbley—CFP). 24 min. Well scored, themes are clearly and vigorously delineated. M-D.

———— *Sonata* II Op.58 D (Cahnbley—CFP; Such—Augener) 26 min. Cello writing comes off better than does most of the piano part. D.

Louis Mennini. *Sonatina* (Bo&H 1955) 15pp., parts. Allegro moderato; Largo; Allegro robusto. Straightforward and soaring melodic ideas, freely tonal, octotonic, strong rhythms and structures, shifting meters. Large span required. M-D.

Friedrich Metzler. *Sonata* 1972 (Lienau) 21pp., parts.

Nikolai Miakovsky. *Sonata* I Op.12 D 1911–35 (USSR) 30pp., parts. Adagio; Allegro passionato. Numerous tempi changes and moods in finale. A remarkable work full of restrained austerity and at places great dynamism. Complex harmonic and contrapuntal writing. Awkward for piano at times, but the musical merits outweigh these few spots. Orchestrally conceived. M-D to D.

———— *Sonata* II Op.81 a 1948–9 (USSR). Three movements of clear melodic lines, lucid harmonic style, outstanding individual instrumental technique. M-D.

Hans Friedrich Micheelsen. *Suite* (W. Müller 1971). Chansonette (Allegretto grazioso); Arietta (Andante cantabile); Amouretta (Allegro). Well written. M-D.

Darius Milhaud. *Sonate* 1959 (Sal) 23pp., parts. Animé, Gai: 9/8, independent lines, skipping left hand, chromatic, rocking figuration, tonal G ending; large span required. Lent, Grave: 4/4, secco style, thin textures mixed with chords, rhythmic shifts, short motives. Vif et Joyeux: 3/4, facile polytonal and free contrapuntal lines, vigorous rhythms, octotonic, d closing. M-D to D.

Charles Mills. *Duo Fantasie* Op.90 (CFE).

Ernest John Moeran. *Sonata* a (Nov 1948) 23½ min.

Albert Moeschinger. *Sonate* Op.61 (Br 2462 1949) 26pp., parts. Modéré; Allegro vivace; Lento; Presto. Freely tonal around E♭, Impressionistic, broad gestures, expressive Lento, octotonic, quartal and quintal harmony. Large span required. M-D to D.

Marius Monnikedam. *Sonate* (Senart).

Xavier Bassols Montsalvatge. *Sonata Concertante* (UME 1974) 31pp., parts. Vigoroso: chromatic; large skips; parallel chords; flowing Allegretto senza rigore section; coda fades away; requires broad span. Moderato sostenuto: striking gestures open movement; chordal, including three-note clusters in both hands; added-note technique. Scherzo: 5/8, alternating hands, repeated octaves over open fifths, short glissando, secco ending. Rondo—Allegro: piano alternates between chordal and linear style; declamatory ending. Very little influence noted. D.

Robert Muczynski. *Sonata* Op.25 (GS).

Konrad Friedrich Noetel. *Sonate* (Br 1806).

Vítězslav Novák. *Sonata* Op.68 g (Artia 1941). Moravian and Slovak folk music influence felt throughout this work. M-D.

Lionel Nowak. *Sonata* I (CFE).
_____ *Sonata* II (CFE).
_____ *Sonata* III (CFE).

Toshitsugu Ogihara. *Duet* (Japan Federation of Composers 1969) 40pp., parts. Andante; Introduction—Allegro. Bitonal, neoclassic lines, some Japanese flavor, beautiful MS. M-D.

Georges Onslow. *Sonata* Op.16/2 c (Uwe Wegner—Br 1972) 41pp., parts. For viola or cello and piano. See detailed entry under duos for piano and viola.

Juan Orrego-Salas. *Duos Concertante* Op.41 1955 (PIC 1963) 52pp., parts. Cantilena; Danza; Egloga; Ditirambo; Triskelion; Himno; Époda. An impressive work with many features to recommend it. Requires thorough musicianship and technical accomplishment. Built along neoclassic lines. Displays a catalogue of pianistic techniques and idioms. Large span required. D.

Hall Overton. *Sonata* (CFE 1960) 21 min.

Manuel Palau. *Cancion de Mar* (UME 1972) 4pp., parts.
_____ *Coplas de mi Tierra* (UME 1972) 7pp., parts.

Paul Paray. *Sonate* B 1919 (Jobert) 40pp., parts. Andantino quasi allegretto;

Andante; Allegro scherzando. Flowing melodies, undulating rhythms, flexible counterpoint, strong harmonies, Impressionistic. D.

Robert Parris. *Cadenza, Caprice, Ricercare* 1961 (ACA) 32pp., parts. Cadenza: solo cello. Caprice: freely tonal, figuration divided between hands, fast half pedals, dissonant counterpoint, dramatic arpeggi figuration, brilliant piano part, glissandi. Ricercare: octotonic, imitation, long lines, theme treated in various ways, pointillistic, expressive sustained conclusion; large span required. D.

Jiří Pauer. *Sonata* Op.45 (Artia 1955) 25 min.

Stephen Paxton. *Sonata* Op.1/1 A (Frank Dawes—Schott 1972) 20pp., parts. Allegro; Adagio; Rondo (tempo di minuetto). Bright and attractive work. M-D.

George Perle. *Concerto* (TP 1Œ66) 32pp., parts. Piano reduction by composer. Introduction and Allegro: a few harmonics called for in piano part. Andante espressivo: lyric, builds to climax, subsides. Finale: large span required; five different tempi indicated by metronome marks. The entire work has numerous Schönbergian overtones. D.

Ivo Petric. *Gemini Music* 1971 (Društva Slovenskih Skladateljev 1971) 7pp., plastic ring binder. Two copies necessary for performance. Explanations in Croatian and English. Reproduced from holograph.

Rudolf Petzold. *Sonata* Op.41 (Gerig 544).

Hans Pfitzner. *Sonata* Op.1 f♯ (Br&H 1892) 27 min. Shows influence of Schumann and Mendelssohn. The first movement treats three themes ingeniously, and the burlesque finale is especially effective. M-D to D.

Gregor Piatigorsky. *Scherzo* (JWC 1939) 12pp., parts. Some changing meters, lyric mid-section, mildly contemporary, tonal. M-D.
_____ *Variations on a Theme of Paganini* (EV).

Gabriel Pierné. *Sonata* Op.46 f♯ 1922 (Durand) 30pp., parts. A skilful technique and light touch are displayed in this one-movement work. It is well proportioned with original formal structure, has varied sonorities, is thoroughly French, and is full of charm and warmth. M-D.

Willem Pijper. *Sonata* I 1919 (JWC) 16 min. Strong dissonant writing with atonal and polytonal treatment. Themes from the opening movement are heard in the Habanera and Finale movements. Cyclic construction. D.

Mario Pilati. *Sonata* A (Ric 1931).
_____ *Theme and Variations* (Ric 124428).

Ildebrando Pizzetti. *Sonata* F 1921 (Ric 119404 1933) 40pp., parts. 31 min. Largo; Molto concitato e angoscioso; Stanco e triste—Largo. Post-Romantic chromatic writing. Some unusual metrical treatment adds the most interest. Pianist is called on to move all over the keyboard with great facility. In the 1920s and 30s this work was very popular. D.

Quincy Porter. *Fantasy* (CFE).

Francis Poulenc. *Sonata* 1948 (Heugel) 44pp., parts. 21 min. Allegro—tempo di marcia: strongly vigorous contrasted with charming and lyric writing. Cavatine: calm, lyric, elegant harmonies, Romantic lyricism, sweet. Ballabile—trés animé et gai: dancelike, brilliant, frivolity romps everywhere. Largo–Presto: refined sensuousness, witty, brisk, unpretentious and thoroughly enjoyable writing in this large-scale work. D.

André Prevost. *Sonata* (Ric 1974) 23pp., parts.

Maria Teresa Prieto. *Adagio y Fuga* (EMM 1953) 13pp., parts. Adagio is freely tonal, chordal. Leads directly to the Fuga, which is properly treated with each instrument having its go with the subject. The Adagio intrudes near the middle of the fugue before the final fugue statement finishes in chordal fashion. M-D.

Sergei Prokofiev. *Ballade* Op.15 c 1912 (MCA). Shows a fine imagination with dramatic expression but is still a student work. M-D.
_____ *Sonata* Op.119 1949 (Rostropovich—IMC; Garbousova—MCA 55pp., parts; CFP 4710) 21 min. Andante grave; Moderato; Allegro ma non troppo. Vigorous lyricism juxtaposed against a gently humorous setting. Three movements, respectively, of narrative, witty and biting diablerie (scherzo), and rather moody but lyric writing. D.

Sergei Rachmaninoff. *Sonata* Op.19 g 1901 (Bo&H; IMC) 49pp., parts. 32 min. Lento—Allegro moderato; Allegro scherzando; Andante; Allegro mosso. One of the most important cello sonatas of the twentieth century. The two instruments are beautifully united in a ripe Romantic, expansive conception. It has much in common with the *Second Piano Concerto,* written about the same time, and is supremely grateful to the performers. D.

Günter Raphael. *Sonata* Op.14 b (Br&H 1926) 15 min.

Alan Rawsthorne. *Sonata* 1949 (OUP 21.006) 15 min. Three closely linked movements. Main theme and secondary theme of the second movement come from the first movement development section. New thematic material is introduced in the final movement; coda returns to the main subject of the first movement. D.
See: M. Cooper, "Current Chronicle," MQ, 35/2, April 1949. Refers to the clarinet *Quartet* and the cello *Sonata*.

Max Reger. *Caprice* a 1901 (UWKR 31 1973) 3pp., parts. Lively melody, accompanied punctuated chords. M-D.
_____ *Sonata* Op.5 f (Schott 1911). One of Reger's finest early works, beautifully displays his creative powers. D.
_____ *Sonata* II Op.28 g (Br&H 1899; UE 1927) 33pp., parts. Agitato; Prestissimo assai; Intermezzo; Allegretto con grazia. Much activity for the pianist, whirlwinds of notes. D.
_____ *Sonata* III Op.78 F (Bo&Bo 1934) 27 min. Arranged Schulz-Furstenberg. Allegro con brio: rhapsodical, improvisatory. Scherzo: short and lively, effective. Andante con variazioni: simple theme, fluctuating harmonies. Finale: gigue-like. D.
_____ *Sonata* IV Op.116 a (CFP 1911) 30½ min.

Frederich Reidinger. *Sonata* Op.9 (Dob).

Aribert Reimann. *Sonata* 1963 (Ars Viva) 21 min.

Karel Reiner. *Sonata Brevis* Op.39 (Supraphon).

Franz Reizenstein. *Sonata* A (Lengnick 1949) 60pp., parts. 27 min. Moderato; Allegro vivace; Adagio—Allegro amabile. Expansive writing requiring virtuoso technique. D.

Hermann Reutter. *Sonata Monotematica* (Schott 6424 1972) or for bassoon (6425) 19pp., parts. A one-movement work based on one subject. The exposition is contained in the Allegro appassionato section and is followed by a Vivace (Scherzo and Trio); the Adagio molto sostenuto section is a monody and is followed by an Allegro assai, a contrapuntal Finale in free fugato style. Freely tonal, neoclassic. M-D.

Ivan Řezáč. *Sonata* 1956 (Artia) 62pp., parts. Allegro moderato; Andante con moto; Presto; Molto allegro. Freely tonal and modal with Hungarian folk music influence, octotonic, octaves in alternating hands, neoclassic orientation. Requires large span. M-D.

George Rochberg. *Ricordanza: Soliloquy for Cello and Piano* (TP 1972) 8pp., parts. A surprising three-section tonal work in post-Romantic tradition. Short cadenza for cello followed by an interesting closing for piano. Lovely Romantic sounds, pre-Wagnerian harmony. Rochberg describes it as a "commentary" on the opening of Beethoven's Cello *Sonata* in C, Op.102/1; and the opening of the central section is a direct quotation, transposed, of the Beethoven theme. A large piece of full-blown Romantic chamber music. M-D.

Jens Rohwer. *Zwei Sätz* (Möseler 1975) 19pp., parts. Explanations in German.

Bernhard Romberg. *Sonata* Op.38/1 e (IMC).
_____ *Sonata* Op.38/2 G (IMC).
_____ *Sonata* Op.38/3 B♭ (IMC).
_____ *Sonata* Op.43/1 B♭ (IMC 10pp., parts; CF B3350; Billaudot). Allegro; Andante; Finale—Allegretto. Classic style, attractive. M-D.
_____ *Sonata* Op.43/2 C (IMC; Billaudot).
_____ *Sonata* Op.43/3 G (IMC; Billaudot).

Joseph Guy Ropartz. *Sonata* I g 1904 (Durand) 34pp., parts. 28 min. Allegro moderato; Quasi lento; Allegro. Franckian influence is present in this well-constructed and expressive work. The slow movement is evocative of folksong usage. Piano writing is most effective. M-D.
_____ *Sonata* II a 1918–19 (Durand).

Miklos Rozsa. *Duo* Op.8 1932 (Br&H) 17 min. Romantic conception with musical and technical difficulties equally divided between the two instruments. Has much audience appeal. M-D.

Edmund Rubbra. *Sonata* Op.60 g 1946 (Lengnick) 31pp., parts. 22 min. Andante moderato: close to rondo form. Vivace flessible: a scherzo. Finale (Tema—Adagio) is a set of seven contrapuntal variations ending with a fugue. Piano writing shows great variety in texture. M-D.

Marcel Rubin. *Sonata* 1928 (Dob 1974) 29pp., parts. 15 min. Molto vivace: octotonic, freely tonal around C, clear textures, linear. Grave: changing meters, mixture of chordal and linear textures, freely tonal around G.

Allegro commodo: melodic counterpoint between the two instruments. Presto: dancelike (waltz), long lines, two contrapuntal lines between instruments, chordal coda. Neoclassic. M-D.

Anton Rubinstein. *Sonata* Op.18 D (Schulz—GS L63; USSR, 7opp., parts; Augener) 26 min.

––––––– *Sonata* II Op.39 G (Br&H). Beautiful and grateful writing. Easily comprehended by lay audiences. M-D.

Witold Rudzinski. *Polonaise-Rapsodie* 1969 (PWM 1971) 16pp., parts.

Armand Russell. *Jovian Sonatina* (Bourne 1974) 9pp., parts. For solo bass clef instruments and piano.

Pierre Ruyssen. *Concertino* 1963 (Delrieu) 23pp., parts. Allegro moderato; Andante; Final. Conservative writing, operatic overtones. M-D.

Camille Saint-Saëns. *Sonata* I Op.32 c (Durand; IMC 2888; USSR). Allegro; Andante; Finale. An elegant and agitated work with clear classical forms. One basic tempo per movement. Recapitulation always displays the ideas in their original order. Piano and cello are combined in intriguing configurations but the independence of each instrument is never overlooked. The short, majestic Andante is treated in a full chorale style that contrasts effectively with the stormy and tempestuous Finale. A truly beautiful work that deserves to be heard more often. M-D.

––––––– *Sonata* II Op.123 F (Durand 1905). A rather serene and graceful opening movement leads to a classical scherzo followed by a Romantic Adagio and a disappointing finale. M-D.

Aulis Sallinen. *Metamorfora* (Fazer 1974) 7pp., parts. Ideas evolve in a freely tonal style with a preference for ninth chords. Sustained sonorities in piano, sectionalized, mildly contemporary. M-D.

Erkki Salmenhaara. *Sonata* 1960 (Fazer) 16pp., parts. Allegro; Adagio; Allegro. Neoclassic orientation. Clear textures, freely tonal, some changing meters, carefully crafted, much imitation in final movement. M-D.

Giovanni Battista Sammartini. *Sonata* G (Nicolas Karjinsky—ESC 1963) 12pp., parts. 12 min. Allegro; Grave; Vivace. The realization contains some sonorities too heavy for this style. M-D.

––––––– *Sonata* G (Moffat—Schott).

––––––– *Sonata* G (Rose—IMC).

––––––– *Sonata* G (Salmon—Ric R101).

_____ *Sonata* G (Stutschewsky—IMC).
_____ *Sonata* G (Senart 5349).
_____ *Sonata* G (Krane—Spratt).
_____ *Sonata* g (Sal—Ric R703).
_____ *Sonata* a (Ruf—Schott).
Some of these sonatas may be duplicates.

Pierre Sancan. *Sonate* 1961 (Durand) 18pp., parts. Allegro deciso; Andante sostenuto; Vif. Disjunct octaves, freely tonal, chordal punctuation, toccata-like passages, octotonic, glissandi, melodic line superimposed in triplets. Expressive sonorities in Andante sostenuto; perpetual-motion and toccata style in Vif. Superb piano writing. Large span required. D.

Luis Sandi. *Sonatina* (EMM 1965) 15pp., parts. Largo–Allegro comodo; Adagio non troppo; Allegro vivo. Colorful writing, some Latin-American rhythmic treatment. M-D.

A. Adnan Saygun. *Sonata* Op.12 1935 (PIC 1961) 31pp., parts. Animato: broken seventh figures in ostinato style, freely tonal, tranquillo second section, modal; dramatic clusterlike sonority concludes movement. Largo: mixture of chordal and arpeggi texture, quartal harmony, recitative-like, brief Allegro and Vivace sections. Allegro assai: shifting meters, large span required, rhythmic, octotonic, brilliant conclusion; large span required. Turkish national flavor mixed with traditional forms. M-D to D.

Alessandro Scarlatti. *Tre Sonate* (G. Zanaboni—Zanibon 1967) 12pp., parts. Published for the first time. Unfigured bass realized. Introductory note in Italian and English. I d, II c, III C. M-D.

Christoph Schaffrath. *Sonate* A (Hans Neemann—Br&H 1942) 11pp., parts. Allegretto; Adagio; Allegro. An attractive work; tasteful continuo realization. M-D.

Xaver Scharwenka. *Sonata* Op.46 e (Augener 9287).

Othmar Schoeck. *Sonata* (Br 3960 1959) 21pp., parts. Fliessend; Schnell; Andantino. This work was intended by the composer to have four movements, but only three were completed when he died. Freely tonal with great doses of chromaticism in the Schnell movement especially. Neoclassic, thin textures. M-D.

Humphrey Searle. *Fantasy* Op.57 1972 (Faber) 7 min. Eight variations and cadenza. Requires a big technique. D.

Roger Sessions. *Six Pieces* (EBM).

Vissarion Shebalin. *Sonata* Op.51/3 C (USSR 2541). Versatile contrapuntal style. Slow movement most appealing with a highly individual technique. D.

Dmitri Shostakovitch. *Sonata* Op.40 1934 (Piatigorsky—Leeds 48pp., parts; Rose—IMC; CFP 4748; USSR) 26 min. One of the most important works in the contemporary repertoire. Moderato: pliable thematic material, contemplative at first, more dramatic later. Moderato con moto: scherzo-like, large structure, peasant humor. Largo: serious, concentrated texture. Allegretto: vivacious, witty. D.

Ezra Sims. *Sonata* (CFE).

Emil Sjögren. *Sonate* Op.58 A (WH 1409) 25pp., parts. Allegro agitato; Romanza; Allegro con spirito. Romantic writing in a Nordic Brahmsian style and idiom. D.

Nikos Skalkottas. *Largo* (UE 1965) 5pp., parts. Turgid, thick chromatic textures. M-D.
———— *Sonatina* 1949 (UE 12387 1955) 24pp., parts. 15½ min. Allegro moderato; Andante; Allegro molto vivace. Freely atonal but resembles the composer's twelve-tone works in sonority. Long lyric lines lend themselves to linear treatment. Novel harmonic idiom. Requires a large span and firm rhythmic control. D.
———— *Tender Melody* 1949 (UE). Brooding, dark lyricism. Piano part consists of various figurations and is built on an ostinato of three four-voice chords. Uses early Schönberg techniques. M-D.

Lucijan Marija Skerjanc. *Capriccio* (Društva Slovenskih Skladateljev & Gerig 1974) 24pp., parts. Cello part edited by Ciril Skerjanc.

Lubos Sluka. *Sonata* (Artia).

David Stanley Smith. *Sonata* Op.59 (GS).

Hale Smith. *Sonata* (CFP) 25 min.

Leopold Spinner. *Sonatina* Op.26 1973 (Bo&H) 20pp., parts. 13 min.

Henk Stam. *Sonatine française* (Harmonia).

Zeev Steinberg. *Six Miniatures* (IMI 1973). A dodecaphony primer similar to Křenek's *Twelve Short Piano Pieces*. Int.

Halsey Stevens. *Hungarian Children's Songs* (PIC 1957) 10pp., parts. The tunes on which these charming pieces are based were chosen from a large collection of children's game songs. (*Gyermekjátékok*) edited by Bartók and Kodály. Many of the games are similar to the round games played in England and America, such as "London Bridge," "Go In and Out the Window," etc. The texts (which are included), like those of "Mother Goose" rhymes, are frequently obscure in meaning and defy literal translation. Six tunes are attractively set in clear textures with the piano having an equal share in the ensemble. Int. to M-D.

———— *Three Pieces* 1947 (CFP 1958) 9pp., parts. 4½ min. For bassoon (cello) and piano. See detailed entry under duos for piano and bassoon.

———— *Intermezzo, Cadenza and Finale* 1949, rev. 1950 (PIC) 12pp., parts. 7½ min. Adagio: *pp* dark, low, sustained chords in piano support a more active yet dolce cello line. A *forte* in piano interrupts briefly what is otherwise a hypnotic and hushed Intermezzo. The Cadenza is mainly for the cello, with the piano making a few chordal and melodic contributions derived from the opening movement. The strong Finale is rhythmically active with contrasting sections. A meno mosso coda returns the Intermezzo mood, and the work closes in delicate and mysterious shadings. Suitelike in many ways, this work also fulfils the esthetics of a fine sonata. M-D.

———— *Music for Christopher* 1953 (PIC 1968) 8pp., parts. 3 min. Four short contrasting movements (Andante; Con moto moderato; Andante con moto; Allegretto) based on folklike material. Appealing. M-D.

———— *Sonatina Giocosa* 1954 (ACA) 7 min. Originally for double bass and piano. See that section for description.

———— *Sonatina* I 1957 (Helios) 11pp., parts. 8 min. Moderato con moto: syncopated chords under a basically diatonic melody, hemiola, ternary design. Poco adagio: octotonic, moving chromatic chords, choralelike; large span required. Allegro: opening rhythmic motif is worked through many guises; brittle and staccato sonorities are interlaced with longer melodic lines supported by sustained chords; contains augmentation, diminution, and a cracking good closing. M-D to D.

———— *Sonata* 1965 (PIC) 27pp., parts. 14½ min. Commodo: freely centered around b, octotonic, octaves, quintal and tertian harmonies mainly with some quartal sonorities, tritone important, free imitation. Poco adagio: piano introduction, subtle metrical shifts from 7/8 to 6/8 keep expressive line constantly alive. Allegro moderato: sprightly rhythmic figures are transformed; cantando, more sustained mid-section brings out longer lines developed from opening figures; moving thirds in piano part; octotonic writing in sixteenth-notes lead to closing. Large span required. M-D to D.

Alan Stout. *Sonata* 1966 (CFP 1975) 25pp., parts. 18 min. Moderato ♩ = 60–63; Moderato ♩ = 104–100; Maestoso ♩ = 56; ♩ = 112. Each movement has other tempi than the one listed at the beginning. "In the Presto section of the second movement, notes without stems are to be played freely, as the visual pattern suggests—within the time stated. Black notes are to be played short, white notes long and somewhat marcato. The absolute duration of the notes depends on the pedal indications, which *must* be followed strictly. . . . It is my hope that a performance of this work will give a sense of improvisation and play (in the highest meaning of that word). The performers should not hesitate to 'bend' the tempo; i.e., use nineteenth-century style rubato to accomplish this expressive aim" (from the Performing Notes). Complex rhythmic procedure, pointillistic, dynamic extremes, expressionistic. Entire range of both instruments used. D.

Richard Strauss. *Sonata* Op.6 F (UE 1007; Rose—IMC). 27 min. The less theatrical slow movement seems to come off best in this youthful piece, although keen regard for the artistic balance of both instruments is shown. Masterly technical skill is revealed, and there are numerous inspired passages. D.

Howard Swanson. *Suite* (Weintraub 1951) 27pp., parts. Prelude; Pantomime; Dirge; Recessional. Fluent writing, flexible meters, freely tonal, clear lines, well worked out. Much facility is required for the Recessional. M-D to D.

Witold Szalonek. *Sonata* (PWM).

Alexander Tansman. *Sonata* C 1930 (ESC) 27pp., parts. 15 min. Allegro moderato: parallel harmonies, chromatic, secco style in lower register; large span required. Largo: ostinato-like figures, tranquil and legato, rich harmonies, works to appassionato climax and subsides to *pp* ending. Scherzo: changing meters in signature: 3/4, 3/8, 4/4, 3/8; octotonic, bitonal, shifting rhythms, unusual conclusion. M-D to D.

Simón Tapia Colman. *Sonata* (EMM 1961) 27pp., parts. Moderato; Largo; Giocoso; Vivo. Serial overtones, syncopation, parallel chordal shifts, some awkward arpeggi in final movement. M-D.

Alexandre Tcherepnin. *Sonata* Op.29 D 1924 (Hekking—Durand) 10 min. Allegro (SA); Cadenza; Allegretto (Rondo). Skilfully written, eclectic style, attractive, contrapuntal Cadenza. M-D.
———— *Sonata* II Op.30/1 1924 (UE 7349) 20pp., parts. 10 min. Moderato: SA, thin textures, chromatic, octotonic; recapitulation is transposed down a

major third. Lento: three free contrapuntal lines. Vivace: Rondo, triplet and duplet figuration, hemiola, unusual rhythmic vitality. M-D.

———*Sonata* III Op.30/2 1919, rev. 1926 (UE 9572 1928) 18pp., parts. 8 min. Allegro moderato; Andantino; Presto. Colorful writing with the piano part thoroughly exploited. Pianistic, as one would suspect, since the composer is an outstanding pianist. M-D.

Georg Philipp Telemann. *Sonata* a (Ruyssen—Delrieu).

——— *Sonata* D from *Der Getreue Musikmeister* (Degen—Br; Upmeyer— Nag 23 8pp., parts; Upmeyer—IMC) Lento; Allegro; Largo; Allegro. In the Upmeyer editions a few wrong notes are found in bars 15–16 in the first Allegro. M-D.

Olav Thommessen. *Duo-Sonata* 1968 (IU) 32pp., parts. Adagio grandioso; Pastorale; Adagio serioso; Intermezzo. Strong, dramatic, unusual writing; unique personal style. Expressionistic, intense. Clusters at conclusion. Complex and very difficult for both instruments. D.

Niso Ticciati. *Sonata* G "Homage to J. S. Bach" (OUP 1963) 12pp., parts. "This sonata is intended to serve as an introduction to the study of the early Italian sonatas and has therefore been composed in a corresponding style" (note in the score). M-D.

Ernst Toch. *Sonata* Op.50 (Schott 1929) 20pp., parts. 12 min. Allegro commodo; Intermezzo: "Die Spinne"; Allegro. First movement opens pandiatonically but evolves into more chromaticism until almost every note has an accidental attached. This clears up and a brief return to the opening mood ends the movement. The last movement has a great dance exuberance about it. Infectious writing. M-D.

Giuseppe Torelli. *Sonata* G (Franz Giegling—HM 69) 7pp., parts. Adagio; Allegro; Adagio; Allegro. Valuable preface by the editor. Elegant and expressive writing. M-D.

Karl Ottomar Treibmann. *Sonate* 1966 (CFP 1971) 23pp., parts.

Donald Tweedy. *Sonata* (MCA).

Ernst Ludwig Uray. *Sonata* f (Dob 1969) 50pp., parts. Kraftvoll, energisch, mässig schnell: highly chromatic; slower and more sustained second tonal area; numerous inner voices; concludes in A at a *ppp* level; requires large span. Nicht schnell, humorvoll: B♭, parallel chords, a dry humor. Sehr langsam, ausdrucksvoll: c, legato, intense, rich harmonies, soaring line, widely spread chords. Rhapsodisch bewegt: f, broken-chord figuration, contrasting sections, dramatic gestures, much activity, closes in f on a *sfz*. D.

Sándor Veress. *Sonatina* C (SZ 1950) 10½ min.

Heitor Villa-Lobos. *Grand Concerto* (ESC) 20 min.
_____ *Sonata* II Op.66 1916 (ESC 1930) 56pp., parts. 23 min. No folklore influences are found in this work. It is built on solid traditional structures. Allegro moderato: extensive piano introduction; freely tonal around a; bold gestures; triplet figure divided between hands; involved rhythms; Presto coda. Andante cantabile: flowing line in cello; subtle syncopation in piano; widely rolled chords require left hand to cross over right hand; some quartal harmony. Scherzo: strong accents; octotonic, hemiola, double glissandi, fast harmonic rhythm. Allegro vivace sostenuto: percussive sonorities; three with four; free counterpoint; large chords; a maze of tonal flux creates a downpour of color; requires large span. D.

Antonio Vivaldi. *Six Sonatas* (Diethard Hellmann—CFP 4938 44pp., parts, second cello ad lib; Nikolai Graudan—GS L1794; Kolneder—Schott; Chaigneau—Senart 5082 45pp., parts; Rose—IMC) 1 B♭, 2 F, 3 a, 4 B♭, 5 e, 6 B♭. The CFP edition is clean and includes tasteful realizations. The Senart edition has some heavy-handed realizations. The GS edition has a preface that describes the editor's procedure: 1. Tempo definitions have been made more specific, and some descriptive terms have been added. 2. Dynamic markings have been provided (Vivaldi left none). 3. Additional bowings have been indicated. "These [four-movement] sonatas deserve a high place in the cellists' concert repertoire, but they are also singularly well suited for teaching purposes because of the many technical and musical problems they offer" (from the Foreword). Tasteful realizations. M-D.
_____ *Sonata* a (Rose—IMC).
_____ *Sonata* B♭ (Rose—IMC).
_____ *Sonata* VI Bs♭ (Ticciati—Hin).
_____ *Sonata* c (Salmon—Ric R691).
_____ *Sonata* e (Salmon—Ric R692).
_____ *Sonata* V e (Rose—IMC "Concerto in e"; Ticciati—Hin).

Hans Vogt. *Elemente zu einer Sonate* 1973 (Bo&Bo) 24pp., parts. 18 min. Contains fourteen separate sections, each involving one or more of the following elements: clusters, pointillistic treatment, unmeasured sections, complex rhythms, changing meters, varied moods and textures, tremolo, percussive use of piano, expressionistic writing. D.

Bernard Wagenaar. *Sonatina* (Benditzky—CF B2448).

George Walker. *Sonata* 1957 (Gen 1972) 30pp., parts. 15 min. Allegro passionato: SA; most involved movement of the work; opens with undulating triplets; contrasting spiky second idea; worked-through development section; slightly varied recapitulation fades away to *pp*. Sostenuto: piano part mainly chordal. Allegro: uses syncopation in a highly dramatic fashion; some of the spiky idea from the opening movement returns; Presto coda adds a brilliant finishing touch. M-D to D.

Ben Weber. *Five Pieces* Op.13 1941 (CFE) 9pp., parts. 7 min. Animato; Allegretto; Largo; Largamente, Misterioso; Alla marcia. Contrapuntal twelve-tone idiom, declarative statements, jaunty rhythms, flexible meters, clever "oompah" basses in Alla Marcia. Requires large span. D.
———— *Sonata* Op.17 (ACA) 9 min. Relaxed twelve-tone idiom; vocal melodic contours almost recall Schubert. D.

Anton Webern. *Two Pieces* 1899 (G. Piatigorsky—CF 1975) 7pp., parts. From the composer's autograph MS in the Moldenhauer Archives.
———— *Cello Sonata* 1914 (Friedrich Cerha—CF 1966) 3pp., parts. Taken from Webern's autograph MS in the Moldenhauer Archives. One sketched-out movement, intense and expressionistic. D.
———— *Three Small Pieces* Op.11 1924 (UE) 2½ min. Thirty-two aphoristic bars of skeletal statements, distilled and delivered through instrumentalized veils. Webern's exclusive esthetic, which balances between sound and its cessation, has reached the end. It is very difficult to make these pithy epigrams comprehensible. D.

Karl Weigl. *Sonata* (CFE).

Charles Whittenberg. *Sonata* (CFE).

Charles-Marie Widor. *Sonate* Op.80 (Heugel).

Jean Wiener. *Sonate* 1968 (Sal) 38pp., parts. Dedicated to Mstislav Rostropovitch. Lent–Vif; Largo; third movement untitled. Freely tonal and chromatic, alternating hands, arpeggi figuration, dancelike rhythms in final movement, strongly bitonal. Large span required. D.

Malcolm Williamson. *Variations* (Weinberger 1964) 13 min.

Thomas Wilson. *Sonata* (Chappell).

Robert Wittinger. *Polemica* Op.29 1974 (Br&H 5028) 30pp., parts. Reproduced from holograph. Instructions in German. Clusters, indefinite repetitions, pointillistic, proportional notation, glissandi, sectional changes in tempi and texture, intense, percussive, nervous, avant-garde. D.

Joseph Wölfl. *Sonate* Op.31 d (Folkmar Längin—Br HM 111 1953) 28pp., parts. Largo; Allegro molto; Andante; Finale–Allegro. Pianistic, much in the classic style (middle Beethoven). The Andante is very touching. A fine and little-known addition to the literature. M-D.

William Wordsworth. *Sonata* Op.9 e 1937 (Lengnick 1946) 47pp., parts. Poco adagio—Allegro moderato; Largamente e molto cantabile; Allegro con brio. Post-Romantic writing, interesting chromatic treatment, big climaxes. M-D to D.

Charles Wuorinen. *Adopting to the Times* (CFP 1968-9) 46pp., 16 min. A first-rate pianist is required to handle the complexities. D.

——— *Duuiensela* 1962 (ACA) 28pp., parts. 9 min. Conventional and tactus-style notation. "The basic principle involved (in tactus-style notation) is that a constant quantity of space (demarked by half-bar-lines) represents a constant quantity of time (in this score, one second). Within this time-space, notes are positioned visually, and must be played so that: their occurrence in time corresponds to their placement in space" (from the score). Contains other directions. Pointillistic, clusters, flexible meters, serial influence, glissandi, dynamic extremes, virtuoso writing for both performers. Mixture of traditional and avant-garde. D.

——— *Grand Union* (CF) 13 min.

Bernd Alois Zimmermann. *Intercomunicazione* 1967 (Schott 6004) 40pp., 2 scores necessary. 12-24 min. Graphic notation; piano adds pitches and chords and other short passages. Only time points are given to indicate ensemble; dynamics are serialized. Avant-garde. For the venturesome only. D.

Johann Rudolf Zumsteeg. *Sonata* B♭ (Folkmar Längin—CFP 4823 1961) 18pp., parts. Allegro; Adagio; Finale—Presto. This attractive work, published two years after Zumsteeg's death, is apparently incomplete, having only two movements and just a "basso" part for accompaniment. The editor has realized the bass part in a simple, early classical style and has added a Finale, the last movement of another cello sonata of Zumsteeg's, still in MS. This last movement may be omitted. M-D.

Duos for Piano and Double Bass

Alain Abbott. *Fusions* 1973 (EMT 1309) 13pp., parts. 6½ min. Concours du Conservatoire National Supérieur de Musique de Paris 1974. Rocking chordal figuration of various intervals, chromatic, cluster-like sonorities, independent lines, some avant-garde notation, proportional rhythmic relationships, tremolo, complex. Requires large span. D.

André Ameller. *Concertino* (IMC 1953) 12pp., parts. One movement with varied tempi and moods, flexible meters, freely tonal, mildly contemporary. Shows off both instruments to good advantage. M-D.
_____ *Sonate* I Op.39 G (Durand 1948) 12pp., parts. Allegro; Lento expressivo; Vivace. Tonal, clear textures, neoclassic. M-D.

Tony Aubin. *Cantilène varié* (Leduc).

Gustavo Becerra-Schmidt. *Sonata* 1964 (LAMC) 13pp., parts. Allegro Giusto; Andante; Allegro tranquillo. Neoclassic, clear, light textures, on quiet side. M-D.

Lennox Berkeley. *Introduction and Allegro* (Yorke 1972) 10pp., parts. Short with freshness and a lack of complexity, neoclassic. Problem of balance is beautifully solved, well crafted. M-D.

Johann Adam Birkenstock. *Sonate* g (D-Boussagol—Leduc 1954) 16pp., parts. Adagio; Allegro; Largo cantabile; Allegro con spirito. Effective keyboard realization. M-D.

Siegfried Borris. *Sonata* Op.117 (Sirius).

Giovanni Bottesini. *Complete Bottesini* (Slatford—Yorke 1974) Preface in English and German. Vol.I: 34pp., parts. Contains *Bolero; Romanza patética (mélodie); Gavotta;* "Ne cor più non mi sento," Tema con variazione Op.23. Vol.II: 52pp., parts. Contains *Allegretto capriccio;*

Romanza drammatica (élégie) Op.20; *Fantasia* "I Puritani"; *Fantasia* "Lucia di Lammermoor."

Auguste Chapuis. *Fantaisie Concertante* (Durand 1907) 11pp., parts. Contrasted sections, late Romantic style, similar to an opera transcription, tuneful. M-D.

Klaus Dillmann. *Sonate* e (Hofmeister 1957) 18pp., parts. Allegro moderato; Adagio cantabile; Allegretto. Mildly contemporary, quartal and quintal harmony, clear lines. M-D.

Domenico Dragonetti. *Adagio and Rondo* C (Yorke 1975) 26pp., parts.
———— *Concerto* A (E. Nanny—Leduc 1925) 19pp., parts. Allegro moderato; Andante; Allegro giusto. Generally well edited. M-D.
———— *Concerto* A (Nanny, Sankey—IMC).

Pierre Max Dubois. *Le gal cascadeur* (Rideau Rouge 1973) 4pp., parts. Variations très faciles.

Henry Eccles. *Sonata* g (F. Zimmerman—IMC 1951) 8pp., parts. Largo; Corrente—Allegro con spirito; Adagio; Vivace. An effective transcription. M-D.

Ferenc Farkas. *Sonatina Based on a Hungarian Folk Song* 1955 (Artia) 11pp., parts for double bass, bassoon, or cello. See detailed entry under duos for piano and cello.

Willem de Fesch. *Übungssonate* (K. Siebach—Hofmeister) 9pp., parts. Same work in d and e. Siciliano; Allemande; Arietta; Menuett I & II. M-D.
———— *Sonata* Op.8/12 G (Sanky—IMC 1965) 8pp., parts. Prelude; Allemande; Sarabande. Effectively transcribed. M-D.

Robert Fuchs. *Sonata* Op.97 (McGinnis & Marx) 23pp., parts. Allegro moderato molto; Allegro scherzando; Allegro giusto. In a Brahmsian style. Good writing for the piano. M-D.

Giovannini [no first name]. *Sonata* a (R. Slatford, C. Tilney—Yorke 1970) 5pp., parts. Adagio; Aria staccato e allegra; Staccato e Arioso; Ballo Arioso e Presto; Sarabanda. M-D.

Reinhold Moritsevich Gliere. *Four Pieces* (USSR 1952) 39pp., parts. *Prelude* Op.32/1, *Scherzo* Op.32/2, *Intermezzo* Op.9/1, *Tarantella* Op.9/2. Fairly attractive writing. M-D.
Available separately from IMC and Forberg.

František Hertl. *Sonata* 1947 (Státní Nakladtelstvi) 36pp., parts. Allegro moderato; Andantino; Rondo—Alla Polka, Moderato. Freely tonal, centers around a, clear lines. Rondo is especially interesting. M-D.

———— *Vier Stücke* (Supraphon 1969) 30pp., parts. *Preludium, Burleska, Nokturno, Tarantella.* Contrasting, colorful, bitonal, dance rhythms, mildly dissonant. Would make an attractive recital group. Large span required. M-D.

Paul Hindemith. *Sonata* 1949 (Schott) 21pp., parts. 14 min. Allegretto: rondo-like. Scherzo: short. Molto adagio—Allegretto grazioso (Lied): simple theme is gradually thickened with more decoration until a sudden interruption of a free recitative leads to the last variation (Lied). D.

Franz Anton Hoffmeister. *Concertino* II (Sankey—IMC).

———— *Concerto* II (Malaric—Schott).

Karel Horky. *Sonatina* 1961 (Panton 1972) 23pp., parts.

Alan Hovhaness. *Fantasy* 1974 (Continuo Music Press) 16pp., parts. 10 min. Six varied sections in mood and tempo. Typical of composer's writing; straightforward with no major difficulties in either part with regard to technique or interpretation. Title completely expresses composer's intent. M-D.

Wilhelm Hübner. *Antaios* (CFP 9397 1973) 28pp., parts.

Rudolf Jettel. *Konzertante Sonate* (Eulenburg GM 36 1971) 32pp., parts. Moderato: syncopated left-hand octaves, parallel chords, freely tonal, chromatic. Allegro scherzando: octotonic, shifting rhythms, runs in major seconds, sprightly, sudden dynamic changes; large span required. Andante moderato: opens with slow dissonant counterpoint between instruments; picks up tempo, and piano part becomes rhythmic and chordal. Allegro: treats piano octotonically and concludes with tremolo pesante chords. Neoclassic. M-D.

Joseph Jongen. *Prelude, Habanera and Allegro* Op.106 1938 (CeBeDeM) 15pp., parts. 16 min. Widespread arpeggiated chords open the Prelude in recitative style. Piano provides harmony and rhythm in the Habanera. The Allegro is mainly chordal with some scalar passages. Colorful and appealing writing. M-D.

Tibor Kazacsay. *Divertimento* (EMB 1968) 27pp., parts. Scordatura tuning for double bass. Preludium: chordal, chromatic. Scherzo: light, flowing.

Ballo dell'orso: sustained, leads to an Allegro vivo with heavy chords. Finaletto: rubato opening moves to Allegro vivo with propulsive driving chords, strong ending, mildly contemporary. M-D.

Milo Kelemen. *Concertino* 1959 (CFP 5876 1961) 14pp., parts. One movement, varied tempi, chromatic, propulsive Allegro vivo section, flexible meters. Large span required. M-D.

Peter Lamb. *Concertante Music* (Galaxy).

Victor Legley. *Ballade* Op.86/4 1975 (CeBeDeM) 10pp., parts.

Theo Loevendie. *Music for Double Bass & Piano* 1971 (Donemus) 8 min.

Otto Luening. *Suite* (Galaxy 1958) 12pp., parts. Moderato con moto: freely tonal around A; linear; low register of piano cleverly used with double bass. Not too slow: chantlike, expressive melodies. Allegro moderato: syncopated chords mixed with linear sections, organum-like, bitonal. M-D.

Elisabeth Lutyens. *The Tides of Time* "Sleep Navigates the Tides of Time" Op.75 1969 (Yorke) 6pp., parts. 6 min. Serial, no bar lines, one pedal for long sections, dynamic extremes, wispy sonorities, ensemble problems. Grasps and holds the attention firmly. D.

Elizabeth Maconchy. *Music* 1970 (Yorke) 8pp., set of 2 performing scores. Contrasting tempi; fondness for quartal harmony noted; sustained qualities of piano emphasized; glissandi for double bass. Mildly contemporary, fundamentally post-Impressionistic. Exploits most of what the double bass can best do; a first-rate piece for this combination. M-D.

Jean Maillot. *Fantaisie* (EMT 1971) 13pp., parts. $7\frac{1}{2}$ min. Freely tonal, frequent major seventh chord usage, tempi and mood changes, pedal points, 2 with 3, repeated bitonal chords, octotonic. M-D.

Benedetto Marcello. *Six Sonatas* Op.1 (A. Bacon, L. Drew—GS 1973) 38pp., parts. For cello or double bass and piano. 1 F, 2 e, 3 a, 4 g, 5 C, 6 G. Excellent literature, multi-movements, "sounds" well for the combination. M-D.
Available separately (Zimmerman—IMC).

Paul Baudouin Michel. *Speleologie—jeu* (CeBeDeM 1976) 8pp., parts. $4\frac{1}{2}$ min.

Adolf Misek. *Sonata* Op.5 A (Hofmeister) 23pp., parts. Allegro; Andante religioso; Finale—Rondo. Chromatic, late nineteenth-century style. M-D.
——— *Sonata* Op.6 e (Hofmeister).

Peter Phillips. *Sonata* (McGinnis & Marx).

Thomas Baron Pitfield. *Sonatina* (Yorke 1974) 16pp., parts. Poco allegro: ostinato figuration exploited. Quodlibet—Moderato grazioso: lyric, based on folk songs. Allegro grazioso: classically oriented, mildly contemporary. Int. to M-D.

William Presser. *Sonatina* (Tritone).

Paul Ramsier. *Divertimento Concertante on a theme of Couperin* 1965 (GS) 23pp., parts. Originally for double bass and orchestra. Piano version by the composer. Barcarolle; March; Dirge; Recitative; Valse Cinématique; Toccata Barocca (Passacaglia). Neoclassic style, fluent idioms, freely tonal, octotonic. Large span required. M-D.

Karel Reiner. *Sonata* (Panton 195Œ) 54pp., parts. Preface in Czech, Russian, German, English, and French by Jiri Valek.

Lucie Robert. *Ostinato pour Contrabass et Piano* (Leduc 1973) 12pp., parts. The low registers in piano are exploited, and these, combined with low double bass sounds, produce rich blurred sonorities, which are not always interesting. Bravura writing for the double bass. M-D.

Bernhard Romberg. *Sonata* Op.38/1 e (Sankey—IMC).

Heinz Röttger. *Concertino* 1962 (DVFM 8122) 14pp., parts. Andante; Allegro molto; Quasi Cadenza (piano tacet); Vivace. Freely tonal, shifting rhythms, short patterns, cluster-like chords, driving rhythms in alternating hands, repeated notes, neoclassic. M-D.

Armand Russell. *Jovian Sonatina* (Bourne 1974) 9pp., parts. For solo bass clef instruments and piano.

Finn Savery. *Sonata* (Dan Fog).

Hans Schmid-Sekyt. *Sonata im Antiken Stil* Op.93 (Dob 1951) 13pp., parts. Allegro; Andante; Menuett; Rondo. Good imitation of older (classic) style. M-D.

Fritz Skorzeny. *Sonatina* I 1961 (Dob) 12pp., parts. One movement, various tempi and moods, mildly contemporary, fairly chromatic. The Sehr lebhaft scherzando section is especially attractive. M-D.

———— *Sonatina* II 1961 (Dob) 20pp., parts. Kraftvoll bewegt; Langsam, quasi recitativo; Sehr lebhaft. Tightly constructed movements, greater mixture of style here than in *Sonatina* I. D.

Johann Matthias Sperger. *Sonata* E (R. Malarić—Dob 1956).

———— *Trinital-Sonaten* I—3 (R. Malarić—Dob 1959–60). Arranged by the editor.

Norbert Sprongl. *Sonata* Op.74 (UE 11683 1953) 28pp., parts. Allegro; Andante cantabile; Allegro molto. Highly chromatic idiom but key signatures are present. Flowing figuration in second movement. D.

———— *Sonata* II Op.132 (Dob 1973) 29pp., parts. Translucent and practical piano writing. Three well-balanced movements. Allegro: many melodic phrases with rhythmic character. Lento: builds to climax and subsides; includes fine dialogue writing between the two instruments. Rondo-like finale exploits a perky melody with fetching rhythm. Highly effective. D.

Halsey Stevens. *Arioso and Etude* (AME).

———— *Sonatina Giocosa* 1954 (ACA) 17pp., parts. 7 min. Also for cello and piano. Allegro moderato ma giusto; Poco lento; Allegro. Combines both cheerful and serious moods. Strong demands made on double bass player. Numerous quotations from other works—Schönberg's *Gurrelieder, Dies Irae,* Ravel's *Bolero*—may be discovered in the score. M-D.

Antonio Vivaldi. *Six Sonatas* (N. Grandan—GS 1959). Double bass part edited by Lucas Drew.

Leopold Matthias Walzel. *Sonata Burlesca* Op.37 (Dob 1964) 22pp., parts. Allegretto burlesco; Moderato cantabile; Allegro burlesco. Clever, attractive writing; chromatic; displays both instruments to best advantage. M-D.

Alec Wilder. *Sonata* (Leonard Carroll) 25pp., parts. Four contrasted movements of light, witty, clear, urbane writing. Last movement is a "tour de force" in changing meters. This is a fun piece to play and hear, but there is also enough serious musical matter to place it in the literature. M-D.

Aleksandr Borisovich Zhurbin. *Sonata* (A. Mikhno—Soviet Composer 1975) 35pp., parts.

Duos for Piano and Flute

Carl Friedrich Abel. *Sonata* e Op.6/3 (Beechey—OUP 1972) Clean edition, interpretation of appoggiaturas. Slurring not indicated but required in keyboard part. A separate basso continuo part is provided. Int. to M-D.
——— *Sonata* D Op.6/6 (Beechey—Br).
——— *Sonatas* D, F, G (Sonntag—CFP).
——— *Sonata* C (Sonntag—CFP).
——— *Sonata* G (F. Brüggen—Br&VP 1960). For violin or flute.
——— *Sonatas* (Bacher, Woehl—Br). Vol.I: Sonatas e, D, G. Vol.II: Sonatas C, A, A. For viola da gamba (violin or flute) and basso continuo.

Tommaso Albinoni. *Sonata* a (Ludwig Schaffler—Nag 74 1931) Grave; Allegro; Adagio; Allegro. First-rate keyboard realization. M-D.
——— *Sonata* b (Scheck, Ruf—Ric).

Joseph Alexander. *Sonata* (Gen). Available in facsimile blueprint on special order.

William Alwyn. *Naiades—Fantasy-Sonata* (Bo&H 1973).

Amalie, Princess of Prussia. *Sonata* F (Gustav Lenzewski—Vieweg 108 1975) 8pp., parts for flute or violin. Adagio; Allegretto; Allegro ma non troppo. Agreeable and effective writing, similar in style to J. C. Bach. M-D.

Louis Andriessen. *Paintings* (Moeck 1965).

George Antheil. *Sonata* (Weintraub 1965) 22pp., parts. Allegro: SA, centers freely around F; sudden dynamic changes; repeated notes and chords; flute cadenza; alternating hand passages, left hand over right, large span required. Adagio: ABA, expressive lyric lines, melody in left-hand octaves, lilting. Presto: bitonal, light and staccato, shifting meters, glissando, rhythmic, broken left-hand figuration similar to first movement. M-D.

Paul Arma. *Douze Danses Roumaines de Transylvanie* 1940 (Lemoine 1959) 27pp., parts. 20 min. 1. Danse funèbre des vieillards. 2. Danse des garçons. 3. Hora. 4. Danse des sages-femmes. 5. Chant d'Adieu; repetition of 4, Allegro molto. 6. Hora. 7. En buvant. 8. Chanson du vagabond. 9. Danse ruthène. 10. Ronde. 11. Danse des garçons. 12. En buvant. Colorful, much rhythmic emphasis, contrasted. A group or the entire collection could be performed. M-D.

Malcolm Arnold. *Sonatina* (Belwin-Mills).
――― *Sonatina* d Op.19 (Lengnick 1948) 16pp., parts. 8 min. Allegro; Andante; Allegretto languido.
Both works are in a light, witty vein and are effective. M-D.

Claude Arrieu. *Sonatine* G 1943 (Amphion 1946) 16pp., parts. Allegretto moderato; Andantino; Presto. Tonal, Impressionistic, parallelism, charming, a fun piece for both performers and audience. Presto has figurations similar to those in the Ravel *Sonatine*. Large span required. M-D.

Georges Auric. *Imaginées* 1968 (Sal) 13pp., parts. One movement with varied tempi and character indications, many abrupt ones. In the opening and closing sections low sonorities are exploited, followed by trills and chromatic figuration in the upper register. One voice in one hand leads voice(s) in the other hand by a sixteenth of a beat. Chromatic thirds, skipping chords. Opening material is recapped. Large span required. M-D.

William Babell. *Sonata* f (Tilmouth—OUP). See description under duos for piano and oboe.
――― *Sonata* g (Michael Tilmouth—OUP 1963) 5pp., parts also for oboe or violin. Allegro; Air; Hornpipe, Giga. Seems best suited for oboe but is effective also on flute or violin. Excellent keyboard realization. Int. to M-D.

Carl Philipp Emanuel Bach. *Sonata* W.83 D 1747 (Gustav Scheck, Hugo Ruf—Ric Sy505 1954) 26pp., parts. Allegro un poco; Largo; Allegro. M-D.
――― *Sonatas* (Kurt Walther—HM 71 & 72) 2 vols. Vol.I: W.123 G, W.124 e. Vol.II: W.128 a, W.131 D.
――― *Sonata* W.85 G (Gustav Scheck, Hugo Ruf—Ric Sy634 1955) 16pp., parts. Allegretto; Andantino; Allegro. M-D.
――― *Sonata* W.87 C (Leeuwen—Zimmerman; Jean P. Rampal—IMC 1955, 11pp., parts; Scheck, Ruf—Ric). 9 min. Allegretto; Andantino; Allegro. M-D.

———*Sonata* W.125 B♭ (Scheck, Ruf—Ric Sy 503) 11pp., parts. Adagio; Allegro; Vivace. M-D.

———*Sonata* W.127 G (Scheck, Ruf—Ric).

———*Sonata* W.133 G, "The Hamburg Sonata" (Walther—Schott 4651) 11pp., parts. Allegretto; Rondo—Presto. M-D.

——— *Four Sonatas* (Walther—Br&H).

——— *Six Sonatas* B♭, D, G, D, B♭, G (Walther—CFP).

——— *Sonata* (D. Waitman—AMP 1974). For alto recorder (flute and harpsichord or piano obbligato with cello or basso continuo) 24pp., parts.

Johann Christian Bach. *Six Sonatas* D, G, C, A, F, B♭ (Wittenbecher—CFP).

——— *Six Sonatas* Op.16 1 D, 2 G, 3 C, 4 A, 5 D, 6 F (Heinrichshofen) 37pp., parts. Facsimile reprint of the first edition (ca.1780). M-D.

——— *Sonata* Op.16/1 D (Küster—Nag).

——— *Sonata* Op.16/2 G (Küster—Nag).

——— *Sonata* Op.16/4 A (Küster—Nag 103).

——— *Sonata* (Schunemann—Concordia).

——— *Sonata* D (Ruf—Nag).

——— *Sonata* I d (Schott).

——— *Sonata* F (Maguerre—Moeck).

Johann Christoph Friedrich Bach. *Six Sonatas* D, G, C, A, F, B♭ (Otto Wittenbecher—Zimmermann 1125a,b,c,d,e,f 1925). Published separately. Keyboard realizations get a little heavy from time to time but they are generally acceptable. M-D.

——— *Sonata* F (Hinnenthal—Br&H).

——— *Sonata* II D (Schott).

——— *Sonata* D (Hugo Ruf—Nag 192). For keyboard and flute or violin; cello ad lib. See description under trios for piano, violin, and cello.

Johann Sebastian Bach. *Three Sonatas* S.1030–32 b, E♭, A (Soldan, Woehl—CFP; Stainer, Geehl—Br&H; Wummer—ST; L. Moyse—GS; Barrère—BMC; Kincaid, Polin—TP).

——— *Three Sonatas* S.1033 C, S.1031 E♭, S.1020 g (Alfred Durr—Br 4418). 1031 and 1020 are for flute and obbligato keyboard, 1022 is for flute and basso continuo.

——— *Three Sonatas* S.1033–35 (David—CFP; Geehl, Stainer—ST; Soldan, Woehl—Br&H; Wummer—Billaudot; Rampal—IMC; L. Moyse—GS; Barrère—BMC; Barge, Spiro, Todt—Br&H; Kincaid, Polin—TP).

——— *Two Sonatas* S.1034–35 e, A (Hans-Peter Schmitz—Br 5022). Comes with *Sonata* S.1030 b and *Sonata* S.1032 A, and Sonata S.1039 G for two flutes and basso continuo.

———— *Sonata* S.1032 A (Samuel Baron—OUP 1975) 27pp., parts. Excellent preface in English and German. This is the least known of Bach's sonatas for flute and harpsichord, not for any lack of quality, but because at some stage 40–50 bars were removed from the original manuscript of the first of the three movements. In this edition the whole work is newly edited by Baron, who has replaced the missing bars in a fine, musically convincing reconstruction. M-D.

———— *Sonatas* Bk. I: S.525 E♭, S.526 c (Waltraut, Kirchner—Br 6801). Bk. II: Sonatas 3, 4. Bk. III: in preparation (1976).

———— *Six Sonatas* (CF; Rampal—IMC).

———— *Seven Sonatas* b, E♭, a, C, e, E, g (Marcel Moyse—Leduc). Published separately.

———— *Sonatas* 1, 2, 3 (LeRoy—Billaudot; Roth—Br&H).

———— *Seven Sonatas* (Lea 10). See detailed description of three of these (S.1027–29) under duos for piano and cello.

———— *Sonatas* 2, 6 (Kurt Soldan—CFP). Two of Bach's most ingratiating works, with the Siciliano movements in each being little masterpieces. Clean urtext edition.

———— *Suite* S.1067 b (L. Moyse—GS 1974) 24pp., parts.

Parker Bailey. *Sonata* Op.3 (SPAM 1928–9) 36pp., parts. Moderato; Allegro non troppo; Andante con moto–Allegro non troppo. Fluent writing with strong reliance on arpeggi and varied figurations. Mildly contemporary but tonal. Ideas not well developed. Facile pianism required. M-D.

Simon Balicourt. *Sonata* II 1750 (Les Editions Ouvrières 1967) 11pp., parts. For flute or violin and basso continuo. Transcribed and realized by François Petit. Andante; Allegro assai; Andante; Allegro. Well written in the style of the period. M-D.

Seymour Barab. *Sonatina* (Bo&H).

Michel de la Barre. *Suite* D (Frank Nagel, Winfried Radeske—Sikorski 784 1973) 15pp., parts. Preface in German and English. Prelude; Allemande; Air (le Badin); Air (l'Espagnol); Gavotte; Air (la Coquette); Allemande; Gigue. M-D.

———— *Sonata* G (Ruf—Ric).

———— *Sonate dit l'Inconnue* (Baron).

Francesco Barsanti. *Two Sonatas* Op.1/2 C, 6 B♭ (Gwilym Beechey—OUP) 24pp., parts. 13 min. For alto recorder and basso continuo. Each sonata has four movements, alternately slow and fast. Skillful and imaginative writing. Continuo well realized by the editor. M-D.

_____ *Three Sonatas* F, d, g (Bergmann—Schott).
_____ *Sonata* B♭ 1727 (Hugo Ruf—HM 184) 12pp., parts. Adagio: non tanto allegro; Sostenuto; Allegro. M-D.
_____ *Sonata* C 1727 (Hugo Ruf—HM 183) 14pp., parts. Adagio; Allegro; Largo; Presto. M-D.
_____ *Sonata* c 1727 (Hugo Ruf—HM 184) 12pp., parts. Adagio; Con spirito; Siciliana; Gavotte. M-D.

Robert Basart. *Fantasy* 1963 (Sal 1972) 15pp., parts. 7 min. Serial, pointillistic, sectional, many tempo changes, expressionistic, dynamic marks on many notes, complex. D.

Stanley Bate. *Sonata* (L'OL 1938).
_____ *Sonatina* (Schott 10040 1950) 16pp., part for tenor recorder or flute and piano. Allegro; Lento; Presto. Piano is treated percussively; harmonic seconds are prevalent; alternating hands. Mildly contemporary, freely tonal around a. Presto is toccata-like with a surprising decrescendo *mp* ending. M-D.

Gustavo Becerra Schmidt. *Sonata* 1953 (LAMC) 17pp., parts. Mosso; Andante; Furioso presto. Neoclassic treatment, clear textures and lines. M-D.

Conrad Beck. *Sonatina* (Schott 5198 1961) 16pp., parts. Moderato–Allegro; Vivo–molto sostenuto; Allegretto; Sostenuto. Chromatic and freely tonal, clusterlike chords, octotonic, neoclassic. Large span required. M-D.

John Ness Beck. *Sonata* (UMP).

Alfred von Beckerath. *Sonata* (Möseler).

Ludwig van Beethoven. *Sonata* B♭ Kinsky, Anhang 4 (Werner Richter—Zimmermann 1975, 23pp., parts; van Leeuwen—CFP; Laube—CF; IMC; Hess—Br&H). Authenticity doubtful. Possibly dates from ca.1790. Allegro moderato; Polonaise; Largo; Allegretto molto con Variazioni. Delightful classical writing. M-D.
_____ *Variations* Op.105 (VU; Br&H). For violin or flute.
_____ *Variations* Op.107 (VU; Br&H). For violin or flute.
Both of these sets greatly favor the piano and contain some most interesting writing. M-D.

Sadio Bekku. *Sonate* 1954 (Ongaku No Tomo Sha 1958) 22pp., parts. Allegro moderato; Vivace. Both movements are in SA design, freely tonal.

Clear and orderly lines reveal a refreshing lyricism. Feeling of moving ahead is necessary in the first movement. M-D.

Franz Benda. *Two Sonatas* C, e (Janetzky—Hofmeister).

_____ *Sonata* G Op.3/1 (Ruetz—Nag; Hugo Ruf—Schott 5574) 16pp., parts. From "Trois Sonates pour le Clavecin Avec l'Accompagnement d'une Flute ou Violin." Allegro; Cantabile; Scherzando. Solid classic writing with attractive figuration for both instruments. M-D.

_____ *Sonata* e (Schoenbaum—Br).

_____ *Sonata* F (EM; IMC).

Georg Benda. *Sonata* G (Manfred Ruetz—Nag 154 1960) 15pp., parts. Allegro moderato; Andantino; Allegro. This work was published in 1942 under the name of Franz Benda, Georg's brother, his senior by thirteen years. It also exists in a slightly different version for violin and keyboard. The quick movements are melodious and lively; the slow movement has a plaintive and tragic character. Keyboard is treated in a competitive melodic way with the flute. M-D.

Niels Viggo Bentzon. *Six Variations on an Original Theme* Op.17 (WH 3406 1943) 11pp., parts. Quartal and quintal harmonies, freely tonal, neoclassic, syncopated theme. Strongly contrasted variations, tremolo, wide dynamic range, chromatic triplets. Var. 4 is a flute solo. Perpetual motion idea in Var. 5. Var. 6 uses the piano percussively in alternating hands. Coda is quiet, with theme returning for a Molto tranquillo closing. M-D.

Jean Berger. *Suite* (BB 1955) 23pp., parts. Allegro commodo; Moderato; Molto moderato; Allegro. Clear lines and textures, chordal. Parallelism in second movement gives an Impressionistic feeling. M-D.

Lennox Berkeley. *Sonatina* a (Schott 10015 1940) 12pp., parts. 10 min. Moderato, Adagio; Allegro moderato. Lyrical and sustained thematic beauty, clear, terse. Alternating chords between hands. Modest in scale. M-D.

Herman Berklinski. *Sonata* (ACA) 13½ min.

Alain Bernaud. *Incantation et Danse* (Rideau Rouge 1973) 15pp., parts.

Wallace Berry. *Duo* 1969 (ST) 19pp., parts. Includes performance directions. Elegiac throughout most of the piece, canonic, chromatic, melodious, large arpeggiated chords, flexible meters; keen sense of rubato necessary. A contemporary tone poem. Pianist must tap knuckles on solid wood of the piano. Large span required. M-D to D.

Thomas Beversdorf. *Sonata* (ST 503 1966) 32pp., parts. Allegro con moto: dramatic marcato opening, canonic, broken octaves, large chords, extreme ranges, chromatic broken-chordal figuration. Andante: repeated notes and chords, long lines; large span required. Allegro ma non troppo energico: fast scales, pesante rhythmic chordal figures, trills, ideas effectively combined, reiterated patterns, broken octaves in alternating hands, brilliant conclusion. D.

Günter Bialas. *Sonata* (CFP).

Diogenio Bigaglia. *Sonata* g (CFP).

Jean Binet. *Sonatine* (Foetisch 1952) 15pp., parts. Lent–Modérément animé; Lent; Assez vif. Chromatic, Impressionistic tendencies. M-D.

Gordon Binkerd. *Sonatina* 1947 (Bo&H 1972) 15pp., parts. Allegro moderato: SA, free counterpoint, chromatic lines. Andantino: flowing piano has a more active mid-section; opening section mood returns. Allegro giocoso: 5/8, 3 + 2 and reverse 2 + 3 provide basis for dancelike quality; effective scalar closing. M-D.

Marcel Bitsch. *Three Sonatines* (Leduc 1949) 19pp., parts. Andante pastorale; Sarabande; Vivo assai. Like a three-movement work. Moves over keyboard, chromatic, not easy. M-D to D.

Martino Bitti. *Four Sonatas* (Ruf—HM) a, c, g, G.

Boris Blacher. *Duo* (Bo&Bo 1972) 12pp., parts. Allegro moderato; Andante; Presto; Andante. Pointillistic, flexible meters, thin textures. M-D.

Michel Blavet. *Six Sonatas* Op.2 1731 (Walter Kolneder—Müller; Bo&H) Bk. I, 36pp., parts: 1. L'Henriette, 2. La Vibray, 3. La Dhérouville. Bk. II, 40pp., parts: 4. La Lumagne, 5. La Chaurel, 6. La Bouget. These multi-movement sonatas show Blavet to be a composer of good taste with a profound command of musical phraseology. In a preface he speaks of "character pieces," which are summed up in the titles of the works. First and family names are used as well as captions like "Gossip," "Goblins," "Regrets," etc., in accordance with French ballet practice of the day. Tasteful basso continuo realizations. M-D.
———— *Two Sonatas* Op.2/2 d, 3 E (Ruf—Schott).
———— *Sonata* Op.3/2 b (Ruf—Br).

Ernest Bloch. *Suite Modale* 1956 (BB 1958) 14pp., parts. 12 min. Moderato; L'istesso tempo; Allegro giocoso; Adagio–Allegro deciso. Modality permeates the entire work, giving rise to interesting scales and chords. M-D.

J. Bodin de Boismortier. *Six Sonatas* Op.91 D, g, G, e, A, c (Marc Pincherle—Heugel 1970) 81pp., parts. Le Pupitre 20. All are multi-movement works that show marked originality. Some gracious and charming writing here. M-D.

Mélanie Bonis. *Sonata* (ESC).

Helmut Bornefeld. *Choralsonate* I "Auf Mienen Lieben Gott" 1957 (Br 3481) 16pp., parts. Keyboard part can be played on piano, harpsichord, or organ. Zart und ruhig fliessend: quartal and quintal chromatic harmony, flowing lines, many sequences; chorale ingeniously worked into texture. In sehr ruhigen Achteln einleitend: fragmentary ideas, non legato figures in keyboard, 3 against 2, chromatic arpeggi figures, tremolo, chords in alternating hands; descending lines provide restful conclusion. Neoclassic. M-D.

Pierre Boulez. *Sonating* 1946 (Amphion 1954) 31pp., parts. One serial movement of complex rhythmic and percussive writing. Series inspires similar thematic motives. Highly varied and fragmentary texture, pointillistic. Varied SA design; development section, beginning at the Scherzando, alludes to material from the exposition. Flexible meters, terribly involved. D.
See: Carol K. Brown, "An Analysis of the Pitch Organization in Boulez's 'Sonatine' for flute and piano," *Current Musicology* 20 (1975): 87–95.

Darijan Božič. *Sonata in Cool I* (Gerig).

Cesar Bresgen. *Sonata* (Schott 4111 1951) 23pp., parts. Fliessend, doch nicht rasch; Lebhaft und sehr leicht; Ruhige Viertel. Strong neoclassic writing, on a par both musically and technically with some of the Hindemith duo chamber sonatas. D.
——— *Sonatine* D (Heinrichshofen/Sirius). For soprano blockflute and piano.
——— *Studies* IV (Dob).

Thomas Briccetti. *Sonata* Op.14 (McGinnis & Marx 1962) 42pp., parts. Moderato: freely tonal, chromatic figuration involving broken octaves, shifting rhythms, flute cadenza, sudden dynamic changes. Andante cantabile: free dissonant counterpoint, effective use of trills, rich sonorities. Prestissimo: fast octotonic sixteenth-note writing; dramatic arpeggi gestures; subtle syncopation; extreme dynamic range; leads directly into an Andante section full of chromatic chords and arpeggi; prestissimo tempo and mood return to wrap up this large and important contribution to the literature. D.

Benjamin Britten. *Gemini Variations* Op.73 (Faber Fo14 1965). Quartet for two or four players for violin, flute, and piano four-hands. If two players are used, it is performed by flute and piano or by violin and piano. Twelve variations and fugue on epigram of Kodály. M-D.

Raynor Brown. *Sonata* I (WIM 107 1975) 25pp., parts. Prelude; Fugue; Rondo. Freely tonal, octotonic, quartal harmony, flowing imitative lines, thin textures, neoclassic. M-D.

Adolf Brunner. *Sonata* (Br 1990) 23pp., parts. 15 min. Allegro leggiero; Adagio rubato; Allegro molto. Neoclassic tendencies but textures are thick at stress points. Freely tonal, long lines. M-D.

Stephen Douglas Burton. *Stravinskiana, Concertino for Flute and Piano* (Sal 1974) 25pp., parts. Maresto: strongly rhythmic; more sustained mid-section; groups of four sixteenth notes spread out over interval of major seventh frequently used. Intensivo: cool upper-register sonorities; flute has a solo section; walking bass octaves under pungent chords make for unusual effect; *pppp* closing. Moto Perpetuo (bongo and snare indicated in piano part—unclear whether to use those instruments or to imitate the effect on the piano): varied figurations from chromatic scale passages to tremolo to long-held low register chords; percussion and timpani indications also seen. A frantic and hair-raising piece of writing. D.

Antonio Caldara. *Sonata* di chiesa (CFP).

Robert Casadesus. *Sonata* Op.18 (Durand 1948) 43pp., parts. Allegro moderato: flowing, lusingando figuration, scalar, added-note technique used in second subject, 3 with 4, seventh chords, fast thirds in right hand, large span required. Andante: 6/8, berceuse-like rocking figures, short trills in inner voice joined by trills in bass line, quiet. Molto vivo: secco, fleeting, trills, shifting rhythms, hemiola, broken octaves, melody embedded in figuration; builds to climax; centers around E. D.
―――― *Fantaisie* Op.59 1959 (Durand) 13pp., parts. Freely tonal around e–E, varied mood and tempi, clever use of grace notes, flowing and undulating lines. M-D.

Jacques Castérède. *Sonata en forme de Suite* (Leduc 1957) 20pp., parts.

Prelude: chromatic alternating lines between hands, freely tonal, long phrases, mordents. Menuet: fifth note, first bar, in flute part should be a C♯, not A; contains some snappy rhythms for a menuet; expanding chordal intervals are frequent. Sarabande: lovely expressive lines over sustained chords. Rondo: dancelike, spirited, *pp* closing. Thorough treatment of both instruments. D.

Norman Cazden. *Sonata* Op.36 1941 (ACA) 14 min.

Charles Chaynes. *Sonatine* (Leduc 1952) 12pp., parts. Très allant: one movement, varied tempi, light, clever but also well written, somewhat in the style of Poulenc. Large span required. M-D.

Barney Childs. *Sonata* (CFE).

Frédéric Chopin. *Variations* E (PWM Vol. XVI of Complete Works 1959; Rampal—IMC; Belwin-Mills). PWM has commentary in English by Ludwik Bronarski. 8pp., parts.

Wen-Chung Chou. *Cursive* 1963 (CFP) 15pp., parts. 11 min. " 'Cursive' refers to the type of script in which the joined strokes and rounded angles result in expressive and contrasting curves and loops. The cursive script represents the essence of Chinese calligraphy as its expressiveness depends solely upon the spontaneous but controlled flow of ink which, through the brush-strokes, projects not only fluid lines in interaction but also density, texture and poise" (from the preface). This piece has been influenced by the cursive concept, mainly in its use of specific but indefinite pitches and rhythm, in regulated but variable tempo and dynamics, as well as various timbres on the two instruments. Pianist must tap, stop, and pluck strings and play glissandi on the strings. Performance directions. Pointillistic fragmentary melodies, virtuoso display of effects. D.

Muzio Clementi. *Three Sonatas for the Piano or Harpsichord with the Accompaniment of a Flute or Violin* Op.2 (Hin 1971). Unchanged facsimile of an Amsterdam edition of the 1780s. These are actually *Sonatas* Op.2/3, 5 and Op.4/4. Misprints of the original have not been corrected but they are easy to spot. M-D.
———— *Sonata* Op.2/3 G (Jean-Pierre Rampal—IMC 1963) 7pp., parts. Moderato: Rondo—Allegretto. Straightforward writing with the two couplets in the Rondo being especially pleasant. M-D.

Arnold Cooke. *Sonatina* 1965, rev. 1961 (OUP 1964) 16pp., parts. Allegro moderato; Andantino; Allegro vivace. Cheerful, bright, witty. Clever syncopation in last movement. M-D.

Paul Cooper. *Sonata* 1964 (JWC 1967) 18pp., parts. 12 min. Strong contemporary writing for both instruments. Pianist is required to play rapid glissandi with finger nail while sustaining keys silently to produce colorful sonorities. Firm rhythmic control necessary for proper ratios in some measures. Form and fabric are uniquely molded together. D.

Aaron Copland. *Duo* (Bo&H 1971) 21pp., parts. Three movements of wide-ranging intervals coupled with propulsive and additive rhythms. Reflective passages recall *Appalachian Spring* but the harmonies and intervallic structure are obviously later vintage. M-D.
———— *Vocalise* (Bo&H 1974) 4pp., parts. Flute part edited by Doriot A. Dwyer.

Michel Corrette. *Sonata* d (Galaxy).
———— *Sonata* e (Ruf-Schott).
———— *Sonata* II (Petit-Galaxy).
———— *Sonatille* b (Laurence Boulay—EMT 1964) 10pp., parts, cello ad lib. Preface in French, English, and German. Allegro moderato; Largo; Allegro. "Sonatille" is a term Corrette invented to designate some short sonatas each subtitled "Solo for the transverse flute or violin with bass . . . oeuvre XIX." Keyboard part is equal in importance to that of the flute. Somewhat Italian in style. Editorial additions indicated. M-D.

Ramiro Cortés. *Elegy* (EV 1952) Poetic, lyric.

Jean Coulthard. *Lyric Sonatina* (Waterloo 1976) 21pp., parts.

François Couperin. *Concert Royal IV* (Rampal, Vernon-Lacroix—IMC 1960) 11pp., parts. Prélude; Allemande; Courante Française; Courante à L'Italienne; Sarabande; Rigaudon; Forland en Rondeau. Mainly because of the ornamentation this work is listed as D.

Adrian Cruft. *Seven Pieces* Op.79 (Chappell 1975). Simple flute tunes progressing in technical and rhythmic problems. The final piece is in 5/4. Int.

Carl Czerny. *Duo Concertante* Op.129 G (F. Vester—UE 1975) 51pp., parts. Allegro; Scherzo—Allegro molto; Andantino grazioso; Rondo—Allegretto. Both instrumental parts are equally difficult. Strong Beethoven influence, excellent structure. M-D.

Ingolf Dahl. *Variations on a French Folktune* 1935 (Boonin) 16pp., parts. 10 min. Based on "Au clair de la lune." Eight contrasting variations, the last one a fughetta. Tonal and graceful writing for both instruments. M-D.

_____ *Variations on an Air by Couperin* 1965 (Boonin) 20pp., parts. 10 min. Theme is "Les Graces Natureles." Five contrasting variations plus an interlude and a fughetta. Separate part for alto recorder. Eighteenth-century theme is incorporated tastefully into a mildly contemporary style. M-D.

Jean-Michel Damase. *Sonata en Concert* Op.17 (Lemoine 1952).

_____ *Scherzo* Op.25 (Lemoine 1957) 14pp., parts. 3½ min. Constant motion in 6/8 and/or 9/8 moves over entire keyboard. Some long lines. Must be sparkling clean to impress properly. Large span required. M-D.

Raphael Dannatt. *Sonata* Op.6 1968 (ST SS-931) 19pp., parts. A one-movement work with contrasting sections, tempi, and mood. Freely chromatic; linear and homophonic mixture; short motifs expanded and developed; inner voices take on added significance; large chords, 3 with 2; careful interplay between instruments; good octave technique necessary, *p* closing. Neoclassic orientation. M-D.

Franz Danzi. *Sonatine* D (W. Lebermann—Schott 6191 1970) 32pp., parts. Larghetto—Allegretto; Larghetto; Polacca. M-D.

_____ *Sonatine* e Op.34 (Müller 82 1048 09). Classical features, linked movements. M-D.

Gyula David. *Sonata Fuvolara es Zongorára* 1954 (EMB z.1867) 27pp., parts. Allegro; Adagio; Vivace molto. Tonal, based on folklike tunes. Octotonic, parallel chords, thin textures. Adagio is quite free (poco rubato). A folkdance with strong rhythms is the basis for the finale. M-D.

Jack Delano. *Sonatina* (PIC 1965) 26pp., parts. Allegro; Adagio; Allegretto grazioso; Allegro. Freely tonal, varied textures, parallel chords, quick figuration alternating between hands, hemiola, neoclassic. M-D.

François Devienne. *Sonata* I e (J. P. Rampal—IMC 1974).

Robert Di Domenico. *Sonata* 1957 (EM) 19pp., parts. Facsimile of composer's MS. One movement, varied tempi, atonal, thin textures, cadenzas for both instruments. Requires large span. M-D.

Emma Lou Diemer. *Sonata* 1958 (ST 1973) 23pp., parts. 9½ min. Moderately fast, gracefully: imitative, trills in inner voices. Moderately slowly, expressively: pastoral, flowing. Joyfully, fast: thin textures, freely tonal. M-D.

Charles Dieupart. *Suite* I C (Hugo Ruf—Moeck 1084 1966) Ouverture; Allemande; Courante; Sarabande; Gavotte; Menuet; Gigue. This is the first of six suites left by Dieupart. J. S. Bach was so impressed with these works that he copied two of them by hand. Tasteful keyboard realization. M-D.
_____ *Suite* IV e (J-C. Veilhan, D. Salzer—Leduc 1974) 9pp., parts for flute or violin and basso continuo.

Charles Dodge. *Duo* (CFE).

Gaetano Donizetti. *Sonata* C 1819 (Raymond Meylan—CFP 1969) 15pp., parts. Largo–Allegro. Opening in c sets somber mood; Allegro is all bright and cheerful. Development section proceeds through some interesting tonalities. M-D.

Sem Dresden. *Sonata* 1918 (Senart) 16½ min.

Pierre Max Dubois. *Sonate* (Leduc 1959) 25pp., parts. 19 min. Allegro: octotonic, freely tonal around C, shifting rhythms, glissando, chords in alternating hands, Gallic wit. Recitative—Andante nostalgico: bitonal, plaintive melody, musette-like mid-section, rich harmonies. Rondo: broken-chord patterns, glissandi, varied meters, subito martelé effects; large span required. The entire work has a kind of Poulencian charm about it. M-D to D.

Henri Dutilleux. *Sonatine* (Leduc 1943) 16pp., parts. 8 min. One large movement of transparent and clear colors, charming writing. Sections are Allegretto, Andante, and Animé, molded together in a strong formal construction. Carefully controlled harmonic dissonance and melodic distortion. M-D.

Helmut Eder. *Sonatine* Op.34/4 (Dob).

Ryan Edwards. *Sonata* Op.10 (Billaudot 1974) 29pp., parts.

Günther Eisenhardt. *Aus dem Indianerleben. Eulenspiegeleien* (DVFM 1974). For recorder and piano.
_____ *Sonatine* (Hofmeister 1972) 16pp., parts for soprano blockflöte and piano.

Manuel Enriquez. *Diptico* I (IU) 3pp., parts. Diagrammatic notation. Numerous directions for performers. Strings to be plucked and struck. Clusters, tremolo clusters, stopped strings, aleatoric, avant-garde. D.

Heimo Erbse. *Sonata* Op.25 1967 (Bo&Bo) 32pp., parts. Con moto; Lento; Quarter note = 138–144; Vivace assai. Serial, expressionistic. D.

Gabriel Fauré. *Fantaisie* Op.79 (Hamelle) 17pp., parts. 5 min. Andantino; Allegro. Lovely, cool, flowing writing. M-D.

Jan Reindert Adriaan Felderhof. *Suite* (Donemus 1974) 18pp., 2 parts (flute and oboe), photostat of MS.

Viktor Fenigstein. *Four Rufspiele* (Eulenburg 1974) 12pp., parts.

Brian Ferneyhough. *Four Miniatures* (CFP).

Giorgio Ferrari. *Sonata* 1957 (EC 1968) 34pp., parts. 10 min. Allegro moderato; Adagio; Allegro vivo. Chordal punctuation, chromatic, octotonic, thin textures. The last two movements contain contrasting tempi and moods. Effective treatment of both instruments. MC. M-D.

Willem de Fesch. *Six Sonatas* (Woehl—HM 1949) Vol.I: 1 D, 2 c, 3 e. Vol.II: 4 G, 5 A, 6 b.

Ronald Finch. *Sonata* (Schott 10723 1959) 12pp., parts. For tenor recorder and piano. Andante piacevole; Presto; Moderato. Tonal, shifting meters, thin textures, neoclassic, attractive. M-D.

Nicolas Flagello. *Concerto Antoniano* 1953 (Gen 1964) 45pp., parts. Originally for flute and orchestra, piano reduction by the composer. Allegro moderato: freely tonal, synthetic scales, sudden dynamic changes, long trill, flute cadenza, large span required. Andante comodo: Ravel-like, triplets, repeated chords, 2 with 3, sinking conclusion. Allegro con brio: disjunct subject; octotonic; concludes with an Alla Fuga; requires good octave technique. Neoclassic. M-D.

Marius Flothuis. *Sonata da Camera* Op.17 1943 (Donemus D40 1951) 16pp., parts. Cadenza: piano part is chordal while flute moves about freely. Sonatina: freely tonal, dissonant counterpoint, broken triplet chord figuration in left hand. Lamento: repeated low notes in left hand, chords in right hand; flute has melody. Rondo alla Francese: octotonic, like a two-part invention between the instruments, surprise *pp* closing; large span required. M-D.

Hendrik Focking. *Sonata* Op. 1/2 (Hans Schouwman—Heuwekemeijer 1956) 7pp., parts. Moderato; Allegro; Presto. A few unusual harmonic characteristics would place this in the Rococo period. M-D.
———— *Sonata* Op. 1/6 G (Wisse—Br&VP 1949).

Jacqueline Fontyn. *Sonate* 1952 (CeBeDeM 1964) 18pp., parts. 15 min. Allegretto, Adagio; Vivo. A mixture of neoclassic and expressionistic writing; becomes very involved at spots. D.

John Vaino Forsman. *Sonatina Divertante* (Br 3301 1955) 15pp., parts. Allegretto moderato; Andante mesto; Allegro animato. Neoclassic, clear textures, taut construction. M-D.

Wolfgang Fortner. *Sonata* 1947 (Schott). In Hindemith idiom. Light, tonal centers apparent. The fourth movement rondo has an extensive second episode made up of a theme, four variations, and a coda. M-D.

Jean Françaix. *Divertimento* (Schott FTR96 1955) 23pp., parts. Toccatina; Notturno; Perpetuum mobile; Romanza; Finale. Delightful, refreshing, witty, much charm. M-D.

Frederick the Great, King of Prussia. *Ten Sonatas* (C. Bartuzat—Br&H 5451) Vol.I: *Sonatas* d, B♭, B♭, D, A. Vol.II: *Sonatas* B♭, e, d, E♭, D. Stylistic keyboard realizations by Paul G. Waldersee and Günter Raphael. Multi-movement works in rococo style. M-D.
———— *Sonata* A (Sonntag—Sikorski).

Hermann L. Freedman. *Sonata* (Thames 1973). Atonal, non-strict serial. M-D to D.

Kurt Joachim Friedel. *Sonata* (Möseler).
———— *Sonatina* (Heinrichshofen/Sirius 1973) 13pp., parts. For alto recorder and piano.
———— *Suite* (Möseler 1973) 19pp., parts.

Kazuo Fukushima. *Three Pieces from "Chū-u"* (CFP 1964) 2 copies required. 7½ min. Pointillistic, major sevenths preferred, dynamic extremes with more use of quieter sonorities. Flutter tonguing and quarter tones required for flute. Second piece is for solo flute. M-D.

Anis Fuleihan. *Pastoral Sonata* 1940 (PIC 1967) 26pp., parts. Allegro: main idea is generated from opening triplet; quartal harmony; second theme is heard in the piano in an octave melody; development utilizes alternating hands in harmonic fourths; staccato style in right hand contrasts with legato flute line; altogether a flowing movement. Andante: ABA; main idea is imitated by both instruments; rocking quartal and quintal chords; octotonic writing and octaves lead to flute cadenza; abbreviated A section returns and concludes with widely spread piano texture. Prestissimo: light perpetual-motion idea in piano is interspersed with sixteenth-note pattern and synco-pated chords; legato, flowing sixths in piano may present a problem; melody, sixteenth-note pattern, and syncopated chords all distilled together in the piano part; chords in alternating hand patterns; brilliant crescendo, decorated arpeggio, and a subito chord conclude this work of gracious writing. M-D.

Jean Gabriel-Marie. *Slovakiana* 1968 (Choudens 1974) 28pp., parts.

Hans Gál. *Concertino* Op.82 (UE).
_____ *Three Intermezzi* Op.103 (Schott 1074) 19pp., parts. For tenor re-corder or flute and piano or harpsichord. Pieces are charming, pose no great technical demands yet they present a full score for sensitive performers. Romantic influence. Int. to M-D.

Johann Ernst Galliard. *Sonata* Op.1/1 C (Gustav Schenk, Hugo Ruf—Ric Sy521 1956) 8pp., parts. Largo; Allegro; Largo; Allegro. M-D.
_____ *Sonata* Op.1/2 d (Gustav Schenk, Hugo Ruf—Ric Sy522 1956) 7pp., parts. Grave; Allegro; Largo; Vivace e affettuoso. M-D.
_____ *Sonata* Op.1/3 e (Gustav Schenk, Hugo Ruf—Ric Sy533 1956).

Philippe Gaubert. *Sonata* (Durand).

Francesco Geminiani. *Sonata* e (Ruf—HM 1961).

Harald Genzmer. *Sonata* 1940 (R&E) 24pp., parts. 11½ min. Lebhaft; Ruhig fliessend; Lebhaft. Neoclassic, strong tonal implications, clear textures. M-D.
_____ *Zweite Sonate* E 1945 (Schott 3881) 21pp., parts. 10 min. For alto-blockflöte and piano. Material well developed, non-lyrical in approach. M-D.

Vittorio Giannini. *Sonata* 1958 (Colombo NY2103 1964) 28pp., parts. Adagio (Introduction)–Allegro; Sostenuto e cantabile; Rondo—Allegro con brio. Neo-Romantic style, long beautiful melodies, pianistic, a rather sunny work. M-D.

Felice Giardini. *Sonate* Op.3 (E. Polo—Fondazioni Eugenio Bravi 1941)

I Classici Musicali Italiani, vol.3. For violin or flute and keyboard. See detailed listing under duos for piano and violin.

Walter Gieseking. *Sonatine* 1935 (Fürstner A8355F) 17pp., parts. Moderato; Allegretto; Vivace. Mildly contemporary chromatic style, flowing, attractive. M-D.

———— *Variationen über ein Thema von Edvard Grieg* (Fürstner A8375 8358F 1938) 23pp., parts. For flute or violin and piano. Theme is from the "Arietta" Op.12/1 by Grieg. Twelve contrasting variations in a freely chromatic style. Attractive writing that almost spotlights the piano more than the other instrument. M-D.

Anthony Gilbert. *The Incredible Flute Music* Op.11 (Schott 1070) 14pp., parts. Pointillistic, dynamic extremes, aleatoric. Pianist whistles; flutist sings; title is true! Avant-garde. D.

Peggy Glanville-Hicks. *Sonatina* (Schott 10029 1941) 12pp., parts. Animato assai; Lento recitativo; Vivace. Neoclassic, clear lines and textures. Slow movement is slightly Impressionistic. M-D.

Alexander Goehr. *Variations* Op.8 1959 (Schott) 15pp., parts. 10 min. Eleven variations. Serial, pointillistic, complex writing. D.

Ernest Gold. *Sonatina* (Simrock 1966) 28pp., parts. 12 min. Allegretto giocoso; Moderato grazioso; Animato. Vitality permeates this entire work, even the slow movement. Texture gets thick but for a short time only. There is nothing here an experienced pianist could not handle. M-D.

Stan Golestan. *Sonata* (Sal).

Harold Gramatages. *Duo* A♭ 1943 (ECIC 1946) 8pp., parts. Allegro moderato; Tranquillo e molto cantabile; Allegro. Imitative, syncopation, freely tonal, clear lines. M-D.

Lewis Granom. *Sonata* G (Fleury—Ric 1921).

Carl Heinrich Graun. *Sonata* D (CFP).

Christoph Graupner. *Two Sonatas* (HM).

Charles T. Griffes. *Poem* 1922 (Barrere—GS). Originally for flute and orchestra.

Camargo Guarneri. *Sonatina* 1947 (Mercury) 19pp., parts. 9½ min. Allegro: thin textures, bitonal, tart. Melancolico: linear, cantabile, staccato middle-voice usage. Saltitante: dance, staccato textures, freely chromatic. M-D.

Jean-Pierre Guignon. *Sonata* Op.1/8 A, ca.1737 (Hugo Ruf—Schott 5883 1971) 14pp., parts. Allegro, poco grazioso; Un poco andante; Allegro poco e grazioso; Allegro molto. Expert continuo realization. M-D.

Louis-Gabriel Guillemain. *Sonata* G 1734 (Hugo Ruf—Schott 5570 1968) 15pp., parts. Adagio; Allemanda; Sarabanda; Allegro assai. M-D.

Jesus Guridi. *Tirana, homenaje a Sarasate* (UME 1973) 9pp., parts.

Joaquín Gutiérrez Heras. *Sonata Simple* (Collecion Arion 1968) 17pp., parts. Allegro non troppo; Andante; Allegro. Thin textures, neoclassic, hemiola, tremolo, effective. M-D.

Reynaldo Hahn. *Variations on a Theme by Mozart* (IMC1796) 10pp., parts. Theme and seven contrasting variations. Only Var.4 changes tonality. M-D.

Karl Haidmayer. *Flötensonate* 1962 (Dob 1971) 26pp., parts. Allegro; Andante espressivo; Animato. Tonal and centered around d, chromatic, repeated clusterlike chords, quartal and quintal harmony, toccata-like finale, mainly thin textures, neoclassic. Punctuating left-hand octaves; large span required. M-D.

Iain Hamilton. *Sonata* 1966 (TP 1969) 21pp., 2 scores necessary. 14 min. One player uses piccolo, flute, alto flute, and bass flute. In nine sections with no breaks. All pedaling is marked although some may be added at pianist's discretion. Serial influence, pointillistic, dynamic extremes, shifting meters (5, 2, 3½, etc.). Chords are increased up to clusters with both hands and arms; large span required. Section 4 is a cadenza for solo piano requiring four staves to notate; tremolo chords, expressionistic. D.

George Frederick Handel. *Chamber Sonatas* (Seiffert—Br&H) published separately. Op.1/1a e, 1b e, 2 g, 5 G, 6 g, 8 c, 10 g, 12 F, 13 D, 14 A, 15 E, 17 a.
———— *Eleven Sonatas* (Schmitz—Br) Handel Ausgabe IV/3: Op.1/1a, 1b, 2, 4, 5, 9, 11.
———— *Sonatas* 1, 2, 3, 4, 5, 6, 7 (CF).

_____ *Ten Sonatas* (Rampal—IMC; Woehl—CFP). CFP edition includes 3 *Halle Sonatas*: a, e, b.

_____ *Eight Sonatas* (Bopp—CFP; Fleury—Bo&H).

_____ *Eight Sonatas* (Georges Barrère—BMC). Vol.I: 1, 2, 3, 4; Vol.II: 5, 6, 7, 8. A few liberties are taken in this edition.

_____ *Seven Sonatas* (Cavally—ST; Schwedler—CFP).

_____ *Four Sonatas* Op.1 (Hillemann—Schott).

_____ *Four Original Sonatas* (Hans-Peter Schmitz—Nag 122) Op.1/2 g, 1/4 a, 1/7 C, 1/11 F.

_____ *Four Sonatas* (Bopp—CFP).

_____ *Fitzwilliam Sonatas* (T. Dart—Schott 1948) Bb, d, d.

_____ *Fitzwilliam Sonatas* 1 Bb, 2 D, 3 G (Klauss Hofmann—Hänssler). A good discussion of each piece is contained in the foreword. M-D.

_____ *Three Sonatas* (Dancker—Nag).

_____ *Three New Sonatas* (Nag).

_____ *Sonatas* Op.1/1, 2 (Heugel 1974) score and parts.

_____ *Sonata* Op.1/7 (Michel Sanvoisin—Heugel 1974) 14pp., 2 parts.

_____ *Sonata* Op.1/4 a (Heugel 1974, 10pp., parts, figured bass realized by Michel Sanvoisin, includes part for viola da gamba; Helmut Mönkemeyer—Moeck). Larghetto; Allegro; Adagio; Allegro. M-D.

_____ *Sonata* b (Fleury—Bo&H).

_____ *Sonata* Bb (Mann—Bo&H).

_____ *Sonata* c (Scheck, Ruf—Ric).

_____ *Sonata* D (W. Hinnenthal—HM 3) 7pp., parts. Adagio; Allegro; Adagio; Menuet. M-D.

_____ *Sonata* e (Fleury—Bo&H).

_____ *Sonata* Op.1/11 F (Helmut Mönkemeyer—Moeck 2012) 7pp., parts. Larghetto; Allegro; Siciliana; Allegro. M-D.

_____ *Sonata* g (Scheck, Ruf—Ric).

See: A. O. Gould, "The Flute Sonatas of G. F. Handel: A Stylistic Analysis and Historical Survey," thesis, University of Illinois, 1961.

Tibor Harsanyi. *Three Pieces* 1924 (Sal) 8pp., parts. Lento: recitative-like opening and closing; Impressionistic chordal sonorities in mid-section. Scherzo: fleeting, short chords in piano with moving flute line are contrasted with legato flowing chords in a short mid-section. Lento: bitonal broken triplet arpeggi figuration throughout in piano with long sustained lines in flute. A lovely group. M-D.

J. P. E. Hartmann. *Sonata* Op.1 (WH).

Johann Adolph Hasse. *Sonata* d Op.1 (B&VP).

_____ *Sonata* D (Nag 99) 8pp., parts. Adagio; Allegro; Larghetto; Minuetto. M-D.

_____ *Sonata* G (Hugo Ruf—Schott 5447 1966) 11pp., parts. Andante; Allegro, Largo; Tempo di Minuetto. M-D.

_____ *Sonata* G (Englander—Hofmeister).

Johann Wilhelm Hassler. *Two Sonatas* (Martin Glöfrt—Nag 11; Rucker— CFP), parts. *Sonata* 1 D 1786: Andantino gracioso; Allegro, quasi presto e scherzando. Keyboard part takes on much more importance than the flute. M-D. *Sonata* 2 G 1787: Allegro; Allegro scherzando. Much use of triplet figuration in the Allegro. M-D.

Hikaru Hayashi. *Sonata* 1967 (Ongaku No Tomo Sha) 26pp., parts. SA design in outer movements, ABA form in slow movement. The third movement is based on a Japanese folktune. Freely tonal, thick sonorities, Impressionistic techniques in slow movement, imitation, and thick repeated chords in finale. M-D to D.

Franz Josef Haydn. *Sonata* No.8 G (IMC; CFP).

_____ *Sonata* G (Perry—Bo&H).

Michael Haydn. *Sonata* G (Beyer—CFP).

Bernard Heiden. *Sonatina* 1958 (AMP) 20pp., parts. Allegro: alternating chords in both hands are interrupted by chorale material, which is the basis for this movement. Andante sostenuto: flowing eighth-note motion. Allegretto: much dialogue between the instruments. Neoclassic. M-D.

Everett Helm. *Sonata* C (Schott 4193 1952; Bo&H) 13pp., parts. 12 min. Allegro; Lento; Aria; Vivo. Neoclassic, freely tonal, many thirds in the Aria; Lento is most expressionistic with some dramatic gestures. M-D.

Hans Werner Henze. *Sonatina* (Schott 1951) Light, well crafted. The tune "The Miller of Dee" is cleverly and amusingly introduced in the finale. M-D.

Willy Hess. *Elf Tonstücke* Op.74 (Eulenburg 1972) 31pp., parts.

Kurt Hessenberg. *Sonata* B♭ Op.38 1947 (Schott) 15 min. Notturno; Rondo; Fantasia. Neoclassic. M-D.

_____ *Suite* Op.77 1963 (Schott) 12 min. Sonatina; Ostinato; Fughetta; Andantino con variazioni. M-D.

Paul Hindemith. *Sonata* 1936 (Schott) 14 min. Heiter bewegt; Sehr langsam; Sehr lebhaft; Marsch. Clear textures and forms, light in style. Final two movements are more cheerful and out-going than the first two. Ends with a crisp march that alludes to the first movement. D.

Franz Anton Hoffmeister. *Sonata* Op.13 C 1795–1805 (Hans-Peter Schmitz—Nag 236 1973). 40pp., parts. 20 min. with repeats. For flute or violin and piano. Three movements. Almost a piano sonata with flute accompaniment. Excellent second-rate music, well written for both instruments. M-D.

Karl Holler. *Sonata* I Op.45 (CFP).
———— *Sonata* II Op.53 C (Schott 4546 1955) 21pp., parts. 11½ min. Con moto e leggiero (4 + 2/4); Vivo capriccioso; Tranquillo cantabile; Presto e giocoso. Freely tonal, exploits resources of the piano. M-D to D.

Alexandru Hrisanide. *Sonata* II 1960–2 (Gerig 1973) 15pp., parts. 7 min. Vivo: one movement, serial, pointillistic, dynamic extremes, uses full keyboard range, some unusual notation. D.

Johann Nepomuk Hummel. *Sonata* Op.2/2 G (Helmut Riessberger—Dob 181 1967) 32pp., parts. Allegro; Romanza (two different versions are included); Rondo—Allegro. Foreword in German and English. Sources and editorial additions identified. An utterly charming work. M-D.
———— *Sonata* Op.50 D (Helmut Riessberger—Dob 148, 27pp., parts; CFP). In Dob edition sources are identified in a Foreword in German, English, and French. A challenge to both instruments is presented by this solidly structured piece. Allegro con brio: SA, unconventional harmonic treatment in the development section. Andante: serene, quiet, Beethoven-like. Rondo: pastoral and swift. M-D.
———— *Sonata* Op.62 A (Helmut Riessberger—Dob 473 1973) 25pp., parts. Urtext; editorial additions identified. Allegro con garbo: especially attractive second subject. Menuetto moderato: effective pianistic figuration. Rondo—Vivace: spirited, appealing. M-D.

Jacques Ibert. *Sonatine* (Jeux) (Leduc 1925) 15pp., parts. Animé: highly chromatic, light, cheerful, feathery; tripartite form; bounces on quintuple pulse. Tendre: more Impressionistic sounds; melodic line woven into figuration; canonic treatment; fades away into nothingness. M-D.

Desiré-Émile Inghelbrecht. *Sonatine en Trois Parties* (Leduc 1920) 23pp., parts. For flute and piano or harp. Préambule; Sicilienne; Rondes. Impressionistic, chromatic, octotonic. Contains some lovely and attractive sonorities. Probably more effective on the harp. Requires large span. M-D.

Hidenao Ito. *Apocalypse* 1965 (SZ 1971) 10pp., parts. 10 min. Four movements consisting of brief fragments that can be rearranged in various formats by the performers. Serial, pointillistic, clusters, avant-garde. D.

Gordon Jacob. *Suite* (OUP 1959) 33pp., parts. 20 min. Originally for tenor recorder and string quartet. Piano reduction by the composer. Prelude; English Dance; Lament; Burlesca alla Rumba; Pavane; Introduction and Cadenza; Tarantella (optional sopranino recorder). Diatonic and straightforward writing in delightfully contrasted movements. M-D.

Philipp Jarnach. *Sonatina* Op.12 (Lienau 1920) 11pp., parts. One movement, varied tempi, serious mood, similar to early Schönberg style. D.

Carlos Jiménez Mabarak. *Cinco Piezas* (Collecion Arion 1968) 20pp., parts. Alegoria del Perejil; La Imagen Repentina; Nocturno; El Ave Prodigiosa; Danza Magica. Serial, astringent style, flexible meters. M-D.

André Jolivet. *Fantaisie-Caprice* (Leduc 1954) 4pp., parts. Tranquil opening, works up to an incisive Allegro climax, drops back, and builds again to the conclusion. Freely tonal; half-step is an important unifying device. M-D.
————*Sonata* 1958 (Heugel) 30pp., parts. Fluide; Grave; Violent. Complex, well-organized writing that will require mature pianism. Intense and taut style throughout. Large span necessary. Very D.

Joseph Jongen. *Sonata* Op.77 1924 (CeBeDeM) 28 min.

Klaus Jungk. *Sonata* (Br 3305 1956) 18pp., parts. Largo–Allegro (Thema) and 6 Variations; Con moto; Vivace. Mildly contemporary neoclassic style, careful formal construction. First movement presents the most problems, holding it together with all the tempo changes being the greatest. M-D.

Paul Juon. *Sonata* Op.78 (Zimmermann 1924) 27pp., parts. Gemächlich; Langsam, doch nicht schleppend; Straff, jedoch nicht zu schnell. Much rhythmic activity, post-Romantic writing, tonal with chromatic coloration, sweeping pianistic gestures. M-D to D.

Pal Kadosa. *Sonatina* Op.56 (EMB 1962) 27pp., parts. Poco allegro; Andante moderato; Molto vivo. No pause between movements. Freely tonal, chords in alternating hands, imitation. Sustained chords in Andante movement, dancelike rhythms in finale reminiscent of Bartók. Attractive. M-D.

László Kalmár. *Sonata* (Bo&H 1971) 5 min. Eight short linked-together sections—sounds like one movement. M-D.

István Kardos. *Scherzo Variato* (Gen 1970) 12pp., parts. 8 min. Scherzo—Tema is strongly rhythmic and is made up of three extensively developed variations. Freely tonal. Hungarian color and rhythms make this a worthwhile work with much involvement for both instruments. M-D.

Sigfrid Karg-Elert. *Impressions Exotiques* Op.134 (Zimmermann).

Homer Keller. *Sonata* (CFE).

Talivaldis Kenins. *Concertante* 1966 (Bo&H 1972) 13 min. Presto furioso—Cadenza; Vivace assai. Explores all the flute technique and sonority. In a concertante dialogue with the piano develops different moods of expression described by the movement titles. Clear textures with much rhythmic vitality. D.

Harrison Kerr. *Suite* 1940–1 (Arrow 1943) 20pp., parts. 9 min. Prelude; Dance; Recitativo; Toccata. Twelve-tone, quartal harmonies, dissonant counterpoint, sudden dynamic changes. Large span required. D.

Piet Ketting. *Preludium e Fughetta* 1970 (Donemus) 12pp., parts. Chromatic; both pieces evolve into a complicated climax before ending quietly. Piano must be careful not to overbalance flute in climaxes, which is easy to do. Well crafted. M-D to D.

Jack Kilpatrick. *Sonata* Op.155 (CFE).

Johann Philipp Kirnberger. *Two Sonatas* G, g (CFP).
_____ *Sonata* G (Bernhard Weigant—Schott 5571 1967) 13pp., parts. Adagio; Allegro; Allegro. M-D.

Charles Koechlin. *Sonata* Op.52 (Sal 1922) 26pp., parts. 15 min. Adagio molto tranquillo; Mouvement de Sicilienne; Final. The outer movements are connected with similar thematic material while the middle movement provides contrast in the form of a lyrical intermezzo. Long, flowing, chromatic lines; parallel chords and broken-chord figuration used frequently. Large span required. M-D.

_____ *14 Pieces* (Sal 1948) 16pp., parts. Short, contrasting, appealing, interesting counterpoint between the instruments. Appropriate for various occasions, including church use. Int. to M-D.

Barbara Kolb. *Figments* (CF 1969) 9 min. One movement. Both instruments are pointillistically oriented with much hopping about. D.

Egon Kornauth. *Sonatine* Op.46a (Dob 1959) 16pp., parts. 10 min. Rondino; Intermezzo; Siciliano. Tonal, chromatic, quartal harmony, thin textures, flowing, appealing neoclassic writing. M-D.

Leo Kraft. *Fantasy* 1963 (Gen 1971) 8pp., parts. Freely: changing tempi, harmonics, serial, long pedal effects with both una corda and sostenuto, clusters, plucked strings. Effective. M-D.

Johann Ludwig Krebs. *Six Chamber Sonatas* (Bernhard Klein—CFP 1962) Vol.I: *Sonatas* A, G, C. Vol.II: Sonatas e, a, D. Multi-movement works with the slow movements having more interest. M-D.
_____ *Sonata* C (Scheck, Ruf—Ric).
_____ *Sonata* D (Ermeler—CFP).
_____ *Sonata* e (Ermeler—Br).

Julian Krein. *Sonata* 1957 (USSR) 46pp., parts. Moderato; Lento; Presto. Key signatures are used but this work is freely tonal and moves through many keys. Kind of Prokofiev style but with more Slavic flavor. Piano part is thoroughly developed. D.

Ernst Křenek. *Suite* 1954 (BB) 11pp., parts. Andante; Allegretto moderato; Andante con moto; Allegro vivace. Serial, sparse textures. M-D.
_____ *Flute Piece* 1959 (Br 3330) 15pp., parts. In nine phases. "Sections A & B may be performed separately. If section A alone is played the piano part is omitted. If section B is played by itself, the piano starts four bars before B" (from the score). Harmonics, pointillistic, serial, complex writing. D.

Conradin Kreutzer. *Sonata* Op.35 G (Eulenburg GM33 1971) 32pp., parts. Andante maestoso–Allegro; Andantino grazioso; Rondo—Allegro molto. Straightforward classic style. M-D.

Ulrich Krüger. *Sonata* (Musikus Busch 1973) 17pp., parts.

Johann Baptist Krumpholz. *Sonata* F (Nag 1933) 10½ min.

Ton de Kruyf. *Pas de Deux* Op.22 1968 (Bo&Bo) 12pp., 10 min. Ostinato; Intermezzo; Giochi. Directions in German. Serial, pointillistic, avant-garde. D.

Friedrich Kuhlau. *Grand Sonate Concertante* A (UMP).
———— *Grand Sonate Concertante* E (UMP).
———— *Introduction and Variations on a Theme from Carl Maria von Weber's Euryanthe* Op.63 1825 (Hans-Peter Schmitz—Br 19111 1971) 23pp., parts. Preface in French, German, and English. Sources identified. Requires a warm and genial performance with elegance and verve. Tempi and dynamics can be treated very flexibly, and contrasts can be emphasized. M-D.
———— *Sonata* Op.83/1 G (CFP).
———— *Sonata* Op.83/2 C (CFP).
———— *Variations on a Scottish Song* Op.104 (Billaudot; Hanssler).
———— *Trois Duos Brillants* Op.110 (Jack Spratt 1960). 1 B♭, 18pp., parts. 2 e, 16pp., parts. 3 D, 18pp., parts.
Billaudot has a large selection of Kuhlau's works for flute and piano.

Felicitas Kukuck. *Sonata* (Möseler 1962) 16pp., parts. Bewegt; Ruhig; Sehr schnell und leicht. Clear neoclassic construction throughout. M-D.

Ezra Laderman. *Sonata* 1957 (OUP) 24pp., parts. 12 min. Moderato; Allegro molto; Fugato; Allegro. Short chromatic figures are important in this freely tonal work. Idioms involved include octotonic writing, broken chords, imitation and syncopation, and sudden dynamic changes. Neoclassic orientation. D.

Yehoshua Lakner. *Sonata* 1948 (Israeli Music Publications 1951) 32pp., parts. 18 min. Allegro energico molto rubato; Adagio; Allegro. Striking instrumental texture with strong oriental atmosphere, logically developed form, varied rhythmic structure, expressive melodic lines. Large span required. M-D to D.

Peter Lamb. *Sonatina* (Bo&H 1074) 16pp., parts. Three movements (fast, slow, fast). Graceful, Prokofiev-like, mainly diatonic with shifting harmonies. Effective neoclassic writing for both instruments. M-D.

Richard Lane. *Sonata* (CF).

Santo Lapis. *Three Easy Sonatas* Op.1 ca.1710 (Hugo Ruf—Schott 4632) 15pp., parts for flute (violin or oboe, cello or bassoon ad lib). I D: Affet-

tuoso; Moderato; Allegro. II A: Spiritoso; Andante e delicato; Allegro. III
e: Vivace; Largo; Allegro assai. Graceful, appealing, fluent keyboard realizations. M-D.

William P. Latham. *Fantasy Concerto* (Spratt 1950) 28pp., parts. Piano
reduction by Joan Seyler. One continuous large movement in varied tempi,
moods, and textures. Mainly neo-Romantic with mildly contemporary
flavor created by colorful rhythms. M-D.

_____ *Sonata* II (Spratt 1965) 6pp., parts. Allegro moderato; Adagio;
Vivace. Like Prokofiev's *Classical Symphony* in style. Int. to M-D.

Philibert de Lavigne. *Six Sonatas* Op.2 ca.1740 (Willi Hillemann—Noetzel)
Published separately. I. La Baussan, 7pp., parts (N3264); II. La d'Acut,
8pp., parts (N3265); III. La Dubois, 7pp., parts; IV. La Beaumont, 10pp.,
parts (N3272); V. La Persan, 7pp., parts (N3273); VI. La Simianne, 7pp.,
parts (N3274). The program descriptions of the individual sonatas and
some of the movements are characteristic of the period. These multi-
movement works can be performed on all of the woodwind instruments in
use during the first half of the eighteenth century, and on the violin. Performance practices are discussed in the preface by the editor. Each work
also includes a cello part ad lib.

Jean Marie Leclair. *Sonata* b (Druilhe—Ric).
_____ *Sonata* b (Ruf—Ric).
_____ *Sonata* C (ESC).
_____ *Sonata* C (Ruf—Ric).
_____ *Sonata* C Op.1/2 (Schott).
_____ *Sonata* e (Bouillard—ESC).
_____ *Sonata* I e (CFP).
_____ *Sonata* G (Bouillard—ESC).
_____ *Sonata* Op.2/5 G (Ruf—Br).
_____ *Sonata* Op.9/2 (Polnauer—JWC).
Also see sonatas for piano and violin.

Jacques Leduc. *Sonate* Op.21 1966 (CeBeDeM) 31pp., parts. 16 min. Mae-
stoso; Andante amabile; Allegro ritmico. Mildly contemporary with strong
French influence. Finale is highly rhythmic with toccata-like sections.
M-D.

Ton de Leeuw. *Sonata* (Donemus).

René Leibowitz. *Sonata* Op.12a 1944 (Boelke-Bomart) 6 min.

Johann Georg Linicke. *Sonata* a (Curt Ruckler—Mitteldeutscher) 12pp., parts. Allegro; Adagio; Villanella. M-D.

Pietro Locatelli. *Three Sonatas* (Gustav Scheck, Walter Upmeyer—Br 626 1944) 19pp., parts. I G: Adagio; Allegro; Largo; Allegro. II D: Vivace; Largo; Allegro. III g: Largo; Allegro; Largo; Allegro. All three are M-D.
_____ *Sonata* B♭ (Ruf—Schott).
_____ *Sonata* II D (Feltkamp—B&VP) 8pp., parts.
_____ *Sonata* F (Alexander Kowalscheff—Hug GH9000 1947) 8pp., parts. Largo; Allegro; Cantabile; Allegro. M-D.
_____ *Sonata* F (CFP).
_____ *Sonata* G (CFP).

Jean Baptiste Loeillet (of London). *Sonata* Op.3/7 e (P. Poulteau—Leduc 1974) 8pp., parts.
_____ *Sonata* Op.3/11 D (P. Poulteau—Leduc 1974) 9pp., parts.

Jean Baptiste Loeillet (of Lyons). *Three Sonatas* Op.1/1, 2, 3 (Hinnenthal—HM 43).
_____ *Sonata* Op.1/1 a (Stave—Moeck; Hinnenthal—Br 1952).
_____ *Sonata* Op.1/2 d (Hinnenthal—Br 1952).
_____ *Sonata* Op.1/3 G (Hinnenthal—Br 1952).
_____ *Sonata* Op.1/4 F (Mönkemeyer—Moeck 1029) 11pp., parts. Largo; Allegro; Vivace; Giga. M-D.
_____ *Sonata* Op.1/6 C (Stave—Moeck).
_____ *Two Sonatas* Op.2/5 c, 4/6 g (Mönkemeyer—Moeck 1032) 15pp., parts.
_____ *Sonatas* Op.3/2 B♭, 3 g, 4 G, 5 c, 6 e, 10 d (Schott). Available separately.
_____ *Three Sonatas* Op.3/9, 4/9, 10 (Hinnenthal—HM 162).
_____ *Three Sonatas* Op.3/12, 4/11, 12 (Hinnenthal—HM 165).
_____ *Sonata* Op.3/8 G (Ruf—Schott).
_____ *Sonata* Op.3/9 B♭ (Ruf—Ric).
_____ *Sonata* Op.4/11 f (Hinnenthal—Br 1960).
_____ *Sonata* V c (Feltkamp—CFP).
_____ *Sonata* Op.5/1 e (Sadie—Musica Rara 1961).
_____ *Sonata* X F (Feltkamp—CFP).
_____ *Sonata* e (Lovering—Bo&H), not Op.5/1.
_____ *Sonata* F (Beon—IMC).
_____ *Sonata* G (Beon—IMC).
_____ *Sonata* g (Beon—IMC).
_____ *Sonata* 14 g (CF).

———*Sonatas* (Heugel 1974). For recorder and basso continuo. Selections. Edited from the Roger edition, Amsterdam, 1705 and 1715. Includes part for viola da gamba. Vol.I: Sonata Op.1/1 a; Sonata Op.1/2 e; Vol.II: Sonata Op.3/2 B♭; Sonata Op.3/8 F.
See: Brian Priestman, "Monograph with Thematic Index," *Revue Belge de Musicologie,* IV.

George Simon Löhlein. *Sonate* G 1765 (Dieter Sonntag—Heinrichshofen 1967) 16pp., parts. Allegro; Amoroso poco Andante; Vivace. The slow movement requires an even trill. M-D.

Armand Lonque. *Sonata* (H. Elkan).

Otto Luening. *Fantasia Brevis* (Highgate 1974) 11pp., parts. Varied sections concluding with a quasi cadenza. Mixture of diatonic and chromatic as well as chordal and linear style, asymmetric phrase structure. Strong F♯ conclusion. M-D.
———*Sonatina* 1952 (Galaxy) 5pp., parts. Andante tranquillo: slight tempo changes, tonal and chromatic, inner voice is important. Mildly contemporary. M-D.
———*Short Sonata* 1952 (Galaxy) 16pp., parts. For flute and piano or harpsichord. Allegro Moderato: freely tonal, changing meters, mainly linear with thickened textures for emphasis. Theme and Variations: no break between variations, contrasting textures for each variation, more tonal than first movement. Neoclassic. M-D.
———*Second Short Sonata* (Galaxy) 7pp., parts. Moderato: linear, imitation. Adagio: chordal, bitonal. Allegro: triplet figuration, melody part of triplet, bitonal. Int. to M-D.
———*Third Short Sonata* (Galaxy) 7pp., parts. Slow and somewhat free in tempo: atonal, chromatic lines divided between hands, chords in low register. Interlude: free in tempo and dynamics, chordal for piano. With fantasy and freedom: opens with flute cadenza; chordal punctuation; widely spread textures; tremolo sevenths; bitonal close. M-D.

Otto Luther. *Sonata* Op.13 (Pro Music).

Charles McLean. *Two Sonatas* Op.1/9, 10 1737 (David Johnson—OUP Musica da Camera 22 1975) 13pp., parts. Parts to each sonata published separately. Italian characteristics mixed with a backward glance at the seventeenth century. Charming, unpretentious short movements. Keyboard realization is very playable. Int.
———*Sonata* Op.1/9 D (Ernest Bullock—OUP 1948).

Antoine Mahault. *Sonata* G VI (Hans-Peter Schmitz—Br 3307) 16pp., parts. Source identified. Adagio; Allegro; Largo; Menuetto (with 8 variations). Excellent basso continuo realization by Max Schneider. M-D.

Peter Mai. *Concertino* (Hofmeister 7468) 18pp., parts. For sopranblockflöte or oboe and piano. Allegro risoluto; Adagio misterioso; Allegro. Thin textures, freely tonal, highly attractive neoclassic style. M-D.

———— *Sonatina* (Hofmeister 1974) 12pp., parts. Mässig bewegt; Ruhig schwingend; Lebhaft. Mildly dissonant Hindemith style. Freely tonal around d. Finale is toccata-like. M-D.

Francesco Mancini. *Sonata* (Marcello Castellanti—HM 220 1974) 14pp., parts. Amoroso; Allegro; Largo; Allegro. Forward-looking harmonies in the Amoroso. Combines contrapuntal with cantabile style. M-D.

Benedetto Marcello. *Twelve Sonatas* (Colombo).

———— *Sonata* Op.1/4 (Wisse—CFP), with Focking *Sonata*.

———— *Sonatas* Op.2/1 F, 2 d (Jörgen Glode—HM 151 1958) 15pp., parts.

———— *Sonatas* Op.2/3 g, 4 e (Jörgen Glode—HM 142 1956) 13pp., parts.

———— *Sonatas* Op.2/6 C, 7 Bb (Jörgen Glode—HM 152 1958) 14pp., parts.

———— *Sonata* Op.3/1 F (Veggetti, Martucci—De Santis 1948) 12pp., parts. Adagio; Allegro; Largo; Presto. M-D.

———— *Sonata* Op.3/2 G (Veggetti, Martucci—De Santis 1948; Slater—OUP 1950; Zanke—Zimmermann 1954).

———— *Sonata* Op.3/3 d (Veggetti, Martucci—De Santis 1948) 12pp., parts.

———— *Sonatas* a, Bb (Ermeler—OUP).

———— *Sonata* Bb (Pearson—OUP).

Frank Martin. *Ballade* 1939 (UE 11318 1944) 16pp., parts. 7 min. Originally for flute, string orchestra, and piano. Piano reduction by composer. Sections marked off by contrasts of rhythm with a cadenza in the middle. Fresh and graceful writing, strong melodic rhythms, asymmetric phrases, quasi-modal harmonies. M-D.

Bohuslav Martinů. *First Sonata* 1945 (AMP 1951) 34pp., parts. 19½ min. Allegro moderato: SA; chromatic triads add shimmering effect; complex rhythms; polyphonic lines. Adagio: free variation form, three variations, theme repeated, short coda. Allegro poco moderato: new material plus brief altered restatements of ideas from previous movements. Rhythmic drive and bubbling vitality. Virtuoso performers required. D.

Johannes Mattheson. *Twelve Sonatas* (van Leeuwen—Zimmermann 1923)

Book I: 1 D, 2 G, 3 A, 4 D, 5 D, 6 e. Book II: 7 A, 8 b, 9 e, 10 A, 11 d, 12 D.

———— *Sonata* A (Schott).

Nicholas Maw. *Sonatine* 1957 (JWC 1611) 12pp., parts. 9 min. Allegro con spirito: syncopated chords, changing meters, freely tonal, harmonic sevenths frequent; flute cadenza ends movement. Lento: sevenths are used again; syncopated rhythms; ostinato-like figures; wide-spread rolled chords; cross rhythms; leads directly to Allegro vivo: alternating hands, octaves, martellato chords, fast repeated notes, octotonic writing, strongly rhythmic, *pp* closing. M-D.

Olivier Messiaen. *Le Merle Noir* (The Blackbird) (Leduc 1951) 8pp., parts. 6 min. Exposition of four short sections is recapped with the last two sections transposed, à la sonata idea. An extended birdlike coda follows with an elaborate twelve-note series accompaniment and its retrograde inversion, repeated four times. Each repetition rises a halfstep. The entire process is repeated with the twelve-note series inverted. Pedal is to be held down throughout this section thereby providing highly interesting sonorities. M-D.

Donal Michalsky. *Partita Piccola* 1962 (WIM 1969) 9 min. The structure of each movement is indicated by its title. Preludio: quasi-rhapsodic, cautious, expository. Toccata: flighty, light, repeated notes, binary form. Variazioni: theme and six variations. Giga alla rondo: contrapuntal imitative rondo in fast triple meter. The title is a historical reference to the four movements of the pre-classical suite (or sonata): slow, fast, slow, fast. The tonality is the result of using a c twelve-tone row (C–E♭–D–A–B♭–F–D♭–A♭–E–F♯–B–G, progressing from tonic to dominant). It is limited to two transpositions and two forms (original and retrograde), except for the third movement, which uses the inversion form. M-D.

Georges Migot. *Sonata* (Leduc 1950) 24pp., parts. Prélufe: upper register favored. Allant—Léger: thin and thicker textures judiciously mixed. Deploration: choralelike; large span required. Allègre: open harmonies, arpeggi figuration, fugal section. Conclusion: chordal and arpeggi figures and unusual chord progression provide colorful movement. M-D to D.

———— *Sonatine* II (Schott 5347 1964) 16pp., parts. Prélude; Allant, comme une danse; Grave; Finale—une danse. Simple; straightforward style; has much charm. Mildly contemporary. M-D.

Darius Milhaud. *Sonatine* 1922 (Durand) 17pp., parts. 9½ min. Tendre: smooth textures, chromatic, difficult skips; seconds are important to piano motif. Souple: barcarolle-like; flowing rhythm is punctuated with jazz characteristics. Clair: brilliant and dramatic, infused with subtle humor, silken *ppp* ending. M-D to D.

Charles Mills. *Sonata* E (ACA) 12 min. For alto recorder and piano.
_____ *Sonata* (ACA) 14 min. For tenor recorder and piano.

Wolfgang Amadeus Mozart. *Six Sonatas* (Bopp—Reinhardt 1959) K.10 B♭, K.11 G, K.12 A, K.13 F, K.14 C, K.15 B♭.
_____ *Six Sonatas* (Louis Moyse—GS 1905 1974) 65pp., parts. Same sonatas as listed above. These two- and/or three-movement sonatas, written by Mozart when he was eight years old, are astonishingly mature works for one this age. "All that will be found in Mozart later on is already potentially here in these works" (from the foreword). These sonatas are more satisfactory on the violin than on the flute. Most of the time the flute part is an accompaniment to the fuller piano part. In this edition the editor has given the flute a more important role by sometimes interchanging the right hand of the piano with the flute part, establishing what he feels is a fairer dialogue between the two instruments. Editorial dynamics are enclosed in parentheses. M-D.

Robert Muczynski. *Sonata* Op.14 (GS 1965) 32pp., parts. Allegro deciso; Scherzo; Andante; Allegro con moto. Skilful writing that is variously energetic, exhilarating, expressive, and convincing. Freely tonal and exceptionally melodic. The entire work affords both performers fine opportunities for displaying musicianship and virtuosity. Requires large span. D.

Herbert Murrill. *Sonata* G (OUP 1951) 11pp., parts. 5½ min. Largo; Presto; Recitativo; Finale. Tonal, neoclassic, hemiola, parallel chords. M-D.

Johann Gottfried Müthel. *Sonata* D (J. Philipp Hinnenthal—Br 3322 1959) 12pp., parts. Adagio: Allegro ma non troppo; Cantabile. Charming and cheerful. Excellent keyboard realization. M-D.

Jean-Jacques Naudot. *Six Flute Sonatas* Op.1 (CFP 1973). Composer is called Jacques-Christophe in this edition. First published in Paris in 1726. These varied and imaginative works consist mainly of dance movements, melodic tunes and frequent use of "Gracieusement." The figured bass, realized by A. M. Gurgel, provides balanced support. A cello/gamba part is included. Would make a good substitute for the overplayed Handel recorder sonatas, which were not written for the flute traversière! Int. to M-D.
_____ *Sonata* Op.9/5 G (Hugo Ruf—HM 182) 12pp., parts. Larghetto; Allegro; Sarabanda; Allegro, ma non presto; Giga I and II. This work could

have been played on the Musette, the fashionable instrument in upper French society of the time. M-D.

Henrik Neugeboren. *Sonata* (TP).

Ngūyên-Thiên-Dao. *Tây Nguyên* (Sal 1969) 15pp., parts. Directions are given in French for preparing the piano. Clusters, timed notation ("play this for so many seconds," etc.), dynamic extremes, serial-like, tempi changes. Pianist must strike and pluck strings, improvise, and use, assorted brushes and tools. Flutist has as many different requirements as pianist. Also uses untuned signals from a shortwave radio, which produces unusual atmospheric and coloristic possibilities. Avant-garde. D.

Walter Niemann. *Kleine Sonate* Op.81 (CFP).

Per Norgaard. *Pastorale* (WH 4287 1975) 4pp., parts. Impressionistic, quiet, rocking accompaniment figure, hemiola. Trills effectively used. Centers around f♯–F♯. Large span required. M-D.

Jean Papineau-Couture. *Suite* (CMC 1944–5) 46pp., parts. 18 min. All three movements begin with the same flute motif, each in a different mood. Prélude: bithematic, a sort of pastorale. Aria: da capo form; in the nature of a prolonged meditation; piano serves more as accompaniment to solo flute in this movement while the outer movements treat both instruments equally. Rondo: lively; complete rhythmic independence retained with each instrument. D.

Ernst Pepping. *Sonata* (Br 3320 1958) 19pp., parts. Allegro cantabile; Quieto; Animato. Clear neoclassic treatment, freely tonal. M-D.

Johann Christoph Pepusch. *Sonatas* 1, 2, 3, 4, 7, 8 (Danckler, Langner—Moeck).
———— *Two Sonatas* (Ruf—Schott).
———— *Two Little Sonatas* G, a (Rucker—CFP).
———— *Sonata* d (Ruyssen—Delrieu).
———— *Sonata* G (Curt Ruckler—Mitteldeutscher) with J. G. Linicke *Sonata* a, 12pp., parts. Adagio; Allegro; Adagio; Allegro. Linicke: Allegro; Adagio; Villanella. M-D.

Giovanni B. Pergolesi. *Sonata* XII (EM).

Piotr Perkowski. *Sonata* (PWM).

Ivo Petric. *Sonata* (Gerig).

Anne Danican Philidor. *Premier livre de pièces pour la flûte traversière ou la flûte a bec alto ou le violon et basse continue* (clavecin ou piano). Restitution de Maurice-Pierre Gourrier, realisation de Colette Teniere (Ouvrières 1972) 10pp., parts. This first book was published in 1712 and contains an overture and six dances, a reflection of contemporary chamber music taste. The continuo realization is excellent. No performance directions but contains information on Philidor's life. M-D.
_____ *Sonata* d (Hugo Ruf—HM 139 1956) 11pp., parts. Lentement; Fugue; Courante; Gracieusement; Fugue. M-D.

Gabriel Pierné. *Sonata* Op.36 (Durand).

Willem Pijper. *Sonata* 1925 (Donemus 1952) 20pp., parts. 11½ min. Achieves a striking balance between the instruments; musical ideas beautifully expressed. Rhythmically and melodically the flute and piano go their own way to form a dual unity of musical ideas. The opening chord in the piano is the nucleus from which the whole work evolves, and the flute theme develops immediately from this chord. Allegro: in three parts with a flute cadenza serving as transition before a short repetition of the opening part. Lento: most important movement, tranquil and poetic in two parts, insistent bass patterns. Presto: colorful polymetric and polytonal combinations bring the whole work to a brilliant conclusion. M-D.

Walter Piston. *Sonata* 1930 (AMP 1933) 27pp., parts. Allegro moderato e grazioso; Adagio; Allegro vivace. Neoclassic lines and treatment. Freely tonal, dissonant. M-D.

Giovanni Platti. *Sonata* A (Ruf—Ric).
_____ *Sonata* A (Phillip Jarnach—Schott 2457) 12pp., parts.
_____ *Sonata* D (Schenk, Ruf—Ric).
_____ *Sonata* e (Phillip Jarnach—Schott 376) 11pp., parts. Allegro non tanto; Larghetto; Minuetto; Giga. Heavy-handed editing. M-D.
_____ *Sonata* G (Phillip Jarnach—Schott 377) 10pp., parts. Grave; Allegro; Adagio; Allegro molto. M-D.
_____ *Sonata* Op.3/6 G (Ruf—Schott).

Ignance Pleyel. *Sonata* III B♭ (Irene Alberti—Eulenburg GM 44 1971) 22pp., parts. Allegro molto; Tema con (6) variazioni.
_____ *Sonata* IV A (Irene Alberti—Eulenburg GM 45 1971) 28pp., parts. Untitled first movement; Andante; Rondo.

_____ *Sonata* VI D (Irene Alberti—Eulenburg GM 46 1971) 29pp., parts. Allegro; Rondo.
All three sonatas are written in a Mozartian style with uniquely individual melodic ideas. The rondos are especially full of charm and freshness. M-D.

Claire Polin. *First Flute Sonata* (ST SS26 1959) 20pp., parts. Andantino: lilting 6/8 displays the virtuosity of the flute while retaining a freely expressive feeling in its cadenza and fantasia passages; chromatic broken-chordal figuration in piano is basic to the movement. Adagio ma non tanto: a study in the production of bell-like tones for both instruments. Presto: climaxes the preceding movements with a brisk march in SA design. Mildly contemporary. M-D.

Francis Poulenc. *Sonata* (JWC 1956–7) 23pp., parts. 12 min. Allegro malinconico; Cantilena—Assez lent; Presto giocoso. Neoclassic orientation, light and witty. The second movement is attractively sentimental. Final movement alludes to both subjects from opening movement. Delicate textures. M-D.

Sergei Prokofieff. *Sonata* Op.94 (Rampal—IMC; Leeds). See discussion of this work under duos for piano and violin.

Daniel Purcell. *Sonata* F (Phillip Jarnach—Schott 3693 1940) 10pp., parts. Andante cantabile; Moderato; Allegro; Adagio; Allegro. Simple realization. M-D.

Henry Purcell. *Sonata* F (Fleury—Ric).
_____ *Sonata* F (Jarnach—Schott).
_____ *Sonata* g (Forst—EM).

Johann Joachim Quantz. *Six Sonatas* Op.1 (Dieter Sonntag—Müller 1965) 34pp., parts. 1 D, 2 G, 3 e, 4 G, 5 D, 6 A. Helpful realizations. M-D.
_____ *Sonata* Op.1/2 B♭ (Nagel—CFP).
_____ *Sonata* Op.1/3 e (Heinz Schreiter—Br&H 4172) 11pp., parts. Adagio cantabile; Presto; Moderato. M-D.
_____ *Sonatas* (Forberg—CFP) available separately: 1 a, 2 B♭, 3 c, 4 D, 5 e.
_____ *Sonata* b (Ruf—Schott).
_____ *Sonata* e (Ruf—Schott).
_____ *28 Variations on "As I Slept, I Dreamt"* (Br&H).

Bertin Quentin. *Sonata* Op.1/2 d (Hugo Ruf—HM 186 1964) 11pp., parts. Allemanda I & II; Corrente; Sarabanda; Giga. M-D.

Marcel Quinet. *Concertino* 1959 (CeBeDeM) 26pp., parts. 11 min. Allegro moderato; Canons; Rondoletto. Well structured, freely tonal with a highly chromatic vocabulary, long-held sonorities. Complex imitative writing in Canons; Rondoletto sparkles and dances. M-D to D.

Irmfried Radauer. *Duo Concertante* 1954–5 (Litolff CF 5871 1960) 26pp., parts. 16½ min. Evolution I; Kontrast; Evolution II. Written in an astringent neoclassic style. Kontrast is slower, recitative-like, while the outer movements are more rhythmically conceived. Flexible meter; moves over keyboard. D.

Gunter Raphael. *Sonata* Op.8 e (Br&H).

Anton Reicha. *Sonata* Op.54 G (CFP).
———— *Sonata* Op.103 D (Walter Lebermann—Schott 5573 1968) 51pp., parts. Lento–Allegro non troppo: rocking 6/8 introduction all on a dominant pedal point, SA in D, colorful development section, numerous varied figurations. Lento: G, expressive, classic patterns, crossing hands; strong punctuated chords outline tonal evolution; busy coda must remain calm and *a piacere*. Finale—Allegro vivace: D, rondo, broken octaves, chromatic figuration, a fun movement to play. M-D.

Carl Reinecke. *Sonata "Undine"* Op.167 (IMC 1757) 31pp., parts. Clarinet may be substituted for flute. Allegro: e, 6/8, SA, overlapping broken chord figuration between hands, chromatic runs. Intermezzo—Allegretto vivace: b, ABA; A sections scherzo-like, B section more cantabile and flowing. Andante tranquillo: G, ABA with final A section beginning on dominant, lyric, sentimental. Finale: e, SA, non-tonic opening, chromatic, broken-chord patterns, arpeggio closing. M-D.

Franz Reizenstein. *Partita* (Schott 10041 1946) 20pp., parts. Entrada: march-like, freely tonal, thin textures. Sarabanda: expressive, lyric, chordal. Bourrée: spirited, neoclassic. Jig: flowing chromatic lines, cheerful. M-D.

Roger Reynolds. *Mosaic* (CFP 6620) 12 min. This work occasionally requires unconventional methods of sound production. It achieves effect as a tile mosaic does, through the Gestalt from many discrete elements of various dimensions, textures, and colors. Segments are characterized by instrumental techniques (grace notes, trills, repeated notes, etc.) as well as by tempo, dynamics, and pitch organization. The work is lyrical but of sparse texture. D.

Verne Reynolds. *Sonata* (CF).

Franz Xaver Richter. *Sonata* G (Zinnbauer—Schott).

Alan Ridout. *Three Nocturnes* (Chappell 1974) 11pp., parts. Short, attractive. M-D.

Ferdinand Ries. *Sonata* Op.169 E♭ 1814 (Hans-Peter Schmitz—Br 19107 1970) 53pp., parts. Allegro moderato; Adagio con moto; Rondo—Allegro. This is the last of Ries's five flute sonatas. Schmitz suggests in the preface that the work should be played with great expression—"Con sentimento," in fact—and that the dynamic contrasts should be strongly marked in accordance with the contemporary concert notice (*Harmonicon* II 1824, 35) of Ries's playing, which remarked on his powerful hand and romantic wildness and praised his strong contrasts of loud and soft. All the cliché figurations and idioms of late Classic and early Romantic writing are present. M-D.

Vittorio Rieti. *Sonatina* (JWC).

Jean Rivier. *Sonatine* (EMT 1956) 18pp., parts. Allegro moderato: many tempo changes, freely tonal. Lento affettuoso: chromatic, expressive. Presto jocando: jaunty, Gallic humor shows throughout. M-D.

Marguerite Roesgen-Champion. *Sonata* F (Leduc 1950) 15pp., Parts. 13½ min. Introduction—Moderato; Adagio; Rondo Final. Impressionistic, chords in alternating hands, flowing lines, chromatic, added sixths. Final is cheerful and very rhythmic. M-D.

Jens Rohwer. *Sonata* (Möseler).

Johan Helmich Roman. *Two Sonatas* (Kurt W. Senn—HM 101 1952). *Sonata* G: 11pp., parts. Largo; Allegro; Larghetto; Andante; Vivace. *Sonata* b: 9pp., parts. Larghetto; Allegro; Non troppo allegro; Grave; Allegro. Clear realizations. M-D.
_____ *Two Sonatas* 4 B♭, 7 B♭ (CFP).
_____ *Two Sonatas* 5 B♭, 8 C (CFP).
_____ *Sonata* b (Erdmann—CFP).
_____ *Sonata* D (Johannes Brinckmann, Wilhelm Moor—Sikorski 218 1954) 11pp., parts. *Sonata* 12 of "XII Sonatas flauto traverso, violine e cembalo." Editorial suggestions in smaller print. Con spirito; Allegro; Con affetto; Allegro. Stylistically correct continuo realization. M-D.

Joseph Guy Ropartz. *Sonatine* 1930 (Durand) 26pp., parts. Très modéré; Très lent; Assez vif. Mildly Impressionistic idiom. Colorful. M-D.

Thomas Roseingrave. *Two Sonatas* 1728 (Richard Platt—OUP, Musica da Camera 21 1975) 14pp., parts, including cello ad lib. Parts to each sonata published separately. Preface in English and German. *Sonata* 4 g and *Sonata* 7 C from a set of twelve solos. Italian in style with a few unexpected progressions. Range of solo part suggests an oboe would be as suitable as the flute. Contains some fine music. A certain rhythmic vitality is needed in the keyboard realizations and should be added by the performer. Int.

Howard Rovics. *Cybernetic Study* I (Okra 1968) 9pp., parts. For alto flute and piano. Harmonics, serial, chromatic clusters. Strings prepared with rubber or felt wedges, plucked stopped and tapped strings. Colorful instrumental interaction. D.
———— *Sonata* (CFE).

Wilhelm Friedrich Rust. *Sonata* A (Janetzky—Pro Musica 1953).

Dimitur Sagaev. *Sonata* Op.49 1966 (Nauka i Izkustvo 1972) 32pp., parts.

Giovanni Battista Sammartini. *Sonata* G (CFP).

Pierre Sancan. *Sonatine* (Durand 1946) 19pp., parts. One movement, Ravel-like in style. Flute cadenza; graceful flowing lines in piano. Three sections of contrasting moods and tempi. M-D.

Claudio Santoro. *Sonata* (Tonos).

Tibor Sárai. *Studio* (Zenemükiadó Vallalat 1965) 10pp., parts. Bitonal, dance rhythms, contrasting moods and tempi. M-D.

István Sárközy. *Sonata da Camera* 1964 (EMB 1972) 16pp., parts. 8 min. Sostenuto: Chromatic chordal sonorities, short–long rhythmic germ. Andante: tonal, simple accompaniment style, interrupted short–long rhythmic germ of Sostenuto. Allegro: Hungarian folkdance-like, attractive writing. Some chords of ninth require large span. M-D.

Andres Sas. *Sonatina-Fantasia* (PIC 1953) 20pp., parts. Fantasia: staccato style, dancelike, changing key signatures, free-form movement. Elegia: expressive, lyric, nocturne-like piano style. Danza: short-long alternates with long-short rhythms, contrasting lyric andante section, coda is a juxtaposition between andante and vivace. Attractive. M-D.

Willy Schneider. *Sonata Serena* (Möseler).

Robert Schollum. *Sonatine* (Dob 1958) 12pp., parts. Energisch: serial, mixed figuration, leads directly to Chaconne: with sixteen variations. Well-constructed atonal writing. M-D.

Franz Schubert. *Introduction and Variations on a Theme from Die Schöne Müllerin* D.802 1824 (Br&H; IMC). One of the most important works from the Romantic era for flute and piano. A virtuoso set of variations, based on the eighteenth song in the cycle, "Trockne Blumen" (Withered Flowers). Introduction is moody. The following variations alternate between great introspection and display figuration for the flute. A mock military march serves as the final variation. The pianist is a full partner throughout, and the second variation presents a whirlwind octave passage for the left hand. D in a few spots. M-D.

Erwin Schulhoff. *Sonata* (JWC 1928) 28pp., parts. 11½ min. Allegro moderato; Scherzo; Aria; Rondo—Finale. Diffusive neoclassic chromatic writing. Requires fine pianistic equipment. D.

Bart Schurink. *Madrigali* 1968 (Donemus) 15pp., parts. 10 min. Seven pieces. Piano is tacet in No.7. Vertical lines are not bar lines but points for orientation in time. Clusters, plucked strings, pointillistic, percussive use of the piano, expressionistic and thorny writing for both instruments. D.

Elliott Schwartz. *Sonata* (TP).

Cyril Scott. *Sonata* (Elkin 1961) 30pp., parts. Tempo molto moderato e sempre poco rubato; Andante tranquillo; Rondo frivolo. Scott was experimenting with a new style in this work. Quartal and quintal harmonies, serial-like in places. D.

Jean Baptiste Senaillé. *Sonata* 1. livre, No.5 c (Dolmetsch—UE 1974) 10pp., parts. For tenor recorder and keyboard. Transposed to g and arranged for recorder in accordance with the composer's comment, "Cette sonate peut se jouer sur la flûte." Edited and arranged by Carl Dometsch, keyboard accompaniment by Arnold Dolmetsch. M-D.

Syoko Shida. *Sonata* (Japan Federation of Composers 1970) 29pp., parts. Based on a Japanese tea-picker's song. Moderato: chromatic patterns, quartal and quintal harmonies, free interplay of ideas between instruments. Allegro (ma non troppo): fast repeated chords interspersed with rolled chords, long pedal effects, chromatic; two lento sections provide contrast. Colorful if not always convincing writing. D.

Makoto Shinohara. *Kassouga* (Leduc 1960) 7pp., parts. Lent, expressif et souple: quintal harmonies in piano, free wistful melodic line in flute. Vif et rythmé: descending chordal sevenths, repeated eighth-note chords, flute cadenza, driving rhythms, recitative ending. M-D.

—————— *Relations* (Moeck 1973) 4pp., notes. 2 playing scores, each has 13 loose leaves, 8 min. Explanations in German and English. Kind of a brilliant catalogue of avant-garde gestures, no development of any type, and short on dramatic sense. D.

Otto Siegl. *Sonate* 1968 (Dob 1971) 25pp., parts. 18 min. Allegro assai; Meditation; Allegro con moto. Strong craft, neoclassic, appealing ländler tempo and style in finale. Tonal with chromatic coloration, imitation, octotonic, hemiola. M-D.

Pavel Šivic. *Sonata* (Gerig).

Harvey Sollberger. *Music for Flute and Piano* 1963-4 (McGinnis & Marx) 26pp. Serial, pointillistic, clusters, highly organized, expressionistic, sumptuous sonorities. Requires large span. D.

Eliodoro Sollima. *Sonata* (Schott). For alto flute and piano.

—————— *Sonata* (Schott). For tenor recorder and piano. 15 min. Three movements. Traditional writing in atonal style. Reminiscent of Bartók. Rewarding for both performers. D.

Giovanni Battista Somis. *Sonata* F (Frank Nagel—Möseler 1973) 8pp., parts. Fine realized figured bass. M-D.

József Soproni. *Sonata* (EMB 1971) 18pp. 2 copies necessary for performance. Andante, senza misura; Sostenuto; Allegro vivace. Serial, repeated notes, pointillistic, clusters, many tempi changes, sudden dynamic changes, rhythmic proportional relationships, strings plucked, strong glissandi, avant-garde. Large span required. D.

Norbert Sprongl. *Suite* Op.98 (Dob 1973). Four movements, somewhat reminiscent of late Carl Nielsen style. M-D.

Edward Staempfli. *Fünf Stücke* (Bo&Bo 1960) 20pp., parts. 1. Ziemlich lebhaft 2. Langsam 3. Leicht bewegt 4. Nicht zu langsam 5. Mässig. Serial, atonal, severe writing. D.

Henk Stam. *Sonata* 1972 (Donemus 1974) 19pp., parts, photostat of MS.

John Stanley. *Complete Works for Flute and Basso Continuo* Op.1 (John Caldwell—OUP 1974). These eight solos are really sonatas. Usually one dance is included within the general pattern of four movements. Well-balanced phrases, functional bass lines. Fine introduction in English and German as well as notes on performance, editorial method, and critical commentary. A wealth of varied material. Nos.3, 5, and 7 are available separately.

_____ *Complete Works for Flute and Basso Continuo* Op.1 (George Pratt—CFP 7108 1971). Each of the eight works is available separately. Contains discreet use of legato and interesting keyboard realizations, tuneful. Excellent preface.

_____ *Six Solos for Flute, Violin or Oboe and Keyboard Instrument* (Concordia).

_____ *Six Solos for a German Flute or Violin and Continuo* Op.4 (George Pratt—JWC 1975) 44pp., parts for flute or violin and viola da gamba or cello. Excellent preface. Solo I: Siciliana; Menuet. Solo II: Adagio; Poco Allegro; Adagio; Menuet. Solo III: Adagio; Allegro; Menuet with 3 variations. Solo IV: Adagio; Poco allegro; Gigg. Solo V: Adagio; Allegro; Gigg. Solo VI: Siciliana; Allegro; Menuet with 2 variations. Keyboard realization of these small suites is a compromise between unimaginative chords and an over-ornate, contrived treatment. The performer may prepare or extemporize his own version. Int. to M-D.

Gitta Steiner. *Jouissance* (CFE).

Halsey Stevens. *Sonatina* 1943 (BB 1947) 15pp., parts. 6 min. Delicate, piquant. Two outer movements (Allegretto; Allegro) lively, contrasting warmth in the slow, middle movement (Andante quasi Siciliano). The Finale uses a twelve-tone theme but the movement is not organized along serial lines. M-D.

_____ *Sonatina Piacevole* 1956 (PIC 1968) 12pp., parts. 4½ min. For alto recorder or flute or violin, and piano or harpsichord. With some modification, transposing the higher passages down an octave, it may also be played on the oboe. Allegro moderato; Poco lento, quasi ciaccona; Allegro. The chaconne is heard in four varied treatments. Neobaroque orientation. M-D.

Richard Stoker. *Sonatina* (CFP H526 1968) 12pp., parts. 8 min. Three untitled, contrasting movements with only tempo markings. Free dissonant counterpoint, neoclassic style, attractive. Large span required. M-D.

William Sydeman. *Duo* (Seesaw).

Antoni Szalowski. *Concertino* (Amphion 1951) 12 min.

Endre Székely. *Capriccio* 1961 (Zenemükiadó Vállalat 1964) 20pp., parts. Lento rubato–(Animato) Andante–Allegro scherzando; Moderato; Allegro. In all outer forms a sonata. Dancelike rhythms, enough Hungarian flavor to make the outside movements interesting. Mildly contemporary. Percussive use of piano, much use of close intervals for rhythmic drive. Large span required. M-D to D.

Tadeusz Szeligowski. *Sonata* (PWM).

Akira Tamba. *Sonata* 1957 (Rideau Rouge 1972) 21pp., parts. Originally for flute and string orchestra as a *Concerto da Camera*. A one-movement work in contrasting sections. Harmonic idiom based on sevenths; chromatic; sweeping gestures move over keyboard; full sonorities; imitation; much activity in both parts; expressionistic. D.

Alexandre Tansman. *Sonatine* (Sal 1926) 15pp., parts. Modéré; Intermezzo; Scherzo (Fox-Trot); Notturno; Finale. Charming and ingratiating Impressionistic writing. Great fun for performers and listeners. M-D.

Georg Philipp Telemann. *Six Partitas* B♭, G, c, g, e, E♭ (W. Woehl—HM 47) For flute (violin or oboe) and continuo.
———— *Twelve Method Sonatas* 1732 (M. Seiffert—Br 2951 1950). Each sonata includes Telemann's own suggested ornamentation. Published separately: Book 1: *Sonatas* g, A. Book 2: *Sonatas* e, D. Book 3: *Sonatas* a, G. Book 4: *Sonatas* b, c. Book 5: *Sonatas* E, B♭. Book 6: *Sonatas* d, C.
———— *Sonata* B♭ (Concordia). From the continuation of the *Method Sonatas*.
———— *Four Sonatas* G, c, B♭, F (Wittgenstein, Wilt—GS).
———— *Four Sonatas* F, B♭, f, C (HM 6). From *Der Getreue Musikmeister*.
———— *Sonatas and Pieces* (D. Degen—HM 7). From *Der Getreue Musikmeister*. For flute (violin or oboe) and continuo. Sonata a, Sonata g, L'hiver, Air Trompette, Niaise, Napolitana. M-D.
———— *Sonata* b (CFP). From *Der Getreue Musikmeister*.
———— *Sonata* C (CFP). From *Der Getreue Musikmeister*.
———— *Sonata* F (E. Dohrn—Nag 8 1931) 7pp., parts. From *Der Getreue Musikmeister*, Hamburg, 1728. Vivace; Largo; Allegro. Realization would be more effective if some of the thicker sonorities were pruned slightly. M-D.
———— *Two Sonatas* d, C (CFP). From *Essercizii Musici*.
———— *Sonata* D (H. Ruf—Schott 5719) 15pp., parts. No.2 from *Essercizii*

Musici. Largo; Vivace; Dolce; Allegro. Excellent keyboard realization. M-D.

_____ *Sonata* a (ST).

_____ *Sonata* b (M. Silver—JWC 1953) 12pp., parts. Continuo Series II. Cantabile; Allegro; Dolce; Allegro. Intelligent editing and realization. M-D.

_____ *Sonata* C (M. Sanvoisin—Heugel 1974) 6pp., parts.

_____ *Sonata* F (M. Sanvoisin—Heugel 1974) 5pp., parts.

_____ *Six Concerti* (J. P. Hinnenthal—Br 2961). For flute and harpsichord; cello ad lib. These concerti can also be played by the following combinations: flute, violin, and cello; violin and cello; or flute, violin, and continuo.
Published separately: *Concerto* D (Br 3341). *Concerto* g (Br 3342). *Concerto* A (Br 3343). *Concerto* e (Br 3344). *Concerto* b (Br 3345). *Concerto* a (Br 3346).

_____ *Solo* b (J. P. Hinnenthal—Br 3537) from *Tafelmusik* I.

Carlo Tessarini. *Sonata* F (Hans-Peter Schmitz—Br 3303 1956) 8pp., parts. Largo; Allegro; Adagio; Vivace. Fine thorough-bass realization by Max Schneider. Attractive period writing. M-D.

Tiet Ton-That. *Vision II* 1966 (Chan Anh 2) (EMT 1968) 17pp., parts. 10 min. Lento tranquillo; Allegro; Moderato; Lento tranquillo. Includes another realized version of the first piece. Strings are plucked; wooden case of piano has to be struck; brush is needed to stroke strings. Complex, pointillistic, expressionistic, avant-garde. D.

Frederico Moreno Torroba. *Dedicatoria* (UME 1973) 9pp., parts.

Joan Tower. *Movements* (ACA 1970) 25pp., parts. Three untitled movements. Serial, pointillistic, stopped strings, dynamic extremes, varied tempi, expressionistic. D.

Jean Louis Tulou. *Solo* Op.82 A (Billaudot 1973) 17pp., parts. Rev. by Robert Heriche.

Danuta Uhl. *Sonatina* (PWM).

Erich Urbanner. *Acht Stücke* 1957 (UE 13026). Short, terse, atonal, serial, acerbic writing. No.4 is for solo flute. D.

Robert Valentine. *Three Sonatas* (Hildemarie Peter—Lienau 1956) 36pp., parts. Ornamentation table. I d: Adagio; Allegro; Adagio; Allegro. II G: Adagio; Allegro; Andante; Allegro. III g: Adagio; Allegro; Andante; Allegro. Valentine worked for several decades in Italy, and these works, with their fertile themes, austere and formal structure, and typically English traits, also show the influence of the Italian school. Musical pieces of charming invention. M-D.

Jacques Vallier. *Sonatine* II (Zurfluh 1973) 16pp., parts.

Johann Vanhal. *Sonata* (B. Tuthill—McGinnis & Marx).

David Van Vactor. *Sonata* (AME).
——— *Sonatina* 1975 (Rhodes) 11pp., parts.

Ralph Vaughan Williams. *Suite de Ballet* ca.1924 (R. Douglas—OUP 1961) 15pp., parts. 6 min. Improvisation; Humoresque; Gavotte; Passepied. Thin textures, folk-like, charming. M-D.

Francesco Veracini. *Twelve Sonatas* (Walter Kolneder—CFP) Vol.I: F, G, D. Vol.II: B♭, C, a. Vol.III: c, F, g. Vol.IV: d, F, c. Contrasting multimovements of great beauty. M-D.
——— *Sonata* I (Paumgartner—Bo&H).
——— *Sonata* II (Paumgartner—Bo&H).

John Verrall. *Sonata* (Tritone 1976) 16pp., parts. Excellent balance between flute and piano, contemporary harmonic treatment, attractive and moving. M-D.

Leonardo Vinci. *Sonata* D (Joseph Bopp—Reinhardt 1949) 12pp., parts. Adagio; Allegro; Largo; Presto; Pastorella. M-D.
——— *Sonata* G (Joseph Bopp—Reinhardt 1955) 14pp., parts. Siciliana—Andante; Allegro; Aria Cantabile; Gavotta, Menuetto Il gusto Italiano—Le Goût Français; Affetuoso. Interesting writing with highly contrasting movements. Fine realizations. M-D.

Antonio Vivaldi. *Six Sonatas* "Il Pastor Fido" Op.13 (HM; IMC) C, C, G, A, C, g.
——— *Sonata* C (M. Silver—JWC 1952) 11pp., parts. Affettuoso; Allegro assai; Larghetto; Allegro. This work comes from a MS in the University Library, Cambridge. Vintage Vivaldi. Fine basso continuo realization. Int. to M-D.
——— *Sonata* C (Giovanni Gatti—Br&H). A relatively simple work, efficient editing, large print, well spaced.

———— *Sonata* C (Frank Nagel—Heinrichshofen 1970) 8pp., parts, cello ad lib. Affettuoso; Allegro; Larghetto; Allegro. Figured bass well realized by Winfried Radeke. M-D.

———— *Sonata* c (Schott).

———— *Sonata* d (Frank Nagel—Heinrichshofen 1970) 7pp., parts, cello ad lib. Preludio; Siciliano; Sarabanda; Allegro. Basso continuo realized by Winfried Radeke. M-D.

———— *Sonata* e (David Lasocki—Musica Rara 1973). Cello ad lib. Found in a Swedish MS. Andante; Siciliano; Allegro; Arioso. Editing and basso continuo realization are excellent. M-D.

———— *Sonata* F (Franz Brüggen—Br&VP 517 1959) 8pp., parts. Siciliano; Allemanda; Allegro. Good realization of basso continuo. M-D.

———— *Sonata* g (Joseph Marx—McGinnis & Marx 1946) 20pp., parts. Vivace; Allabreve—Fuga da Capella; Largo; Allegro ma non presto. Figured bass is finely realized by Erwin Bodky. M-D.

Roman Vlad. *Sonatina* (SZ 1956) 18pp., parts. Allegretto, con spirito: many tempo and texture changes, tremolo, dynamic extremes (*pppp*). Allegro comodo: rhythmic, thin textures, repeated notes, dancelike. D.

Georg Christoph Wagenseil. *Sonata* D ca.1765 (Rudolf Scholz—Dob 1972) No.536 in DM. 14pp., parts. Allegro; Adagio; Allegro. "In its gallant–sentimental style, the work is typical of the Viennese Rococo: nimble, rippling triplets and sixteenth-note figures over a simple bass line, with an extremely economical use of harmony so that the solo instrument's pre-eminence is never endangered; melodic lines with florid embellishments and sighing suspensions; rhythmically pronounced sixteenth-note triplets and 32nd-note runs" (from the preface). M-D.

Karl Heinz Wahren. *Frétillement* (Bo&Bo 1972) 15pp., parts. Allegro con moto; Allegro agitato. Serial, atonal, complex rhythms, pointillistic. D.

Adam Walacinski. *Dichromia* (PWM 1970) 7pp. Clusters, harmonics, pointillistic, dramatic gestures, avant-garde. Directions in German and Polish. D.

Lloyd W. S. Webber. *Sonatina* D (Hin 76 1941) 15pp., parts. 8 min. Allegretto piacevole; Larghetto. Freely tonal but never moves too far from tonic. The Larghetto leads into a delightful Presto giocoso with arpeggi triplets and syncopated rhythms. A Larghetto e allargando section provides contrast with the final Presto giocoso, which is marchlike in character. M-D.

Jaromir Weinberger. *Sonatine* (CF W1811 1941) 13pp., parts. Con moto; Menuet; Rondo. Thin textures throughout, mildly contemporary. Kind of a contemporary Clementi Op.36 *Sonatina*. Int.

Jean Baptiste Wendling. *Sonata* G from Op.1 (Erich Ade—Ichthys 231) 12pp., parts. Allegro; Adagio; Presto. Musical, worthy, cleanly realized figured bass. M-D.

Lawrence Widdoes. *Sonatina* 1963 (TP 1967) SPAM 46 12pp., parts. Two untitled movements. Serial, atonal, pointillistic, questioning conclusion. Presents some rhythmic ensemble problems. D.

Florian Wiefler. *Sonatine* Op.15/1 (Dob 1974) 15pp., parts. Fliessend; Sehr ruhig. Characteristics of Hindemith, frequent tempo changes, free serial treatment and triadic atonality make for an interesting style. The second movement is a combination of slow–fast sections. On p.10 and at the bottom of p.14 a treble clef should be added to the right hand of the piano part. M-D.

Alec Wilder. *Sonata* I 1964 (Margum) 24pp., parts. Untitled first movement; Andante; Scherzo; Rubato. Written in a light, clear, semi-Poulencian style. Freely tonal with flexible meters. D.
————— *Sonata* II 1965 (Sam Fox 1970) 20pp., parts. 12 min. Allegretto; Adagio ma non tanto; Scherzando; Molto cantabile. Foreword by Samuel Baron. A successful work that affords a gratifying range of expressive possibilities to the performers. Each movement contains leading clues to the interpretation, more from the emotional ramifications of a single mood than from a formalistic analysis of motives and keys. "The restlessness of the first movement, the dreamlike introspection of the second, the humor of the third, and the full-throated outpouring of the fourth are all expressed in free forms, forms that have their unexpected twists and turns as well as modulations that seem to take us to the 'wrong' key" (from the preface). D.

Geoffrey Winters. *Sonatina* Op.28 (Thames 1965) 20pp., parts. Outer movements have humorous characteristics. Middle movement, Andante, utilizes chordal motion in the piano under the flute melody, which exploits the interval of a fourth. Int. to M-D.

Stefan Wolpe. *Piece in Two Parts for Flute and Piano* 1960 (McGinnis & Marx 1969) 72pp., parts. In two large movements, the first untitled, the second titled, "Spirited." Complex writing that includes changing meters, sudden dynamic extremes, pointillistic treatment, proportional rhythmic relationships, serial organization, exploitation of extreme ranges, harmonics, fast chromatic figuration, tremolo chords. Intricate, requires a large span and thorough pianistic equipment as well as much ensemble experience. D.

Boleslaw Woytowicz. *Sonata* (PWM).

Charles Wuorinen. *Sonata* (CFE) 15 min.

Isang Yun. *Garak* 1963 (Bo&Bo) 11pp., parts. Cluster-like percussive chords, serial influence, expressionistic, complex atonal patterns, *ppppp* closing. D.

Luigi Zaninelli. *Canto* (EV 1973) 7pp., parts. Opens with a Con malinconia, row-like flute solo. At Con movimento, ma non troppo the piano enters with full *pp* mildly dissonant chords. A Tranquillo section gives the piano more melodic flexibility. The full *pp* chords return, and these two basic ideas make up the form of the piece. The row seems to unwind gradually with assistance by the piano and a calm a piacere settles over the concluding two bars. A true contemporary extended character piece. D.

Julien François Zbinden. *Sonatina* Op.5 (Schott 1951).
_____ *Fantaisie* Op.22 1954 (Br&H 6200) 11pp., parts. 6 min. Contrasting sections, flute cadenza, bitonal, octotonic, shifting meters, freely tonal, some jazz influence. M-D.

Hans Zender. *Musik für Flöte und Klavier* 1950 (Bo&Bo 1953) 27pp., parts. 20 min. Mässig schnell; Sehr langsam und ruhig; Scherzo; Ruhig und langsam; Rondo. This suite follows neoclassic lines, is somewhat more dissonant than Hindemith, and develops naturally. D.

Friedrich Zipp. *Au clair de la lune Variations* (CFP).
_____ *Fantasia, Pastorale e Fuga* 1969 (Willy Müller 1973) 12pp., parts. For tenor recorder (flute) and piano (harpsichord), cello or viol ad lib.
_____ *Sonatine* Op.23a (Schott).
_____ *Suite* Op.35a (Litolff 14011 1956) 20pp., parts. 15 min. Transcription by the composer of the original work for flute and string orchestra. Giocoso; Andante; Molto vivace; Introducktion—Declamato e espressivo—Allegro ritmico. Spontaneous writing, neoclassic orientation. M-D.

Duos for Piano and Oboe

Hendrik Andriessen. *Ballade* 1952 (Donemus) 10pp., parts. Bitonal, quasi-recitative sections, arpeggi figures. Romantic rolled-chord sonorities end this poetic tone poem *pp*. Requires large span. M-D.

Malcolm Arnold. *Sonatina* (Lengnick 1951) 15pp., parts. 8 min. Leggiero: Andante con moto; Vivace. Light, jocular style. M-D.

William Babell. *Sonata* f (Tilmouth—OUP 1963) 8pp., parts. For oboe, violin, or flute and keyboard. Adagio; Vivace; Largo; Presto. Slightly more difficult than the *Sonata* g. M-D.
_____ *Sonata* g (Tilmouth—OUP 1963) 5pp., parts. For oboe, violin, or flute and keyboard, but best suited for oboe. Allegro; Air; Hornpipe; Giga. Int.
Both sonatas are attractive to performers and listeners.

Carl Philipp Emanuel Bach. *Sonata* W.135 g (K. Walther—Br&H 1953; G. Schreck, H. Ruf—Ric SY506 1954, 14pp., parts). Adagio; Allegro; Vivace (with 3 variations). Both editions have stylistically correct realizations. M-D.

Johann Sebastian Bach. *Sonate* g (R. Meylan—CFP 1972) 28pp., parts. This is probably the well-known *Sonata* S.1030 b for flute and keyboard, transposed by Bach to the new key to suit the oboe's characteristics more adequately. It is an important addition to the oboe repertoire. M-D.

John Bavicchi. *Sonatina* Op.30 (OUP 1970) 12pp., parts. 10 min. Moderato: freely tonal around G; varied mood and tempi changes using different figuration; widely spread textures; octotonic; requires good octave technique. Poco Adagio: imitation; piano has more solo part. Con Spirito: thin textures, repeated octaves, broken-chord figuration. Natural writing for both instruments. M-D.

Conrad Beck. *Sonatine* (Schott 4449 1957) 12pp., parts. 10 min. Allegro moderato; Larghetto; Allegro vivace. Freely tonal, neoclassic. M-D.

Peter Benary. *Sonatine* (Möseler). Sensitive, clear neoclassic lines, straightforward. Int. to M-D.

Richard Rodney Bennett. *Sonata* 1961 (Belwin-Mills) 26pp., parts. Vivace; Lento espressivo; Leggiero e ritmico; Agitato. Dissonant, careful thematic development. Requires large span. D.

Jean Berger. *Sonata da Camera* (BB 1037a 1957) 20pp., parts. 12 min. Moderato; Allegro; Lento; Animato. Parallel chords, changing meters, chromatic figuration, octotonic. Neoclassic with Impressionistic influences. M-D.

Lennox Berkeley. *Sonatina* (JWC 1964) 16pp., parts. Molto moderato; Andante; Allegro. There are technical problems for both performers, but the piece wears well and is worth the effort. The outer movements are written in a mildly contemporary flowing style, while the Andante is more sustained and serious. M-D.

Alessandro Besozzi. *Sonata* C (E. Rothwell—JWC 1956) 12pp., parts. Andante; Allegro; Larghetto; Allegretto. Delightful and interesting writing in classic style. M-D.

Edward Boguslawski. *Szkice* (Sketches) (PWM 1965) 10pp., parts. Preludium; Scherzino; Notturno; Postludium. Attractive contemporary writing with subtle mood contrasts in each piece. A colorful and short suite that would add interest to any program. M-D.

Edith Borroff. *Variations and Theme* (Sam Fox 1963) 15pp., parts. Introduction and Waltz Interlude; Romp; Story; Promenade; Interruption and Theme–Finale. Serial, thin textures, clever; contrasting movements that finally arrive at the attractive theme. M-D.

Maurice Bouchor. *Fantaisie Concertante* 1932 (Costallat).

Roger Boutry. *Sonatine* 1958 (Sal) 20pp., parts. Allegro; Andante; Allegro. Freely tonal with much chromatic color, oboe cadenza in first and second movements. The finale is dancelike. Generally thin textures predominate. 3 with 2. Requires a large span. M-D.

York Bowen. *Sonata* Op.85 D (JWC 1944) 16½ min.

Pierre de Bréville. *Sonatine* E♭ 1924 (Rouart-Lerolle) 20pp., parts. 10½ min. Allègre; Très calme; Vite. A well-crafted work that is pianistic and is slightly contemporary sounding. Alternating hand usage and added-note technique seem to be favorite devices. Flowing, musical, careful attention to details, some Franck influence present. M-D.

Jacques Castérède. *Sonate* 1959 (Leduc) 26pp., parts. 21 min. Moderato pastorale: chromatic figuration, varied tempi, basically pastoral mood throughout. Scherzando—Non troppo presto: broken left-hand octaves with right-hand chords, freely tonal, flexible meters, repeated notes, a few tricky spots. Adagio: repeated chords, some are tenths; constant eighth-note pulsation. Moderato tranquillo: flowing, chromatic, French neoclassic style. D.

Pierre Chédeville (the eldest). *Sonatille* Op.6/3 c (G. Favre—Siècle Musical 1949) 11pp., parts. Tendrement; Allemande; Rondeau; Gigue. Keyboard realization and oboe converse in a rhythmical and melodious counterpoint that is both charming and ingenious. M-D.

Frederick Chopin. *Variations on a Theme from Rossini's Cenerentola* 1824 (J. P. Rampal—IMC 1960) 5pp., parts. Finale of No.12 in the *Cenerentola* score serves as theme. Graceful, elegant; cleverly conceals a rather primitive harmonic scheme. M-D.

Johann Cilenšek. *Sonate* 1960 (Litolff 5248) 17pp., parts. Allegro; Lento assai; Molto vivace. Well-contrasted moods, dissonant style, ideas developed naturally, some neoclassic characteristics, freely tonal. M-D.

Arnold Cooke. *Sonata* 1957 (Nov) 34pp., parts. 20 min. Andante: wistful quality; short cadenza leads to an Allegro vivace: martial opening idea contrasted with flowing sections. Andante: sustained, more rhythmical second idea. Rondo: dancelike, "patter" chords at Poco più mosso, chromatic coloration, long lines at closing. M-D.

Elizabeth Sprague Coolidge. *Sonata* (CF 1947) 35pp., parts. Introduction and Allegro; Reverie; Theme and (5 contrasted) Variations. Mildly contemporary. Flowing quality with many triplets. Final movement has a different character for each variation: Gigue, Fugato, 3-voice Canon, etc. M-D.

Henry Cowell. *Three Ostinati with Chorales* (Music Press 1946) 16pp., parts. For oboe or clarinet and piano. Written for oboe and piano but Cowell considers them equally suitable for clarinet and piano. Each chorale is followed by its ostinato, which is more elaborate. All have fresh and attractive ideas, simply conceived and containing melodic appeal. M-D.

Robert Cundick. *Turnabouts* (Bo&H 1964) 24pp., parts. Four contrasting pieces very effectively written for this combination. Ideas are well developed, and the entire suite is attractive. Mildly contemporary with flowing lines. M-D.

Martin Dalby. *Sonatina* 1969 (Nov 1975) 8pp., parts. $4\frac{1}{2}$ min. Allegretto-molto rubato: atonal, pointillistic, chromatic. Adagio: piacevole, thin textures. Leggiero e quasi presto: serial influence, mainly secco style. M-D.

John Diercks. *Sonata* (TP 1966) 26pp., parts. Allegro: SA, flexible meters, buoyant themes; pianist uses light touches of pedal for color; arpeggiated chords contrast more transparent staccato section. Andante cantabile: ABA; diatonic theme in oboe treated in duet fashion with left-hand piano part; B section more active but mainly employs softer dynamic levels. Allegro con brio: changing meters, dancelike, more chromatic lines; Cantando section provides contrast before opening ideas return. A cracking good ending and an outstanding contribution to this literature. M-D.

Stephen Dodgson. *Suite D* (OUP 1974) 15pp., parts. 9 min. Prelude; Ground; Canzonet; Dance. Key signatures are no help. Instruments treated equally in thoroughly contemporary neoclassic settings; fairly relaxed moods. Keyboard writing is guitar-like at places while the oboe is treated melodically (Dodgson is a guitarist). Experienced performers required. D.

Henri Dutilleux. *Sonata* (Leduc 1947) 23pp., parts. 11 min. Aria—Grave: curling ostinato-like chromatic figures underlie a more diatonic melody; three layers of sound; works up to cadenza-like conclusion. Scherzo: staccato chords, flexible meters, imitation, colorful; sustained chords fade away and movement ends *ppp*. Final—Assez allant: contrasting figurations and moods; requires firm rhythmic control and exact dynamics. Strong formal construction in all movements. D.

Alvin Etler. *Introduction and Allegro* 1952 (AMP 1958) 16pp., parts. 8 min. Sustained syncopated harmonies; piano bass line very important. The Allegro 5/4 has much rhythmic mobility, is freely tonal, and contains a few dynamic surprises. M-D.

Peter Evans. *Sonata* (JWC 1953) 23pp., parts. $14\frac{1}{2}$ min. Moderato; Variations; Rondo—Allegro con brio. Post-Romantic chromatic writing. Piano part contains much interest. M-D.

Jan Reindert Adriaan Felderhof. *Suite* (Donemus 1974) 18pp., 2 parts (flute and oboe), photostat of MS.

Félicien Foret. *Sonata* G (Lacour 1945) 25pp., parts. Allegro moderato; Andante, poco lento; Menuet; Vif. Witty and facile, à la Poulenc. Mildly contemporary. M-D.

Géza Frid. *Caprices Roumains* Op.86 (Donemus 1975) 18pp., parts. 8½ min. Based on Rumanian folk melodies, sectional, varied rhythms and moods, chromatic, modal, whole-tone scales used. Mildly contemporary. M-D.

Friedrich Theodor Frohlich. *Pastorale and Rondo* 1824 (H. Steinbeck—Eulenburg 1974) 20pp., parts. Pastorale: gentle dotted rhythms; subdominant relationships; has some of the pseudo-qualities of Beethoven's "Pastorale" *Symphony*. Rondo: two episodes with three statements of the refrain, Chopinesque, syncopation, ornamental lines. M-D.

Pierre Gabaye. *Sonatine* (Leduc 1957) 19pp., parts. Assez vif: B, moving parallel chords, contemporary Alberti-bass treatment, large span required (tenths). Lent, avec douceur: A♭, wistful, more active mid-section. Très vif: B, 6/8, forward motion throughout, hemiola, chromatic in mid-section. Witty, pleasing and attractive writing. M-D to D.

Francesco Geminiani. *Sonata* e (H. Ruf—Br HM 178 1961) 8pp., parts. Adagio; Allegro; Largo; Vivace. High notes, passages difficult for breath control, double fingerings avoided in this work. It is especially suitable for the oboe. Excellent keyboard realization. M-D.

Jaap Geraedts. *Jan Klaassen—Serenade* (Donemus 1953, rev. ed. 1973) 5pp., parts. Photostat. Quartal harmony exploited in an Allegro grazioso setting. M-D.

Walter Girnatis. *Sonate* (Sikorski 1955) 12pp., parts.

Cornelis Willhelmus De Groot. *Deux Figures* (Donemus 1974) 16pp., parts.

John Hall. *Sonata* Op.19 (Chappell 1968–9). Three movements, changing meters, rhythmic problems. D.

George Frederick Handel. *Sonata* Op.1/6 (Stade—CFP; Scheck, Ruf—Ric SY513 1954, 11pp., parts; Bleuzet—Costallat). Larghetto; Allegro; Adagio; Allegro. Ric edition gives original text in addition to the editor's suggested realization for the oboe. M-D.

_____ *Sonata* Op.1/8 (Stade—CFP; Scheck, Ruf—Ric 1954; Bleuzet—Costallat).
_____ *Fitzwilliam Sonata* B♭ (Dart, Bergmann—Schott 1948).

Howard Hanson. *Pastorale* Op.38 1949 (CF) 9pp., parts. 6 min. Freely tonal, Poco più mosso mid-section, molto espressivo ending, flowing, effective. M-D.

Christopher Headington. *Sonatina* 1960 (Bo&H 1973) 20pp., parts. Three movements in mildly contemporary idiom that centers around E♭, triadic sonorities, not for beginners. M-D.

Johann David Heinichen. *Sonata* g (Müller).

Willy Hess. *Drei Tonstücke* Op.71 (Eulenburg 1969) 12pp., parts.
_____ *Sonate* Op.44 C (Amadeus 1975) 27pp., parts.

Paul Hindemith. *Sonata* 1938 (Schott) 23pp., parts. 12 min. Cheerful: short opening motive is thematic germ for entire work. Lively: same theme serves as basis for alternating slow and fast sections. Very slow: mid-section displays theme harmonized in a caricature version of *Tristan!* Last two movements are telescoped into one. Fluctuating tonal polarity, clever rhythms, fugal textures. D.

Stanley Hollingsworth. *Sonata* Op.2 B♭ (GS 1954) 22pp., parts.

Joseph Horvath. *Sonatina* Op.3 1949 (Belwin-Mills) 7½ min. Clean, transparent, concise, and economic in style. First movement bubbles over with high spirits and perky rhythms. A short slow movement leads directly to the extremely lively finale. Harmonic idiom has a sharp edge to it, and cross-accentuation of rhythms lend it a spicy and invigorating wit. M-D.

Jacques Ibert. *Escales II Tunis Nefta* 1922 (Leduc 1924) 5pp., parts. Arranged by the composer. Modéré, très rythmé: tritone is integral part of left hand; opens *pp*, builds to a climax, subsides, ends *ppp*. Colorful and attractive writing in a mildly contemporary style. M-D.

Pierre Israel-Meyer. *Portrait d'un Masque* (Technisonor 1973) 7pp. 2 copies necessary. Notes in French only.

André Jolivet. *Sérénade* 1945 (Billaudot 3153) 31pp., parts. Originally for wind quintet with oboe principal. Piano reduction by the composer. Cantilèna; Caprice; Intermède; March burlesque. Intense chromatic style, freely dissonant, atonal. M-D.

Willem Kersters. *Sonatina* Op.63 (CeBeDeM 1974) 12pp., parts. 5½ min. First two movements untitled; Scherzando. Thin textured, mild pointillistic technique, secco style, interesting pedal effects. M-D.

Johann Philipp Kirnberger. *Sonata* B♭ (H. Töttcher—Sikorski 269 1954). Fine keyboard realization. M-D.

Kenneth Blanchard Klaus. *Theme and (3) Variations* (MS available from composer: % School of Music, Louisiana State University, Baton Rouge, LA 70803) 8pp., parts. Freely tonal, parallel chords, dramatic and sweeping arpeggi gestures, disjunct melodic line, mixture of linear and homophonic styles. Large span required. M-D.

Charles Koechlin. *Sonata* 1915–16 (ESC) Over 20 min. The largest of all oboe sonatas. Moderato: pastoral, evokes a calm countryside where people work. Dance of the Fauns: a difficult scherzo. Evening in the Countryside: printed separately in the *La Revue Musicale*, June 1923. A House in the Country: this was the original title but in the definitive version there is no name for this movement. Popular songlike character. D.

Peter Jona Korn. *Sonata* Op.7 (Simrock Elite Edition 3230 1964) 39pp., parts. Moderato; Romanza; Rondo. Neoclassic style, fondness for triplets noted. Romanza uses many juxtaposed major and minor thirds. Rondo concludes with a fugue plus a more chordal coda. D.

William Latham. *Sonata* I (Spratt 1949) 24pp., parts. Grave: quartal and quintal harmonies in piano support oboe melody and lead to Commodo section, which is more rhythmically oriented; piano has undulating quartal harmonies in left-hand vriplets against two eighths in right hand; chordal punctuation ends the movement. Andantino: pastoral feeling with both instruments contributing melodic ideas. Allegro: dancelike, broken octaves, bright closing. Mildly contemporary. M-D.

Philibert de Lavigne. *Six Sonatas* Op.2 ca.1740 (Willi Hillemann—Noetzel). Published separately. These multi-movement works can be performed on all of the woodwind instruments in use during the first half of the eighteenth century, and on the violin. See detailed listing under duos for piano and flute.

Theodor Leschetizky. *Variationen über ein Thema van Beethoven* (Schott 1937). The theme is from Beethoven's "Andante Favori."

Jean Baptiste Loeillet (of Lyons). *Sonata* Op.5/1 e 1717 (Sadie—Musica Rara 1961) 7pp., parts. Allemanda; Sarabanda (ornamented version, which may be used in repeats); Gavotta; Gigue. Dynamic marks have been added by the editor, and other editorial markings are identified. Excellent continuo realization. M-D.

Otto Luening. *Three Nocturnes* 1958 (Galaxy) 17pp., parts. Nights in the Garden of Chopin: E♭, flowing oboe line, chromatic broken chordal figuration in piano; B section has more elaboration in the piano line. Nights in the Garden of a "Night Club": blues and jazz influence, rich harmonies, full of chords, freely tonal around C. Nights in the Garden of Paganini: C, toccata-like and brilliant, dance influence, syncopated melody. A colorful set. M-D.

Robert McBride. *Workout* 1936 (AMP) 16 min. Fast; Slow; Medium. Both instruments collaborate in a carefree session of musical exercise, passing germinal themes from one to the other. Witty, jazzy, rhythmical construction. Virtuoso, idiomatic, and urbane writing. D.

John McCabe. *Dance–Prelude* (Nov 1971) 8pp., parts. 4 min. Bold piano part, expressive oboe treatment. Two bell-like sonorities worked over in numerous ways provide basis for this piece. Dissonant harmonic idiom. M-D.

Elizabeth Machonchy. *Three Bagatelles* (OUP 1974) 15pp., parts. 8 min. For oboe and harpsichord or piano. Allegro; Poco lento; Vivo. Imaginative writing, with the keyboard part mainly consisting of chromatic chords. Trills, broken chordal figures used for rhythmic punctuation, some melodic usage. Contemporary musical language throughout, eloquent gestures, tart dissonances, neoclassic–post-Stravinsky. M-D.

Peter Mai. *Concertino* (Hofmeister 7468) 18pp., parts. For sopranoblock-flöte or oboe and piano. See detailed entry under duos for piano and flute.

Riccardo Malipiero. *Sonata* 1959 (SZ) 14pp., parts. Moderato: calm, sustained, ends with ninth chords. Veloce e grottesco: varied figures. Deciso: accented chords, Più tranquillo mid-section, *a tempo* Deciso returns. Neoclassic style. Thin textures never overbalance oboe. M-D.

Ursula Mamlok. *Five Capriccios* 1968 (CFP 1975) 7pp. 6½ min. Pointillistic, serial (including dynamics), plucked and stopped strings, clusters, long pedals in No.5, thorny. D.

Robert P. Manookin. *Sonata* 1976 (MS available from composer: 275 East

200 South, Orem, UT 84057) 22pp., parts. With vigor; Very slowly, freely and expressively; Lively. Harmony is frequently quartal and filled with sevenths. Thin textures; instrumental independence produces effective sonorities. Rocking bitonal chords in Lento; finale has a charming and flowing infectious quality about it. Mildly contemporary. M-D.

Bohuslav Martinů. *Concerto* (ESC 1960) 27pp., parts. 16½ min. Originally for oboe and orchestra, piano reduction by the composer. Moderato; Poco Andante; Poco allegro. Chromatic style, some tremolo, rhythmic problems prevalent in first movement. Obviously comes off better with orchestra, but a fine pianist can make this a stunning-sounding piece. D.

Darius Milhaud. *Concerto* (Heugel 1958) 34pp., parts. 18½ min. Originally for oboe and orchestra, piano reduction by the composer. Animé; Avec sérénité; Animé. Large span required; difficult to make all parts sound. D.
———— *Sonatine* (Durand 1955) 20pp., parts. Charme et vivacité; Souple et clair; Entrain et gaité. Light, attractive to play and hear. M-D.

Charles Mills. *Sonata* (ACA) 15 min.

Otto Mortensen. *Sonata* (WH 1953) 19pp., parts. Moderato; Allegro vivace. In Poulencian style, light, witty, appealing. M-D.

Carl Nielsen. *Fantasiestücke* Op.2 (WH 1959) 11pp., parts. 5½ min. Romance; Humoresque. Contrasted, chromatic. These early works date from before Nielsen's mature style had developed, but they nevertheless make an attractive group. M-D.

Peter S. Odegard. *Sonatina and Cadenza* 1965 (McGinnis & Marx) 8pp., parts. Very slowly: serial, tremolo, linear, attacca to Fast: shifting meters, rubato, many crescendi and decrescendi. Cadenza: each instrument has twelve fragments adding up to 52 beats at a given tempo; aleatoric, secco, ringing sonorities, expressionistic, thin but thorny textures; large span required. D.

John Paynter. *Three Pieces* (OUP 1972) 7pp., parts. Estampie: chordal (quartal) for first part, linear and chordal for second part. Lamento: piano lid is opened and the oboist directs his sound towards the strings to excite the sympathetic resonance; white-key clusters depressed silently. Saltarello: cluster-like chords in left hand with octaves in right hand, counter-melody with oboe. M-D.

Ivo Petric. *Sonatina* 1955 (Drustva Slovenskih Skladateljev 1975) 17pp., parts.

Karl Pilss. *Sonata* e (Dob 1974) 32pp., parts. In Richard Strauss and Pfitzner idiom; late-Romantic academicism. First movement: SA, coda joins opening material to second group material in an accelerando to the end. Second movement: slow, ABA; songlike A, agitated B section. Third movement: a terse scherzo. Fourth movement: aggressive tarantella. Well written for both players though it is no masterpiece. M-D.

Walter Piston. *Suite* 1931 (ECS) 15pp., parts. Prelude; Sarabande; Minuetto; Nocturne; Gigue. Sure draftsmanship, fine sense of proportion, dry wit, simplicity of mood. M-D.

Thomas B. Pitfield. *Sonata* a (Galaxy 1948) 21pp., parts. 9 min.

Giovanni Platti. *Sonata* c (G. Hausswald—Müller 1975) 12pp., parts.

Francis Poulenc. *Sonata* 1962 (JWC) 22pp., parts. 13 min. Elégie; Scherzo—Très animé; Déploration—Très calme. A mixture of moods with all the best-known Poulencian characteristics present, from lush harmonies to wistful tunes. A major work. D.

William Presser. *Sonata* 1966 (Tenuto) 20pp., parts. 13 min. Neoclassic style. Allegretto: opens with ostinato figues that evolve into a melody; Più mosso section with forward motion; opening idea returns to close movement. Adagio: sustained, active melodic lines in piano, ends *pp*. Allegro: hemiola, much rhythmic vitality; ends *pp*. M-D.

György Ránki. *Don Quijote y Dulcinea* (EMB 1961) 12pp., parts. For piano or harpsichord and oboe. Andantino espressivo e rubato: arpeggiated seventh chords, chromatic *pp* ending. Allegretto grazioso e capriccio: 5/8, dancelike, mordents, turns, short oboe cadenza, extreme ranges of keyboard near conclusion; sprightly idea concludes this attractive piece. M-D.

Sam Raphling. *Sonata* (Spratt 1967) 16pp., parts. One continuous movement with varied tempi, moods, and idioms. The style is generally flowing, and the textures are clear and thin. Freely tonal around F♯. M-D.

Franz Reizenstein. *Sonatina* (Lengnick 1942) 21pp., parts. 12 min. Allegretto; Cantilène; Vivace. Attractive, effective, melodic charm, cheerful and sometimes witty (for Reizenstein!). Last movement requires a fine octave technique. M-D.

Verne Reynolds. *Three Elegies* (MCA 1970) 11pp., parts. Contrasted, solid contemporary style. Effective individually or as a group. No.2 needs much facility from the pianist. Large span required. M-D.

Alan Richardson. *Aria and Allegretto* (JWC 1965) 8pp., parts. 6 min. Contrasting, mildly contemporary, tonal but highly colored style. M-D.
_____ *French Suite* (OUP 1949) 26pp., parts. 14 min. Rendezvous; Les Peupliers; Passepied; Causerie; Les Moulins. Mildly contemporary, careful balance between the instruments. M-D.

Jean Rivier. *Improvisation & Finale* 1943 (Costallat).

Thomas Roseingrave. *Two Sonatas* 1728 (Richard Platt—OUP, Musica da Camera 21 1975) 14pp., parts. Range of solo part suggests an oboe would be as suitable as the flute. See detailed entry under duos for piano and flute.

Edwin Roxburgh. *Images* (UMP 1973) 10pp. 2 playing scores necessary. Sectional, pointillistic, clusters, aleatoric, strings played inside the piano. D.

Edmund Rubbra. *Sonata* Op.100 C (Lengnick 1959) 12½ min. Three movements, the first two lyrical, with flowing harmonies and florid melodic line. The cheerful and witty finale is a brilliant Presto with dashing scales for the pianist. Key signatures of three flats for the first movement and four flats for the last movement in spite of the title page that proclaims this is a "Sonata in C"! M-D.

Marcel Rubin. *Sonatine* 1927 (Dob 1973) 12pp., parts. 11 min. Three movements, "Gallic" sounding, mildly contemporary, flexible meters. Int.

Camille Saint-Saëns. *Sonata* Op.166 D (Durand 1921) 19pp., parts. 11 min. Andantino; Allegretto; Molto allegro. Facile writing throughout, graceful Andantino, beautifully flowing Allegretto introduced with an ad libitum oboe recitative. One of the most outstanding works in the repertoire, full of ingenious charm. M-D.

Giuseppe Sammartini. *Sonata* G (E. Rothwell, A. Gibilaro—JWC 1951) 12pp., parts. 9 min. Andante; Allegro assai; Andante lento; Allegro. Tasteful figured bass realization. M-D.

Peter Schickele. *Gardens* 1968 (A. Broude 1975) 8pp., parts. 6 min. Morning: "Because each player is to proceed independently at his own tempo, the score alignment of the oboe and piano parts has no bearing on how the instruments will sound together" (note in score); diatonic and chromatic scale figuration in upper register with pedal held throughout; repeated notes and sequences. Noon: traditional rhythmic alignment, gentle, thin textures. Night: damper pedal held down throughout until final bar; shifting rhythms; left hand repeats low D in quarter notes throughout; varied sixteenth-note figuration in right hand for duration of the movement. M-D.

Gunther Schuller. *Sonata* 1948–51 (McGinnis & Marx) 33pp., parts. 22 min. An early work showing broad sweeping melodic lines. Some Schönberg and Hindemith influence detected. Schuller is always aware of the performer and shows, even at this early stage, a personal language and fine sense of compositional judgement. M-D.

Robert Schumann. *Three Romances* Op.94 1849 (Br&H). Exquisite long lines. M-D.

Mátyás Seiber. *Improvisation* 1957 (Schott 1958) 7pp., parts.

David Stanley Smith. *Sonata* Op.43 e (SPAM 1925–6) 37pp., parts. Allegro moderato; Vivace; Andante sostenuto–Allegro giocoso. Fluent writing that is mainly conceived in Romantic idiom and style. A few mildly contemporary sounds are encountered. M-D.

John Stanley. *Six Solos for Flute, Violin or Oboe and Keyboard Instrument* (Concordia).

Halsey Stevens. *Sonatina Piacevole* 1956 (PIC 1968) 12pp., parts. 4½ min. For alto recorder or flute or violin, and piano or harpsichord. With some modification, transposing the higher passages down an octave, it may also be played on the oboe. See detailed entry under duos for piano and flute.

William Grant Still. *Incantation and Dance* (CF 1955) 9pp., parts. Recitative-like opening, arpeggiated chords. Dance: increased tempo and more rhythmic push; slower, sustained mid-section before rhythmic section returns. Attractive and conservative style. M-D.

Alan Stout. *Music for Oboe and Piano* (CFP) 12 min.

William Sydeman. *Variations* 1959 (Ione 1969) 20pp., parts. 12 min. For oboe and harpsichord or piano. Dynamic indications for piano are included. Marchlike theme punctuated with chromatic chords. Var.I: frenetic motion, ends with punctuated chords from theme. Var.II: quietly, expressive, long lines with chromatic and rhythmic quirks. Var.III: dancelike, large span required. Var.IV: keyboard alone. Var.V: with energy, forceful, moves over keyboard. Theme returns extended. Concludes with a Presto coda. D.

Antoni Szalowski. *Sonatina* 1946 (Amphion 1948) 15pp., parts. 9 min. Allegro non troppo; Adagio; Allegro. Three characteristics describe this work: neoclassic style, Impressionistic, and a little Poulenc wit included. Attractive with much audience appeal. M-D.

Georg Philipp Telemann. *Sonata* a (Degen—Br; Bleuzet—Leduc 1955) 6pp., parts. From *Der Getreue Musikmeister.* Siciliana; Spirituoso; Andante; Vivace. Tasteful keyboard realization by P. Ruyssen. M-D.

———— *Sonata* e (R. Lauschmann—Sikorski 1955) 12pp., parts. Largo; Allegro; Grave; Vivace. Good realizavion although the Largo has almost too much activity. M-D.

———— *Sonata* g (Ruyssen, Bleuzet—Leduc 1952) 11pp., parts. 8 min. Ouverture; Vivo; Sans Souci; Hornpipe; Gavotte; Passepied; Irlandaise. Very attractive. M-D.

———— *Sonata* g (Degen—Br). From *Der Getreue Musikmeister.*

———— *Sonata* g (Hinnenthal—Schott 1948).

———— *Sonatas and Pieces* (D. Degen—HM 7). From *Der Getreue Musikmeister.* For flute (violin or oboe) and continuo. Sonata a, Sonata g, L'hiver, Air Trompette, Niaise, Napolitana. M-D.

———— *Six Partitas* B♭, G, c, g, e, E♭ (W. Woehl—HM 47). For flute (violin or oboe) and continuo.

Ton-That Tiet. *Cinq Pièces* 1965 (EMT 1967) 16pp., parts. Lento tranquillo; Vivo giocoso; Allegro moderato; Lento; Allegro. Strong expressionistic style; moves over keyboard; serial overtones; complex spots; rhythmic problems. D.

Fisher Tull. *Fantasy on L'homme armé* (Bo&H 1976) 12pp., parts.

Burnet Tuthill. *Sonata* Op.24 (Spratt 1946) 20pp., parts. Allegro: short motivic ideas in first section contrasted with more sustained theme in second tonal area; tonal with three different key signatures; requires large span. Slowly: expressive, linear with some harmonic thirds and sixths, flowing. Rondo: gaily, vivacious rhythms, freely tonal around D, *pp* ending. M-D.

Robert Valentine. *Sonata* I F (Lefkovitch, Bergmann—Schott 1952).

———— *Sonata* VIII G 1730 (Lefkovitch, Bergmann—Schott 1951).

Antonio Vivaldi. *Sonata* c (Schlövogt—Schott 1951).

Jacques Christian Michel Widerkehr. *Duo Sonata* (James Brown—Musica Rara 1974) 29pp., parts. Transposed to e, taken from Widerkehr's *Trois duos pour piano et violin ou hautbois* (Paris: Erard, 1817). M-D.

Stefan Wolpe. *Sonata* 1938–41 (McGinnis & Marx).

Charles Wuorinen. *Composition for Oboe & Piano* (CFP 1965) 34pp., parts. 15 min. Durational serialization, canonic writing, qualitative notation, difficult demands on both performers. Extreme registers exploited, numerous tempo and expression markings. D.

_____ *Cycle of Elaborations* I (ACA) 11 min.

Duos for Piano and English Horn

Niels Viggo Bentzon. *Sonata* Op.71 (WH 3976 1955) 16pp., parts. 10 min. Hindemithian influence, poetic, reflective writing. Moderato: moving chromatic chords with a pedal-point, chromatic scales and figuration, flexible meters, strong compositional gestures. Moderato: quasi-recitative; rhythmic freedom in both instruments; serves as introduction to short Largo that closes the movement; large span required. Allegro molto: non-legato triplets, dancelike, alternating hands; Moderato coda with sustained chords in piano moving underneath a flowing English horn line. M-D.

Elliott Carter. *Pastoral* (NME 1945) 15pp., parts. For viola, English horn, or clarinet and piano. See description under duos for piano and viola.

Norman Cazden. *Sonata* Op.104 1974 (MS available from composer: % Music Department, University of Maine, Orono, ME 04473) 15pp., parts. One movement in three sections with outer sections more sustained and mid-section more rhythmic with triplet followed by duplet figuration. Freely tonal around a with liberal use of chromaticism. Excellent craft throughout and extremely well conceived for the combination. A major work for this limited repertoire. M-D to D.

George Frederick Handel. *Sonata* g (IMC).
——— *Sonata* 4 D (IMC).

Frantisek Hertl. *Sonata* (Artia).

Paul Hindemith. *Sonata* 1941 (Schott) 19pp., parts...11 min. One movement with 6 sections: Langsam, Allegro pesante, Moderato, Schnell (scherzo), Moderato, Allegro pesante. These sections serve as alternating variations on themes, somewhat similar in construction to the Haydn f *Variations* (H. XVII: 6) for piano solo. Melancholy atmosphere balanced with a brighter outlook. D.

Hans Huber. *Romanze* 1919 (Eulenberg 1973) 4pp., parts. Romantic harmonies, flowing lines for both instruments, expressive dynamic usage. Int. to M-D.

Ulrich Krüger. *Sonata* (Musikus/Busch 1972) 11pp., parts.

William Latham. *Sonata* No.2 (Spratt).

Charles Mills. *Sonata* (ACA) 20 min.

Humphrey Searle. *Gondoliera* Op.19 (Schott 1950) 4pp., parts. A rocking left hand in 6/8 broken-chord form provides the basic accompaniment. This idea is based on Franz Liszt's "La Lugubre Gondola," first version. Chords in the right hand are gradually added to the melody already provided by the English horn. The unresolved final sonority adds color to this enigmatic little work. M-D.

Richard Stoker. *Three Epigrams* 1968 (Leeds 1971) 7pp., parts. Succinct, related pieces in atonal series idiom. Fast-changing dynamics, pointillistic. No.II is more cantabile and sustained. Large span required. M-D.

Burnet Tuthill. *A Little English* (Tenuto 1973) 8pp., parts.

Duos for Piano and Clarinet

Ella Adaievsky. *Sonata greque* (Tischler & Jangenberg 1913). Greek atmosphere, effective. M-D.

Josef Alexander. *Sonata* (Gen 1972). Three movements. Available in facsimile blueprint on special order.

William Alwyn. *Sonata* 1962 (Bo&H 19145) 25pp., parts. 12 min. One movement. Varied tempi and moods, tertial and quartal harmonies, ideas carefully worked over, freely tonal around E♭, martellato octaves, instrumental color strongly emphasized. M-D.

Hermann Ambrosius. *Sonatina* Op.63 C (C. F. Kahnt 192—) 18pp.

Hendrik Andriessen. *Sonata* 1971 (Donemus).

Violet Archer. *Sonata* (Waterloo 1972). Neoclassic, challenging, convincing. D.

Paul Arma. *Divertimento VI* (Lemoine 1956) 17pp., parts. 11 min. Allegretto: much imitation, colorful "alla zappa" broken seventh sonorities. Poco lento e rubato: recitative-like with piano mainly in a sustaining role. Allegro ben ritmato: toccata-like motion is contrasted with two meno mosso sections. Colorful writing. M-D.

Thomas Arne. *Sonata* B♭ (Craxton—OUP 1950). Two movements, appealing. Arrangement of a harpsichord sonata. M-D.

Charles Arnold. *Sonata* Op.7 (Andre). Pleasant.

Malcolm Arnold. *Sonatina* Op.29 (Lengnick 1951) 16pp., parts. 8 min. Three short movements, some interesting areas, light and witty. M-D.

Larry Austin. *Current* (CPE 1967) 11 min. New notation, avant-garde. Durations of single notes and/or groups of notes are determined in general by the visual space between notational indications. Pitch symbols for quarter tone higher and lower, clusters on black and white keys. Pointillistic, indications where ensemble is simultaneous. D.

Jacob Avshalomoff. *Sonatina* (Music Press 1947) 28pp., parts. Originally for viola, separate part for clarinet. Allegro appassionato: alternating open fifths, arpeggi, mainly diatonic. Lento: moving chords, pochissimo più mosso mid-section. Allegro con brio: driving rhythms with repeated octaves and chords; broken chromatic figuration; Tempo II is più mosso. M-D.

Eduard Bagdasarian. *Sonata* (Yerevan—USSR Epietrat 1953). Charming, tuneful, folk-like. Int.

Jesus Bal y Gay. *Sonata* 1946–7 (EMM 1953) 33pp., parts. Allegro; Adagio; Adagio–Allegro. Contains some glittering writing. Freely tonal, imitation, neoclassic orientation. Large span required, some left hand octave technique necessary for finale. M-D.

Jacques Bank. *Last Post* (Donemus 1975). For bass clarinet and piano. 2 scores, each 13pp., Photostat of composer's MS. Based on a text from *The Observer Review,* June 15, 1975.

Don Banks. *Prologue, Night Piece and Blues for Two* 1968 (Schott 11092) 9pp., parts. A third-stream work (traditional composition and performance concepts combined with those of jazz). Banks has had much experience as a jazz pianist and arranger. Prologue: trills, repeated chords, atonal, thin textures. Night Piece: arpeggio figuration sustained by pedal, expressive, *pp* dissonant chords. Blues for Two: rhythmic with a jazz feeling, syncopated chords, clarinet cadenza, clever left-hand bass treatment. M-D.

Ramón Barce. *Siala* (Editorial de Música Española Contemporanea 1975) 15pp., parts.

Lubor Barta. *Sonata* (Artia).

John Bavicchi. *Sonata* I Op.57 (MS available from composer, Box 182 Astor Station, Boston, MA 02123). Challenging, rewarding. M-D.

Arnold Bax. *Sonata* (Murdoch 1935) 20pp., parts. $12\frac{1}{2}$ min. Two movements with the second more interesting than the first. Thick piano scoring. M-D.

Alban Berg. *Four Pieces* Op.5 (UE 1913) 10pp., parts. 8 min. Mässig—Langsam; Sehr langsam; Sehr rasch; Langsam. Highly sensitive expressionistic writing. Includes characteristics of Berg's mature style even though these are somewhat early works. A major work in this medium. D.
See: L. East, "A Background Study and Extended Analysis of Alban Berg's *Four Pieces for Clarinet and Piano,* Op.5, thesis, King's College (London), 1971.

James Bernard. *Sonatina* (OUP 1958) 8 min. Mattinata; Notturno; Danza. Loose development but contains some clever ideas. M-D.

Leonard Bernstein. *Sonata* (Witmark 1943) 20pp., parts. 11 min. Two movements in neoclassic idiom, both rhythmically interesting. 5/8 meter in finale with shifting rhythms from bar to bar. Enough dissonance to produce a stimulating effect; catchy tunes; last movement is pandiatonic. M-D.

Wallace Berry. *Fantasy in Five Statements* (CF W2447 1971) 8pp., parts. Larghissimo, con affetto: serial, quiet dynamic range, expressionistic, harmonics, pointillistic, ethereal sonorities. Allegro molto e scorrendo: nimble fingers required for this fleeting piece. Come un imagio fantastico: expressive, changing tempi and meter. Scherzoso: quiet and quick except for some shocking interruptions. Agitato–tempestoso: dramatic gestures, climactic for entire work, dynamic extremes. All five are Webernesque in style. D.

Harrison Birtwistle. *Verses* (UE 1966) 6pp., parts. Piano part is sempre una corda throughout entire work, which consists of 8 very short pieces. No.1 is one line long, No.2 is two lines, No.3 is one line while Nos.4–8 are also short, no more than one page each. Pointillistic, serial, abstract. D.

Bruno Bjelinski. *Sonata* (Gerig 1966). Thoroughly contemporary, well-organized, strong thematic material. D.

Vladimir Blok. *Sonatina* (USSR 1965). Two movements, shifting harmonies, facile writing, mildly contemporary. M-D.

John Boda. *Sonatina* (Delevan 1966). Two expertly crafted movements for both instruments. M-D.

François-Adrien Boieldieu and Giovanni Battista Gambaro. *Sonata* (M. Schlesinger 1820; McGinnis & Marx 1965). The opera composer Boieldieu was assisted by the clarinetist Gambaro. Allegro; Theme and Variations. Effective period writing. M-D.

Dimitri Bortiniansky. *Sonata* (USSR 1955). One movement, pleasant. M-D.

Eugene Bozza. *Sonatine* Op.27 (Leduc 1955). A delightful work with plenty of *joie de vivre!* M-D.

Johannes Brahms. *Sonaten* für Klavier und Klarinette oder Viola, Op.120 (Monica Steegman—Henle 1974). Fingering for piano by Hans-Martin Theopold. 55pp., parts. Preface in German, English, and French. (Br&H; Bo&H; GS; Augener).
Available separately: Op.120/1 f 21 min., Op.120/2 Eb 20 min. (Hans-Christian Müller, Jost Michaels, Emil Seiler—VU 1973).
First published in 1895 together with an arrangement of the clarinet part for viola. VU edition contains critical notes and corrections and explains the variations between the original edition and the engraver's copy. Unfortunately these corrections and variations are not similarly noted in the score. Very good page turns in the piano part. These are the greatest sonatas in the repertoire for the instrument.
_____ *Two Sonatas* (Lea 7).

Victor Bruns. *Sonata* Op.22 (E. H. Elsberg 1951). A well-written work that is brilliant if played quickly, lengthy. M-D.
_____ *Vier Stücke* Op.44 (Br&H 1972). Serious, sincere writing. D. Bruns's career as a bassoonist gives him a special insight for writing for wind instruments.

Francis Burt. *Duo* 1954 (UE 12946 1962) 12pp., parts. 8½ min. In two large sections: Adagio–Allegro moderato and Allegro molto with Adagio coda. Solid contemporary writing with numerous twentieth-century idioms and devices effectively used, such as quartal harmony and free dissonant counterpoint. Piano is treated as an equal partner. Requires large span. M-D.

Ferruccio Busoni. *Elegie* (Br&H 1921) 4½ min. Rocking piano part with a few runs, tremolo, tonal in Eb. M-D.
_____ *Reverie Pastorale* (Ric).

Charles Camilleri. *Divertimento* II 1957 (Fairfield 1973) 35pp., parts. 16 min. Three movements, jazz idioms. Preface and notes for the performer are supplied by Jack Brumer, the dedicatee. D.

Frank Campo. *Kinesis* 1950 (WIM 1969) 20pp., parts. This work, divisible in three parts, is a rondo in spirit if not in form. The first part consists of several more or less closely related subsections; the second part is contrasting; the third consists of a modified return of the first followed by a coda.

The title is very appropriate in view of the motoric force (almost moto perpetuo) that propels the music on its course. Thin textures, freely tonal figuration and chords. Large span required. M-D.

Elliott Carter. *Pastoral* (NME 1945) 15pp., parts. For viola, English horn, or clarinet and piano. See description under duos for piano and viola.

Romeo Cascarino. *Sonata* 1947 (Bo&H) 12pp., parts. For bassoon or clarinet in A. See description under duos for piano and bassoon.

Jacques Castérède. *Sonate* (Leduc 1956) 22pp., parts. Con Moto: excellently crafted counterpoint, freely tonal, tremolo chords between hands with melody riding in top voice, octotonic. Scherzo: 6/8 2/4, bitonal, profuse use of triplets. Elegie: wistful melody, full sonorities in midsection, chromatic, large span required. Allegretto tranquillo: poetic, long lines, clear textures, *pp* closing on E♭. M-D to D.

Liviu Comes. *Sonata* (Editura Muzicală a Uniunii Compozitorilo 1967) 18pp., parts. For clarinet in A or B♭ and piano.

Dinos Constantinides. *Impressions* 1975 (MS available from composer, % School of Music, Louisiana State University, Baton Rouge, LA 70803) 20pp., parts. Slow introduction with the clarinet playing some indeterminate pitches. Piano part calls for harmonics, plucked strings, clusters. Cluster-like sonorities freely repeated; waltz tempo is important. Colorful, atonal. M-D.

Arnold Cooke. *Sonata* (Nov 1962). Mildly contemporary, pleasant. May not wear well. M-D.

Henry Cowell. *Six Casual Developments for Clarinet and Piano* (Merion 1949) 16pp., parts. Nos.II, IV, V, and VI are versions of Cowell's *Suite for Woodwind Quintet.* I. Rubato: syncopated; single line in left hand juxtaposed against right-hand chords. II. Andante: flowing arpeggiated figuration with melodic line embedded in piano texture, hemiola. III. Andante: no dynamics indicated, flexible meters, jazz rhythms, chromatic chords. IV. Allegro: jig-like, chromatic, sustained left-hand octaves throughout. V. Adagio cantabile: chromatic chorale treatment; requires a fine legato; 7/4 5/4 alternating meters. VI. Allegretto con moto: fugal, thin textures throughout, changing meters cleverly concealed. M-D.
See: Bruce C. Trible, "The Chamber Music of Henry Cowell," thesis, Indiana University, 1952, 116pp.

———— *Three Ostinati with Chorales* (Music Press 1946) 16pp., parts. See detailed entry under duos for piano and oboe.

Ingolf Dahl. *Sonata da Camera* 1967–70 (Alexander Broude 1973) 27pp., parts. Alla Marcia; Romanza; Intermezzo Nuvoloso; Introduzione e Giga Finale. Chromatic and freely tonal but tonalities firmly controlled. Chords in alternating hands, open textures, flexible rhythms. Virtuoso instrumental writing for both performers, glissandi on strings with fingernail, crossed hands, large span required. D.

Faraele D'Allessandro. *Sonatina* (Sidem Verlag 1956). Waltz; Habanera; Guagira; Rhumba. Four rhythmically interesting, light dance movements. M-D.

Peter Maxwell Davies. *Hymnos "Ymnos esperinos"* 1967 (Bo&H 1970) 2 scores, each 21pp. Nine sections in groups of three. Dramatic treatment, pointillistic, avant-garde, complex, harmonics, dynamics and pitch serialized, bell-like sonorities. Palm and arm clusters splash around the keyboard; piano frequently overshadows clarinet; ensemble problems in No.4. Large span required. D.

Claude Debussy. *Première Rapsodie* (Durand 1910) 12pp., parts. 8 min. Flexible 2 with 3, tremolo octaves. Shimmering mood must be captured. Most complex problem is ensemble. Requires much experience of both players. M-D to D.

René Défossez. *Sonatina* (Editions Metropolis). Imaginative writing with a highly rhythmic finale. M-D.

Anthony Donato. *Sonata* (ST 1967) 20pp., parts. Allegro moderato: minor seconds and major sevenths preferred, some imitation. Andante: pointillistic, rhythmic flexibility needed. Allegro: strong rhythmic writing. Contemporary dissonantal treatment. First-rate pianism required throughout. D.

Matt Doran. *Sonata* 1963 (WIM 1967) 43pp., parts. Allegretto: Andante; Allegro vivace. Doran writes about this work on WIM Records WIMR.1: "It develops along ratjer conventional lines—in contrast with many of today's trends—and uses themes, motives, transitions, modifications of previously presented ideas and even such formal ideas of the old school as development sections and recapitulations." Freely tonal, shifting meters, quartal and quintal harmony, imitation. Bold, forceful writing. Large span required. D.

Pierre Max Dubois. *Sonatina* (Leduc 1956) 16pp., parts. Misterioso: much activity for the pianist, myriad notes! Vif et leger: humorous; triplets used profusely. Calmo: more impressionistic, parallel chords, *pp* closing. Witty and decorative chromatic writing. M-D to D.

Clyde Duncan. *Sonatina* (E. H. Morris 1955) 20pp., parts. Entertaining, fluent, bright and tuneful writing, a well-made piece. Int. to M-D.

Alvin D. Etler. *Sonata* 1952 (AMP) 15 min. Four well-written and contrasted movements. M-D.
————— *Sonata* No.2 (AMP 1960). Thoroughly contemporary treatment with much dissonance, difficult ensemble problems. D.

Robert Evett. *Sonata* 1948 (ACA) 10 min.

Richard Faith. *Two Sea Pieces* (MS available from composer, 1032 East Adelaide, Tucson, AZ 85719). Nocturne: flowing, arpeggi, changing meters, neo-Romantic. Capriccio: ABA design, eighth-note chordal figuration prominent in A section, B section more sustained; short ''spurting'' motive permeates A section; clever closing with long pedal and crescendo. M-D.

Václav Felix. *Sonata da Requiem* Op.30 1969 (Panton) 24pp., parts. For horn or bass clarinet and piano.

Grant Fletcher. *Sonata* (AME 1958). Fluent contemporary writing. M-D.

Arthur Roland Frackenpohl. *Sonatina* (GS 1970). Good structural sense, consistent musical style and substance. M-D.

Jean Françaix. *Tema con variazioni* (ESC 1974) 15pp., parts. 7 min. Delightful, clever, witty, successful. M-D.

Gunter Friedrichs. *Hommage à Anton Webern. Variationen* (Bo&Bo). Serious, intense, pointillistic, complex. D.

Witold Friemann. *Quasi una Sonata* (PWM 1953). Solid post-Romantic style with an expressive, lyric slow movement and a Polish dance finale. M-D.

Monique Gabus. *Sans-souci* (Lemoine 1972) 4pp., parts.

Niels W. Gade. *Fantasias* Op.43 (JWC) 19pp., parts for clarinet and (violin). 13 min. Andantino con moto; Allegro vivace; Ballade—Moderato; Allegro molto vivace. Lush, Romantic writing for both instruments. M-D.

Hans Gál. *Sonata* Op.84 (Hin 1965). Post-Romantic with some mildly contemporary sonorities. M-D.

Antony Garlick. *Sonata* (Seesaw 1970). Polytonal, clever, tart. M-D.

Harald Genzmer. *Sonatina* (Litolff 1968) 14 min. Introduction and three mildly contemporary movements. Interesting melodic writing. M-D.

Edwin Gerschefski. *Sonatine* Op.18 (CFE 1935). Two short movements. Thin textures. M-D.

Anthony Gilbert. *Spell Respell* Op.14 (Schott 1973) 2 playing scores, 16pp. each. In three cycles. Long silences between chords characterize the first cycle; second is highly embellished (respelt); third is very thick in texture. Written for a clarinet with an extended lower range down to C, a "bassett clarinet." Effective suggestions for amplification given. M-D.

Alexander Goehr. *Fantasias* Op.3 1952 (Schott 10509) 18pp., parts. 12 min. Three pieces in post-Schönberg tradition. Concentrated, dense, many details, pointillistic, atonal, complex rhythms, dynamic extremes. Large span required. D.

Jack C. Goode. *Sonatina* 1946 (MS available from composer: % Department of Music, Wheaton College, Wheaton, IL 60187). Atonal, free construction, strong lines. D.

Alexander T. Gretchaninov. *Sonata* Op.161 (USSR).
———*Sonata* Op.171 (USSR 1949). Delightful writing with a colorful set of variations. Satisfying conclusion. Facile pianism required. M-D.

Günter Habicht. *Sonatine* 1969 (Br&H 1975) 10pp., parts.

Iain Hamilton. *Three Nocturnes* Op.6 (Schott 10194 1951) 19pp., parts. 12 min. Adagio mistico: bitonal, major seventh chords over moving octaves in left hand, arpeggi gestures, cadenza-like figuration; contemporary Romantic idiom noted in the outer pieces. Allegro diabolico: syncopated chords in piano support unraveling chromatic fiorituras in clarinet; piano figuration includes melody line; chords in alternating hands; tremolo; percussive treatment of piano; large span required. Lento tranquillo: solo clarinet opening in a free style; low pedal-octaves in piano plus some melody ornamented with atonal figures; tranquil mood dominates. Strong sense of proportion and design. M-D.

Heinz Friedrich Hartig. *Sonata* Op.7 (Bo&Bo 1952) 12pp., parts. Praeambulum; Scherzo; Molto moderato; Rondo. Well-crafted neoclassic writing throughout. M-D.

Bernard Heiden. *Sonatina* 1935 (AMP 1957) 17pp., parts. 10 min. Charming, straightforward, some brilliance. M-D.

Samuel Frederich Heine. *Sonata* Op.13 ca.1805 (Lyle Merriman—ST). One of the earliest sonatas in the literature. Three movements, classical style, lengthy. Solid keyboard writing. M-D.

Edward Burlingame Hill. *Sonata* Op.32 1927 (SPAM). Attractive and tuneful if somewhat dated writing. For A clarinet. M-D.

Paul Hindemith. *Sonata* 1939 (Schott) 28pp., parts. 18 min. Mässig bewegt; Lebhaft; Sehr langsam; Kleines rondo. Fine energetic writing in Hindemith's later expressive style. Strong mood contrasts. Each movement ends at a quiet dynamic level. D.

Alun Hoddinott. *Sonata* Op.50 1967 (OUP) 24pp., parts. 11 min. Cadenza; Aria; Moto Perpetuo. Complex rhythmically and technically. The finale involves fast chromatic octotonic writing, alternating hands, and long sustained chords. Large span required. D.

Richard Hoffman. *Sonatas* Op.48/1,2 (Siegel 1885).

Franz Anton Hoffmeister. *Sonata* (Musica Rara) for A clarinet. Charming and captivating. M-D.

Arthur Honegger. *Sonatine* A 1921–2 (Rouart Lerolle 1925) 11pp., part for A clarinet. Also available for cello and piano. Modéré: chromatic, well crafted. Lent et soutenu: intense individual writing. Vif et rythmique: uses jazz idioms; fun to play. This work seems to be more effective in the piano–clarinet version. See further description under duos for piano and cello.

Herbert Howells. *Sonata* 1946 (Bo&H 1954) 19 min. Con moto, dolce e con tenerezza; Allegro, ritmico, con brio. Brilliant writing for both instruments; requires imaginative projection. Fresh, attractive, spontaneous. Has a rhythmic springiness about it. D.

Karl Hoyer. *Sonata* Op.55 (Friedrich Portius 1934). A Romantic work worthy of performance.

Alexandru Hrisanide. *Sonata* (Editura Muzicală a Uniunii Compozitorilor din RPR 1964) 18pp., parts. Mosso: folk idiom influence felt in colorful rhythms and melodies, sprinkled with dissonance; pianist has main workout. Calmo ma assai mosso: for solo clarinet; a virtuoso display. Lento, rubato molto precipitato: great freedom, musical sonorities; very short, only two pages. M-D.

Johann Nepomuk Hummel. *Sonata* Op.104 A (CFP).

John Ireland. *Fantasy-Sonata* (Bo&H 1943) 22pp., parts. 14 min. One movement that exploits the wide range of the clarinet. Superb piano writing. M-D.

Gordon Jacob. *Sonatina* (Nov 1949) 22pp., parts. 12 min. For viola or clarinet (in A) and piano. See detailed entry under duos for piano and viola.

Gustave Jenner. *Sonata* Op.5 (Br&H 1900). For A clarinet. In tradition of Brahms, with whom Jenner studied. M-D.

Rudolph Jettel. *Sonata* (Hofmeister 1953) 30 min. Solid post-Romantic writing. M-D.

Thomas Arnold Johnson. *Scherzo* (British & Continental 1973) 8pp., parts. Bucolic, short, a good encore. Int.
_____ *Pastorale* (British & Continental) 3 min. M-D.

André Jolivet. *Sonatina* (Bo&H 1964).

Miroslav Juchelka. *Sonatine* (Artia 1965).

Paul Juon. *Sonata* Op.82 (Schlesinger 1925). One long movement of interesting but busy writing. M-D.

Sigfrid Karg-Elert. *Sonata* Op.139b (Zimmermann 1924) Expressive, incisive writing, many notes! D.

Donald Keats. *Sonata* 1948 (MS from composer: % Lamont School of Music, University of Denver, Denver, CO 80210) 32pp., parts. Allegro con spirito; Andante; Presto. Freely tonal around C, octotonic, frequent use of harmonic fourths and sevenths, song-like Andante, strong driving rhythms in Presto, quiet ending. M-D.

Talivaldis Kenins. *Divertimento* (Bo&H). Three movements of effective and imaginative writing. Piano part is reminiscent of Kabalevsky. D.

Stefan Kisielewski. *Sonata* 1972 (PWM) 26pp., parts.

Charles Koechlin. *Sonata* I Op.85 (l'OL 1947). Distinctive and sensitive writing. D.

Ellis Kohs. *Sonata* (Mer 1956). For A clarinet. Excellently crafted, thoroughly contemporary. M-D.

Leo Kraft. *Five Pieces* 1962 (Gen 1970) 16pp., parts. Prelude; Intermezzo; Capriccio; Fantasia; Tarantella. Serial. Titles capture mood of individual pieces. Flexible meters, abstract serious style. Large span required. M-D.

Mikhail Krein. *Two Pieces* (MCA 1957) 16pp., parts. Nocturne: chromatic, serious cantabile style, freely tonal; large span required. Scherzo: outer sections mainly rhythmic; moderato mid-section gives some dynamic and melodic contrast. Style à la Prokofiev. M-D.

Ernst Křenek. *Sonatine* 1938–9 (Belwin-Mills). For bass clarinet.
———— *Suite* (BB 1955) 5 min.

A. F. Kropfreiter. *Aphorismen* (Dob 1970) 11pp., parts. Five pieces. Simultaneous seconds (major and minor) featured in piano part; free-flowing clarinet part. M-D.

Gail Kubik. *Sonatina* (MCA 1971). Mildly contemporary, neo-Romantic characteristics, enchanting writing. Contains a few ensemble problems. M-D.

Jos Kunst. *No time at All* (Donemus 1973). For bass clarinet and piano. 2 playing scores, 17pp. each. Reproduction of composer's MS. "My aim was to organize meanings and formal effects in such a way that these combinations would produce radical changes in as many elements, details and long-distance effects as possible" (composer in *Key Notes* 2 (1975): 50).

Osvaldo Lacerda. *Valsa-Choro* 1962 (IU) 8pp., parts. A kind of *tour de force* treatment in waltz style, chromatic idiom, much hemiola, convincing writing. M-D.

Ezra Laderman. *Sonata* (OUP 1970) 11½ min. Strong formal structure, inventive thematic material, simultaneous major and minor triads. D.

Paul Ladmirault. *Sonate* (Leduc 1949) 18pp., parts. 14 min. Allegro: begins in f, other sections in C, e, F, and returns to f; flowing lines; free counterpoint between clarinet and upper voice of piano part. Andante: Ab, chorale-like, variations. Intermède: C, wistful melody, attacca. Finale: f–F, short motifs developed. Refined and poetic writing with folksong influence throughout. M-D.

Henri Lazarof. *Adieu* (Merion 1976) 11pp., parts. The first portion of the work is to be played on the bass clarinet, the remainder on the B♭ clarinet. D.

Roman Semenovich Ledenev. *Sonata* Op.1 (USSR 1960). Three movements of robust writing, special rhythmic treatment. M-D.

Jean Xavier Lefevre. *Sonata* B♭ Op.12/1 1804–5 (Georgina Dobrée-OUP 1973) 16pp., parts. 12 min. Allegro moderato; Adagio; Rondo. Displays graceful bravura and melodic charm. M-D.
———— *Sonata* e (Edition du Siècle Musical 1949).
———— *Sonata* III B♭ (Borrel—Richli 1951).
———— *Sonata* V d (Viollier—Richli 1949) 5 min.
———— *Sonata* VII g (Marie Claude—Billaudot 1974) 10pp., parts.

Victor Legley. *Sonata* Op.4/3 (CeBeDeM 1959). Well-developed writing with strong ideas. M-D.

Frank Levy. *Sonata* (Seesaw 1968). Emphasis on intervallic development. Strong dissonant writing. D.

Otto Luening. *Fantasis Brevis* (Merion 1937) 6pp., parts. One movement, neoclassic influence. Slowly, piano gives out rhythmic motif in chords, imitation. Più mosso section introduces repeated chords in piano. Varied tempi, pedal through last four bars diffuses closing. D.

Witold Lutoslawski. *Dance Preludes* (PWM 1956; JWC 1972) 19pp., parts. 7 min. Five contrasting dance pieces using many contemporary compositional techniques. Effective writing for both instruments. An outstanding group. D.

Elisabeth Lutyens. *Valediction* (Dylan Thomas, Dec. 1953) Op.28 (Belwin-Mills 1958) 9pp., parts. 10 min. Lento appassionato, quasi fantasia: serial, heavy chords, atonal, changing dynamics, rhythmic and textural sonorities. Tema—Lento tranquillo, quasi variazione: intense, concentrated writing, tremolo, on the quiet side, ingenious and complex. M-D to D.

George F. McKay. *Sonata* (Mer).

Tomás Marco. *Jetztzeit* (Moeck 1972) 12pp., parts.

Bohuslav Martinů. *Sonatine* 1956 (Leduc) 15pp., parts. 10½ min. Moderato; Allegro; Andante; Poco Allegro. Well written in an accessible pleasant style, but there are difficult spots. French influence is strong; Czech dance rhythms appear in last section. Pandiatonic usage. D.

Daniel Gregory Mason. *Sonata* Op.14 c (SPAM 1920) 59pp., parts. Con moto, amabile; Vivace ma non troppo; Allegro moderato. Strong post-Romantic style, broad sweeping melodies, Brahmsian idiom with influence of Vincent d'Indy. Scherzo is based on the whole-tone scale. Effective writing for both instruments. D.

Felix Mendelssohn. *Sonata* E♭ (MCA 1941; Simon—GS 1951). Good ensemble piece but not too exciting. M-D.

Paul-Baudoin Michel. *Delitation I* 1968 (CeBeDeM). For bass clarinet and piano. 11 min.
———— *Sonatine* 1960 (CeBeDeM) 10 min.

Marcel Mihalovici. *Sonata* Op.78 (Heugel 1959) 16½ min. Hindemith influence. Requires fine rhythmic ensemble. D.

Darius Milhaud. *Sonatine* 1927 (Durand 1929) 15pp., parts. 9 min. Très rude: fiercely dissonant, terse and crisp. Lent: most appealing movement. Très rude: outer movements are thematically related. An exciting work for both performers. M-D.
———— *Duo Concertant* 1956 (Heugel) 11pp., parts. 7 min. A short one-movement work in basically a dry, humorous style. Parallel chords, scales in sixths, freely tonal. M-D.

Albert Moeschinger. *Sonatina* Op.65 (Bo&H 1947). Finale is the strongest movement. M-D.

Roger North. *Sonata* 1951, rev. 1953 (JWC 1959) 24pp., parts. 12 min. Allegro; Larghetto; Allegro di molto. Complex, rhythmic problems, flowing dissonant counterpoint. Thorough musicianship required in this neoclassically oriented work. D.

Léon Orthel. *5 Pezzettini* Op.46 (Donemus 1974) 11pp., parts. Photostat of MS.

Juan Carlo Paz. *Composicion en los 12 Tonos* Op.32 (NME 1943) 12pp., parts. 1. Toccata; 2. Tema con variaciones; 3. Canción; 4. Tempo di giga. Twelve-tone techniques explored, serious, taut construction. Tema contains the most interest. M-D.

Krzysztof Penderecki. *Three Miniatures* 1956 (PWM 1959) 10pp., parts. Allegro: scherzando, chromatic. Andante cantabile: flowing, large span required. Allegro ma non troppo: energetic, rhythmic, full chords, fast repeated chords, driving. M-D.

George Perle. *Sonata quasi una fantasia* (TP 1972) 23pp., 10½ min. 2 copies required. One continuous movement. Clarinetist required to use a mute at one place. A few multiple sounds are also indicated. Many meter changes. Beautifully printed score. Written in a kind of non-serial Stravinsky style. Tricky and brittle writing but not overly difficult for pianist. M-D.

Ivo Petric. *Sonata* 1956–7 (CFP 1975) 23pp., parts.

Boris Pillin. *Sonata* 1965 (WIM 1968) 30pp., parts. Numerous high notes for clarinet, good linear writing, freely tonal, conceived along classical lines. The principal element in the work, more salient than any individual theme, is the quasi-cyclic transformation in the outer movements of a "motto" consisting of an easily identified bitonal harmonic progression. Allegro: strict SA; second subject differs in tempo from the first. Adagio: ABA; first section broadly lyric, second more animated and dancelike. Allegro molto: combination of Scherzo—Finale, rondo, jagged and disjunct in character. Large span required. D.

Daniel Pinkham. *Sonata* (ACA 1946, rev. 1949) 10 min. Contains an outstanding finale. D.

Paul A. Pisk. *Sonata* Op.59 1947 (CFE 1951). Serious, angular writing with much dissonance. D.

Ignaz J. Pleyel. *Sonata* Op.1 (Imbault 1801).
———— *Sonatas* Op.2, 3 (Leduc 1791; Darmstadt Library).

Marcel Poot. *Sonatine* (Leduc 1965) 14pp., parts. 8 min. One movement, contrasting sections, octotonic, freely tonal, parallel chords, concerto style, neoclassic. M-D.

Hans Poser. *Sonata* Op.30 1956 (Sikorski 1973) 20pp., parts.

Francis Poulenc. *Sonata* (JWC 1962) 5th rev. ed. 1974. 24pp., parts. 13

min. Allegro Tristamente; Romanza; Allegro con fuoco. All of Poulenc's powers of charm and entertainment are brought together in this work. D.

Ebenezer Prout. *Sonata* Op.26 (Augener 1886). For A clarinet. Brilliant and graceful, late classic style. M-D.

Francis J. Pyle. *Sonata* E♭ "From the Middle Border" (WIM 1969) 31pp., parts. Allegretto con Moto; Andante; Allegro e brilliante. Strong formal structure, serious and effective writing. Ensemble problems especially in the slow movement. Wide dynamic range, freely tonal, neoclassic. Large span required. D.

Priaulx Rainier. *Suite* 1943 (Schott 1949). For A clarinet. 25pp., parts. 16 min. Vivace: harmonic seconds, octaves in alternating hands, hemiola, freely tonal, cross-rhythms, repeated notes against quick rhythmic figures, octotonic, driving climactic close. Andante come da lontano: freely tonal melody in clarinet over repeated rhythmic patterns in piano used repetitively and cumulatively. Spiritoso: driving repeated patterns built on augmented fourths and fifths. Lento e tranquillo: individual use of triadic tonality, sustained low octaves under moving varied figuration. Allegro con fuoco: driving rhythmic repeated patterns, parallel chords, percussive piano texture. M-D.

Nicolai Rakov. *Sonata* 1956 (USSR 1958). Two movements, the first well-developed, the second not as effective. Fast tempo helps second movement. M-D.

Gunther Raphael. *Sonata* Op.65/3 (Br&H 1951) 22pp., parts. Requires humor and strong projection. Final movement is preceded by a verse: "Not for the cat—but for a duck did I compose the final movement." M-D.

Max Reger. *Sonata* Op.49/1 A♭ (UE 1901). For A clarinet.
_____ *Sonata* Op.49/2 f♯ (UE 1903). For A clarinet. 35pp., parts. Four movements.
_____ *Sonata* Op.107 B♭ (Bo&Bo 1909) 35pp., parts. 28 min. Four movements.
Three outstanding works that deserve more hearing. In the class of the Brahms sonatas. Advanced musicianship and pianism required. D.

Hendrik de Regt. *Musica per clarinetto basso e pianoforte* Op.24 (Donemus 1973) 18pp., parts.

Carl Reinecke. *Sonata "Undine"* Op.167 (IMC 1757) 31pp., parts. Clarinet may be substituted for flute. See detailed entry under duos for piano and flute.

Joseph Rheinberger. *Sonata* e♭ Op.105 (Wolfgang Stephan—Schott 1971) 36pp., parts. Allegro non troppo; Andante molto; Non troppo allegro. Late nineteenth-century style that requires advanced pianistic ability. Piece has a fine "sound" to it and is due to be heard again in the interest of nineteenth-century Romanticism. D.

Norman Richardson. *Sonatina* (Bo&H 1973) 16pp., parts. Three movements. Piano part slightly more difficult than clarinet part, slightly academic. M-D.

Ferdinand Ries. *Sonata* Op.29 (Simrock 1820). Solid musical writing, brilliant piano part. M-D.

Gioacchino Rossini. *Fantasia* (Bodini, Zappatini—SZ 1972).

Johann Joseph Rainer Rudolph, Archduke of Austria. *Sonata* Op.2, A 1822 (H. Voxman—Musica Rara 1973) 35pp., parts. Written for Count Ferdinand Troyer (Schubert's clarinetist). Equal demands made on both performers. Long first movement has touches of Beethoven style, such as subito dynamics, quick key changes. Slow Minuet and Trio followed by an elaborate set of variations, varied mainly by harmonic changes. M-D.

Zbigniew Rudzinski. *Sonata* 1958 (AA 1974) 43pp., parts.

Camille Saint-Saëns. *Sonata* Op.167 E♭ 1921 (Durand 1924) 23pp., parts. Allegretto; Allegro animato; Lento; Molto allegro. Effective concert work. Light attractive melodies, facile writing, interesting interplay in finale. M-D.

Pierre Sancan. *Sonatine* (Durand 1963) 7 min. Three connected movements. Excellent, light. D.

Istvan Sarkozy. *Sonata da Camera* (EMB 1974) 19pp., parts.

William Schmidt. *Rhapsody* I. 1955 (WIM 1969) 16pp., parts. Two intransitive motifs are the germinating materials for this work: a three-note figure suggesting a minor mode, and the leaping-upward interval of the minor ninth. After a slow introductory statement a basic sixteenth-note rhythm develops the music at a moderately fast tempo. The proportions of what has now become an A section are dissolved into a slower and more lyrically

expressive B section characterized by a dialogue of the clarinet against an ever-descending tremolo in the piano. This crescendos into a return of the sixteenth-note figures, and a short coda ends the work. Astringent dissonances, octotonic, cluster-like chords. Tremolando chords in alternating hands; large span required. D.
_____ *Sonatina* (WIM 1969) 24pp., parts. Allegro; Adagio; Allegro con brio. Challenging dissonant and rhythmic writing, imitation, neoclassic. Chords in alternating hands; large span required. M-D.

Othmar Schoeck. *Sonata* Op.41 1928 (Br&H 1959). For bass clarinet and piano. 26pp., parts. Gemessen; Bewegt; moves directly into the third movement, which is untitled. Complex post-Romantic writing in a Regerian style. D.

Robert Schollum. *Sonatine* Op.42/1 (Dob 1969). Well crafted. M-D.
_____ *Sonata* Op.55/4 (Dob 1956). Twelve-tone, complex. D.

Robert Schumann. *Fantasiestücke* Op.73 1849 (Bading, Barmas—CFP 1950; Simon—GS 1951) 9 min. Zart und mit Ausdruck: tender, expressive melodies. Lebhaft, leicht: light, many triplets used in various ways. Rasch und mit Feuer: much motion and activity; Schneller and brilliant conclusion. M-D.

Humphrey Searle. *Suite* Op.32 1956 (Schott 1957) 19pp., parts. 11 min. Prelude; Scherzo–fugue; Rhapsofy; March; Hora. Mildly contemporary throughout, well crafted. Hora is especially appealing. M-D.
_____ *Cat Variations on a Theme from Prokofiev's Peter and the Wolf* 1971 (Faber Music 1974) 8pp., parts. For A clarinet and piano. Eight comic pieces. Growltiger's Serenade is a study of up and down glissandi. Tape is used in the Allegro molto Finale. Piano part not technically difficult but requires good chordal tremolos and fast off-beat chord leaps. D.

Giacomo Setacciola. *Sonata* Op.31 1921 (Ric 1958) 41pp., parts. Three movements. Well written with some unusual effects, similar in style to Respighi. M-D with a few spots D.

Mordecai Seter. *Elegy* 1954 (IMI 1968) 11pp., parts. This work "takes the form of a poem in five stanzas. Each stanza opens with a variation on the interval of the third—a basic interval of the work—and develops into a free melodic recitative. The last stanza serves as an epilogue" (from the score). Colorful, effective. Hebraic modality permeates the piece. M-D.

Christopher Shaw. *Sonata* (Nov 1953) 15 min.

Dane Skerl. *Sonatina* (Društva Slovenskih Skladateljev 1972) 10pp. 2 copies necessary for performance.

Leo Sowerby. *Sonata* 1938 (SPAM) 54pp., parts. A serious and superior work. Third movement is a canon. Fourth movement arrives at an exciting musical climax, is mildly dissonant. Requires thorough musicianship and mature pianism. D.

Leopold Spinner. *Suite* Op.10 1955 (Bo&H 1962) 12pp., parts. Moderato; Allegro. Serial, frequent tempi changes, pointillistic, thin textures, expressionistic. M-D.

Charles Villers Stanford. *Sonata* Op.129 (St&B 1918) 40pp., parts. $18\frac{1}{2}$ min. Three movements of convincing writing, especially the slow movement. Post-Romantic style. M-D.

François Steenhuis. *Sonatina* Op.3 1945 (Donemus 1958) $7\frac{1}{2}$ min.

Walter Steffens. *Hommage II* Op.16 (Bo&Bo 1973) 6pp., parts. Persiflage; Akklamation; Konklusion.

Halsey Stevens. *Serenade* 1944 (Helios 1971) 4pp., parts. For viola or clarinet and piano. See detailed entry under duos for piano and viola.
——— *Suite* 1945, rev. 1953 (CFP 1959) 16pp., parts for clarinet and viola. $9\frac{1}{2}$ min. Allegretto: terse, closely knit modal dialogue between the two instruments. Adagio: a broad-shaped movement, rich harmonies, alternates 2/4 and 3/4. Bucolico, pesante: subtle asymmetric rhythms 4 + 7/8, propulsive and well unified, more chordal than most of Stevens's writing. Moderato con moto: expressive long lines, recurring hemiola usage, flowing, develops naturally. M-D.
——— *Dittico* 1972 (Helios) 14pp., parts. 6 min. For sax (or clarinet) and piano. See detailed entry under duos for piano and saxophone.

Richard Stoker. *Sonata* (Leeds 1972) 9pp., parts. Allegretto; Largo mesto; Presto. Pleasant and freely tonal writing for both instruments. M-D.

Robert Suter. *Sonatina* 1937 (Henn 1957). One movement. Twelve-tone, clear, musical. D.

William Sydeman. *Duo* (PIC 1966) 32pp., parts. 11 min. Two abstruse (Adagio; Allegro) dissonant movements, excellent motivic development, unusual rhythmic divisions, tremolo, trills. Requires large span. D.

Antoni Szalowski. *Sonatina* (Omega 1948) 16pp., parts. 9 min. Allegro non troppo; Larghetto; Allegro. Attractive, clever but musical style, a modern classic. Has a great deal of audience appeal. M-D.

Germaine Tailleferre. *Arabesque* (Lemoine 1973) 4pp., parts.

Jenö Takács. *Fantastic* Op.88a (Dob). For A clarinet. A one-movement work marked Andante, molto rubato. Free style, bar lines used only to cancel accidentals. M-D.

Louise Talma. *Three Duologues* 1967–8 (EM) 16pp., parts. 10½ min. Lento–Allegro: freely tonal, ornamental melody, Allegro section more rhythmic, repeated notes, long trills, linear; requires large span. Tranquillo: proportional rhythmic relationships, chromatic, harmonics, serious, expressionistic. Presto: pointillistic, left-hand skips, thin textures, independent lines. D.

André Tchaikowsky. *Sonata* Op.1 (Weinberger).

Alec Templeton. *Pocket Size Sonata* (MCA 1949) 12pp., parts. Three short, attractive movements in jazz style. M-D.
_____ *Pocket Size Sonata II* (SP 1964) 12pp., parts. Three brief movements in light, popular style. M-D.

Hector A. Tosar. *Sonata* (IU) 28pp., parts. 18 min. Allegro ma non troppo; Lento e mesto; Allegro vivace e scherzando. Chromatic, dense. Numerous layers of simultaneous sounds must be projected in the separate voices; "squirts" of notes in the Lento. A major work for the medium. Demands investigation and performance. D.

Donald F. Tovey. *Sonata* Op.16 B♭ 1906 (Schott 1912). Three movements. A neglected late-Romantic work in Brahms tradition. Virtuoso piano part. D.

Burnet C. Tuthill. *Fantasy Sonata* Op.3 (CF 1936) 9 min. Basically a four-movement work distilled into one movement. Based mainly on materials of the first and second subjects. Rhapsodic and atmospheric, requiring thorough musicianship of both performers. M-D.

Jan Baptist Vanhal. *Sonata* B♭ 1806 (B. Tuthill—McGinnis & Marx 1948) 31pp., parts. 13½ min. Extensive preface by Joseph Marx. Allegro moderato; Adagio cantabile; Rondo allegretto. This appears to be one of the earliest clarinet sonatas available in a modern and carefully edited edition. Classic style, clear balance of parts. M-D.

——— *Sonata* B♭ II (Musica Rara 1973) 20pp., parts. Preface in English by Georgina Dobrée. Originally published in 1805. Charming, highly interesting musically, maintains stylistic consistency. M-D.

George Walker. *Perimeters* 1966 (Gen 1972) 14pp., parts. 9 min. Three untitled movements. Serial, terse, mainly linear with a few chordal sonorities that mainly function cadentially. D.

James Walker. *Sonátina* (GS 1974) 11pp., parts. Allegro moderato semplice; Andante Mesto; Allegro. Mildly contemporary tonal writing that is full of charm, humor, and wit. In spite of its popular orientation the music has classical structure and form. M-D.

Carl Maria von Weber. *Grand Duo Concertante* Op.48 (Schlesinger; Lemoine; Simon—GS 1951; Roth—Bo&H) 18 min. Brilliant, sonata design. Tuthill says it is the "best show piece in the literature for both instruments, using all the resources of the clarinet. Weber's best music for clarinet" (*Journal of Research in Music Education* 20, Fall 1972, 327).

——— *Introduction, Theme and Variations* 1815 (Bo&Bo 1962) 9 min.

Jaromir Weinberger. *Sonatine* (CF 1940). Good teaching literature. Int.

Leo Weiner. *Ballade* Op.8 (Rozsavölgyi 1955) 15pp., parts. 10½ min. Sectionalized work in post-Brahms–Dohnanyi idiom. Chromatic, tremolo, runs and arpeggi figuration. M-D.

Fleming Weis. *Sonata* (K&S 1935).

Egon Wellesz. *Zwei Stücke* Op.34 1922 (UE 1258) 5pp., parts. Moderato; Andante appassionato. Atonal, fluent writing, expressionistic, Schönberg idiom. Requires large span. M-D.

Friedrich Wildgans. *Sonatina* b (Dob 1963). Three short movements, thin textures, folk influence. Delightful finale. M-D.

Johann Hugo Worzischek (Vorisek). *Sonata* (Rovnost 1957).

Yehudi Wyner. *Short Sonata* 1949 (ACA). Good ideas well worked out. M-D.

——— *Cadenza* 1969 (AMP). For clarinet and harpsichord or piano. Cadenza; Canzona; Dodecadenza; Decadenza. D.

Isang Yun. *Riul* 1968 (Bo&Bo 1969) 21pp., parts. 14 min. Highly intense writing that sounds like a combination of late Alban Berg and middle Karlheinz Stockhausen. Terribly involved for both performers. Great "spurts" of sound are contrasted with less activity. Only for the most adventurous. D.

Daniele Zanettovich. *Suite* (Leduc 1974) 13pp., parts. 10½ min. Preludio: freely tonal around b, parallel chords, subtle syncopation. Passepied: strong rhythms, staccato chords. Musette: added-note technique prevalent, Ravel-like. Rigaudon: toccata-like passages in alternating hands, ideas from Preludio appear, vigorous conclusion. Neoclassic. M-D.

Friedrich Zehm. *Sonatina Giocoso* (Schott 1976) 7pp., parts.

Friedrich Zipp. *Sonatine* 1970 (Noetzel N3377) 15pp., parts. Allegro giusto; Andante con moto; Allegro energico. Strong quintal harmony, parallel chords, octotonic, more freely tonal second areas, vigorous finale, neoclassic. Large span required. M-D.

Duos for Piano and Bassoon

Joseph Bodin de Boismortier. *Sonata II* a (Ronald Tyree—Musica Rara 1975) 8pp., parts.
———— *Sonata V* g (F. Oubradous—Siècle Musical 1950).
———— *Sonata* Op. 26/2 a (Ronald Tyree—Musica Rara 1975) 14pp., parts.

Victor Bruns. *Sonata* Op.20 (Pro Musica 1952).
———— *Sonata II* Op.45, 1969 (Br&H 1975) 29pp., parts.

Romeo Cascarino. *Sonata* 1947 (Bo&H) 12pp., parts. This work is equally adapted for clarinet and piano. Part for clarinet in A included. Allegretto Moderato: flexible meters, shifting rhythms. Andante Cantabile: broken seventh chords in left hand, flowing motion. Allegretto Giocoso: corky rhythms, delightful style. Mildly contemporary, thoroughly pianistic. M-D.

Barney Childs. *Sonata* (TP).

Arthur Custer. *Divertimento* 1961 (Duchess) 9 min.

Henri Dutilleux. *Sarabande et Cortège* (Leduc 1942) 8pp., parts. Opens slowly, builds to a Mouvement de Marche. Moves over keyboard, chromatic. Cadenza for bassoon, coda for both instruments brings the piece to a blazing conclusion. M-D.

Alvin Etler. *Sonata* 1952 (AMP) 28pp., parts. 14 min. Moderately slow; Fast; Slow; Fast. Well crafted, precise and deft neoclassic writing. Resources of both instruments are thoroughly exploited. Ensemble experience required of both instruments. Salty and unsentimental style, moody atmosphere. M-D.

Ferenc Farkas. *Sonatina Based on a Hungarian Folk Song* 1955 (Artia)

11pp., parts for double bass, bassoon, or cello. See detailed entry under duos for piano and cello.

Johann Friedrich Fasch. *Sonata* C (J. Wojciechowski—CFP 5893) 12pp., parts. For bassoon (cello) and basso continuo; second cello part ad lib. Foreword in German and English. Largo; Allegro; Andante; Allegro assai. Virtuoso bassoon writing, more homophonic in style than most of Fasch's other works. Dynamics, phrasing, and ornamentation are editorial. Simple and effective keyboard realization. M-D. Another edition by (Brian Klitz, L. Seeber—McGinnis & Marx 1963) 14pp., parts. "Tempo, expression, and dynamic markings in this edition have been inserted simply as a guide for those who may need aid in formulating a finished performance within the musical idiom of the late Baroque" (from the score). Excellent keyboard realization.

Jindrich Feld. *Sonatine* (Schott 1971) 22pp., parts. 10 min. Allegro: clever syncopation, many harmonic seconds, Impressionistic. Andante tranquillo: close texture, cadenza for bassoon, intense melodies, colorful closing. Allegro molto: martial quality, figuration from first movement returns. Effective. M-D.

Johann Ernst Galliard. *Six Sonatas* (E. Weiss-Mann—McGinnis & Marx 1946) Vol.I: *Sonatas* 1–3. Vol.II. *Sonatas* 4–6. Multi-movements, more like suites. Int. to M-D.

Harald Genzmer. *Introduktion und Allegro* 1966 (CFP 5920) 12pp., parts. 6½ min. Adagio opening with arpeggi and trills, chromatic figures, leads to Allegro molto: rhythmic skipping left hand, intervals of tenths between hands, bassoon provides melody. Adagio material returns briefly before the Allegro molto mood and a slowing-down chromatic chord sequence concludes the piece. M-D.

Karl Friedrich Grimm. *Sonata* Op.113 E♭ (Otto Wrede—Regina 1956) 14½ min.

Paul Hindemith. *Sonata* 1938 (Schott) 12pp., parts. 8½ min. Leicht bewegt: short, pastoral, expressive, barcarolle-like. Langsam, Marsch, Pastorale: soon moves to march with trio, then to a coda that vaguely recalls the graceful pastoral opening. D.

Ellis Kohs. *Sonatina* (Merrymount 1953) 20pp., parts. 10 min. I: quarter note = 76; II: eighth note = 76; III: Alla marcia. The third movement consists of a theme, three variations, and a coda. Writing for the piano involves movement over the entire keyboard, mildly contemporary, neoclassic, effective combining of the instruments. M-D.

Otto Luening. *Sonata* (Highgate 1970) 11pp., parts. Andante: linear, chromatic, centers around C. Allegro: perpetual motion idea in sixteenth notes, like a two-part invention. Larghetto: sustained, linear, a few chords. Fast: a quick 6 or a rollicking 2, broken octaves, quartal harmony, dancelike, ends firmly in C. M-D.

Benedetto Marcello. *Sonata* (Bo&H).

Marcel Mihalovici. *Sonata* Op.76 (Heugel 1958) 10½ min.

William Presser. *Suite* (TP 1967) 8pp., 2 scores required. 7 min. Fantasy: opening chord to be played when asterisk appears—"somewhere during that measure at the dynamic indicated." Waltz: à la Prokofiev. March: contrapuntal treatment. Habanera: piano provides rhythm, right hand plays only the final three bars. Scherzo: contrapuntal. Neoclassic, thoroughly convincing and entertaining. M-D.

Einojuhani Rautavaara. *Sonata* Op.26, 1965–68 (Weinberger) 8 min.

Hermann Reutter. *Sonata Monotematica* (Schott 6425 1972) 19pp., parts. See detailed entry under duos for piano and cello.

Armand Russell. *Jovian Sonatina* (Bourne 1974) 9pp., parts. For solo bass clef instruments.

Camille Saint-Saëns. *Sonata* Op.168 G 1921 (Durand) 21pp., parts. 10½ min. Allegretto moderato; Allegro scherzando; Molto adagio—Allegro moderato. Logical ideas developed to perfection in the classical sense. Facile pianistic treatment throughout. M-D.

Gustav Schreck. *Sonate* Op.9 (Hofmeister).

Elie Siegmeister. *Contrasts* (MCA 1970) 8pp., parts. Lively, briskly: cheerful and vivacious. Slow, with sentiment: Tempo I (lively) returns and rushes to the closing, only to be met with a slow final two bars. Neoclassic style, flexible meters. The instruments compliment each other. M-D.

Halsey Stevens. *Three Pieces* 1947 (CFP 1958) 9pp., parts. 4½ min. For bassoon (cello) and piano. Allegro moderato: ABA, flowing diatonic lines colored with chromaticism; in 3/4 6/8; metric divisions of 2 + 3/8 + 3 add interest; pedal point. Andante: thin textures mixed judiciously with chords; inner voices important. Allegro: ABA; opening short thematic figure is inspiration for entire piece; rhythmic vigor, 3 + 3/8 + 3. Functional dissonant harmonies. Large span required. M-D.

_____ *Sonata* 1949 (ACA) 12½ min. Allegro: SA, linear, terse writing infused with highly effective rhythmic patterns. Lento moderato: passacaglia format uses flowing counterpoint against fixed figurations. Allegro: thematic germ of this rondo-like finale comes from the concluding idea of the second movement. Original rhythmic treatment, spontaneous. M-D.

Alexandre Tansman. *Sonatine* (ESC 1952) 11pp., parts. Allegro con moto: driving secco chords; some melodic answering by the right hand; bassoon quasi-recitative finishes the movement. Aria: large span required for numerous ninth chords. Scherzo—Molto vivace: rhythmic element is most important, secco chords, *pp* chromatic chords close out this colorful work. M-D.

Alexandre Tcherepnin. *Sonatine Sportive* 1939 (Leduc) 10pp., parts. Lutte (Boxing); Mi-temps (Rest Period); Course (Race). Short, effective, attempts to adapt to music the surprise elements of sports. M-D.

Georg Philipp Telemann. *Sonata* f (Ronald Tyree—Musica Rara 1975) 10pp., parts.

Heitor Villa-Lobos. *Ciranda das Sete Notas* 1933 (PIC 1961) 15pp., parts. Originally for bassoon and orchestra but the composer has made this highly effective arrangement for bassoon and piano. Varied figurations; tempo changes add contrast. Low broken 10ths provide unusual sonorities in a tempo do Andante section. Flowing chords of fourths require facility. Large span required as tenths must be played solidly. M-D.

Alec Wilder. *Sonata II* 1969 (ST 880) 23pp., parts. Four untitled movements with only tempi listed. Movements I and III are active with many chromatic runs and changing rhythmic patterns. Movements II and IV provide contrast in more restful moods; flowing open fifths over ostinato-like figures; octotonic; chromatic chords; *p* ending. Appealing and well written for both instruments. Large span required. M-D.

Julien-François Zbinden. *Ballade* Op.3 (Br&H 1961) 7 min.

Duos for Piano and Trumpet (Cornet)

George Antheil. *Sonata* C (Weintraub 1953) 26pp., parts. Allegretto; Dolce–espressivo; Scherzo; Allegretto. Freely moving harmonies, chromatic, flowing lines, secco style, satiric, sardonic humor in Scherzo, refreshing with a mildly contemporary flavor. Requires large span. M-D.

Franz Benda. *Sonata* F (EM 1957) 7pp., parts. Andante con moto; Moderato; Presto. Flowing, graceful and appealing writing. M-D.

Niels Viggo Bentzon. *Sonata* Op.73 (WH 1970) 24pp., parts. Allegro moderato; Adagio; Allegro. Piano is thoroughly exploited, moving over entire keyboard. Neoclassic writing that requires complete pianistic equipment and ensemble experience. D.

Thomas Beversdorf. *Sonata* (ST 1963) 18pp., parts. Allegro decisivo: SA, chromatic, chordal; large gestures conclude movement. Largo: wide range of piano used; octaves employed melodically; strong climax; *ppp* closing; trumpet cadenza leads directly to Allegro: dancelike, much rhythmic figuration; arpeggi in final section; neoclassic overtones throughout the entire work. M-D.

Ernest Bloch. *Proclamation* 1955 (BB 1959) 8pp., parts. 6 min. Piano reduction by Bloch. Stirring, attention-getting, sectionalized into Allegro energico, Poco meno mosso, Poco più animato, Andante, Più calmo ending. Freely tonal around C. Sections hold together, integral chromaticism. M-D.

John Boda. *Sonatina* (ST). For cornet.

David H. Cope. *Sonata* (CF) 12 min. Three movements. M-D.

Peter Maxwell Davies. *Sonata* 1955 (Schott). Experiments with a rhythmic series. Full of motoric energy and clean, lean writing. M-D to D.

Maurice Emmanuel. *Sonate* (Leduc 1951) 11pp., parts. For cornet or bugle in B♭ and piano. Adagio; Allemande; Aria; Gigue. Suitelike, facile writing with touch of humor. Mildly contemporary. M-D.

Georges Enesco. *Légende* (Enoch) 7pp., parts. Lent et grave: chordal, chromatic, arpeggi, some tempi variation, sweeping lines in mid-section, builds to *fff* climax, *pppp* closing. Authoritative Romantic writing. M-D.

Arthur Frackenpohl. *Sonatina* (GS 1974) 10pp., parts. Based on *Sonatinas* Op.20 and Op.55 by Friedrich Kuhlau. Tempo di marcia; Adagio e sostenuto; Rondo. The piano part stays rather close to the original Kuhlau, with the trumpet line fitted in stylistically correctly. Int. to M-D.

Jean Français. *Sonatina* 1950 (ESC 1952) 12pp., parts. Prélude; Sarabande; Gigue. Light neoclassic writing. Requires strong rhythmic emphasis. M-D.

Harald Genzmer. *Sonatine* 1965 (CFP 5989) 16pp., parts. 8 min. Allegro; Andante tranquillo; Saltarello. Octotonic, parallel chords, alternating hands, freely tonal, bitonal, vigorous finale. M-D.

Iain Hamilton. *Capriccio* (Schott 1952) 5 min.
———— *Five Scenes* 1966 (Schott) 13pp., parts. 10 min. Wild; Nocturnal; Declamato; Nocturnal; Brilliant. Strongly contrasted movements that use tremolo, pointillism (single notes and chords), long pedals, dynamic extremes, clusters. Large span required for these striking pieces. M-D.

Willy Hess. *Sieben Tonstücke* Op.80 (Amadeus-Paüler 1974) 16pp., parts. Intrata; Impromptu; Ecossaise; Menuett; Siziliano; Trauermarsch; Fanfaren und Romanze. Short, well written, attractive mildly contemporary pieces for the young trumpeter and pianist. Int.

Paul Hindemith. *Sonata* 1939 (Schott) 24pp., parts. 11 min. Forceful; Moderately fast–Lively; Music of Mourning–Chorale. Similar in sturdy quality to the clarinet sonata. Authoritative character. Second and third movements are based on alternating tempi with a tune in the second movement similar to "Ach du Lieber Augustin." The third movement is a funeral march. A middle section marked Ruhig bewegt provides contrast. The coda has the trumpet playing the chorale "Alle Menschen müssen sterben." D.

Alun Hoddinott. *Rondo Scherzoso* Op.12/1 (OUP 1958) 3½ min. Thin textures, freely tonal, glissando, colorful, *fff* closing. Would make an effective encore. M-D.

Theodore Holdheim. *Sonata* 1958 (IMI 1966) 43pp., parts. 10 min. Allegro con brio: SA, changing meters, percussive chords, Grave: ABA, expressive. Allegro vivace: rondo, strong rhythms, brilliant closing. Entire work is written in an extended or free tonality. Neoclassic characteristics. M-D to D.

Paul Holmes. *Sonata* (SP 1962) 11pp., parts. 10 min. Allegro: SA, ostinato-like treatment. Adagio: ABA, melodic emphasis in both instruments; Con Moto mid-section has more activity. Allegro: rhythmic; opening idea from first movement returns; requires a good octave technique. Neoclassic orientation. M-D.

Arthur Honegger. *Intrada* (Sal 1947) 7pp., parts. Maestoso: chordal, low sonorities, melody in octaves, large span required. Allegro: vigorous rhythms, syncopation, repeated notes. Maestoso: uses material similar to that of beginning. Freely tonal and appealing writing. M-D.

Alan Hovhaness. *Haroutin* Op.71 (Resurrection) (CFP 6576a 1968) 11pp., parts. 10 min. Originally for trumpet and string orchestra. Piano reduction by the composer. Aria: diatonic, parallel moving thirds and chords; trumpet has melodic emphasis with some embellishment. Fugue: long subject, extensive solo piano writing, scalar passages prevalent, *ppp* Largo misterioso conclusion on A. M-D.

Jean Hubeau. *Sonate* 1943 B♭ (Durand) 18pp., parts. 12½ min. Sarabande; Intermède; Spiritual. Chordal, added-note technique. Martellato brittle style in Intermède. Spiritual is written in a "Tempo di Blues," followed by a Tempo più animato section based on broken-octave figuration, *ffff* closing. Requires large span. M-D.

Kent Kennan. *Sonata* (Warner Brothers 1951) 24pp., parts. 13 min. With strength and vigor: a cracking good opening, has a more legato dolce contrasting second subject. Rather slowly and with freedom: varied sections and moods; ostinato-like treatment in Poco più mosso part; both performers need a good sense of feeling the bar line. Moderately fast, with energy: opens with a fugally conceived idea, followed by shifting rhythms in piano part while trumpet is mainly treated in rhythmic fashion; meno mosso (Simply, in the manner of a chorale) recalls second subject of first movement. Combination of ideas is worked through. Pianistic throughout. M-D.

Morten Lauridsen. *Sonata* (King 1973) 20pp., parts. 12½ min. Allegro vivace: markedly rhythmic, octaves, free dissonant counterpoint, trill important, linear, clear textures. Largo: legato and sustained, freely tonal, Allegro mid-section followed by solo cadenzas for both instruments, contrary synthetic scales. Presto con fuoco: vigorous, dancelike, changing meters, Adagio section recalls mood of Largo movement, neoclassic orientation. M-D to D.

Otto Luening. *Introduction and Allegro* (CFP 66013 1972) 7pp., parts. 2½ min. For trumpet in C and piano. Short, two-page atonal introduction, thin textures, requires large span. Allegro uses imitation; cadenza passage for trumpet; contrasting touches in each hand; chord and single note in alternating hands provide rhythmic drive. M-D.

Peter Mai. *Sonata Breve* (Philharmusica 1975) 12pp., parts. Rhythmisch bestimmt; Ruhig, gesangvoll; Lebhaft. Tonal in a mildly contemporary way, thin textures, well-contrasted movements. M-D.

Bohuslav Martinů. *Sonatine* (Leduc 1957) 15pp., parts. Allegro moderato. A Poco Andante brings the work to a close. Highly pianistic throughout with traditional keyboard idioms used in a mildly contemporary fashion. M-D.

Paul Baudouin Michel. *Capriccio* 1976 (CeBeDeM) 14pp., parts. 6½ min.

M. Milman. *Sonata* (Philharmusica 1973) 23pp., parts. Allegro Molto risoluto Energico. This one-movement work contains many contrasts. Freely tonal, strong syncopation, toccata-like conclusion. Requires large span. M-D.

Vaclav Nelhybel. *Golden Concerto on a Twelve Tone Row* (EM 1960) 12pp., parts. One sectionalized movement. Toccata-like figuration, expressive and sustained section, octotonic, broad conclusion. Row undergoes various treatment. M-D.

Andrzej Panufnik. *Concerto in Modo Antico* (Gothic Concerto) (Bo&H 1956) 20pp., parts. 15 min. Based on old Polish themes. Originally for trumpet and string orchestra, harp, and kettledrums. Piano reduction by the composer. M-D.

Flor Peeters. *Sonata* Op.51 (CFP 1961) 27pp., parts. 13 min. Allegro: B♭, freely flowing, colorful, con fuoco ending. Aria—Adagio: melodic emphasis, piano accompaniment in parallel chords. Finale—Toccata: motoric, alternation of hands in chords, piano has some melodic treatment but mainly provides rhythmic drive throughout. M-D.

Henry Purcell. *Sonata* g (Lumsden—Musica Rara 1962) 7 min. Originally for trumpet and strings but this is an effective keyboard arrangement. M-D.

Robert Russell. *Sonatina* Op.23 1967 (Gen) 11pp., parts. Lento–Allegro; Adagio; Vivo. Freely tonal around B♭, slow contrary octaves, figuration in alternating hands, fast repeated notes. The trumpet bell is placed inside the piano to produce harmonics at end of Adagio. Neoclassic orientation. M-D.

Dimitur Sagaev. *Sonata* Op.64 1969 (Nauka i Izkustvo 1973) 31pp., parts.

Pierre Sancan. *Rapsodies* (Rideau Rouge 1970) 18pp., parts.

Florent Schmitt. *Suite* Op.133 (Durand 1955) 23pp., parts. 16 min. Originally for trumpet and orchestra. Piano reduction by the composer. Gaiment: sprightly, scherzo, contrasting calmer section. Lent sans excès: parallel chords, melodic line worked into fabric, mildly Impressionistic. Vif: chords in alternating hands, dancelike, chromatic. M-D.

Harold Shapero. *Sonata* 1940 (PIC 1956) 23pp., parts. For C trumpet. Slow; Fast. Strong rhythmic language, lyric element always present, logical formal treatment. Final section is marked Slower; neoclassic. Large span required. M-D.

Walter Skolnik. *Sonata* 1971 (Tenuto T126) 23pp., parts. 10 min. Allegro moderato; Lento; Allegretto giocoso. Mildly contemporary, formally well constructed, disjunct melodic material. M-D.

Harvey Sollberger. *Iron Mountain Song* 1971 (Columbia University Press 1974) 24pp., set of 2 scores. Changing meters, expanding intervals, proportional rhythmic relationships, tightly organized, atonal, pointillistic, linear, serial influence. Large span required. D.

Halsey Stevens. *Sonata* 1956 (CFP 1959) 23pp., parts. 15 min. Allegro moderato: incisive theme developed into a stimulating dialogue with the piano; thin piano part heightens brilliance of trumpet part with dissonance and lively rhythmic accents. Adagio tenero: slow, muted trumpet, broadly conceived theme, superimposed intervals, modal elements. Allegro: brilliant, variable meters, bouncy theme, Bartók influence. M-D.

William Sydeman. *The Affections* (AMP 1968) 30pp., parts. 14 min. For C trumpet. Determination; Frenzy; Quiet Dignity; Good Humour; Patriotism;

Urgency; Yearning and Fulfillment. Complex, pointillistic writing throughout. Colorful sonorities. In the final piece the pianist is asked to play all extreme upper register notes as hard as possible. Requires mature pianism and strong hands! D.

Jan Tausinger. *Sonatina Emancipata* 1968 (Panton 1973) 11pp., 2 copies necessary for performance. Explanations in Czech, German, and English.

Alec Templeton. *Sonia* (Bo&H 1935).

Antoine Tisne. *Héraldiques* (Billaudot 1976) 15pp., parts. Explanations in French.

Burnet Tuthill. *Sonata* Op.29 (Warner Brothers 1951) 23pp., parts. Allegro ben marcato: E♭; dramatic chordal and octave opening; mid-section slower and more sustained, leads to an Agitato section, Tempo I, Slower, Agitato ending. Slowly: f; chromatic chords lead to a Vivace mid-section; Tempo I character and varied opening section returns. Rondo—Vivace: contrasting episodes in different keys and character; concludes in B♭. Mildly contemporary. M-D.

David Uber. *Sonata* Op.34 (PIC 1969). For trumpet or trombone and piano. See description under duos for piano and trombone.

James Walker. *Sonatina* (GS 1974) 17pp., parts. Allegro moderato; Andante mesto; Allegro. Freely tonal; much charm, humor, and wit. Popular orientation but strong classical structure and form. Pianist is kept busy. Neoclassic, phrases extended by irregular rhythmic interruptions. The middle movement is a highly expressive Passacaglia. M-D.

Donald H. White. *Sonata* (King 1967) 28pp., parts. Fast and Marked: octotonic, bitonal, undulating quartal and quintal harmonies, triplets, firm rhythms, freely tonal around B♭. Slow: expressive, free dissonant counterpoint, sustained chords in piano support melodic line in trumpet, chordal climax, relaxes and closes *pp*. Spirited: driving rhythms, many harmonic seconds and fourths, parallel chords, motivic generation, octaves in alternating hands, strong finish, freely tonal around B♭. M-D.

Richard Willis. *Sonatina* (ST 1972) 11pp., parts.

Charles Wuorinen. *Nature's Concord* (CFP 66380 1969) 21pp., parts. 11 min. Serial, pointillistic, spatial relationships. D.

Duos for Piano and Trombone

Haim Alexander. *Shur Dodi* (IMI 1969) 16pp., parts. D.

Joseph Alexander. *Sonata* (Gen 1967) 20pp., parts. 12 min. Allegro moderato; Andante con moto; Vivace. A vigorous and robust work. The middle movement contains some expressive sonorities. Interplay of meters and rhythms is of special interest. Neoclassic orientation. M-D.

Leslie Bassett. *Sonata* (King 1967) 24pp., parts. 9½ min. Three movements with first movement (Allegro moderato) SA, a small scherzo (Moderato cantabile) for the middle movement, and a marchlike extensive finale (Allegro marziale). Freely chromatic, flowing lines. Contrapuntal writing is beautifully exploited. M-D.

Niels Viggo Bentzon. *Sonata* Op.277 (WH 1971) 10 min. A large three-movement work with well-developed material. Humor, wit, and satire are characteristic of the moods. D.

John Boda. *Sonatina* 1954 (King) 14pp., parts. 7½ min. First movement is a moderate 2; fast, crisp, modified SA. The second movement is more linear and is in ABA design. Neoclassic style, freely tonal, pandiatonic at times. Mildly contemporary. M-D.

Henry Cowell. *Hymn and Fuguing Tune* No.13 1960 (AMP) 10pp., parts. 6 min. Hymn: chordal, freely tonal around D, strong counterpoint between both instruments. Fuguing Tune: linear textures, freely tonal around C, chromatic runs, Poco più mosso final section leads to closing. M-D.

John Davison. *Sonata* 1957 (SP 1966) 23pp., parts. 11 min. First movement: monothematic, fantasia. Second movement: scherzo and song combination. Third movement: rondo using Advent carol "O Come, Emanuel." Modal throughout. M-D.

Wilhelm Domroese. *Sakura. Japanese Impressions for Trombone and Piano* (Leduc 1974) 12pp., parts. Theme and five variations plus coda. Includes all techniques of trombone playing including singing into mouthpiece. Freely tonal, quartal and quintal harmonies are exploited, octotonic, fast alternating hand passages. M-D.

_____ *Les Ours* (The Bears) Metaphorical suite for trombone and piano (Leduc 1974) 11pp., parts. 7 min. "This easy suite is a musical interpretation of the typical gestures of bears. For all the different movements the same material is used. The first movement symbolizes the clumsy walking of the bear which is glossed by continuous syncopation. The sorrowful resignation of the she-bear in the second movement changes into merry glee in the final dance of the third movement. A skilful distribution of musical tension and its culmination as well as a clear choice of glissandi will intensify the musical expression and place this work within easy reach of the young musician" (from the score). Mildly contemporary. M-D.

Pierre Max Durand. *Parcours* (Rideau Rouge 1975) 10pp., parts.

Henri Dutilleux. *Choral, Cadence et Fugato* (Leduc 1950) 8pp., parts. Choral: E, Lent, good melodic line necessary over chordal accompaniment, chromatic. Cadence: piano provides tremolo and broken-octave gestures. Fugato: staccato, very rhythmic subject worked over and developed, sonorous closing. M-D.

Maurice Franck. *Fanfare, Andante et Allegro* 1958 (Sal) 15pp., parts. Parallel chords, bitonal, seventh chords, large skips, octotonic chromatic writing. M-D.

Harald Genzmer. *Sonata* (CFP 8194 1974) 19pp., parts. Allegro; Adagio; Finale. Genzmer continues the neoclassic emphasis in his writing while gradually extending the harmonic resources. Cluster-like sounds are exploited in the slow movement while trills add effectively to the sonority. Traditional forms are still much in evidence, and a superb craft glows in every measure. M-D.

Walter Hartley. *Sonata Concertante* 1956–8 (Interlochen Press 1968) 10 min. Exposition followed by a chaconne with seven variations and a scherzo that serves as a development, recapitulation, and coda. Synthetic scale, major and minor sonorities juxtaposed between instruments. Mature pianism required. D.

Paul Hindemith. *Sonata* 1941 (Schott) 11 min. A direct thematic relationship links the heavy and festal opening Allegro moderato maestoso and the closing sections in this one-movement conception of quadruple parts. A light Allegretto grazioso, mainly for the piano, and the third part, entitled "Lied des Rauffolds" (Swashbuckler's Song), provide much contrast to the outer sections. Widely spaced intervals show off the trombone as a prancing instrument in this enthusiastic work. D.

Emil Hlobil. *Canto Emozionante* Op.43 1967 (Panton 1972) 15pp., parts.
———— *Sonata* Op.86 1973 (Panton No.1821) 32pp., parts.

Warner Hutchinson. *Sonatina* (CF 1968) 12pp., parts. 8 min. For baritone horn or trombone and piano. See detailed entry under duos for piano and miscellaneous instruments.

Joseph Jongen. *Aria and Polonaise* . .Op.128 (Gervan).

Robert Kelly. *Sonata* Op.19 1951 (Tritone 1970) 22pp., parts. 10 min. Moderate: SA, freely tonal, octotonic. Moderately Slow: ABA, flowing, subtle syncopation. Fast: rondo variations, ragtime and jazz influence. M-D.

Jan Koetsier. *Sonatina* (Donemus 1970) 12pp., parts. Thematic material is not worked out, ABA design for each movement. Exciting short work. M-D.

Otto Luening. *Sonata* 1953 (Highgate) 15pp., parts. 8 min. Short movements. Introduction; Dance; Hymn; Lively—March tempo. Unusual sonorities; rhythmic treatment of melodic writing is of interest. Presents no difficult problems. Neoclassic. M-D.

George F. McKay. *Sonata* (Warner Brothers 1951) 18pp., parts. Allegro moderato—Joyfully expressive, with elasticity and animation: tempo and mood changes in con moto assai and Pastoral sections. Andante poetico: built around contrasting Andante cantabile and Un poco più moto sections; added sixths and sevenths. Allegro ritmico e vigoroso: tempo changes are also present here; unison writing, parallel chords and some imitation for piano part provide limited interest. Mildly contemporary. M-D.

Arthur Meulemans. *Rhapsodie* (Gervan).

Richard A. Monaco. *Sonata* 1958, 1964 (Autograph Editions) 25pp., parts. Allegro: consists of contrasting thematic groups heard inverted, rhythmically altered, or augmented. Andante: loosely constructed and lyrical; rubato style in which both piano and trombone take the lead. Allegro molto:

violence contrasted by flowing sections; both instruments work closely in a
rhythmically unstable atmosphere. Neoclassic orientation. M-D.

Claude Pascal. *Pastorale Héroique* (Durand 1952) 12pp., parts. 6 min.
Required piece for the 1952 Paris Conservatory competition. Strong
chords, octaves, key changes and freely tonal. Trombone cadenza, *ppp*
closing. M-D.
———— *Sonate en 6 minutes 30* (Durand 1958). Bright French harmonic
palette. M-D.

Jean Perrin. *Introduction et Allegro* (Billaudot 1973) 9pp., parts. D.

William Presser. *Sonatina 1961* (Tenuto) 16pp., parts. 11 min. Allegretto;
Scherzo; Andante; Rondo. Simple folk-idiom style is more difficult than it
looks. Musical, linear. *Dies Irae* is used in the scherzo; pianist required to
tap on wood. M-D.

Jean Paul Rieunier. *Silences* (Leduc 1976) 10pp., parts.

William H. Rivard. *Sonata 1955* (Tenuto 1969) 26pp., parts. 15 min.
Smoothly: SA, octotonic. Grave: aria and scherzo, requires large span.
Presto agitato: toccata-like, changing meters, neoclassic. M-D.

Klaus George Roy. *Sonata* (King 1954) 19pp., parts. 10 min. Andante con
moto: freely tonal, chromatic, terse, intense writing. Interludio—Allegro
Scherzando: cheerful, ebullient, may be repeated without pause if desired.
Passacaglia—Moderato, con brio assai: crafted in a masterful manner.
Strong neoclassic writing. M-D.

Anton Ruppert. *Vier Stücke für Posaune und Klavier über B A C H* (Orlando
1973) 13pp., photostat of MS. 2 copies necessary for performance. Explanations in German only.

Robert Russell. *Sonata* Op.24 1967 (Gen) 13pp., parts. 8 min. A one-
movement work in four contiguous sections developed from a three-note
(opening) motive. Octotonic, thin textures, toccata-like figuration divided
between hands. Contrasting mood and tempi. Convincing and well-written
work for both instruments. M-D.

Carlos Salzedo. *Pièce Concertante* Op.27 (Leduc 1958). Largo: f, chordal,
arpeggi figuration. Molto più lento: more chromatic and melodic for piano.
L'istesso tempo: 3/4 then 6/4, chromatic, closing in F major. M-D.

Robert L. Sanders. *Sonata* E♭ (Warner Brothers 1948) 31pp., parts. 16 min. Rather fast: SA, rocking motion in first idea contrasted with more chordal and rhythmic second theme. Scherzo—Lively: a little slower mid-section is more sustained. Chorale—Solemnly: chordal chorale in piano, poco movendo mid-section. Finale—Very fast: 5/8, rondo, piano part treated thematically in unison and octaves. Ascending octaves to close out the movement. Mildly contemporary. M-D.

Svend David Sandström. *Inside* (NMS 1975) 12pp. 2 copies necessary for performance. For bass trombone and piano.

Elliott Schwartz. *Archeopteryx* 1976 (MS available from composer: % Music Dept., Bowdoin College, Brunswick, ME 04011) 12pp. 11 min. Trombonist needs three mutes; pianist must prepare ten notes with coins, rubber, or pencils and mark six strings for muting. Pianist also needs a large wooden mallet, i.e., the sort used for striking tubular chimes, and an ashtray (heavy glass) or coke bottle to press heavily on strings for shrill, ghostly, high overtones. Notation is spatial—each system equals fifteen seconds, contains other performance directions. Pointillistic. Trombonist leans into piano and plays directly over strings; pianist has clusters, slaps under keyboard, finger tremolo on piano case. Strings are scraped, mallet is struck on different ribs of piano, etc. Unusual sonorities, avant-garde. D.

Kazimierz Serocki. *Sonatina* (PWM 1955) 12pp., parts. 7 min. Three movements with shifting meters and tonalities. M-D.

Halsey Stevens. *Sonatina* 1960 (PIC) 20pp., parts. 9 min. Moderato con moto; Andante affettuoso; Allegro. Rhythmic treatment is similar to the Sonata discussed below. Middle movement is chorale-like and needs an expressive legato; large span required. M-D.

———— *Sonata* 1965 (PIC) 28pp., parts. 15 min. Allegro; Adagio; Allegro moderato ma giusto. Continuous development throughout all three movements. Diatonic, shifting meters, neo-baroque style. Rhythmic subdivisions in last movement are most effective. M-D.

Richard Trevarthen. *Sonata* 1966 (Autograph Editions) 12pp., parts. 8½ min. Three movements based on a light and popular style. Int. to M-D.

David Uber. *Sonata* Op.34 (PIC 1969) 24pp., parts. For trombone or trumpet and includes parts for both. Maestoso–Andante tranquillo; Poco lento e lamentando; Rondo. Freely tonal, rhapsodic, light popular style. Parallel chords, no development procedures, mildly contemporary. M-D.

Walter Watson. *Sonatina* 1960 (SP) 8pp., parts. 6 min. Allegro; Adagio; Allegro. Three short movements that display stylistic variety. Lyric qualities are emphasized. Frequent use of seventh chords. M-D.

Stanley Weiner. *Fantasia* Op.42 (Billaudot 1973) 21pp., parts. Les Cuivres/The Brass Instruments: Trombone, level 6: virtuoso.

Paul W. Whear. *Sonata* 1963 (King) 15pp., parts. 12 min. Three movements. Quartal harmonies. Thematic material is rearranged in the outer movements. M-D.

Donald H. White. *Sonata* (ST 1967) 27pp., parts. 14 min. Quietly and sustained: SA; potent tone-row opening subject with eighth- and sixteenth-note figuration followed by chords has many developmental possibilities; dramatic piano writing that uses most of the keyboard; meno mosso for second subject; well worked out movement; dissonance develops naturally. Andante sostenuto: ABA, low chords open followed by chromatic intervals (small and large); syncopated mid-section, opening ideas return; low chords close movement; Impressionistic. Very spirited: rondo; strongly rhythmic and dissonant; low chords of second movement are here moved to the middle and upper registers. Highly effective for both instruments. D.

Alec Wilder. *Sonata for Bass Trombone and Piano* (Margun Music).

Henri Zagwijn. *Esquisse* 1947 (Donemus) 5 min.

Duos for Piano and French Horn

Samuel Adler. *Sonata* 1951 (King) 16pp., parts. 9½ min. Andante con moto: C, freely tonal, flowing melodies, linear writing. Allegro scherzando: C, 6/8, much rhythmic vitality, harmonic interval of the fourth favored, invigorating contrary motion. Molto ma con appassionata: B♭, chromatic, lines always have motion. Allegro con fuoco: B♭, dancelike, ideas well developed. Linear conception that fits the hands. M-D.

Violet Archer. *Sonata* 1965 (CMC) 16pp., parts. 12½ min. Andante energico: serial, Largo cadenza for horn. Interlude—Largo, serioso: colorful sonorities. Arioso—Largo con poco moto: expressionistic. Serially organized, pointillistic treatment at places, difficult ensemble problems. Effective writing. D.

Leslie Bassett. *Sonata* 1952 (King) 20pp., parts. Allegro moderato: rhythmic opening subject followed by chorale-like second subject in Lento and Andantino espressivo mood and tempo; Tempo I returns; and movement closes *ppp*. Andante cantabile: freely tonal around e, nocturne-like. Allegro, ma non troppo: inspired by rhythm from first subject in opening movement; more sustained un poco meno mosso section provides contrast; *ppp* closing similar to first movement. M-D.

Ludwig van Beethoven. *Sonata* Op.17 1800 (Br&H; M. Wolff—Bo&H 1949) 19pp., parts. 13½ min. Shows great maturity and fine balance between horn and piano. Many Beethoven characteristics, such as muscular piano writing, distantly related key changes. Similar in style to the first and third piano concerti. M-D.

Niels Viggo Bentzon. *Sonata* Op.47 (WH 1959) 27pp., parts. Moderato ma non troppo: rising and descending lines both chromatic and diatonic come to a *ppp* cadence; an Allegro employing triplet figuration brings the movement to a final sustained close. Quasi menuetto—allegretto: ABA, an active subject makes this movement very "busy"; mid-section in constant chromatic sixteenths for piano adds much unrest. Rondo—Allegro ma non troppo: toccata-like until a sustained eleven-bar Andante gives relief before toccata activity resumes. Written in an individual style that is strongly chromatic. D.

Thomas Beversdorf. *Sonata* 1949 (ST) 19pp., parts. Scherzo: freely centered around a–A. Andante sostenuto: E–e, horn sings, piano provides harmonic structure and rhythmic interest. Allegro moderato: a–A, upper register of piano effectively used; scales; most dramatic of the movements. Solid pianistic equipment required. M-D to D.

Marcel Bitsch. *Variations sur une chanson Française* (Leduc 1954) 12pp., parts. Four variations and coda. Simple theme treated with mildly contemporary harmonies. Var.III contains a cadenza for horn. Clever and appealing writing. M-D.

Edith Borroff. *Sonata* 1970 (King) 32pp., parts. 14 min. Rhapsody: Impressionistic arpeggi figuration; syncopation; Agitato e più mosso section utilizes octaves in piano part against developing line in horn part; Tempo I returns to conclude movement. Scherzo—Allegro Vivo: triplet treatment, chordal syncopations between the hands. Sarabande: open chordal texture, melodic line tucked in inner voices, Impressionistic. Estampie—Energico ma non presto: sprightly opening leads to a molto meno mosso espressivo section; opening idea returns to speed itself to a Più vivace closing. M-D.

Norman Cazden. *Sonata* Op.33 (Spratt) 8½ min.

David H. Cope. *Sonata* (Seesaw) 23pp., parts. 12 min. Three untitled movements. Freely tonal, changing meters. The second movement relies heavily on arpeggiation in the mid-section. The finale is a highly rhythmic gigue-like conception. Strong thematic material that develops naturally. Large span required. D.

Bernard de Crepy. *Synopse* (EMT 1972) 10pp., parts. 6 min. Avant-garde idiom for horn. Piano part looks simple but contains difficult passage work. M-D to D.

Franz Danzi. *Sonate* Op.28 E♭ (G. Hausswald—Hofmeister) 29pp., parts. For waldhorn and piano. Critical commentary in German. Adagio—Allegro; Larghetto; Allegretto. Classical style, attractive melodies. M-D.
———— *Sonate Concertante* Op.44 (J. Wojciechowski—Sikorski 458 1957) 28pp., parts. For waldhorn and piano. Allegro; Larghetto; Allegretto. A few glimpses of nineteenth-century harmony appear in this work. M-D.

Jean-Michel Defaye. *Alpha* (Leduc 1973) 10pp., parts. 6½ min. Slow and fast sections are contrasted. Lento section is recitative-like with arpeggi figuration and long pedals; octotonic. This leads to a faster section that is dancelike with large syncopated chords (needs a large span). A horn cadenza interrupts before dance idea continues. A colorful fantasy. M-D.

John Diercks. *Fantasy* 1952 (Tenuto 1962) 10pp., parts. Freely tonal, contrasting sections (flowing, poco marcato, with light bits of pedal, etc.), parallel chords, builds to large climax, mildly contemporary, pianistic. M-D.

Anthony Donato. *Sonata* (Warner Brothers 1950) 23pp., parts. Briskly with abandon: clear textures, freely centered around b. Very slowly: piano part provides chords and contrasting counterpoint with horn. Boldly: ostinato figuration, chromatic chords, a faster section serves as coda. Writing for the piano is expert. D.

Richard Faith. *Movements* 1965 (SP) 11pp., parts. 5½ min. Andante; Allegro; Andante espressivo. Short, relatively simple, melodic, rich harmonies. Each movement portrays a definite character or mood. Special care has been given to the idiomatic treatment of both instruments while preserving a coherence of sound and form. Mildly contemporary. M-D.
Two other *Movements,* Lento espressivo and Allegro vivace, are available from the composer at 1032 East Adelaide, Tucson, AZ 85719. Large span required. M-D.

Václav Felix. *Sonata da Requiem* Op.30 1969 (Panton) 24pp., parts. For horn or bass clarinet and piano.

Giorgio Ferrari. *Sonata* (Zanibon 1973) 25pp., parts.

Jean Françaix. *Divertimento* (EMT 1959) 12pp., parts. Introduzion: sixteenth-note figuration with embedded melody, staccato left hand, contemporary Alberti bass, cadenza-like passages for horn at end of movement. Aria di cantabile: chromatic lines in piano with more diatonic melody in horn. Canzonetta: toccata-like with octaves and chords alternating between hands, chromatic chords and runs in mid-section. Witty, delightful, fun for performers and audience. M-D.

Peter Racine Fricker. *Sonata* Op.24 1955 (Schott 10473) 27pp., parts. Con moto: SA, with short development section; leads directly to Presto: scherzo in ABABA design. Invocation: rondo-like form with extensive episodes. Versatile pianistic figuration throughout. M-D to D.

Harald Genzmer. *Sonatine* 1968 (CFP 8025) 10 min.

Don Haddad. *Sonata* (SP 1966) 15pp., parts. 9 min. Allegro moderato; Largo; Allegro moderato. Written predominantly in the Lydian mode, which seems to lend itself particularly well to the unique character of the French horn. Rehearsal suggestions included. Mildly contemporary. Percussive treatment of piano in last movement. Large span required. M-D.

Iain Hamilton. *Aria* 1951 (Schott) 5 min.
_____ *Sonata Notturna* 1965 (Schott) 10pp., parts. 10 min. Lento: thick buildup of low chromatic sonorities; Allegro mid-section explodes with pointillistic chromatic chords and figuration; Lento returns with a Brutale hammered style, including a silent cluster in the lowest register for the harmonic effect. Largo: serial figuration collects into chords before unwinding again; Lento section concludes movement. Scherzando: similar procedures used in first two movements, *pp* closing. Unusual and hypnotic sonorities. M-D.

Walter S. Hartley. *Sonorities II* 1975 (Tenuto) 4pp., parts.

Bernhard Heiden. *Sonata* 1939 (AMP 1955) 23pp., parts. 12 min. Moderato; Tempo di Minuetto; Rondo—Allegretto. Centers freely around B♭, is neoclassically oriented, has much attention-getting power and fascinating qualities. M-D.

Paul Hindemith. *Sonata* 1939 (Schott) 32pp., parts. 16 min. Three large movements: Moderately fast; With quiet motion; Allegro. Excellent fusion of the two instruments, lyrical. Piano part is especially thorny in the final movement, with sixteenth-note triplets embedded with inner voices. Thorough pianistic equipment required. D.
_____ *Sonata* 1943 (Schott) 11 min. For alto sax (or alto horn, or French horn) and piano. See detailed entry under duos for piano and saxophone.

Alun Hoddinott. *Sonata* (OUP 1972) 30pp., parts. 11 min. The first movement, lyrical and shaped with long lines, provides the thematic material for the complete sonata. An elegiac second movement is followed by a three-sectioned scherzo. M-D.

Mark Hughes. *Sonata* (Tritone 1966) 16pp., parts. 16 min. Allegro: rhythmic, octotonic, bitonal, chromatic chords and runs, thinner sonorities in mid-section. Adagio: sustained, widely spread chords require large span; chromatic counterpoint between instruments. Fugue and Cadenza: well-developed fugal textures, chromatic runs in cadenza, Presto coda, *ppp* effective close. M-D.

Kenneth B. Klaus. *Sonata* 1966 (MS available from composer: % School of Music, Louisiana State University, Baton Rouge, LA 70803). Allegro ma non troppo: freely tonal, octotonic, octaves used in texture for punctuation, free dissonant counterpoint, large span..required. Post Script—Lento, quasi Senza misura: cadenza-like; free tempi between instruments; an Allegro subito in arpeggi figuration quickly ends the work. M-D to D.

Charles Koechlin. *Sonata* Op.70 (ESC 1970) 26pp., parts. 13 min. Moderato, très simplement et avec souplesse; Andante très tranquille, presque adagio; Allegro moderato, assez animé cependant. Cool flowing Impressionistic sonorities, triplet figuration, parallel chords. M-D.

Peter Jona Korn. *Sonata* Op.18 (Simrock 3063 1959) 35pp., parts. Allegro tranquillo ma bene mosso: piano part is a study in various types of idiomatic neoclassic figurations while the horn part continually unfolds. Andante con moto: a Hindemithian lullaby. Rondo à la Gigue: rhythmic drive in a unique manner, including a long stubborn and highly effective pedal point before closing. M-D.

Miroslav Krejci. *Sonatina* Op.31c 1950 (Panton 1972) 20pp., parts.

Ernst Lévy. *Sonata* 1953 (Seesaw 1060) 23pp., parts. Adagio; Agitato; Andante; Tempo Giusto; Allegretto; Tempo Giusto. This six-movement work has no meters, and is written in a chromatic and linear freely tonal style. The fifth movement is for solo horn, while the sixth (with a key signature of two sharps) devotes about half of the movement to the piano in fugal textures; firm D tonal conclusion. D.

Ignaz Moscheles. *Duo* Op.63 (Introduction and Rondeau Ecossais) (H. Voxman—Musica Rara 1974) 20pp., parts. Ingratiating and convincing writing in a somewhat eclectic style of the day. Ample dextrous passage work for the pianist. M-D.

Thea Musgrave. *Music for Horn and Piano* (JWC 1967) 27pp., parts. 9½ min. Changing tempos, character. Unmeasured passages are to be played at the indicated speed. Arrows mark places where the ensemble should be exact. Piano part has frequent spidery figurations. First-rate ensemble players required. D.

Carl Nielsen. *Canto Serioso* 1928 (SM 1944) 4pp., parts. ABA, centered freely around F, chordal and scalar figuration, chromatic chords, triplets singly and in harmonic thirds and fourths, tempi changes in mid-section. Lovely writing for both instruments. M-D.

Paul Pisk. *Sonata* Op.77 1953 (CFE) 30pp., parts. Allegro moderato; Adagio; Allegro, ma non tanto. Atonal, contrapuntal, rhythmic. D.

Quincy Porter. *Sonata* 1946 (King) 22pp., parts. Lento introduction leads to Allegro moderato followed by a Poco meno mosso before the Lento mood concludes the movement. Largo espressivo: unbarred, chromatic, rubato. Allegro molto: 2/4, cross-phrasing in piano with driving rhythmic motif; Poco meno mosso section continues to rework the cross-phrasing idea; Poco più mosso returns to Tempo I in 6/8; final statement of the opening motif unwinds to the end; this movement seems to have a difficult time settling down. M-D.

Francis Poulenc. *Elegie* (JWC 1957) 8 min. Technically and emotionally influenced by Benjamin Britten's *Canticle III.* Opening twelve-note melody followed by a questioning theme with hammered sixteenth-notes. Following a slightly varied repetition of these two short sections, a flowing melodic line based somewhat on the opening twelve-note melody evolves and continues to the end. A final cadence states the twelve-note theme again. This piece has some of the same flavor as Poulenc's opera *The Carmelites.* Sweet but serious writing. M-D.

Primož Ramovš. *Sonatine* (Društvo Slovenskih Sktadateljev 1962) 23pp., parts. Allegro–Largo–Allegro vivace. Octotonic, chromatic, linear. Large span and fine octave technique required. M-D.

Hermann Reutter. *Theme Varié* (Leduc 1957) 3pp., parts. Andante theme E♭, three contrasting variations, theme returns slightly changed. Mildly contemporary. M-D.

Verne Reynolds. *Sonata* (ST 1971) 31pp., parts. Moderately; Slow; Fast. Difficult but well written, serially oriented, broad gestures, expressionistic. D.

Ferdinand Ries. *Sonata* Op.34 F (W. Lebermann—Schott 5670 1969) 42pp., parts. Larghetto–Allegro molto; Andante; Rondo—Allegro. Built on many conventional figurations of the period, i.e., scales, octaves, arpeggi, extended Alberti basses, triplets, etc. Still has interest, and a stunning performance would be exciting for performers and listeners. M-D.

————— *Introduction and Rondo* Op.113/2 (G. Meerwein—Musica Rara 1973) 18pp., parts. Piano part requires fine and sensitive fingers if the work is not to sound labored. M-D.

Keith Roper. *Triptych* (Thames 1972) 19pp., parts. Photostat of MS. Both parts are difficult, atonal, fussy rhythmic and textural problems. Horn requires a few unusual effects. D.

Gioacchino Rossini. *Prelude, Theme and Variations* (R. de Smet—CFP 1972) 20pp., parts. 9 min. Available for horn in F (P-7173a) and for horn in E♭ (P-7173b). "Rossini composed this work in Paris in 1857 and dedicated it to his friend E. Leone Vivier (1817–1900), a famous horn soloist, who performed it at Rossini's famous Saturday evening parties, which were a feature of Parisian social and artistic life at that time" (from the score). Tuneful, pianistic, contains some interesting harmonies. M-D.

Robert Russell. *Sonata* (Gen).

Theodor Sack. *Sonata* 1956 (Amadeus 1975) 24pp., parts.

Robert L. Sanders. *Sonata* B♭ 1958 (King 1963) 32pp., parts. 11 min. Allegro cantabile; Tempo di Valse scherzando; Lento, leads directly into Vivace. Mildly contemporary, most interesting sonorities occur in the Lento. The Valse has a kind of Richard Straussian chromatic coloring. M-D.

Robert Schumann. *Adagio and Allegro* Op.70 (Br&H) 11pp., parts. 10 min.

Humphrey Searle. *Aubade* Op.28 (Schott 1956).

Walter Skolnik. *Sonatina* (Tenuto 1976) 18pp., parts.

Klement Slavický. *Capricci* (Supraphon 1969) 21pp., parts.

Halsey Stevens. *Sonata* 1953 (King) 23pp., parts. 12 min. Allegro moderato; Poco adagio; Allegro. Melodic and attractive linear writing. Tonalities are clear with pedal points in the Poco adagio. Hunting call references are heard in the finale. Neoclassic style with economy of thematic material. Thematic transformations are genuinely inspired. Has much audience appeal. M-D.

Richard Strauss. *Andante* Op. posth. 1888 (Bo&H 1973) 5pp., parts. In rich, Romantic, Brahmsian style. M-D.

Eugene Ulrich. *Sonata* (Tritone 1963) 12pp., parts. For baritone horn and piano. One movement. Chordal, freely tonal and dissonant, octotonic, basically same tempo throughout, neoclassic. Requires large span. M-D.

Alec Wilder. *First Sonata* 1964 (Margum Music) 23pp., parts. Allegro—Forcefully: a♭, strong, syncopated chordal gestures. Andante—Slow: G♭, "Rock it sweetly," light style writing. Allegro Giocoso: ostinato-like chordal figures evolve; most excitement is given to the piano; finally arrives at opening tonality of a♭. M-D to D.

——— *Suite* (C.G.F. 1964) 20pp., parts. Dans Quixotic; Slow and Suite; Song; Epilogue; Suitable for Dancing. A semi-light style permeates the writing but it is handled in a professional manner. Obviously Wilder knows the piano and its capabilities very well. M-D.

Christian Wolff. *Duet* 2 1961 (CFP). Includes extensive instructions for performance. One page of diagrammatic notation. Avant-garde. D.

Duos for Piano and Tuba

William Bardwell. *Sonata* 1968 (King) 12pp., parts. 10 min. Dialogue—
Moderato, quasi recitativo: serial, piano part is mainly chordal with some
melodic statement. Scherzo: mostly linear, some left-hand chordal activity.
Passacaglia: piano part is in 30/8, tuba in 5/2, sonorous, chromatic, intense.
D.

Thomas Beversdorf. *Sonata* (ST 1962) 20pp., parts. 15 min. Allegro con
moto; Allegretto grazioso e espressivo; Allegro con brio. A major work
with dramatic gestures for both instruments. Flexibility, plenty of technique
and interpretive abilities required. M-D.

John Boda. *Sonatina* 1967 (King) 15pp., parts. Two untitled movements. I:
sustained chords in piano move gradually from upper to lower register;
parts then switch and piano has active moving line against longer note
values in tuba line; chromatic; short SA movement. II: ostinato-like chords;
more linear section; tuba has a solo Recitative; movement works to large
climax, then quickly subsides to a closing *pp*. Neoclassic orientation. M-D.

Will Gay Bottje. *Concerto* 1973 (ACA) 21pp., parts. 15 min. Very Quietly:
veiled and muffled sonorities, chromatic, chordal alternation between
hands, *ppp* ending. Syncopated—Dance-Like, Generally Light in Character: dance variations, flexible meters, vigorous. Dramatic, But Rubato:
pointillistic tendencies, cadenza for tuba, changing meters, warm lyric
mid-section followed by intense writing, very broad closing. A first-rate
work that requires first-rate performers. One of the finest works in the
medium. D.

Jacques Castérède. *Sonatine* (Leduc 1963) 12pp., parts. 7½ min. For tuba or
saxhorn. Défilé: robust and martial. Sérénade: rocking 6/8, Fauré style.
Final: figuration between alternating hands, repeated discords, trills, octotonic, martellato piano part. M-D.

John Diercks. *Variations on a Theme of Gottschalk* (TP 1968) 12pp., parts. 4½ min. Theme is from "Le Bananier," in C; opens with tuba playing it complete. Piano enters in low register followed by tuba in imitation. Opening motif of theme is expanded and leads to Var.II, in E♭, with more counterpoint in the piano and a *ff* climax to end this section. A tag emphasizing the raised sixth (A natural) moves into Var.III, which exploits the raised sixth degree in a cantando style in both instruments. Var.IV centers around C and becomes poco marcato and for the piano, secco; motivic interplay makes this one of the most attractive variations. Var.V plays around d with more contrapuntal thrusts from the piano. A cadenza-coda utilizes both instruments and descends to a *ppp* before the final burst of activity that brilliantly concludes the piece. Highly attractive writing for both instruments. M-D.

Arthur R. Frackenpohl. *Variations* (The Cobbler's Bench) (SP 1973) 11pp., parts. 5½ min. After a short introduction the well-known theme is heard. Var.I: chordal, octaves. Var.II: legato, slower. Var.III: a fast waltz using cross-rhythms and the interval of the third. Var.IV: a funeral march in minor. Var.V: syncopated and leads to a solo cadenza. Concludes with a codetta similar to the introduction. Clever, attractive writing. Int. to M-D.

James Garrett. *Sonata* (MS available from composer: Royal Oak Drive, Rt. 3, Columbia, TN 38401). 10 min.

Don Haddad. *Suite* (SP 1966) 16pp., parts. 8 min. Allegro maestoso; Andante espressivo; Allegro con brio. Sensible and effective writing that displays the flexibility, sonority, and artistic capability of the instruments. Contains rehearsal suggestions. Mildly contemporary. M-D.

Adolphus C. Hailstork. *Duo* 1973 (IU) 14pp., parts. Expressionistic abstract writing, flexible meters, well structured. Moves over entire keyboard; exploits upper registers in unusual way that effectively blends with the tuba. M-D.

Walter Hartley. *Aria* (EV 1968) 7pp., parts. 2½ min. Expressive. M-D.
_____ *Sonatina* 1961 (Interlochen Press) 9pp., parts. 6 min. Allegretto; Largo maestoso; Allegro moderato. Excellent piano writing that moves over the keyboard, requires much control and careful balance. M-D.
_____ *Sonata* 1967 (Tenuto) 19pp., parts. 12 min. Andante–Allegro agitato; Allegretto grazioso; Adagio sostenuto; Allegro moderato, con anima. Mildly contemporary writing in this major work for the instrument; chromatic vocabulary. Attacca between third and fourth movements. Thematic material lends itself readily to thorough development. M-D.

_____ *Sonorities* 1972 (Philharmusica) 4pp., parts. Quartal and quintal harmonies, ninth chords, freely tonal. M-D.

Paul Hindemith. *Sonata* 1955 (Schott) 20pp., parts. 11 min. The joggy piano part is animated with much harmonic wit as the composer plays with a twelve-note idea. Allegro pesante: fantasy-like, develops freely, short recapitulation. Allegro assai: ABA, scherzo character, short passacaglia for trio. Variationen: ABA, twelve-note idea announced by tuba then immediately by the piano; idea disappears for two variations but appears in the codetta that concludes the "exposition"; semi-development mid-section has a variation "Scherzando" for the piano; then the tuba has a recitative cadenza accompanied by chord progressions containing the twelve-note idea; the "exposition" is repeated a third lower with added decorations for the right-hand piano part. D.

Gordon Jacob. *Tuba Suite* (Bo&H 1973) 23pp., parts. Exploits the tuba's possibilities thoroughly without being difficult. In eight short movements, one for solo piano. Another called "Jacob's Dream" is a ground bass in which the piano progresses step by step to heaven. The last movement is a Galop with cadenza. M-D.

Jan Koetsier. *Sonatina* 1970 (Donemus) 7 min. Allegro; Tempo di minuetto; Allegro moderato. Piano overshadows tuba in the opening of the first movement. The last movement needs a strong sense of continuity between various sections. Solid writing for both instruments. Audience appeal. M-D.

Vaclav Nelhybel. *Concert Piece* (E. C. Kerby 1973) 7pp., parts. 4 min. Originally for tuba and band. Piano reduction by the composer. A dramatic dialogue between the two instruments. Three sections, tonal, much rhythmic thrust, repeated notes between hands, cluster-like sonorities, mildly contemporary. M-D.

_____ *Suite* (Gen 1966) 11pp., parts. 6 min. Allegro marcato; Quasi improvisando; Allegretto; Slow; Allegro con bravura. Syncopated and highly stylized, mildly contemporary. M-D.

William Presser. *Sonatina* 1972 (Tenuto) 20pp., parts. 10 min. Allegretto; Allegro; Adagio–Presto. A poem by Robert Herrick is included in the Adagio section, not to be sung but to help the players interpret the movement. The measure three bars before the end of the work is to be repeated several times. The pianist may play the last repetition one-half step higher. Thin textures. M-D.

_____ *Second Sonatina* 1973 (Tenuto) 16pp., parts. 8½ min. Three

movements with a neoclassic slant. Adagio movement is very poignant.
M-D.

Verne Reynolds. *Sonata* (CF 1969) 13 min. Moderately fast; Slow; Variations. A large work requiring two experienced performers. M-D.

Peter A. Sacco. *Fantasy* (WIM 1971) 6 min. A one-movement work in contrasting lyric–dramatic sections; twelve-tone. D.

Robert Sibbing. *Sonata* 1963 (TP 1070) 32pp., parts. 11 min. Allegro moderato; Larghetto; Allegro giocoso. Thoroughly contemporary writing in a mainly linear style with chordal punctuation used at important cadence and formal points. Solid pianism required. Easy-to-read MS. M-D.

Leo Sowerby. *Chaconne* (CF 1938). Concentrated writing in a mildly contemporary style. M-D.

James Stabile. *Sonata* (WIM 1970) 22pp., parts. 8 min. Allegro vivace; Moderato; Più mosso. Many sevenths, chords in alternating hands, colorful. Last two movements are to be played attacca. First movement is not difficult to unravel. Large span required. M-D.

Halsey Stevens. *Sonatina* 1959–60 (PIC 1968) 20pp., parts. 9 min. Moderato con moto; Andante affettuoso; Allegro. Highly interesting rhythmic usage. Vitality permeates entire work. Extremely well written. Piano part requires thorough equipment. M-D.

Jeno Takács. *Sonata Capricciosa* Op.81 (Dob 1965) 18pp., parts. 9 min. Multi-sectional one-movement work. Mildly contemporary, attractive. M-D.

Alec Wilder. *Sonata* (Mentor Music 1963) 19pp., parts. 10 min. Four movements. Jazz influence, partial linear style, short motivic usage, chromatic. Blends the two instruments effectively. Solid musicianship and pianistic equipment required. M-D.

Duos for Piano and Saxophone

Garland Anderson. *Sonata* 1968 (ST) 23pp., parts. For tenor sax and piano. Adagio–Allegro con brio; Scherzo–Presto; Andante con moto; Allegro ma non troppo. Misterioso opening, driving octotonic writing in the Allegro con brio. Tonal and Impressionistic treatment in the Andante con moto. Pianistic, mildly contemporary, attractive. M-D.

———— *Sonata* (ST 1968) 22pp., parts. For alto sax and piano. Allegro; Andante sostenuto (Chorale); Allegro agitato. Freely tonal, parallel chords, arpeggiation, subtle sonorities, colorful writing. M-D.

Leslie Bassett. *Music for Saxophone and Piano* 1968 (CFP) 17pp., parts. 10 min. Fast: dramatic gestures, extreme ranges exploited, tremolos, trills, "stopped" notes. Slow: more chordal, rhythmic problems, chromatic. Moderato: pointillistic, many dynamic marks, long pedals effective. Fast: chromatic, sweeping gestures, "stopped" notes, Presto coda; large span required. D.

Jean Pierre Beugniot. *Sonata* (Billaudot 1975) 22pp., parts. For alto sax and piano.

Rayner Brown. *Sonata Breve* 1970 (WIM M76) 24pp., parts. Allegro; Passacaglia; Vivace. Octotonic, thin textures, long lines, freely tonal, neo-classic. M-D.

Paul Creston. *Suite* Op.6 1935 (SP) 16pp., parts. 8 min. For E♭ alto sax. Scherzoso; Pastorale; Toccata. Freely tonal, Pastorale meter is 9/8 6/8 9/8. Toccata meter is 4/4 3/4 2/4 3/4. Metrical subdivision is effective in this well-contrasted work. M-D.

———— *Sonata* Op.19 (SP 1945) 35pp., parts. 13 min. With vigor: freely chromatic; driving rhythms; juxtaposed against calmer lines; repeated short patterns; parallel chords; requires large span. With tranquillity: expressive line over chordal substructure, arpeggi figuration, rich harmonies. With gaiety: like a two-part invention for piano; dancing line in saxophone, shifting rhythms; fun for performers and listeners. M-D.

Claude Debussy. *Rapsodie* 1903–5 (Durand 1919) 10 min. For alto sax and piano. Orchestral reduction for piano. A delectable morceau with syncopated Hispanic flavor, sensual languor, and a strange coda that seems to be inspired by Albeniz's *Iberia*. M-D.

Edisson Vasil'evich Denisov. *Sonate* (Leduc 1973) 34pp., parts. 12 min. For alto sax and piano. Both parts are difficult and highly organized. The character is one of agitation and up-beat rhythmic drive, especially in the faster outer movements, where increasingly faster passage work abounds. Half steps, major sevenths, and minor ninths are prevalent. Flexible meters—6/16, 9, 10, or 11/32—require utmost rhythmic precision. In the middle movement the piano mainly has a few arabesques. The saxophonist is asked to play multiphonics, quarter tones, and unusual shakes. A valuable addition to the repertoire. D.

Robert Di Domenico. *Sonata* (MJQ 1968) 26pp., parts.

John Diercks. *Suite* (TP 1972) 12pp., parts. 6½ min. Chase; Barcarolle; Plaint; Gig. Beautifully contrasting movements in tempi and mood. Piano part is a joy to play and presents no major problems, but the Gig in particular needs plenty of projection to bring out the Strepitoso character. Mildly contemporary. M-D.

Henri Dillon. *Sonate* 1949 (Sal 1954) 12pp., parts. Allegro con . .brio; Andante; Vivace. Outer movements are strongly rhythmic while the Andante is calm, legato, and melodious and makes interesting use of inner voices. Mildly contemporary with Impressionistic influences. M-D.

Pierre Max Dubois. *Pièces Caracteristiques en Forme de Suite* Op.77 (Leduc 1962) Five pieces published separately. A l'Espagnole; A la Russe; A la Française; A la Hongroise; A la Parisenne. Attractive writing with resources of piano thoroughly used. M-D.
_____ *Sonata* (Leduc 1956) 21pp., parts. 21 min. Allegro vivo: SA, scalar, chordal, tremolo, freely in C. Andante: chromatic chords; sax cadenza; mid-section builds to vigorous climax before returning to opening mood and ideas. Tempo di Gavotto: piano part is mainly rhythmic. Rondo: giocoso, light Gallic humor, chromatic, scales, piquant conclusion. M-D.
_____ *Sonatine* (Leduc 1966).

George J. Fiala. *Sonata* (CMC 1970) 20 min.

Jean Françaix. *Cinq Danses Exotiques* 1961 (Schott 4745) 15pp., parts. 5½ min. Pambiche; Baiao; Mambo; Samba lenta; Merengue. Clever rhythmic realizations of each characteristic dance. M-D.

Peter Racine Fricker. *Aubade* 1951 (Schott 10235) 4pp., parts. Elegant, freely tonal (almost atonal), grateful writing. M-D.

Hans Gál. *Suite* Op.102b (Simrock 1973) 29pp., parts. This work is identical with Gál's *Suite* Op.102a for viola and piano, except for transcribing the viola to the saxophone part. A long work in four movements in late-Romantic style and idiom. Rhapsodic phrases of the first movement and the playful theme of the finale are especially noteworthy. M-D.

Walter Hartley. *Duo* 1964 (Tenuto T10) 17pp., parts. 5½ min. For alto sax and piano. Octotonic; arpeggi figuration; toccata-like section; Lento section more chordal and sustained; Tempo I returns opening idea. Freely tonal, dramatic conclusion. M-D.

Bernhard Heiden. *Solo* (AMP 1969) 12pp., parts. For alto sax and piano. Slow introduction leads to a toccata-like main section interspersed with a lyrical interlude. Concludes with a recap of the slow material and a short coda based on the toccata material. Hindemithian in style with dissonant harmonies and angular melodies. Piano part is grateful to play; virtuoso approach avoided for sax. M-D.

———— *Sonata* 1937 (Schott) 32pp., parts. 15 min. Allegro; Vivace; Adagio–Presto. Written in a neoclassic style, liberally sprinkled with chromaticism, freely tonal. Exciting writing for both instruments. D.

Paul Hindemith. *Sonata* 1943 (Schott) 11 min. For alto sax (or alto horn, or French horn) and piano. Four abbreviated movements, similar to a Handel violin sonata. Ruhig bewegt: lyric, prelude-like. Lebhaft: SA, elaborate development section. Sehr langsam: ascends to a considerable climax (fourteen bars only) and leads to Das Posthorn (Zwiegespräch)—Lebhaft: a fairly extensive text outlines the mood of the movement, in three sections: a fast piano solo, a slower dancelike horn tune, and a recap of these two ideas simultaneously. D.

Jacques Ibert. *Mélopée* (Lemoine 1973) 4pp., parts. "D'après une vocalise extraite de L'Art du chant de Rose Caron." Modal melody in the sax is supported by color chords with inner voice in the piano. Requires large span. M-D.

Gordon Jacob. *Variations on a Dorian Theme* (June Emerson 1972) 8pp., parts. 8 min. Piano part is in three flats and centers around F. Five variations: allegro, waltz, a rhapsodic variation, adagio, and a lively finale. Grateful writing. M-D.

Frederick Jacobi. *Sonata* (Bourne).

Gregory Kosteck. *Mini-Variations* (Media Press 1971) 6pp., parts. For tenor sax and piano. Harmonics, chromatic chords tossed between hands, detached scalar passages, sustained chords, pointillistic, expressionistic. M-D.

Bernhard Krol. *Sonate* Op.17 (Hofmeister) 23pp., parts. 13 min. Presto; Maestoso—Patetico; Allegro assai. Neobaroque writing in Hindemith style. Middle movement, with dramatic contrast, is most interesting. D.

Meyer Kupferman. *In Two Bits* (Gen 1969) 5pp., parts. For alto sax and piano. Lento: chromatic, pointillistic, dynamic extremes. Scherzando: same characteristics in faster tempo; complex rhythms. D.

Richard Lane. *Suite* (Bo&H 1962) 11pp., parts. For alto sax and piano. Prelude; Song; Conversation; Lament; Finale. Attractive mildly contemporary writing. Piano writing is handled in a polished manner. Int. to M-D.

Jean Marie Londeix. *Tableaux Aquitains* (Leduc 1974) 2pp., parts for each volume. Quatre morceaux séparés (in four volumes). 1. Bachelette, 2. La Gardeuse, 3. Le Traverseur de Landes, 4. Le Raconteur d'Histoires. Short colorful character pieces. Int. to M-D.

Marcel Mihalovici. *Chant Première. Sonate* Op.103 1973 (Heugel) 26pp., parts. 15 min. For tenor sax and piano. One movement. Varied tempi, textures, and moods. Highly chromatic, atonal, octotonic, shifting meters, agitated and intense, expressionistic, complex writing. Nothing short of virtuoso performers will "bring this work off!" Requires large span. D.

Edvard Moritz. *Sonata* Op.96 1939 (ST) 44pp., parts. For alto sax and piano. Allegro molto; Molto andante; Scherzo—Presto; Finale—Quasi allegro. Mildly contemporary style; nineteenth-century pianistic idioms. Well crafted. M-D.
_____ *Sonata* II Op.103 1963 (ST) 32pp., parts. For alto sax and piano. Allegro; Molto Andante; Un poco presto: Vivace. Characteristics similar to those found in Sonata Op.96, plus more flexible meters. Solid writing. Requires large span. M-D.

Robert Muczynski. *Sonata* Op.29 (GS 1972) 15pp., parts. Andante: serious, effective. Allegro energico: virtuosic. D.

Claude Pascal. *Sonatine* b 1948 (Durand) 16pp., parts. A l'aise: syncopated figure in piano part moves over keyboard; cadenza for sax. Lent: chordal sonorities support line in sax; presses forward to Vif: freely tonal, much rhythmic vitality, arpeggi figuration for piano. M-D.

Sam Raphling. *Sonata* II (Gen 1968) 7pp., parts. One movement. Moderately slow, chromatic, bitonal, mysterious quasi-recitative opening, sudden dynamic changes. Moves through various tempi and figurations. Molto agitato leads to a rhythmic conclusion. Neoclassic. M-D.

Hermann Reutter. *Pièce Concertante* 1968 (Schott 5893) 16pp., parts. For alto sax and piano. Exposition; Berceuse; Combination. Highly disciplined neoclassic writing. Fugal textures appear in the last movement. Thoroughly pianistic. M-D.

Lucie Robert. *Cadenza* (Editions Française de Musique 1974) 23pp., parts. _____ *Sonata* (Editions Françaises de Musique 1974) 23pp., parts. 11 min.

Albert Charles Paul Roussel. *Vocalise* (Lemoine 1973) 4pp., parts. For alto, tenor, or soprano sax and piano. D'après une vocalise extraite de "L'art du chant" de Rose Caron.

William Schmidt. *Sonata* (WIM).
_____ *Sonatina* (WIM 1967) 19pp., parts. March; Sinfonia; Rondoletto. Outer movements are more rythoic in nature with strong syncopation, while the Sinfonia is sustained and melodic. The written-out turn is important to the melody in the Sinfonia. Mildly contemporary. M-D.

Albert D. Schmutz. *Sonata* (PIC 1969) 26pp., parts. Allegro; Andante sostenuto; Rondo. Freely tonal, with key signatures. Highly chromatic. The slow movement is especially lovely, with well-balanced textures in both instruments. Displays a facile craft. M-D.

Walter Skolnik. *Sonatina* 1962 (Tenuto 1971) 11pp., parts. 6½ min. Allegro molto; Lento; Allegretto. Linear, freely tonal. Chordal and linear textures combined in the Lento; flowing *pp* closing. Large span required. M-D.

Leon Stein. *Sonata* 1967 (ST) 28pp., parts. For tenor sax and piano. Allegro vivace; Adagio; Allegro. Strong chromatic and atonal writing, octotonic, highly organized. Requires large span. D.

Halsey Stevens. *Dittico* 1972 (Helios) 14pp., parts. 6 min. For sax (or clarinet) and piano. Notturno: flowing chromatic lines; interplay with melody between instruments; builds to climax then subsides to a dark *p* closing. Danza arzilla: a 6/8 Allegro with hemiola intrusions propels this highly effective movement to a brilliant conclusion. This suite is one of the finest works for the combination yet encountered by this writer. M-D.

Jenö Takács. *Two Fantastics* Op.88 (Dob 1972) 25pp., parts. 11 min. Tempo rubato: extreme-range sonorities created with long pedals; night music that is tranquil and expressive; certain parts do not necessarily need to be together; some rapid pedal changes; dramatic arpeggi gestures; cadenza-like. Tempo giusto: opening grows out of low-register secco sonorities; cadenzas for both instruments; repeated clusters. Both Fantastics make one musical entity. Bartók and jazz influences, strong rhythmic drive, imaginative writing. M-D.

Alexander Tcherepnin. *Sonatine Sportive* (Leduc 1943) 10pp., parts. "As its title indicates, this Sonatine attempts to adopt to music the surprise elements of Sports" (from preface by the composer). Each movement has program notes. Boxing (Allegro); Mi-temps (Larghetto); Race (Vivace). Colorful writing for both instruments with a few surprises here and there. M-D.

Marshall W. Turkin. *Sonata* 1958 (TP 1969) 26pp., parts. Allegro con moto; Adagio; Allegro con spirito. Traditional forms, octotonic, freely tonal, hemiola, movements compliment each other, ostinato-like figure in Adagio, large span required. M-D.

Burnet C. Tuthill. *Sonata* Op.20 (ST 1966) 24pp., parts. Allegro giocoso: SA; sixteenth-note figuration; Un poco tranquillo contrasting section has rocking quality and becomes more rhythmic; centers around c with a key signature of two flats. Andante, un poco adagio: highly romantic, cantabile. Presto molto vivace: 6/8, long arpeggi-like lines in piano, trills, chordal punctuation, Prestissimo closing. M-D.

Alec Wilder. *Sonata* (Sam Fox W110 1970) 23pp., parts. 11½ min. I: moving lines; freely tonal; changing meters; moves to a *pp* closing but final note is subito *ff*. II: chromatic chords, waltz-like. III: triplets frequent; syncopation in piano; thin textures mixed with chords. IV: piano part more chordal while the sax is melodically oriented; large span required. Neoclassic. M-D.

Duos for Piano(s) and Miscellaneous Instruments
Audience, Baritone Horn, Euphonium, Guitar, Harmonica, Harp, Metronome, Ondes Martenot, Organ, Percussion, Unspecified

William Ames. *Guernica* (ACA). For piano and cymbal.

Paul Arma. *Deux Resonances* (Lemoine 1974) 25pp., parts. 12 min. For percussion (one player) and piano. I: serial; piano begins clangorously; clusters; very little melodic emphasis. II: impetuous skips plus chordal punctuation dominate this piece; clusters appear near conclusion. A tour de force for the percussionist. M-D.

James Beale. *Pisces Ascending* (ACA). For piano and percussion.

William Bolcom. *Frescoes* (EBM 1975) 32pp. For 2 pianos, harmonium, and harpsichord. Two performers. Each player has a piano; one also has a harmonium, the other a harpsichord. Wildly bombastic music; amazing handling of the four instruments. Bolcom draws on the *Book of Revelation, Paradise Lost,* and the *Aeneid* for visions of death, destruction, and apocalyptic war. Reminders of old battle-pieces and rags are interspersed. In 2 parts: 1. War in Heaven, 2. The Caves of Orcus. D.

Carlos Cruz de Castro. *Llamalo como quieras* (Editorial de Música Española Contemporánea 1974) 11pp. For piano and metronome. Includes performance instructions in Spanish, English, and French.

Anton Diabelli. *Sonatina* Op.68 (K. Scheit—OBV 1951) 7pp., parts. For guitar and piano. Andante sostenuto; Rondo—Allegro ma non troppo.

Pianist must generally keep the dynamics down. Subtleties of the work must be followed. Int. to M-D.

François Dupin. *Myriades* (Leduc 1973) 27pp., parts. 10 min. For percussion and piano. Five pitches (timbales) are required for percussion. Lent: intense introduction, freely tonal, varied rhythmic figuration. Vif: shifting meters, chordal, repeated notes, chromatic runs, glissando two-hand clusters, octave and chords in alternating hands. Lent: free, recitative-like. Vif: ostinato bass, chordal punctuation, waltz-like, bitonal, two linear lines, feverish finish. M-D.

Harold Farberman. *Variations for Percussion with Piano* (BB 1960) 8pp., parts. 5 min. Contemporary Composers Study Score Series, No.17. Percussion required: cymbal, tam tam, timpani, snare drum, tambourine, triangle, glockenspiel, xylophone, 2 bongos, tom-tom, wood blocks, antique cymbal, bass drum, sleigh bells, congo drum. If three or four players are used, there are extra possibilities. Clusters; martial character to theme. Evolves through a waltz, glissandi, repeated chords, syncopated clusters. M-D.

Harald Genzmer. *Concerto* (CFP 8349 1976) 45pp., parts. For piano and percussion. 21 min.

Vinko Globokar. *Drama* 1971 (Litolff 1975) 17 leaves. 2 copies necessary for performance. For piano and percussion. Explanations in French, German, and English. Notes in the score are in German only. Each performer is equipped with microphones, a ring modulator, and amplifiers. Seven scenes, may be played in any successive order. Chance composition, avant-garde. D.

Jan de Graaf. *Three Pieces* (Molenaar 1974) 8pp., parts. For percussion and piano.

Juan Hidalgo. *Milan Piano* (Editorial de Música Española Contemporánea 1974) 15pp. For piano and any kind of instruments or objects with which one can produce undetermined sounds. Avant-garde. M-D.

Alan Hovhaness. *Seven Greek Folk Dances* Op.150 (CFP) 7 min. For harmonica and piano.

Warner Hutchinson. *Sonatina* (CF N4356 1966) 12pp., parts. 8 min. For baritone horn or trombone and piano...Moderately fast; Slowly; March style. Freely tonal, first movement requires a good left hand octave technique. Slowly: colorful, tempo changes add interest. Attractive and flexible writing. M-D.

Marcel Jorand and François Dupin. *Sept Pièces* (Leduc 1974) Book I: I. Pata-Caisse, II. Drôlerie (for snare drum and bass drum). Book 2: III. Ta-ras-tata, IV. Danse (for 2 cymbals, 1 suspended cymbal, triangle, snare and bass drum, tambourine). Book 3: V. Rapsodie, VI. La petite écossaise (for all percussion already listed plus timpani with pedals and kettledrum). Book 4: VII. Variétés (for all percussion already listed plus woodblock, vibraphone, xylophone, 2 tom toms, glockenspiel). Each book is more difficult than the last. All the piano writing is mildly contemporary and helps display the percussion instruments. Large span required in Book 4. M-D.

Mauricio Kagel. *Unguis Incarnatus Est* (UE 15621 1972) 7pp. For piano and . . . (the choice of the second instrument is free). Based on a phrase from Franz Liszt's "Nuages Gris" (1881). Range of the second instrument is listed. Contains directions for the performers. Piano part is either a single line (Liszt melody) or chords based on the melody, or tremolo octaves. Silence is pedalled. Sudden dynamic changes; Pianist must scream "Liszt" *fff* at conclusion. Avant-garde. Requires large span. M-D.

Robert Kelly. *Diacoustics* Op.48 (ACA). For piano and percussion.

Ellis B. Kohs. *Sonata* (M. M. Cole Publishing Co.) 5½ min. For snare drum and piano.

David Lumsdaine. *Kangaroo Hunt* 1971 (UE 29017A) 2 separate sheets, 1 for each player. For piano and percussion. Percussion required: 2 maracas, 2 bongos, 2 hi hat cymbals, vibraphone, xylophone, bells, glockenspiel, pitched instruments ad lib. Includes directions for performance. A mobile work with the performers choosing from nine "blocks" of materials. Pointillistic, widely spread chords, repeated notes, glissando on strings, extreme ranges. Avant-garde, aleatoric. D.

Gilberto Mendes. *Blirium C9* 1965 (Ric Brazil) 7 sheets including one page of musical series. For one, two, or three keyboard instruments: one organ, three pianos, harpsichord and accordion, etc. Or, for three, four, or five different instruments of the same family. Detailed instructions are given for the melodic plan or tessitura—pitch variations. Transitions between groups of notes, aleatoric. Instructions for fragmentation and mounting of the quotations. No two performances ever the same. Avant-garde. D.

Ignaz Moscheles and Mauro Giuliani. *Grande Duo Concertante* Op.20 1814 (S. Behrend—Simrock Elite Ed. 2709 1973) 68pp., parts. Moscheles added the piano accompaniment to Giuliani's guitar part. Allegro maestoso; Scherzo; Largo; Pastorale. This is the most elaborate work of this combination composed during the first half of the nineteenth century. Written by two outstanding virtuosi, the piano part is a charming catalogue of Moscheles's style and idioms; consists of glittering runs, octaves, and generally facile writing throughout. This edition, when compared with the first edition, contains numerous errors (197 in the guitar part and 41 in the piano part). M-D.

Marlos Nobre. *Variações Rítmicas* Op.15 1963 (Tonos) 14 min. For piano and percussion.

———— *Sonancias* Op.37 1972 (Tonos) 12 min. For piano and percussion.

Tadeusz Paciorkiewicz. *Duet Concertante* (AA 1974) 43pp., 2 scores needed for performance. For piano and organ. General registration suggestions for the organ are listed. I. Comodo: melody in octaves, freely tonal, secco style, glissandi; requires fine octave technique. II. Largo quieto: imitative, chromatic undulating lines, *ppp* closing. III. Giocoso e scherzando: moving harmonies around pedal point, left-hand octave punctuation, many harmonic seconds used in figuration. IV. Adagio deciso: melody in octaves, secco style with expanding and contrasting figures, brilliant passage work (in octaves ad lib) at conclusion. M-D to D.

Flor Peeters. *Concerto for Organ and Piano* Op.74 (HWG 1958) 58pp., 2 scores necessary for performance. Introduzione ed Allegro: forceful octaves; triplet figures lead directly to the Allegro (SA), which contains much octotonic writing; freely tonal around e; chords interspersed with figuration; recapitulation approached by a glissando; movement ends in a blaze of tremolo full chords in upper register. Arioso: ABA; rolled seventh and ninth chords in piano while organ has modal melody; second idea more chromatic; when A returns, piano has melody and organ the chords. Cadenza e Finale: chordal punctuation; trills in upper register; toccata figuration begins at the Allegro vivo e fermo; Andantino section uses rich harmonies; toccata figuration returns; brilliant scales and chords end movement. The success of this work (and any work in this combination) depends in part on the ability of the performers to allow for the time it takes the organ to "speak." The piano responds faster in most cases, and this ensemble problem can only be solved by familiarity with the room and the instruments involved. M-D.

Nicole Philiba. *Recit* 1973 (EMT) 16pp., parts. 7 min. For ondes martenot and piano. Sectionalized, varied tempi and moods, low register exploited, freely tonal, arch form, *pppp* closing. M-D.

Boris Pillin. *Duo* (WIM 1971). For percussion and piano. Allegro: SA except that the recapitulation and development are combined; two themes, both of which recur in various transformations in the second and third movements. Andante: roughly an arch form, i.e., it consists of several short sections which are recapitulated in (approximately) reverse order; general character of the movement is a gradual coalescence, out of sparse fragments, into a long-lined theme, followed by a return to fragmentation. Maestoso–Allegretto risoluto: overall AA' form with coda; ironic and scherzo-like in character; at end of coda there is a return to material from beginning of the first movement. Primitivistic style, depending more upon rhythmic momentum and ostinato repetition than sophisticated material development. Dissonant but freely tonal; frequently uses clusters coloristically. M-D.

Marta Ptaszynska. *Little Mexican Phantasy* (PWM 1974) 10pp., parts. Percussion required: xylophone, 2 campanelli, 3 tom toms, snare drum, triangle, small drum, suspended cymbal. M-D.

Sam Raphling. *Suite for Solo Percussion and Piano* 1968 (Bourne). In two parts, published separately. I: 1. Tambourine, 2. Wood Blocks, 3. Cymbals, 4. Castanets; Encore: Toccata (solo utilizing 4 instruments). II: 5. Triangle, 6. Bass Drum, 7. Temple Blocks, 8. Snare Drum; Encore: Theme and Variations (solo utilizing 8 instruments). Freely tonal style liberally laced with dissonance. Effective ensemble writing. M-D.

Edwin Roxburgh. *Dithyramb II* (UMP). For percussion and piano.

Carlos Salzedo. *Sonata* 1922 (SPAM) 37pp., 2 copies necessary for performance. For harp and piano. In one movement: Luminous–Lento subito–langorously–Lento. Highly chromatic, tremolos, trills, Impressionistic coloring throughout. Unusual combination produces some unusual sonorities. D.

Claudio Santoro. *Diagrammas Ciclicos* 1966 (Tonos 1971). For percussion and piano. 2 scores. Pianist has to play inside the piano. Clusters, improvisation, avant-garde. D.

Dieter Schnebel. *Abfälle I: Reactions* (Schott 1971). 7pp. 8 min. Concerto for one instrumentalist (piano) and audience, or instrumental group. Chance composition.

———— *Modelle* (Schott 1974) 4pp. of explanations in German and English, 13pp. on 6 folded loose leaves. For one pianist and audience. This is a worked-out version of the above *Abfälle I: Reactions.*

Karlheinz Stockhausen. *Mantra* 1970 (Stockhausen Verlag) 59pp. For 2 pianos, each with cymbals, wood blocks, and electronic modulators built to the composer's specifications (operated by the pianists). Includes prefatory notes and instructions for performance in German, English, and French. Avant-garde. D.

Koji Takeuchi. *Five Improvisations* 1965 (UE 14275) 19pp., parts. For piano and vibraphone. Allegro moderato; Andante; Vivace; Moderato; Presto, ma non troppo. Serial, atonal, contrasting, pointillistic, clusters. M-D.

Geoffrey Tomlinson. *Concourse* (Bo&H 1973). For percussion and piano.

Joaquin Turina. *Ciclo Plateresco—Tema y Variaciones* Op.100 (UME 1947) 17pp., 2 copies necessary for performance. For harp and piano. Lento introduction leads directly into the Theme (Andante). Three variations and a Majestuoso closing. Colorful and seductive sonorities that seethe with Spanish dance rhythms and cantando melodies. The two instruments complement each other. M-D.

Donald H. White. *Lyric Suite* (GS). For euphonium and piano. Four movements, supplied in both bass and treble clefs. Piano part is well written but difficult; preference for intervals of a second and a fourth. Well laid-out with a good sense of climax and rhythmic drive. D.

Henri Zagwyn. *Mystère* 1942 (Donemus) 17pp., 2 copies required. For harp and piano. In two parts. I: Prélude; Evocation; Sabbat infernale. II: Intermède; Invocation; Apotheose. A chromatic and colorful style requiring fine pianistic ability. M-D.
———— *Van de Jaargetijden* 1945 (Donemus) 23pp., 2 copies required. For harp and piano. Zomer; Herfst; Winter; Lente. Same style as described above. D.

Duos for Piano, Another Instrument, and Tape

Gilius van Bergeijk. *Sonate* (Donemus). For English horn, piano, and tape.

Lukas Foss. *Ni Bruit Ni Vitesse* (Sal 1972) 22pp. For piano, one percussionist, and tape recorder. Requires 1 grand piano, 2 cowbells, 2 Japanese bowls, 2 triangle beaters, 1 tape recorder, loudspeakers on stage. Tape can be rented from the publisher or the two performers can make their own tape. Score contains all the necessary instructions. The pianist plays inside the piano. There are 21 short sections all timed to the second with extensive performance directions. Some highly unusual sonorities. Avant-garde. D.

Werner Heider. *Kunst-Stoff* (CFP 1973). For amplified clarinet, prepared piano, and stereo twin-track tape. $13\frac{1}{2}$ min. A separate score is necessary for each performer. The tape recorder can be operated by the pianist. Includes notes for performance and an explanation of symbols and abbreviations in English and German. In part, graphic notation. Reproduction of the composer's original MS. Avant-garde. D.

Lejaren Hiller. *Machine Music* 1964 (TP). For piano, percussion, and two-channel tape recorder. 28pp., 3 scores necessary for performance. 11 min. Tape available on rental only from publisher. Large complement of percussion required. Includes a suggested stage plan. Eleven movements: 1. First Trio (piano, percussion, and tape); 2. First Solo (piano); 3. First Duo (tape and percussion); 4. Second Solo (piano); 5. Third Solo (tape); 6. Second Duo (percussion and piano); 7. Fourth Solo (tape); 8. Fifth Solo (percussion); 9. Fifth Solo (percussion); 10. Sixth Solo (percussion); 11. Second Trio (piano, percussion, and tape). Contains extensive notes for use of the tape recorder. Some possible performance variations and additions include: the pianist (if (s)he desires) may blow up a balloon during the Fourth Solo and explode it precisely on the downbeat of the Fifth Solo. The pianist, rather than the percussionist, may run around the piano with the roller toy in the Second Trio, etc. Large clangorous chords, pointillistic treatment, extreme registers exploited, clusters, long pedal effects. Generally fun to perform. Avant-garde. Large span required. D.

Dieter Schoenbach. *Canzona da Sonar* III (Moeck 1971). For soprano recorder, piano, and tape. 17pp., parts.

Elliott Schwartz. *Music for Napoleon and Beethoven* (on their 200th Birthdays) 1969 (Bowdoin). For piano, trumpet, two tapes, and assistant. 3 scores needed for performance. 11pp. Each system is equal to 15 seconds; notation is proportional within that context. Notes in boxes indicate play material rapidly, any order, repeated as you wish for duration of box. Fill up box entirely with sound, i.e., no silences. Pianist has clusters, plucked and muted strings; needs two drumsticks; must "prepare" certain indicated pitches; uses erasers, thick screws, tobacco pouches, clips, coins, pencils, etc.; extensive tape directions. Pointillistic, sudden dynamic changes, full chords. Pianist intones certain sounds ("ah," creates melisma on any sung pitch); stamps foot; snaps fingers; clasps hands. Two-handed glissandi, chromatic scales, contrary motion. Includes fragment of Beethoven to be played *ppp*. Trumpeter also has to speak; fades to silence. Avant-garde. D.

Music for Three Instruments

Trios for Piano, Violin, and Cello

Karl Friedrich Abel. *Six Sonatas* Op.5 (Reprint of the London edition: R. Bremmer 1764) in 2 vols. For violin, cello, and harpsichord (piano). Nos.4 and 5 available from CFP. The slow movements are more weighty than many other slow movements from this time. Details of articulation, dynamics, and ornamentation show a definite polish. Keyboard parts range from Int. to M-D.

Jean Absil. *Trio* Op.7 1931 (CeBeDeM 1962) 43pp., parts. 30 min. Allegro energico; Nocturne; Intermezzo; Final. Bold pianistic gestures, chromatic, subtle sonorities in Nocturne, French influence. Requires facile octave technique. D.

Samuel Adler. *Trio* 1964 (OUP) 45pp., parts. 14½ min. Allegro con fuoco: rhythmic chromatic theme, changing meters, hemiola, flowing figuration, clear lines. Largo: the opening section consists of two contrasting ideas juxtaposed—broken chordal sustained low harmonies and sprightly short motif in upper register—main idea is longer and treated two octaves apart in piano; *pp* closing. Allegro ma non troppo: syncopated opening motif, imitation. The whole work is built on neoclassic lines and is freely tonal. Rhythmic vigor, flow of melodic ideas, and clarity of texture make this a distinctive work. M-D.

Karl Ahrendt. *Trio* 1972 (MS available from composer: 5 Old Peach Ridge Road, Athens, OH 45701) 31pp., parts. Allegro deciso e dramatico; Adagio; Allegro. Some aleatoric procedure with given glissando figures, bell-like sonorities, large gestures for piano in particular. Mildly contemporary. Clearly focused writing in all parts. D.

Tomaso Albinoni. *Tre Sonate* Op.6/4, 5, 7 (W. Reinhart—Hug 1959). Each sonata is a unique piece in itself and contrasts with the others. M-D.

Alexander A. Aliabev. *Trio* E♭ 1817 (USSR 1952) 37pp., parts. Unfinished. Attractive writing in post-Mozart style. It is possible that Aliabev studied with John Field when Field was in Moscow. Allegro moderato: SA; opening idea shows Aliabev's indebtedness to John Field; development moves through numerous keys, ending in E; a chromatic slide-slip returns to E♭ Cantabile style; movement is complete by itself and would make a delightful program opener. No evidence has been presented to contradict the possibility that Aliabev may have intended it to be only a one-movement work. M-D.

See: Carol A. Green, "Style in the Instrumental Chamber Music of Alexander A. Aliabev," thesis, Indiana University, 1969, 72pp.

David Amram. *Dirge and Variations* 1962 (CFP) 14 min. Tonal, skillfully conceived for each instrument. Quiet opening, full presentation of the extended Dirge, upper timbres explored in one variation for all instruments. Despite its title, there is much bright sound and motion. Fluent and natural lyric writing. M-D.

Volkmar Andreae. *Trio* Op. 1 f (Schott 1901) 43pp., parts. Displays youthful sincerity and Romantic charm. Liszt and Wagner influence is strong. Three contrasting movements that were considered very modern when they appeared at the turn of the century. M-D.

Hendrik Andriessen. *Piano Trio* (Donemus 1939) 20 min. Fully exploits the possibilities this combination offers. Written in a very personal style. Mainly mildly contemporary with the exception of some polytonal usage. M-D.

Violet Archer. *Trio* II 1956 (CMC) 50pp., parts. Allegro; Largo tranquillo; Allegro con brio, energico. Thin textures, thoroughly contemporary treatment of all instruments. D.

Anton Arensky. *Trio I* Op. 32 d 1894 (CFP 4315; USSR 1971: Augener; K; IMC) 51pp., parts. 29 min. Four movements that foreshadow Rachmaninoff's style, especially the subject of the last movement. Striking features include the arresting main theme of the first movement and the Scherzo with its fast scales in the piano part. Cyclic thematic material. M-D.

———— *Trio II* Op.73 f (USSR; Bosworth) 56pp., parts. Allegro moderato; Romance—Andante; Scherzo; Tema con (6) Variazioni. More characteristic of Arensky's mature style, but Schumann's spirit seems to hover over the first movement. The Romance also seems to come from the same origin that inspired Schumann's piano *Romances*. The Scherzo is a waltz in both tempo and style. Waltz influence is also seen in the third and fifth variations of the finale. M-D.

Isabel Aretz. *Trio* 1965 (IU) 28pp., parts. Andante: complex metric treatment, pointillistic, serial, barless. Theme and Variations: seven variations, thorny. Allegretto: toccata-like in places. Final: bar lines, very advanced and difficult writing in a strongly dissonant style. Linear conception. D.

Richard Arnell. *Trio* Op.47 (Hin). Essentially diatonic writing but interlaced with contemporary idioms. Pure melodic writing comes through in all parts. Music is effectively written and well laid-out for the medium. M-D.

Malcolm Arnold. *Trio* Op.54 (Paterson 2714). Basically diatonic style coupled with touches of humor and a direct simplicity. There is both a light and a serious quality about this piece. Transparent textures and clever handling of the piano part add to its attractiveness. Strong propulsive quality. M-D.

Claude Arrieu. *Trio* (Amphion 1958) 53pp., parts. Moderato; Lento; Scherzo; Toccata. Neoclassic style infused with seriousness of purpose and facile handling of all three instruments. The Lento especially has some beautiful sonorities. M-D.

Arno Babadjanian. *Piano Trio* f♯ 1952 (USSR) 36pp., parts. Largo–Allegro espressivo; Andante; Allegro vivace. Contains much Romantic excitement and dramatic pathos, sweeping lines, very colorful, Rachmaninoff influence but original idiom. Folksong tradition of Armenia, composer's native country, is also present. D.

Andre Babayev. *Trio* (USSR).

Victor Babin. *Trio* (Augener 1956) 56pp., parts. Largo; Allegro ritmico e ben accentuato. Well written throughout, especially the piano part. Mainly in a diatonic style with some mildly contemporary sonorities. M-D.

Carl Philipp Emanuel Bach. *Sonata* W.90/3 C 1776–7 (Oberdörffer—HM 46) 20pp., parts. This is a model for Haydn's Piano Trios. The piano part is completely emancipated from the strings. Allegro di molto: SA; piano part by far the most interesting, with runs, skips, and chords. Larghetto: A, second half moves to a, cadences on dominant of C. Allegretto: piano and violin are in duet much of the time; after much activity the movements ends in a *pp* whisper. M-D.

———— *Three Trios* Op.2 (Schmid—Br 305). Attractive if a little "cool" writing. Second ideas are often more appealing than the first. Keyboard part is completely involved. M-D.

Johann Christian Bach. *Trio* D (Riemann—IMC).
———— *Two Trios* A, C (Möseler). Charming and technically interesting. Clear homophonic textures with little or no imitation. Int. to M-D.

Johann Christoph Friedrich Bach. *Sonata* C (F. Oberdörffer—HM 46). Cello ad lib. Allegro di molto; Larghetto: Allegretto. Belongs to the same genre as the piano trios of Haydn, which developed later. In this sonata the strings are only supplementary to the keyboard part, which is far more interesting, even if their participation does lend variety and a characteristic note to the sonority. M-D.
———— *Sonata* D (H. Ruf—Nag 192) 27pp., parts. Cello part ad lib. Allegro con spirito: much sixteenth-note figuration. Andante: elegant binary movement. Rondo Scherzo: delightful, invigorating. Charming and sometimes rather delicate writing. M-D.
———— *Trio Sonata* (Frotscher—Sikorski). Cello ad lib.

Henk Badings. *Trio I* 1934 (Schott 3169) 31pp., parts. 20 min. Allegro; Adagio; Scherzo; Allegro vivace. Broadly conceived melodies developed contrapuntally. Serious, almost tragic overtones permeate this work, especially the Adagio. Badings is a Romantic modern who continues the Brahms–Reger–Hindemith line. Polytonal writing a favorite harmonic device. Large span required. M-D to D.

Esther W. Ballou. *Trio* 1955 (CFE) 40pp., parts. Allegro con brio; Andante con moto; Allegro. Freely tonal, octotonic, changing meters, effective texture and dynamic contrasts within movements, bold figurative gestures, neoclassic. Dissonant counterpoint creates strongly independent lines. D.

Josef Bartoš. *Piano Trio* (Hudební Matice 1947) 31pp., parts. One movement. ABA, chromatic, fast harmonic rhythm, varied pianistic idioms, contrasting più tranquillo mid-section with Allegro appassionato outer sections. M-D.

Arnold Bax. *Trio* B♭ (Chappell 1946) 41pp., parts. 22 min. Allegro con brio; Adagio; Tempo moderato e molto ritmico. Shows a mastery and grasp of this combination in Bax's Romantic style. Subtle sense of beauty. M-D.

Mrs. H. H. A. Beach. *Trio* Op.150 (Composers Press 1939) 41pp., parts. 15 min. Allegro con brio; Lento espressivo–Presto; Allegro. Finely adjusted sonorities make for an ideal balance in this work. The piano is not overly loaded and forms the binding partnership that is necessary for successful trio writing. The work might be considered overly sweet by today's standards but it is sincere writing by one of America's most outstanding women composers. It is well worth reviving. M-D.

James Beale. *Trio* Op.5 1947 (CFE) 55pp., parts. Reproduction of the MS. Adagio–Allegro–Adagio–Allegro; Allegro; Lento. A large-scale work that integrates the three instruments in a most efficient manner. Neoclassic style provides the framework. The piano is called upon to utilize most of the keyboard; arpeggi figuration. The composer makes suggestions in a preface concerning tempi in the Lento movement. Score is easy to read. Large span required. M-D.

Ludwig van Beethoven. *Piano Trios* (E. Planten—Henle) Vol.I: Op.1/1, 2, 3; Op.11. Vol.II: Op.70/1, 2; Op.97; Op.121. Vol.III: (contains the less-known compositions): Op.44Eb; WoO37 G for piano, flute, and bassoon; WoO38Eb; WoO39 Bb; Op.38 Eb for piano, clarinet (violin), and cello (Beethoven's own arrangement of *Septet* Op.20); and Hess-Verzeichnis 48 Eb. This last-named trio movement is an integral work in itself found in a sketch book of Beethoven's containing compositional sketches between 1784 and 1800. Beethoven did not specify the violin or the cello (but did specify the piano) in this movement, but he probably had them in mind. All sources in this edition were carefully checked. Practical and scholarly edition.

———*Thirteen Trios* (CFP) Vol.I: Op.1/1, 2, 3; Op.11; Op.70/1, 2. Vol.II: Op.44; Op.97; Op.121a "Kakadu" Variations; Op. posth. *Trios* in Bb and Eb. Vol.III: Op.36 after *Symphony* II; Op.38 after *Septet*. Lea has same volumes in study scores.

——— *Six Celebrated Trios* (IMC). Op.1/1, 3; Op.11; Op.70/1, Op.97; Op.121a.

——— Available separately: *Trio* Op.1/1 Eb (Br&H; Adamowski—GS L1421; Augener 7250a). *Trio* Op.1/2 G (Br&H; Adamowski—GS L1422; Augener 7250b); *Trio* Op.1/3 c (Br&H; Adamowski—GS L1423; Augener 7250c); *Trio* Op.11 Bb (Br&H; Adamowski—GS L1424; Augener 7250d; IMC; CFP 7064). *Trio* Op.70/1 D (Br&H; Adamowski—GS L1425; Augener 7250e). The first movement is lively and outstanding for great clarity in the treatment of the three instruments. The second movement has a remarkable piano part with trills and runs but does not overbalance the strings. The third movement suggests a humorous folksong. *Trio* Op.70/2 (Br&H; Adamowski—GS L1426; Augener 7250f). A cheerful piece throughout with a set of variations for the second movement that display advances over earlier examples of this form. *Trio* Op.97 Bb "Archduke" (Br&H; Adamowski—GS L1427; Augener 7250g). This symphonically conceived work makes great demands on both players and instruments. The first two movements are especially notable for their clarity, the scherzo in particular. The last two movements are a revelation of technical and expressive power. *Trio* Op.121a (Br&H) 10 Variations on "Ich bin der Schneider Kakadu." *Trio* Op.38 (IMC) arranged by the composer from the *Septet* Op.20. It should be remembered that Beethoven made his debut as a composer with the three Piano Trios Op.1, published in 1795. The Op.70 and the "Archduke" *Trio* Op.97 represent Beethoven's mature works in this form. Much territory is covered between Op.1 and Op.97 and the form must have been a favorite with the composer.

———— *Two Trios* Op. posth. Bb, Eb (Augener 7250h).

———— *Allegretto* Eb ca.1783 (Werner—Elkin 1955).

———— *Rondo* D (Werner—Chappell).

See: Elfrieda F. Hiebert, "The Piano Trios of Beethoven: An Historical and Analytical Study," Ph.D. diss., University of Wisconsin, 1970.

Peter Benary. *Trio* (Möseler 1974) 15pp., parts. Hausmusic No.113. Adagio; Più mosso, molto agitato; Grazioso, non troppo allegro; Adagio. Free serial style, great variety of pianistic figuration, intense. M-D to D.

William Sterndale Bennett. *Piano and Chamber Music* (G. Bush—St&B 1972) Musica Britannica Vol.37. Introduction, facsimilies, 23pp.; commentary, 5pp. Includes *Chamber Trio* Op.26 of 1839, which is probably the finest work in the collection. It is slender but graceful. The second movement, a Serenade, provides pizzicato for both strings throughout while the piano supplies flowing lines in contrast. The entire work has many Mendelssohn characteristics. It is not known if this edition has separate parts. M-D.

Franz Berwald. *Trio* I Eb 1849 (GM) 33pp., parts. Introduction—Allegro con brio; Andante grazioso; Finale. M-D.

———— *Trio* II f 1851 (GM) 41pp., parts. Introduzioni—Allegro molto; Larghetto; Scherzo. Conceived as one extensive movement. M-D.

———— *Trio* III d 1851 (GM) 45pp., parts. Allegro con molto; Adagio quasi largo; Finale. One extensive movement. M-D.

———— *Trio* IV C (GM). M-D.

Solid classical writing in all four trios with Romantic characteristics appearing more frequenlty in the later works.

Philip Bezanson. *Trio* (CFE).

Boris Blacher. *Trio* (Belaieff 1973) 27pp., parts. Short rhythmic motifs, structurally integrated, thoroughly contemporary style, variable meters, economy of texture, wiry, individual style. D.

Christopher Bochmann. *De Profundis—Meditation for Violin, Cello and Piano* 1970 (OUP) 14pp., parts. 6½ min. "The work takes its title from the opening of Psalm 130: 'Out of the deep have I called unto thee, O Lord: Lord, hear my voice' " (from composer's note). The work is an interaction of four separate arc forms: the minor thirds in harmonics that mark the divisions between the four main sections form one of these arcs, the first and fourth main sections together form another, and the second and third each another. All thematic material is derived more or less closely from a pattern of seven notes and its combinations with itself. The title purposely avoids the designation "piano trio" because the way in which the instruments are used seems to be insufficiently close to that of the piano trio literature: here the violin and cello are treated nearly as one instrument in contrast to—almost in opposition to—the piano. Serial, proportional notation, dynamic extremes, changing meters, chords in tremolo, pointillistic, avant-garde. Large span required. D.

Leon Boëllmann. *Trio* Op.19 (Hamelle) 64pp., parts. An unusual form is used in this work: the first section comprises the introduction, allegro, and andante; the second combines the scherzo and finale. Modal and Romantic harmonic characteristics. M-D.

René de Boisdeffre. *Trio II* Op.32 (Hamelle 1882) 45pp., parts. Prelude—andante maestoso; Scherzo; Andante (with a grandiloquent conclusion); Finale—allegro energico (rondo form). Boisdeffre wrote mainly chamber music. This piece is well written along traditional lines for all instruments. M-D.

Joseph Bodin de Boismortier. *Trio* Op.50/6 D 1734 (P. Ruyssen—Nag 143) 11pp., parts. Largo; Allegro; Larghetto; Allegro. Tuneful, technically simple, reflects the popular lighthearted and charming taste of the day. Tasteful keyboard realization. Int.

Siegfrid Borris. *Trio* Op.90/1 (Sirius).

Johannes Brahms. *Trios* (E. Herttrich—Henle 1972) 212pp., parts. Piano fingering added by H.-M. Theopold. Contains Op.8b (includes first and second versions with textual comparisons collated); Op.87 C; Op.101 c.
——— Op.9, first version (CFP; Br&H; GS; IMC). This early work already displays Brahms's consummate mastery of balance between the piano and strings. A complete revision took place in 1889, and this new version is the one usually heard. Shows slight influence of Schumann and Mendelssohn but displays supreme mastery of the chamber music idiom. A rich thematic, harmonic, and rhythmic substance is apparent from the broad opening

lyrical theme. Crisp cross-rhythms come across in the Scherzo. This is the most Romantic of the first three trios.

——— *Trio* Op.40 E♭ (Br&H; CFP 3899b; K; IMC; Augener 5117; EPS 249). For piano, violin, and horn or viola or cello. First movement is in ABABA rondo form. Similar themes quoted in third and fourth movements as a unifying device. D.

——— *Trio* Op.87 C (Br&H; CFP 3899C; GS L1768; Augener 9301; IMC). One of the great works in this form; full of inspiration; has perhaps the broadest appeal. Strong thematic relationship between the first (a good-humored, busy SA) and last movements. The separation of theme and development becomes less clear, especially in the opening of this work. Frequently the strings combine for vigorous chords alternating and contrasting with chords on the piano. The second movement is a set of variations on a melody of a vaguely Hungarian or gypsy character. The Presto section of the Scherzo is built on a large sweeping melodic arc. D.

——— *Trio* Op.101 c (Br&H; CFP 3899D, Adamowski—GS L1510; IMC). In the intense and dramatic first movement, all exposition material is contained in bar one. The nobility of the thematic material and the superlative manner in which it is developed are perfection exemplified. The second movement is light and delicate with an almost ghostly quality to it. The third movement, with its multiple rhythms, is mainly a dialogue between strings and piano. This is the greatest of the first three trios. D.

——— *Trio* Op.114 a (Br&H; CFP 3899E; K; IMC; EPS 250). For clarinet or violin or viola, cello, and piano. Strong thematic relationships between the first and last movements. The third movement is in ABACA rondo form. D.

——— *Trio* A (Bücken, Haase—Br&H).
The trio for piano, violin, and cello reached its full bloom with Brahms.

Cesar Bresgen. *Trio* 1972 (Dob 07217) 20pp., parts. Two short movements with chromatic harmonies and enormous rhythmic drive. The second movement makes much out of the interval of the fourth. Throughout there are continual changes of mood and tempo as well as of rhythm. Astringent dissonances abound, similar to middle-period Bartók. Piano textures are carefully handled. Ensemble will require much thought. D.

Tomás Bretón. *Four Spanish Pieces* (ESC). Also published separately. 1. Dance Orientale, 2. Boléro, 3. Polo Gitano, 4. Scherzo Andalou. These effective display pieces were very popular in the early part of this century but their brilliance has somewhat faded. M-D.

Frank Bridge. *Phantasie Trio I* (Augener 1908) 31pp., parts. The form corresponds to an SA design with an andante replacing the usual development and a scherzo providing a contrasting mid-section to the andante. Abrupt ending. Main ideas treated in a broad, dignified manner. There are few ensemble problems in this well-crafted and highly Romantic work. M-D.

———— *Trio II* (Augener 1930) 75pp., parts. Allegretto ben moderato; Molto allegro; Andante molto moderato–Allegro ma non troppo. Post-Romantic writing of a high order. A catalogue of pianistic clichés and idioms in this style. D.

Earle Brown. *Music for Violin, Cello and Piano* 1952 (UE 15443 1972) 7pp., parts. Explanations in English and German. One movement. Short, highly contrasted dynamics (serialized?), dissonant pointillism, post-Webernesque technique. Bar lines only indicate points at which all three parts have the same number of sixteenth-note units, for ensemble synchronization. The general conception of the work is of a kind of spontaneous "pulseless" energy. In rehearsing this piece it is more important to develop a sense of the time values of the durations and figurations at the various tempi than it is to count the rhythm in the usual way. Dynamic marks are attached to most notes. D.

Max Bruch. *Trio* Op.5 c 1857 (Br&H; Hamelle) 39pp., parts. Andante molto cantabile: broadly laid out and attractive. Allegro assai: same serious mood as the Andante. Presto: fiery, opening melody of the first movement returns in a short Andante section before the clangorous Prestissimo ending. Modeled on classical lines. M-D.

Willy Burkhard. *Trio* Op.43 (Br 2093) 20pp., parts. One movement. Extended, free design. A subtle rhythmic pulse is combined with a linear style. M-D.

Adolf Busch. *Trio* Op.15 a (Simrock 1920). Reger's influence shows through but the writing is distinguished in many ways, in spite of its lack of motion and polyphony. The work gains by Busch's intimate knowledge of ensemble music. D.

Alan Bush. *Three Concert Studies* Op.31 1947 (Nov) 18 min. Sturdy pieces, vitality of No.1 and inventiveness of No.3 (in use of harmonics and rhythmic expertise) are of special interest. Impressive, inventive, original,

Dietrich Buxtehude. *Trio Sonata* Op.1/1 F (B. Grusnick. A. Wenzinger—Br 1151; Peyrot, Rebuffat—Senart 2721) 15pp., parts. M-D.

———— *Trio Sonata* Op.1/2 G (Br 1152, 12pp., parts; Senart 2918). M-D.

———— *Trio Sonata* Op.1/3 a (Br 1153; Schott). M-D.

_____ *Trio Sonata* Op. 1/4 B♭ (Br 1154). M-D.

_____ *Trio Sonata* Op. 1/7 e (K&S; IMC) 15pp., parts. Allegro; Presto; Poco presto; Prestissimo. M-D.

_____ *Trio Sonata* Op. 2/2 D (Br&H; K&S; IMC). M-D.

_____ *Trio Sonata* Op. 2/6 E (Nag; IMC). M-D.

_____ *Trio Sonata* D (Döbereiner—Br&H). M-D.

_____ *Sonata à Trois* (Crussard—Foetisch). M-D.

These works have an average of five to eight contrasting movements with the outer movements normally fast. The slow movements are usually short and transitional. For a more thorough discussion of these pieces see SBE, 250–54.

Charles Camilleri. *Trio* (Fairfield 1975) 60pp., parts. 23 min. Libero: serial movement; violin and cello open and are followed by piano in a Recitative section; all instruments come together in an Andante Sostenuto (calmo) section that works through the opening material. Allegro vivace: much rhythmic drive in all instruments. Lento: Impressionistic sonorities with piano having a highly elaborate right-hand figuration. Allegro molto vivace: triplet figuration in all instruments leads to dramatically punctuated chromatic chords; these ideas continue to the second part of the movement, where we are told that "tempo is left to the discretion of each player. Familiarity with the material and style will eventually produce a serenity and depth of feeling surpassing the basic rhythmic excitement apparent at first"; Tempo I of this movement brings the work to a brilliant conclusion. D.

Alfredo Casella. *Sonata a Tre* Op. 62 1938 (Ric 124383) 50pp., parts. Introduzione—Allegro ma non troppo; Andante cantabile, quasi Adagio; Finale (Tempo di Giga). The piano provides rhythmic and harmonic functions while the lyric strings are treated melodically. All movements are extensive. The second movement opens with a canonic twelve-note idea but it is not developed. D.

Mario Castelnuovo-Tedesco. *Piano Trio* G 1928 (Ric 121053) 78pp., parts. Allegro con baldanza; Litanie (Tema con 5 Variazioni); Allegretto; Rondo all'Ungherese. Strong melodies, rich harmonies, undulating lines, broad pianistic gestures. D.

René de Castéra. *Trio* Op. 5 D (Rouart Lerolle 1904). Closely related themes in this four movement work. The first movement, in SA design, is overflowing with bold ideas. An introduction includes an important theme that returns in the slow conclusion of this movement. The second movement, a divertissement in rondo form, presents a Basque dance in 5/8 meter. The third movement (assez lent) is a song in ABA design. The finale (très-animé) is in SA and glitters with color. The piano carries much of the interest in this piece, especially in the finale. M-D.

Alexis de Castillon. *Trio* Op.4 B♭ (Durand 1871) 45pp., parts. Prelude et Andante; Scherzo; Romance; Finale.

—— *Trio* II Op.17 d (Heugel 1872) 67pp., parts. Allegro moderato; Allegretto non vivo; Scherzando vivace; Adagio–Allegro con fuoco.

Auguste Caune. *Trio* (Hamelle) 57pp., parts. Allegro moderato; Scherzo; Adagio; Final. Fine sense of form, traditional harmonic and rhythmic vocabulary. M-D.

Josef Ceremuga. *Trio* e (Artia).

Sergio Cervetti. *Fünf Episoden* 1965 (Moeck 5032) 31pp., parts. 15 min. I. Molto agitato, II. Come improvvisando, III. Misterioso, IV. Molto lento con fantasia, V. Molto flessibile e leggiero. Abstract, expressionistic, pointillistic, serial, avant-garde techniques such as damping strings with hands, clusters. D.

Luciano Chailly. *Parametri per 3 strumenti* (Bèrben 1973) 24pp., parts.

Cécile Chaminade. *Piano Trio I* Op.11 (Durand 1900) 45pp., parts. Allegro; Andante; Scherzo; Finale. The Scherzo shows off the piano in a Mendelssohnian brilliance. The outer movements are well written but not as spontaneous sounding as the Scherzo. M-D.

—— *Piano Trio II* Op.34 (Enoch 189?) 61pp., parts. Allegro moderato; Lento; Allegro energico. D.

Auguste Chapuis. *Trio* G (Durand 1912). Animé, pas trop, et très espressif: vigorous, developed fugally then melodically with a big G conclusion. Assez vif, spiritual et chantant: scherzo, lively, light, flexible trio in G. Calme sans lenteur: a Lied; slow march rhythm of quasi-religious character; expressive theme that is developed in a calm, then strong manner. Gaiment, dans l'allure d'une ronde populaire: vivacious, joyful conclusion. Franck influence; solidly constructed. M-D.

Ernest Chausson. *Trio* a 1882 (Rouart Lerolle).

—— *Trio* Op.3 g 1882 (Rouart Lerolle 1919) 69pp., parts. 31 min. Pas trop lent; Vite; Assez lent; Animé. Strongly influenced by Franck, with some Wagner influence here and there. Great ingenuity in piano writing is coupled with a delicate and sensitive approach to the instrument. Long lines and lush sonorities provide much sensual beauty but the individual movements leave a great deal to be desired with their loose formal construction. D.

Camille Chevillard. *Trio* Op.3 F (Durand 1884). Franck influence seen here but there is a certain amount of originality and a fine sense of form. The most unusual feature of this work is a piano cadenza, just before the finale coda, that incorporates not only the subjects of this finale but also the main idea from the first movement. The finale is brilliant and full of *joie de vivre*. M-D.

Raymond Chevreuille. *Trio* Op.8 1936–47 (CeBeDeM 1963) 34pp., parts. 17 min.

Frédéric Chopin. *Trio* Op.8 g 1828 (Br&H; Balakirev—CFP 48pp., parts; PWM, Vol.16 of *Complete Works;* Litolff; K&S) 25 min. Allegro con fuoco: SA; coda; tonic key is over-used. Scherzo—Con moto, ma non troppo: lively and flowing. Adagio sostenuto: nocturne-like, charming. Finale—Allegretto: cheerful and vivacious. "Its classicism may be disputed, nevertheless it contains lovely music" wrote Huneker. Chopin, in August of 1830, wrote: "Last Saturday I tried the trio, and, perhaps because I had not heard it for so long, was satisfied with myself. 'Happy man,' you will say, won't you? It then struck me that it would be better to use the viola instead of the violin, as the first string predominates in the violin, and in my trio it is hardly used at all. The viola would, I think, accord better with the cello." D.

Francesco Ciléa. *Trio* (EC 1963) 69pp., parts. Allegro sostenuto; Scherzo; Andante molto espressivo; Allegro con fuoco. Nineteenth-century style. M-D.

Rebecca Clarke. *Piano Trio* 1921 (Winthrop Rogers) 41pp., parts. Moderato ma appassionato; Andante molto semplice; Allegro vigoroso. The three movements are based on a central idea that is used in different forms throughout the work. A work of sweeping lines, unusual power, and passion; displays a great deal of brilliant writing for the piano. D.

Muzio Clementi. *Trio* Op.22/1 D. See detailed entry under trios for piano, one stringed instrument, and one wind instrument.
———— *Trio* Op.28/2 D 1791 or 1792 (Casella—EC; Casella—GS 1936) 23pp., parts. Allegro amabile; Polonaise; Rondo. Revised and elaborated on by Casella. The piano part is original but the string parts have been completely reworked. This is a lustrous and delectable trio with clear, limpid, and flowing musicality. The original edition is contained in the

Collected Works of Muzio Clementi (New York: Da Capo Press, 1973), Vol.4, pp.65-75. M-D.

Dinos Constantinides. *Trio* 1967 (MS available from composer: % School of Music, Louisiana State University, Baton Rouge, LA 70803) 31pp., parts. Allegro: frequent use of seconds, varied figuration, octave tremolo in left hand, dramatic conclusion; large span required. Largo: ABA, sustained, repeated syncopated chords, works to broad climax then subsides. Allegro vivo: driving rhythms, freely tonal, repeated chords, dissonant counterpoint, effective conclusion. M-D to D.

Aaron Copland. *Vitebsk* 1929 (Bo&H) 18pp., parts. Study on a Jewish Theme. Contains Copland's only use of quarter tones, which are used coloristically rather than structurally. The opening contains highly grating sonorities. A granitically conceived, expressive, and impressive work. D.

Henry Cowell. *Trio* 1964-5 (CFP) 29pp., parts. 19 min. Nine short movements based on comon melodic and rhythmic materials. Largo tenuto; Allegretto; Andante; Allegro; Andante sostenuto; Allegro; Allegretto; Adagio cantabile; Allegro assai. "The piano functions by and large as an independent entity of the tonal texture with strings playing either soloistically or in duet. Musical material is treated in widely varied fashion—as sheer melody (1st movement), arpeggio etude (2nd and 7th movements), chromatic study in oblique motion (4th movement), chorale (5th movement), or fantastic scherzo (6th movement). The finale, of almost Webernian brevity, seems to break off almost before getting started, the intent being to create the feeling common to much Indian and Indonesian music of infinite continuity beyond the span of actual sound" (from the preface). Cowell's last completed work. M-D.

Ram Da-Oz. *Trio* 1963 (Israeli Music Publications) 36pp., parts. One serial movement divided into three parts. Opens slowly and meditatively; tempo increases to allegro ma non troppo. Here begins a rondo-like section. Tempo and tension further increase until a climax is reached with the piano part having a percussive character, persistently repeating rhythmical figures. Second part opens with a piano subito (bar 226). Short introduction, then piano has a narrative theme. A series of free variations follow. Third part (begins bar 311) presents rhythms that become more complex until the climax of the whole work is reached. Piano is here performing the task of several percussive instruments playing various rhythms. Tempo and tension decrease gradually, and trio closes as it began, lento. D.

Ingolf Dahl. *Trio* 1962 (PIC 1971) 58pp., parts. Allegretto grazioso; Notturno I; Rondino Cantabile; Notturno II; Finale: Variazioni (5), Recitativo e

Coda. Open textures, pointillistic, strong abstract writing. Well-controlled free tonal usage, supple rhythms, melodic and harmonic materials serialized, versatile writing for all instruments. Rhythmic problems, parts play together independently of each other. Large span required. D.

Gyula David. *Trio* (EMB 1974) 32pp., parts.

Mario Davidovsky. *Chacona* 1972 (EBM) 16pp., parts. 10 min. Pointillistic, flexible meters, at one point the pianist must pluck strings and strike the keys simultaneously. Abstract, expressionistic. Requires large span. D.

Helmut Degen. *Piano Trio* (Br 2095 1948) 39pp., parts. Andante espressivo–Allegro; Adagio cantabile; Allegro. Moderate modernism infused with a Hindemithian flavor, neoclassic. M-D.

Edisson V. Denisov. *Trio* Op.5 1954 (USSR C1755K) 60pp., parts. Moderato; Allegro; Largo; Allegretto. Freely tonal, colorful, pianistic, mildly contemporary with a Russian flavor. M-D.

David Diamond. *Piano Trio* 1951 (PIC 1956) 46pp., parts. Clear structures, SA procedures, intense lyric writing tinged with Romantic feeling, freely chromatic harmonic usage. M-D.

John Diercks. *Serenade* (Tritone 1962) 10pp., parts. MS reproduction.

Gaetano Donizetti. *Trio* (B. Päuler—CFP 8116 1972) 20pp., parts. Largo–Allegro; Largo; Andantino. These movements have been merged into a trio and published here for the first time. Preface by the editor describes editorial policy. Clear classic writing, tuneful. M-D.

Richard Donovan. *Trio* 1937 (Bo&H) 32pp., parts. One movement. One of Donovan's best works. Shows fine command of formal structure in particular. Mildly contemporary. M-D.
———— *Trio* II 1963 (CFE) 45pp., parts. 23 min. Andante tranquillo; Variations; Allegro energico. Introspective, neo-Romantic, yet contains a certain kind of transparency. Freely tonal with varying harmonic pungency. Finale is especially vigorous and straightforward. D.

James Drew. *Almost Stationary* (TP 1976) 4pp., parts. Parts in score format.

Anton Dvořák. *Trio* Op.21 B♭ 1875 (Artia; Adamowski—GS L1524; Lienau) 58pp., parts. 29 min. Allegro molto; Adagio molto e maestro; Allegretto scherzando; Finale. An early work that does not reflect the true personal touch of the composer, but the form is most delightfully worked out. M-D.

———— *Trio* Op.26 g 1876 (Artia; IMC) 27 min. Displays an economy of thematic material plus a character of intense yearning. M-D.

———— *Trio* Op.65 f 1883 (Artia; Simrock; IMC) 41 min. All three instruments are well knit in their interaction. The music varies in character from grave and gloomy to passionate. The piano adds a symphonic grandeur. A peaceful resignation arrives only at the end of the work. D.

———— *Dumky Trio* Op.90 1890–1 (Artia; Mercury; Simrock; IMC) 44pp., parts. 30 min. Dvořák's most famous work in this combination; very typical of his chamber music; Bohemian in character. There are six *dumka* (alternation of yearning melancholy and wild gaiety) movements in this work, each thematically independent and separate from each other. Piano is accorded brilliant treatment; higher registers of cello exploited. Excellent counterpoint infuses all three parts; much vitality that comes from the national rhythms and melodic styles. D.

John Eaton. *Piano Trio* (SP) 18pp., parts. One extended movement. First string on the violin is tuned down a quarter step and notes are written at sounding pitch. An arrow (accent) system is used in the piano part that means "bring out the notes preceded by the arrows." Expressionistic, atonal, shifting meters and rhythms, irregular tremolo, spread-out sonorities, harmonics, slowly large arpeggiated chords, clusters combined with melody. Pencil to be pressed into strings at one point; one large arpeggiated chord is given and pianist is to improvise up the keyboard in similar arpeggios, splashing clusters around keyboard. Avant-garde, impressive sonorities and writing. Large span required. D.

Horst Ebenhöh. *Einigen Minuten für Klaviertrio* Op.32/1 1973 (Dob) 20pp., parts. All performers indulge in contemporary techniques such as instrumental slides. New signs are explained (in German only). Varied piano writing includes short phrases of broken-chord figures, legato major thirds in the bass, extended trills, much syncopation. Rhythmic complexities provide major ensemble problems. Many contrasting elements do not fit together well. D.

Anton Eberl. *Trio* (Sonata) c (Litolff). Formerly attributed to Mozart (K.291) but now considered to be the work of Eberl. M-D.

Klaus Egge. *Trio* Op.14 1941 (EMH). Dramatic, tender, and brutal sounds; strong emotional overtones. Written under the influence of the war between Finland and the USSR. D.

Heimo Erbse. *Trio* Op.8 1953 (Bo&Bo) 57pp., parts. 16 min. Allegro; Scherzo; Larghetto; Vivace giocoso. Complex rhythmic treatment, neo-classic melodic style, chromatic and freely tonal, effective handling of all three instruments. D.

Gabriel Fauré. *Trio* Op.120 d (Durand 1923) 40pp., parts. 21 min. Allegro, ma non troppo; Andantino; Allegro vivo. Three lofty movements filled with Fauré's incomparable grace and elegance. Thin textures (especially for the period), serene, tenderly persuasive, freely tonal. The second movement projects the piano cantando espressivo spontaneously. Requires more musicianship and refined sensibility than a brief look at the score would suggest. M-D.

Václav Felix. *Trio* Op.5 C 1956 (Artia) 34pp., parts. Allegro; Lento; Moderato; Presto. Freely tonal, folk influence, dance qualities, colorful. M-D.

Oscar Lorenzo Fernández. *Trio Brasileiro* Op.32 1924 (Ric BA6113) 57pp., parts. Allegro maestoso; Cancão; Dansa; Final. Much Brazilian melodic inspiration (some folk themes, some original themes in folksong style) with contemporary rhythmic vitality. This work won an international competition. Piano supplies much of the rhythmic interest. M-D.

Georgio Ferrari. *Trio* (Zanibon 1973) 50pp., parts. Photostat of MS.

Ross Lee Finney. *Trio II* A (CF 1958) 47pp., parts. 19½ min. Brightly colored opaque sounds, powerful rhythmic drive, strong tonal functions always freely present, idiomatic writing for all instruments. M-D.

César Franck. *Trio* Op.1/1 F♯ 1840 (CFP 3745; Durand; Hamelle) 55pp., parts. Andante con moto (in 5 sections); Allegro molto (Scherzo and 2 trios); Finale—Allegro maestoso (SA design). The piano part is so massively scored that ensemble balance is almost impossible. Requires a fire-breathing virtuoso to handle the cascading octaves and numerous repeated chords. Cyclic in form and hints at the later Franck. This trio is far superior to the other two in this opus number. D.
_____ *Trio* Op.1/2 B♭ 1840 (Hamelle; Schuberth).
_____ *Trio* Op.1/3 b 1840 (Hamelle; Schuberth).
_____ *Trio* Op.2 B 1842 (Hamelle; Schuberth). In one movement. This is the rewritten last movement of the Op.1/3, for Franz Liszt. Contains interesting moments (the recapitulation begins with the second subject), but it is nowhere near the equal of Op.1/1. M-D.

Géza Frid. *Trio* Op.27 1947 (Donemus) 17 min. Frid's Hungarian origin can still be felt in the themes and spirit of this work, but French influence is also strong. The piano part is especially well written, in part because of Frid's outstanding ability as a concert pianist. D.

James Friskin. *Phantasie* e 1908 (Nov) 15pp., parts. Serious intimacy of expression in this work, especially the melodic writing. Post-Romantic characteristics of the highest order are integrated into a well-crafted work. Contrasted sections. M-D.

Gunnar de Frumerie. *Trio II* (NMS). Brilliant neoclassic writing showing strong free rhythms and brittle harmonies, freely tonal. A highly polished work of a fastidious craftsman who has contributed a composition of genuine substance; completely unostentatious. M-D.

Sandro Fuga. *Trio* 1941 (SZ) 52pp., parts. 28 min. Allegro con fuoco; Mosso, con semplitita; Grave—Sostenuto (Novembre 1939). Neoclassic, clear and transparent textures, freely tonal, colorful and idiomatic writing for the piano. M-D to D.

Niels W. Gade. *Trio* Op.42 F 1863 (Br&H; Augener) 35pp., parts. 20 min. Allegro animato; Allegro molto vivace; Andantino; Finale. A good work for amateurs who enjoy Romantic poetic sounds. Grateful writing for all instruments. M-D.
———— *Noveletten Trio* Op.29 a 1853 (Costallat) 35pp., parts. Allegro scherzando; Andante con moto; Moderato; Larghetto con moto; Finale. This Scandinavian pioneer of the Romantic school writes with an individual touch. Both Mendelssohn and Schumann influenced him and a great deal of the former shows in both these trios. The string writing appears to be more successful than that for the piano. M-D.

Renaud Gagneux. *Trio* (Jobert 1976) 6pp., parts. 7 min. Explanation of signs in French. One untitled movement. Long pedals, harmonics, repeated patterns, xylophone mallet used on piano strings, pointillistic, expressionistic. M-D to D.

Hans Gál. *Variations on a Viennese Popular Tune* Op.9 1921 (Simrock 843) 11pp., parts. Genuine Viennese music although it is a little short on gaiety and sensuous charm. M-D.
———— *Trio* Op.49b 1948 (OBV) 16pp., parts. Violin can be replaced by an oboe or flute. Moderato e tranquillo; Pastorale; March Burlesque. Written in the best chamber music style with an ensemble of independent individu-

als whose function of leading, counterpointing, accompanying parts is changing perpetually. Mildly contemporary. M-D.

Fritz Geissler. *Trio* 1970 (DFVM) 55pp., parts. Trauermarsch: fluid rhythmic figures, serial influence, expressionistic dynamic extremes, cluster-like percussive chords, graphic and traditional notation, strongly chromatic. Intermezzo: scherzo, light and elegant, pointillistic, best-organized movement. Passacaglia: lugubrious subject built on tritone; three variations and reprises expose the subject to various treatment; thin textures. Finale: shifting meters; left hand is chordal; right hand has fluid figures similar to opening movement; accented chromatic chords; tremolo clusters; improvisation; short section in Walzer tempo; intense percussive ending. Mixture of neoclassic and avant-garde techniques. D.

Armando Gentilucci. *Crescendo* (Ric 1971) 15pp. on 2 folded loose leaves, photostat of MS. 3 copies necessary for performance. 12 min. Pointillistic, takes the form of one long crescendo from *ppp* beginning to *fff* ending. D.

Harald Genzmer. *Trio* 1943 F (CFP 5025) 14 min. Hindemith influence is strong. This work is otherwise freely tonal, contains some polyrhythmic interpolations, and combines contrapuntal textures with expressive coloring. M-D.
_____ *Trio* 1964 (CFP 5990) 33pp., parts. 20 min. Allegro con brio; Tranquillo; Burleske; Finale. Octotonic, shifting meters, repeated harmonic seconds, alternating hand figuration, quartal and quintal harmony, effective trill usage, freely tonal with plenty of chromaticism, large arpeggiated chords. Large span required. Neoclassic. D.

Roberto Gerhard. *Trio* 1918 (Senart) 32pp., parts. 26 min. Modéré; Très calme; Vif. Attractive and accomplished tonal writing that shows strong French influences. M-D.

Edwin Gerschefski. *Rhapsody* Op.46 (CFE) 22pp., parts. Contrasting tempi, moods, and textures; freely tonal; tremolo; octotonic; figuration interestingly dispersed between hands; parallel chords; intense Andante cantabile section; bold gestures; dramatic conclusion. D.

Oswald Gerstel. *The Nightingale and the Rose* (Israeli Music Publications 1975) 25pp., parts.

Mikhail Gnessin. *Trio* Op.63 (USSR MI8733G 1947) 34pp., parts. Draws on Arab–Semitic sources, with their luxurious ornamentation, but at the same time preserves a strong bond with Russian musical culture. M-D.

Benjamin Godard. *Trio I* Op.32 G (Heugel) 49pp., parts. Allegro; Tempo di Minuetto moderato; Andante quasi adagio; Allegro vivace. M-D.

———— *Trio II* Op.72 F (Durand 1884) 59pp., parts. Allegro moderato; Adagio; Vivace; Allegro vivace. M-D.

Both works are delightfully written in the Romantic style of the day and are recommended to amageur performers. Godard knew how to turn a good melody but there are places marked by an over-sentimentality.

Alexander Goehr. *Piano Trio* Op.20 1966 (Schott 11004) 20pp., parts. 20 min. Con anima: players required to play in different meters; in these places the relationship of meters is proportional and the bar lines (strong beats) do not synchronize; each player must express his own meter and not be hampered by the need of precise ensemble. Lento possibile e sostenuto: free, grace notes to be played as if anticipating (syncope) next indicated value; this long slow movement is the glory of this trio. Free use of motivic elements; repetition employed to help clarify formal structures; concentrated dense idiom; unusual development of texture; Bartók influence. D.

Hermann Goetz. *Trio* Op.1 g 1863 (UWKR 14 1976) 40pp., parts. Langsam–Feurig; Sehr ruhig; Flüchtig, erregt; Mässig rasch–Ziemlich lebhaft. Influenced by Mendelssohn, Schumann, and Brahms. Even though this work is listed as Op.1, it displays expressive and effective writing for all instruments. M-D.

Carl Goldmark. *Trio* Op.4 B♭ (K&S) 57pp., parts. Schnell; Adagio; Scherzo; Finale. Pronounced Romanticism; lyric sections the most convincing. Spontaneous melodic and harmonic treatment is mainly diatonic. Abundant craft is evident in the conscientious development of this work. The Adagio is especially effective with its introductory improvisation that recalls Hungarian gipsy tunes. M-D.

———— *Trio* Op.33 (Schweers & Haake) 53pp., parts. Allegro con moto; Scherzo; Andante sostenuto; Allegro. One of Goldmark's finest works. D.

Alexander Gretchaninov. *Trio I* Op.38 c 1906 (Belaieff) 59pp., parts. Allegro passionato; Lento assai; Finale—Allegro vivace. Nineteenth-century sweeping chromatic pianism throughout. The style is comparatively sustained and homophonic. D.

———— *Trio II* Op.128 G (Belaieff) 18 min.

Odd Grüner-Hegge. *Trio* Op.4 (WH 2288 1923) 51pp., parts. Allegro energico; Andantino, molto tranquillo; Allegro giocoso; Andante; Lugubre maestoso. This youthful work exhibits a fine technique and sense of form. Nordic flavor cast in post-Wagnerian harmonic vocabulary. M-D to D.

Joseph Guy-Ropartz. *Trio* a (Durand 1919) 69pp., parts. Modérément animé; Vif; Lent–Animé. Somewhat austere writing with a Franckian tinge (Guy-Ropartz studied with Franck). The style is eclectic-Romantic with Breton folktunes serving as some of the inspiration. Overextended. M-D.

Elizabeth Gyring. *Trio Fantasy* 1954 (CFE) 11pp., parts. 9 min. One movement, sectionalized with contrasting tempi. Expressionistic and intense, freely tonal and chromatic, many dynamic changes, short motivic lines, dramatic climax. D.

Adalbert Gyrowetz. *Sonata* F (M. Munclinger—Supraphon MVH No.30 1973) 25pp., parts. Preface in Czech and German. Allegro moderato; Andante con moto; Rondo. Classical style, clear forms, charming. M-D.

Karel Hába. *Trio* Op.24 1940 (Hudební Matice) 29pp., parts. Allegro moderato; Andante cantabile; Allegro scherzando. Written in a chromatic, Regerian style with strong lyrical elements. The piano is treated to many late nineteenth-century idioms. D.

John Hall. *Trio* (Chappell 1968) 21 min. Three movements; Presto coda concludes the work. Tonal feeling is present in a highly chromatic style. The piano writing is more difficult than the other parts. D.

Iain Hamilton. *Trio* Op.25 (Schott 10590 1956) 36pp., parts. 15 min. Allegro giojoso; Intermezzo; Presto. Neoclassic harmonic treatment although the scoring is dark-tinged and dense. Disciplined writing with serial influence. Technical and expressive capacities of individual instruments are explored. Large span required. M-D to D.

George Frederick Handel. *Chambertrio* XXIII g (M. Seiffert—McGinnis & Marx 1974) 12pp., parts. Largo andante; Allegro; Largo; Allemande; Allegro. This work has an interesting history, explained in an insert by Marx. In g throughout with a key signature of one flat. A very beautiful and enduring work with fine keyboard realization. M-D.

Jan Hanuš. *Trio* (Frescos) Op.51 1961 (Artia) 53pp., parts. 23½ min. Andante mesto; Molto allegro, fantastico e feroce; Adagio non troppo; Allegro molto e tempestuoso. Designed in a formally classical layout with alternating slow and quick movements, the finale being in SA form. The descriptive title indicates the composer's intention to create four musical pictures, but there is no definite extra-musical program. All are dramatic in character, and their essential mood or atmosphere is in keeping with the tempo and character indications of the individual movements. Mildly contemporary with a certain Czech national flavor. D.

Roy Harris. *Piano Trio* 1934 (TP) 31pp., parts. Allegro con bravura: strong tonal elements embedded in polyharmonic structures; bold lines; imitation important; rhythmic canons with close range entries prominent. Andante religioso: low descending slow octaves provide harmonic substructure; piano adds melodic and cross-phrasings. Fugue–Grave–poco più mosso: builds to enormous sonorous conclusion. D.

Tibor Harsanyi. *Trio* 1926 (Heugel 29665) 34pp., parts. Allegro; Lento; Presto; Allegro con fuoco. The first and last movements are in SA design, each with three subjects. Straightforward and clear writing throughout. Classical and national influences are at work in this freely tonal composition. The lyrical slow movement and the dramatic finale are especially effective for the piano. M-D.

Franz Joseph Haydn. *Piano Trios* (H. C. R. Landon—Dob). Complete edition in process (1977), 45 trios to be published separately. Not fingered; editorial indications are in brackets. These trios contain some of Haydn's most glorious music, and they cover most of his composing career. The large majority are unknown to most pianists and only in the last few years, with more complete editions becoming available, have we had the opportunity to become familiar with this great literature. A piano trio was, for Haydn, more an accompanied keyboard solo than a work for three independent instruments. Frequently the cello duplicates the bass of the keyboard part. H. C. R. Landon tells us in his preface that Haydn's 45 trios may be conveniently divided into three groups: the early works (Nos.1–16) composed in or before ca.1760, of which several were never published at all; the middle works (Nos.17–30), of which all except one (No.17, an arrangement made ca.1784 of a baryton piece composed about 1772) were composed between 1784 and 1790; and the London trios (Nos.31–45) written in or for Britain between 1793/4 and 1796. This third group especially contains profundities and an imaginative, lean style.
_____ *Piano Trios* (W. Stockmeier—Henle) in the Complete Edition of the Joseph Haydn Institute. Fingered by Jörg Demus; preface in German, French, and English; critical commentary in German. Vol.I (contains all the early works): Hob.XV: 1, 2, 34–38, 40, 41, Cl, fl; Vol.II: Hob.XV: 5–14; Vol.III (separate edition of the Flute Trios—for piano, flute, and cello): Hob.XV: 15–17. This series is to be continued; see chart below.
_____ *Trios* (F. Hermann—CFP) 3 vols.
_____ *Trios* (David—Br&H) 29 trios, published separately.
_____ *Divertimento* E Hob. XV:34 (Landon—Dob DM22).
_____ *Divertimento* F Hob. XV:37 (W. Weismann—Leuckart) No.11 in Alte Musik. Cello ad lib.
_____ *Divertimento* B♭ Hob. XV:38 (W. Weismann—Leuckart) No. 10 in Alte Musik. Cello ad lib.

Haydn's Keyboard Trios
As Numbered in Hoboken Catalogue and Four Editions

Key	Doblinger (H.C.R. Landon)	Haydn Werke (Stockmeier—Henle)	Hoboken Catalogue	Peters (Hermann)	Breitkopf & Härtel (David)
F	1	3	XV:37		
C	2	2	XV:C1		
G	3		XIV:6, XVI:6		
F	4		XV:39		
g	5	9	XV:1	19	16
F	6	8	XV:40		
G	7	7	XV:41		
D	8 (lost)	Appendix	XV:33		
D	9 (lost)	Appendix	XV:D1		
A	10	10	XV:35		
Eb	11*	5	XV:34		
Eb	12*	1	XV:36		
Bb	13*	4	XV:38		
f	14*	6	XV:f1		
D	15				
C	16		XIV:C1		
F	17	11	XV:2, XIV:2	26	25
G	18	12	XV:5	28	28
F	19	13	XV:6	25	23
D	20*	14	XV:7	10	21
Bb	21*	15	XV:8	24	22
A	22*	16	XV:9	15	9
Eb	23*	17	XV:10	20	17
Eb	24*	18	XV:11	16	11
e	25*	19	XV:12	7	10
C	26*	20	XV:13	14	8
Ab	27*	21	XV:14	11	24
D	28*	22	XV:16	30	30
G	29*	*Flute Trios* 23	XV:15	31	31
F	30*	24	XV:17	29	29
G	31*		XV:32		
A	32*		XV:18	13	7
g	33*		XV:19	17	14
Bb	34*		XV:20	9	13
C	35*		XV:21	21	18
Eb	36*		XV:22	23	20

Key	Doblinger (H.C.R. Landon)	Haydn Werke Stockmeier— Henle)	Hoboken Catalogue	Peters (Hermann)	Breitkopf & Härtel (David)
d	37 *		XV:23	22	19
D	38 *		XV:24	6	6
G	39 *		XV:25	1	1
f♯	40 *		XV:26	2	2
e♭	41 *		XV:31	18	15
E♭	42 *		XV:30	8	12
C	43 *		XV:27	3	3
E	44 *		XV:28	4	4
E♭	45 *		XV:29	5	5

Appendix

Key	Doblinger (H.C.R. Landon)	Haydn Werke Stockmeier— Henle)	Hoboken Catalogue	Peters (Hermann)	Breitkopf & Härtel (David)
C			XV:3	12	26
F			XV:4	27	27

An asterisk (*) indicates works available in the Doblinger edition as of January 1977. See: A. Craig Bell. "An Introduction to Haydn's Piano Trios," MR 16 (1955): 191–97; A. Peter Brown. "A Re-introduction to Joseph Haydn's Keyboard Works," PQ 79 (Fall 1972): 42–47.

———— *Klaviertrio* F Hob. XV:40 (H. Heussner—Dob DM4).

———— *Capriccio* A Hob. XV:35 (EMB). Based on the National Széchényi Library Budapest copy.

Bernhard Heiden. *Trio* 1956 (AMP) 64pp., parts. 19 min. Allegro agitato; Adagio; Vivace; Allegretto. Cohesive writing with much variety that shows a masterful skill. In spite of the strong influence of Hindemith this work displays marked individuality, with much emotional power in the melodic inspiration. The piano carries no excessive weight and is used to advantage. Large span required. D.

Hans Werner Henze. *Kammersonate* 1948, rev.1963 (Schott 5382) 15pp., parts. 15 min. Allegro assai; Dolce, con tenerezza; Lento; Allegretto; Epilogo. Strong rhythmic style, lyric cantabile lines, intellectual refinement. Instrumental colors imaginatively explored in this serially influenced work. Henze reveals an expressive and direct contemporary language. M-D.

Kurt Hessenberg. *Trio* Op.53 1950 (Wilhelmiana) 41pp., parts. 23 min. Allegro con fuoco; Adagio; Variationen. Classical leanings are present but the work is mainly Romantic in style and conception and employs a mildly contemporary harmonic and rhythmic setting that is freely tonal around F. A sense of humor comes through, especially in the finale, a large set of variations. M-D.

Alun Hoddinott. *Trio* Op.77 (MS available from the composer: % Music Department, University of Cardiff, Wales). Schoenberg influence; written in a type of international style. The Andante has a kind of *Erwartung* mood. Twelve-tone; well worked-out; anguished and nervous atmosphere about this piece. D.

E. T. A. Hoffmann. *Trio* E (H. Schulze—DVFM 8303 1971) 49pp., parts. Allegro moderato: SA, very colorful development. Scherzo: ABA. Adagio: introductory, expressive, leads directly to Allegro vivace; straightforward writing with both Classical and Romantic overtones. M-D.

Vagn Holmboe. *Trio* Op.64 (Viking). Spontaneous eclectic style, thematically interesting, expansive yet concentrated and distinctive writing. Organically integrated; subtlety of motivic organization is superb. D.

Alan Hovhaness. *Trio* Op.3 e (CFP 1971) 18pp., parts. 9 min. Allegro moderato: SA, repeated figures, traditional development techniques. Adagio espressivo con doppio canone: sustained chordal opening followed by doppio canone treatment in mid-section; short coda uses imitation with sustained chordal closing. Fuga—Allegro ma non troppo: fugal textures. This early piece does not have the usual later Hovhaness characteristics but is written in a strictly neoclassic style. M-D.

Johann Nepomuk Hummel. *Trio* Op.12 E♭ (CFP, 24pp., parts; UE). Original ideas, piano is particularly favored. M-D.
_____ *Trio* Op.22 F (Litolff, 14pp., parts; Haslinger). Technique outweighs artistry. Contains some delightful variations on a pleasing theme. Unusual treatment of the cello. Concludes with a cheerful alla turca movement. M-D.
_____ *Trio* Op.35 G (Litolff, 18pp., parts; Haslinger). Influenced by Mozart.
_____ *Trio* Op.65 G (Litolff) 18pp., parts.
_____ *Trio* Op.83 E "Grand Trio" (CFP). Extremely well written; shows real progress in Hummel's technical ability. Much virtuosity displayed in brilliant passage work of the finale. D.
_____ *Trio* Op.93 E♭ (CFP). This "Grand Trio" gives the piano highly preferential treatment. Brilliant opening movement, an emotional larghetto, and whirling rhythms are apparent in the rondo finale. M-D to D.

_____ *Trio* Op.96 E♭ (Litolff). Catchy rhythms and spirit in opening movement. Slow movement is more classically oriented, with some obvious defects. The allegro vivo finale is a delightful piquant dance with much appeal. M-D.

Andrew Imbrie. *Trio* 1946 (SP 1963) 28pp., parts. Allegro energico: linear, octotonic, freely tonal around G, rich in ideas, cleverly proportioned; contains a section for solo piano; large span required. Lento: opens with cantabile section for solo piano; haunting in its strange and lyric appeal; freely tonal around E♭. Presto con fuoco: quasi-cadenza for solo piano, many chromatic harmonic sixths, octaves in alternating hands, rhythmic drive. Colorful in its dynamic twists of rhythm and melody. Clear textures, parts balanced. D.

Vincent d'Indy. *Piano Trio II* Op.98 En forme de suite 1929 (Rouart Lerolle) 30pp., parts. 1. Entrée, en Sonate; 2. Air; 3. Courante; 4. Gigue en rondeau, sur une chanson Française. Written in a lighter, simpler, and more transparent style than d'Indy's earlier works. Economical use of material coupled with an intellectuality that sometimes overwhelms; expressive inspiration makes this an attractive but somewhat dated work. Rhythmic vitality displayed in the Gigue en rondeau gives this movement the most appeal. M-D.

John Ireland. *Phantasie* a 1908 (Augener 15202) 23pp., parts. 12½ min. An extended SA design in a Classic–Romantic style. M-D.
_____ *Trio* II e 1917 (Augener 15219) 20pp., parts. 14 min. One movement. Martial atmosphere influenced by the period in which it was composed (World War I). Based on thematic material that is progressively metamorphosed in the manner of free variations. M-D.
_____ *Trio* III E 1938 (Bo&H) 62pp., parts. 25 min. Allegro moderato; Scherzo; Andante cantabile; Finale. Written in a crisp Romantic idiom using material from 1913; reveals a happy balance between the three instruments. M-D.

Charles Ives. *Trio* 1904–11 (PIC 1955) 28pp., parts. 20 min. Andante moderato: no dynamic marks indicated; collage of polyrhythms and polyharmonies plus superimposed themes. Tsiaj: title signifies "This Scherzo Is a Joke"; contrasting tempi; traces of "Marching Through Georgia," "Jingle Bells," "My Old Kentucky Home," "Long, Long Ago," and other tunes are embedded in the vigorous contrapuntal texture. Moderato con moto: varied tempi; last part of this movement quotes from "Rock of Ages." All the Ives trademarks are found in this work. It is one of the most important American chamber compositions. Meditative, richly lyric, one of Ives's most profound artistic statements. D.

Gordon Jacob. *Trio* (J. Williams 1959) 28pp., parts. Adagio; Scherzo allegro; Molto adagio e mesto; Allegro. Well crafted, clear lines, clever rhythms. Economy and astringent brusqueness of expression are characteristic of this work. Jacob knows how to exploit his musical materials and is a master at involving all instruments equally. M-D.

Tadeusz Jarecki. *Trio–Fugato e Aria* Op.11 (JWC 1943) 11pp., parts. 7½ min. See detailed entry under trios for piano, violin, and viola.

Joseph Jelinek. *Trio* Op.10 (Artia). Written in the accessible fashionable style of the day. Attractive and fluent melodies and harmonies pour forth at every turn. M-D.

Knud Jeppesen. *Little Summer Trio* 1957 (WH 4016) 26pp., parts. 15 min. See detailed entry under trios for piano, one stringed instrument, and one wind instrument.

Paul Juon. *Trio I* Op.17 a (Schlesinger 1901) 35pp., parts. Allegro; Adagio non troppo; Rondo. Combines a blend of Russian and German influences with a Slavic character. Homogeneous thematic material. The Adagio is refreshing in its lyrical simplicity. M-D.

———— *Trio II* Op.39 D Trio Caprice on Selma Lagerlöf's *Gosta Berling*. (Schlesinger) 55pp., parts. 27 min. Moderato non troppo; Andante; Scherzo; Risoluto. Inspired by the novel *Gösta Berling,* which made a profound impression on Juon. Brahms-like in treatment with well-developed melodic ideas and clever rhythmic treatment, this work is an adventure in highly colored tone painting. M-D.

———— *Trio* Op.60 (Zimmermann 1915) 35pp., parts. Moderato assai; Andante cantabile; Risoluto, ma non troppo allegro. M-D.

———— *Suite* Op.89 (Birnbach 1932) 24pp., parts. Moderato; Giocoso; Andantino; Allegretto; Allegro giusto. Displays a fine sense of form and rhythmic power. M-D.

Pal Kadosa. *Trio* Op.49 1956 (Kultura) 24pp., parts. Moderato quasi andante, poco rubato; Vivo; Allegro ben marcato. Free metric treatment, strong accents, folksong influence present but not obvious, elaboration of short concise motifs. Sinewy contrapuntal textures and a percussive piano approach make this an exciting piece for performers and listeners. M-D.

Armin Kaufmann. *Trio* Op.57/2 (Dob 1958) 11pp., parts. 8 min. Andante; Allegro sereno. Striking thematic technique, Balkan folk influence, thin textures. A fresh sounding and musicianly work; mildly contemporary. M-D.

Rudolf Kelterborn. *Fantasia a Tre* 1967 (Br 4138) 22pp., parts. One large movement with contrasting sections. Strong feelings of structure even in a piece entitled "Fantasia." An expanded tonal system and certain neoclassic elements infuse this work with a sturdy, but at places, lively vitality. Large span required. M-D.

Harrison Kerr. *Trio* 1938, rev. 1949–50 (CFE) 33pp., parts. 15 min. Allegro; Grave; Allegro. Vivid chromatic writing, freely tonal, austere, fine flow of ideas that unfold naturally. Highly active finale with only a short respite in a Meno mosso section. D.

Leon Kirchner. *Trio* 1954 (AMP) 22pp., parts. 15 min. Eighth note = 92; Largo. Strong Romantic lines and emotional excitement in all three instruments. Rhapsodic elements throughout, chromatic, violently dissonant, restless, clear design, strongly guided motion, unquenchable vitality, tempo fluctuations. Advanced pianism required. D.

Giselher Klebe. *Elegia Appassionata* Op.22 1955 (Bo&Bo) 22pp., parts. One movement. Tart vocabulary; twelve-tone influence; various elements amalgamated into a personal harmonic system. Piano writing is thorny and uncompromising at spots. Varied moods and tempi; expressionistic. D.

Richard Rudolf Klein. *Fantasia* (Möseler 1974) 15pp., parts. Varied tempi and moods, sectionalized, shifting meters, neoclassic orientation, thin textures preferred. M-D.

Joonas Kokkonen. *Trio* Op.1 1948 (Finnish Music Information Centre) 37pp., parts. 20 min. Un poco adagio leads to Allegro moderato, ma energico, SA: trills in piano move into a chromatically colored, rhythmically driving opening section; movement develops excitingly and closes sempre appassionato. Andante tranquillo e semplice: 5/4; melodic treatment of all instruments; piano provides full chordal sonorities (tenths are used); chorale-like. Allegro molto e giocoso: rhythmic, changing meters, à la Prokofiev, contemporary Alberti-bass treatment, freely tonal. M-D.

Paul Kont. *Klaviertrio 1964* (Dob 1974) 25pp., parts. 14 min. Based on the *Trio 1948* for flute, harp, and cello and differs from it in character although the musical material is the same. The older work emphasized color and softness of the texture whereas the 1964 trio emphasizes the rhythmic concertante element. Three movements (Vivace; Lento; Allegro) in a light neoclassic style. The finale abounds in syncopations, arpeggi, and scales. A pleasurable piece for performers and listeners. M-D.

Egon Kornauth. *Trio* Op.27 b (CFP 1921) 39pp., parts. Allegro moderato ma energico: piano has introduction alone, strings join in, and the piano then announces the first subject (Brahmsian); a short development follows. Andante molto rubato: follows attacca and uses the same ideas from the first movement; allegretto scherzando mid-section introduces new material. Allegro moderato ma energico: begins like the first movement but takes a different journey; theme from the scherzando (second movement), heard in piano, gently closes the movement while the strings hold the pedal note B for the last eleven bars. Mildly contemporary style and fluent manipulation of the piano writing make this still an attractive piece today. D.

Erich Wolfgang Korngold. *Trio* Op.1 D 1909 (UE 2996) 51pp., parts. 26 min. Allegro non troppo, con espressione; Scherzo; Larghetto; Finale. The influence of Richard Strauss is very strong—complex modulatory procedure; strong contrasts; excessive changing of harmonic, rhythmic, and thematic direction—but characteristics of the future composer are seen even in this very early but astonishingly mature work of a twelve-year-old. Over-elaborate writing with thick textures for the piano especially. M-D to D.

Leopold Anton Koželuch. *Sonata* Op.12/1 B♭ (K&S) 35pp., parts. Organum series III/54. Mainly a piano sonata with violin obbligato, as the piano carries most of the musical material. About the same difficulty as a Haydn or Mozart piano sonata. A good introduction to Classic period style and form. M-D.

———— *Trio* Op.12/2 A (H. Albrecht—K&S) 35pp., parts. No.54 in Organum Series. Allegretto; Adagio; Allegro. Editorial tempo suggestions. Foreword in German.

———— *Trio* Op.12/3 g (K&S) 38pp., parts. No.41 in Organum Series. Allegro; Adagio: very florid; Allegro. Editorial tempo suggestions. Foreword in German. Pleasant and easy-flowing melodies with period harmony make these agreeable and attractive pieces. Effective instrumental idioms. M-D.

Jaroslav Křička. *Trio* Op.38 "Doma" (At Home) On a Czech Church Tune 1923-4 (Artia) 31pp., parts. 20 min. Sectionalized with such titles as: Prologo, Fuga, Intermezzo, Cantabile (Trio), Presto, Andante religioso, Epilogo. Influences of folksong, the Russian School (Rimsky-Korsakov in particular), and Vítězslav Novák are all felt in this work. Melodic lyricism, spontaneous invention, technical facility, fluent expression, and naivety all shine through in various degrees. M-D.

Toivo Kuula. *Trio* Op.7 A 1908 (WH 1925) 72pp., parts. Moderato assai; Scherzo; Andante elegico; Finale. SA design; mechanical and over-extended developments; piano part highly decorative. Long lyrical phrases, broad climaxes, Romantic Brahmsian tradition. M-D.

Osvald Lacerda. *Trio* 1969 (IU) 27pp., parts. 10 min. Lento: SA, dissonant, linear construction. Movido: Rondo, ABA^{1}CA^2, hemiola, clusters, generally thin textures throughout. M-D.

Ezra Laderman. *Trio* 1959 (OUP) 38pp., parts. 14 min. Adagio espressivo; Andante con moto; Molto allegro, leggiero. Three contrasting movements evolve from one basic idea. Freely tonal. The "Come una danza" section from the first movement is especially appealing. M-D to D.

Edouard Lalo. *Trio* Op.7 c (Costallat) 45pp., parts. Allegro moderato; Romance; Scherzo; Final. M-D.

———— *Trio* II b (Hamelle 187?) 33pp., parts. Allegro maestoso: piano enters at the second section; opening theme treated canonically with piano; brilliant coda. Andante con moto: mainly two melodic ideas worked out. Menuetto allegretto: charming and fresh. Allegretto agitato: begins suddenly; two bold and sonorous ideas are mounted with restless rhythms. M-D to D.

———— *Trio* III Op.26 a 1880 (Durand 2740) 43pp., parts. 26 min. Allegro appassionato: a discussion of thematic material grows more heated to the end of the movement. Scherzo: d, all fire and vitality in a galloping 6/8 meter. Très lent: E, meditative and spiritual character. Allegro molto: A, explodes like a bomb in a furious marchlike character. Probably Lalo's finest and most finished chamber work. Intense rhythms and color. D.

Noël Lee. *Deux Mouvements* 1959, rev. 1970 (MS available from composer: 4 Villa Laugier, 75017 Paris, France) 19pp., parts. Intermède: rhythmic and cantabile, chromatic, syncopation, short chordal sections, harmonics; large span required; effectively contrasts with Marche: low staccato bass versus upper register, clusters, misterioso P conclusion. Unusual endings for both movements. Neoclassic. M-D.

René Leibowitz. *Trio* Op.20 1950 (Boelke-Bomart) 12 min. Strict twelve-tone writing with a dramatic quality that leans toward Berg. Complex rhythms, wide leaps, thin textures and full harmonies in the piano writing. D.

Guillaume Lekeu. *Trio* 1890 (Rouart Lerolle) 59pp., parts. Lent-Allegro; Très lent; Très animé–Lent–Très vif–Lent–Très vif; Lent. Franck influence. Admirable ideas in long lines treated in a heroic and sometimes passionate manner. Romantic virtuoso approach. D.

John Lessard. *Trio in Six Parti* 1966 (Joshua). Strong neoclassic lines. Well constructed. M-D.

Peter Tod Lewis. *Trio* 1960 (CFE) 16pp., parts. One movement. Expressionistic, sectionalized, parallel sonorities, strong rhythms, tremolo, thin textures, freely tonal and serially influenced. Large span required. M-D.

Otto Luening. *Trio* (Galaxy) 28pp., parts. One movement. Allegro agitato: strong asymetrical melody, freely tonal, triplet broken-chord figuration and octaves, more chordal and sustained second tonal area, tremolo chords in alternate hands, imitation. Varied tempi, moods, and meters. Neoclassic. M-D to D.

Enrico Mainardi. *Trio* 1939 (SZ).
———*Trio* 1954 (Schott 4770) 40pp., parts. Andante sostenuto; Intermezzo; Finale. Chromatic style, mildly Romantic. M-D.

Artur Malawski. *Trio* 1953 (PWM) 66pp., parts. 30 min. Lento–Allegro moderato: chromatic, alternating hands, many triplets, expansive lines; chordal sections contrast with linear sections. Andante sostenuto: right hand provides counterpoint with strings while the left hand provides a contemporary Alberti-bass; chromatic duplets and triplets; appassionato mid-section with trills moves to great climax before returning to opening mood and ideas. Scherzo: agitato and non-legato alternating hand figuration, parallel chords, octotonic. Rondo: octotonic, moving full-octave chords, hands crossing, chromatic runs; Andantino section is more chordal and sustained; strong dramatic conclusion. D.

Gian Francesco Malipiero. *Sonata a Tre* 1927 (UE 9519) 32pp., parts. 24½ min. Allegro impetuoso: for cello and piano alone. Ritenuto: for violin and piano alone. Lento–Allegro vivace: for all three instruments. All movements are sectional with varied tempi. Finale has a recapitulation of material from the first two movements. Colorful writing. M-D.

Franco Margola. *Trio* II (Zanibon 3712).

Frank Martin. *Piano Trio on Popular Irish Melodies* 1925 (Hug) 35pp., parts. 21 min. French influences seen in the harmonic and rhythmic treatment. Opening Allegro moderato is full of Gaelic spirit, while the more Impressionistic Pastoral Adagio suggests an Irish landscape. The finale Gigue is more French than Irish and presents technical and interpretative problems for all instruments. M-D.

Maria de Lourdes Martins. *Trio* 1959 (Gulbenkian Foundation) 40pp., parts. Lento–Allegro–Lento: fluid rhythms that continually change; second theme is a canon between the violin and cello; development is divided into two parts. Tempo di Minuetto: nine variations on Minuetto theme suggests an eighteenth-century atmosphere. Vif: rondo, strong rhythms, canon used, recitative-like wide arpeggiated chords. Neoclassic. M-D.

Bohuslav Martinů. *Bergerettes* (PIC 1963) 44pp., parts. Poco allegro: has a trio, Poco meno mosso. Allegro con brio: mid-section exploits alternating hands and tremolo. Andantino: A sections are more chordal; B section is more linear. Allegro: corky rhythms plus long phrases. Moderato: parallel chords, sixteenth-note triplets, Poco allegretto Trio contrasts. M-D.

———— *Trio* 1930 (Schott 2183) 20pp., parts. Five short pieces. Allegro moderato; Adagio; Allegro; Allegro moderato; Allegro. Written in a highly chromatic style. No.5 has an extensive solo part for piano. M-D.

———— *Trio II* d 1950 (ESC) 39pp., parts. 16 min. Allegro moderato; Andante; Allegro. Contrast plus superb balance is the hallmark of this work with equally balanced outer movements and an andante half again as long. It has a Czech folklike flavor with flowing themes and development. The finale evolves completely from the opening idea; this kinetic movement is one of the most exciting in all trio literature. D.

———— *Trio III* C 1951 (ESC) 51pp., parts. Allegro moderato; Andante; Allegro. Dissonant and polytonal setting with well-defined melodies. Sonorities are crucially important; climaxes underlined with strong densities. Motoric drive in the last section with asymmetrical phrase divisions brings this significant neoclassic work to a sonorous conclusion. D.

Joseph Marx. *Trio–Phantasie* g 1910 (UE) 74pp., parts. Four movements. Highly chromatic and rhapsodic idiom with some imaginative writing. Displays a well-developed craft. Seems long-winded today but does contain some inspired moments. See especially the Adagietto movement. For a full discussion of this work see CCSCM, II, 122.

Yori-aki Matsudaira. *Variazioni* 1957 (SZ) 31pp., parts. 14 min. Serial in dynamics and pitch, pointillistic, atonal, shifting meters, complex rhythms, solo variation for piano, involved and complicated. D.

Felix Mendelssohn. *Trios* (S. Grossmann—Henle 1972) 131pp., parts. Fingering for piano part added by H.-M. Theopold. Contains Trio Op.49 d

(1839), 32 min; Trio Op.66 c (1845) 27 min. The autograph of Op.49 differs greatly from the final printed version. This publication is based on the two earliest editions. Except for a youthful work from 1820, which so far has not been published, these are the only works of Mendelssohn in this category. Symbols placed in brackets are not in the sources, from which they have clearly been omitted through oversight. Preface contains other pertinent information. The piano is treated felicitously and pianistically and does not overpower the strings. Op.66 is especially well proportioned, and Op.49 is one of the treasures of the Romantic chamber literature. D.
Other editions: *Two Trios* (CFP 1740). *Trio* Op.49 (Br&H; Adamowski—GS L1458; Augener 7267a). *Trio* Op.66 (Adamowski—GS L1459).

Georges Migot. *Trio ou Suite à Trois* 1935 (Leduc) 46pp., parts. Prélude; Allègre; Danse; Final. Strong contrapuntal lines that develop their own modal harmony. Rhythm derives from an intertwining of melodic lines. Broad, expansive, individual style. D.

Darius Milhaud. *Trio* (Heugel 1968) 37pp., parts. Strong polytonal and contrapuntal lines with an overall supple feeling and spirited animation. The product is a brilliant and virtuosic sounding work but does not require virtuosity from its performers. Solid and logical construction. M-D.

Charles Mills. *Trio* (ACA) 22 min. Mainly diatonic writing in a neoclassic style, full of fine melodies and shifting chord progressions. Forceful and expressive writing, highly idiomatic, modern and imaginative. M-D.

Douglas Moore. *Trio* 1953 (Galaxy 1963) 48pp., parts. Allegro molto marcato; Adagio; Allegro vivace. Tonal with dissonant contrasts used to create tension; traditional formal schemes; fundamentally lyric. The musical substance explores with firm assurance the inherent possibilities of all three instruments. Mildly contemporary. M-D.

Ennio Morricone. *Distanze* (Distances) 1958 (Sal 1973) 28pp., parts. 5 min. Pointillistic, sudden dynamic changes, wide dynamic range *pppp—ffff*, non-tonal, frequent tempo changes, continuous development in a kind of variation technique, pedal used for sonority effects, expressionistic. Large span required. D.

Harold Morris. *Trio II* 1937 (SPAM 1952) 32pp., parts. Passacaglia: moderately slow. Scherzo: brisk and sprightly; slow–quick–Tempo I–very slow. Fugue: not too fast. Exploits much of the keyboard in a mildly contemporary style. Deserves to be revived. M-D.

Wolfgang Amadeus Mozart. *Trios for Piano, Violin and Cello* (G. Lorenz—Henle 1972) 190pp., parts. Fingering for piano added by H.-M. Theopold. Includes K.254 B♭ (Divertimento), K.496 G, K.498 E♭, K.502 B♭, K.542 E, K.548 C, K.564 G. All but K.254 are sheer masterpieces. Most material is shared between the piano and the violin, although the cello does make a subtle and unique contribution. This excellent edition is based on autographs. Text is most carefully reproduced. In K.498 the score includes both the original clarinet part (from the autograph) and the violin arrangement of it. Some interesting variants turn up.

———— *Klaviertrios* (W. Plath, W. Rehm—Br 4545). Includes K.10–15, K.254, K.496, K.498 "Kegelstatt," K.502, K.542, K.548, K.564, Fragment K.442, Anhang 52, 51.

———— *Seven Trios* (CFP 193; David—IMC). K.254, K.496, K.502, K542, K.548, K.564, and K.498 for clarinet or violin, viola, and piano. Available separately: *Trio* K.254 B♭ (Br&H; CFP; GS L1607; Augener 7268f) 16 min. *Trio* K.496 G (Adamowski—GS L1602; CFP; Br&H; Augener 7268a) 25min. *Trio* K.502 B♭ (Br&H; GS L1603; Litolff; Augener 7268b). *Trio* K.542 E (Br&H; GS L1604; Augener 7268c; Litolff; Drei Masken Verlag—a facsimile of Mozart's MS). *Trio* K.548 C (Br&H; GS L1605; Litolff; Augener 7268d) 16½ min. *Trio* K.564 G (Br&H; GS L1606; Litolff, Augener 7268e). *Trio* K.498 E♭ (GS L1403) originally for piano, violin or clarinet, and viola.

———— *Trio* K.442 d (Br&H; Litolff; GS L1608).

Dika Newlin. *Trio* Op.2 1948 (CFE) 71pp., parts. Introduction; Largo; Liberamente; Quasi cadenza. A highly organized serial work, with contrasting tempi and moods, and shifting meters. Intense and expressionistic. Includes two Trios. D.

Marlos Nobre. *Trio* Op.4 1960 (Tonos) 16 min. Influence of Villa-Lobos and Milhaud noted but serial tendencies are also evident; more in the "Latin" tradition of Dallapiccola and Berio. The piano part carries a great deal of the piece. In some instances it is more like a concerto for piano with string accompaniment. D.

Ib Nørholm. *Trio* Op.22 1959 (Samfundet til Udgivelse Af Dansk Musik) 20 min. Andante; Allegretto; Moderato; Adagio; Allegro. Fresh and subtle coloristic writing in serial style. D.

Vítězláv Novák. *Trio* Op.1 g (Urbanek 1187) 51pp., parts, Allegro moderato; Allegro giusto; Andante sostenuto e mesto; Allegro non troppo.

———— *Trio quasi una Ballata* Op.27 1902 (Artia; Simrock 31pp., parts; UE) 16 min. One movement with contrasting tempi and moods. In the

Brahms–Dvořák tradition with Slovakian folk music inspiration. Contains four rhapsodic, linked movements in the manner of the ballad with monothematic treatment. M-D.

Lionel Nowak. *Trio* 1954 (CFE).

Juan Orrego-Salas. *Trio* (PIC).

Andrezej Panufnik. *Trio* 1934 (PWM 1950) 40pp., parts. Three untitled movements. Freely tonal, mildly contemporary, flowing lines, syncopation. Fine balance achieved between feeling and intellect, heart and brain, impulse and design. Large span required. M-D.

Vincent Persichetti. *Serenade III* Op.17 (PIC 1952) 14pp., parts. Moderato grazioso; Andante sostenuto; Moderato. Lyrical melodic lines based on seminal motivic materials rooted in diatonic harmony. A contrapuntal compactness and rhythmic drive combined with a personal and practical touch make this one of Persichetti's most successful Serenades (he has written eight Serenades for various instruments). Gratifying piano writing. M-D.

Rudolf Petzold. *Trio* Op.39 1961 (Gerig 435) 19pp., parts. 17 min. Introzione; Adagio ben sostenuto; Prestissimo. Serial, intense, expressionistic, dynamic extremes, trills effectively used, short–long rhythmic idea prevalent, combination of linear and homophonic writing, brilliant and dramatic conclusion to entire work. D.

Hans Pfitzner. *Trio* Op.8 F (Simrock 1898) 67pp., parts. Movements are related with one fundamental theme serving as the basis of each. Kräftig und feurig, nicht zu schnell: begins in a high-spirited mood; cello has main theme, which is later fully developed. Langsam: Romantic, deeply expressive. Mässig schnell, etwas frei im Vortrag: piano opens with a vivacious and rhythmic idea; strings add their own dance theme, and the combination of these ideas provides the basis of the movement. Rasch und wild: fast and tempestuous, has the most pitfalls for the pianist. Strong dramatic contrasts add effectively to success of this piece. D.

Gabriel Pierné. *Trio* Op.45 (Durand 1922). One of Pierné's finest works; displays characteristics of clarity, elegance, and a fine sense of proportion. Color and variety permeate the harmonic language. Thoroughly French writing of a refined artistic nature. Highly pianistic. M-D.

Willem Pijper. *Trio* Op.7 e 1914 (Donemus). Diatonic themes, freely polyphonic, bitonal combinations, Mahler and Debussy influence noted. M-D.

―――― *Trio II* 1921 (Donemus) 24pp., parts. 14 min. Andante, molto rubato; Vivo; Allegretto giocoso. Polytonal treatment provides harsh dissonance; changing meters with overlapping contrapuntal lines. Germ-cell provides most material for this strongly knit work. D.

Georg Pirckmayer. *Transition 56/71* 1956 (Dob 1975) 17pp., parts. Allegro moderato; Andante; Allegro vivace. Expressionistic. Requires large span.

Filipe Pires. *Trio* (EC 1960) 23pp., parts. Lento assai: contains a mid-section Presto before returning to opening tempo and mood; leads directly into final movement, a Passacaglia with the cello taking the lead with the subject. Equal treatment of instruments throughout entire work. Freely tonal, mildly contemporary. M-D.

Walter Piston. *Trio* 1935 (Arrow Press) 43pp., parts. 17 min. Allegro: SA unraveled in an almost Mendelssohnian circumspection. Adagio: short ABA. Allegro con brio: in a lively 6/8, full of verve and inventiveness. Allegro moderato: much contrapuntal interplay between the three instruments. Tonality is in evidence throughout although it is not usually obvious. Simplicity of form and a highly finished contrapuntal texture are its main characteristics. M-D.

―――― *Trio II* 1966 (AMP) 26pp., parts. Facsimile of composer's autograph. Molto leggiero e capriccioso; Adagio; Vigoroso. Displays a disciplined harmonic and contrapuntal technique with great manipulation of ideas. Freely dissonant; transparent textures, closely knit ensemble writing. D.

Ildebrando Pizzetti. *Trio* A (Ric 119896 1925) 71pp., parts. 30 min. Mosso e arioso; Largo; Rapsodia di Settembre. Sensitive writing in an expansively lyric character. The final movement has the two strings playing in 3/2 (calmo e contemplativo) while the piano part has a 3/4 × 3 time signature (Vivace—non presto). As the movement develops these rhythmic differences become less noticeable although the pianist retains the obvious opening eighth-note figuration throughout the movement. D.

Ignaz Pleyel. *Klavier-Trios* (W. Stockmeier—Henle 292 1976) 39pp., parts. Fingering for the piano part added by Jörg Demus. Trios in C, Hob.XV: 3 and in F, Hob.XV: 4. Both works have undergone a strange set of circumstances. There is now conclusive evidence that they were written by Haydn's pupil Pleyel, not by Haydn. This situation is discussed in the preface. As regards form and style, both works deviate from the authentic

Haydn trios to such an extent that if one ignores any philological consideration it would seem certain that they did not originate with Haydn. Editorial
additions made to conform to analogous passages are distinguished by
square brackets. Excellent urtext and practical edition. M-D.

Robert Pollock. *Trio* 1972 (Boelke-Bomart) 11 min.

Marcel Poot. *Trois Pièces en Trio* (ESC 1935) 23pp., parts. 12 min. 1.
Allegro Marziale, 2. Adagio in stilo antico, 3. Impromptu. Clever rhythmic
treatment and arresting sonorities are mixed with gaiety, wit, and sophistication. Grateful piano writing; Impressionistic influences felt in the second
piece. M-D.

Hans Poser. *Variations on "The Cuckoo and the Donkey"* (Möseler).

Sergei Rachmaninoff. *Trio Elégaique I* g 1892 (USSR 1973; Bo&H) 34pp.,
parts.
_____ *Trio Elégaique II* Op.9 d 1893 (Gutheil; IMC) 64pp., parts. 43 min.
Moderato–Allegro moderato; Quasi variazione—Andante; Allegro risoluto.
Composed in the form of SA and a set of variations. The piano, as might be
expected, dominates more than true chamber music style dictates. Written
in honor of Tschaikowsky, who died while it was being composed. Strong
emotional quality, melancholy. Sequences of hymnlike character are interspersed with brilliant piano passages. Powerful melodic gift already seen
in this early and somewhat diffuse work. D.

Josef Joachim Raff. *Trio* Op.102 c (Schuberth 1864).
_____ *Trio* II Op.112 G 1866 (Rieter-Biedermann).
_____ *Trio* III Op. 155 a "Grand Trio" (Bo&Bo 1872; Hamelle).
_____ *Trio* IV Op.158 D (R&E 1871; Hamelle).
These works are not the best of Raff's compositions as they are somewhat
diffuse and lack strong self-criticism. But there are good ideas and basically
a fine understanding of the instruments. They are full of a special spirit of
Central European Romanticism. No.3 is the finest of those listed above.
Raff demands a good deal from all the performers. M-D to D.

Erhard Ragwitz. *Trio* Op.10 1965 (DVFM 8311) 35pp., parts. Allegro;
Lento appassionato; Allegro agitato. Freely tonal around d, generally thin
textures, octotonic, toccata-like finale, neoclassic. M-D.

Jean Philippe Rameau. *Pièces de Clavecin en Concerts* 1742 (E. Jacobi—Br
1970) 63pp., parts. For violin or flute and viol (gamba) or a second violin
and keyboard. Five concerts (suites), which are first and foremost keyboard

pieces. They can all be played on the keyboard alone. "The term 'en concert' means 'for ensemble playing,' the ensemble being formed by the addition of parts for melodic instruments which 'accompany' the obbligato keyboard" (from preface, which gives much more information). Includes Rameau's "Notice to Performers" and "Notice for the Harpsichord, Flute and Viole," all in French, German, and English. Beautiful urtext and performing edition. D. (Saint-Saens—Durand). Somewhat over-edited.
Each suite available separately (Peyrot, Rebuffat—Senart).

Maurice Ravel. *Piano Trio* a (Durand 1914) 35pp., parts. 28 min. exudes warmth and is full of rich harmonic color, especially in the piano part. Long undulating melodic lines are often heard in octaves or double octaves in the violin and cello. All instruments are perfectly deployed. The rhythmically intricate Pantoum movement requires a crispness in touch. All movements are closely related thematically. The opening movement (Modéré) has a broad sweeping melody in 8/8 (3 + 2 + 3/8). The second movement (Pantoum) is breathless and fast with a grand tune in the second middle section. Passacaille (Très large): a dignified passacaille. The Final is elaborate and exciting. The outer movements are noble and highly expressive. D.
See: Brian Newbould, "Ravel's Pantoum," MT, 116 (March 1975): 228–31. Clarifies the background of the title "Pantoum" used by Ravel in the Piano Trio.

Alan Rawsthorne. *Trio* 1962 (OUP) 32pp., parts. 14 min. Introduction—poco lento: freely tonal, clear lines, subtle writing, leads directly to the Capriccio—Allegro deciso: theme is given out in octaves and quickly followed by a poco misterioso section in 5/8; flowing chromatic triplets; large chordal gestures; movement unfolds fluently with these basic elements. Theme and Variations—Allegretto: no separation between variations; following the modal and mainly diatonic theme are nine contrasting short variations; there is a consistency of texture and nervous intensity about the movement that is projected with lively figuration. The entire piece "communicates" well. M-D.

Max Reger. *Trio* Op.102 e (Bo&Bo 1908) 92pp., parts. Allegro moderato, ma con passione; Allegretto; Largo; Allegro con moto. Strong, sweeping and impassioned, influenced by J. S. Bach. Seriousness and expressive qualities in the outer movements are notable. The piquant and shapely scherzo and trio are masterfully crafted. D.

Carl Reinecke. *Trio II* Op.230 (Br&H) 43pp., parts. Allegro; Adagio sostenuto; Scherzo; Finale. Reinecke's works have not withstood the test of time very well, but there is some solid musical writing in this trio that should see it revived from time to time. M-D.

Otto Reinhold. *Piano Trio* (Br 1915 1952) 23pp., parts. Sehr heftig; Intermezzo; Sehr erregt. Freely tonal, repeated chords, quintal harmony. Outer movements have much rhythmic drive while the Intermezzo rides gracefully on flowing melodies. Neoclassic orientation. Requires large span. M-D.

Franz Reizenstein. *Trio* Op.34 1957 (Lengnick) 30pp., parts. 10 min. One movement. Reizenstein studied with Ralph Vaughan Williams but there is not much English influence in this work. Reizenstein was a natural and fine pianist, and the piano part is idiomatically conceived in every aspect. Freely tonal, diffuse. M-D.

Josef Rheinberger. *Trio* III Op.121 B♭ (Forberg 1881) 59pp., parts. Allegretto amabile; Romanze; Scherzo; Finale.
_____ *Trio* IV Op.191 F (Leuckart 1899) 47pp., parts. Moderato; Adagio molto; Tempo di minuetto; Finale.
Both of these works, while strongly Romantic, do show the influence of Mozart, Beethoven, and Schubert. Formally and in developmental skill (his canonic weaving in particular), Rheinberger is a real craftsman. Hungarian influence is also heard in Op.121. Both trios are highly recommended to amateur chamber groups. M-D.

Wallingford Riegger. *Trio* Op.1 1919 (SPAM 1933) 60pp., parts. Allegro moderato; Larghetto misterioso; Allegro. This early work is effective; leans toward a pre-Impressionist style with contrapuntal techniques, uses traditional formal schemes. M-D.

George Rochberg. *Piano Trio* 1963 (TP) 29pp., 3 scores necessary for performance. 18 min. Rochberg's last twelve-tone work. Each instrument has a solo section that alternates with an ensemble section. These contrasting sections delineate the formal structure of the piece. Materials are passed from one part to another. The climax near the end displays the most instrumental interaction. All the techniques associated with twelve-tone technique are present: pointillistic treatment, extreme dynamics that also appear to be serialized, expressionistic style. D.

Albert Roussel. *Trio* Op.2 E♭ 1902 rev. 1927 (Rouart Lerolle) 53pp., parts. 29 min. Modédére, sans lenteur; Lent; Très lent. Cyclic theme that appears in the Introduction and first movement takes on more importance in the slow movement and returns in the brisk and highly rhythmic finale. Varied tempi, especially in the finale. Fondness for triplet figuration and arpeggi is apparent. Lent movement is the most Impressionistic. D.

Edmund Rubbra. *Piano Trio* Op.68 1950 (Lengnick) 27pp., parts. 20 min. Andante moderato, e molto flessibile; Episodio scherzando; Prima Meditazione–Seconda Meditazione–Terza Meditazione. One-movement form but actually in three without a break. Cyclic treatment, seems to prefer lower registers of the piano. Written for the Rubbra–Gruenberg–Pleeth Trio of which the composer was a member from 1945 to 1956. D.

_____ *Piano Trio* II Op.138 1970 (Lengnick) 27pp., parts. Two movements, the second being a delightful scherzo with a syncopated main theme. Dignified writing showing development through the Brahms tradition. Solid craft, rich harmonies. D.

Anton Rubinstein. *Trio* I Op.15/1 F (Hofmeister) 47pp., parts. A good piece for amateurs looking for an accessible and M-D work, but there are many hurdles for the pianist.

_____ *Trio* II Op.15/2 (Hamelle; Hofmeister; UE 49pp., parts). Moderato; Adagio; Allegro assai; Moderato.

_____ *Trio* III Op.52 B♭ (Hamelle; Bartholf Senff) 51pp., parts. Moderato assai; Andante; Allegro moderato.

_____ *Trio* IV Op.85 (Hamelle).

_____ *Trio* V Op.108 (Hamelle).

As might be expected, the piano parts of all these works are effectively written in a Romantic-eclectic style and require fine technical facility.

Camille Saint-Saëns. *Trio* Op.18 F 1863 (Hamelle) 53pp., parts. 26 min. One of Saint-Saëns' most inspired early works. The opening movement is one of gaiety and alluring joy. The scherzo turns this gaiety into humor with pizzicato effects and cross-rhythms. The Andante is beautifully molded with an expressive theme in ballad style. M-D to D.

_____ *Trio* Op.92 e 1892 (Durand) 32 min. Five movements that display great craft and inspiration. Unexpected episodes are introduced between the main subjects, and phrases return to the tonic in sinuous ways. At times all three instruments move with great freedom, then are heard in unison passages. 5/4 interrupts 5/8 at one point and adds interest. Logical development supports perfect balance. M-D to D.

These works display brilliant piano writing that does not overbalance the strings. They are models of style and have strong emotional appeal.

Allen Sapp. *Trio* I (CFE).

Karl Schiske. *Sonatine* Op.34 1952 (Dob) 20pp., parts. Andante; Allegro; Adagio. Constantly shifting meters, freely tonal around a, neoclassic. M-D.

Johann Schobert. *Trio* Op.6/1 E♭ (A. Karsch—Nag 197) 18pp., parts. Allegro; Andante; Tempo di Menuetto. Schobert is one of the forefathers of modern chamber music for the piano. This trio is written in a style close to that of the Mannheim school. The keyboard part, with its figuration, is interesting on its own as well as combining effectively with the other instruments. The dark coloration of the Andante, with its extensive cantilene, looks forward to Beethoven. M-D.

Franz Peter Schubert. *Trios* (E. Badura-Skoda—Henle 1973) 156pp., parts. Fingering for the piano part added by H.-M. Theopold. Contains *Trio* Op.99 B♭, D.898, 31 min.; *Trio* Op.100 E♭, D.929, 39 min.; Sonata movement B♭, D.28; Adagio E♭, Op. posth.148, D.897. Preface in German, English, and French. Critical commentary in German. Beautifully printed and thoroughly reliable performing edition. Based on the most authentic sources. These and the background of all four works are discussed in the preface. The inspiration and delicacy as well as restraint exhibited in the development of thematic material make D.898 and D.929 some of the most successful of this great lyricist's chamber music. See especially the exposition and development of the first movement of D.898. The scherzo of D.100 is constructed from a canon that receives amazing treatment.

———— *Werke für Klavier und mehrere Instrumente* (A. Feil—Br 1975) 302pp., parts, 8 facsimilies. Contains *Trio* B♭, D.28 (1812); *Trio* E♭, D.929/Op.100 (1827); *Trio* B♭, D.898/Op.99 (1828?); *Trio* E♭, D.897/Op. posth.148 (1828?); *Quartett* F (Adagio e Rondo concertante) D.487 (1816); *Quintett* A, D.667/Op. posth.114 (1819?); Anhang: *Trio* E♭, D.929/Op.100 (Entwurf, 1827). Introduction, preface, and critical commentary (with 23 musical examples) in German.

———— *Complete Chamber Music for Piano and Strings* (I. Brüll—Dover) 2 vols. A reprint of the Breitkopf and Härtel complete edition. Includes *Quintet* Op.114 ("Trout"), *Quartet* (Adagio and Rondo Concertante F), and *Trios* Op.99, Op.100, Op.148 (a Notturno in B♭). Reasonably priced but no mention is made of separate parts.

Available separately: *Trio* D.898/Op.99 (Br&H; CFP; UE 4851; Schott; Adamowski—GS L1471; Augener 7277). *Trio* D.929/Op.100 (Br&H; CFP; Adamowski—GS L1472; Augener 7278; EPS).

Clara Schumann. *Piano Trio* Op.17 g (W. Wollenweber UWKR 16) 35pp., parts. Allegro moderato; Scherzo—Tempo di Menuetto; Andante; Allegretto. Shows influence of Haydn, Mendelssohn, Weber, and Robert

Schumann, but the composer's own style displays interesting rhythms and fresh modulations that are sometimes abrupt and more delicate than forceful. The work is thoroughly musicianly and well crafted even if more imitative than innovative. Simple straightforward writing, charming. M-D.

Robert Schumann. *Three Trios* (CFP).

_____ *Trio* Op.63 d 1848 (CFP; Adamowski—GS L1476; Augener) 28 min. Tumultuous opening movement, vivacious Scherzo, emotional intensity, anguished dynamism. Poetic and highly inspired with the piano part occasionally unduly overemphasized. All three instruments are called upon to supply virtuosic effects. Schumann's finest trio. D.

_____ *Trio* Op.80 F 1847 (CFP; Adamowski—GS L1477; Augener) 26 min. Molto animato; Con espressione intima; In tempo moderato; Non troppo vivo. Although written at about the same time as the first trio, in a letter to Carl Reinecke, Schumann said this work "makes a quicker and more ingratiating appeal." Has the warmth and Romantic style that characterize many of his other works. D.

_____ *4 Phantasiestücke* Op.88 1842 (Br&H 25pp., parts; CFP 27pp., parts; IMC). Romanze a; Humoreske d; Duett d; Finale a. Highly sensitive writing. M-D.

_____ *Trio* Op.110 g 1852 (CFP; Adamowski—GS L1478; Augener; Eulenburg) 25 min. Schumann is seen at his most dramatic in this work. Steady rise and fall of parts, contrary direction of lines, doublings not offensive. D.

Paul Schwartz. *Trio* Op.10 (CFE).

Ralph Shapey. *Trio* (CFE). Much internal play of energies that constantly sets up tension and release. Overlapping ideas in broad phrases. Shapey's own description of his compositional procedures is appropriate here: "imposed discipline by ritualistic reiteration." There is much expressive power and emotional impact in this complex music. D.

Seymour Shifrin. *Trio* 1974 (Boelke-Bomart) 11 min. Neoclassic, clear formal outlines, ambiguous tonal usage achieved by chromatic writing, fast harmonic motion. Strongly contrasted materials such as lyric and pointillistic lines; short dynamic upbeat figures combined with broad sustained downbeats. Dramatic and tense writing make for difficult listening. D.

Dmitri Shostakovich. *Trio* Op.67 e 1944 (CFP; MCA; USSR 63pp., parts; IMC) 27 min. First movement: strange opening in harmonics, unusual tonal quality, folk-like melody, disquieting. Second movement: impetuous, frenetic, relentless. Third movement: sombre, elegiac; piano carries harmonic color. Fourth movement: angular and menacing Jewish-flavored main subject; dancelike grotesquerie; moves with a contrapuntal mechanical, rhythmical motion; coda recalls theme of first movement. Anxious, tense, disturbing; achieves a profound result. Tragic moods of the time are reflected in this trio, one of the most brilliant and effective Soviet chamber works. D.

Nikos Skalkottos. *Trio* 1936 (UE 14149). Light, transparent, introspective writing. Serial influence felt but not used in any strict manner. Long lyric lines lend themselves to contrapuntal development. D.

———*Eight Variations on a Greek Folk Song* 1938 (UE 12735 1957) 21pp., parts. 12 min. Modal chromatic harmonic idiom; contrasting variations provide both interest and unity. Effective expressionistic treatment of folk material. M-D.

Dane Skerl. *Trio* 1973 (Društva Slovenskih Skladateljev) 19pp., parts.

Bedřich Smetana. *Trio* Op.15 g 1855 (Artia; CFP 4238; UE 46pp., parts; IMC; Eulenburg 52pp., parts) 27 min. Moderato assai: SA; melancholy theme; piano has sustained chords until bar 17, when it gives out the main idea; octaves; vigorous but gloomy ending. Allegro, ma non agitato: has two contrasting alternativos (or trios): rhythmic motion of piano accompanies lament of strings; a doloroso scherzo. Finale—Presto: energetic; arpeggio figures; a grave martial quality gives idea of a funeral procession; Tempo I returns and brings the movement to a close. Written while Smetana was suffering from the loss of his first child, who was $4\frac{1}{2}$ years old. Liszt appreciated this work. D.

Julia Smith. *Trio-Cornwall* (Mowbray 1966) 39pp., parts. $14\frac{1}{2}$ min. Allegro giusto; Theme with (7) Variations; Allegro quasi rondo. The title refers to Cornwall-on-the Hudson, New York, where the composer first heard the bird calls that provide thematic material for the first movement. The second movement presents a few outside glimpses, including Puerto Rico and the Virgin Islands. Third movement is back in Cornwall and uses the familiar street sound (c–e–g–e auto horn call) as a first theme and a syncopated melody as a second theme. First and last movements are in SA design. Mildly contemporary. M-D.

Leland Smith. *Trio* (CFE 1947) 25pp., parts. See detailed entry under trios for piano, one stringed instrument, and one wind instrument.

Jose Soler. *Trio* 1963 (Seesaw) 23pp., parts. Serial, pointillistic, broad atonal gestures, dynamic extremes, piano cadenza. One extended movement, varied tempi, moods, thorny and complex writing. D.

Leopold Spinner. *Trio* Op.6 1955 (TP) 19pp., parts. Andante; Allegro moderato; Allegro poco vivace. Strong Webern influence, possibilities of twelve-tone technique exploited. Changing tempi, pitch, and dynamics serialized; pointillistic. D.

Louis Spohr. *Trio* Op.119 e (Litolff) 27 min.

———*Trio* Op.123 F 1843 (Br 48pp., parts; Litolff).

———*Trio* Op.124 a 1844 (B. Mersson—KaWé 1973, 43pp., parts; Litolff). Allegro moderato; Andante con Variazioni (highly figurative for the piano); Scherzo; Finale.

———*Trio* Op.133 B♭ 1848 (O. Leinert—Br 19106 48pp., parts; Litolff). Br edition has a preface and critical notes in German, French, and English. Allegro: shows a preference for chords in both hands and a full piano part, and even though Spohr was not a pianist, there is a remarkable versatility in the use of purely pianistic idioms. Menuetto—Moderato: sparkling passage work is required from the pianist in the trio. Poco Adagio: has the character of an Intermezzo; uses widely spread chords and harplike idioms, and serves as a link to the lively closing Rondo. Finale—Presto: pleasant lightness, transparency, and rhythmic pithiness; Spohr called this movement the *Sprudelsatz* (hot spring movement) as a facetious pun in remembrance of the Karlsbad hot springs, where he was staying when he composed the movement. One of the most grateful chamber works of the Romantic period. M-D to D.

———*Trio* Op.142 g 1852 (Leinert—Br; Litolff).

These works are somewhat dated by today's standards but there is a sturdy character streaked with tenderness that makes the writing highly interesting at places.

Aloiz Srebotnjak. *Diary* 1972 (Društva Slovenskih Skladateljev) 35pp., parts.

Patric Standford. *Trio* (Nov 1970) 34pp., parts. 25 min. Frequent octave passages and string tremolos provide much of the basic material for this one-movement work. Compelling and intense writing. D.

Christopher Steel. *Trio* Op.23 (Nov 1968) 34pp., parts. 10 min. Allegretto; Molto moderato; Presto. Freely tonal, flowing lines, octave imitation and syncopation, octotonic, parallel chords. Presto is toccata-like with harmonic seconds, repeated chords; grand pause before coda leads to brilliant closing. Large span required. M-D.

Halsey Stevens. *Trio* III 1953-4 (ACA) 42pp., parts. 14½ min. Allegro non troppo, marcato; Con moto moderato; Vivace. Freely tonal, dissonant

counterpoint, thin textures, modal, toccata-like finale with contrasting episodes. Material unfolds naturally. Large span required. M-D to D.

Wolfgang Strauss. *Trio* Op.58 1971 (DVFM) 29pp., parts.

Georgy V. Sviridov. *Trio* Op.6 (USSR 1963) 79pp., parts. Allegro
moderato; Allegro vivo; Andante; Allegretto. Has a full-blooded Russian
Slavic sound. Large nineteenth-century pianistic gestures in a slightly contemporary idiom. Thorough integration of all instruments. D.

Sergey Ivanovitch Taneyev. *Trio* Op.22 D (Simrock 101pp., parts; USSR).
Allegro: condensed SA design, elegant and well-crafted writing. Allegro
molto: Scherzo with the addition of a theme and variations; returns to
opening tempo. Andante espressivo: connected with a violin cadenza that
leads directly to the Finale—Allegro con brio: animated and fast. Shows a
masterful use of counterpoint coupled with unusual formal construction. D.

Alexandre Tansman. *Trio* II 1938 (ESC) 31pp., parts. Introduction et Allegro; Scherzo; Arioso; Finale. Strong lyric melodic inventiveness,
rhythmic dynamism, subtle melancholy. Construction elements carefully
worked out. Piano part displays complete understanding of the instrument.
Chromatic; Impressionistic tendencies. M-D.

Alexander Tcherepnin. *Trio* Op.34 (Durand 1925) 15pp., parts. 8 min.
Moderato tranquillo; Allegretto; Allegro molto. Economic writing in all
movements. The first movement, in SA design, has an extensive development section. The finale, highly rhythmic, is the most serious, and concludes with a perpetual motion idea. Lines are frequently passed from one
instrument to another in the composer's "interpoint" approach. M-D to D.
———— *Triple Concertino* Op.47 1931 (UE 15772 trio version 1972) 36pp.,
parts. 15 min. Originally for violin, cello, piano, and orchestra. This version
made by the composer. Allegro marciale: chordal with many seconds included, freely tonal, triplets, repeated notes; large span required. Lento: low
register exploited; tremolo; rhythmic and melodic elements contrasted. Allegro: 7/4, ostinato-like, alternating hands, heavy chords, chromatic figuration. Presto: quintal harmony, strong rhythms, 3 with 4; coda slows to a
Lento closing. Colorful and pianistic writing. M-D.

Georg Philipp Telemann. *Six Concerti* (Br 2961). See detailed entry under
duos for piano and flute.

Antoine Tisné. *Musique en Trio* (Billaudot 1973) 68pp., parts. Fervent;
Hallucinant "Vision Fantastique"; Elégiaque; Violent. Chromatic, ex-

pressionistic, serial influence, wide dynamic range, octotonic, harmonics, pointillistic. The Elégiaque movement is made up of twelve contrasting "Structures" similar to variations. Percussive treatment of the piano in last movement. Virtuoso writing and instrumentation. Requires large span. D.

Donald Francis Tovey, *Trio* Op.1 b (Schott 28638 1910) 53pp., parts. Maestoso, quasi andante, ma con moto; Menuetto; Rhapsodie; Finale. M-D.

———— *Trio* Op.8 c (Schott 27833 1906). Originally for piano, clarinet, and horn. Separate parts for violin and cello. M-D.

———— *Trio* Op.27 D 1910 (Schott) 36pp., parts. Allegro con brio; Larghetto maestoso; Allegro energico, non presto. Spacious; broad writing; firm technical handling; influence of late Beethoven and Brahms discernible in the construction of this work. Classically oriented. M-D.

Peter I. Tschaikowsky. *Trio* Op.50 a 1882 (CFP 3777, 91pp., parts; USSR; IMC; Augener 7285). Written in memory of Nicolas Rubinstein. Pezzo elegiaco: SA; melancholy opening idea; Russian Allegro giusto second subject; third idea brought in and worked out with the other two main ideas; concludes with heavy minor chords in the piano. Theme and Variations: beautiful swaying theme in Russian character is the basis for this movement with eleven variations; eighth variation, a fugue, is frequently omitted in performance; short coda (lugubre) brings back the elegiac main theme in the strings with a slow rhythm funeral march in the piano. Strongly emotional and stirring. D.

Joaquin Turina. *Trio I* Op.35 d (Rouart Lerolle 1926) 32pp., parts. 23 min. In the nature of a 3-sectioned fantasy: Prélude et Fugue; Theme et (5) Variations; Sonata. Written in a style that blends Spanish and foreign elements. Has much charm and interesting timbre. The variations movement has the most interest, with each variation adapted to a different Spanish rhythm. M-D.

———— *Trio II* Op.76 b (Rouart Lerolle 1933) 28pp., parts. 14 min. Lento–Allegro molto moderato: much rhythmic drive, ideas contrasted, not developed. Molto vivace: 5/8; a short Lento mid-section is chordal and Impressionistic; 5/8 returns. Lento: solid and broken chordal figuration; moves to a dancelike Allegretto followed by a meno mosso that pulls it back to a Moderato before a quickening of pace continues to the end. Varied tempi could cause ensemble problems, cyclic. M-D.

———— *Circulo* Op.91 (Fantasia) 1936 (UME) 19pp., parts. 9½min. 1. Amanecer, 2. Mediodio, 3. Crespúsculo. Spanish color and glitter. M-D.

Alfred Uhl. *Kleines Konzert* (Dob 1975) 44pp., parts. Serially organized in a very personal style. D.

Fartein Valen. *Trio* Op.5 1924 (NMO) 37pp., parts. 22 min. Moderato; Scherzo; Largo; Finale. Harmonies occur in passing notes that are highly chromatic and treated in a linear fashion. Distinct, personal style that is complex, yet the music develops imaginatively. D.

Antonio Veracini. *Sonata à Tre* Op.1/10 (F. Polnauer—Hug 1973) 16pp., parts. Four movements—slow, fast, slow, fast—using same tonal vocabulary as Veracini's contemporary Corelli. Veracini is a careful craftsman. M-D.

————*Sonata da Camera* Op.3/2 C (F. Polnauer—JWC 1970) 20pp., parts. Continuo Series No.1. Slow, fast, slow, fast outline; spacious printing. Int. to M-D.

Heitor Villa-Lobos. *Premier Trio* c 1911 (ESC 1956) 63pp., parts. 20 min. Allegro non troppo; Andante sostenuto; Scherzo; Allegro troppo e finale. Contains big splashes of color throughout. The finale anticipates Villa-Lobos's later experimentation with the blending of Bach's style and Brazilian musical elements in the *Bachianas Brasileiras*. D.

————*Deuxième Trio* 1915 (ESC 1928) 64pp., parts. 20 min. Allegro moderato; Berceuse–Barcarolla (in 10/16); Scherzo; Finale—Molto allegro. Requires enormous technique as well as stamina. Romantic–Impressionistic sonorities with rather heavy-handed piano writing. D.

————*Troisième Trio* 1918 (ESC 1929) 71pp., parts. 25 min. Allegro con moderato; Assai moderato; Allegretto spirituoso; Finale—Allegro animato. Requires virtuoso pianism with tremendous strength. D.

These three trios are almost a catalogue of twentieth-century (to that time) pianistic techniques and idioms. D.

Ernst Vogel. *Trio* 1971 (Dob) 22pp., parts. 14 min. Three untitled contrasting movements. Written in a dissonant neoclassic style. Thematic material is pale. D.

Robert Volkmann. *Trio* Op.3 F (Litolff 1917). Light in character. M-D.

————*Trio* Op.5 b♭ (Litolff 1914; Br&H 44pp., parts). Three movements but gives the impression of having only two, as the last two movements are connected. Opening movement is virile and passionate, while the second is pleasant with ritornello usage. A wild tempestuous finale ends rather quietly. Uses all the pianistic techniques common to the period. This work made Volkmann well-known. It was dedicated to Liszt, and he was fond of it. M-D.

————*Musikalisches Bilderbuch* Op.11 (WH).

Alex Voormolen. *Trio* C 1918 (Rouart Lerolle) 26pp., parts. 13½ min. Lent; Pavane; Très modéré–Animé et spirituel. Strong Ravel and late Debussy influence. Aristocratic, picturesque writing combined with harmonic vitality. Voormolen studied with Ravel and Roussel. M-D.

George Walker. *Music for Three* 1970 (Gen) 7pp., parts. 5 min. Terse, abstract, serial, pointillistic, effective. Demands high level of ensemble experience for all players. D.

Karl Weigl. *Trio* 1939 (Joshua).

Louis Weingarden. *Things Heard and Seen in Summer* (OUP 1974) 17pp., parts. 7 min. 11 short pieces: 1. Grazioso (violin, piano), 2. Andante (piano), 3. Andantino (cello, piano), 4. Lento (violin, piano), 5. Organum—Allegretto (violin, cello, piano), 6. Lento (cello), 7. Largo (violin, piano), 8. Ostinati (cello, piano), 9. Andante (violin, cello, piano), 10. Andantino (violin), 11. Vivace (violin, cello, piano). Expressionistic writing. Piano employs clusters, plucked strings, glissandi with finger nail. Solid pianistic equipment required throughout. D.

Charles Marie Widor. *Trio* Op.19 B♭ (Hamelle 1875) 56pp., parts. Allegro: flexible writing, elegant second subject. Andante con moto quasi moderato: siciliano rhythm; contains some powerful moments; quiet ending. Scherzo—Vivace: piano announces well-marked theme; lively dialogue; a curious false entry of the trio before its normal appearance, then scherzo is repeated complete. Finale—Presto: rondo, followed by flowing and fresh writing; then all three instruments make strong statements before rondo returns. M-D.

Dag Wiren. *Trio* I Op.6 1933 (MG) 32pp., parts. 15 min. Allegro; Adagio; Fughetta. Fresh and lightly characterized melodic style; Nordic outlook but also shows influence of Prokofiev and Honegger. Freely tonal, centers around c♯. M-D.
———— *Trio* II Op.36 (MG 1963) 27pp., parts. 15 min. Andante–Allegro molto; Intermezzo; Lento espressivo; Molto allegro. Metamorphosis technique used (a musical motif derived from a basic theme forms the point of departure for the whole work). Lucid and polished tonal language. M-D.

Ermanno Wolf-Ferrari. *Trio* Op.7 F♯ 1901 (Rahter) 31pp., parts. Sostenuto; Largo; Lievemente mosso, e tranquillo sempre. Cobbett says this work "contains fine and interesting ideas, and there is an impression of independence in all three movements, the last of which is a very skilfully developed canon" (CCSCM, II, 590). Romantic writing that is heavily chromatic and sounds somewhat dated. Lyrical expression flows unchecked. D.

Russell Woollen. *Trio* Op.29 1957 (CFE) 77pp., parts. Andantino; Vivo; Adagio; Allegro deciso. Well-ordered and balanced forms, octotonic, freely tonal, poignant and expressive Adagio, dance influence in finale, neoclassic. Requires large span. M-D.

Isang Yun. *Trio* (Bo&Bo 1976) 14pp., parts. 11 min.

Mario Zafred. *Trio* III 1955 (Ric 129607) 52pp., parts. Photo of composer's MS. Moderatamente mosso; Lento; Scherzando; Sostenuto. Neoclassic, clear textures, thorough use of all instruments. M-D.

Trios for Piano, Violin, and Viola

Carl Philipp Emanuel Bach. *Trio* I W.94 D (G. Picciolo—IMC 1955) 19pp., parts. Allegretto; Adagio; Allegro molto. M-D.

—————— *Trio* II W.93 a (Piccioli—IMC 1955) 16pp., parts. Andantino; Largo e sostenuto; Allegro assai. M-D.

—————— *Trio* III W.95 G (Piccioli—IMC 1955) 16pp., parts. Allegretto; Adagio; Presto. M-D.

These works were probably written for keyboard, flute, and viola but they sound equally well in the piano, violin, and viola combination. All three realizations border on the fussy.

Arnold Bax. *Trio* Op.4 1906 (JWC) 33pp., parts. 14½ min. In one movement. Strong Richard Strauss and Dvořák influence noted in this early work. Demonstrates high proficiency and facility in writing for this combination. Thick harmonic decoration; requires strong pianistic equipment to sort the more important from the less important. D.

Johannes Brahms. *Trio* Op.40 E♭. See detailed entry under trios for piano, violin, and cello.

—————— *Trio* Op.114 a. See detailed entry under trios for piano, violin, and cello.

John Diercks. *Diversion* (Tritone). MS reproduction.

Johann Ladislav Dussek. *Notturno Concertante* Op.68. See detailed entry under trios for piano, one stringed instrument, and one wind instrument.

Hans-Georg Görner. *Concertino* Op.31 (Hofmeister). See detailed entry under trios for piano and two woodwinds.

Erich Hamann. *Trio* Op.38 (Dob 1964) 28pp., parts. Allegro con moto: SA, octotonic, broken octaves, freely tonal, linear; large span required. Allegro molto: ABA, imitation, repeated and chromatic octaves, chordal sonorities spread over keyboard. Thema con Variationi: folk-like theme, 8 contrasting variations; Presto coda returns to opening idea of second movement; mildly contemporary. M-D.

Tadeusz Jarecki. *Trio–Fugato e Aria* Op.11 (JWC 1943) 11pp., parts. 7½ min. For piano, violin, and cello or viola, includes viola part. Allegro agitato section centered around f♯ opens the work. Left hand arpeggi figuration supports melodic full-chord octaves in right hand. Contrasting subdued material follows. Imitation is heard between the strings. The Aria centers around b and involves all instruments in contrapuntal melodic treatment. The opening fugato section returns to conclude the work con forza and *fff*. Mildly contemporary. M-D.

Joseph Jongen. *Trio* Op.30 f♯ (Durand 1909) 51pp., parts. Prélude: two subjects intertwine in much chromatic figuration and chordal treatment; interlude leads to the Theme and Variations: freely developed in varied treatment; last variation serves as the Final: expanded and further development of variation idea preceding brilliant conclusion. Cobbett says this work "is the first important contribution since Mozart to the repertoire for piano, violin and viola, and demonstrates convincingly the effectiveness of the combination" (CCSCM, II, p. 40).

Robert Kelly. *Theme and Variations* Op.11 1947 (CFE) 29pp., parts. 14 min. Based on theme "Nobody Knows de Trouble I Seen." Nine variations of contrasting mood, texture, and tempi. Imaginative writing. Basically tonal with some chromaticism. The vigorous final variation is the most extensive and demanding. Effective and unpretentious. M-D.

Aram Khachaturian. *Trio* 1932 (CFP; Bo&H; MCA; Musica Rara; Anglo-Soviet Press) 41pp., parts. 16 min. See detailed entry under trios for piano, one stringed instrument, and one wind instrument.

Ignaz Lachner. *Trio* Op.37 B♭ (Hofmeister) 27pp., parts. Allegro moderato; Andante con moto; Scherzo; Finale.
_____ *Trio* Op.45 G (Hofmeister) 62pp., parts. Allegro moderato; Andante; Allegretto; Finale.
_____ *Trio* Op.58 D (Hofmeister) 50pp., parts. Allegro con spirito; Andante; Scherzo; Finale.
_____ *Trio* Op.89 (Hofmeister) 35pp., parts. Allegro giusto; Andantino, quasi Allegretto; Scherzo; Allegro Molto.
_____ *Grand Trio* Op.102 E♭ (Augener 5277) 27pp., parts. Andante con moto; Andante; Allegro con spirito.

These pieces are well constructed but sound old fashioned today. Nevertheless, they are melodically charming and admirable for amateurs looking for works in this rather unusual combination. M-D.

Jean Marie Leclair. *Sonata* D (David—IMC 1943) 11pp., parts. Adagio; Allegro; Sarabande–Andante; Allegro assai. Sarabande is especially attractive. M-D.

Georges Migot. *Trio* 1918 (Senart) 21pp., parts. Modéré; Un peu lent; Lent. Same theme is presented in each movement. Independent melodic lines produce polytonal and sometime strong dissonances (especially for 1918). Modéré is improvisational, has no virtuoso effects, uses syncopated octaves between hands. The whole work gives a static impression since all movements are somewhat slow. M-D.

Rudolf Moser. *Suite* Op.99 A (Gertrud Moser 1970, through O. Harrassowitz) 26pp., parts. For violin, viola, and piano or for flute, clarinet in A, and harpsichord.

Wolfgang A. Mozart. *Trio* K.498 E♭ (Henle; CFP; Eulenburg; Adamowski—GS 31pp., parts) for piano, violin or clarinet, and viola. Andante; Menuetto and Trio; Allegretto. Perhaps the greatest masterpiece for this combination. M-D.

Ignaz Pleyel. *Three Trios* Op.44 (Hermann—Augener 5280).

Max Reger. *Trio* Op.2 b (Schott 1004; Augener) 38pp., parts. Allegro appassionata ma non troppo; Scherzo; Adagio con variazioni. Not as chromatic as the late works but Reger's personal style is already present. The (5) variations movement is the most effective. Technical problems are solved with great skill. M-D to D.

Robert Schumann. *Märchenerzählungen* (Fairy Tales) Op.132 (Br&H 27pp., parts; CFP 19pp., parts; IMC) for piano, violin or clarinet, and viola. 1. Lebhaft nicht zu schnell: scherzando, fast broken chords. 2. Lebhaft und sehr markiert: accented chords, some moving very quickly; more melodic mid-section; opening returns. 3. Ruhiges Tempo, mit zartem Ausdruck: restful, cantabile, sixteenth-note inner accompaniment figure difficult to control. 4. Lebhaft, sehr markiert: strong chords; good octave technique required; many repeated chords in mid-section; opening returns. An effective group. M-D.

Georg Philipp Telemann. *Six Trios* 1718 (K. Schultz-Hauser—Vieweg

1973) No.5 is for violin, viola da gamba (viola), and continuo. 14pp., parts. Some of Telemann's finest works. This fine set is richly contrapuntal with profound slow movements. No.5 is a good example from the set. The realization will probably need some elaboration. M-D.

———— *Triosonate* a (H. Ruf—Heinrichshofen 1973) 12pp., parts. No distinction between original and editorial additions. The simple continuo realization will need some elaboration. Both this work and No.5 above are first modern editions. Int. to M-D.

————*Pyrmonter Kurwoche Scherzi Melodichi* 1734 (M. Ruhnke—Br 1974) 123pp., 8 facsimiles. Vol.XXIV of *Musikalische Werke*. For violin, viola, and continuo. Also contains the *Corellisierende Sonaten* for two violins or flutes and continuo. Preface and critical commentary in German.

———— *Scherzi Melodichi* (Hoffmann—Nag 246 1975) 62pp., parts. 2 vols.

Trios for Piano and Two Violins (Including Trio Sonatas)

[Most of the trio sonatas can be played by two violins and a keyboard instrument, with cello ad lib.]

Evaristo Felice dall'Abaco. *Trio Sonata* Op.3/2 (A. Egidi—Vieweg V34) 8pp., parts. Adagio; Allegro; Largo; Allegro. Charming writing, tasteful keyboard realization. M-D.

Henrico Albicastro. *XII Sonate a Tre* Op.1 (S. Kind—UE 1949) 4 vols., 3 sonatas in each vol. Preface in German.

———— *12 Triosonaten* Op.8 (M. Zulauf—Br 1974) Schweizerische Musik-denkmaler, vol.10. Critical commentary in German.

———— *Dritte Sonate* b (R. Moser—Vieweg) 11pp., parts. Adagio; Allegro; Adagio; Allegro. Good keyboard realization. M-D.

Tomaso Albinoni. *Trio Sonata* Op.1/3 1694 (Upmeyer—Nag 34) 12pp., parts.

———— *Trio Sonata* Op.1/6 a (E. Schenk—Dob; OBV).

———— *Trio Sonatas* Op.1/10–12 (Kolneder—Schott). 2 vols.

———— *Trio Sonata* Op.8/4a 1720 (E. Schenk—Dob 1952) 19pp., parts. Allemanda: prelude-like. Giga: delightful. Sarabanda: quick; this type of sarabanda was frequently encountered in the middle baroque period. This *Sonata da Chiesa* shows a more personal, intense kind of writing. Large leaps, more ornamentation, and some chromaticism appear. M-D.

———— *Trio Sonata* Op.8/4b B♭ (Schenk—OBV) 11pp., parts. Grave, Adagio: powerful, reminiscent of Handel. Allegro: active, motoric. Larghetto: subtle, siciliano-like. Allegro: delicate winding flourishes. Dynamics are editorial and are only suggestions. M-D.

Albinoni's earlier works are generally of the four-movement, slow-fast-slow-fast design with fairly stereotyped harmonic schemes.

Thomas A. Arne. *Trio Sonata* Op.3/1 A (Langley, Seiffert—Br&H) 16pp., parts.

_____ *Trio Sonata* Op.3/2 G 1739–40 (H. Murrill—Hin 1950) 13pp., parts. 8 min. Largo; Con spirito; Largo; Allegro. Only the Con spirito movement might present problems, with its trills. M-D.

_____ *Trio Sonata* Op.3/3 E♭ (H. Murrill—Hin 1950) 16pp., parts. 8 min. Grave; Allegro moderato; Giga. Int. to M-D.

_____ *Trio Sonata* Op.3/4 f (H. Murrill—Hin 1960) 8pp., parts. 7 min. Largo; Vivace; Largo; Presto. Int. to M-D.

_____ *Trio Sonata* Op.3/5 D (H. Murrill—Hin 1960) 7pp., parts. 6 min. Largo; Andante; Largo; Allegro. Int.

_____ *Trio Sonata* Op.3/7 e (Hin).

_____ *Trio Sonata* e (Nov).

All these pieces contain charming melodies in a variety of moods.

Charles Avison. *Trio Sonata* e (Moffat—Simrock 893) 8pp., parts. Adagio espressivo; Allegro ma non troppo; Largo; Allegro, ma grazioso. Effective writing in the style of the day. M-D.

Carl Philipp Emanuel Bach. *Trio Sonata* A (Dürr—Moeck 1073).

_____ *Trio Sonata* a (Dürr—Moeck 1072).

_____ *Trio Sonata* B♭ (Schumann—Leuckart).

_____ *Trio Sonata* B♭ (IMC).

_____ *Trio Sonata* B♭ (L. Landschoff—CFP 4237) 31pp., parts. Allegro; Adagio ma non troppo; Allegretto. Excellent realization. M-D.

_____ *Two Trio Sonatas* F (CFP 4288).

_____ *Trio Sonata* G (H. Riemann—Br&H 1829a/b) 17pp., parts. No.16 in Collegium Musicum series. Allegretto; Andantino; Allegro. Highly edited. M-D.

_____ *Trio Sonata* G (IMC).

Most of these sonatas are also suitable for flute and violin with keyboard.

Johann Christian Bach. *Trio-Sonata* G (F. Nagel—Möseler 1976) 12pp., parts.

Johann Sebastian Bach. *Four Trio Sonatas* (Landschoff—CFP 4203A,B). Vol.I: No.1,S.1037 C; No.2,S.1039 G. Vol.II: No.3,S.1038 G for flute, violin, and basso continuo; No.4,S.1079 c for two flutes and basso continuo (from *The Musical Offering*).

_____ *Three Trio Sonatas* C, G, c (CFP 237) from *The Musical Offering*. No separate bass part.

Available separately: *Trio Sonata* c (Kirnberger—CFP 237A).

_____ *Two Trio Sonatas* S.1037, S.1038 (David—Br&H) 22pp., parts. S.1037: Adagio; Fuge; Canon; Gigue. S.1038: Largo; Vivace; Adagio; Presto. Highly edited.

_____ *Trio Sonata* S.1036 d (Nag 49) 16pp., parts.

_____ *Trio Sonata* S.1037 C (Schott; David—IMC) no separate bass part. Adagio; Fuge; Canon; Gigue.

_____ *Konzert* S.1043 d (D. Oistrakh—CFP 9032) 23pp., parts. Piano reduction by Wilhelm Weismann. Foreword in German and Russian. Vivace; Largo, ma non tanto; Allegro. Excellent piano reduction; beautiful edition. M-D.

Wilhelm Friedemann Bach. *Trio Sonata* D (Zimmermann). No separate bass part.

_____ *Trio Sonata* F (H. Buys—B&VP) 14pp., parts. Largo; Allegretto; Allegro assai e Scherzando. The Largo presents the most problems. M-D.

Michel de la Barre. *Sonata* V g (Viollier—Noetzel). Cello ad lib.

Giovanni Battista Bassani. *Sonata a tre* Op.5/2 d (Zanibon 4440).

_____ *Sonata a tre* Op.5/7 A (Zanibon 4441).

_____ *Sonata a tre* Op.5/9 C (Schenk—OBV 461) 10pp., parts. Cello ad lib. Presto; Grave; Allegro; Largo; Presto. In Corelli style. The five movements are bound to an earlier point of view. Imaginative writing. M-D.

Alfred von Beckerath. *Sonatine* 1937 (Moeck 1018) 11pp., parts. For 2 violins or other treble instruments and piano. Allegro moderato; Andante; Lento; Molto allegro. First two movements center around F although no key signature is present. Accidentals are added. Neoclassic, mildly contemporary sonorities. Int. to M-D.

Jan Jiri Benda. *Trio Sonata* (Artia). No separate bass part.

Jiri Antonin Benda. *Trio Sonata* E (V. Nopp—Artia MAB vol.2) 11pp., parts. Moderato; Largo; Allegro. Imbued with a feeling of spontaneity and freshness. M-D.

Gerard Bertouille. *Trio* 1955 (CeBeDeM) 16 min.

Heinrich Ignaz Franz von Biber. *Sonata a tre* (Janetzky—Pro Musica).

_____ *Sonata a tre* (Musica Rara).

Luigi Boccherini. *Sonata a tre* c (A. Moffat—Simrock Elite Edition 1143)

11pp., parts. Cello ad lib. Allegro; Andante espressivo; Allegro con spirito. Clear classic style. M-D.

Giovanni Maria Bonocini. *Sonata a tre* Op.1/6 d (Schenk—OBV). Cello ad lib.

_____ *Sonata a tre* C (Moffat—Simrock). Cello ad lib.

William Boyce. *Trio Sonata* II F (H. Murrill—Hin 55) 14pp., parts. Andante vivace; Adagio; Allegro; Allegro ma non troppo.

_____ *Trio Sonata* III A (Jensen—Augener 7432).

_____ *Trio Sonata* VI B♭ (Hin 733).

_____ *Trio Sonata* VII d (Moffat—Nov).

_____ *Trio Sonata* VIII E♭ (Hin 641).

_____ *Trio Sonata* IX C (Hin 642).

_____ *Trio Sonata* XI c (Moffat—Simrock) 11pp., parts. Adagio; Fuga; Andante affettuoso; Allegro.

_____ *Trio Sonata* XII G (Hin 643).

These sonatas, issued in 1747, are magnificent pieces, extraordinarily varied in dimensions and style.

Domenico Brasolini. *Sonata da Camera* g (K. Fellerer—Müller 33 1956) 6pp., parts. Balletto—Vivace; Corrente—Largo; Giga—Prestissimo. Dance quality permeates the entire piece. M-D.

Benedictus Buns. *Sonata* Op.8/3 d (Heuwekemeijer EH 803) 11pp., parts. Cello part ad lib. Foreword in Dutch. Adagio; Allegro; Adagio; Allegro. Continuo part well realized by Hans Schouwman. M-D.

Giovanni Battista Buonamente. *Sonata "La Monteverde"* (D. Stevens, Y. Menuhin—Hin 680) 5pp., parts. Cello part ad lib. The two violins are in strict canon throughout. This is the first sonata in Buonamente's Seventh Book of Sonatas and is dedicated to Monteverdi. M-D.

Antonio Caldara. *Sonata a tre* Op.1/4 B♭ (Upmeyer—Nag). Cello part ad lib.

_____ *Sonata a tre* Op.1/5 e (Schenk—OBV). Cello part ad lib.

_____ *Sonata a tre* Op.1/6 c (Upmeyer—Nag). Cello part ad lib.

_____ *Sonata a tre* Op.1/9 (Schenk—OBV). Cello part ad lib.

_____ *Sonata da Chiesa* b (Vieweg 99). No separate bass part.

_____ *Sonata da Camera* g (UE 10677–8). Cello part ad lib.

Placidus von Camerloher. *Four Sonatas* (Schott) 2 vols. Cello part ad lib.

Maurito Cazzati. *Trio Sonata* Op.18/9 1656 (W. Danckert—Br HM 34) 7pp., parts. Largo; Grave con Tremolo; Vivace; Allegro. In a Corelli-like style with freely flowing lines in the last two movements. Int.

———— *Capriccio* a 3 Op.50/29 "Il Guastavilani" (E. Schenk—OBV DM 444) 9pp., parts. Preface in English and German. Cello part ad lib. Largo; Allegro; Grave; Allegro. Noble lines in the Largo. Moody and playful echoes occur in the Grave. Cazzati wrote fifty Capriccios for church and chamber music. Each one bears a name—in this case, that of a senator from Bologna. Int. to M-D.

Louis Nicolas Clérambault. *Sonate* VII e (Peyrot, Rebuffat—Senart 266). Cello part ad lib.

———— *Sonate* G (Lemoine). Cello part ad lib.

Arcangelo Corelli. *48 Sonatas* Op.1/4 (W. Woehl—Br 701–16 1939) 16 vols. bound as one or available separately. Sources are identified. Includes preface and a discussion of the ornaments. Vols.1–4: *12 Sonate da Camera,* Op.2. Vols.5–8: *12 Sonate da Camera,* Op.3. Vols.9–12: *12 Sonate da Camera,* Op.4. Vols.13–16: *12 Sonate da Camera,* Op.1.

———— *12 Sonatas* Op.1 (W. Woehl—IMC) rev. W. Lyman.

———— *12 Sonatas* Op.2 (L. Schaeffler—IMC) rev. W. Lyman, 3 vols. of 4 sonatas each.

———— *12 Sonatas* Op.3 (Kolneder—Schott) 4 vols.

———— *6 Sonatas* Op.4 (H. Sitt—IMC).

These sonatas are unrivaled as examples of the trio sonata. Most of them are short and occupy only three or four pages. The sonata a tre occupies the same position in the chamber music of the thorough bass period as the string quartet did in the classical period. Br&H, Schott, CFP, Augener, and Senart have a number of these sonatas separately.

Paul Creston. *Partita* Op.12 1938. See detailed entry under trios for piano, one stringed instrument, and one wind instrument.

Hugo Distler. *Sonate* Op.15a über alte Deutsche Volkslieder (Br 1091) 28pp., parts. I. Taglied: based on "Es Taget vor dem Walde." II. Legende: based on "Ach Elslien, Liebes Elslein." III. Maienkurante: based on "Wie Schön Blüht uns der Maien." Neoclassic, thin textures, imitation between all parts, delightful. M-D.

Karl Ditters von Dittersdorf. *Concerto* A 1779 (W. Upmeyer—Nag 41 1968) 43pp., parts. Allegro molto; Larghetto; Rondeau—Allegretto. The original score is intended for more than one string player to a part, but an intimate music-making session would require only one player to a part. Cadenzas are left to the discretion of the keyboard player. Charming period writing. Int. to M-D.

Thomas Alexander Eskine, Earl of Kelly. *Trio Sonata* IV C (D. Johnson— OUP 1973) 8pp., parts. 7 min. Musica da Camera No.5. First published in 1769. Editorial additions identified. Includes critical commentary. Andante; Minuetto. Adequate keyboard realization. Pianist could add more interest. M-D.

Johann Friedrich Fasch. *Trio-sonata* c (CFP 1974) 14pp., parts. Cello ad lib. Preface in German and English. Critical commentary in German.
_____ *Three Trio Sonatas* a, F, G (Br&H 1904).
_____ *Trio-sonata* D (F. Nagel—Eulenburg 1974) 12pp., parts. In four short movements like a sonata da chiesa. Affetuoso; Allegro; Largo; Allegro. Should be played as two pairs of movements: one and two together, and three and four together. Charming writing, rather plain continuo realization that should be added to. Int.
_____ *Sonata* a 3 (Kranz—Leuckart).
_____ *Trio* a (Riemann—Br&H).
_____ *Trio* D (Hausswald—Nag).
See: David Alden Sheldon, "The Chamber Music of Johann Friedrich Fasch," Ph.D. diss., Indiana University, 1968, 243pp. Bach thought so highly of Fasch's music that he copied out five of his orchestral suites.

Willem de Fesch. *X Sonata a Tre* (B&VP) 4 vols. For 2 flutes or 2 violins and keyboard. See detailed description under trios for piano and two flutes.
_____ *Three Sonatas* Op.12 1748 (Heuwekemeijer 802 1957) 28pp., parts. Introduction by Willem Noske. 1 D: Largo; Allemanda; Menuetto I and II. 2 g: Largo; Alla Breve; Giga. 3 G: Largo; Allemanda; Menuetto. Outstanding melodies, splendid unbroken melodic lines. The allemandes are the most involved movements. M-D.

Johann Joseph Fux. *Sonata Pastorale* K.397 F (E. Schenk—Dob DM 420 1953) 4pp., parts. Preface in English and German. Adagio; Un poco Allegro. A lovely Christmas piece that symbolizes in a charming manner the Austro–Italian cultural synthesis of the baroque period and clearly reflects Fux's style. Frequent dynamic changes and full harmony comply with the espressivo-style, pervaded by the deeply felt emotion related to the birth of Christ. M-D.
_____ *Sonata a tre* d (Noetzel).

Christoph W. Gluck. *Eight Trio Sonatas* (F.-H. Neumann-Croll—Nag 205–208 1963). Vol.I: C, g. Vol.II: A, B♭. Vol.III: E♭, F. Vol.IV: E, F. Gluck was Sammartini's pupil from 1737 to 1741. In these early works, Sammartini's influence is seen, especially in No.3. Short skipping motifs of a buffo character treated in canon and sentimental sighs add special interest to these works. They form a link between the instrumental music of the baroque and classical periods. Editorial additions are indicated by brackets and are printed in smaller type. Valuable preface. Carefully realized bass but can be added to if desired. M-D.

———— *Triosonate* VI F (G. Beckmann—Br&H 1972). No.37 in Collegium Musicum series. Figured bass realized. Includes part for cello. M-D.

———— *Trio Sonata* F (Moffat—Simrock).

———— *Trio Sonata* g (Bouvet—ESC).

———— *Trio Sonata* g (Möbius—Nag).

Joseph Haas. *Chamber Trio* Op.38 (Schott).

George Frederick Handel. *Sonate en Sol Mineur* Op.2/2 (J. Peyrot, J. Rebufat—Sal 2723 11pp., parts; M. Seiffert—Br&H 15pp., parts). Andante; Allegro; Largo; Allegro. Tasteful realizations. M-D.

———— *Sonata* Op.2/4 B♭ (H. Sitt—IMC). Andante; Allegro; Larghetto; Allegro.

———— *Trio Sonata* Op.2/5 (S. Flesh—Nag 240 1974) 19pp., parts. Based on the Halle Handel Edition. Larghetto; Allegro; Adagio; Allegro. M-D.

———— *Sonata* Op.2/8 (H. Sitt—CFP). Andante; Allegro; Arioso; Allegro.

———— *Seven Sonatas* Op.5/1–7 (W. Serauky—Br 1973) 73pp. Vol.10,2 in Series IV: Instrumentalmusik of the Halle Handel Edition. Continuo realization by Max Schneider. Based on the most reliable sources available.

———— *Sonata en Re* Op.5/2 (J. Peyrot, J. Rebufat—Sal 3116) 9pp., parts. Cello ad lib. Adagio; Allegro; Musette; Allegro; Musette; March; Gavotte. Careful realizations. M-D.

———— *Trio Sonata* C (Nag 230).

———— *Trio Sonata* g (S. Flesch—Nag 235).

———— *Trio Sonata* g (J. A. Parkinson—OUP 1969) 15pp., parts; cello ad lib. See detailed entry under trios for piano and two flutes.

Josef Matthias Hauer. *Hausmusik* (F. Blasl, E. Stricz—UE 20031 1971) 15pp., 3 copies necessary for performance. Extensive introduction in German by Nikolaus Fheodoroff describes structure of the work. Twelve-tone, octotonic, cleverly worked out, tricky rhythms, does not contain a single rest. M-D.

Franz Joseph Haydn. *Six Sonatas* Op.8 (A. Gülzow and W. Weismann—CFP 4376A,B). Cello ad lib. Vol.I: 37pp., parts. 1 E♭: Allegro; Adagio; Presto. 2 G: Allegro; Menuetto; Presto. 3 b: Adagio; Allegro; Tempo di Menuetto. Vol.II: 39pp., parts. 4 E♭: Allegro; Menuetto; Presto. 5 G: Allegro, Menuetto; Presto. 6 A: Allegro moderato; Andante; Menuetto; Fuga. Most markings are editorial. These delightful early pieces, composed between 1750 and 1756, are interesting in style and full of charm. Int. to M-D.

Kurt Hessenberg. *Trio* Op.26 G 1942 (CFP) 17 min. Moderato; Menuetto; Introduktion und Finale. Neoclassic, mildly contemporary. M-D.

Gustav Holst. *A Fugal Concerto* Op.40/2 (Nov 1923) 17pp., parts. See detailed entry under trios for piano and two miscellaneous winds.

Arthur Honegger. *Petite Suite* 1934 (Philharmusica 1974). Le chant du Monde. Three short, somewhat whimsical tonal movements with only the first and third using the piano. French Gebrauchsmusik. Written for the composer's niece and nephew and can be performed by any two treble instruments and piano. Int. to M-D.

Johann Ludwig Krebs. *Trio Sonata* b 1743 (L. H.-Erbrecht—K&S 1961) 19pp., parts. No.62 in Organum Series. Andante; Allegretto; Un poco allegro; Vivace. A fine example of Krebs's gallant style. M-D.

Jean Marie Leclair. *Sonata* Op.4/1 d (H. Majewski—Heinrichshofen).
———— *Sonata* Op.4/2 B♭ (H. Majewski—Heinrichshofen) 18pp., parts. Preface. Adagio; Allegro ma non troppo; Largo cantabile; Allegro assai.
————*Sonata* Op.4/3 d (H. Majewski—Heinrichshofen) 22pp., parts. Preface. Adagio; Allegro; Aria; Sarabanda.
————*Sonata* Op.4/4 F (H. Majewski—Heinrichshofen 1973) 22pp., parts. Preface.
————*Trio Sonata* B♭ (A. Moffat—Lengnick) 18pp., parts. Adagio; Allegro ma non troppo; Andante cantabile; Allegro.
These sonatas unite French formal understanding with the German art of contrapuntal composition and the malleable Italian feeling for melody. Rich thematic invention, ingenious polyphonic arrangement, versatility in the forms, and a refined sense of harmony identify Leclair as one of the most important French composers of the eighteenth century. All these works are approximately M-D.

Pietro Locatelli. *Trio Sonata* Op.3/1 G (Riemann—Br&H).

———— *Trio Sonata* Op.5/1 G (H. Albrecht—K&S 1954) 23pp., parts. No.52 in Organum Series. Andante; Largo andante; Allégro; Vivace. Tempi and other suggestions contained in the preface. M-D.

———— *Trio Sonata* Op.5/4 C (H. Albrecht—K&S 1951) 9pp., parts. No.46 in Organum Series. Largo; Allegro. Tempi and other suggestions contained in the preface. M-D.

———— *Trio Sonata* Op.5/5 d (H. Albrecht—K&S 1953) 11pp., parts. No.50 in Organum Series. Largo; Vivace; Pastorale—Andante. Tempi and other suggestions contained in the preface. M-D.

———— *Sonata* E (Ruf—Schott).

Jean Baptiste Loeillet (of Lyons). *Sonata* Op.1/2 G (Ruf—Schott).

———— *Sonata* Op.1/4 D (Ruf—Schott).

———— *Sonata* Op.1/6 e (Ruf—Schott).

Bohuslav Martinů. *Sonata* (Deiss 1933) 24pp., parts. Allegro poco moderato: octotonic, chromatic, syncopated chords, thin textures prevail. Andante: scalar, staccato octotonic, tremolo; brief cadenza with all instruments participating leads directly to Allegretto: arpeggi and syncopated chordal gestures, trills, shifting accents; Allegro vivo coda. Freely tonal, neoclassic. M-D.

———— *Sonatine* (Leduc).

Arthur Meulemans. *Sonata* 1954 (CeBeDeM) 25pp., parts. 18 min. Allegro non troppo; Adagio; Allegro. Extension of the Franck–Jongen style; chromatic and with varied idioms and devices. Lack of direction produces a "busy" quality, especially in the first movement. D.

Darius Milhaud. *Sonata* 1914 (Durand) 35pp., parts. Pastoral: easy flowing, Impressionistic, transparent. Vif: rhythmic and motoric; relieved by a Moins vif singing section; only four bars of the Vif section return before the Moins vif mood ends the movement. Lent: freely unwinding melodic line, parallelism in piano part, some ostinato treatment, elastic writing. Tres vif: motoric opening leads to a dramatic (choral, arpeggi) intrusion; opening mood returns; five octave arpeggiated chords interspersed with broken octaves lead to a less active bridge to the coda; a rather strange movement that fortunately sounds better than it looks on the score. M-D.

Jean-Joseph Mondonville. *Sonatinas en Trio* Op.2 1734 (R. Blanchard—Heugel) 103pp., parts. No.3 in Le Pupitre series. Introduction in French. 1 e: Adagio; Allegro Aria; Presto. 2 B♭: Adagio; Fuga; Gratioso; Allegro. 3

G: Largo; Fuga; Cantabile; Giga. 4 F: Largo; Fuga; Gratioso; Presto. 5 D: Allegro; Fuga; Largo; Allegro. 6 c: Adagio; Fuga; Largo; Allegro.

—— Sonata Op.2/3 G (J. Peyrot, J. Rebuffat—Senart 2657) 9pp., parts. Frequent exchanges between all parts, idiomatic and resourceful writing. M-D.

See: Edith Borroff, "The Instrumental Works of Jean-Joseph Casanéa Mondonville" 2 vols., Ph.D. dissertation, University of Michigan, 1958.

Leopold Mozart. *Sonata a 3* IV G (Schenk—OBV) 11pp., parts. Allegro; Adagio (g); Presto. Fine realization. M-D.

Andrzej Nikodemowicz. *Improvvisazione* (PWM 1973) 14pp., 6 min. Part for both violins in one score.

John Christopher Pepusch. *Six Trio Sonatas* 1710 (L. Hoffmann-Erbrecht—Br&H 2001 1954) Vol.I: 18pp., parts. 1 e, 2 g, 3 G. Vol.II: 20pp., parts. 4 Bb, 5 d, 6 F. Excellent keyboard realizations. M-D.

—— *Trio Sonata* C (G. Hausswald—Schott) 9pp., parts. Largo; Allegro; Adagio; Presto. Unobtrusive keyboard realization.

—— *Trio Sonata* D (L. Hoffmann-Erbrecht—K&S) 11pp., parts. No.57 in Organum Series. Preface in German. Largo; Allegro; Adagio; Allegro.

—— *Trio Sonata* F (K&S) 15pp., parts. No.56 in Organum Series. Preface in German. Largo; Allegro; Adagio; Allegro.

—— *Trio Sonata* G (K&S 1961) 8pp., parts. No.61 in Organum Series. Preface in German. Allegro; Adagio; Allegro.

All the sonatas in the Organum Series have stylistically correct keyboard realizations.

—— *Trio Sonata* g (CFP 4556).

Giovanni Battista Pergolesi. *Sonate a Tre* (Gli Amici Della Musica da Camera 1940; Franco Columbo) 136pp. Preface in Italian by F. Caffarelli. 1 G, 2 Bb, 3 c, 4 G, 5 C, 6 E, 7 g, 8 Eb, 9 A, 10 F, 11 d, 12 E, 13 g, 14 C. Most of these sonatas are in three movements: Fast–Slow–Fast. Simple and tasteful realizations. M-D.

—— *2 Trio Sonatas* (T. W. Weiner—Nag 107) 16pp., parts. Preface in German. 5 c: Allegro; Adagio; Allegro. 10 Eb: Allegro non tanto; Andantino; Allegro fugato.

—— *Trio Sonata* I G (Riemann—Br&H).

—— *Trio Sonata* III G (CFP 4888A).

—— *Trio Sonata* IV Bb (CFP 4888B).

—— *Trio Sonata* C (CFP 4557).

Ignaz Pleyel. *Three Trios* Op.44 (Augener 5334).

Jaromir Podesva. *Concertino* (Panton 1973) 20pp., parts.

Henry Purcell. *Music for Strings and Keyboard* (Nov). Reprint from the complete edition published as a practical collection for the performer. This volume contains three-part Pavans, a four-part Pavan, three Overtures, Chacony, and a reconstruction of the *Suite* in G. Separate parts.

———— *Two Trio Sonatas* (H. David—Schott 2312) 20pp., parts. Preface in French, German, and English. 1 g, 2 B♭. Masterful contrapuntal skill, short themes, unique harmonic language with unusual harmonic progressions, deeply expressive. Excellent keyboard realizations. M-D.

———— *Trio Sonatas* (CFP 4649A) 1 g, 2 B♭.

———— *Trio Sonatas* (CFP 4649B) 3 a, 4 g, Chaconne.

———— *Trio Sonatas* (CFP 4242A) E♭, F ("The Golden Sonata").

———— *Trio Sonatas* (CFP 4242B) D, d.

Johann Joachim Quantz. *Trio Sonata* a (L. Hoffmann-Erbrecht—K&S) 19pp. parts. No.65 in Organum Series. Preface in German. Andante moderato; Allegro; Affettuoso; Vivace. Keyboard realization is stylistically outstanding. M-D.

———— *Trio Sonata* c (Zimmermann).

———— *Trio Sonata* d (Schroeder—Br&H).

———— *Trio Sonata* D (Forberg).

———— *Trio Sonata* D (Ruf—Symphonia SY650).

Jean Philippe Rameau. *Pieces de Clavecin en Concerts* 1742 (E. Jacobi—Br 1970) 63pp., parts. For violin or flute and viol (gamba) or a second violin and keyboard. See detailed entry under trios for piano, violin, and cello.

Johan Helmich Roman. *Seven Trio Sonatas* (Vretblad—MG).

———— *Six Trio Sonatas* (Vretblad—MG).

Edmund Rubbra. *Fantasy* Op.16 1925 (Lengnick). Loose pastoral SA marked "flowing" in 6/8 with three main subjects treated in a variety of ways. After a codetta the recapitulation begins with the third subject followed by the first two subjects. Music dies away to a close. M-D.

Giuseppe Sammartini. *Concerto* I A (H. Illy—Br 1971) No. 196 in HM. 40pp., parts. Organ probably works best as solo instrument but another continuo instrument should also be used. All parts written out. Andante spiritoso; Allegro assai; Andante; Allegro assai. M-D.

———— *Concerto* II (H. Illy—Br HM 197).

———— *Sonata* Op.1/3 E♭ (H. Riemann—IMC).

Cyril Scott. *Sonata* (Elkin 1964) 41pp., parts. Poco tranquillo: flowing, chromatic, rubato. Elegy: alternating chordal figure at beginning used frequently; haunting feeling; parallelism. Finale Frivolo—Energico: rhythmic push throughout; a few rhythmic tricky spots for the pianist; arpeggi figuration introduces the final romp. M-D.

Josep Soler. *Trio* (PIC).

Johann Wenzel Anton Stamitz. *Orchestral Trio* Op.1/1 C (H. Riemann—Br&H) 21pp., parts. Cello ad lib. Allegro; Andante ma non adagio; Menuet; Prestissimo. Over-edited. M-D.
_____ *Orchestral Trio* Op.1/2 A (H. Riemann—Br&H) 19pp., parts. Cello ad lib. Allegro assai; Andante poco Adagio; Menuet; Prestissimo. Over-edited. M-D.
_____ *Orchestral Trio* Op.1/3 F (Riemann—Br&H).
_____ *Orchestral Trio* Op.1/4 D (Riemann—Br&H).
These pieces provide some interesting music.
_____ *Sonata* a 3 G (Moffat—Simrock).

Giuseppe Tartini. *Trio Sonata* Op.8/6 D (E. Schenk—Dob DM 438 1954) 7pp., parts. Preface in German and English. Largo andante; Andante; Presto. A clean edition. M-D.
_____ *Trio Sonata* D (H. Dameck—IMC 1943) 8pp., parts. Andante; Menuetto; Allegro assai. Octave bass line in last movement needs careful control. M-D.

Georg Philipp Telemann. *Six Trio Sonatas* (Kolneder—Schott) 2 vols.
_____ *Corellisierende Sonaten* (A. Hoffmann—Nag 248 1975) Vol.I: Sonatas F, A, b. Score and parts. Vol.II not yet available.
_____ *Trio Sonata* a (W. Woehl, rev. W. Lyman—IMC 1952) 12pp., parts. Cello ad lib. Largo; Vivace; Affettuoso; Allegro. M-D.
_____ *Trio Sonata* c (W. Woehl, rev. W. Lyman—IMC 1952) 15pp., parts. Cello ad lib. Largo; Vivace; Andante; Allegro. M-D.
_____ *Trio Sonata* e (Moffat—Simrock).
_____ *Trio Sonata* g (Ruf—Schott).

Antonio Veracini. *Sonata* Op.1 c (Jensen—Augener 7415).
_____ *Sonata* Op.1/10 (F. Polnauer—Schott 1973) 16pp., parts. Four movements, slow–fast–slow–fast, using same tonal vocabulary as Veracini's contemporary Corelli. Veracini is a careful craftsman. Distinction between original and editorial markings is shown. Simple continuo realization is effective. Int.

Antonio Vivaldi. *12 Sonate da Camera* Op.1 1705–9 (W. Upmeyer—Br 351–2) Vol.I: Sonatas in g, e, C, E, F, D; 32pp., parts. Vol.II: Sonatas in E♭, d, A, B♭, b, d. Editorial additions indicated by brackets. Excellent realizations. M-D.

Available separately: Op.1/1 (Peyrot, Rebuffat—Senart 2717). Op.1/2 (Senart 2720). Op.1/3 (Senart 2913). Op.1/4 (Senart 3118).

———— *Two Sonatas* Op.5/5,6 (Upmeyer—Nag).

———— *Sonata a tre* Op.5/6 g (E. Schenk—Dob DM 418 1949) 6pp., parts. Preface in German and English. Preludio: rococo theme, rich and expressive harmony. Allemanda: powerful polyphony. Air menuet: profound, shows French spirit. Ternary form (written out) is unusual for the period. M-D.

George Christoph Wagenseil. *Sonata a Tre* Op.1/3 B♭ 1755 (E. Schenk—Dob DM 443 1953) 10pp., parts. Preface in German and English. Allegro; Allegro molto; Minuetto I, II: Molto Allegro. This work illustrates in a charming manner the style and spirit of Austrian rococo music: graceful themes, preference for repetition of short motifs and for syncopated rhythms, concise form, and witty subtle harmonic language. M-D.

———— *Trio Sonata* F (K. Geiringer—UE 1067–8) 12pp., parts. Preface in German, English, and French. Allegro; Andante; Minuetto; Allegro assai. Editorial additions not indicated. M-D.

Gregorius Joseph Werner. *Sonatina* D (EMB with Dob DM 391 1974) 7pp., parts. Larghetto; Allegro.

———— *Sonatina* F 1759 (EMB with Dob DM 392 1974) 8pp., parts.

———— *Symphoniae sex Senaeque Sonatae* 1735 (R. Moder—Dob DM 401 1971) 20pp., parts. Foreword in German and English. A collection of six pairs of works, each pair consisting of a three-movement symphonia (Spirituoso; Larghetto e sempre piano; Allegro assai) and a four-movement sonata da chiesa (Largo; Allegro; Largo; Allegro). In most of the pairs the symphonia and the sonata are related by key but each can stand alone, as there is no other cyclic cohesion. The symphonias are fresher sounding and more lively, while the sonatas demonstrate more contrapuntal strictness. M-D.

Trios for Piano(s) and Miscellaneous Strings

Carl Philipp Emanuel Bach. *Six Sonatas* (G. Piccioli—IMC) 16pp., parts. For viola, cello, and piano or for clarinet, bassoon, and piano. 1. E♭, Allegretto. 2. E♭, Allegro molto. 3. E♭, Allegro. 4. B♭, Allegro. 5. E♭, Andante. 6. B♭, Allegro. These short pieces sound more like the style of Johann Christian Bach than that of C. P. E. Bach. M-D.
_____ *Trio* F (Piccioli—IMC) 12pp., parts. For viola, cello, and piano. Un poco Andante; Allegretto; Allegro. Clear and neat realizations. M-D.

Arthur Berger. *Trio* 1972 (Boelke-Bomart) 27pp., parts. 10 min. For piano, guitar, and violin. Includes instructions for performance. One movement, Gentilmente e sotto voce: serial influence, pointillistic, shifting meters, long pedals, varied tempi and moods, repeated accented notes, silent clusters for harmonics, two notes prepared with a screw, removed from one pitch during the piece and another pitch is prepared. Grazioso section is dancelike. Final Calmo utilizes long pedals for spread-out sonorities, dolcissimo and *pp* conclusion. Contains some lovely and sensitive sonorities as well as it being a thoroughly integrated piece of writing. M-D.

Gaetano Donizetti. *Trio* E♭ (B. Pauler—CFP). For piano, viola, and cello.

George Frederick Handel. *Double Concerto* C (F. Ronchini—ESC) 20pp., parts. For 2 cellos and piano. Originally for 2 cellos and orchestra. Allegro; Largo; Allegro. Interesting spacing of the cellos. Keyboard reduction is over-edited. M-D.
_____ *Sonata* C (Delrieu). For 2 cellos and piano.
_____ *Sonata* g (Feuillard—Delrieu). For 2 cellos and piano.

Edino Krieger. *Sonancias* 1975 (Sonorities) (MS available from composer: Rua Itambi 20, Apt. 707, Botafogo, 20.000 Rio de Janeiro, GB Brazil) 11pp., parts. For violin and 2 pianos. Uses clusters, highest and lowest pitches possible, repetition ad lib, harmonics. Notes are lengthened indefinitely. Avant-garde. D.

George Frederick McKay. *Suite* (B. Turetzky—McGinnis & Marx 1962) 7pp., parts. For 2 double basses and piano. Night Scene: Impressionistic, melody in upper register of piano, thin chordal accompaniment. Canonic Capriccio: piano provides a delicate, thin-textured accompaniment to the two double basses in canon. Mother Elephant's Lullaby: moderato espressivo, chordal, added-note technique, unresolved final chord. Folk Dance: rhythmic, modal, clever. Attractive writing throughout entire suite. Int. to M-D.

Benedetto Marcello. *Two Sonatas* (Glode—Moeck 1056). For 2 cellos and piano.

David Noon. *Fantasy* Op.28 (CF 1974) 26pp. 2 scores necessary for performance. For violin and piano four-hands. Facsimile of MS.

Claudio Spies. *Viopiacem* 1965 (Bo&H) 12pp., parts. 9 min. For viola, piano, and 2-manual harpsichord. The title is derived from the first syllables of the names of each of the instruments in their order of entry. One player seated on a revolving piano stool can handle both the piano and the harpsichord parts. Twelve-tone, pointillistic, little barring, low registers exploited, complicated rhythms and ensemble problems, long pedals, fascinating sonorities. D.
For a full discussion of this work see: Paul Lansky, "The Music of Claudio Spies; An Introduction," *Tempo* 103 (1972): 38–44.

Giuseppe Tartini. *Sonate* (Bazelaire—Leduc). For 2 cellos and piano.

Antonio Vivaldi. *Six Sonatas* (CFP 4938). For 2 cellos and piano. Many basic patterns are similar but within the restricted framework Vivaldi constantly and delightfully varies the details. M-D.

Trios for Piano, One Stringed Instrument, and One Wind Instrument

Karl Friedrich Abel. *Trio Sonata* C (Möbius—Moeck). For flute, violin, and basso continuo. Weighty slow movement, concentrated treatment of ideas, polished craftsmanship, especially in the ornamentation and articulation. Basso continuo has interesting figurations and rich harmony for the period. M-D.

Dieter Acker. *Glossen, Trio II* (Bo&Bo 1974) 8pp., parts. For clarinet (flute), cello, and piano (harpsichord). Explanations in German and English. Austero; Animato, senza rigore; Faceto, senza rigore; Grave, senza rigore. Meter-free measures, duration in seconds of a section. Clusters, pointillistic, avant-garde.

Jurriaan Andriessen. *Trio II* 1955 (Donemus) 37pp., parts. For flute, viola, and piano. Allegro moderato: octotonic contemporary Alberti-bass, chromatic sequence and figuration, repeated harmonic thirds, dancelike character, bitonal, alternating hands. Andante cantabile con espressione: charming bitonal waltz, short motifs, à la Poulenc. Allegro vivace: expanding intervals, rhythmic, syncopation, running figures tossed from one hand to another, hemiola, acrobatic finish. Subtle French influence. M-D.

Edward Applebaum. *Montages* (JWC 1968) 16pp. 3 copies required for performance. 9 min. For clarinet, cello, and piano. Serial; piano part erupts then holds sustained chords. Thorny ensemble problems. D.

Paul Arma. *Divertimento* II 1951 (EMT 1967) 22pp., parts. 17 min. For piano, flute, and cello. Also available in a version for flute or violin, cello, and harp. Rubato; Con moto, scherzando; Poco lento; Robusto. Chromatic, secco, rhythmic finale, colorful. Certain sections feature two of the three instruments. M-D.

Richard Arnell. *Trio* Op.64 (Hin) 5 min. For flute, cello, and piano. Eclectic, efficient writing that communicates with its audience immediately. M-D.

Carl Philipp Emanuel Bach. *Trio* I D (IMC) for flute, viola, and piano.
———— *Trio* II a (IMC). For flute, viola, and piano.
———— *Trio* III G (IMC). For flute, viola, and piano.
———— *Trio* W.161 B♭ (L. Landshoff—CFP 4237) 31pp., parts. For flute, violin, and keyboard, or for two violins and keyboard; cello part ad lib. Allegro; Adagio ma non troppo (with ad lib cadenza); Allegretto. Tasteful realization. M-D.
———— *Trio* F (IMC). For viola, bassoon, and piano.
———— *Triosonata* D (G. Braun—Hänssler) 28pp., parts. For flute, violin, and piano.
———— *Trio Sonata* W.147 C (Ruf—Br). For flute, violin, and basso continuo.
———— *Trio Sonata* W.148 a (K. Walther—Zimmermann) 14pp., parts. For flute, violin (oboe), and continuo.
Also see listing of trios for piano and two violins.
———— *Quartett* W.93 a 1788 (E. F. Schmid—Nag 222; IMC) 19pp., parts. For piano, flute (violin), viola, and cello. Preface in German and English. Andantino; Largo e sostenuto; Allegro assai. In Viennese classical style, Beethoven-like; keyboard writing has freed itself from thoroughbass principles and is fuller and richer than in earlier works of Bach. Delightful coloristic effects produced between interplay of instruments. M-D.
———— *Quartett* W.94 D 1788 (E. F. Schmid—Nag 223; IMC) 19pp., parts. For flute (violin), viola, cello, and harpsichord (piano). Usually listed as a trio. Preface in German and English. A bright and ingenious piece. M-D.
———— *Quartett* W.95 D (Schmid—Br 2675). For piano, flute, viola, and cello. Usually listed as a trio. M-D.
These three *Quartetts* are usually listed as trios.

Johann Christian Bach. *Six Sonatas* Op.2 1764 (Smith—Dob). For flute, cello, and piano. Published separately. Nice runs, hands exchange, a few hand-crossings, fluent passage work. M-D.
———— *Sonata* C (Nagel—Schott). For flute, violin, and piano.
———— *Trio* B♭ (Nagel—WIM). For flute, violin, and basso continuo.
———— *Trio Sonata* B♭ (Koelbel—CFP). For flute, violin, and piano.
———— *Trio* II (Schünemann—K&S). For flute, violin, and piano.

Johann Sebastian Bach. *Three Trio Sonatas* (L. Moyse—GS 45815) 46pp., parts. For flute, violin, and piano; cello ad lib. I. G: Largo; Vivace;

Adagio; Presto. II. c: Largo; Allegro; Andante; Allegro. III. G: Adagio; Allegro ma non presto; Adagio e piano; Presto. The fine realizations by the editor are aimed at performance on the piano. M-D to D.

_____ *Two Sonatas* C, D (David—Br&H). For flute, violin, and piano.

_____ *Trio Sonatas* III G, IV c (Landshoff—CFP). For flute, violin, and keyboard.

_____ *Trio Sonata* G (IMC). For flute, violin, and basso continuo. No separate bass part.

Wilhelm Friedemann Bach. *Sonata* B♭ (Seiffert—IMC). For flute, violin, and piano; cello ad lib. Strong motivic process at work; ideas fragmented. Ornaments, rests, and triplets present. M-D.

_____ *Sonata* F (Br&VP). For flute, violin, and piano.

_____ *Trio* B♭ (Br&H). For flute, violin, and piano; cello ad lib.

Sven-Erik Bäck. *Sentire* 1969 (WH) 7pp., 3 copies necessary for performance. For flute, cello, and piano. Explanations in English. Five short movements. Pianist uses soft vibraphone sticks, hand-mutings, and some scratchings on strings. Cleverly put together. M-D.

Béla Bartók. *Contrasts* 1938 (Bo&H) 34pp., parts. $17\frac{1}{2}$ min. For clarinet, violin, and piano. Three movements: 1. Verbunkos (Recruiting Dance), 2. Pihenö (Relaxation), 3. Sebes (Fast Dance). Piano part is antiphonally featured in the second movement. Composed for the combined talents of Benny Goodman and Joseph Szigeti. A display piece for the three instruments in a pure Hungarian idiom. Virtuosity required. D.

Leslie Bassett. *Trio* 1953 (CFE) 36pp., parts. For clarinet, viola, and piano. Adagio: piano figuration serves as main thread of the movement while the other instruments counterpoint against it. Allegretto, ma ben marcato: syncopated dance movement, contrasting quiet sections. Adagio, ma non troppo: strong linear writing for all instruments, buildup of chords from time to time. Allegro moderato: ABA; outer sections use continuous sixteenth notes and dotted thematic ideas; mid-section employs eighth-note motion with legato themes. Neobaroque, freely tonal with chromatic texture, clear tonal centers. M-D.

Marion Bauer. *Trio Sonata* I (CFE). For flute, cello, and piano.

Gustavo Becerra-Schmidt. *Trio* (PAU 1958) 23pp., parts. For flute, violin, and piano. Allegro moderato: octotonic, bitonal textures, open fifths; large span required. Adagio: extreme registers used, repeated cluster-like chords in accompaniment, sequences. Allegro giusto: contrapuntal, chromatic lines, repeated harmonic sixths, thin textures, neoclassic orientation, mildly contemporary. M-D.

Alfred von Beckerath. *Sonatine* 1937 (Moeck 1018) 11pp., parts. For 2 violins or other treble instruments and piano. See detailed entry under trios for piano and two violins.

Ludwig van Beethoven. *Trio* Op.11 Bb 1798 (Br&H; CFP 7064; GS L1424; CF; Augener 7250d; IMC). For clarinet, cello, and piano. Extensive development of contrasting melodic fragments in first movement. Adagio: highly ornamented with piano providing the most atmosphere. Finale: ten undistinguished variations based on a tune from Joseph Weigl's opera *The Corsair*. M-D.

———— *Trio* Op.38 Eb (IMC). For clarinet or violin, cello, and piano. Arranged by Beethoven from his *Septet* Op.20.

Richard Rodney Bennett. *Commedia* II 1972 (Nov) 16pp., parts. 8½ min. For flute, cello, and piano. Four related sections are bridged by duet or solo passages. D.

Alban Berg. *Adagio* from *Chamber Concerto* (UE 12242 1935) 24pp., parts. 13 min. For violin, clarinet, and piano, arranged by Berg. Full of twelve-tone idioms but technical adroitness is balanced with emotional perception. Heart as well as brain are present. M-D.

Wilhelm Reinhard Berger. *Trio* Op.94 g (Musica Rara 1974; CFP) 55pp., parts. For clarinet, cello, and piano. The pianist is overly worked, with Brahms being the model for this composition. An A clarinet is required for the slow movement, Bb for the other movements. M-D to D.

Lennox Berkeley. *Trio* Op.44 (JWC 1956) 33pp., parts. 26 min. For piano, French horn, and violin. Allegro; Lento; Tema and (10) Variations. Neoclassic writing infused with lyrical and gentle witty elements. Terse and clear forms. D.

Antonio Bertali. *Sonata a 3* a (R. Wigness, R. P. Block—Musica Rara 1975) 8pp., parts. For 2 violins, bassoon (or trombone) and basso continuo.

Thomas Beversdorf. *Suite* 1947 (IU) 30pp., parts. For clarinet, cello, and piano. Andante: piano opens in octotonic treatment of the main diatonic idea; triplets follow, interspersed with octaves; trills; open sonorities. Allemande: chromatic, sixteenth-note figuration, repeated octaves and patterns. Sarabande: piano provides chords that bind together the two other instruments; G closing. Menuetto I: fugal. Menuetto II: more imitation, DC Menuetto I. Gigue: rhythmic drive; chords and runs bounce along at a sprightly pace. A fine neoclassic suite. M-D.

Heinrich Ignaz Franz von Biber. *Sonata a 3* (Kanetzky—Musica Rara). For two violins, trombone, and continuo.

Karl-Birger Blomdahl. *Trio* (Schott 10508 1956) 36pp., parts. For clarinet, cello, and piano. Tranquillo: serial; opening quiet sonorities soon explode; leads to a moderato, fluente e grazioso that develops with thin textures, imitation, independent octave lines; spins itself out to a whisper. Tranquillo, ma non troppo lento: thicker sonorities for the piano with help of the pedal; chromatic lines unravel. Allegro giocoso: rhythmic and light; short repetitive patterns grow to climax and subito drop back to *pp;* same procedure is followed again freely reworked. Tranquillo: similar to opening; piano finishes alone. M-D to D.

Philipp Friedrich Böddecker. *Sonata* sopra "La Monica" 1651 (K&S). For violin, bassoon, and keyboard. Four variations on the binary tune "La Monica." Violin repeats tune while the bassoon creates elaborate variations. M-D.

Sebastian Bodinus. *Sonata* E♭ (Vieweg 193). For two oboes or flutes, cello, and basso continuo. Slow; Fast; Siciliana. Strong harmonies and lines, clear forms. M-D.

András Borgulya. *Trio* 1964 (EMB 1974) 15pp., parts. For piano, clarinet, and violin.
_____ *Trio* (Gen). For flute, violin, and piano.

Johannes Brahms. *Trio* Op.40 E♭ 1865 (Br&H; CFP 3899b; Augener 5117; IMC; K). For French horn, violin, and piano. Andante: quiet; in a five-part form (not SA) with two contrasting themes that alternate; fluid and melancholy writing. Scherzo: wonderful energy and driving rhythm. Adagio mesto: sustained, deeply emotional; the recapitulation is one of Brahms's greatest. Finale—Allegro con brio: beautifully prepared for in the Adagio; has characteristics of a bouncing hunt. D.
_____ *Trio* Op.114 a 1891 (Br&H; CFP 3899E; K; IMC). For clarinet, cello, and piano. Allegro: SA; piano adds rhythmic punctuation along with thorough participation; broad Romantic writing. Adagio: elegiac theme; beautiful coloring of the instruments produces wonderful harmonies. Andantino: a minuet with two trios; ingenious scoring. Finale: SA, alternates 2/4 and 6/8 meter. D.

Benjamin Britten. *Gemini Variations* Op.73 (Faber F014 1965). Quartet for two or four players for violin, flute, and piano four-hands. If two players are used, performed by flute and piano, or by violin and piano. Twelve variations and fugue on epigram of Kodály. M-D.

Rudolph Bubalo. *Soundposts* (Ludwig 1975) 15pp., parts. For violin, clarinet, and piano. 6½ min. Part of the Cleveland Composers Guild publication series.

Barney Childs. *Trio* 1972 (Basheva Music, 23149 Oakbridge Lane, Newhall, CA 91321). Also contained in Vol. 4 of American Society of University Composers Journal of Music Scores. 10pp. For clarinet, cello, and piano. Cello opens, inflects quarter tones; piano enters lyric and drowsy with pedal; repeated patterns. Vertical alignment of parts is unimportant except where specifically cued: "Play your own tempo, ignore other players." "Stemless pitches once each only, in given order at any point during time of bar, any rhythms." Contains harmonics, long pedals. Piece fades out and the performers all read listed poetry on cue. Avantgarde. M-D.

Muzio Clementi. *Trio* Op.22/1 D (I. Sauer, U. Harnest, H. Meier—Müller 1972) 21pp., parts. For flute, cello, and piano. Violin can replace flute. Based on an 1809 André edition. Allegro di molto: SA; piano shares greatly in melodic material in addition to providing rhythmic (broken octaves, triplets, etc.) interest. Allegretto innocente: charming ideas, Minore midsection. Finale—Vivace assai: dancelike, unusual modulations, third relationships, brilliant conclusion. Classic style with thin textures throughout. Int. to M-D.

François Couperin. *Concerts Royaux* 1722 (D. Lasocki—Musica Rara 1974). For flute (oboe), violin (viola da gamba), and basso continuo. Vol.I: 8pp., 3 parts. Vol.II: 11pp., 2 parts. Vol.III: 16pp., 3 parts. Vol.IV: 14pp., 3 parts. These pieces are really "French" suites of dances with Italian influence seen in the lyrical structure of their melodies. No instruments were specified in the original editions. Contains groups of contrasting, charming airs and dances. Beautiful, pliant, and full of iridescent writing. This edition is helpful concerning problems of French ornamentation. Interesting continuo realizations.

Paul Creston. *Partita* Op.12 1938 (MCA) 46pp., parts. For flute, violin, and piano or for two violins and piano. Originally for flute, violin, and string orchestra. Piano reduction by Creston. Preamble; Sarabande; Burlesk; Air; Tarantella. Contemporary treatment of Baroque and dance forms. M-D.

_____ *Suite* Op.56 1953 (SP 1972) 66pp., parts. 25 min. For flute, viola, and piano. Prelude; Quasi-Sarabande; Scherzino; Arioso; Rondo. A well-contrasted work written in a grateful mildly contemporary style that is extremely pianistic. Rich harmonies and strong melodic writing add to its effectiveness. Large span required. M-D to D.

George Crumb. *Vox Balaenae for Three Masked Players* 1971 (CFP) 10pp., parts. 18 min. For electric (electrically amplified) flute, electric piano, and electric cello. Vox Balaenae (Voice of the Whale) was inspired by the singing of the humpback whale. Performers should wear black half-masks throughout the performance of the work. They are intended to give a symbolic representation of the powerful impersonal forces of nature (nature dehumanized). All three instruments are electrically amplified with a minimum of distortion. Thorough performance directions are included. Pianist needs a paper clip, a chisel, and a solid glass rod, and harmonics are called for. A suggested form for program listing is: Vocalise (. . . for the beginning of time): flautist sings and plays the notes simultaneously; Variations on Sea-Time; Sea-theme; Archeozoic (Var.I) Proterozoic (Var.II); Paleozoic (Var.III); Mesozoic (Var.IV); Cenozoic (Var.V); Sea-Nocturne (. . . for the end of time). A tightly unified work with some incredible sonorities, slow pacing throughout. Avant-garde. D.

Norman Dello-Joio. *Trio* 1944 (CF). For flute, cello, and piano. Unpretentious writing with spirit and grace and clear formal structures. Key signature for each movement but free modulation is frequent. Vivacious rhythmic usage. D.

Friedheim Döhl. *Sotto Voce* 1973 (Gerig) 20pp. For flute, cello, and piano. 3 scores required for performance. Explanations in German and English. Avant-garde.

Pierre Max Dubois. *Suite* 1968 (Maurer) 28pp., parts. Photostat of MS. For piano, violin, and clarinet.

Maurice Durufle. *Prélude, Récitatif et Variations* Op.3 1928 (Durand) 27pp., parts. 11 min. For flute, viola, and piano. Parallel chords, arpeggi figuration, subtle syncopation, crossed hands, varied tempi. Folk-like tune is basis for the four variations and extensive closing section. In style of Fauré–Ravel; strong colors. M-D to D.

Johann Ladislav Dussek. *Grand Sonata* Op.65 F 1808 (D. Lasocki—Musica Rara 1975) 45pp., parts. For flute, cello, and piano. Preface in English.

One of Dussek's finest chamber works. First movement presents a lovely melodious opening idea; a colorful and varied harmonic scheme in the development is especially unusual. The second movement, a Larghetto, is mainly notable for its lyrical beauty and versatile and imaginative use of small motifs. The opening four bars of the Rondo are based on dominant-seventh harmony, which sounded very fresh at the time it was written; the rest of the movement unfolds naturally and effectively. Although built around the piano, the entire work shows a fine awareness of chamber music dialogue and counterpoint. M-D.

————— *Notturno Concertante* Op.68 (C. D. S. Field—Br 1972) 44pp., parts. 4pp. of notes. For piano, violin, and horn (viola). Mainly a brilliant duo for piano and violin with horn accompaniment. Long rondo (424 bars) is followed by a shorter minuet and trio. Broad cantabile melodies, arpeggiated accompaniment, colorful modulations—all molded into a lyrical and dramatic piece of Romantic writing. Viola part is provided by editor as an alternate to the horn. Articulation and dynamics are discussed in the preface. D.

Anton Eberl. *Grand Trio* Op.36 E♭ (H. Voxman—Musica Rara 1973) 44pp., parts. For piano, clarinet, and cello. Dramatic, long lines, unusual harmonic shifts. Form is well developed; piano is the most important part. Probably one of the most valuable trios in this combination written during the classical period. M-D.

Halim El-Dabh. *Thulathiya* 1955 (CFP) $7\frac{1}{2}$ min. For viola, oboe, and piano. Thoroughly original in its Eastern inflection, ingenious timbres, highly logical dissonance. M-D.

Richard Faith. *Trio* 1967 (MS from composer: 1032 East Adelaide, Tucson, AZ 85719) 65pp., parts. For piano, violin, and French horn. Moderato: contrasted ideas, chromatic. Andante espressivo: piano treated more harmonically. Allegro scherzando: some meter changes, rhythmic subtleties. Presto: alternating hands, requires strong fingers. Neoclassically oriented. D.

Morton Feldman. *Durations III* 1962 (CFP 6903) 6pp., parts. For piano, tuba, and violin. Instruments begin simultaneously and are then free to choose their own durations within a given general tempo. The sounds themselves are designated. Sonorities are thinned and thickened, thereby keeping the basic image intact. Avant-garde. M-D.

Benjamin Frankel. *Trio* Op.10 (Augener). For clarinet, cello, and piano. Written in a sustained and intensely introspective melancholy style. Has an affinity with Ernest Bloch. Displays great technical versatility and eclecticism. Freely tonal with much dissonance. D.

Paul Walter Fürst. *Petitionen* Op.51 (Dob 1975) 17pp., parts. For piano, clarinet, and viola. Allegro assai; Langsam; Improvisierend—Langsam; Vivace; Langsam–Allegro. Neoclassic, bitonal, parallel chords, cluster harmonics and clusters, glissando, mildly contemporary. M-D.

Johann Joseph Fux. *Sonata a Tre* d (Hillemann—Heinrichshofen). For flute, violin, and piano. Polyphonic lines are beautifully woven into a fine texture for all three instruments. M-D.

Hans Gál. *Trio* Op.49b 1948 (OBV) 16pp., parts. See detailed entry under trios for piano, violin, and cello.
_____ *Trio* Op.97 (Simrock Elite Edition 3145 1971) 32pp., parts. For piano, clarinet, and violin. Moderato assai; Andantino capriccioso poco sostenuto; Tema con Variazioni. Written in a fairly accessible style with no twentieth-century "Second Viennese School" accoutrements. Freely tonal, mildly contemporary, and "sounds" well. M-D.

Mikhail Glinka. *Trio Pathétique* d 1832. For clarinet, bassoon or cello, and piano. See detailed entry under trios for piano and two miscellaneous woodwinds.

Joseph Goodman. *Trio* 1967 (AMP 96528-55) 55pp., parts. 20 min. For flute, piano, and violin. Moderato; Allegro molto; Lento (fugue). The first two movements are composed in such a way that formal structures and speeds of development unfold simultaneously on different levels. In the Moderato, three levels are formed in this way: flute: Introduction and Rhapsody, violin: SA design, piano: Etude and Trio. In the Allegro molto there are two levels, the flute and violin forming one (Rondo à la Tarantella), the piano another (Theme and Variations). Freely tonal, neoclassic orientation. D.

Elizabeth H. Gyring. *Trio* (CFE). For piano, clarinet, and viola.

Louis Haber. *Parade, Blues and Allegro* (Gen 1971) 16pp., parts. For flute, piano, and violin. Parade: clusterlike chords, martial rhythms, bitonal, chords in alternating hands; large span required. Blues: seventh and ninth chords, alternating octaves, octotonic. Allegro: syncopated, subito dynamic changes, imitation, octotonic, arpeggi figuration, contrary chromatic chords. M-D.

John Hall. *Trio III* (Chappell). For violin, French horn, and piano. Prelude; Scherzo; Night Interlude; Rondo. Equality of all parts achieved. Changing meters, effective contemporary treatment. D.

George Frederick Handel. *Kammertrio VII* (M. Seiffert—Br&H). For flute, piano, and violin; cello ad lib. This is Trio-Sonata Op.2/1 c. Over-edited. M-D.

—— *Trio* (Kolneder—Schott). For oboe, violin, and basso continuo.

—— *Trio Sonata* Op.2/5 F (Hinnenthal—Br). For oboe, violin, and basso continuo. M-D.

Roger Hannay. *Fantôme* 1967 (CFP 66486 1976) 22pp., parts. 12 min. For clarinet, viola, and piano. The pianist requires the following auxiliary percussion: 2 xylophone sticks, 2 timpani sticks, 2 wire brushes, metal rod with blunt tip, claves. Special piano notation indicates fingernail glissando on strings next to piano brace, arm clusters. Long pedals; strings must be struck with hands; sounding board must be tapped through sound hole. Pointillistic, harmonics, cadenza passage, improvisatory section, avant-garde. Large span required. D.

Franz Joseph Haydn. *Cassation* H IV: D2 (F. Nagel—Litolff 1973) 20pp., parts. For flute, violin, and piano.

—— *Trio* Op.2/4 (Bergmann—Schott). For flute, violin, and piano; cello ad lib.

—— *Three Trios* (Rampal—IMC). For flute, cello, and piano.

—— *Trio* No.29 F (CF) 17pp., parts. For violin or flute, cello or bassoon, and piano. Allegro; Finale—Tempo di Menuetto. First movement contains elaborate figuration while the last movement is an elegant menuetto. M-D.

—— *Klaviertrio* No.30 D (David—Br&H). For flute, cello, and piano.

—— *Trio* No.31 G (CF) 25pp., parts. For flute or violin, cello or bassoon, and piano. Allegro; Andante; Finale—Allegro moderato. Contains some bold modulations. M-D to D.

Nos.29–31 are basically sonatas for piano with an accompaniment by the other instruments.

—— *Trios* (W. Stockmeier—Henle 284 1976) Vol.III. 67pp., parts. For flute, cello, and piano. Contains *Trio* D Hob. XV:16, *Trio* G Hob. XV:15, *Trio* F Hob. XV:17. It is possible to play all three trios replacing the flute part by the violin. Fingering for the piano part has been added by Jörg Demus. Excellent urtext and practical edition. M-D.

Paul Hindemith. *Trio* Op.47 1928 (Schott) $12\frac{1}{2}$ min. For viola, heckelphone, and piano. Solo, Arioso, Duette (first movement): opens with a three-part invention-like section; followed by a slow arioso for heckelphone and piano inspired by a fragment from the Solo; leads to the lively Duette: viola and heckelphone accompanied canonically by the piano. Potpourri: four sections all thematically independent. One of Hindemith's most important chamber works, too seldom heard. D.

Mogens Winkel Holm. *Transitions II* (WH 4256 1973) 43 loose leaves. 3 copies necessary for performance. For flute, cello, and piano. This entire work is to be played *pp*. It is a series of repetition and shifting principles, and the effects of these in interplay between the instruments. "The music could perhaps be compared to three sonorous whirls or spirals that move, quietly interlocking, by turning about themselves a couple of times in slow motion. This demands a certain amount of the performers. Perhaps first and foremost what one could call unshakable confidence in an 'a-personal' form of expression, a *non-espressivo,* in which the musician, instead of seeking solo brilliance, balances and interlaces the sound in order to achieve a perfect blend between the instruments (not more than *pp*), aiming at 'objective' phrasing without crescendo, stringendo, vibrato and other so-called expressive effects. I would like a great deal of the strength of the work to lie in these omissions" (from the foreword). Score is printed on separate pages to help solve page turning. Atonal, pointillistic, many repeated notes, tremolo, complex rhythms, alternating hands, avant-garde. Requires great control. D.

Arthur Honegger. *Petite Suite* 1934 (Philharmusica 1974). See detailed entry under trios for piano, one stringed instrument, and one wind instrument. Int. to M-D.

Klaus Huber. *Ascensus* (Ars Viva No. 1979) 3 playing scores (piano has 31pp., flute and cello each have 23pp.). Instructions in German. Avant-garde.

Johann Nepomuk Hummel. *Adagio, Variations and Rondo on "Schöne Minka"* Op.78 1819 (N. Delius—Musica Rara 1968; B. Pauler—Amadeus 1975) 30pp., parts. For flute, cello, and piano. Introduction; Thema, 7 Variations and Finale. Facile writing by a skilled hand, with the piano being especially favored. Treatment of the variations might be considered shallow but it is at least superficially effective. M-D.

Andrew Imbrie. *Serenade* 1952 (SP). For flute, viola, and piano. 20 min. 40pp. Lively ideas with clear shape and direction, chromatic, lyric and expressive. Rhythmic vitality, rich and inventive harmonic texture. Large-scaled formal logic; clever interplay of motifs; concludes with a slow movement whose mood lives on after the music has ended. D.

———— *To a Traveler* 1971 (SP) 3 scores necessary, 24pp. each. 9 min. For piano, violin, and clarinet. Takes its title from Rexroth's translation of a poem by Su Tung P'o. "From a very quiet, transparently scored introduction, two chief melodic ideas soon emerge; the first for clarinet, the second, a little faster, for violin. This general rise in energy and pace is carried further by the passage which follows and moves to a rapid climax through the use of quickly moving figurations. The texture suddenly dissolves and the initial quiet motion is resumed. The much faster tempo and agitated figuration soon re-assert themselves, and they lead to an extended development. This culminates in a kind of brief cadenza for all three instruments at a still faster tempo. The effect of this is to consume most of the remaining energy, allowing for a final return to the peaceful character of the introduction, which is now combined with the reminiscent strains of the clarinet playing an expanded version of its original melody" (from the score). Long pedals, chromatic motifs, chords with four different dynamic levels, tremolando effects, cluster-like chord at conclusion. Large span required. D.

Vincent d'Indy. *Trio* Op.29 B♭ 1887 (Durand; Hamelle; IMC) 66pp., parts. For clarinet, cello, and piano. Ouverture: B♭; second section in F♯; third section in A♭; followed by a bridge theme with further modulations and then returns to B♭. Divertissement: E♭, has two intermèdes with the second in e♭. Chant élégiaque: D♭, ABA, expressive melody. Finale: B♭, rondo, highly pianistic. D'Indy's first mature chamber work. The cyclic principle unifies the work remarkably well, and it is beautifully laid out for the pianist. D.

Charles E. Ives. *Largo* 1901–2 (PIC 1953) 8pp., parts. For clarinet, cello, and piano. Broken chords over ostinato-like bass, freely tonal. Quasi allegretto section elaborates the bass line with cross-accents; full chords in right hand; climax; ritard; and returns to opening idea. Ends on a G triad with an added b♭. M-D.

Wolfgang Jacobi. *Trio* 1946 (Edition Kasparek) 26pp., parts. 17 min. For flute, violin, and piano. Allegro; Larghetto; Fugue—Allegro. Neobaroque style, similar to Hindemith. M-D.

Arthur Jannery. *Three Fantasies* 1974 (MS available from composer: 1010 Sutton St., Radford, VA 24141). For flute, cello (or bass clarinet), and piano. Fast: piano serves mainly as supporting instrument though some melodic use is incorporated; white-key glissandi. Quite Slow, and expressively: Impressionist sonorities in piano aided by liberal use of pedal. Allegro: bright cheerful writing, imitation, two-note figuration prominent, chromatic, brilliant conclusion. D.

Knud Jeppesen. *Little Summer Trio* 1957 (WH 4016) 26pp., parts. 15 min. For flute, cello, and piano. Violin can be substituted for flute. Allegretto leggiero: sprightly, freely tonal, G key signature, passages in tenths, contrasted lines, witty. Adagio: lyrical, centers around D, chromatic, syncopated pedal point closing. Allegro animato: jaunty rhythms, thin-textured opening, becomes more chordal, some imitation; a good-humored finale. Infused with Impressionist tendencies; mildly contemporary harmonies. M-D.

Wilfred Josephs. *Trio* Op.76 (Nov 1975) 49pp., parts. 18 min. For horn, violin, and piano.

Harrison Kerr. *Trio* 1936 (Merion) 22pp., parts. For clarinet, cello, and piano. Allegro; Largo; Vivace–Scherzando; Allegro Vivace–quasi presto. Chromatic, quartal harmonies, dissonant counterpoint especially in the third movement, parallel chords, changing meters. Twelve-tone influence present but not used in a strict sense. Kerr is basically a Romantic, and that quality is never entirely lost in this work. M-D to D.

Aram Khachaturian. *Trio* 1932 (CFP; Bo&H; MCA; Musica Rara; Anglo-Soviet Press) 41pp., parts. 16 min. For clarinet (or viola), violin, and piano. Andante con dolore, con molto espressione: begins in g, ends in c; a poetic duet between the clarinet (imitating a zurna, a Transcaucasian wind instrument) and the violin while the piano mainly supports. Allegro: dance rhythms, transparent tonal coloring. Moderato: a set of variations based on an Uzbek folk tune; colorful harmonic and timbre contrasts. The composer's stylistic idiosyncrasies are already stamped on this early work, which explores most of the keyboard. M-D to D.

Karl Kohn. *Trio* (CF 1975) 26pp., parts. 23 min. For violin, horn, and piano. Facsimile edition.

Franz Koringer. *Sonata Profana 5*: quasi divertimento ungherese (L. Krenn 1974) 22pp., parts. 10 min. For clarinet, viola, and piano.

Johann Krebs. *Trio* e 1743 (F. Nagel—Müller). Four movements. For 2 flutes and piano; second flute part can be played on oboe or violin. M-D.

Ernst Křenek. *Trio* 1946 (AMP 1955) 15pp., parts. For violin, clarinet, and piano. Allegretto moderato comodo; Allegro agitato–Allegro deciso–Andante. Partial twelve-tone technique incorporated into Křenek's spiky style; varied figuration and rhythmic treatment. Last movement is highly sectionalized. M-D.

Konradin Kreutzer. *Trio–Grande Sonate* Op.28/2 G (I. Sauer, U. Harnest, H. Meier—Müller 2064 SM 1972) 56pp., parts. For piano, flute, and cello. Allegro con moto; Adagio; Finale. Kreutzer had a distinguished reputation in Germany during the nineteenth century but this work shows more skill and experience than inspiration. Traditional classic idioms and techniques are used. M-D.

Rudolphe Kreutzer. *Trio* Op.28/2 G (Müller). For flute, cello, and piano. Viennese classical style, Beethoven influence noted, not especially idiomatic. M-D.

Friedrich Kuhlau. *Trio Concertante* Op.119 G (Simrock). For flute, cello, and piano. Strong melodies, reminiscent of Schubert and Weber, independent parts, forceful command of formal structures. M-D.

John Lessard. *Trio* (Gen 1968) 31pp., parts. For flute, cello, and piano. Allegretto: freely tonal, serial influence, thin textures contrasted with fuller sonorities; large span required. Lento: chordal punctuation, dry staccato treatment in lower register. Andante: chordal, sustained, contrasted with short fragments. Presto: fugal textures, neoclassic orientation. M-D.

Ernst Levy. *Trio* 1968 (Seesaw) 17pp., parts. For clarinet, viola, and piano. Andante: sustained octave syncopation, chromatic patterns. Moderato: octotonic, quartal and quintal harmonies, chromatic inner voices. Moderato: transfer of line between instruments, chromatic sixteenths, sequence; gradually unwinds to a *ppp* conclusion. Moderato: solo piano elaborates previous ideas. Presto: similar to earlier material, upper register, fugal, left hand broken-octave pattern in low register. Mildly contemporary. M-D.
———— *Second Trio* 1970 (MS at LC) 36pp., parts. For clarinet, cello, and piano. Four untitled movements in a freely tonal, highly chromatic style. Unusual symbols used are explained on final page. More dissonance here than in the first trio. M-D to D.

Robert Hall Lewis. *Trio* 1966 (Dob 1974) 20pp., parts. 10 min. For violin, clarinet, and piano. "[My] earlier music was concerned with a basic linear-developmental process in the serial manner. In recent years I have abandoned this approach for a music embracing larger and more varied conceptual gestures. Hence, the interplay of continuity–discontinuity, subtle contrasts of timbre and rhythm, and structural flexibility are more characteristic of my present style" (DCM, 423). This atonal work is in one movement and contains cadenzalike passages for the three instruments. Similar texture throughout. Varied tempi, meters, melody, and rhythm do not display much continuity, and many notes have to be scrambled for! On p.13, right hand in piano part requires a bass clef, not a treble clef. D.

Otto Luening. *Trio* 1973 (CFP) 39pp., parts. For flute, cello, and piano. Shifting meters, freely tonal, pointillistic, 7 with 5, arpeggi figuration, clusters, tremolo, strong individual writing, some neoclassic characteristics. M-D.

_____ *Trio II* (Highgate 1974) 22pp., parts. For flute, violin, and piano; cello or bassoon, ad lib. Larghetto; Allegro; Largo; Allegro. Freely tonal, tertial harmony, shifting meters, free counterpoint, highly expressive Largo, interesting triplet use in finale. A very beautiful and flowing work. M-D.

Elisabeth Lutyens. *Horai* Op.67/4 (Olivan Press 1968). For violin, horn and piano.

John McCabe. *Dance Movements* (Nov 1967). For horn, violin, and piano. Plenty of dissonance in the piano part. A Lento moderato provides a quiet opening, followed by contrasting quick, slow, quick movements. A final upward rush of scale figuration at the end concludes the piece. D.

_____ *Sonata* (Nov 1969). For clarinet, cello, and piano. One continuous movement. Well constructed; very effective vivo section. Pianist is required to strike strings with rubber beaters and to pluck them. M-D.

Roger Marsh. *Sweet and Short* (Nov). For clarinet, piano, and double bass.

Donald Martino. *Trio* 1959 (ECS 2069 1970) 24pp., parts. For violin, piano, and clarinet. Seven contrasting sections to be felt as a unit and played without pause. Six varied types of attack are included as well as a description of special signs. Also includes "Special Notes to the Pianist." Dynamic extremes, pointillistic, tightly organized, plucked and damped strings, clusters, expressionistic. D.

Bohuslav Martinů. *Madrigal Sonata* 1936 (AMP) 28pp., parts. 9 min. For piano, flute, and violin. Poco Allegro; Moderato. Piano has largest share of the chromatic neo-Romantic writing. Syncopation in certain spots will require the most careful counting by all performers. Virtuosic and dramatic treatment. D.

―――― *Sonata* 1936 (Br 3326 1959) 36pp., parts. For piano, violin, and flute. Allegro poco moderato: freely tonal, rhythmic drive, chromatic runs with chords, chordal syncopation, octotonic, cross-rhythms. Adagio: sustained and expressive; large span required. Allegretto (Scherzo): piano has rhythmic introduction with a bouncy left hand, chords in alternating hands, solo piano episode, varied gestures in coda. D.

―――― *Trio* F 1944 (AMP) 44pp., parts. 19 min. For flute, cello (or viola), and piano. Poco allegretto; Adagio; Andante–Allegretto scherzando. Essentially conservative writing in a whimsical mood. Transparent and concentrated lyricism. D.

Karl Julius Marx. *Trio* Op.61 (Hänssler 16.014 1972) 36pp., parts. For flute, cello, and piano. Fantasia; Scherzo; Introduzione e Rondo. Coherent whole, mildly contemporary writing, instruments treated equally. Scherzo would make a fine encore or short movement; a fine contribution to the limited repertoire. M-D.

Toshiro Mayuzumi. *Metamusic* (CFP 1964) 2pp., parts. For piano, violin, and saxophone. "This piece is to be performed *only on the stage,* as the piece has been written for both visual and acoustic effects. None of the parts (scores) is connected at any point with any of the other parts. Each performer is to play his part independently, though the performances should be started at the same time. The total duration of the performance may be decided freely by the performers. Namely, the piece can be played as a whole, in repetitions, or in part, according to the performers' desire" (from the composer's instructions for performance). The pianist uses clusters; must shut the keyboard lid with a bang and get up, then sit down slowly and open it again. Everything must be performed as written *but only with animated gestures and without any sound!* Exceptions are the clusters, pizzicati, and the banging of the keyboard lid. Avant-garde.

Wilfred Mellers. *Trio* 1962 (Nov) 23pp., parts. For flute, cello, and piano. Eclogue: changing meters, freely tonal, skipping harmonic sixths, chromatic figuration, trills. Estampie: quick and rhythmic, chords in alternating hands, melodic emphasis in sections, harmonics. Threnody: cantabile, chordal sonorities, involved rhythms, melodic *pp* closing. Mildly contemporary style throughout. M-D.

Pavle Merkù. *Astrazioni* Op.23 1956 (Društvo Slovenskih Skladateljev 1963) 25pp., parts. For clarinet, cello, and piano. Introduzione Allegretto:

short figures, freely tonal, sustained section leads to fugato textures, rhythmic conclusion. Contrasto—Allegro non troppo: chromatic harmonic thirds in ostinato-like patterns in an eight-bar group; this grouping evolves through various (5) treatments. Distensione—Lento: further elaboration on Introduzione opening short figures. Conclusione—Allegro mosso: incisive rhythmic treatment, hemiola, chromatic triplets, marcato and crescendo to final *ff* conclusion. A folk flavor permeates this mildly contemporary work. M-D.

Georges Migot. *Le Livre des Danceries* 1929 (Leduc) 37pp., parts. For flute, violin, and piano. Introduction; Gai; Religieux; Conclusion. Highly individual part-writing that produces free counterpoint and strong dissonance with a profusion of polytonalities, all conceived in a modal harmonic vocabulary. Migot's techniques are inspired by Debussy. His mystic interests are reflected in the Religieux movement. Resources of all three instruments are thoroughly explored. M-D.

Darius Milhaud. *Suite* (Sal 1936) 20pp., parts. For piano, violin, and clarinet. 1. Ouverture: light and cheerful, span of tenth required, centers freely around D, colorful textural shifts. 2. Divertissement: animated, 4/4 Moins animé uses some 3 + 3 + 2 rhythms for clever effect. 3. Jeu: for violin and clarinet alone. 4. Introduction et Final: 5/4 Modéré, chordal, leads to Vif, 6/8, colorful light chords with added seconds, glissandi, much vitality, *pp* ending. Charming and gracious writing. M-D.

Akira Miyoshi. *Sonate* (Ongaku No Toma Sha 1966) 29pp., parts. No.40 in Contemporary Japanese Music Series. For flute, cello, and piano. Modéré: octotonic, flexible meters, chromatic figuration, alternating hands; large span required. Passacaille: extensive gestures, repeated notes, subject fragmented. Finale: fast triplets, chordal punctuation interspersed with scalar and arpeggi figures, dramatic conclusion. Written in an international style with French influence noted. M-D.

Wolfgang Amadeus Mozart. *Trio* K.498 E♭ (Br&H; Adamowski—GS L1403; Augener 7268g; Lienau; IMC). For piano, clarinet, and viola. Andante: monothematic; turn-figure of the opening bar is charmingly varied. Menuetto: contrapuntal, animated; highly interesting trio. Allegretto: a rondo that continually sings; melody and contrapuntal technique distilled towards end of the movement; an enchanting conclusion. M-D.

Robert Muczynski. *Fantasy Trio* Op.26 (GS 1971) 24pp., parts. For clarinet, cello, and piano. Four movements. Well written, attractive but not easy, freely tonal with frequent bitonal clashes. Rhythmic variety is very adroit. The finale makes clever play out of changing meters. The piano part is very demanding in some places. Stravinskyesque. M-D.

Joseph Myslivecek. *Trio* Op.1/4 B♭ (H. Riemann—IMC) 11pp., parts. For flute, violin, and piano. Three contrasting movements with a minuet. Not difficult and very effective. This has become a popular and fairly well known work. M-D.

Stefan Niculescu. *Triplum* 1971 (Sal) 15pp., parts. For flute, cello, and piano. Hétérophonie I, II, and III. Homophonie I, II. Polyphonie I, II. Contains elaborate performance directions. Improvisation, traditional and avant-garde notation, pointillistic, dynamic extremes, mobile form. Avant-garde. D.

Per Norgaard. *Trio* Op.15 (JWC 4033 1958) 35pp., parts. For clarinet, cello, and piano. Sostenuto–Allegretto: flexible meters, freely tonal, triplet usage, thin textures. Larghetto: sustained opening, expressive, widespread textures; half step is thematically important; builds to chordal climax; tremolando; subsides; *pp* closing. Con moto: 6/8, trills, subito dynamic changes, chromatic, rhythmic drive, alternating hands, octotonic, two groups of four eighths in 6/8; half step still integral to motivic construction. Poco allegro, con affetto: intense; figures and patterns; grace notes used for rhythmic precision and color; *fff* climax; recedes; *pp* closing; half step used constantly. This work shows a fine talent searching for a consistent style. M-D.

Lionel Nowak. *Trio* 1951 (CFE). For clarinet, cello, and piano.

Toshitsugu Ogihara. *Concerto for Flute, Violin and Piano* 1961 (Japan Federation of Composers 1973) 51pp., parts. Allegro: SA; material well developed; pentatonic scale influence slightly felt. Andantino: ABA; triplet figure prominent; graceful chordal syncopations give a dance feeling. Allegro: free SA design; pentatonic influence mixed with chromatic usage; minor seconds plentiful; bitonal; equal interest in all parts; calm, slow coda capped with a strong, lively finish. D.

Jean Papineau-Couture. *Trio en Quatre Mouvements* (CMC 1974) 20pp., parts. For clarinet, viola, and piano. Four movements have metronome marks. Directions for performers in French. Clusters, harmonics, contrary-motion glissandi. Virtuoso writing for all instruments. The framework for the piece is logical and well planned. D.

Robert Parris. *Trio* 1959 (ACA) 22 min. For clarinet, cello, and piano.

Gabriel Pierné. *Sonata da Camera* Op.48 (Durand) 32pp., parts. For violin, clarinet, and piano. Prélude; Sarabande et Finale. The sarabande is based on the name Louis Fleury, to whose memory the piece is dedicated. Well crafted; has qualities of grace, refinement, and sensitivity; supple writing that shows Pierné was well grounded in counterpoint. M-D.

Ignaz Pleyel. *Sonate* Op.16/1 G (H. Albrecht—K&S 35) 32pp., parts. For flute, cello, and piano. Allegro; Adagio; Rondo. Facile, charming. Especially lovely Adagio. M-D.

_____ *Sonate* Op.16/2 C (H. Albrecht—K&S 36) 31pp., parts. For flute, cello, and piano. Allegro vivace; Rondo; Presto. Lively. M-D.

_____ *Sonate* Op.16/5 e (H. Albrecht—K&S 37) 28pp., parts. For flute, cello, and piano. Allegro molto; Andantino; Rondo. Minor key is used to advantage. M-D.

_____ *Grand Trio* Op.29 (Musica Rara; Simrock 15pp., parts). For flute, cello, and piano. Allegro; Andante; Rondo. Mozartian grace, high classic style, fluent, melodious.
The general effect of all these pieces suggests a diffuse but harmonically rich Haydn style.

Elizabeth Posten. *Trio* (JWC 1960). For flute, clarinet (or viola), and harp (or piano). See detailed entry under trios for piano and two miscellaneous woodwinds.

Johann Joachim Quantz. *Trio Sonata* c (Schultz, Hauser—Schott). For flute violin, and basso continuo.

_____ *Trio Sonata* C (W. Bergmann, L. Lefkovitch—Schott 10652) 20pp., parts. For flute, violin, and continuo; cello ad lib. Allegro; Adagio; Allegro. Preface by editors. Tasteful realizations. M-D.

_____ *Trio Sonata* D (M. Seiffert—K&S) 15pp., parts. For flute (oboe), violin, and basso continuo. Adagio; Allegro; Largo; Allegro. More appropriate realization than many of this editor's. M-D.

_____ *Trio Sonata* D (Ruf—Ric). For flute, violin, and basso continuo.

_____ *Trio Sonata* g (Br&H). For flute, violin, and continuo. Imaginative outer movements, Siciliana middle movement. M-D.

_____ *Trio Sonata* G (Schott 11254). For oboe, cello (bassoon), and piano. See detailed entry under trios for piano and two miscellaneous woodwinds.

Jean Philippe Rameau. *Pièces de Clavecin en Concerts* 1742 (E. Jacobi—Br 1970) 63pp., parts. For violin or flute and viol (gamba) or a second violin and keyboard. See detailed entry under trios for piano, violin, and cello.

Günther Raphael. *Trio-Suite* Op.44 (Müller WM1611SM 1968) 27pp., parts. For flute, cello, and piano. Praembulum; Courante; Sarabande;

Menuett; Gigue. Neobaroque style, freely tonal. The Menuett is by far the most extensive movement. Requires solid pianism throughout. M-D.

———— *Trio* Op.70 1950 (Br&H 6206) 39pp., parts. 15 min. For clarinet, cello, and piano. Allegro: strong rhythms and syncopation; harmonic seconds, fourths, and fifths; large span required. Andante: long lines with embellishments; sustained. Allegro molto: toccata-like, alternating hands, sustained and lyric episodes, driving coda. Neoclassic. M-D.

Hendrik de Regt. *Musica per flauto, violoncello e clavicembalo* Op.29 (Donemus 1973) 24pp., parts.

———— *Circe* Op.44 (Donemus 1975) 36pp., parts. For clarinet, violin (or viola), and piano. Photostat of MS.

Carl Reinecke. *Trio* Op.264 A 1904 (Br; Simrock 39pp., parts; IMC). For clarinet, viola, and piano. In a refined Mendelssohn style with an appealing Legend slow movement. M-D.

Karel Reiner. *Loose Leaves* (Panton 1972) 43pp., parts. For clarinet, cello, and piano. Free atonal style; melodic ideas varied by using mainly dissonant intervals—seconds, sevenths, and ninths. M-D.

Roger Reynolds. *Acquaintances* (CFP 6611 1963) 13pp., parts. 7 min. For flute, double bass, and piano. The disparate qualities of the flute and the double bass are combined through the mediation of the piano. Two atypical cadenzas separate the three characterized sections—Abrupt, Antic, and Acceptance. Short, continuous and freely developing, the work moves through a spectrum of mood from slapstick to severity. Plucked strings; pointillistic; in the Interlude the pianist is asked to ad lib if more support is necessary. Sense of humor will help the performance. D.

Ferdinand Ries. *Trio* Op.28 (D. Klöcher—Musica Rara 1969) 40pp., parts. For clarinet, cello, and piano. Allegro; Scherzo—Allegro vivace; Adagio; Rondo. Beethoven influence is obvious and reflects the transition from Classicism to early Romanticism. M-D.

Bernard Rogers. *Ballade* (PIC 1966) 15pp., parts. For piano, viola, and bassoon. Piano opens a long Vivace section alone, joined by the viola and bassoon at Deciso. Other sections are Deliberato, Andante moderato, ma agitato, Cadenza and Andante tranquillo, and quasi adagio, all played without break. Lovely sonorities and excellent ensemble writing. M-D.

Ned Rorem. *Trio* 1960 (CFP 6430 1966) 26pp., parts. 18 min. For flute, cello, and piano. Largo misterioso–Allegro: interesting flute cadenza at beginning over sustained chords in the piano; Allegro section contrasts with running chromatic figuration. Largo: a melancholy, intermezzo-like, bittersweet slow movement. Andante: cello cadenza; piano part has repeated chords in left hand and melodic line that intertwines with cello and flute. Allegro molto: clear lines, French flavor, instruments used to fine advantage. M-D.

Archduke Johann Joseph Rainer Rudolph. *Trio* (Musica Rara). For clarinet, cello, and piano. A fine example of amateur composition; written in a pseudo-Beethoven style with some effective moments. M-D.

Dieter Salbert. *Kammermusik* 1971 (Möseler) 12pp. 3 copies are necessary for performance. For piano, clarinet, and violin.

László Sáry. *Image* (EMB 1974) 10pp., 3 copies necessary for performance. For clarinet, cello, and piano.

Herman Schroeder. *Zweites Klavier-Trio* Op.40 (Schott 5651 1967) 35pp., parts. For violin, horn, and piano. Andante sostenuto–Allegro; Adagio; Presto scherzando.
_____ *Piano Trio III* Op.43 (Schott 6008 1969) 42pp., parts. For clarinet, cello, and piano. Allegro animato; Largo; Poco vivace.
Both works are written in an atonal and dissonant neoclassic style based on the techniques of Hindemith. M-D.

Robert Schumann. *Fairy Tales* Op.132 1853 (Br&H; CF; IMC). For clarinet, viola, piano. See detailed description under trios for piano, violin, and viola.

Elliott Schwartz. *Trio* 1964 (CF 1972) 17pp., parts. 11 min. Facsimile edition. For flute, cello, and piano. Not too rapidly; Very slowly, but with tension; Very lively. Serial influence, wide skips, sudden dynamic changes, percussive use of piano. The sustained second movement uses only one piano stave. The exciting finale contains shifting meters and requires great agility on the part of the pianist. Large span required. D.

Klement Slavický. *Trialog* 1966 (Panton) 40pp., parts. For piano, violin, and clarinet.

Leland Smith. *Trio* (CFE 1947) 25pp., parts. For flute (or violin), cello, and piano. Fast, but not too much; Slowly, with expression; Scherzo—Fast; Very Fast. Freely tonal, octotonic. Fast movements are infused with dance qualities; slow movement is somewhat Impressionistic but highly intense. Requires fine octave technique and large span. D.

Harvey Sollberger. *Divertimento* 1970 (ACA). For flute, cello, and piano. Unusual timbral and virtuosic writing. D.

Carl Stamitz. *Trio* Op.14/1 (W. Upmeyer—Nag 38) 13pp., parts. For flute, violin, and continuo. Moderato; Andante moderato; Rondo—Moderato. The last two movements contain minore sections. Keyboard part is mainly chordal. M-D.
_____ *Triosonate* Op.14/5 F (Hillemann—Br&H). For flute, violin, and continuo.

Robert Starer. *Trio* (PIC). For B♭ clarinet, cello, and piano.

Wolfgang Steffen. *Trio* Op.37 (Bo&Bo 1973) 19pp., parts. 12 min. For flute, cello, and piano. Directions for all instruments in German. Pointillistic, clusters, dynamic extremes, proportional rhythmic relationships, highly organized, complex. Strings are to be strummed. D.

Leon Stein. *Trio Concertante* 1961 (CFE) 49pp., parts. For piano, violin, and alto sax. Allegro con brio: SA, extensive development, Impressionistic; sonorities handled in a neoclassic style. Siciliano—Andante moderato: rocking mood in opening section; middle section has more activity (runs, arpeggi) but is generally kept subdued; opening mood returns briefly. Scherzoso—Allegro vivace: much rhythmic drive couched in a Gallic humorous style; clever ending. M-D.

Igor Stravinsky. *Suite from L'Histoire du Soldat* (JWC 1918; IMC) 28pp., parts. For clarinet, violin, and piano. Arranged by the composer. March du Soldat; Le violon du Soldat; Petit concert; Tango–Valse–Rag; La danse du Diable. Highly effective arrangement. Retains the main ingredients and many of the sonorities from the original. D.

Richard Swift. *Trio* Op.14 (CFE). For clarinet, violin, and piano. Swift "describes his music as influenced by the Viennese twelve-tone school; by the work and thought of Stravinsky, Babbitt, Perle, and Sessions; and by the analytical methods of Heinrich Schenker" (DCM, 723).

William Sydeman. *Trio* 1961 (Seesaw). For oboe, viola, and piano. Sydeman describes himself as "a musical hybrid, split between the traditional urge to 'say something' and twentieth-century materials, which have so long been associated with impersonality and abstraction" (DCM, 725).
_____ *Fantasy and Two Epilogues* 1964 (Okra) 17pp., parts. 9 min. Reproduced from holograph. For flute, cello, and piano. Serial; the flute and cello play together much of the time without the piano. When the piano

enters in the Fantasy it is to play in a "wild" manner, grabbing low-pitched notes and chords. About the middle of the first epilogue the following direction is given: "From here on to the end of the epilogue the piano dominates completely!" The second epilogue uses the piano in a "fleeting" manner and has figuration that is to be played "as if a three-note trill." Contains some stunning sonorities but is a very complex piece. D.

Elias Tanenbaum. *Trio* (CFE). For clarinet, cello, and piano.

Phyllis Tate. *Air and Variations* 1957 (OUP) 29pp., parts. For violin, clarinet, and piano. 14 min. Air; Variations; Aubade; Tempo di Valse; Serenade; Tarantella; Fugal March (Finale). Piano is silent for the Tarantella variation. Strong neoclassic style. M-D.

Georg Philipp Telemann. *Essercizii Musici. Trio Sonata* XII E♭ (H. Ruf—Schott 1974) 19pp., parts. For oboe, harpsichord (piano), and continuo. Sounds best when performed by oboe, harpsichord obbligato, a continuo instrument such as cello, viola da gamba, or bassoon and a continuo chordal instrument such as another harpsichord or lute (guitar). The affecting mesto slow movement and the following brilliant Allegro are especially fine. M-D.
———— *Six Concerti* (Br 2961). See detailed entry under duos for piano and flute.
———— *Trio Sonata* e (K. Hofmann—HM 224). For oboe, violin, and basso continuo. 10pp., parts.
———— *Trio Sonata* g (Ruf—Ric). For oboe, violin, and basso continuo.
———— *Sonata* e (K. Hofmann—HM 219) 14pp., parts. For flute, oboe (or violin), and basso continuo. Largo; Allegro; Affettuoso; Vivace. Clean realization. M-D.
Numerous other trios are available from Br, Heinrichshofen, Schott, and IMC.

Siegfried Thiele. *Proportionen* 1971 (DVFM) 27pp., parts. For oboe, cello, and piano. Explanations in German.

Alfred Uhl. *Kleines Konzert* (Dob 7744 1938) 32pp., parts. For clarinet, viola, and piano. Allegro con brio: chromatic, staccato style, chordal, octaves. Grave, molto tranquillo: ostinato-like figures, arpeggiated accompaniment, inner voices important. Vivo: scherzo-like, octotonic, sequences, secco style, chordal buildup, drops back, sudden *ff* closing. Neoclassic. M-D.

Hermann Josef Ullrich. *Trio-Fantasy* Op.20 1946 (Dob) 21pp., parts. For horn, violin, and piano. One movement. Freely tonal with heavy doses of accidentals, frequent tempo changes, expressionistic. Some Impressionistic influence noted in parallel chords and added sixths. Arpeggi figuration, tonal conclusion. Piano part relies heavily on chords; large span required. M-D.

Jan K. Vanhall. *Trio* Op.20/5 E♭ (Weston, Bergmann—Schott). For clarinet, piano, and violin. Graceful and melodious writing. M-D.

———— *Trio* E♭ (Musica Rara). For clarinet, cello, and piano. Haydn and Mozart influence here. M-D.

Carl Maria von Weber. *Trio* Op.63 1813–9 (Musica Rara; CFP 1473; IMC). For flute, cello, and piano. Formal perfection and admirable contrapuntal treatment abound in this work, but the outer movements are over-worked with too much lively figuration. The scherzo has two sections; the concise Andante espressivo has the subtitle "Shepherds Lament," an apt description. M-D to D.

Adolph Weiss. *Trio* 1955 (CFE). For flute, violin, and piano.

Stefan Wolpe. *Trio* 1963 (McGinnis & Marx) 63pp., parts. For flute, cello, and piano. Dense textures with much activity, but the work gives the feeling of great clarity! Similar to a high-speed virtuoso conversation. Exhilarating but complex writing. D.

Hugh Wood. *Trio* Op.3 (UE 12945 1961) 21pp., parts. 12 min. For flute, viola, and piano. Vivace; Tema and (8) Variations. The final variation is a cadenza. Serial, individual style, pointillistic, M-D.

Charles Wuorinen. *Trio* I 1961 (ACA) 4 min. For flute, cello, and piano.

———— *Second Trio: Piece for Stefan Wolpe* 1962 (CFP) 9 min. For flute, cello, and piano.

———— *Third Trio* (CFP) 16½ min. For flute, cello, and piano.

———— *Trio Concertante* (ACA) 12 min. For violin, oboe, and piano.

István Zelenka. *Trio* (Edition Modern, Musikverlag Hans Wewerka). For horn, violin, and piano.

Trios for Piano and Two Flutes (Including Trio Sonatas)

Evaristo Abaco. *Trio Sonata* Op.3/2 F (CFP).

Carl Philipp Emanuel Bach. *12 Little Pieces* W.81 (K. Walther—Zimmermann; Mitteldeutscher) 5pp., parts. Menuet; Polonaise; Allegro; Andantino, etc. Short, attractive. Int.
———— *12 Kleine Stücke* W.82 (Johnen—CFP).
———— *Trio* Eb (Zimmermann).

Johann Sebastian Bach. *Sonatas* for two flutes and continuo arranged from *Sonatas* for viola da gamba and harpsichord, S.1028, S.1029 (J. Bopp, E. Müller—Reinhardt 1973) 40pp., parts. Preface in German and French.
———— *Trio* G (Müller).
———— *Trio Sonata* S.1039 (H.-Peter Schmitz—Br 4403 25pp., parts; M. Seiffert—Br&H 23pp., parts; CFP). Adagio; Allegro ma non presto; Adagio e piano. The Seiffert edition is over-edited; the Schmitz edition is based on the *Neue Bach-Ausgabe* and has a preface in French, German, and English. This work also exists in a version by Bach himself for viola da gamba, keyboard, and basso continuo (S.1027). There is a common denominator between the four movements: the eighth notes of the Adagio become the quarter notes of the Allegro ma non presto, and the eighth notes of the Adagio e piano become the half notes of the Presto. D.

Wilhelm Friedemann Bach. *Trio* I D (M. Seiffert—Br&H 5651 10pp., parts; IMC). Andante; Allegro; Vivace.
———— *Trio* II D (M. Seiffert—Br&H 5652 10pp., parts; IMC). Allegro ma non tanto; Larghetto; Vivace.
———— *Trio* III Bb (M. Seiffert—Br&H 5653) 10pp., parts. Largo; Allegro ma non troppo; Vivace.
———— *Trio* IV a (M. Seiffert—Br&H 5654) 7pp., parts. Allegro; (Larghetto) unfinished.

Michel de la Barre. *Sonate* V G (R. Viollier—Pegasus PE 1069 1964) 12pp., parts. Preface in French and German. Prelude; Gigue; Gavotte; Fugue. Beautiful realization, many opportunities for ornamentation. M-D.

Joseph Bodin de Boismortier. *Trio Sonata* F (Ruf—Schott).
_____ *Trio Sonata* G (Ruf—Schott).

William Corbett. *Sonata* C 1705 (H. Ruf—HM 216 1973) 10pp., parts. In Vol.I of the two-volume collection *Trio Sonatas by Old English Masters.* Largo; Fuga; Adagio; Jigga. Fine clean realizations. M-D.

Archangelo Corelli. *Sonate da Camera* Op.2 (D. Degen—CFP 4567 1943) 12pp., parts. 1 F: Adagio; Allemanda; Corrente; Gavotta. 5 B♭: Adagio; Allemanda; Sarabanda; Tempo di Gavotta. 7 F: Adagio; Allemande; Corrente; Giga. All three sonatas have short movements. Fine edition. M-D.
_____ *Sonata* II (Moeck—Schott).

Veit Erdmann. *Mobile I, II, III* (Möseler 1973) 16pp., 3 copies necessary for performance. Avant-garde.

Willem de Fesch. *3 Sonaten* Op.7 (J. R. Le Cosquino de Bussy—B&VP 1947) 23pp., parts. 2 D: Largo; Allemanda. 4 g: Largo; Presto. 8 e: Andante; Tempo di Gavotte.
_____ *Sonaten* Op.12 (W. Noske, H. Schouwman—Br 802 1957) 28pp., parts. 1 D: Largo; Allemanda; Menuetto 1 and 2. 2 g: Alle breve; Giga. 3 G: Largo; Allemanda; Menuetto. Strong melodic lines, a kind of instrumental bel canto. M-D.
_____ *X Sonata a Tre* (B&VP) 4 vols. For 2 flutes or 2 violins and keyboard. Sonata II D: Largo; Allemanda; Giga. 8pp., parts. Sonata IV g: Largo; Presto. 9pp., parts. Sonata VIII e: Andante; Allemanda; Tempo di Gavotte. 6pp., parts. All are M-D.

Harald Genzmer. *Sonate* 1954 (Schott 4091) 12pp., parts. For 2 altoblockflutes and piano. Allegro molto; Andante; Vivace. All three movements are freely centered around C, with the Andante more chromatically colored. Superb neoclassic writing, appealing. M-D.

Carl Heinrich Graun. *Triosonate* D (L. Stadelmann—Leuckart 1973) 12pp., parts. Leuckartiana No.41. Probably intended for Graun's master, Frederick the Great. A somewhat run-of-the-mill work but worth looking at. Int. to M-D.
_____ *Sonata* E♭ (H. Kölbel—HM 211) 21pp., parts. Continuo realized by Ernst Meyerolbersleben. Preface in German and English. Adagio; Allegro

non molto; Allegro. "The musical grandeur of the sonata is technically easy to achieve, thanks to the motto of the composer: 'One must not, without special cause, make unnecessary difficulties'" (from the preface). M-D.

_____ *Triosonate* F (Moeck).

George Frederick Handel. *Trio Sonata* e (Nagel—Schott).
_____ *Chamber Trio* XIII g (M. Seiffert—Br&H).
_____ *Chamber Trio* IXX (M. Seiffert—Br&H).
_____ *Trio Sonata* g (J. A. Parkinson—OUP 1969) 15pp., parts; cello ad lib. 11 min. This work is attributed to Handel. Editorial additions are identified. Adagio; Allegro; Siciliano; Allegro. Suitable for violins or oboes or treble recorders. Excellent keyboard realization. M-D.
_____ *Triosonaten* Op.5 (Schneider—Barnhouse).
All these pieces remain an unalloyed delight.

Johann Adolph Hasse. *Trio Sonata* Op.3/6 D (E. Schenk—Dob DM 435 1973) 12pp., parts. Preface in German and English. Allegro moderato; Andante amoroso; Fuga. "Our work has all the musical charm of the Rococo; in it, Hasse proves himself to be a mediator between Pergolesi (in the three-movement formal scheme with fugal finale) and the Classic era, the tonal language of which is present in elements of unmistakably Mozartian nature" (from the Preface). M-D.
_____ *Trio Sonata* e (Ruf—Schott).

Johann Krebs. *Triosonate* b (Erbrecht—K&S).
_____ *Triosonate* b (Ruf—Schott).
_____ *Trio* D (H. Riemann—Br&H No.1865a/b) 17pp., parts. Ouverture à la française; Rejouissance; Menuet; Bourrée; Gigue. Over-edited. M-D.
_____ *Trio* e 1743 (F. Nagel—Müller). Four movements. Second flute part can be played on oboe or violin. M-D.

Jean Marie Leclair. *Sonate à trois* (Harmonia Uitgave). The keyboard part is impressively integrated into the ensemble. M-D.

Pietro Locatelli. *Trio* Op.3/1 G (Riemann—Br&H; IMC).
_____ *Trio Sonata* Op.5/1 G (H. Albrecht—K&S; H. Kolbel—Heinrichshofen 1261 16pp., parts; C. Crussard—Foetisch 7784 19pp., parts). Andante; Largo; Andante; Allegro; Vivace. The Kolbel realization is more stylistically acceptable. M-D.
_____ *Trio Sonata* Op.5/3 E (Ruf—Schott).
_____ *Trio Sonata* Op.5/4 C (H. Albrecht—K&S 1951) 9pp., parts. No.46

in Organum Series. Foreword in German includes tempo suggestions. Largo; Andante; Allegro. Clean edition. M-D.

———— *Trio Sonata* Op.5/5 d (H. Albrecht—K&S 1952) 11pp., parts. No.50 in Organum Series. Foreword in German includes tempo suggestions. Largo; Vivace; Pastorale. Clean edition. M-D.

Jean Baptiste Loeillet (of Lyons). *Trio Sonata* OP.1/2 (Ruf—Schott).

———— *Trio Sonata* Op.1/4 D (Ruf—Schott).

———— *Trio Sonata* Op.1/6 (Ruf—Schott).

———— *Trio Sonata* Op.2/12 (Ruf—Schott).

———— *Trio Sonata* e (A. Beon—IMC 1511) 15pp., parts. Largo; Allegro; Largo; Allegro. M-D.

———— *Sonata* g (A. Beon—IMC 1265) 12pp., parts. Adagio molto sostenuto; Allegro con brio; Largo; Allegro. Realization is somewhat heavy. M-D.

———— *Sonata* g (A. Beon—IMC).

Daniel Purcell. *Sonata* F ca.1710 (H. Ruf—HM 217 1973). In Vol.II of the two-volume collection *Trio Sonatas by Old English Masters.* 9pp., parts. Largo; Allegro; Vivace. Fine and clean realization. M-D.

———— *Trio-Sonate* d (Ruf—Schott).

Johann J. Quantz. *Sonata* D (O. Fischer, O. Wittenbecher—Forberg 1921) 9pp., parts. Andante; Allegro; Affetuoso; Vivace. Over-edited. M-D.

———— *Sonata* G (Fischer, Wittenbecher—Forberg).

———— *Trio* a (Koch—Mösler).

———— *Trio Sonata* D (Ruf—Ric).

———— *Trio Sonata* a (Erbrecht—K&S).

———— *Trio Sonata* G (Ruf—Br).

———— *Trio Sonata* C (W. Birke—HM 60 1959) 16pp., parts. Affettuoso; Alla breve; Larghetto; Vivace. All editorial additions identified. Clean realization. M-D.

———— *Trio Sonata* c (C. Blumenthal—Zimmermann 11495) 15pp., parts. Andante moderato; Allegro; Larghetto; Vivace. Over-edited. M-D.

Giovanni Battista Sammartini. *Six Sonatas* Op.6 (Rampal—IMC) 2 vols. Bright, engaging, beautifully inventive writing. M-D.

———— *12 Sonatas* (Giesbert—Schott) 3 vols.

Georg Philipp Telemann. *Sonata* A (H. Schreiter—Br&H No.1970) 12pp., parts. Cantabile; Alla breve; Lento; Allegro. M-D.

———— *Sonata* F (Fussan—Schott).

_____ *Sonata* g (Monkemeyer—Schott).

_____ *Sonata* (Schreiter—IMC).

Robert Valentine. *Sonata* c 1721 (H. Ruf—HM 217 1973). In Vol.II of the two-volume collection *Trio Sonatas by Old English Masters*. 7pp., parts. Adagio; Allegro; Adagio; Giga. Fine, clean realization. M-D.

Samuel Wesley. *Trio* F (H. Cobbe—OUP 1973) 33pp., parts. This work dates from 1826. Two long movements; the first in SA design is preceded by an Andante somewhat in the style of J. S. Bach. The second movement is a set of graceful variations in the style of Mozart. M-D.

William Williams. *Sonata* a 1703 (H. Ruf—HM 216 1973). In Vol.I of the two-volume collection *Trio Sonatas by Old English Masters*. 10pp., parts. Adagio; Vivace; Allegro. Fine, clean realization. M-D.

Trios for Piano and Two Miscellaneous Woodwinds

John Addison. *Trio* (Augener 18167R 1952) 30pp., parts, 13 min. For flute, oboe, and piano. Allegro; Lento con moto; Scherzo. Light film style, added-note technique frequently used, mildly contemporary, octotonic, linear, witty. M-D.

Jurriaan Andriessen. *Trio* I 1955 (Donemus) 39pp., parts. For flute, oboe, and piano. Allegro giusto; Andante; Allegro giocoso. Freely tonal with chromaticism, scales in ninths, octotonic, generally thin textures, neoclassic. Large span required. D.

Jorge Antunes. *1.6 − 1.6 × 10 Coulombs* 1967 (SDM). For flute, bassoon, and piano with amplifier.

Carl Philipp Emanuel Bach. *Six Sonatas* W.92 (G. Piccioli—IMC 1955) 16pp., parts. For clarinet, bassoon, and piano. Six short one-movement pieces. Allegretto; Allegro di molto; Allegro; Allegro; Andante; Allegro. In Johann Christian Bach style! Acceptable realizations. M-D.
———— *Six Pieces* (E. Simon—ST 1972) 20pp., parts. For clarinet, bassoon, and piano.
———— *Trio* I D (IMC). For flute, clarinet, and piano.
———— *Trio* II a (IMC). For flute, clarinet, and piano.
———— *Trio* III G (IMC). For flute, clarinet, and piano.
———— *Trio Sonata* W.148 a (K. Walther—Zimmermann) 14pp., parts. For flute, violin (oboe) and continuo.

Johann Sebastian Bach. *Trio Sonata* S.1079 c (from *The Musical Offering*). For two flutes and basso continuo. In Vol.II of *Four Trio Sonatas* (Landschoff—CFP 4203B).

Jacques Bank. *Die Ouwe* (Donemus 1975) 13pp. 3 copies required for performance. For bass recorder, bass clarinet, and piano. Photostat of composer's MS. Note in Dutch.

Ludwig van Beethoven. *Trio* G Kinsky37 ca.1786–90 (P. Badura-Skoda—Br&H 6604 1970) 27pp., parts. For piano, flute, and bassoon. Allegro; Adagio; Thema andante variazioni. Early and delightful writing. Piano has more than its share of the action. M-D.

──────*Trio* Op.38 (Musica Rara; IMC) 40pp., parts. For clarinet, bassoon or cello, and piano. Arranged by Beethoven from his *Septet* Op.20. Adagio–Allegro con brio; Adagio cantabile; Tempo di menuetto; Tema con (5) Variazionen; Scherzo; Andante con moto–Alla marzia–Presto. M-D.

Andras Borgulya. *Trio for Flute, Bassoon and Piano* (Gen 1973) 14pp., parts. Moderato: serial influence, thin textures, broken *ppp* secco octaves. Allegretto giocoso: piano mainly punctuates with chords and broken chordal figuration. Lento: sustained, changing meters, percussive grace notes. Allegro, ma non troppo: octotonic chromatic chords treated in ostinato-like fashion; Meno mosso section uses pesante chords and short figures; coda returns to opening idea of the movement. Neoclassic style. M-D.

Geoffrey Bush. *Trio* (Nov 1955) 11 min. For oboe, bassoon, and piano. Many thirds, many octaves, little development; much repetition but contains some interesting harmonic usage. M-D.

David Diamond. *Partita* 1935 rev. 1956 (PIC 1961) 16pp., parts, 8 min. For oboe, bassoon, and piano. Neoclassic orientation, mildly contemporary, most effective part is for the piano. Allegro vivo; Adagio espressivo; Allegro molto (3 + 2/4). M-D.

Gaetano Donizetti. *Trio* (Musica Rara). For clarinet, bassoon, and piano.

Pierre Max Dubois. *Les Tréteaux* (Choudens 1966) 29pp., parts. For flute, sax, and piano. Prologue en Fanfare: piano punctuates with chords; runs and passages for alternating hands. Romantica: nocturne-like style; broken triadic chords in left hand spread over interval of a tenth. Valse Vulgaire: piano provides rhythmic push and some melodic answering; somewhat like style of Jean Françaix. All glitter and fun. M-D.

Maurice Emmanuel. *Sonata* 1907 (Lemoine 1929) 23pp., parts. For flute, clarinet, and piano. Allegro con spirito; Adagio; Molto allegro e leggierissimo. A rousing and, at times, romping, fun-filled work in a pre-Poulenc style. Requires a large span and facile pianism. M-D to D.

Peter Racine Fricker. *Trio* (Serenade II) Op.35 1959 (Schott 10739) 26pp., parts. For flute, oboe, and piano. Andante moderato; Scherzo—Allegro; Slow—Poco Allegro. Free and occasional use of serialism. This work shows that involved processes are part of Fricker's musical thinking, which has strong emotional qualities. Textures generally clear. Piano writing, even though serialistic, fits the hand appropriately. M-D.

Baldassare Galuppi. *Triosonate* G (Ruf—Br). For flute, oboe, and basso continuo. Lyrical and tuneful writing, skillful but traditional harmony with occasional chromatic inflexion. A few ideas are thoroughly treated. M-D.

Mikhail Glinka. *Trio Pathétique* d 1832 (Musica Rara 1957; EMT; IMC; 29pp., parts). For clarinet, bassoon or cello, and piano. Allegro moderato; Scherzo—Vivacissimo; Largo; Allegro con spirito. An attractive period piece from Glinka's early years in Italy. Full piano treatment in Romantic style with a preference displayed for external refinement and outward polish. M-D.

Hans-Georg Görner. *Concertino* Op.31 (Hofmeister 7246) 20pp., parts for all instruments. For two saxophones (alto and tenor) and piano, or for violin, viola and piano. Allegro moderato; Moderato, all' antico; Rezitativo cantando. Freely tonal, traditional forms, Hindemith style, careful balancing of all parts. M-D.

Elizabeth Gyring. *Trio* 1951 (CFE) 40pp., parts. For oboe, clarinet, and piano. Allegro con fuoco–Molto vivace: driving rhythms, intense, Poco Andante second tonal area, chromatic. Larghetto: chordal, syncopated accompaniment in left hand, serious and somber. Scherzo: lively but expressive; highly chromatic; canon appears in Trio; extensive coda. Finale—Rondo: vigorous, complex figures, strong, colorful, unique style. D.
———— *Trio* (CFE). For clarinet, bassoon, and piano.

George Frederick Handel. *Trio Sonata* g (J. A. Parkinson—OUP 1969) 15pp., parts; cello ad lib. 11 min. Attributed to Handel. Editorial additions identified. Adagio; Allegro; Siciliano; Allegro. Suitable for violins or oboes or treble recorders. Excellent keyboard realization. M-D.

Franz Joseph Haydn. *Trio* No.29 F (CF). For flute, bassoon, and piano.
———— *Trio* No.31 G (CF). For flute, bassoon, and piano.
See detailed entries under trios for piano, one stringed instrument, and one wind instrument.

Johann D. Heinichen. *Trio Sonata* F (Nov). For flute, oboe, and continuo. Four movements. Int. to M-D.

———— *Trio Sonata* F (Janetzky—Müller).

———— *Sonata* G (Hausswald—Br&H).

Gustav Holst. *A Fugal Concerto* Op.40/2 (Nov 1923) 17pp., parts. For flute, oboe, and piano, or for two violins and piano. Moderato: octotonic, secco style, in D. Adagio: cantabile line in all three instruments, wistful melody. Allegro: staccato; shifting accents; old English dance tune "If All the World Were Paper" appears near conclusion; jiglike; good left-hand octave technique required; short cadenza passages for woodwinds. M-D.

Arthur Honegger. *Concerto da Camera* 1948 (Sal) 22pp., parts, $16\frac{1}{2}$ min. For flute, English horn, and piano. Originally for flute, English horn, and string orchestra. Piano reduction by composer. Allegretto amabile; Andante; Vivace. Conceived in the classical sense, virtuosity of all three instruments is intertwined in a refined polyphony. All movements are related to the eighteenth century in their natural rhythms and flowing pulses. Repeated chords, driving rhythms in outer movements, parallelisms. Large span required. M-D.

Arthur Jannery. *Three Fantasies* 1974. See detailed entry under trios for piano, one stringed instrument, and one wind instrument.

Hunter Johnson. *Trio* 1954 (J. Kirkpatrick—Galaxy 1972) 28pp., parts, 23 min. For flute, oboe, and piano. Allegro con fuoco: main idea is the syncopated figure announced in octotonic fashion by the piano; freely tonal and centers around d; shifting meters; textures thicken at the coda. Adagio serioso: flexible meters; independent lines evolve; entire closing section is chordal and sustained for the piano; utilizes most of keyboard; requires large span. Allegro molto: chromatic lines begin in low register and work up the keyboard; imitation; reworks ideas from the other movements into one gigantic maelstrom. First-rate writing throughout. Deserves more hearings. D.

Piet Ketting. *Sonata* 1936 (Donemus) 41pp., parts, 26 min. For flute, oboe, and piano. Praembulum: dramatic skipping chords open movement; freely tonal; thin textures; short–long motif is frequent. Ciaconna: piano opens with eight-bar subject; other instruments provide counterpoint; varied treatment evolves into complex figuration before thinning out near closing. Fuga: short–long idea is integral to subject; flute and oboe open with piano announcing subject in octaves; asymmetrical phrasing; *pp* closing. Neoclassic orientation. M-D.

Johann Krebs. *Trio* e 1743 (F. Nagel—Müller). Four movements. For 2 flutes and piano; second flute part can be played on oboe or violin. M-D.

Jean-Baptiste Loeillet (of London). *Sonata* c (EV; A. Beon—IMC) 11pp., parts. For flute, oboe, and piano. Grave; Poco largo; Adagio–Andante; Allegro. Highly edited. M-D.

—————— *Sonata* d (EV; IMC). For flute, oboe, and piano.

—————— *Trio Sonata* Op.1/1 F 1722 (Ruf, Bergmann—Schott; Moeck 1076 11pp., parts). For flute, oboe, and piano. Grave; Allegro; Adagio; Gavotte; Aria; Allegro. M-D.

—————— *Trio Sonata* Op.2/2 F (Ermeler, Kluge—Heinrichshofen).

—————— *Trio Sonata* Op.2/4 d (Ruf—HM 181; A. Mann—Music Press MPI 513) 12pp., parts. Largo; Allegro; Adagio; Allegro.

—————— *Trio Sonata* Op.2/6 c (Ruf—Br).

Elisabeth Lutyens. *Fantasie Trio* Op.55 1963 (Olivan Press) 19pp., parts, $10\frac{1}{2}$ min. For flute, clarinet, and piano. Three untitled contrasting movements. Serial, pointillistic, shifting meters, expressionistic. Photostat of composer's MS, not easy to read. D.

—————— *Music for Three* Op.65 (Olivan Press 1966). For flute (alto flute), piccolo, oboe, and piano.

William Mathias. *Divertimento* Op.24 (OUP 07.022 1966) 23pp., parts. 10 min. For flute, oboe, and piano. Allegretto: contrary-motion arpeggi, short buoyant motifs, fast repeated chords. Andante comodo: longer lines, chordal texture mixed with sixteenth-note staccato figuration with pedal, written-out trills. Allegro ritmico: fugal; varied textures; bimodal passage concludes work on D. A light-hearted work, crafted with great skill and imagination. M-D.

Felix Mendelssohn. *Konzertstück* I Op.113 f 1832 (Br&H 9pp., parts; McGinnis & Marx; Sikorski; IMC). For clarinet and basset horn or two clarinets and piano.

—————— *Konzertstück* II Op.114 d (Br&H 11pp., parts; McGinnis & Marx; Sikorski; IMC). For clarinet and basset horn or two clarinets and piano. Each work has three movements played without a break. The Br&H edition gives no alternative part for a second clarinet in lieu of the basset horn; has good page turns and cues. M-D.

Rudolf Moser. *Suite* Op.99 A (Gertrud Moser 1970, through O. Harrassowitz) 26pp., parts. For violin, viola, and piano or for flute, clarinet in A, and harpsichord.

Thea Musgrave. *Trio* (JWC 1960) 19pp., parts, 10 min. For flute, oboe, and piano. One movement. Short motif appears in various guises; serialism used to investigate textural problems and sonorities. Displays intelligence, resolution, and clarity of purpose. D.

Elizabeth Posten. *Trio* (JWC 1960) 29pp., parts, 12½ min. For flute, clarinet (or viola), and harp (or piano). Piacevole; Pastorale nostalgica—Molto moderato; Fileuse—Dolce delicato; Vivace scherzando. Tonal; clear, concise writing. More effective, separate parts written for piano at a few spots. Colorful, programmatically conceived. D.

Francis Poulenc. *Trio* (JWC 1926) 34pp., parts. For oboe, bassoon, and piano. Lent–Presto; Andante; Rondo–Tres vif. A thoroughly effective work; dry humor marvelously exploited in the two wind instruments. Limpid style, except for final part of the last movement, which is a merry gigue. M-D.

Johann Joachim Quantz. *Trio Sonata* C (Bergmann—Schott). For flute, oboe, and basso continuo.
_____ *Trio Sonata* c (C. Blumenthal—Zimmermann ZM95) 15pp., parts. For flute, oboe, and piano. Andante moderato; Allegro; Larghetto; Vivace. M-D.
_____ *Trio Sonata* D (Ruf—Ric). For flute, oboe, and basso continuo.
_____ *Trio Sonata* G (Ruf—Heinrichshofen). For flute, oboe d'amore, and continuo. The oboe d'amore part is alternately for violin. (Schott 11254). For oboe, cello (bassoon), and piano. An attractive Italian-style trio with lively outer movements and a gracious middle Largo movement. Int. to M-D.

Alan Rawsthorne. *Sonatina* 1936 (OUP 1968) 30pp., parts, 11 min. For flute, oboe, and piano. Allegretto: no time signature, flexible number of counts in each bar; dotted barlines, with regular barlines at structural points; freely tonal; varied textures; large span required. Lento ma non troppo: thin chromatic lines; *ppp* triplet figure adds unusual sonority. Presto: like a two-part invention in texture; shifting accents; octotonic; con brio quasi cadenza for piano near conclusion; strong rhythmic ending. Neoclassic. M-D.

Franz Reizenstein. *Trio* Op.25 A 1945 (Lengnick 1953) 61pp., parts, 21 min. For flute, oboe, and piano. Allegro tranquillo; Andante; Scherzando— Fughetta; Allegro vivo. Hindemith influence is strong. Various tonal centers are present, giving a kind of Romantic polytonal effect. Tune of "Daisy Bell" is used in the last movement. Superb pianistic writing. D.

Norbert Rosseau. *Rapsodie* Op.81 1958 (CeBeDeM) 23pp., parts. 12 min. Lento; Presto; Lento; Presto; Lento. Strong broken-octave gestures and quiet sonorities represent the Lento, while the Presto parts utilize shifting rhythms in octotonic style. Flowing triplet figuration. Neoclassic style. M-D.

Howard Rovics. *Cybernetic Study II* 1968 (Okra) 9pp., parts. For clarinet, bassoon, and piano. Serial, changing meters, pointillistic, expressionistic dramatic gestures, harmonics, abstract. Large span required. D.

Florent Schmitt. *Sonatine en Trio* Op.85 1934–5 (Durand) 13pp., parts. For flute, clarinet, and piano. Assez animé; Assez vif; Très lent; Animé. Post-Romantic rhetoric with a few Impressionist mannerisms; technically coherent if diffuse. Strong chromatic usage in the second movement presents a few complex pianistic problems. M-D.

William Sydeman. *Trio* 1968 (Seesaw). For bass clarinet, bassoon, and piano.

Georg Philipp Telemann. *Sonata* a (IMC). For flute, oboe, and piano; cello part ad lib.
———— *Sonata* c (IMC). For flute, oboe, and piano; cello part ad lib.
———— *Sonata* c (K. Hofmann—HM 195) 12pp., parts. For flute, oboe, and basso continuo. Adagio; Allegro; Adagio; Allegro. Preface in English and German. M-D.
———— *Sonata* d (Ruf—Br 3332) 14pp., parts. For flute, oboe, and basso continuo. Trio XI from the *Essercizii Musici*. Largo; Allegro; Affettuoso; Presto. Excellent basso continuo realization. M-D.
———— *Sonata* e (K. Hofmann—HM 219) 14pp., parts. For flute, oboe (or violin), and basso continuo. Largo; Allegro; Affettuoso; Vivace. Clean realization. M-D.
———— *Trio Sonata* e (M. Ruetz—HM 25) 16pp., parts. For flute, oboe, and keyboard; cello ad lib. Affettuoso; Allegro; Grave; Allegro. Intelligent realization. M-D.
———— *Trio Sonata* XII E♭. See detailed entry under trios for piano, one stringed instrument, and one wind instrument.

Heitor Villa-Lobos. *Fantaisie Concertante* 1953 (ESC) 34pp., parts. 15 min. For piano, clarinet in C, and bassoon. Allegro non troppo; Lento; Allegro impetuoso. Colorful chordal sonorities chromatically enriched; entire keyboard utilized; seventh chords in triplets; inner lines to be brought out; syncopation; 3 with 2; contrary scales. Large span and stamina required! D.

Antonio Vivaldi. *Trio* a F.XV/1 (N. Deluis—Musica Rara 1967) 16pp., parts. For treble recorder (flute), bassoon (cello), and basso continuo; cello ad lib. Largo; Allegro; Largo cantabile; Allegro molto. The realization is a little plain and regular. M-D.

———— *Trio Sonata* g (Musica Rara). For 2 oboes and continuo.

Henri Zagwijn. *Trio* 1952 (Donemus). For oboe, clarinet, and piano.

Trios for Piano and Two Brass Instruments

Hubert Arnold. *Sonata* (ST). For 2 trumpets and piano.

Richard Benger. *Miniature Suite* (JWC 1972) 22pp., parts. For two B♭ trumpets and piano. Moderato: much ostinato in piano. Andante: complementing melodies in trumpets. Presto: staccato technique used in all parts. Maestoso: piano part is chordal, under syncopated trumpets. Allegro: broad dramatic sweeps in piano while trumpets are more rhythmically treated. Thin textures, neoclassic influence, mildly contemporary. M-D.

Boris Blacher. *Divertimento* Op.31 (Bo&Bo 1958) 18pp., parts. For trumpet, trombone, and piano. Allegro: chordal, span of ninth required. Andantino: rocking 6/8 quality. Presto: triplets, chromatic chords. Moderato: melody interspersed with chords. Allegretto: for trumpet and trombone alone. No. 6 (no title); for piano alone; melody punctuated with chords in left hand; quiet. Presto: 5/8, flowing, *ppp* ending. M-D.

Helge Jung. *Concertante Suite* Op.9 (Hofmeister 1972) 20pp., parts. For two trumpets and piano. Five movements of challenging writing for all three players. A complete trumpet score is provided both trumpet performers. M-D.

Rudolf Mayer. *Sonata* (ST). For two French horns and piano.

Vaclav Nelhybel. *Suite* (Gen 1966) 12pp., parts. For two trumpets and piano. Vivo; Molto espressivo; Marcato con bravura; Slow; Allegro marcato. Effective mildly contemporary neoclassic writing. M-D.

Johann Pezel. *Sonatinas* (Bicinia) (R. P. Block—Musica Rara 1972) Nos.63, 64, 67, 69, 70, 72, 73. For two cornetti and continuo. Score and parts for each sonatina.

——— *Sonatinas* 1675 (Bicinia) (R. P. Block—Musica Rara 1969) Nos.71, 74. For two clarini (trumpets) and basso continuo. 6pp., parts. Playable on C trumpet. Short pieces in binary form. Attractive, excellent foreword. Int.

Primoz Ramovs. *Con Sordino* (Društva Slovenskih Skladateljev 1974). 3 copies necessary for performance. For trumpet, trombone, and piano. Explanations in Croatian and English.

David Uber. *Sonata* (PIC). For trumpet, trombone, and piano.

Alec Wilder. *Suite* (Sam Fox 1971) 31pp., parts. 14 min. For French horn, tuba, and piano. Maestoso; Pesante; In a Jazz manner; Berceuse; Alla caccia. Distinctive jazz idioms and chamber music are blended with a restrained nonchalance. Strong melodies, excellent balance between all instruments, a valid combination. The style is close to neoclassic and results in some mildly contemporary and unusual sonorities. M-D.

Trios for Piano, One Brass Instrument, and One Woodwind

Jacobo Ficher. *Sonatina* Op.21 1932 (NME) 19pp., parts. For piano, alto sax, and trumpet. Allegro, quasi alla breve: SA, linear style punctuated with chromatic chords, moves directly to Lento: chromatic harmonic thirds in right hand move over broken triplet augmented octaves in left hand; moves immediately to Presto: more linear than opening movement but chromatic chords are still present; rhythmic drive. M-D.

Godfrey Finger. *Sonata* C (R. L. Minter—Musica Rara 1974) 10pp., parts. For trumpet, oboe, and keyboard. Preface in English. M-D.

Walter Hartley. *Double Concerto* 1969 (J. Boonin) 16pp., parts. 7 min. For alto sax, tuba, and piano. Originally for alto sax, tuba, and wind octet. Piano reduction by the composer. Allegro con brio: piano has counterpoint to other parts and provides rhythmic punctuation. Andante: unfolding linear lines. Presto: integrally and equally related to the other parts with fine balance between all three instruments. Interesting sonorities. M-D.

Heinrich von Herzogenberg. *Trio* Op.61 D (H. Truscott—Musica Rara 1972) 38pp., parts. For oboe, French horn, and piano. Allegretto; Presto; Andante con moto; Allegro. Written in a general Brahmsian style but independent thought is present at all times. Expert handling of the three instruments, especially in the thoughtful Allegretto and the final rondo. Worthwhile music that deserves reviving. Valuable preface by the editor. M-D.

Noël Lee. *Commentaries on a Theme from Aaron Copland* 1966 (MS available from composer: 4 Villa Laugier, 75017 Paris, France) 19pp., parts. For trumpet, clarinet, and piano. Slow and Tranquil; With Motion; Very Slow and Majestic; Moderate and Rhythmic; Slow and Tranquil. "This work, based on the opening measures of the third movement of the *Quartet* for piano and strings by Copland, is designed for moderately-advanced performers. If the pianist's hands are small, the notes in brackets may be omitted; certain octaves may be split between the two hands'' (from the score). Written in a neoclassic style that is chromatic and generally thin-textured. Clear formal structures. Effective balancing of the instruments. M-D.

Johann Pezel. *Biccinia 75* (R. P. Block—Musica Rara 1972) 18pp., parts. For clarino (trumpet in C), bassoon, and keyboard.

Carl Reinecke. *Trio* Op.188 a (Br&H; IMC) 33pp., parts. For oboe, French horn, and piano. Allegro moderato; Scherzo—Molto Vivace; Adagio; Finale—Allegro ma non troppo. M-D.
———— *Trio* Op.274 B♭ (Br&H; Musica Rara; WIM) 16pp., parts. 7 min. For clarinet, French horn, and piano. A one-movement Allegro. M-D.

Elliott Schwartz. *Divertimento* 1963 (Gen) 15pp., parts. 10 min. For clarinet, French horn, and piano. Humoreske; Dirge; Dance (piano tacet); (4) Variations. Neoclassic, mildly contemporary. Instruments are well integrated. M-D.

Trios for Piano(s), Percussion, and Another Instrument

Zbigniew Bargielski. *Servet* (AA 1975) 14pp., parts. 7 min. For violin, viola, or cello; or for violin and viola; or for viola and cello; or for all 3 stringed instruments, percussion, and piano. The pianist performs some of the percussion parts. Avant-garde.

Henry Brant. *5 and 10¢ Store Music* 1932 (ACA) 5 min. For violin, piano, and kitchen hardware. As early as 1921 Brant was playing homemade instruments in a backyard orchestra for which he composed his first experimental music. *5 and 10¢ Store Music* is an extension of this experiment. M-D.

———— *Ice Age* (NME 1954) 18pp., parts. For piano, clarinet, and glockenspiel. Sparkling. Aleatoric (called "independent" by Brant) and "coordinated" writing. Piano plays in upper or lower registers through much of the piece. Key signatures are present. "Glistening" sounds reinforce the title. M-D.

Henry Cowell. *Set of Five* (CFP 1968) 43pp., parts. 18 min. For piano, violin, and percussion. One skilled player can handle all the percussion instruments. Largo sostenuto: requires five muted gongs of various sizes; has a definite oriental flavor (open fifths); octotonic; chromatic lines. Allegro: xylophone in staccato passages with piano produces parallel moving thirds. Andante: lyrical; requires five small-to-medium tom tom drums. Presto leggiero: perpetual motion; a modern "Flight of the Bumble Bee"; six glass, metal, or porcelain bowls of different pitches may be used. Vigoroso: arpeggiated tone clusters using forearm; glissando harmonics on the strings; uses the same set of drums as in third movement. Skill and virtuosity, both intellectual and technical, are called for from all three performers. M-D to D.

Harold Farberman. *Trio* (Gen 1966) 20pp., parts. For piano, violin, and percussion. Two percussion players are preferred but one can play the part with the proper set-up. Requires large percussion complement; directions for percussion set-up included. Five movements. Serial construction, pointillistic, clusters, plucked and stopped strings, fingers must be rubbed over strings. Piano cadenza follows the third movement. Fourth movement requires everyone to play *pp;* parts may be played in whatever rhythm the players wish, but notes must follow the order given. Each player selects his own tempo. Avant-garde. D.

Ross Lee Finney. *Two Acts for Three Players* (CFP 1975) 46pp., parts. 15½ min. For piano, clarinet, and percussion. Act I, Scene 1: Sweet and Low, Scene 2: The Plot Thickens; Intermezzo; Act II, Scene 1: Romance, Scene 2: The Chase. Clever treatment of all instruments. The pianist, by careful pedaling, contrasts rich sonorities with "dry." "Memory of the silent films that gave so many hours of pleasure in the early decades of this century— figures such as Buster Keaton, Fatty Arbuckle and Charlie Chaplin—forms the basis of this work.... *Two Acts for Three Players* should sound as though accompanying a film, reflecting the pacing, the humor and the bathos. The performers are also actors to be watched by the audience as well as heard" (from the preface). Extensive directions, un-metered spatial sections, special instrumental notation explained. Traditional techniques mated with avant-garde. D.

Steven Gerber. *Variations* (ACA). For piano and 2 percussionists.

Elizabeth Gyring. *Two Marches* (ACA). For 2 pianos, timpani, and triangle.

Werner Heider. *Musik im Diskant* 1970 (Hänssler 11.403) 13pp., parts. 5½ min. For piccolo, piano (or harpsichord), and percussion. Traditional and proportional notation, dynamic extremes, clusters, glissando on strings, pointillistic, highly organized. To be spoken at conclusion: "genug." Avant-garde. D.

Alan Hovhaness. *Suite* Op.99 (CFP 6047 1957) 20pp., parts. 14 min. For piano, violin, and percussion (celesta, tam tam, xylophone). Prelude: pedal held throughout; low-register sonorities. Pastoral: pedal held throughout; a low-register harmonic second is to be played on the strings with a timpani stick. Allegro: repeated scale figures in upper register divided between the hands. Pastoral: same requirements as first Pastoral. Canon: octotonic writing two octaves apart. Allegro: pedal held throughout; figure consisting of triplet in left hand with alternating B♭ A♭ is repeated almost continuously; rests and a low C♯ sounding for two measures break it up; *ppp* conclusion. Effective if a little monotonous. M-D.

Bertold Hummel. *Ludi a Tre* (Schauer). For oboe, piano, and percussion.

Nikolai Lopatnikoff. *Sonata* Op.9 1926 (Edition Russes de Musique) 35pp., parts. For piano, violin, and snare drum. Allegro Energico: parallel chords coupled with melodic elements, staccato octaves, repeated fourth, seventh, and ninth chords, freely tonal. Andante: Impressionistic, asymmetrical phrase lengths, large span required. Allegro Vivace: octotonic, driving rhythmic sixteenths, syncopated chords, contrary-motion triplets, melodic emphasis in episode; vigorous rhythmic element returns to close out movement in a brilliant display for all instruments. M-D to D.

Alain Louvier. *Houles* (Leduc). For piano, percussion, and Ondes Martenot. Stormy, free in construction. Frantic explosions of quotes from Beethoven and Chopin intrude from time to time. Avant-garde. D.

Franco Mannino. *Epitaffio* Op.86 (EC 1974) 6pp., parts. For piano, flute, and percussion.

Paul-Baudouin Michel. *Colloque* 1967 (CeBeDeM) 54pp., parts. 16 min. For piano, trumpet, and percussion. Performance instructions in French, including placement of instruments. Introduzione–Adagio–Allegretto; Lento; Allegretto. Freely tonal, tremolando, octotonic, percussive treatment of piano, secco style. Lento is intense, and dramatic gestures are important; octaves in alternating hands; contrast in tempo changes are part of this movement. The finale uses contrary chromatic runs and brilliant chordal skips, breathtaking finish. Solid craft is demonstrated in this mildly contemporary, neoclassic work. Large span required. D.

Marcel Mihalovici. *Improvisations* Op.83 1961 (Heugel) 20pp., parts. 8 min. For 2 percussionists and piano. Varied sections, tempi, and moods. Added-note technique, shifting meters, freely tonal style, mildly contemporary. Percussion required: gong, vibraphone, timbales, marimba, 3 tom toms, tambour militaire, kettle drum with pedals, 3 Chinese blocks. M-D.

Robert Nagel. *Finale* Op.17 (ACA). For piano and 2 percussionists.

Lejos Papp. *Impressioni* (EMB). For piano, flute, and gong.

Ödön Partos. *Agaga* (A Legend) (IMI 1962) 33pp., parts. 12 min. For piano, violin, and percussion. Serial, oriental character. Source for the work is the oriental technique of improvisation based on developing variations. In five movements to be played without a break. The first movement is an image–cadenza; the second, a quasi-theme; the third, a set of variations in accelerating tempo; the fourth, a reprise of the theme in modal variation; the fifth, a variant of the third movement. Pointillistic, flexible meters. Row dictates development. Contains a diagram and performance directions. D.

Francis Pyle. *Sonata for Three* (Leblanc 1964) 22pp., parts. 10 min. For piano, clarinet, and percussion. Aria; Quasi Pastorale; Quasi Recitativo; Vivo. One sectionalized movement that is played without stop. Key signatures are present; mildly dissonant and mainly linear style; wide dynamic range. Requires a large span. M-D.

William Schmidt. *Septigrams* 1956 (WIM AVI 28 1967) 34pp., parts. For flute, piano, and percussion. Percussion required: snare drum, medium tom tom, low tom tom, and suspended cymbal. Written in the form of a suite with seven short movements. Introduction: a fife and drum march. Quartal Blues: slow brooding "blues" style that uses piano harmonics and soft brushes. Syncophrases: lively, syncopated 12/8. Polyjazz: a mid-twentieth-century interpretation of American jazz. Improvisational Variant: a cadenza in free, unbarred style, without percussion. The Percussive Fugato: rondo, a three-bar motif imitated in a quasi-fugal style using all three instruments. Finale: a slow chorale. The piano is handled in numerous ways, including percussive syncopated chords, figuration in alternating hands, bitonal octaves, "blues" seventh chords, harmonics, contrary chromatic triads. Many jazz sonorities. Requires a large span. M-D.

Robert Schollum. *Mosaik* Op.75 1968 (Dob) 15pp., 3 copies necessary for performance. For piano, oboe, and vibraphone. Rasch; Rasch, im Charakter etwa eines Geschwindmarsches; Ruhig fliessende; Rausch und leicht. Free twelve-tone usage. Clusters, pointillistic, dynamic extremes, glissandi on white and black keys together, free repetition. "His use of timbres derived originally from Debussy and Milhaud. The later austerity in his style is related in part to his interest in the world's folk musics" (DCM, p.662). D.

Gunther Schuller. *Music* 1957 (AMP) 18 min. For piano, violin and percussion.

Giora Schuster. *Accenti* (IMI 1965) 31pp., 3 copies required for performance. For 2 pianos and percussion. One player can handle all the percussion parts. First section untitled; Intermezzo; Andante—molto ritmico. Includes notes for performance and diagram for grouping the instruments. Percussion required: 3 timpani, xylophone, side drum with snares, suspended cymbal, bass drum, triangle, tam tam, 3 tom toms, 2 temple blocks, claves. Major sevenths are important; freely serial, pointillistic, some strings prepared by rubber wedges. Abstract. Requires seasoned ensemble players. D.

Kazimierz Serocki. *Fantasmagoria* (PWM 1971) 18 unnumbered leaves. 11–14 min. Instructions for performance (7pp.). 3 scores required for performance. Diagrammatic notation in part. Aleatoric. D.

Ralph Shapey. *Evocation* 1959 (IU) 37pp. For piano, violin, and percussion. Recitative—with intense majesty; With humor; With tenderness; With intense majesty. Serial, profound writing. The slow movement (With tenderness) and finale are unusually haunting and moving. Contains placement instructions for the percussion battery. Percussion required: low gong, high medium and low tom toms, bass drum, cymbals high and low, high wood block, medium gamelan, snare drum, 3 different kinds of sticks. Bar lines are used only as visual aids to the performers; they do not refer to any conception of metric or phrase division. Clusters, pointillistic. D.

Wolfgang Steffen. *Triplum 72* Op.39 (Bo&Bo 1973) 23pp. 4 copies required for performance. 14 min. For flute (alto recorder ad lib), piano, and percussion. Performance directions in German. Pointillistic, dynamic extremes, harmonics, improvisation, cluster tremolos, avant-garde. D.

Karlheinz Stockhausen. *No.11 Refrain* (UE 13187 1961) 3pp., including one of instructions. For piano, celesta, and vibraphone. Pianist needs 3 wood blocks; celesta player requires 3 antique cymbales; vibraphonist needs 3 cow bells and 3 glockenspiel plates. Six systems (each consisting of two or three staves) are to be read from left to right and from top to bottom. An extensive set of rules is given. Six degrees of loudness are indicated by the thickness of the dots and lines. There are six different signs for durations and five different types of pauses. Performers, on indication, produce a click with the tip of the tongue on the upper inside gum; five different pitches are to be made by changing the position of the mouth. Shouted syllables, glissandi, clusters, etc. A quiet and spaciously composed continuity of sounds is disturbed six times by a short refrain consisting of glissandi and clusters, trills, bass notes (in the piano), and brief snatches of melody. Players choose the points at which the refrain is played, and these change from one performance to the next. Avant-garde. D.

Alan Stout. *Fantasy* Op.62/4 (ACA). For 2 harpsichords or pianos and percussion.

Roger Tessier. *Vega* (Editions Françaises de Musique 1973) 16pp., parts. For piano, percussion, and Ondes Martenot. Part of series "Hommage à

Copernic.'' Reproduced from holograph. Graphic notation in part. Avant-garde. D.

Alain Weber. *Variantes* (Leduc 1972) 16 min. For piano and 2 percussionists. Eleven variations of highly complex writing, severe chromaticism, some avant-garde notation, aleatoric sections. Only for the most adventurous with plenty of pianistic equipment and perseverance. D.

Charles Wuorinen. *Trio* III (CFP 1974) 52pp., parts. For piano, flute, and percussion. D.

Trios for Piano, Other Instruments, and Tape

Will Gay Bottje. *Interplays* 1970 (ACA) 30pp., parts. For piano, harpsichord, horn, and tape. Tape available from composer: % School of Music, Southern Illinois University, Carbondale, IL 62901. 1. Piano and horn: pointillistic, length of sound decay indicated. Tape Interlude 1. 2. Horn and harpsichord: chordal, uses alternating hands. Tape Interlude 2. 3. Piano and tape: extensive directions, long pedals, strings damped, unusual sonorities. 4. Horn and tape. 5. Harpsichord and piano: playful pointillism. Tape Interlude 3. 6. Piano, harpsichord, tape: "In memory of certain E flat Pieces," playfully rondo-like. Tape Interlude 4. 7. Horn, piano, harpsichord, tape: chordal, very broad, quodlibet. Avant-garde. D.

Roger Reynolds. *Traces* 1968 rev.1969 (CFP 66247) 18pp. For flute, cello, piano, signal generator, ring modulator, and 6 channels of taped sound. This work "is concerned not only with events, but with their residue. The pianist makes a series of nine statements in the form of three interrelated groups of three short pieces. The flute and cello draw upon materials in these pieces, extending them (without recourse to development or elaboration). In the second and third set of three, long taped sounds overlap the pianistic events as well as flute and cello traces, suggesting the coexistence of several time frames and the resonance of memory. The work is of variable length" (from the score). Taped sounds are supplied with rental materials. Directions for performance and stage set-up are given. Piano techniques range from pointillistic treatment and playing AFAP (as fast as possible) to harmonics and long pedals. Graphic and ratio notation combined with traditional notation. Avant-garde. D.

Karl Heinz Wahren. *L'art pour L'art* 1968 (Bo&Bo). For flute, cello, piano, and tape.

Music for Four Instruments

Quartets for Piano and Strings

[Piano, violin, viola, and cello unless otherwise noted.]

Jean Absil. *Quartet* Op.33 1938 (CeBeDeM 1962) 47pp., parts. 22 min. Allegro moderato: chromatic chordal opening, alternating hands, fleet 32nd-note arpeggi and scales, emphatic octaves. Intermezzo: broken octaves, 3 with 2, arpeggi triplet patterns; piano has a quasi cadenza. Fileuse: an unending stream of steady sixteenths in one instrument or another. Recit et Final: piano opens with a rising dramatic gesture; important inner voices; hand crossings; chromatic thirds; exciting closing; large span required. D.
———— *Fantaisie* Op.40 1939 (CeBeDeM) 22pp., parts. 10 min. Chromatic vocabulary, arpeggi and scalar gestures, short cadenza for piano, octaves in alternating hands. M-D.

William Alwyn. *Rhapsody* 1939 (OUP) 20pp., parts. 10 min. Romantic and well-crafted writing with Impressionistic touches. The outer, driving rhythmic Moderato e deciso sections are contrasted with a più tranquillo mid-section. Freely tonal, strong conclusion. M-D.

William Ames. *Quartet* (CFE).

Carl Philipp Emanuel Bach. *Quartets* W.93 a, W.94 D, W.95 G 1788 (Schmid—Nag 222, 223, 224). See detailed entry under quartets for piano(s), strings, and winds.

Johann Christian Bach. *Quartet* G (W. Bergmann—Schott 4151) 34pp., parts. Allegro; Rondo: piano part is obbligato except for the places (indicated by figures) that have been supplemented by the editor. Because of the pianistic style and Bach's preference for the piano, the use of that instrument, rather than a harpsichord, is historically justified. M-D.

Henk Badings. *Quartet* 1973 (Donemus) 40pp., parts. Reproduced from MS.

Badings favors an intense, chromatic harmony more in tune with German thinking than with French. A distant similarity to Hindemith. D.

Leonardo Balada. *Cuatris for Four Instruments* (Gen 1970) 18pp., parts. 8½ min. For flute or violin, clarinet or viola, trombone or cello or bassoon with prepared piano or harpsichord. Five movements that involve clusters, *pp* chromatic figuration, prepared strings using chains or metal, improvisation with clusters ad lib in bravura fashion, repeated notes, crossed hands, pointillistic treatment, striking strings and glissandi on strings. Large span required. Avant-garde. D.

Arnold Bax. *Quartet* (Murdoch 1924) 27pp., parts. In one movement, Allegro moderato. Dramatic, impulsive, explosive mood, chromatic. M-D to D.

Ludwig van Beethoven. *Quartets* (S. Kross—Henle 1973) 110pp., parts. Op.16, WoO36/1–3. Piano part fingered by H.-M. Theopold. The three piano quartets WoO36 were written when Beethoven was 15 years old. The style of these works and the fact that he reached back into these quartets for thematic material for his first piano sonatas (Op.2/1 and 3) speak strongly for their genuineness. While not comparable with his later string quartets, they are lovely compositions and have much to teach about ensemble work. The pianist needs to be able to handle octaves with some facility. Op.16 E♭ (1796–7) was originally written for piano, oboe, clarinet, bassoon, and horn. All the following publishers have Op.16 for violin, viola, cello, and piano as arranged by Beethoven: Br&H; F. A. Roitzsch—CFP 8431 54pp., parts; GS L1623; Augener 7198; EPS; IMC. Both versions have the same opus number.
_____ *Quartet* II D Op. posth. (Br&H).
_____ *Quartet* III C Op. posth. (Br&H).

Warren Benson. *Capriccio* (CF). 15 min.

Sebastian Bodinus. *Sonata* E♭ (H. Fischer—Vieweg 1939) 11pp., parts. For 2 oboes or violins, bassoon or cello, and piano. Adagio; Allegro; Siciliana; Allegro assai. Attractive, good realization. M-D.

Léon Boëllmann. *Quatuor* Op.10 (Hamelle). Four movements: spirited allegro, delicate scherzo, sombre andante, breezy and cheerful finale. Mildly contemporary modal harmonies, Franckian influence. M-D.

René de Boisdeffre. *1er Quatuor* Op.13 g (Hamelle) 82pp., parts. Allegro ma non troppo; Scherzo; Andante expressivo; Finale. M-D.

———— *2me Quatuor* Op.91 E♭ (Hamelle) 91pp., parts. Andante espressivo—Allegro con brio; Scherzo; Andante; Finale. M-D to D. Both works display above-average Romantic writing.

Mélanie Bonis. *Quatuor* Op.72 1905 (Hamelle) 70pp., parts. Moderato; Intermezzo; Adagio; Final. Chromatic, numerous key signatures. Franck influence present; traditional late turn-of-the-century pianistic treatment. M-D to D.

Johannes Brahms. *Quartet* Op.25 g 1861 (H. Krellmann—Henle 79pp., parts; Schumann—CFP 3939A; Br&H; GS L1624; Simrock; Schroeder—Augener; EPS; IMC) 39 min. The Henle edition is based on the autograph and the most reliable sources. Allegro; Intermezzo—Allegro (ma non troppo); Andante con moto; Rondo alla Zingarese. Full of contrasts and majestic themes, this quartet is one of the most exciting pieces in all chamber music literature. It is probably the most popular of the three piano quartets because the Rondo is reminiscent of Brahms's *Hungarian Dances*. The Intermezzo displays unusual coloring and delicacy. D.

———— *Quartet* Op.26 A 1861–2 (H. Krellmann—Henle 67pp., parts; Br&H; CFP 3939C; GS L1626). The Henle edition has fingering for the piano part added by H.-M. Theopold and also contains a preface in German, English, and French. Allegro non troppo; Poco adagio; Scherzo—Poco allegro; Finale— Allegro. The first movement demonstrates Brahms's fine contrapuntal skill with a theme easily expressed by strings or piano. Serene melodies in the slow movement, the finest in this work, plus a flowing scherzo (with the trio written in canon) and the sustained drive of the finale show Brahms at his best. D.

———— *Quartet* Op.60 c 1874–5 (H. Krellmann—Henle 55pp., parts; CFP 3939C; Br&H; GS L1626; IMC). 31 min. The Henle is an excellent practical urtext with a preface in French, German, and English. Allegro non troppo; Andante–Allegro commodo. This piano quartet was the earliest one conceived but Brahms reworked it later, hence the completion date of 1874–5. It shows youthful impulsiveness as well as characteristics of the mature, poised master. Displays great despair and is gloomier than Op.25 and Op.26. D.

See: Henry Cope Colles, *The Chamber Music of Brahms* (New York: AMS Press, 1975; reprint of London, 1933 edition); Henry S. Drinker, *The Chamber Music of Brahms* (New York: AMS Press, 1974; reprint); Ivor Keys, *Brahms Chamber Music* (London: BBC Music Guides, 1974); Robert Pascall, ''Ruminations on Brahms's Chamber Music,'' MT 1590 (August 1975):697–99.

Frank Bridge. *Phantasy* f♯ (Augener 1911) 32pp., parts. Many contrasted sections in an extended andante con moto enclosing a central allegro vivace and followed by a concluding retrospective tranquillo. Much arpeggiation, sombre, reflective mood. M-D.

Edvard Hagerup Bull. *Sonata con spirito* 1970 (Editions française de musique, Technisonor) 87pp., parts.

Clement Calder. *Quartett* 1968 (Bo&Bo) 12pp., parts. Three untitled movements with metronome indications only. Serial, flexible meters, pointillistic, abstract writing. D.

Alexis de Castillon. *Quatuor* Op.7 g 1871–2 (Hamelle). Larghetto–Allegro deciso: SA; introduction plays an important part in the movevent. Scherzando: a minuet with curious rhythmic effects. Larghetto, quasi marcia religiosa: ABA. Allegro: rondo, dancelike, flowing Romantic writing for all instruments. M-D.

Ernest Chausson. *Quartet* Op.30 A 1897 (Rouart Lerolle; IMC 95pp., parts). Animé: SA. Très calme. ABA. Simple et sans hâte: AB. Animé: SA. A mature work that presents an unusually fine balance in the motivic interplay between piano and strings. Superb piano writing, sweeping gestures, cyclic constituents. D.

Aaron Copland. *Quartet* 1950 (Bo&H) 36pp., parts. 21 min. Adagio serio: eleven-note row, two mutually exclusive whole-tone groups; expressive polyphony. Allegro giusto: great rhythmic variety of the row, but steady meter throughout; witty, appealing. Non troppo lento: soliloquy-like; linked to original row by whole-tone scales; near the conclusion ten notes of the row are heard in descending whole-tone scales in parallel major sixths. This was Copland's first attempt at serial technique, and the motivic and rhythmic organization is almost too tight and stiff in places. Sonata and fugue elements are synthesized. D.

Arcangelo Corelli. *Trio Sonata* Op.1/1 F (E.P. Biggs—Music Press MPI 30–12). For 2 violins, cello, and organ or piano. Grave; Allegro; Adagio; Allegro; Adagio. Graceful and flowing ideas organized into perfect structural designs; unity of musical logic and beauty of melody. Excellent keyboard realization. A perfect example of the Sonata da Chiesa. M-D.
_____ *Trio Sonata* Op. 3/2 D (E.P. Biggs—Music Press MPI 34-10). For 2 violins, cello, and organ or piano. Grave; Allegro; Adagio; Allegro. M-D.

Ingolf Dahl. *Quartet* 1957 (J. Boonin) 50pp., parts. 18½ min. Melodic and harmonic materials are serialized. Fantasia Appassionata: pointillistic, martellato passage work, capricious and molto staccato, dry and brittle writing. Antiphon: flexible meters; more lyric and longer lines; section for solo piano; contrast range from dolcissimo, misterioso to energico and feroce; tremolo. Rondo alla Campanella: piano is mainly used percussively, with strongly accented sonorities colored with grace notes; alternating hands; fragmented ideas; effective arpeggio figures pedalled; widely spread gestures; solo piano part; harmonics. Melodic and harmonic materials are serialized. D.

Albert Delvaux. *Vijf Stukken* (Five Pieces) 1964 (CeBeDeM) 51pp., parts. Allegro spiritoso: freely serial, melodic, duplet and triplet figuration, alternating hands. Adagio: molto espressivo, chordal, syncopated melody, broken-chord figuration. Allegretto scherzando: dancelike; antiphonal writing between piano and strings. Larghetto: mainly chordal and sustained. Vivo: rocking triplet pulsation, punctuated chords. Mildly contemporary serial treatment throughout. D.

Emma Lou Diemer. *Quartet* 1954 (Seesaw) 23pp., parts. 12 min. Agitated: freely tonal, repeated octaves and quartal harmonies, dialogue between strings and piano, octotonic, shifting rhythms in repeated patterns. Rather slow, pensive: trills and long unfolding lines. Jocose: uses sharp, precise and staccato figures; bouncing motifs, effective coda. M-D.

Théodore Dubois. *Quartet* a (Heugel 1907) 61pp., parts. Allegro agitato; Andante molto espressivo; Allegro leggiero; Allegro con fuoco. The last movement is based on thematic ideas from the other movements and serves as a summary of the whole work. M-D.

Antonín Dvořák. *Quartet* Op.23 D 1875 (Artia; Litolff; Schlesinger) 26 min. Clarity of style, vitality of thematic material. Treatment of piano fairly simple but highly effective, in spite of some obvious sequential modulation. Much short-sectioned exchange between instruments. The third and final movement, in two sections, combines the functions of scherzo and finale. M-D.

———— *Quartet* Op.87 Eb 1889 (Artia; Simrock; IMC) 28 min. More commanding, with rich style, yet concise and expressive with greater emotional intensity than Op.23. The first theme of the opening movement (SA) is heard with great clarity and power. Later on the cello maintains pedal points augmented by the viola (both playing pizzicato) while the violin follows the piano figurations. The Lento is one of Dvořák's loveliest lyrical and atmospheric movements. The melodious first and last sections of the scherzo enclose a monotonously harmonized motif, oriental in character. An energetic finale in clear SA design closes the work. D.

Anne Eggleston. *Piano Quartet* (Jaymar 1954–5) 38pp., parts. 22 min. Moderately with expression; Allegro scherzando; Lento; Allegro. The four movements, although not connected thematically, have in common the relationship between the piano as an individual and the strings as a group. All movements have passages in which these two elements are either united or contrasted. Influences of Bloch are evident in the first and third movements; of Bartók in the alternating rhythms of the Scherzo; and of Hindemith in the first movement, written in concerto grosso form, which builds to a four-part fugue before the final statement of the theme. M-D.

Georges Enesco. *Quartet II* Op.30 d 1944 (Editura Muzicală a Uniunii Compozitorilor din Republica Socialista Romania) 79pp., parts. Allegro moderato; Andante pensieroso ed espressivo; Con moto moderato. Unusual harmonic vocabulary, fluid and complex rhythms, surprising sonorities. D.

Robert Evett. *Quartet* 1961 (ACA) 23 min.

Gabriel Fauré. *Quartet I* Op.15 c 1879 (Hamelle 85pp., parts; IMC) 32 min. Allegro molto moderato: opens with an unusual unison passage for strings accompanied by syncopated piano chords. Scherzo—Allegro vivace: piano states the main theme, in 6/8; remarkably original writing that treats the piano like a harp. Adagio: breathes long lines and is of great intrinsic beauty. Allegro molto: flows ever forward. D.
_____ *Quartet II* Op.45 g 1886 (Hamelle 91pp., parts; IMC) 36 min. Allegro molto moderato; Allegro molto; Adagio non troppo; Allegro molto. One of Fauré's most powerful works; combines highly interesting thematic material with a more closely woven texture. The fiery Scherzo has more sharply defined outlines than does *Quartet I*. A noble slow movement is followed by an impetuous finale, and the whole work reveals an intensity and a diversity of sentiment infrequently heard in Fauré's writing. D.

Zdeněk Fibich. *Quartet* Op.11 e 1874 (Artia; Urbanek 51pp., parts). In three movements, with only five themes in the entire piece. Allegro moderato: two themes, rolled chords, tremolo, octave runs, alternation of hands. Tema con variazioni: one theme, eight contrasting variations, coda. Finale—Allegro energico: two themes with all five themes from the entire work combined at the end. Romantic, nationalistic, flowing piano writing. Fibich's chef d'oeuvre is notable for its closely woven ensemble technique. M-D to D.

Benjamin Frankel. *Quartet* Op.26 (Nov 1962) 24pp., parts. Moderato: declamatory; fast chordal skips; seconds prevalent; octotonic; moves over entire keyboard; atonal. Allegretto: octaves and chords in alternating hands;

poco meno mosso mid-section contrasts secco and sustained writing; large span required. Lento: freely dissonant; cantando; many harmonic sevenths; intense build-up; *pp* closing. Sensitive writing throughout. D.

Isadore Freed. *Triptych* (SPAM 1945) 63pp., parts. Risoluto: chordal, some melodic emphasis. Andante sostenuto: ostinato treatment; Animato mid-section. Allegro, ben ritmato: rhythmic emphasis with chords, brief melodic sections for piano. Mildly contemporary, mainly treated in homophonic style. M-D.

Gunnar de Frumerie. *Quartet* 1942 (NMS). Rich sonorities tinged with Romanticism; firm formal control; flowing counterpoint between instruments; broad gestures. Piano writing effective throughout. M-D to D.

Hermann Goetz. *Quartet* Op.6 E (Wollenweber UWKR 15 1974) 60pp., parts. Rasch und feurig; Langsam (theme and 4 variations); Scherzo; Sehr langsam–Frisch und lebendig. Shows a mastery of style. Instances of profound sadness and inspiring energy permeate the work. Emotional theme of the variations and the melancholy introduction to the finale show Goetz at his best. A three-part canon in the trio of the scherzo points up the composer's fine craft. Brahmsian in style. Worth reviving. D.

Francesco de Guarnieri. *Quartetto* (Carisch 1942) 68pp., parts. 34 min. Allegro moderato; Cantabile; Finale. Chromatic, sequences, traditional pianistic approaches, mildly contemporary. M-D.

Reynaldo Hahn. *Quartet III* G (Heugel 1946) 53pp., parts. Allegretto moderato; Allegro assai; Andante; Allegro assai. Flexible and light writing, clear harmonies, numerous easy-fnowing melodies. Gallic clarity in the tradition of Saint-Säens mixed with style of Massenet, Hahn's teacher. The slow movement is especially melodious and beautiful. M-D.

Franz Joseph Haydn. *Quartet* Op.5/4 G (W. Upmeyer—Nag 129) 12pp., parts. For 2 violins, viola, and piano; cello ad lib. Originally a Divertimento for woodwinds, strings, and basso continuo. Hob.II: 1. This arrangement here can also be performed by flute, violin, viola, and piano. Vivace; Andante moderato; Menuetto; Fantasia (with 5 variations). Delightful writing, appealing format. M-D.
———*Divertimento* Hob.XIV: 2 C ca.1760 (H.C.R. Landon—Dob DM 325 1966) 5pp., parts. For 2 violins, cello, and piano. Allegro moderato; Menuet. A genuine miniature in two tiny movements; charming and gracefully written. Int.

———— *Divertimento* Hob.XIV: 9 F (L. Kalmar—Litolff 1972) 10pp., parts. For piano, 2 violins, and cello.

———— *Divertimento* C (G. Balla—Litolff). For 2 violins, cello, and piano. Written before 1766. Moderato; Minuetto; Finale. The finale (Scherzo) is by far the best movement, truly vintage Haydn wit. Piano writing is quite easy. Int. to M-D.

———— *Concertini* (H. Walter—Henle 1969) 47pp., parts. Fingering for piano added by H.-M. Theopold. From the Complete Edition of the Joseph Haydn Institute. Contains four concertinos: 1. Hob.XIV: 11 C, Moderato; Adagio; Allegro. 2. Hob.XIV: 12 C, Allegro; Adagio; Finale. 3. Hob.XIV: 13 G, Allegro moderato; Adagio; Finale. 4. Hob.XVIII: F2 F, Moderato; Adagio; Allegro assai. These all date from the early 1760s when Haydn wrote concerted music with keyboard within the technical range of amateur performers. Contains preface and remarks about the individual sources. An excellent practical and urtext edition. Int. to M-D.

Kurt Hessenberg. *Quartett* Op.10 C 1935 (Müller) 21 min. Written in a mildly contemporary style with a Hindemith flavor. Full of admirable individual traits that show that Hessenberg is a superb craftsman. M-D.

Emil Hlobil. *Quartette* Op.23 1943 (Hudební Matice 1948) 59pp., parts. 22 min. Allegro vivace: C, SA, bitonal usage; piano provides figuration and harmonic structure. Lento: E♭, ABA, lyric with B section more lively. Allegro assai: C, SA; piano has short ostinato-like figurations and stays busy but has little or no melodic emphasis. Piano or harpsichord can be used but the work seems to be conceived more for the piano since numerous crescendo and decrescendo marks are used. M-D.

Arthur Honegger. *Rhapsody* 1917 (Sal 1923) 13pp., parts. For 2 flutes, clarinet, and piano, or for 2 violins, viola, and piano. See detailed entry under quartets for piano and three woodwinds.

Herbert Howells. *Piano Quartet* Op.21 a 1916, rev. 1936 (St&B). 27 min. Allegro moderato, tranquillo: the hill is reflected at dawn. Lento, molto tranquillo: hill seen during a day in mid-summer. Allegro molto, energico: the hill in the month of March. Programmatic references "to the Hill at Chosen and Ivor Gurney who knows it." Intensely moving and gripping; one of the finest works of the period. "English" style, modal, inspired by folk tunes. M-D.

Johann N. Hummel. *Quartet* Op. posth. G (K. Stierhof—Dob DM 538 1976) 37pp., parts. Two movements. Over-elaborate figuration in the piano part, somewhat superficial and showy. Not easy. M-D.

Vincent d'Indy. *Quartet* Op.7 a 1878 (Durand). Opening movement: SA design with some interesting modulations in the second tonal area but the style is mainly reserved and conservative. Andante: an expressive ballade, no complexities. Rondo: main idea not used at the conclusion, but principal subject from the second episode assumes supremacy. Clever rhythmic inventiveness adds to the interest of this work. D.

Gordon P. Jacob. *Quartet* (Nov 1972) 64pp., parts. 22 min. Opens majestically with a short Andante that leads to a lively Allegro section. Eight tempo changes are encountered in the Scherzo, in which the pianist has fast octave passages. The third movement is an expressive Variations and Epilogue. The pianist needs plenty of agility. D.

Joseph Jongen. *Quatuor* Op.23 E♭ 1902 (Durand). Cyclic in form, close affinity to Franck. Themes have a sustained beauty and are expressed in a unique way. Classical format, with the different parts of each movement built on two themes with traditional development procedure. No overexuberant display in any of the instruments. Lengthy work. M-D to D.

Léon Jongen. *Divertissement en forme de variations sur un thème de Haydn* 1955 (CeBeDeM 1962) 32pp., parts. 11 min. Moderato; Nocturnal Pastoral; Tempo di Marcia; Vivamente. Based on tune from finale of the Haydn "Surprise Symphony." Clever and effective mildly contemporary writing. M-D.

Jan Kapr. *Rotazione 9* (Supraphon 1967) 27pp. Full score required for each player. Includes passages in indeterminate notation. Three series used provide a nine-angled crystal for Kapr to manipulate. Some controlled improvisation by prescribed pitches. Requires much rehearsal time. D.

Willem Kersters. *Quatuor* Op.53 1970 (CeBeDeM) 28pp., parts, 12½ min. Moderato; Andante (in memoriam Henri Koch); Allegro molto. Octotonic, chromatic, photostat of MS is difficult to read, thin textures, eclectic style. M-D.

Ellis B. Kohs. *Quartet* 1962 (Cameo Music) 20 min. Studies in Variation, Part II. This is part of a larger work: Part I, for woodwind quintet; Part III, for piano; Part IV, for solo violin. "The grand design . . . is that the four compositions are variations of each other and have a measure-for-measure correspondence. That is to say, if we understand it correctly, the basic material remains the same and recurs in the same order, but on each appearance is varied in texture, dynamics, rhythm, melodic direction and special effects. In style, according to the composer, he has 'attempted a synthesis or reconciliation of certain elements of newer compositional techniques with traditional concepts of tonal order and structure.' As an ambitious project Mr. Kohs' work is probably unique. Countless composers have produced variations of one kind or another, but we can think of none who has utilized the variation principle on such a large and complicated scale'' (Albert Goldberg in the *Los Angeles Times*, May 7, 1963).

Egon Kornauth. *Quartet* Op.18 c (Dob). Written in a mildly contemporary idiom with strong Romantic influences, such as those of Brahms, Schumann, and Reger. M-D to D.

Hans Kox. *Quartet* 1959 (Donemus). Thematic material is developed in a convincing and conscious manner. Striking rhythmic procedure. M-D to D.
———— *Pianokwartet II* 1968 (Donemus) 7 min.

Guillaume Lekeu. *Quartet* (Rouart Lerolle 1909). Unfinished; revised by Vincent d'Indy, who added an admirable conclusion to the second movement (lento e con passione), a highly expressive nocturne. Lengthy development in first movement, rich sonorities. Contains some moving and impassioned pages from a strong Romantic personality. D.

Daniel Lesur. *Suite* 1943 (Amphion 140) 29pp., parts. Nocturne; Ricercara; Berceuse; Tarantella. Elegant writing, modal. Some Impressionist influences and a little dissonance produce some subtle harmonies. The work shows Lesur to be a composer whose refined style displays both lyrical and poetic qualities. M-D.

Jean Baptiste Loeillet (of Lyons). *Sonata* Op.2/11 D (H. Ruf—Schott 5393) 12pp., parts. For 2 violins, cello, and keyboard. Adagio; Allegro; Largo; Allegro. Excellent and stylistic realization. M-D.

Gustave Mahler. *Quartet* g 1876 (P. Ruzicka—Sikorski 800 1973) 31pp., parts, facsimile. First edition. Introduction in German and English, critical commentary in German. This 234-bar movement was written when Mahler was a student in Vienna, but the thematic ideas already have a personal profile. The form and treatment clearly show the influence of Brahms, Schumann, and Schubert on the young Mahler. Triplet figuration is relied on heavily in the exposition and recapitulation. An agitato-like development works to a suspenseful climax. The subdued, muted, intermezzo-like section just before the recapitulation is very moving; and the melancholy, sinking closing in a negates any conventional exterior one might expect to find in a sixteen-year-old. An appendix contains a 24-bar sketch for a scherzo movement. D.

Bohuslav Martinů. *Quartet I* 1942 (AMP) 52pp., parts. 22 min. Poco allegro; Adagio; Allegretto poco moderato. Spontaneous pulse patterns produce a strong and virile rhythmic fabric. Wide harmonic range includes simple progressions as well as biting dissonance. Fluid and transparent polyphony plus vivid tonal sonorities add to the integral unity. Great variety of traditional pianistic techniques and idioms in a contemporary setting. D.

Felix Mendelssohn. *Quartet* Op.1 c 1822 (CFP; Br&H) 25 min. M-D.

———— *Quartet* Op.2 f 1823 (CFP; Br&H) 22 min. The melody in the Adagio movement is especially fervent, and its bold enharmonic modulations as well as the melodic invention in the intermezzo (Allegro moderato) show great originality for a fourteen-year-old. M-D.

———— *Quartet* Op.3 b 1825 (CFP; Br&H) 30 min. In this compelling piece, the piano part requires lightness and transparency to balance the string writing. The Adagio is in the nature of an expressive "Song Without Words." A noble quality permeates both outside movements. With this work, Mendelssohn finishes his apprenticeship and becomes a composer in his own right. M-D.

These three early quartets, modeled on Weber and early Beethoven, show an extraordinary precocity. The strings are skillfully pitted against the piano in some places, but the piano part is much more important than the string complement in Op.1 and Op.2. All three quartets consist of four movements and contain scherzi in duple meter.

See: John Horton. *The Chamber Music of Mendelssohn* (London: Oxford University Press, 1946), pp.10–15.

Darius Milhaud. *Quartet* 1966 (Durand) 29pp., parts. Strongly characterized melodies in both shape and rhythm; chords of 9ths, 11ths, and 13ths are present and enrich the harmony. Milhaud utilizes maximum capacities for colorful sonorities in all four movements. M-D.

Wolfgang Amadeus Mozart. *Quartets* K.478 g 1785, K.493 E♭ (E. Herttrich—Henle 1974) 67pp., parts. This edition is based on the autograph, the first edition (1787), and the André edition (1809). Fingering for the piano part has been added by H.-M. Theopold. Clear printing, high urtext standards continued here as in other Henle editions. Preface in German, English, and French, Most authorities seem to agree that K.478 is the finer of the two quartets. Its passionate first movement, melancholy Andante, and exuberant finale with exquisite melodies make it a catalogue of Mozart's finest art. D.

Available separately: *Quartet* K.478 (H. Federhofer—Br 1957) 52pp., parts. A fine preface includes background on the work as well as editorial procedures and sources used. Allegro; Andante; Rondo—Allegro moderato.

Virtuoso demands are made on the pianist but the strings are completely integrated into the texture. This work is unjustly neglected.

Other editions of both quartets by CFP; Br&H; Augener; BMC.

———— *Chamber Concertos—Piano Quartets* 1765 (A. Hoffmann- Möseler) K.107/1 D (Corona 121); K.107/2 G (Corona 122); K.107/3 E♭ (Corona 123). For 2 violins, cello, and continuo. The continuo part is the solo piano. These are early concerto arrangements after Johann Christian Bach's *Sonatas* Op.5. Mozart played K.107/1, 2 not only in his prodigy days but also in later years. M-D.

———— *Chamber Concerto—Piano Quartet* K.246 C (Corona 125) (Möseler). M-D

Wolfgang Amadeus Mozart (The Son). *Quartett* Op.1 g 1802 (H. Riessberger—Dob 1966) 43pp., parts. Molto vivace; Adagio, ma non troppo; Theme con Variazioni (9 variations and coda). Reveals a noteworthy musical talent. Classic style with traditional pianistic idioms and figurations. M-D.

Vítězslav Novák. *Quartet* Op.7 c 1894, rev. 1899 (Artia; Simrock 39pp., parts). Andante; Scherzino; Rondo. In the Brahms–Dvořák tradition; expert writing with Slovak folk materials making a distinguished contribution to this work. M-D.

Robert Palmer. *Piano Quartet* 1947 (J. Kirkpatrick—SPAM 1950) 80pp., parts. Allegro e molto energico: oriental scale of half and whole steps is used for main subject while contrasting subject is constructed on wide intervals. Andante con moto e semplice: chromatic possibilities exploited from alternating major and minor triads. Molto allegro e dinamico: tonal, pandiatonic. Presto: clean lines, driving rhythms, cross-rhythms; evolves from small motifs. Neoclassic, modal, unusual scales. D.

Walter Piston. *Quartet* 1964 (AMP 1974) 28pp., parts. 18 min. Facsimile of composer's autograph. Leggero e scorrevole; Adagio sostenuto; Allegro vivo. Classical sonata form is the basis for this work. Baroque polyphonic textures are welded together with harmony, key relationships, and rhythms of the twentieth century. Neoclassic qualities permeate every bar of this work by a master craftsman. D.

Marcel Poot. *Quartet* 1932 (ESC) 39pp., parts. 24 min. Allegro giocoso; Menuetto; Finale. Stravinsky-like in rhythms and dissonance with some Prokofiev influence noted. Finale is especially dancelike with the exception of one Impressionistic episode (Quasi moderato). D.

Almeida Prado. *Ex itinere* 1974 (Tonos 10316).

Marcel Quinet. *Quartet* 1957 (CeBeDeM) 52pp., parts. 16 min. Allegro moderato; Adagio; Allegramente. Neoclassic in structure and atonal harmonic treatment. Frequent alternation of hands. Large span required. D.

Max Reger. *Quartet* Op.133 a 1914 (CFP 3977; Simrock) 51pp., parts. Allegro con passione; Vivace; Largo con gran espressione; Allegro con spirito. This autumnal work is an impressive masterpiece. It contains a passionate first movement, a genial scherzo à la Beethoven, and a festive, lighthearted finale. Rich polyphonic lines and abrupt changes of mood underlie its construction. D.

Josef Rheinberger. *Quartet* Op.38 E♭ 1870 (Hamelle; Augener). This work sounds dated today but in its time it proved to be interesting to pianists and string players. "This is one of those quartets which has provided amateurs, who are not all high-brows (myself among the number), with a transition stage, and for that reason alone deserves to be rated highly" (CCSCM, II, p.294).

Jean Roger-Ducasse. *Quatuor* g 1910 (Durand). First movement: ternary and binary rhythm alternated; second theme has a Fauré flavor; powerful coda, abrupt ending. Andantino ma scherzando: fantasy-like theme, with variations. Third movement: dark, mysterious, connected by a pedal point to the Finale: main ideas are combined with themes from previous movements; strong movement. M-D to D.

José Rolón. *Cuarteto* E♭ (EMM 1967) 82pp., parts. Allegro molto con brio; Adagio; Molto vivace; Allegro giocoso vivace. Post-Romantic writing, style of late nineteenth-century French school. A little Impressionistic in places. Might be mistaken for Dubois or his contemporaries. M-D.

Anton Rubinstein. *Quatuor* Op.55 (Hamelle). Also published as a quintet for piano, flute, clarinet, horn, and bassoon. Eclectic writing with very little contrapuntal development. Most interesting are the melodies with a hint of Russian melos. Beautiful musical writing (for its day) but not terribly original. M-D.
———— *Quatuor* Op.66 (Hamelle; Simrock).

Camille Saint-Saëns. *Quartet* Op.41 B♭ (Durand). Allegretto: serene, with a slow march entering near the end. Andante: effective melodic and contrapuntal writing, great variety of figuration and devices. Scherzo: 6/8; a nocturnal dance with 2/4 meter intruding near the conclusion; two recitatives also interrupt the movement. Finale: vigorous, thematics from previous movements are brought together to unify the work. Ingenious treatment of the subjects. M-D to D.

Franz Schubert. *Quartet* D.487 F, Adagio and Rondo Concertante 1816 (CFP 1347; Br&H) 35pp., parts. 14 min. The Adagio serves as an introduction and builds anticipation and suspense. The Rondo is a brilliant. .and colorful movement built on a number of contrasting ideas in different tonalities. An unusual pattern of ABCD–development–ABCD–coda is the result. Schubert incorporates all his unique pianistic idioms into this highly effective work, which is in many ways a miniature concerto for piano with strings. D.

Also available in the Dover reprint of the I. Brull—Br&H edition in *Complete Chamber Music for Pianoforte and Strings*. This volume also contains the "Trout" quintet and the three trios for piano, violin, and cello.

Robert Schumann. *Quartet* Op.47 E♭ 1842 (A. Dörffel— CFP 53pp., parts; Br&H; Bauer—GS L1711; Augener; IMC). 27 min. Sostenuto assai–Allegro ma non troppo; Scherzo—molto vivace; Andante cantabile; Vivace. One of the most important works in the literature for this combination. Equal division of interest between the four instruments. Unsurpassed in Romantic fervor and beauty. D.

Richard Strauss. *Piano Quartet* Op.13 c 1884 (Aibl; UE 65pp., parts; IMC) 35min. Requires a taut and lively performance with a good sense of Romantic stylistic traditions. All four movements effective. Striking and sweeping lyrical melodies; post-Brahmsian in its exuberant musical language. Brilliant coda in first movement (Allegro) and the spirited Scherzo require virtuosity of all interpreters. The Andante has an expressive melody and concludes like a delicate serenade. A syncopated Schumannesque opening announces the finale in which the themes are ingeniously combined and the coda is as effective as the one in the opening movement. D.

Rezsö Sugár. *Quartetto* (Zenmükiadó Vállalat 1964) 28pp., parts. For 2 violins, cello, and piano. Allegro; Andante; Vivo. Colorful Hungarian flavor, mildly contemporary. M-D.

Carlos Surinach. *Quartet* (PIC 1944) 56pp., parts. 20 min. Three movements that are full of Spanish color and rhythmic vitality. Fresh and evocative writing. Little development and unashamed tunes, but the splashes of color and passionate treatment add up to a direct and charming work. The cross-rhythms of the third and final movements are intoxicating. M-D.

Sergei I. Taneiev. *Quartet* Op.20 E 1902–6 (USSR 1974) 94pp., parts. First published by Belaieff in 1907. Brilliant and sonorous Romantic writing for the piano. Cobbett considers the work "profound and sublime in conception" (CCSCM, II, p.487). Three movements with the outer movements written in SA design while the second, an Adagio tosto largo, is in ABA form. D.

Alexander Tansman. *Suite-Divertissement* (ESC 1930). Neoclassic approach and construction; strong rhythmic emphasis does not detract from the lyricism of the work. Lightness and charm shine through at all times, even when textures become complex. M-D.

Georg Philipp Telemann. *Quartet* G (Hinnenthal—Br 3534). For oboe or violin, violin, cello, and basso continuo.

Joaquin Turina. *Quatuor* Op.67 a 1931 (Rouart Lerolle). Iberian poetic style throughout with strong rhythmic and coloristic effects. Chromatic idiom, some cyclic elements. Thematic opposition with repetition varied by timbre is preferred over large structures with organic development. D.

Antonio Vivaldi. *Sonata* g (G. F. Ghedini—IMC 1240) 19pp., parts. For flute (violin I), oboe (violin II), bassoon (cello), and piano. Allegro ma cantabile; Largo; Allegro molto. Unencumbered realizations. M-D.

William Walton. *Piano Quartet* 1918–9 (St&B 1924; rev. ed. OUP 1976) 74pp., parts. 26 min. Allegramente; Allegro scherzando; Andante tranquillo; Allegro molto. This early work displays stylistic distinctiveness and great technical assurance for a sixteen-year-old. Modal flavor, transparent textures. Ravel's influence is noted especially in the second movement, a rhythmic scherzo and rustling fugati. Noble and effective writing. Large span required. M-D to D.

Donald Waxman. *Quartet* (Galaxy 1966) 43pp., parts. Allegramente: SA; piano introduction; freely tonal but centers around D; subito trills; unusual coda; large span required. Adagietto: ABA, varied use of triplet figure, quintal harmony, flowing melody in mid-section. Introduction, Theme, Variations: chromatic figuration; piano gives out the bright theme by itself; six contrasting variations (piano is tacet in Var.4) with the final one extended by a coda. Gallic influence permeates this well-written work; a kind of Poulencian charm adds real interest to this basically neoclassic-inspired composition. M-D.

Carl Maria von Weber. *Quartet* Op.8 1810 (CFP 2177 41pp., parts; IMC). Allegro: piano gives opening vigorous statement; second subject is given to strings while the piano weaves an intricate design around it; thorough development. Adagio: smooth beginning but soon becomes more agitated to a più moto e con fuoco; opening character returns but is disturbed by coda figuration. Minuet: highly agitated with some relief in the peasant dance trio. Presto: a versatile fugue subject that opens the movement is followed by a jaunty theme that takes on an operatic and potpourri character. Serene and sunny writing throughout. D.

Charles-Marie Widor. *Quatuor* Op.66 a (Durand 1892). Learned and accomplished writing, very much in the style of Saint-Saëns. Plenty of vitality. D.

Russell Woolen. *Quartet* A 1961 (CFE) 110 pp., parts. Allegro deciso: freely tonal; octotonic; emphatic octaves; imitation; large span required. Andante: flowing; chantlike lines; more active mid-section that includes sweeping arpeggi. Allegretto: rondo; rhythmic hemiola lines; uses extremes of keyboard; pesante chromatic chordal section; basically thin textures; neoclassic. D.

Iannis Xenakis. *Morsima-Amorsima (ST/4-1,030762)* 1962 (Bo&H) 28pp., parts. $10\frac{1}{2}$ min. For violin, cello, double bass, and piano. Stochastic, pointillistic. Enormous dynamic extremes; every note has a dynamic mark attached. Avant-garde. D.

Quartets for Piano(s), Strings, and Winds

Jurriaan Andriessen. *Suite de Noel* 1944 (Donemus). For flute, violin, viola, and piano. Easy to listen to, uncomplicated, breathes something of the spirit of the eighteenth-century divertimento. M-D.

Theodore Antoniou. *Quartetto Giocoso* Op.26 1965 (Br) 15 min. For oboe, violin, cello, and piano. Ten short movements of ironic character, each of which is a miniature caricature of a well-known form, to be played amusingly, exaggerating the form. Explores abstract relationships between motivic ideas and the movements of sounds, possible combinations of dialogue, several ways of playing the instruments, and problems of space. Some of the pieces are Introduzione; Notturno; Duettino; Ostinato; Perpetuo; Rondoletto; Tollatino; Terzino; Finale. M-D.

Carl Philipp Emanuel Bach. *Quartet* W.93 a 1788 (Schmid—Nag 222) 19pp., parts. For flute, viola, celno, and piano.
_____ *Quartet* W.94 D 1788 (Schmid—Nag 223) 19pp., parts. For flute, viola, cello, and piano. Allegretto: scales, dramatic figures, trills, alternation of hands. Sehr langsam und ausgehalten: more melodic, lovely harmonies. Allegro di molto: highly rhythmic, sixteenth-note figuration, driving conclusion. Represents a complete breakthrough to the Viennese classical style, Beethoven-like. The keyboard part has freed itself considerably from the thoroughbass principles and shows fuller and richer writing. Bach probably meant this work to be performed on the hammerklavier. M-D.
_____ *Quartet* W.95 G 1788 (Schmid—Nag 224) 20pp., parts. For flute, viola, cello, and piano. Allegretto: many trills, arpeggiation. Adagio: chordal and scalar passages, effective ending. Presto: motoric, driving sixteenths. M-D.
In all three quartets, a violin may substitute for the flute, and the cello part is ad lib.

Johann Christian Bach. *Quartet* C (Ruf—Heinrichshofen). For flute, violin, viola, and basso continuo.

———— *Quartet* Op.6/8 E♭ (W. Radeke, F. Nagel—Schott 5989) 21pp., parts. For flute, violin, viola, and basso continuo. Largo: chordal sonorities with some melodic interest. Allegro spirituo: rhythm emphasized, some development. M-D.

Johann Sebastian Bach. *Sonata à 3* (GS). For flute, violin, cello, and piano.
———— *Trio Sonata* ("Musical Offering") (H. Eppstein—Henle 1976 23pp., parts; Br&H). The Henle edition has an excellent preface and continues the superb standards of that publishing house. D.
———— *Trio Sonata* S.1039 (Seiffert—Br&H). For 2 flutes, cello, and piano.
———— *Trio Sonata* b (Hindermann—Br). For 2 oboes, cello, and basso continuo.

Leonardo Balada. *Cuatris for Four Instruments* (Gen 1970) 18pp., parts. 8½ min. For flute or violin, clarinet or viola, trombone or cello or bassoon with prepared piano or harpsichord. See detailed entry under quartets for piano and strings.

Jochen Beck. *Quartett* 1971 (Möseler) 19pp., parts. For flute, violin, cello, and piano.

Niels Viggo Bentzon. *Mosaique Musicale* Op.54 (WH 3912 1951) 27pp., parts. One large movement with three contrasting sections. The following influences are felt: jazz, popular music, Hindemith, Schönberg, and Bartók. Neobaroque style. Large span required. M-D.

Lennox Berkeley. *Concertino* Op.49 (JWC 1956) 33pp., parts. 11½ min. For recorder (or flute), violin, cello, and harpsichord (or piano). Aria I—Lento; Aria II—Andante; Vivace. Neoclassic style, especially apparent in outer movements. Aria I, for recorder and cello alone is built on a twelve-note chaconne theme accompanied by serial melodic variations, five statements. This movement fits nicely in a work that has close ties with the eighteenth century. Traditional pianistic treatment. D.

Sebastian Bodinus. *Sonata* E♭ (H. Fischer—Vieweg 1939) 11pp., parts. For 2 oboes or violins, bassoon or cello, and piano. Adagio; Allegro; Siciliana; Allegro assai. Attractive, good realization. M-D.

Charles Boone. *Quartet* 1970 (Sal) 15pp., parts. For piano, violin, cello, and clarinet. Performance instructions in French and English; numerous directions in the score. Uses harmonics, clusters, stopped strings. "The end of each phrase is indicated by its time in seconds. The time of each individual phrase is proportional to its linear disposition of the notes, but the time-space ratio is not necessarily the same in all phrases'' (from the score). Static sound blocks; extremes of instrumental timbre explored. Avantgarde. D.

Benjamin Britten. *Gemini Variations* Op.73 1965 (Faber F014) Twelve Variations and Fugue on an Epigram of Kodály. 37pp., parts. Quartet for 2 or 4 players. Written for twelve-year-old twins, each of whom played the piano; one also played the violin, the other the flute. May be performed by 2 players (flute–piano, violin–piano) or by 4 players (violin, flute, and piano duet). Contains performance directions. The theme is No.4 of *Epigrams* (1954) by Zoltán Kodály. Written for varied combinations: Theme (piano duet with ad lib. flute and violin); Var.I (piano solo); II (violin and piano); III (violin solo); IV (flute and violin); V (flute and violin); VI (flute and violin); VII (flute solo); VIII (flute and piano); IX (piano solo); X (piano duet with ad lib. flute and violin); XI (piano duet); XII (piano solo); Fugue (flute, violin, and piano duet, with ad lib. flute and violin). M-D.

Willy Burkhard. *Lyrische Musik* Op.88, in memoriam Georg Trakl (Br 2495) 23pp., parts. For flute, viola, cello, and piano. Poco lento; Allegro agitato; Lento; Allegro moderato; Allegro agitato. Highly linear and contrapuntal writing, neobaroque style. Large span required. M-D.

René de Castéra. *Concert* 1922 (Rouart Lerolle) 51pp., parts. For piano, cello, flute, and clarinet. Paysage; Intermède—Lent et Grave; Rondeau Varié. Folksong flavor noted in themes. Flexible style, fresh sounds for the time when they were written, tonal, mildly Impressionistic. M-D.

George Crumb. *Eleven Echoes of Autumn* (CFP 1965) 11pp., parts. 16 min. For violin, alto flute, clarinet, and piano. Pieces to be performed without interruption: Eco 1. Fantastico (for piano alone). Eco 2. Languidamente, quasi lontano (''hauntingly''). Eco 3. Prestissimo. Eco 4. Con bravura. Eco 5. Cadenza I (for alto flute). Eco 6. Cadenza II (for violin). Eco 7. Cadenza III (for clarinet). Eco 8. Feroce, violento. Eco 9. Serenamenti, quasi lontano (''hauntingly''). Eco 10. Senza misura (''gently undulating''). Eco 11. Adagio (''like a prayer''). Each of the echi exploits certain timbral possibilities of the instruments. A ''bell-motif'' generates much of the music played on the piano as fifth-partial harmonics. Descending whole-tone interval is important. Substantial musical material produces sonic effects and a ghostly atmosphere; improvisatory quality. D.

Carl Czerny. *Grande Sérénade Concertante* Op.126 E♭ (Musica Rara) 55pp., parts. For clarinet, horn, cello, and piano. Plenty of tricky turns in the elaborate piano part illuminate this extensive and delightful work. D.

Martin Dalby. *Commedia* (Nov) 13 min. For clarinet, violin, cello, and piano.

Robert Di Domenica. *Quartet for Flute, Violin, Horn and Piano* 1959 (Margun Music).

Emma Lou Diemer. *Movement for Flute, Oboe, Clarinet and Piano* 1976 (Seesaw) 26pp., parts. 10 min. Serial influence, patterns are to be repeated varying the number of times and the order in which groups of notes are played; some sections are not to be synchronized. Varied sections, moods, and tempi. Glissandi on strings with finger and rubber eraser, harmonics, tremolo. Well constructed, avant-garde. D.

Gottfried von Einem. *Reifliches Divertimento* Op.35a (Bo&H 1974) 8pp., parts. For violin, viola, horn, and piano. Two short variations on a theme from Act III of Von Einem's opera *Der Besuch der alten Dame* (The Visit of the Old Woman). Transparent and contrapuntal textures. M-D.

Johann Friedrich Fasch. *Sonata* B♭ (W. Woehl—HM 26) 15pp., parts. For recorder, oboe, cello, and basso continuo. Largo; Allegro; Grave; Allegro. Efficient continuo realization. M-D.
_____ *Sonata* D (R. Gerlash—HM 207) 20pp., parts. For flute, violin, bassoon, and basso continuo. Largo; Allegro; Largo; Allegro. Continuo realization is adequate and is only an editorial suggestion. M-D.
_____ *Sonata à 4* (H. Töttcher, C. Spannagel—Sikorski 241) 11pp., parts. For violin, oboe, horn, and basso continuo. Andante; Allegro; Andante; Allegro. M-D.
Fasch's music shows the flowing and amiable handwriting of the Telemann School.

Morton Feldman. *Durations I* 1960 (CFP 6901) 5pp., For violin, cello, alto flute, and piano. Sonorities are the most important; technique is secondary. The duration of each sound is chosen by the performers. Numbers between sounds indicate silent beats. Low dynamics. Avant-garde. M-D.

Godfrey Finger. *Sonata* C (R.L. Minter—Musica Rara 1974) 18pp., parts. For trumpet, violin, oboe, and continuo. Fluent but traditional handling of the then-popular Italian idiom. M–D.

Ross Lee Finney. *Divertissement* 1964 (Bowdoin College Music Press) 70pp., parts. 25 min. For clarinet, violin, cello, and piano. Facsimile of composer's MS. Avant-garde techniques used for musical purposes. Allegro energico: much activity; pianist hits strings with flat of hand, plucks strings with hand or plectrum; dampens string with fingers. Adagio misterioso: sonority-oriented for piano; dynamic extremes; pianist produces rasp along string wiring with plectrum. Allegro giocoso: pianist scrapes wire of string with hard object, produces harmonics by touching string while striking key, and uses snare drum stick to pluck string (ad lib.); pedal effects. Cadenzas: pianist may improvise discreetly using only sounds that can be produced inside the piano while the other instruments improvise freely following durations and contours suggested; (the object is to achieve a virtuosity and rhythm that notation might inhibit, and to have fun!); Adagio misterioso returns and concludes with pianist playing a cadenza of harmonics only. Allegro energico: has much of the activity and excitement of opening movement. D.

Tommaso Giordani. *Quartet* Op.3/1 G ca. 1775 (S. Sadie—Musica Rara 1966) 15pp., parts. For flute, violin, cello, and piano. Allegro; Rondo–Allegro. The piano's role is partly continuo and partly obbligato. This early example of a piano quartet contains some charming classical style figurations and rhythms. Tommaso was the son of Giuseppe Giordani. M-D.

Arsenio Giron. *Quartet* 1963 (CF) 45pp., parts. For flute, clarinet, viola, and piano. Facsimile edition. Allegro; Largo; Presto. Serial, pointillistic, sudden dynamic changes, clusters, last two movements attacca. D.

David Gow. *Quartet* Op.28 1967 (Musica Rara) 38pp., parts. 13 min. For flute, oboe, cello, and piano or harpsichord. A one-movement work with varied tempi and changing meters, tremolo chords, rushing arpeggi gestures, broken chromatic chords, arpeggiated chords, alternating hands. Piano is used more for color and for its unifying capacity than melodically. Freely tonal. M-D to D.

Johann Gottlieb Graun. *Concerto* F (Schroeder—Moeck). For flute, 2 violins, and basso continuo. Expressive lines dotted with rests suggest more gallant style than Corelli sustained style. Some contrapuntal treatment. M-D.

Ray Green. *Holiday for Four* (AME 1949) 40pp., parts. 14 min. For viola (includes an alternate clarinet part in place of viola), clarinet, bassoon, and piano. Includes other suggested instrumentation. Fugal Introduction; Prairie Blues; Festive Finale. Contrasting movements, mildly contemporary, many seventh chords, effective suite. Blues and folksong elements permeate the second movement. M-D.

Jean Guillou. *Colloques No. I* (Leduc 1966) 17pp., parts. 13 min. For flute, oboe, violin, and piano. A one-movement, sectioned work. Lento: dotted rhythms in piano, harmonic sevenths and ninths. Allegro: quick chromatic figurations in all instruments. Lento: character like that of opening movement; piano part ostinato-like. Allegro: rhythmic drive. Lento: ideas from both earlier Lentos. Moderato e misterioso: staccato right hand, *pp* line over sustained low chordal sonorities in left hand. M-D.

Jacques Guyonnet. *Polyphonie III* 1964 (UE 13550) 23pp., parts. For 2 pianos, flute, and viola. Explanations in French, German, and English, including placement of the instruments. Highly organized (pitch, dynamics, etc.), harmonics, expressionistic, percussive treatment of the pianos, dynamic extremes, shifting meters, pointillistic, avant-garde. D.

George Frederick Handel. *Concerto I* d (Zobeley—Schott). For flute, violin, cello, and basso continuo.
_____ *8 Psalmouverturen* (H. Monkemeyer—Pelikan 748–9) 2 vols. For oboe (soprano or tenor recorder, or violin), 2 violins, and basso continuo. Contains the overtures to Nos.1–5, 7, 10, and 11 of the *Chandos Anthems*. M-D.
_____ *Kammertrio* No.19 G (Br&H). For 2 flutes, cello, and piano.
_____ *Kammer Trios* II d, IV F, VI D. For 2 oboes, bassoon (cello), and piano. See detailed entry under quartets for piano and three woodwinds.

Charles Haubiel. *In Praise of Dance* (H. Elkan). For oboe, violin, cello, and piano.
_____ *Masks* (Seesaw). For oboe, violin, cello, and piano.
_____ *Partita* (Seesaw). For oboe, violin, cello, and piano.

Franz Joseph Haydn. *Quartet* Op.5/4 G 1770 (W. Upmeyer—Nag 129) 12pp., parts. For flute, violin, viola, and piano; cello ad lib. Vivace; Andante moderato; Menuetto; Fantasia with 5 Variations. A little-known but charming and accessible work. M-D.

Johann David Heinichen. *Concerto* G (H. Fischer—Vieweg 1938) 11pp., parts. For flute, 2 violins, and basso continuo. Vivace; Allegro; Largo; Allegro. M-D.
_____ *Concerto* G (K. Janetzky—Hofmeister 1972) 16pp., parts. For flute (oboe), cello (bassoon), cello, and basso continuo. Andante; Vivace; Adagio; Allegro. This keyboard realization is more interesting than the Fischer realization listed above. M-D.

John Heiss. *Quartet* 1971 (Bowdoin College Music Press) 10pp., parts. 7 min. For flute, clarinet, cello, and piano. Combines nonstandard and standard notation, pointillistic, numerous dynamic marks, proportional rhythmic relationships, changing meters, many performance directions, varied tempi, expressionistic and avant-garde. D.

Paul Hindemith. *Quartet* 1938 (Schott) 49pp., parts. For clarinet, violin, cello, and piano. Mässig bewegt: SA; freely tonal around F; piano leads out with main theme; lyric second subject follows in all instruments; dynamic climax marks the beginning of the recapitulation. Sehr langsam: ABA; leisurely flowing melody, accompanied by subdued harmonies; dramatic turbulent mid-section rises to a *ff* climax, then a calm transition passage brings back the opening material. Mässig bewegt: three sections, each with different tempo markings, and a coda; first section is moderately paced; followed by a fast, brilliant, dancelike part interlaced with complex rhythms and counterpoint; tempo relaxes while piano has staccato figurations in the upper register; barbaric rhythmic figure in the piano introduces the coda, which moves to a swift conclusion. D.

Alan Hovhaness. *Quartet II* Op.112 (CFP 6436). For flute, oboe, cello, and piano.

Ilja Hurnik. *Sonata da Camera* 1952 (Artia). For flute, oboe, cello, and piano. Neoclassic style combined with baroque forms and Czech folk music. M-D.

Johann Gottlieb Janitsch. *Sonata da Camera* Op.4 C (D. Lasocki— Musica Rara 23pp., parts 1970; B&VP). For flute, oboe, violin, and basso continuo. Andante e molto; Allegro; Allegro assai. Both editions are excellent. M-D.
——— *Chamber Sonata* Op.8 "Echo" (Wolff—Br&H). For flute, oboe (or violin or flute), viola, and keyboard. Fine counterpoint and unusual harmonies. M-D.
——— *Quadro "O Haupt voll Blut und Wunden"* (K. Hofmann— Hänssler 1973) 26pp., parts. 2 pages of notes. For oboe, violin, viola, and basso continuo. Largo; Allegretto; Adagio; Vivace. A chorale melody in the oboe is used as a cantus firmus in third movement while other instruments are involved in separate dialogue. Editorial additions are identified. M-D.
——— *Quartet* c (Winschermann—Sikorski 617). For oboe, violin, viola, and basso continuo. M-D.
The influence of C. H. Graun is seen in all these works.

Heinrich Kaminski. *Quartet* Op.1B 1912 (UE 8333) 39pp., parts. For clarinet, violin, cello, and piano. Frisch; Ruthenisches Volkslied (4 variations on a charming folksong); Scherzo (Var.5); Finale (Var.6). Neobaroque style, polyphonically oriented, a few tangled spots. M-D.

Wilhelm Kempff. *Quartet* Op.15 (Simrock 1925) 74pp., parts. For piano, flute, violin, and cello. Andante–Allegro; Adagio con melancolia, semplice (based on an old Swedish folksong); Menuett; Introduzione e Finale. Smooth writing, technically facile, broad pianistic gestures. M-D to D.

Peter Jona Korn. *Fantasy* Op.28 1955 (Simrock—through Bo&H in U.S.). For horn, piano, violin, and cello.

Ernst Křenek. *Hausmusik* (Br 1959) Seven Pieces for the Seven Days of the Week. 13pp., parts. For piano, violin, guitar, and blockflute. 1. Moderato: for piano, four-hands. 2. Allegretto: for blockflute and guitar. 3. Andantino: for 2 blockflutes and a third instrument. 4. Allegro: for violin and guitar. 5. Animato: for blockflute and violin. 6. Andante con passione: for violin and piano. 7. Allegretto: for piano, alto blockflute and guitar. Minor problems for each instrument, logically worked out, intellectually satisfying. Int. to M-D.

Meyer Kupferman. *Infinities Thirteen* (Bowdoin College Music Press 1965) 54pp., parts. A quartet for 8 instruments: flute–piccolo–alto flute, clarinet–bass clarinet, violin–viola, and piano. Part of a "Cycle of Infinities," all based on the same twelve-tone row. Pointillistic, percussive use of piano, splashing dramatic gestures, flexible meters, complex ensemble problems. Requires four virtuoso performers. D.

Noël Lee. *L'Ami, L'Adoré* (Anecdotes) (MS available from composer: 4 Villa Laugier, 75017 Paris, France) 15pp., parts. For horn, violin, cello, and piano. Allegretto con grazia; Largo. Neoclassic orientation, thin textures. Gallic wit and humor comes through; extreme ranges of keyboard exploited; ostinato-like figures. Large span required. M-D.

Gerhard Maasz. *Concertino* (Br 3331 1960) 23pp., parts. For piano, flute, violin, and cello. Fantasia: quartal harmony, freely tonal, arpeggi figuration. Allegro: light staccato in right hand over sustained single note in left hand; second half more chordal. Andante: peaceful and flowing. Rondo: thin textures; octotonic; cadenzas for flute, violin, piano; contemporary Alberti-bass treatment. Neoclassic. M-D.

Bohuslav Martinů. *Quartet* 1947 (ESC 1961) 12 min. For oboe, violin, cello, and piano. Rhythmic energy is in abundance. Wide harmonic range with simple progressions and harsh dissonances. D.

Toshiro Mayuzumi. *Metamusic* (CFP 6357). For piano, violin, saxophone,

and conductor. See detailed entry under trios for piano, one stringed instrument, and one wind instrument.

Olivier Messiaen. *Quatuor pour la fin du temps* 1941 (Durand) iv + 52pp.,
parts. For violin, clarinet, cello, and piano. Contains a condensed quotation
from verses 1–6 of the book of Revelation, which was the inspiration for
this piece. Study score, which includes an outline of the religious "pro-
gramme of the work," is also available. 1. Liturgie de cristal: piano has an
ostinato progression of 29 chords, repeated five times, while clarinet and
violin have florid figurations. 2. Vocalise, pour l'Ange qui annonce la fin
du Temps: ABA; B section has the "impalpable harmonies of the heavens"
with a plainsong-like melody, accompanied by *pp* cascades of chords that
represent drops of water in a rainbow. 3. Abîme des Oiseaux: ABA for solo
clarinet. 4. Intermède: a scherzo, piano tacet. 5. Louange à l'Éternité de
Jésus: piano and cello alone; calm, sweet chords of the piano accompany a
ternary melody for the cello. 6. Danse de la fureur, pour les sept trompetts:
all four instruments in unison; involved formal and metrical construction;
gongs and trumpets are suggested. 7. Fouillis d'arcs-en-ciel, pour l'Ange
qui annonce la fin du Temps: thematic references to first, second, and sixth
movements; involved archlike form. 8. Louange à l'Immortalité de Jésus:
piano and violin alone; related to fifth movement; a two-part movement in
two stanzas that begin identically and change directions halfway through;
piano accompanies the violin's "expressif, paradisiaque" melody; sweet,
succulent chords. Written while Messiaen was a prisoner of war; one of his
most striking and beautiful works. Displays a wide range of instrumental
textures and variety. D.
See: David Stephen Bernstein, "Messiaen's Quatuor pour la fin du temps: an
analysis based upon Messiaen's theory of rhythm and his use of modes of
limited transposition," Ph.D. diss., Indiana University, 1974, 133pp. Contains an analysis of each movement.

Otto Mortensen. *Quatuor Concertant* (WH 3850a). For piano, flute, violin,
and cello.

Ignaz Moscheles. *Fantasy, Variations and Finale* Op.46 (Musica Rara). For
violin, clarinet, cello, and piano. Much decorative figuration, frequent
empty gestures. M-D to D.

Johann Gottlieb Naumann. *Quartet* Op.1/5 E♭ (P. Bormann—Sikorski 275)
15pp., parts. For piano, flute, violin, and cello. Andante: flowing style.
Grazioso; should have a dancing swing to it. Idiomatic keyboard writing in
a conservative style. There is charm, a certain delicacy in the rhythmic

treatment, and some originality in the piece that reminds one of Johann Christian Bach's works. M-D.

Stephen Oliver. *Ricercare* (Nov 1973). For piano, clarinet, violin, cello. See: Jane Glover, "Stephen Oliver," MT, December 1974; 1042ff.

Vittorio Rieti. *Sonata* 1924 (UE). For flute, oboe, bassoon, and piano. Lean textures; dance influence felt with much rhythmic motion. Key changes and frequent modulations are present along with strong lyrical lines. M-D.

George Rochberg. *Contra mortem et tempus* 1965 (TP) 39pp., 4 copies needed for performance. For flute, clarinet, violin, and piano. Uses open-score notation; basically unmeasured; permits maximum flexibility of performance. Notes to the performers explains other notation signs. Gradual changes of speed, harmonics on piano, arm clusters, long pedals, pointillistic. The performer with the best deep voice should sing–speak "con-tra mor-tem et tem-pus" at the very end. "Rochberg's most recent compositions incorporate Ivesian simultaneities of original and preexisting materials. The beautifully textured 'Contra mortem et tempus' juxtaposes snatches from Boulez, Berio, Varèse, and Ives as well as Rochberg's own somewhat Bergian 'Dialogues' for clarinet and piano (1958)" (Alexander L. Ringer, DCM, p.629). Avant-garde. D.

Antonio Salieri. *Triple Concerto* D (Wojciechowski—Sikorski). For oboe, violin, cello, and piano.

Giovanni Battista Sammartini. *Sonata* D (Noetzel). For flute, 2 violins, and piano; cello ad lib.

Alessandro Scarlatti. *Quartet* F (W. Woehl—CFP 4558) 10pp., parts. For recorder, 2 violins, and piano; cello ad lib. Untitled first movement; Allegro; Grave; Allegro. Basso continuo realization is somewhat bland and could be reworked. M-D.

Hans Ludwig Schilling. *Concerto Piccolo* 1964 (Br&H 6468) 37pp., parts. 14 min. For flute, English horn, viola, and piano. Proposta—sehr schnell; Ruhig (piano tacet); Rondo—lebhaft bewegt. Neoclassic, colorful chromaticism, freely tonal. Large span required. D.

Johann Heinrich Schmelzer. *Sonata a 3* (Musica Rara 1974). 12pp., parts. For violin, trombone, bassoon, and basso continuo.

Florent Schmitt. *Pour presque tous les temps (2/4 3/4 3/2 6/8 5/4)* Op.134

(Durand 1956) 25pp., parts. 10 min. For piano, violin, flute, and cello. Alerte; Au clair de la R-IV; Lent mais non languide; Vif. Sonorities and rhythms of intrinsic beauty, straightforward idiom, effusive lyricism, Impressionistic influence. Requires large span. M-D to D.

Elliott Schwartz. *Soliloquies* 1965 (Bowdoin College Music Press) 26pp., 4 copies required. 9 min. For flute, clarinet, violin, and piano. Two untitled pieces. Four notes must be prepared on the piano by inserting objects (a metal screw or nail, a dime, some tightly wadded paper, bits of wood, rubber jar-lid liner, etc.), which should create a separate different sound. Requires a soft timpani stick for pianist to strike low strings. At times the piano itself is struck with the palm, not knuckles or fist, on described areas. Sonority-oriented with some unusual musical results. Sections marked "Free" indicate times when players are asked not to synchronize their parts with one another. Avant-garde. D.

Kazimierz Serocki. *Swinging Music* (Moeck 1970) 4 min. For clarinet, bassoon, cello or double bass, and piano. Strong rhythmic feel, nondoctrinaire use of compositional techniques, fluctuating dynamics. Some graphic notation allows a certain amount of interpretive freedom. M-D.

Akio Shiraishi. *Anagram* (Ongaku No Tomo Sha 1966) 18pp., parts. For clarinet, violin, cello, and piano. Four untitled pieces. Serial, pointillistic, dynamic extremes, tremolo, atonal. D.

Yngve Sköld. *Kvartett* (Eriks Musikhandel). For 2 flutes, cello, and piano.

Robert Starer. *Concertino* 1948 (Israeli Music Publications) 27pp., parts. For 2 voices or 2 instruments (oboe or trumpet, bassoon or trombone), violin, and piano. The two "voice" parts may be sung or they may be played by the suggested instruments. It is also possible to have one part sung and the other played. The concertante element dominates the entire work. The first movement (Cantamus) praises the joy of singing, the second is a tender lament, and the third a jubilant Allelujah. Mildly contemporary with Judiac flavor. Octonic. Large span required. M-D.

William Sydeman. *Quartet* 1963 (Okra) 15 min. For flute, clarinet, violin, and piano.
———— *Quartet* (Seesaw). For clarinet, violin, cello, and piano.

Georg Philipp Telemann. *Concerto a 4* (Veyron-Lacroix—IMC). For flute, oboe, violin, and piano.
———— *Concerto* B♭ (EMT). For 2 flutes, cello, and piano.

_____ *Concerto* D (Richter—Schott). For flute, violin, cello, and piano.

_____ *Parisian Quartet I Concerto Primo* G (W. Bergmann—Br 1967) 34pp., parts. For flute, violin, viola da gamba or cello, and basso continuo. Grave; Allegro; Largo; Presto; Largo; Allegro. Written for four virtuosi in Paris with Telemann at the keyboard. Two different sets of figured bass, both Telemann's, from 1730 and 1736, present much contrast. One of Telemann's best pieces of chamber music. M-D.

_____ *Quartet* b 1733 (E. Dohrn—Nag 24) 27pp., parts. For flute, violin, cello, and basso continuo. From "Nouveaux Quatuors en Six Suites," Paris. Prélude (with a B section "Flatteusement"); Coulant; Gay; Vite; Triste; Menuett. M-D.

_____ *Quartet* b (Nag). For flute, violin, cello, and piano; second cello ad lib.

_____ *Quartett* d (Tafelmusik 1733 II, No.2) (Seiffert—Br&H 1910) 19pp., parts. For recorder (bassoon or cello), 2 flutes, and basso continuo; cello ad lib. Andante; Vivace; Largo; Allegro (with a cantabile mid-section). Effective, if slightly over-edited. M-D.

_____ *Quartet* D (Zimmermann). For flute, violin, cello, and piano.

_____ *Quartet* e 1733 (E. Dohrn—Nag 10) 23pp., parts. For flute, violin, cello, and basso continuo. No. 6 from "Nouveaux Quatuors en Six Suites," Paris. Prélude; Gay; Vite; Gracieusement; Distrait; Modéré. A highly interesting work. M-D.

_____ *Quartet* e (Seiffert—Br&H). For violin, flute, cello, and keyboard.

_____ *Quartet* G (H. Tsöttcher, K. Grebe—Sikorski 473) 24pp., parts. For flute, oboe, violin, and basso continuo. Part I, No.2 of Telemann's *Tafelmusik*, 1733. Largo; Allegro; Largo (with a Moderato section); Grave; Vivace. M-D.

_____Quartet G (Hinnenthal—Br 3534). For oboe or violin, violin, cello, and basso continuo.

Other works in these combinations are available from CFP; IMC; Foetisch.

Douglas Townsend. *8 X 8 Variations on a Theme of Milhaud* Op.3/1 (CFP 6094 1957) 7pp., parts. For soprano recorder or flute or piccolo, trumpet or clarinet or oboe, cello or bassoon, and piano. An alternate oboe part in C is provided. From the film *8 X 8* by Hans Richter. Theme, four contrasting variations and coda. Piano has a two-line Interlude between variations 3 and 4. Mildly contemporary, attractive. M-D.

Ben Weber. *Variations* Op.11a 1941 (ACA) 16pp., parts. 5 min. For violin, clarinet, cello, and piano. Basically this theme and the seven contrasting variations are conceived in a contrapuntal twelve-tone idiom with strong tonal implications. Declarative gestures and corky rhythms give an air of witty exuberance. Requires a large span. D.

———— *Serenade* Op.39 1954 (ACA) 19pp., parts. 9 min. For flute, violin, cello, and piano or harpsichord. Alla marcia; Andante espressivo; Adagio teneramente; Moderato Allegro poco maestoso. Atonal and intense but not too harmonically complex. "Mr. Weber's *Serenade* is a hale and jolly four-movement piece . . . the work is neither agonizingly atonal nor harmonically complex. When it is not being playful, moreover, a highly selective romantic impulse chisels its lyric lines into a state of intensity that is always natural, never labored. In sum, the work is a fine one; it has gumption and it has charm. And it makes a lovely sound" (Jay S. Harrison, *New York Herald Tribune*, January 27, 1954). D.

Anton Webern. *Quartet* Op.22 1930 (UE 10050) 13pp., parts. 5 min. For tenor saxophone, clarinet, violin, and piano. Sehr mässig: motivic development by themes branching out, intertwining, moving forward and backward; canonic narrative in pointillistic application. Sehr schwungvoll: extreme, sparse texture that is characteristic of all Webern's later works; pointillistic; sense of wider-spread sonorities; more settled than first movement but still represents a rarefied style. Carefully mixed instrumental colors. Canonic technique throughout. D.

Zbigniew Wiszniewski. *Quartet* 1972 (AA 1974) 21pp., 4 copies necessary for performance. For piano, flute, horn, and double bass. Explanations in Polish and English.

Quartets for Piano and Three Woodwinds

Leonardo Balada. *Cuatris for Four Instruments* (Gen 1970) 18pp., parts. $8\frac{1}{2}$ min. For flute or violin, clarinet or viola, trombone or cello or bassoon with prepared piano or harpsichord. See detailed entry under quartets for piano and strings.

George Barati. *Quartet* (CFP). For flute, clarinet, bassoon, and piano.

Sebastian Bodinus. *Sonata* E♭ (H. Fischer—Vieweg 1939) 11pp., parts. For 2 oboes or violins, bassoon or cello, and piano. Adagio; Allegro; Siciliana; Allegro assai. Attractive, good realization. M-D.

Frank Campo. *Concertino* 1965 (WIM). For 3 clarinets (E♭, B♭, and bass) and piano. This work pits two instrumental groups against one another in a manner similar to that of the concerto grosso. The clarinets provide a strong color contrast for the piano. The work is in three motivically related movements performed without pause. The first movement is a Rondo in which both the rondo theme and the contrasting musical idea return each time in altered fashion (A–B–A^1–B^1–A^2). A brief rhapsodic interlude for solo piano leads to the Tarantella finale, which utilizes various types of fugal imitation while maintaining the robust spirit of this southern Italian dance. M-D.

Jean Marie Depelsenaire. *Concertino* (Philippo—Combre 1972) 12pp., parts. For 3 clarinets and piano. Andantino; Larghetto; Andante–Allegretto. Octotonic, tonal with some chromaticism. Second movement is for the clarinets alone. Thin textures. M-D.

Peggy Glanville-Hicks. *Concertino da Camera* 1946 (L'OL) 24pp., parts. For flute, clarinet, bassoon, and piano. Allegretto; Adagio; Finale. Neoclassic, freely tonal, toccata-like rhythm in finale, mildly contemporary. Large span required. M-D.

Roger Goeb. *Concertant* IB (CFE). For flute, oboe, clarinet, and piano.

Ray Green. *Holiday for Four* (AME 1949) 40pp., parts. 14 min. For viola (or clarinet), clarinet, bassoon, and piano. See detailed entry under quartets for piano(s), strings, and winds.

George Frederick Handel. *Kammer Trio* I B♭ (Seiffert—Br&H). For 2 oboes, bassoon, and piano. M-D.
_____ *Kammer Trio* II d (Seiffert—Br&H 1912). For 2 oboes, bassoon (cello), and piano. Adagio; Allegro; Affettuoso; Allegro. M-D.
_____ *Kammer Trio* IV F (Seiffert—Br&H 1914) 15pp., parts. For 2 oboes, bassoon (cello), and piano. Adagio; Allegro; Largo; Allegro. M-D.
_____ *Kammer Trio* VI D (Seiffert—Br&H) 17pp., parts. For 2 oboes, bassoon (cello), and piano. M-D.
_____ *Kammer Trio* VIII g (Seiffert—Br&H). For 2 oboes, bassoon, and piano; cello ad lib.
_____ *Kammer Trio* XIV g (Seiffert—Br&H). For 2 flutes, bassoon, and piano; cello ad lib.
The Seiffert realizations are somewhat thick but are always usable. There are 22 Chamber Trios in this series.

Vagn Holmboe. *Quartetto Medico* Op.70 (JWC 4069A 1962) 18pp., parts. 11 min. For flute, oboe, clarinet, and piano. Andante medicamento: bitonal implications, alternating hands, parallelism, octotonic, freely tonal, clean-edged lines. Allegro quasi febrilo: seventh chords, syncopation, chromatic scalar passages, patterns. Intermedico I (Andante senza pianisticitis): without piano. Intermedico II (sans marais): for solo piano; alternating hands, patterns similar to those in first movement, nontonal harmony, subtle, dancelike rhythms. Allegro con frangula: alternating hands with broken patterns in right hand, tremolo, nervous vitality, thin textures, sixteenth-note patterns and scales, clever ending. Radiant woodwind writing throughout; luminous piano writing. Finely worked out piece, neoclassic style. M-D.

Arthur Honegger. *Rhapsody* 1917 (Sal 1923) 13pp., parts. For 2 flutes, clarinet, and piano, or for 2 violins, viola, and piano. Larghetto–Allegro–Larghetto. An early work with strong Impressionistic tendencies in the outer sections. Tripartite structure, with the mid-section a rhythmic march. Rhapsodic more in the sense of sonorities than of form. Quartal harmonies, parallel seventh chords, octotonic, broken octaves. M-D.

Darius Milhaud. *Sonate* 1918 (Durand) 36pp., parts. For flute, oboe, clarinet, and piano. Tranquille: ABA, abstruse piano writing, pastoral. Joyeux: chordal, broken chords, widespread sonorities provide striking polytonal mixtures. Emporté: emphatic rhythmic treatment, free tonal exploitation, *ffff* climax. Douloureux: langorous; funereal; expressive; *pppp* closing; final C major tonic is meaningful. M-D to D.

Marcel Quinet. *Concertino* 1960 (CeBeDeM) 33pp., parts. 11 min. For oboe, clarinet, bassoon, and piano. Allegro giocoso; Sostenuto; Vivace. Seventh chords, chromatic, repeated open fifths and seconds in Vivace movement, neoclassic in structure, freely tonal. Requires large span. M-D to D.

Georg Philipp Telemann. *Quartett* d (Tafelmusik 1733 II, No.2) (Seiffert—Br&H 1910) 19pp., parts. For recorder (bassoon or cello), 2 flutes, and basso continuo; cello ad lib. Andante; Vivace; Largo; Allegro (with a cantabile mid-section). Effective, if slightly over-edited. M-D.
_____ *Quartett* d (Hinnenthal—Br&H). For 2 flutes, bassoon, and basso continuo; cello ad lib.

Antonio Vivaldi. *Sonata* g (G.F. Ghedini—IMC 1240) 19pp., parts. For flute (violin I), oboe (violin II). bassoon (cello), and piano. Allegro ma cantabile; Largo; Allegro molto. Unencumbered realizations. M-D

Quartets for Piano, Woodwind(s), and Brass and for Piano and Brass

Franz Berwald. *Klavierquartett und Klavierquintette* (Br 4913 1973) 233pp., parts. Vol.13 of the Complete Edition, edited by Ingmar Bengtsson and Bonnie Hammar. Includes *Quartet* for piano, woodwinds (clarinet, bassoon) and horn, Op.1 E♭. The *Quartet* is available separately (Br 43pp., parts; GM). Introduzione—Adagio, Allegro ma non troppo; Adagio; Finale. The piano part contains some moments of highly original and poetic writing, although Mendelssohn's influence looms large. The piano takes the lead through most of this work. Berwald replied to a critic, following the first performance of this work: "I had anticipated the rather unfavourable impression these works would make, written as they are in an altogether individual style," this in particular since they are "experiments, based upon a rather unusual system, a new treatment of the instrumentation and its employment" (from the preface of the Br edition, which is an urtext edition with all editorial additions identified). M-D.

Charles Ives. *Scherzo—All the Way Around and Back.* See detailed entry under quintets for piano(s), percussion and/or tape, and other instruments.

Meyer Kupferman. *Curtain Raiser* (Gen). For flute, clarinet, horn, and piano. In preparation (1976).

Daniel Manneke. *Diaphony for Geoffrey* (Donemus 1973). For trumpet, horn, trombone, and piano.

Nikos Skalkottas. *Quartet* (UE). For oboe, bassoon, trumpet, and piano.

Robert Starer. *Concerta a Tre* 1954 (MCA 1966) 48pp., parts. 18 min. For clarinet, trumpet, trombone, and piano. Originally for clarinet, trumpet, trombone, and strings; reduction by the composer. Allegro: has elements of the concerto grosso in the juxtaposition of the winds against the piano.

Andante: lyrical, treats the instruments more in their individual capacities. Finale: each instrument has its own thematic material derived from its own particular quality in sound and technique; in a cadenza-like section called Trialogue, they enter into purposeful conversation with each other. M-D.

Quartets for Piano(s), Percussion, and Other Instruments

David Amram. *Discussion* (CFP 1965) 20pp., parts. 10 min. For flute, cello, piano, and percussion. Theme and four variations. Jazz elements breathe naturally in this piece, which combines a strong lyric quality with genuine excitement and dissonant counterpoint. D.

Gilbert Amy. *Inventions* (2) (Heugel PH261 1965) 39pp., parts. $15\frac{1}{2}$ min. For flute, piano/celesta, harp, and vibraphone/marimba. Directions in French and English. Serial, pointillistic, dynamic extremes, changing meters, improvisation required, traditional plus graphic notation, mobile form. Avant-garde. D.

Béla Bartók. *Sonata for Two Pianos and Percussion* 1937 (Bo&H). 2 (or 3) players required for the percussion ensemble: 3 timpani, xylophone, 2 side drums, bass drum, cymbals, suspended cymbal, triangle, tam tam. Assai lento–Allegro molto: contains the most complexities. Lento ma non troppo: great color in this "night music" movement. Allegro non troppo: a lively dance movement that disappears in a C tonality. Traditional designs are used in the three movements (SA, ABA, and rondo) but they are given new dimensions and perspectives by the varied colorful instrumentation. Percussive qualities of all instruments emphasized. The timpani and the xylophone have important thematic parts while the other percussion provide colorful and somewhat heavy sonorities plus rhythmic emphasis. Thematic unification is not an aim of this work. Ensemble difficulties. D.

Luciano Berio. *Linea* (UE). For 2 pianos, vibraphone, and marimba. Opens slowly, soft with slipping overlaps, decorative. The title refers to the music's concern with lines and not to the struggle-game of Linus and Apollo in Xenakis's piece of the same name. M-D to D.

Antonio Gino Bibalo. *Autumnale* (Autumn Music) Suite de concert pour 4 instruments 1968 (WH 4261 1974) 36pp., parts. 20 min. For flute, piano, vibraphone, and double bass. 1. Musique nocturne (Prélude): three short sections; a short transition leads to the actual night music and a coda; bitonal; through-composed; piano opens with sustained arpeggi chords, virtuoso effects for piano; a little serenade is presented reminiscent of the night music movements in Bartók's string quartets Nos.4 and 5. 2. Pas de quatre (pour insects): scherzo, ABA, dancelike, bitonal, ostinato-like treatment in the piano's lower register, amusing, clever writing. 3. Melancolique (élégie): ABA; double bass has melody; pointillistically shaped transition; introductory material returns distributed between the double bass, flute, and vibraphone; coda. Dans les plateaux verts du Congo (On the Green Congo Meadows) (Invention): ABA; opening flute solo is a Congolese folk tune; Invention here is used in the sense of contrivance, not in the Bach context; A-sections are treated like passacaglias; figurations derive from folksongs; double canon in B-section between double bass and bass of piano part; piano is treated percussively. 5. Introduction et toccata (Etude–Finale): a brilliant "tour de force" in which all instruments are displayed in relation to each other; piano concludes movement with an octave chromatic cadenza. Well-written and highly interesting music. D.

Boris Blacher. *Two Poems for Jazz Quartet* 1957 (Bo&Bo) 11pp., parts. For vibraphone, double bass, drums, and piano. First Poem uses piano in chordal syncopation. Second Poem uses it more melodically with some chordal syncopation. Delightful sonorities. M-D.

Philippe Boesmans. *Sur Mi* (Jobert 1974) 7 leaves., 13 min. For 2 pianos, electronic organ, and percussion. Explanations in French. 4 copies necessary for performance. Percussion required: cymbals, tam tam. Spatial and traditional notation, complex chords and rhythmic problems, pointillistic, dense textures, dynamic extremes. Contains almost insurmountable ensemble problems; only for the best equipped avant-garde performers. D.

William Bolcom. *Session 3* (Merion 1975) 27pp., parts. For E♭ clarinet, violin, piano, and percussion.

Claude Bolling. *Sonata for Two Pianos, Percussion and Double Bass* (Les Editions Bleu Blanc Rouge 1973) parts. Piano I (classic) 30pp. Piano II (jazz) 34pp. Percussion required: cymbal, hi-hat, snare drums, small tom tom, big tom tom, bass drums. This sonata "has been composed to allow two pianists of different styles to play together. It is not necessary for the classical pianist to be versed in jazz, nor the jazz pianist to have studied his classics. Even, it's heartily recommended that each of the two styles retain their individuality, and thereby accentuate the contrast'' (from the score). The work is divided into three contrasting sections. The "classical" pianist's part has elements of Chopin and Rachmaninoff mixed with a Gershwin flavor. The "jazz" pianist's part reflects the influence of Duke Ellington, while the formal structure of the work depends on traditional forms and resources. The work holds together remarkably well in spite of its opposite styles. M-D.

––––––– *Suite* (Les Editions Bleu Blanc Rouge 1973) 70pp., parts. For flute, piano, percussion, and double bass. Percussion required: cymbal, hi-hat, snare drums, small tom tom, big tom tom, bass drums. 1. Baroque and Blue; 2. Sentimentale (pianist can improvise in this movement); 3. Javanaise (Java in 5); 4. Fugace (Allegro fugato); 5. Irlandaise; 6. Versatile; 7. Veloce. Bolling acquired a reputation in France as a jazz piano prodigy at the age of fourteen. He has had formal training and has performed with many jazz greats. "This Suite in 7 parts is composed for a 'classic' flute and a 'jazz' piano. The style of writing for each instrument is somewhat different. It should be interesting to bring out those oppositions in the interpretation. The first half of the 6th movement, 'Versatile,' is written for the bass flute. It is possible to play the whole piece with only flute and piano, but it is (more) complete with double bass and percussion" (from the score). Clever, effective amalgamation of the two styles that produces some surprising results. D.

Paul Bowles. *Music For a Farce* 1938 (Weintraub 1953) 34pp., parts. For piano, trumpet, percussion, and clarinet. Allegro rigoroso; Presto (Tempo di Tarantella); Allegretto (Tempo di Quickstep); Allegro; Lento (Tempo di Valse); Allegro (Tempo di Marcia); Presto; Allegretto. Clever, whimsical, mildly contemporary. M-D.

Cesar Bresgen. *Bilder des Todes* (Dob 1973) 44pp., 19 min. Score and parts for 2 pianos and 2 players on kettledrums and percussion. Toccata: fast-moving, chromatic sixteenths in both piano parts; mid-section becomes more lyric and sustained; an agitato section concludes the movement with a strong punch; large span required. Variationen: staccato and marcato figuration are contrasted with octotonic melody, syncopation, and triplet figuration in crescendo. Intermezzo I: melody is accompanied with secco chords; serious. Ricercare I: linear treatment of ideas. Intermezzo II: grace-note octotonic melody; short. Ricercare II: unraveling eighth-note figuration in one piano while other comments and amplifies line. Epilog: free, long pedals, maestoso ending. Exciting writing in this suite. D.

David Cope. *Koosharem, a Ceremony of Innocence* (MS available from composer: c/o School of Music, Miami University, Oxford, OH 45056) 17pp., parts. For clarinet, percussion, string bass, and piano.

George Crumb. *Dream Sequence* (Images II) 1976 (CFP). For violin, cello, piano, and percussion, including suspended cymbals, crotales, Japanese temple bells, sleigh bells, maracas, Thai buffalo bell, glass harmonica (tuned crystal goblets). Crumb states that ''The form might be described as cyclical movement within a prevailing stasis'' and also suggests that perhaps this is ''indeed the proto-typical 'form' of dreams and nature.'' Characterization in the score reads, ''Poised, timeless, 'breathing': as an afternoon in late summer.'' Timeless effect created by ethereal drone of the glass harmonica, repetitive rhythms in piano and percussion, and free melodic fragments interpolated by strings. Forceful articulation in piano part terminates cyclical repetition. Short closing section fades away as goblets stop ringing one by one. D.

Edison Denisov. *Concerto* 1963 (UE 14301) 23pp., parts. For flute, oboe, piano, and percussion. Ouverture: flexible meters, octotonic, tritone important, light toccata-like passages, contrapuntal treatment of harmonic sevenths, shifting rhythms, fugal texture. Cadenza: flute cadenza; then oboe, piano, and finally the percussion follow, each with their own cadenza. Coda: pointillistic, changing meters, crescendo to end, *ffff* conclusion. Exacting writing. D.

Morton Feldman. *Four Instruments* 1965 (CFP) 6pp. For violin, cello, chimes, and piano. Durations of simultaneous single sounds are extremely slow. All sounds are connected without pauses unless notated. Dynamics are exceptionally low, but audible. Avant-garde. M-D.

Paul Fetler. *Cycles for Percussion and Piano* (Schott Bat 14 1973) 30pp., parts. Requires three percussion players and one pianist. Includes distribution, symbols, and notation instructions. Large percussive complement required. Also contains symbols for the percussion sticks. Piano part includes glissandi produced inside piano with thumbs or soft mallets and approximate pitches plucked inside piano. Widely spread sonorities, clusters, pointillistic treatment. Partially avant-garde. Large span required. M-D.

Lukas Foss. *Echoi* 1961-3 (CF and Schott). For clarinet, cello, percussion, and piano. A children's tune introduced into this piece. Stochastic techniques. The work is controlled by the drummer striking the anvil to redirect the musical activity, banging on the strings of the piano to stop the pianist, etc. Avant-garde. M-D to D.

_____ *Ni Bruit Ni Vitesse* ("Neither Noise Nor Haste") (Sal 1972) 21pp., parts. For 2 pianos and 2 percussionists. Careful explanations in English. Exploits sonorities on the keys and strings and requires in addition 2 cow bells, 2 Japanese bowls, and 2 triangle beaters. Percussionists play inside the pianos. Delicate percussive and timbre effects provide gamelan-like sonorities. Visual element of watching activity of performers provides much interest. Aleatoric. Hangs together remarkably well. M-D.
See: Eric Salzman, "The Many Lives of Lukas Foss," *Saturday Review*, 25 (February 1967): 73–76.

Juan Guinjoàn. *Cinco Estudios* (Alpuerto 1974) 17pp., parts. For 2 pianos and 2 percussionists. Explanations in Spanish, French, and English.

Arne Mellnäs. *Capricorn Flakes* (CFP 1970) 4 large sheets. For piano, harpsichord, vibraphone, and glockenspiel. Aleatoric throughout. Twenty-two thematic fragments on one large sheet for each instrument constitute the score. Clever, funny directions in English such as, "Nothing is too boring for you to tackle," or "Desire for Seclusion," "Produces the maximum effect with the minimum effort" (from instructions in the score). A fun piece. Avant-garde. M-D.

Francis Miroglio. *Réfractions* (UE 14796 1973) 6 loose leaves. For flute, violin, percussion, and piano. Reproduction of composer's MS. Explanations in French, German, and English. Percussion required: glockenspiel, vibraphone, temple blocks, bongos, caisse claire, ton grave, cimbale chromatique, cymbale cloutée, cymbale aigu, cymbale grave, tam tam, triangle, wood block, glass chimes. Extensive performance directions. Six sections are arranged in an interchangeable manner. The violin and flute play standing up and move according to the specifications given in one of the schemes provided. The instrument notated in the middle of the page and marked with a black line should be given prominence. Piano part includes clusters, playing on the string, rapid glissandi, pointillistic chords, long pedal effects. Aleatoric, avant-garde. D.

Marlos Nobre. *Canticum Instrumentale* Op.25 1967 (Tonos) 35pp., parts. 10 min. For flute, harp, piano, and percussion. Contains notation directions. Free rhythms; notes are to be played with irregular rhythms ·as long as the line lasts in the prescribed tempo. Long pedals, pointillistic, dynamics serialized, cascading gestures, harmonics, fascinating sonorities. Avant-garde. D.

Robert Parris. *Concerto* 1967 (ACA) 38pp., parts. 14 min. For percussion, violin, cello, and piano. Percussion required: xylophone, celesta, bells, tam

tam, side drum, bass drum, traps. Grave: freely tonal and dissonant; varied tempi; clusters; large and brittle chords move over keyboard; changing meters; toccata-like figuration; octave tremolo between hands; wide dynamic range; wispy staccati; requires large span. Allegro: virtuosic piano part with grand gestures moving over entire keyboard; conclusion subsides and fades away. D.

Urs Peter Schneider. *Kirchweih* (Moeck 1964–71) Five Reductions. I. Kreuge (1964–7), nach Heinrich Seuse, for xylophone, piano, flute, and harmonium. The other Four Reductions are for different instrumentation.

Elliott Schwartz. *Multiples* (Cole 1975) 7pp. 4 scores necessary for performance. For piano, 3 percussionists, films, and tapes. Extensive performance directions. Pianist has special notational symbols. This piece is to be performed together with tapes, films, and slides of previous performances, not simply as a "live" piece on stage. For a first performance, make tapes, slides, etc., of rehearsals. Each percussionist has the following instruments: one capable of producing specific pitches; groups of instruments in "graduated" sizes offering four relatively "pitched" sounds from high to low; one or two middle-to-large-sized instruments capable of producing a sustained resonance. Each performer begins anywhere on the page and follows boxes in any circular path chosen. All performers are synchronized to a steady rhythmic metric pulse. Performance begins off-stage. In addition to other requirements, the pianist has to yell, scream into piano, and call out a name of a composer or an instrument. Avant-garde.

Milan Stibilj. *Condensation* 1967 (Br 6101) 25pp., parts. For 2 pianos, trombone, and percussion. Percussion required: 2 bongos, 3 tom toms, bass drum, 2 cymbals, tam tam. "Considered from a formal point of view, the composition is constructed on the principles of simple harmonic motion, which are represented in the note-values. Because the precisely determined rhythmic elements pass from one instrument to another, the underlying structure of the form remains fixed, despite the simultaneous use of improvised passages, which allow each interpreter to maintain his independence" (from notes in the score). Pointillistic, serial, avant-garde. Extreme ensemble problems in precision. D.

Karlheinz Stockhausen. *Kreuzspiel* (Crossplay) 1951, rev. ed. 1960 (UE 13117) 32pp., 10 min. For oboe, bass clarinet, piano, and percussion. Pointillistic, "music in space." The idea of an intersection (crossing) of temporal and spatial phenomena is presented in three stages. Pitches are gradually shifted from one register to another. Careful directions are given for the grouping of the instruments and the heights at which players should stand or sit. Every note has a dynamic mark attached. The first of the composer's avant-garde pieces. D.

Morton Subotnick. *Serenade II* (McGinnis & Marx) 18pp., parts. For clarinet, horn, piano, and percussion. Performance directions concerning notation: bar lines indicate beats at the designated tempo; the spacing of the notes within the measure designates the way the notes fall in relation to the beat; notes are short unless otherwise indicated. The percussionist who works only inside the piano needs woven marimba mallets, using woven part for soft sounds, stick for hard sounds. All performers play from left to right together; however, they choose freely within each beat. A cadenza is made of two phrases, marked A and B, and the players decide on the patterns to use at each performance. The horizontal line indicates the middle of the range for each instrument. The number at the left of each group indicates the number of beats at M.M. 60 for that group. The number to the right indicates the length of the pause between groups. The groups are chosen at random during the pause. Big notes indicate loud, small notes soft, etc. Clusters, pointillistic, avant-garde. D.

Stefan Wolpe. *Quartet I* 1950 rev.1954 (McGinnis & Marx) 63pp., parts. For tenor saxophone, trumpet, piano, and percussion. Lento: loose, mournful and fanfare-like ideas, flexible asymmetrical meters, complex rhythms, cluster-like sonorities. Con moto: jazzy ideas and suave structures brought together; suspended conclusion. Intense expressionistic nontonal writing with numerous ensemble problems. Only for the most venturesome groups. Short and calculated attacks and timbres. D.
———— *Quartet* (McGinnis & Marx). For oboe, cello, piano, and percussion. In preparation (1976).

Hans Zender. *Quartet* 1964–5 (Bo&Bo 22027) 19pp., parts. For flute, cello, piano, and percussion. Directions for performance in German. Three movements with various directions for different realizations. Complex writing in a serial and strongly atonal style. D.

Quartets for Piano, Other Instruments, and Tape

Robert Ehle. *Five Pieces for Instruments with Prepared Electronics* (CF). For clarinet, violin, piano, percussion, and tape.

Karel Goeyvaerts. *Quartet* 1972 (CeBeDeM) 10 leaves. 10 to 30 min. For piano quartet and tape. Explanations in Dutch, French, and English. 4 copies necessary for performance. "On the day of the performance, a recording is to be made of the broadcast news, preferably from different languages. . . . This recording is to be heard during the performance, with a suitable amplification for the space where the performance takes place. . . . A performance plan shall be prepared that will fit the recording of the day" (from the score). Fragments are given, improvisation required. Avant-garde. M-D.
See: Karel Goeyvaerts. "The Sound Material of Electronic Music," *die reihe,* English ed., I: 35–37.

Jonathan Harvey. *Inner Light I* (Nov) 30 min. For flute/piccolo, clarinet, percussion, piano, and tape.

Elliott Schwartz. *Multiples.* For piano, 3 percussionists, films, and tapes. See detailed entry under quartets for piano(s), percussion, and other instruments.

Morton Subotnick. *Serenade No.3* (Bowdoin College Music Press 1965) 24pp., parts. For flute, clarinet, violin, piano, and tape. Alternates between exact notation with spatial notation. No tempo indication means the players are to follow the cues. Where tape cues exist, players should play as closely as possible with the tape; where no cues exist, no exact relationship is intended. The piano part moves over the keyboard in pointillistic fashion, with extreme dynamic ranges and clusters. Aleatoric. Subotnick has an uncanny ability to "blend" the tape part into the ensemble. There are moments when the ear is only aware of a unique ensemble that works! M-D.

Music for Five Instruments

Quintets for Piano and Strings

[Piano, two violins, viola, and cello unless otherwise specified.]

Charles Henri Valentine Alkan. *Rondo Brillant* Op.4 (Lemoine) 19pp., parts. Copy at LC. For piano, 2 violins, viola, and cello/double bass. Adagio (Introduction)–Largement; Rondo—Allegretto grazioso. Elegant salon style, all glitter and sparkle for the piano with the other instruments coming along only for the ride! D.

Anton Arensky. *Quintet* Op.51 D 1900 (USSR 1958) 67pp., parts. Allegro moderato: SA design. Andante: a set of variations on "Sur le pont d'Avignon," with shifting harmonies. Scherzo—Allegro vivace: SA with two scherzi. Finale—Fuga: free double fugue. Effective, full Romantic style writing for the piano throughout. The fugue requires a fine octave technique. D.

Grażyna Bacewicz. *Quintet I* 1952 (PWM) 25 min.
_____ *Quintet II* 1965 (PWM 3975) 57pp., parts. 18 min. Moderato–Allegro–Molto Allegro: the half step and tritone are very important; alternating hands, bitonal figuration, glissandi, simultaneous trills in extreme registers, chromatic passage work, tremolo, clusters. Larghetto: sustained section, long pedal effects; large span required. Allegro giocoso: rhythmic figuration, chordal punctuation, repeated patterns; similar devices used in other movements. D.

Johann Christian Bach. *Quintet* Op.11/4 E♭ (Nag). For 3 violins (or flute, oboe, and violin), viola, and basso continuo; cello ad lib.
_____ *Quintet* Op.11/5 A (Steglich—Br; Musica Rara). For flute or violin, oboe or violin, violin, viola, cello, and basso continuo.
_____ *Quintet* Op.11/6 D (Nag). For 3 violins (or flute, oboe, and violin), viola, and basso continuo; cello ad lib.

Henk Badings. *Pianokwintetten* 1952 (Donemus) 24 min.

Béla Bartók. *Quintet* 1904 (D. Dille—EMB 1970) 172pp., parts. Preface by editor in English, German, and Hungarian. Andante: freely tonal around C; chordal; flowing arpeggi figuration mixed with arpeggiated chords; chromatic scalar passages; tremolo; syncopated triplets; octotonic; broken figuration in triplets; long scalar passages used as dramatic gestures; fluent octave technique and large span required. Vivace–Scherzando: dancelike; centers around f♯; Hungarian gipsy flavor; spread-out Alberti-bass figuration; imitation; lush Romantic chords in Moderato section; glissandi. Adagio: chromatic; lyric; syncopated chords lead to Adagio molto, where there is much instrumental reaction between piano and strings; sweeping arpeggi gestures, Romantic descending chromatic chords à la *Rosenkavalier*; some changing meters; leads directly to Poco a poco più vivace: Hungarian dance flavor; many octaves used to propel rhythm; tempo increases; concludes after a breathtaking pace in C. Virtuoso writing somewhat reminiscent in style of Bartók's *Rhapsody*, Op.1. D.

Leslie Bassett. *Quintet* 1962 (CFE) 50pp., parts. 20 min. Moderately slow: twelve-tone; dramatic gestures; chordal punctuation; tremolo; requires large span. Fast: repeated harmonic seconds; rhythmic drive; short chromatic lines. Slow: intense; varied figuration; low register of piano treated effectively. Slow–Faster: hammered chordal sonorities; widely spread texture; strong driving rhythms in final section. D.

Mrs. H. H. A. Beach. *Quintet* Op.67 f♯ 1909 (A. P. Schmidt) 47pp., parts. Adagio–Allegro moderato; Adagio espressivo; Allegro agitato. This dreamy, sensuous work in a Brahmsian vein contains effective writing for all the instruments, but the piano part seems by far to be the most important. The second movement has a rich Strauss-like melody, yet it has its own unique integrity and style. Many Romantic idioms, handled in a thoroughly crafted manner. Deserves reviving. D.

Arrigo Benvenuti. *Folio, diferencias sobre cinco estudios* (Bruzzichelli).

Franz Berwald. *Klavierquartett und Klavierquintette* (Br 4913 1973) 233pp., parts. Vol.13 of the Complete Edition edited by I. Bengtsson and B. Hammar. Preface in German and English, critical commentary in English. Includes *Quartet* Op.1 E♭ for piano, woodwinds, and horn, and *Quintet* Op.6 for piano and strings. The piano writing contains moments of highly original and poetic treatment, although Mendelssohn's influence looms large. The *Quintet* was composed during the 1850s, 1857 at the latest. Appendix: Larghetto and Scherzo for piano and string quartet from an earlier piano quintet in A (composed during the latter part of the 1840s or about 1850). M-D.

Henrich Ignaz Franz von Biber. *Serenade* (P. Nettl—Nag 112) 12pp., parts. For 2 violins, 2 violas, and basso continuo; cello ad lib. Serenada; Allamanda; Aria; Ciacona (based on chorale "Der Nachtwächter); Gavotte; Retirada. A fine suite in period style. M-D.

Ernst Bloch. *Quintet* 1921–3 (GS) 129pp., parts. 35 min. Agitato; Andante mistico; Allegro energico. Quarter-tone usage. picturesque exoticism, mildly contemporary modal flavor, massive opening movement. D.

_____ *Quintet II* 1957 (BB 1962) 40pp., parts. Animato: two twelve-tone sections; the second is an exact transposition of the first, used only melodically; no other serial rules incorporated; the falling fifth outlines a tonic feeling; tritone frequently used. Andante: theme and variations; rich sonorities. Allegro; rondo with lyric interludes; bitonality plays an important part. Strong thematic ideas. Not as virtuosic as the first *Quintet*. D.

See: Dika Newlin, "The Later Works of Ernst Bloch," MQ, 33 (1947): 443–59. Contains a general discussion of Bloch's compositional style and an analysis of *Piano Quintet I*.

Luigi Boccherini. *Quintet* Op.57/1 A (S. Sadie—Musica Rara 1962) 27pp., parts. Allegro moderato; Menuetto; Andantino con un poco di moto; Allegro giusto. The piano quintet was a rare form when this work was composed. Interesting classic figuration and some unusual harmonies are used. M-D.

_____ *Quintet* Op.57/2 B♭ (GS; CFP B73; B&VP) 35pp., parts. Allegretto moderato; Menuetto tempo giusto; Finale. The piano part assumes some individuality. M-D.

_____ *Quintet* Op.57/6 "Military Night Watch in Madrid" (IMC). Boccherini came close to Haydn's and Mozart's style in this work. Foreshadows some of the later developments of the piano concerto. M-D.

René de Boisdeffre. *Quintet* Op.11 d 1883 (Hamelle) 77pp., parts. Allegro con brio; Scherzo; Andante ma non troppo; Final. Undistinguished writing by today's standards. M-D.

_____ *Quintet* Op.25 D 1890 (Hamelle) 85pp., parts. For piano, violin, viola, cello, and double bass. Allegro con brio; Intermezzo; Marche; Pastorale. Well written, pianistic. Traditional harmonic, melodic, and rhythmic treatment. M-D to D.

_____ *Quintet* Op.43 B♭ (Hamelle).

Alexander Borodin. *Quintet* c 1862 (Br&H 5718; USSR 1968, 55pp., parts). Andante: graceful flowing lines, cantabile and legato. Scherzo: large skips in left hand; chordal; some imitation; Trio uses octotonic writing and melody refers to the opening movement. Finale: short motifs contrasted with larger lines, broken-octave triplets, arpeggiation, syncopated chords, octave passages. M-D.

Siegfried Borris. *Quintet* Op.99/3 (Heinrichshofen/Sirius 1973) 33pp., parts. Photostat of MS. For piano, violin, viola, cello, and double bass. Allegro con brio; Largo; Largo–Vivace alla burlesca. Hammered repeated syncopated octaves, harmonic seconds, fourths, major sevenths, octotonic, chords in alternating hands, freely tonal, linear and thin textures, flowing lines in second movement, corky rhythmic subject for burlesca movement, shifting meters, neoclassic orientation. M-D.

Johannes Brahms. *Quintet* Op.34 f (H. Krellmann—Henle 1971; Br&H; CFP 3660; GS L1646; Heugel 188; EPS). Henle edition (75pp., parts) uses the autograph and Brahms's own marked copy of the first edition as sources; contains fingering of piano part by H.-M. Theopold; includes brief remarks on each movement. Allegro non troppo; Andante, un poco Adagio; Allegro; Allegro non troppo. This work began as a string quintet, the fifth instrument being a second cello. It was rearranged as a sonata for two pianos (IMC), and finally emerged in its present form in 1865. This quintet is probably one of the ten greatest masterpieces in the chamber music repertoire. It is a big, muscular work for small forces, and has features in common with Beethoven's *Quartet* Op.95. In both compositions the finales have slow introductions followed by long, binary main sections, which lead into faster, lengthy codas. Thematic metamorphosis takes place in the first and third movements. The slow movement is rather difficult to sustain. D. See: Thomas F. Dunhill, "Brahms' Quintet for Pianoforte and Strings," MT, 72 (1931): 319–22. Each movement is discussed and analyzed.

Frank Bridge. *Quintet* 1904–12 (Augener) 68pp., parts. Adagio–Allegro moderato: d; chord in right hand with fast chromatic figuration in left hand and the reverse is a pattern frequently found in this work; bold arpeggiated strokes; lyric second theme in F; tremolo. Adagio ma non troppo: B; nocturne-like in style; chromatic; Allegro con brio mid-section in d; works to great octave climax; opening section and mood return. Allegro energico: driving rhythmic figuration; legato and staccato triplets; frequent modulation; alternating hands; dramatic scalar and chordal gestures bring work to a close. Strong post-Romantic writing. D.

Adolf Busch. *Quintett* Op.35 (Br&H 5370 1927) 52pp., parts. Sostenuto; Adagio cantabile; Finale—Molto appassionato. Slight Reger influence, violent dynamic changes, some complex polyphonic spots. D.

Roberto Caamaño. *Quinteto* 1963 (IU) 72pp., parts. 19 min. Allegro: serial;

opens with octaves in extreme registers that move close together and begin again, but moves directly into a sciolto figuration that embraces the main idea; triplet atonal (row) figuration spread over keyboard; punctuated chords (ninths and tenths) and whole-note chords bring the movement to a close. Allegro: the row is run through quickly in pointillistic fashion. Lento: piano provides sustaining sonorities and marked chordal pulsation. Molto allegro: row is octotonically treated in various registers; chordal rhythmic punctuation. Thin textures throughout most of the work. D.

John Alden Carpenter. *Quintet* 1934 (GS) 60pp., parts. Moderato–Allegro: chromatic themes, pedal point under parallel moving chords, a few meter changes, Impressionistic tendencies. Andante: sustained, low register exploited, broken arpeggi figurations, sweeping climax, seventh harmonies. Allegro non troppo: driving rhythms, chordal seconds frequently used, dancelike syncopations, contrasting sections. D.

Mario Castelnuovo-Tedesco. *Quintet* 1932 F (Forlivesi) 60pp., parts. Lento e sognante–Vivo e appassionato: chromatic broken chordal figuration, grandiose chords, scalar. Andante: parallel chords; builds to a large climax then subsides; triplets are frequent. Scherzo: broken octaves, scales, repeated chords, contrary-motion figures. Vivo e impetuoso: alternating hands; sustained chords; arpeggi; dramatic piano part has a short quasi-recitativo section that leads to a Moderato (alla marcia funebre) before returning to opening tempo and idea; brilliant conclusion. D.
———— *Second Piano Quintet* 1951 (Forlivesi).

Alexis de Castillon. *Quintette* Op.1 E♭ (Durand) 59pp., parts. Allegro; Scherzo; Adagio et Final. The spirit of Saint-Saëns hovers over this work. M-D.

Alexandre Cellier. *Quintette II* b (Senart 1922) 43pp., parts. Allegro ben moderato; Ben moderato e tranquillo; Lento recitativo; Allegro con fuoco. Strong Franck influence. M-D.

George W. Chadwick. *Quintet* E♭ (A. P. Schmidt 2569 1896) 69pp., parts. Copy at LC. Allegro sostenuto; Andante Cantabile; Intermezzo; Final. Brahms and Franck influences are felt here although the work does display a solid craft for the period. M-D to D.

Boris Chaikovsky. *Quintet* 1962 (USSR) 82pp., parts. Moderato: SA; proceeds almost from beginning to end in quarter notes; octotonic; modal; freely chromatic; dramatic development section leads to a mirror recapitulation with the climax at the beginning. Allegro: free rondo; lyrical refrain alternates with episodes; contrasting timbres of the piano and strings are underlined; abrupt tempo changes. Allegro: a poignant scherzo; toccatalike; SA characteristics; driving and impetuous; tense and dramatic main theme with a resilient rhythm. Finale: an Adagio in SA design without a development; progression of chords serves as the main theme, like a solemn procession; sombre and melodious secondary theme. Emotions soar in this quintet but it gives an impression of being well knit, clear, and precise in its expression. A worthy work in a style best described as a mixture of Prokofiev and Khachaturian. M-D to D.

Camille Chevillard. *Quintette* Op.1 E♭ (Durand) 80pp., parts. Allegro ma non troppo; Tempo di Marcia; Molto vivace; Allegro molto appassionato. Traditional writing but exploits the piano admirably. M-D.

Barney Childs. *Music for Piano and Strings* (ACA 1965). For piano, violin, viola, cello, and double bass. Parts. The solo piano part is composed of 27 individual sheets assembled in the order decided by the performer. There is no stipulated length on many of the sheets, this direction being left up to the soloist. A page turner is required. Soloist may rehearse with or without the strings—that is, a performance may be carefully worked out, so that all performers know just what will be happening when, or it may be completely spontaneous. Some of the directions for the pianist are: "This section is made up of these 4 chords (chords, 1 note) played in any order or repeated as you wish." "Using a piece of heavy aluminum foil or light sheet metal, crinkled or smooth, place over strings in middle register, after normal sound. Soft-drink bottle caps may be placed on top of the foil or metal if you wish. Music played during this section should be busy, linear, wandering." Contains unusual and original directions that produce some fascinating sonorities. The strings portion contains six "movements" to be played in any order. Four of them contain a solo for one of the string players. Requires a fine imaginative pianist to make this piece work, but the effort would be worthwhile. D.

Tudor Ciortea. *Cvintet Cu Pian* c♯ (Editura Muzicală 1961) 92pp., parts. Larghetto–Allegro non troppo ma deciso: introduction, SA, chromatic and interesting rhythmic structure, figuration in alternating hands. Molto vivace: Scherzo, ABA, coda. Adagietto: ABAB form, warm cantabile treatment of main A idea, contrasing B sections, coda. Vivace: rondo, freely tonal (but highly chromatic) and pianistic writing. D.

Halfdan Cleve. *Quintett* Op.9 E♭ (Br&H), In Brahms style and tradition. D.

Johann Baptist Cramer. *Quintuor* Op.9 E (Probst 321) 17pp., parts. Copy at LC. For piano, violin, viola, cello, and double bass. Largo—assai gioioso; Adagio; Allegretto vivo. Also available in an arrangement for piano and flute (or violin) by the composer. M-D.

Ernst Dohnányi. *Quintet* Op.1 c 1902 (Dob) 63pp., parts. Allegro; Scherzo; Adagio, quasi andante; Finale—Allegro animato. Written in the grand European tradition; sings and soars with the spirit that imbued the music of Dohnányi's masters, who closed the nineteenth century and ushered in the twentieth. Brahms-like, broad, lyric, impassioned writing. Dohnányi played the piano part at his debut as a composer. D.

———— *Quintet* Op.26 e♭ 1919 (Simrock) 43pp., parts. 20 min. Allegro non troppo; Intermezzo; Moderato. One of Dohnányi's most impressive works. Strong contrapuntal techniques; form and drama interact closely; sombre colors except for the scherzo (in the middle of the Intermezzo); Romantic but economical scoring. D.

Theodore Dubois. *Quintette* F. For oboe (or second violin or clarinet), violin, viola, cello, and piano. See detailed entry under quintets for piano(s), strings, and winds.

Johann Ladislav Dussek. *Quintett* Op.41 f (UWKR 39 1975) 23pp., parts. For piano, violin, viola, cello, and double bass. Allegro moderato ma con fuoco; Adagio espressivo; Finale. Contains some interesting harmonic innovations through the use of chromaticism. Effective finale with some brilliant figuration. Concludes with ascending melodic form of scale. M-D.

Antonín Dvořák. *Quintet* Op.5 A (Artia).

———— *Quintet* Op.81 A (Artia; Simrock 59pp., parts; GS L1627; EPS 305) 28 min. The piano part is fuller than in Dvořák's *Piano Quartets*. First movement exploits submediant in the recapitulation and coda. National dance characteristics are found in the second movement (Dumka) and in the Furiant, which takes the place of a scherzo. A radiant rondo concludes the quintet. Intoxicating melodies, vital rhythms, colorful scoring, and contrasts in mood are present in abundance. D.

See: Sir Henry Hadow, "Dvořák's Quintet for Pianoforte and Strings (Op.81)," MT, 73 (1932): 401–404. An analysis compares the work and stylistic traits of Dvořák with those of Schubert and Beethoven.

Oleg Eiges. *Quintet* 1961 (USSR) 60pp., parts. Pesante–Moderato Allegro: SA; theme of the introduction plays an important part in further development; driving and dynamic main subject is followed by a lyrical second idea; development builds on the introduction and main subjects; recapitulation presents the second subject and a coda based on material derived from the first subject. Andante con moto: SA; calm; melodious; first theme resembles a Russian folk song; second subject is in the nature of a slow march; an element from the first movement introduction is encountered in the more lively development section; the slower motion returns in the recap. Allegro vivace: SA; combines a scherzo and fast waltz; an extensive coda is based on a theme from the introduction of the first movement; the finale lends its bright and vigorous coloring to the whole work. Idiomatic and kaleidoscopic writing. Mildly contemporary. M-D to D.

Edward Elgar. *Quintet* Op.84 a 1918 (Nov) 67pp., parts. Moderato: chromatic, chordal, octotonic, arpeggi figuration, sixteenth-note octaves in left hand, 3 with 4. Adagio: broken chordal figures move over keyboard. Andante–Allegro: sweeping arpeggi patterns, chorale-like section, wide dynamic range. Artistic writing but not always pianistically conceived. D. See: H. C. Colles, "Elgar's Quintet for Pianoforte and Strings, Op.84," MT, 60 (1919): pp.596–600. A discussion of the work from a formal, harmonic, and developmental point of view.

Georges Enesco. *Quintet* Op.29 (Editura Muzicală a Uniunii Compozitorilor 1968; Sal) 86pp., parts. Con moto molto moderato; Vivace, ma non troppo. Involved, highly chromatic although key signatures are present. Second movement is very long and includes varied tempi (Più tranquillo provides a needed contrast). Individual and unique style that includes some wild and impassioned writing. Requires thorough musicianship throughout. D.

Robert Evett. *Quintet* 1954 (ACA) 20 min.

Gabriel Fauré. *Quintet I* Op.89 d (GS 1907; Hamelle) 28 min. Molto moderato; Adagio; Allegretto moderato. Three movements of refined expression with a perfect sense of balance. The Adagio uses all instruments in a canonic workout with excellent effect and is the most successful movement. The finale develops from a single figure and is a masterpiece of delicate writing. D.

———— *Quintet II* Op.115 c 1921 (Durand) 76pp., parts. 30 min. Allegro moderato: sixteenth-note patterns, swaying dancelike chromatic movement, thin textures, imitation. Allegro vivo: scalar; broken octaves; broken double notes accompany melody in other hand; themes get tangled; triplets embedded with important bass line; flowing passage work; clever and vivacious. Andante moderato: important half-step melodic idea; added-note and syncopated chords; rotary motion required; deeply emotional; arpeggi; melancholy mood. Allegro molto: triple-time bass with the piano accenting duple rhythm; long lines; octave-apart melodic writing; alternating hands;

thematic transformation. A searching work of commanding proportions and great profundity. Shows the 71-year-old composer's fresh and youthful enthusiasm. D.

Richard Felciano. *Aubade* (ECS) 13pp., parts. For violin, viola, cello, harp, and piano. Sustained sonorities; long pedals; right foot is to come down hard on damper pedal from a distance of about six inches above, so that impact sounds. Sharp strokes on keys, pointillistic, glissandi, harmonics. Expressionistic. M-D.

John Field. *Quintet* A♭ (Br&H 859) 17pp., parts. One beautiful movement that is Andante con espressione, nocturne-like throughout. The piano carries the largest part of the ensemble. M-D.

Ross Lee Finney. *Piano Quintet* 1953 (Henmar) 52pp., parts. Adagio sostenuto: chordal, sustained, leads to Allegro marcato: chords interspersed with octotonic disjunct figuration moving over keyboard; sustained slow section with references to the introduction interrupts from time to time, and these two basic ideas form the bulk of the movement. Allegro scherzando: continuous filigree figuration contrasted with rhythmic melodic idea; melodic idea is extended and accompanied by tonal repeated chords; long semi-chromatic runs; repeated A in piano part for final four bars concludes movement. Nocturne, Adagio sostenuto: freely flowing tonal lines. Allegro appassionato: serpentine chromatic right-hand triplets with eighth-note octaves in left hand; independent lines in both hands; much rhythmic push. Clear textures throughout. M-D.

———— *Piano Quintet II* (Columbia University Press 1974) 54pp., parts. Introduction–Larghetto: serial, dramatic, chordal, trills, quick melodic spurts in 32nds; uses most of keyboard. Allegretto moderato: secco style; piano has cadenza-like section that exploits runs, chromatic thirds, and large skipping gestures. Allegro drammatico: piano has marked melodic line; octotonic; pointillistic effects; hammered repeated chords at end. Epilogue—Adagio cantabile: tranquil row unfolds; various layers of sound; final row statement heard in bell-like tolling tones; hypnotic conclusion. D.

Arthur Foote. *Quintet* Op.38 (H. W. Hitchcock—Da Capo) 60pp. Allegro giusto—appassionato; Intermezzo; Scherzo; Allegro giusto. Schumannesque and Brahmsian qualities. Whimsical themes throughout. Intermezzo (the finest movement) contains some real surprises in its instrumental color. Eminently worth reviving. M-D to D.

César Franck. *Quintet* f (CFP 79pp., parts; Hamelle; BMC; IMC; EPS). Molto moderato quasi lento–Allegro; Lento, con molto sentimento; Allegro non troppo, ma con fuoco. Although this is a fairly early work (1878–9), it is a fine, impassioned piece, full of Romantic sensibility. Economy of musical material and ability to create a coherent whole are beautifully illustrated in this dramatic work. One of the three or four greatest works in the form; represents the epitome in musical expression of which the combination is capable. D.

Peter Racine Fricker. *Concertante V* 1971 (MS available from composer: c/o Music Dept., University of California at Santa Barbara) 28pp., parts. $9\frac{1}{2}$ min. Declamato—Scherzoso: piano has much chromatic staccato activity in unisons two octaves apart; leads to a broader (Solemne) section, where the piano is treated more legato and chordally (lirico); short accelerando moves into più mosso before a Molto Allegro section juxtaposes long lines with short motivic ideas; cadenza for piano brings together much of the material already exposited; Alla marcia section brings back the Declamato—Scherzo material from the opening; a final accelerando brings the work to an exciting conclusion. The style is mainly linear with a transparent clarity, serially inspired, with free key centers lurking in the background. Fricker knows how to write idiomatically for instruments so that they sound their best. M-D.

Ignaz Friedman. *Quintett* c (WH 1918) 66pp., parts. Allegro maestoso; Larghetto, con somma espressione; Epilog. Contains some fluent and beautiful writing, somewhat in a post-Brahms–Reger style. The second movement is highly eclectic with changes of mood and tempi. M-D to D.

James Friskin. *Quintet* Op. 1 c 1907 (St&B) 79pp., parts. Allegro risoluto; Allegro molto; Adagio sostenuto; Molto sostenuto e maestoso. Written in a heroic Brahms-like style. M-D.
———— *Phantasy* f 1910 (St&B 1024) 43pp., parts. One large sectionalized movement in post-Romantic style. M-D.

Anis Fuleihan. *Quintet* 1964 (Bo&H) 71pp., parts. Allegro: flexible meters, serial, octotonic, trills; row is inventively treated. Andante con moto: more lyric, even in the Animato section; enfático added-note chords are effective. Allegro giusto: sempre staccato style, alternating hands; leads directly to Andante: long piano introduction moves through a Molto vivace and picks up rest of instruments; chords in fourths and fifths lead to a 7/4 section, where the melodic idea is hammered out with arpeggiated accompanied chords; rhythmic pulsation increases to a subito Largamente coda that ends in A; *pp*. Clear textures. D.

Blas Galindo. *Quintetto* 1960 (IU; LC) 43pp., parts. Commissioned by the

Sprague Foundation of the Library of Congress. Allegro; Lento; Allegro. Freely tonal writing that is at some points very tonal. Generally clear lines, some imitation and parallelism, alternating hands, cross-relations, seventh chords, and use of the tritone combine to make this neoclassic work both accessible and exciting. D.

Edwin Gerschefski. *Quintet* Op.16 (ACA 1961) 54pp., parts. Maestoso; Allegro leggiero (rev. version); Adagio; Allegro con brio. Tremolo, oc- totonic, linear, glissandi, neoclassic, hemiola. Low register of piano effec- tively exploited. Large span required. M-D.

Vittorio Giannini. *Quintet* 1932 (SPAM) 96pp., parts. Allegro con spirito; Adagio; Allegro. Virtuoso post-Romantic writing that constantly keeps the pianist involved. Extension of idiomatic pianism in the Brahms tradition. D.

Alberto Ginastera. *Quintetto* 1963 (Bo&H 19251) 52pp., parts. 16 min. Introduzione; Cadenza I per viola e violoncello; Scherzo fantastico; Cadenza II per due violini; Piccola musica notturna; Cadenza III per pianoforte; Finale. Strong, freely chromatic, wide dynamic range, clusters, tremolo, alternating hands. The piano cadenza is *ff* and dramatic, with large percussive chords. *Ppp* figuration builds and leads (octotonically) to a large cluster that opens the Finale. Large span required. D.

Roger Goeb. *Quintet* (CFE).

Eugene Goossens. *Quintet* Op.23 1918 (JWC) 35pp., parts. One large movement with varied tempi and moods. Dramatic and flamboyant writing with chromatic octaves and figuration most consistently used. M-D to D.

Enrique Granados. *Quinteto en sol menor* 1898 (UME 1973) 41pp., parts. Allegro: SA; marcato unison opening; chromatic thirds; arpeggi; much statement and answer between piano and strings. Allegretto quasi andanti- no: chordal opening in piano while the violin has rhythmic figure, piano then takes this figure; undulating thirds and sixths. Largo–Molto presto: vigorous rhythmical figures alternate with more langorous idea from second movement. M-D.

Sofia Gubaidulina. *Quintet* C 1957 (USSR) 78pp., parts. Allegro: SA; aus- tere and virile; short exposition is almost exclusively based on an intense development of the main subject from an initial motif; second subject, grotesque and full of restrained sarcasm, is stated polyphonically; abrupt and startling contrasts appear in the development; simple textures with scales in parallel and contrary motion. Andante: scherzo-like, simple timbres; based on a naive marchlike theme that, in further development, leads to combinations of weird, uncanny sonorities. Larghetto sensibile: warmly lyric; a cantabile theme flows like a calm narrative. Presto: rondo; toccata-like; full of energy; themes pursue one another in an irresistible torrent. Colorful writing in a mildly contemporary idiom. M-D.

Reynaldo Hahn. *Quintet* (Heugel 28175 1923) 65pp., parts. Molto agitato e con fuoco; Andante; Allegretto grazioso. Flowing lines, Impressionistic, beautifully pianistic. M-D.

Roy Harris. *Quintet* 1938 (GS) 74pp., parts. Strongly polyphonic, full of elaborate canonic devices and subtle thematic development, rich melodic invention. Passacaglia: not a true passacaglia, but has a strong central pattern that is used throughout; piano part develops into a quasi-toccata; six variations on the "theme." Cadenza: the piano is most effectively used in this movement, a multiple cadenza that employs sharp percussive writing, melodic passages in octaves, and intense polyharmonies; each instrument solos the "theme" rhapsodically. Fugue: a triple fugue on three subjects that has built-in toccata-like episodes. A strong spirit of classicism permeates this entire work. Strongly polyphonic, full of elaborate canonic devices and subtle thematic development, rich melodic invention. D.
See: Arthur Mendel, "The Quintet of Roy Harris," MM, 17/1 (November-December 1939): 25–29.

Josef Matthias Hauer. *Zwölftonspiel (2. Juni 1948)* (Fortissimo 1971) 12pp., parts. Photostat of MS. For piano and string quartet, with a twelve-tone row by Wolfgang Kammerlander.

Peter Herrmann. *Klavierquintett* (DVFM 8517a 1970) 57pp., parts. Allegro moderato; Lento; third movement untitled (dotted half note=80). Syncopated harmonic seconds, octotonic, secco style, melody in lower register, chromatic thirds and octaves, contrasting ideas and moods in all movements, traditional forms, bitonal. Finale contains fugal textures and figuration in alternating hands, *ppp* closing. Neoclassic Hindemithian style, D.

Heinrich von Herzogenberg. *Quintett* Op.17 C (Br&H) 58pp., parts. Allegro moderato, un poco maestoso; Adagio; Allegro; Presto. Masterly writing from the technical viewpoint and also intellectually interesting. Skillful use of the tone color of all instruments. Worth reviving. M-D.

Alun Hoddinott. *Quintet* Op.78/4 (OUP 1972) 32pp., parts. A one-movement work of six thematically linked sections. Sparse textures in all parts, nebulous clusters, much octave writing for the piano. M-D.

Alan Hovhaness. *Piano Quintet* Op.9 (CFP 6568 1963) 10 min. Andante: pianist must hold down pedal throughout the movement; short ornamental figures in upper register. Lento: mainly *p* arpeggio figuration mixed with short chromatic crescendo–decrescendo sections. Adagio: clusters, short chromatic runs, clusters return. Allegro molto: clusters in alternating hands. Allegretto: long pandiatonic chordal lines in the piano part. Very little drama but interest is sustained by sheer continuity and evocative sonorities. M-D.

Johann Nepomuk Hummel. *Quintet* Op.87 E♭ (UWKR 25, 41pp., parts; CFP; McGinnis & Marx). For violin, viola, cello, double bass, and piano. Allegro e risoluto assai: SA; main theme martial; triplets; unusual tonal progressions; uneven number of notes in a bar of chromatic runs (à la Chopin); piano has melodic line part of the time. Menuetto: animation and exuberance mixed with melancholy; great fluidity in moving through keys; Schubert-like; scalar runs in the bright Trio. Largo: short; free cantabile style; almost a cadenza for the piano. Finale: agitated but cheerful mood prevails; driving rhythms; facile pianistic figuration; brilliant and effective closing. One of Hummel's greatest chamber works; great fun for the pianist. D.

Vincent d'Indy. *Quintette* Op.81 g 1924 (Senart) 42pp., parts. Assez animé: broken chordal figuration; melody is taken over by the piano in full-octave chords; fully worked-out development; un peu plus lent coda; *pp* closing. Assez animé: 5/4; piano provides much syncopation; freely chromatic; strong *ff* closing. Lent et expressif: lightly flowing, sustained lines, rich harmonies. Modérémente animé: three layers of sound in the piano opening, broken figuration in alternating hands, sustained mid-section, brilliant closing. D.

Charles Ives. *Adagio Cantabile* (The Innate) 1908 (PIC 1967) 5pp., parts. 3 min. For piano, string quartet, and double bass (optional). Chromatic, chordal, left hand over right, parallel chords. Concludes on quartal harmony. M-D.

———— *Hallowe'en* 1912 from *Three Outdoor Scenes* (Boelke-Bomart) 7pp., parts. 3 min. Contains three separate movements, all available separately: *In Re Con Moto Et Al* (PIC), *Largo Risoluto No. I* (PIC), *Largo Risoluto No. II* (PIC). The piano part is atonal in this cacophonic takeoff on Halloween and April Fools' Day jokes. It may be repeated three or four times; the last time a drum can be added to the general confusion, to be played "as fast as possible without disabling any player or instrument." M-D.

Frederick Jacobi. *Hagiographa* 1938 (Arrow) 59pp., parts. 26 min. A set of three musical biblical narratives. 1. Job: broken chordal figuration; sustained section; at meas. 14 piano has melodic idea supported with mild dissonant chords; syncopation; chordal f♯ closing. 2. Ruth: melodic; expressive; parallel chords; sixteenth-note figuration; syncopated chords; *ppp* dolcissimo ending; large span required. 3. Joshua: rhythmic and furious chordal opening; staccato broken octaves contrasted with long pedalled sonorities; flowing octaves in parts; climactic strepitoso ending. Tends toward seriousness and meditation. Colorful writing even if it sounds a little tame to today's audiences. M-D.

Ulysses Kay. *Piano Quintet* 1949 (ACA) 25 min. First movement: striking themes achieve a powerful climax; piano used contrapuntally. Second movement: slow; eloquent; derives its appeal from the slow rise of a beautiful melodic idea; resounding combination of instruments in vertical lines gives it life. M-D to D.

Kent Kennan. *Quintet* (GS 1940) 84pp., parts. Allegretto; Lento; Vivace; Andante–Allegro. Mildly contemporary with strong melodic writing. Sweeping arpeggi, sturdy chords, quartal and quintal harmonies, octotonic, syncopated melodies, alternating hand patterns, feroce conclusion. Large span required. D.

Giselher Klebe. *Quintett "quasi una fantasia"* Op.53 (Br 4150 1967) 32pp., parts. 16 min. Allegro molto; Andante mosso. Serial, atonal, pointillistic, expressionistic, concludes with same six bars that opened the work. Second movement has varied tempi and moods. Chords, chromatic figuration and arpeggi, repeated notes, varied tempi in last movement, unresolved final chords. D.

Erich W. Korngold. *Quintet* Op.15 E 1920 (Schott) 57pp., parts. 18½ min. Mässiges Zeitmass, mit schwungvoll blühendem Ausdruck; Adagio (9 variations on Korngold's "Lieder Des Abschieds" Op.14); Finale. Extraverted writing that constantly moves the pianist over the keyboard. Accidentals are plentiful, à la Reger. D.

Rudolphe Kreutzer. *Quintet* (R.P. Block—Musica Rara 1974) 85pp., parts.

Kenneth Leighton. *Quintet* Op.34 (Nov 1962) 98pp., parts. 29 min. Allegro con moto: chromatic; shifting meters; punctuated chords; quartal harmony. Adagio sostenuto e molto espressivo: octotonic; trills embedded in unwinding chromatic figures; works to a broad climax; large span required. Scherzo: fleeting, brilliant, syncopation, repeated chords, reiterated patterns. Passacaglia: quiet expressive opening builds and drops back; varied treatment of the passacaglia idea, including changed tempi, shifted meters, scalar intrusions, martellato figures in alternating hands, augmentation; *fff* conclusion in C. D.

John McCabe. *Nocturnal* Op.42 (Nov 1967) 46pp., parts. 13 min. Introduction; Nocturne I; Cadenza I; Interlude; Cadenza II; Nocturne II; Epilogue. Strong contemporary treatment of all instruments. D.

Riccardo Malipiero. *Quintetto* 1957 (SZ) 35pp., parts. 18 min. Moderato: freely chromatic, changing meters, varied figuration. Molto veloce: octaves in alternating hands, chordal punctuation. Large span required. Adagio: piano has melodic and chordal treatment; animated section gives piano more rhythmic thrust; alternating perfect and diminished fifths close the movement. Mosso: octaves, repeated chords, skipping left hand, dramatic conclusion. D.

———— *Sonata a Cinque* 1934 (Ric). For flute (violin), violin, viola, cello, and piano. See detailed entry under quintets for piano(s), strings, and winds.

Frank Martin. *Quintette* 1920–1 (Henn) 53pp., parts. Andante con moto; Tempo di Minuetto; Adagio ma non troppo; Presto. This piece is marked by classical form, finely developed themes, and a predilection for delicately shaded sonorities. Idiomatic writing for all the instruments, chromatic melodies, ostinato-like patterns, and a rich mellow expressiveness make this a highly deserving work. The piano writing is a pleasure throughout. D.

Bohuslav Martinů. *Quintette* (La Sirène Musicale 1933) 28pp., parts. 18½ min. Poco allegro: octotonic, parallel chords, chromatic, scalar, varied use of triplets. Andante: scales; more sustained writing; large span required. Allegretto: changing meters; repeated octaves and notes; duplets into triple meter; alternating hands. Allegro moderato: chromatic chords alternate with scales; brilliant closing; good octave technique required. M-D to D.

———— *Piano Quintet II* 1944 (AMP) 60pp., parts. 18 min. Poco allegro: infectious; injects jazz into an old hymn tune "The Son of Man Goes Forth to War"; highly chromatic. Adagio: great serenity; staccato *p* repeated sixteenth-note chords. Scherzo—Poco allegretto: lively scherzo, much octotonic writing. Largo–Allegro: dramatic, opens with strings alone; in the Allegro the piano uses hand alternation and broken octaves. Engaging writing throughout. D.

See: Joseph Kerman, "The Chamber Music of Bohuslav Martinů," MQ: 35 (1949): 301–305. Includes an analysis of *Piano Quintet II*.

Toshiro Mayuzumi. *Pieces for Prepared Piano and Strings* (CFP 1957) 17pp., parts. 13 min. Prologue: Interlude; Finale. Materials required for preparation include pieces of rubber, a bolt, and a screw. Imaginative sonorities; uses variation of serial technique; neo-Impressionistic; makes unique use of blending piano sounds with strings, especially in the repeated notes of the piano. A cadenza for prepared piano is included. Prepared and unaltered tones mixed. Mayuzumi is regarded as the Messiaen of Japan. D.

Nicolas Medtner. *Quintet* C 1950 (Zimmermann) 54pp., parts. Rachmaninoff influence is present in this strong idiomatic and articulate writing for the piano. It is an effective work, very playable, and it would be rewarding for performers who like their music to sound as though it were written in a comfortable and familiar style of the 1920s. Plenty to challenge the pianist. D.

———— *Chamber Music*. (USSR 4127) Vol.8 of *Complete Works*.

Georges Migot. *Quintette, Les Agrestides* (Senart 1920) 85pp., parts. Un peu lent–Allegro; Rude, comme une danse agreste; Modéré. Difficult writing in Migot's unique style. Unusual harmonic shifts brought about by continuous superimposed melodic lines; moves over keyboard; flexible tempi; sudden dynamic changes permeated with a certain archaic flavor; architectural forms. All add up to an unusual work. D.

Darius Milhaud. *Piano Quintet* 1951 (Heugel) 36pp., parts. 16½ min. Avec Vivacité; Avec Mystère; Avec Douceur; Avec Emportement. Melodically oriented but the themes are sometimes fragmented and juxtaposed amid much figuration. It is easiest to hear the themes and lines in the third movement. Small fragments build larger structures; homophonic and contrapuntal elements. Some polytonality, octotonic, quartal harmonies, parallel chords. Large span required. D.

Zygmunt Mycielski. *Five Preludes* 1967 (PWM 1973) 16pp., parts. Reproduction of the composer's MS.

Vítězslav Novák. *Quintet* Op.12 (Simrock 1904) 46pp., parts. Allegro molto moderato; Andante (based on an old Bohemian song from the 15th century); Slovakisch. Colorful writing with Bohemian folksong influence in a Brahms idiom. M-D.

Stephen Oliver. *Music for the Wreck of the Deutschland* (Nov 1972). An analogue that exploits the restrained sound of the string quartet with the piano. Concentrated and complex writing. D.
See: Jane Glover, "Stephen Oliver," MT, December 1974: 1042–43.

Tadeusz Paciorkiewicz. *Piano Quintet* 1972 (ZAIKS) 60pp., parts. Allegro ben moderato; Andante; Con moto. Linear, freely tonal, ostinato figures, harmonic seconds and fourths used in secco style, trills used extensively in final movement, tremolo, basically neoclassic style. M-D.

Robert Palmer. *Piano Quintet* 1950 (CFP 6003) 61pp., parts. Allegro moderato; Scherzo; Aria; Lento Maestoso–Allegro. This entire work focuses mainly on rhythmic and metrical materials. Brackets are used to denote rhythmical groupings that depart from the normal meter. Highly saturated with rich dissonance. A cyclic theme appears in all movements. This work is consistent in style and substance and shows a highly developed craft. The Phrygian pastoral theme in the Aria is especially effective. Strong organic unity. D.

Vincent Persichetti. *Piano Quintet* Op.66 1954 (EV) 41pp., parts. 23 min. Reproduction of the composer's MS., easy to read. In one long, compactly organized movement but with frequent tempo and character changes. Economic style is austere, rhythmically vigorous, and contrapuntal. Piano textures are sparse and generally clear. Freely dissonant with some polytonal moments, yet the piece is tonally integrated. D.

Hans Pfitzner. *Quintet* Op.23 C 1908 (CFP 2923) 64pp., parts. Allegro, ma non troppo; Intermezzo; Adagio; Allegretto commodo. Strong influences of Wagner, Schumann, and Richard Strauss are felt in this work. It is Romantic and Germanic through and through, and seems somewhat overblown today, but is superbly written for the pianist. Full of expansive lyricism and rich chromatic harmonies, the thematic transformations involve dissonant counterpoint and unconventional rhythmic intricacies. D.

Gabriel Pierné. *Quintet* Op.41 1916–7 (Hamelle) 93pp., parts. Moderato molto tranquillo; Sur un rhythme de Zortzico; Lent–Allegro vivo ed agitato. Repeated chords, some shifting meters in the second movement, broad pianistic gestures, parallel chords, chromatic. D.

Walter Piston. *Quintet for Piano and String Quartet* 1949 (AMP) 44pp., parts. 20 min. Allegro comodo: poetic; neo-Romantic mood; flowing harmonic figurations; main idea juxtaposed against this backdrop; more tension in the mid-section which uses fourths and fifths, tonality is G. Adagio: light, dissonant harmonies over pedal point; bold dissonance of consecutive sevenths; *pp* to *ff* and back to *pp*. Allegro vivo: ABA; a Pistonian dance with a quasi-contrapuntal B section; opens with a tricky rhythmic figure; the A section has a coda in G and drops the third in the final chord. Highly crafted writing with tasteful elegance. D.

Mel Powell. *Piano Quintet* 1957 (Bo&H) 49pp., parts. I. Fantasia: varied tempi, shifting meters, short motifs, controlled improvisation. II. Intermezzi: piano tacet. Presto Figurato: chromatic figures in alternating hands; chordal punctuation; Alla Stretta climax is capped with a glissando and quickly subsides to a Cantilena lento that contains much diaglogue between instruments and finally diminishes to a *pp* closing. III. Allegro cantabile: figuration (chromatic, octotonic) moves over keyboard; additive meters (3/8 + 2/4). Entire work has serial overtones. Requires experienced performers. D.

Väinö Raitio. *Quintet* Op.16 (Fazer) 66pp., parts. Adagio espressivo–Allegro non tanto; Lento, ma non troppo; Finale. Impressionistic influences, clear traditional forms, bold and dramatic gestures. Pianistic techniques are based on an extension of those used by Richard Strauss and Maurice Ravel. Mildly contemporary. Large span required. D.

Günter Raphael. *Quintett* Op.6 c♯ (Br&H No.1934a/g 1925) 72pp., parts. Allegro molto appassionato; Allegretto; Andante sostenuto; Allegro con fuoco. In Brahms–Reger tradition. Dramatic gestures for the piano. D.

Max Reger. *Quintet* Op.64 c (CFP 8853) 72pp., parts. Con moto e agitato; Vivace; Lento addolorato e con gran affetto; Allegro risoluto. Complicated harmonic system with great modulatory freedom. Shows a colossal craft. The pianist must constantly be moving from one complex situation to another. Slow movement is one of great beauty, in spite of its complexities. D.

Franz Reizenstein. *Quintet* Op.23 D (Lengnick 1948) 30 min. A noble four-movement work with the piano writing by far the most interesting. Written in the tradition of Brahms, Fauré, and Elgar in a mildly contemporary but effective style. The first movement is tense and stringently constructed; the second is slightly more relaxed and beautiful. An enchanting (if somewhat helter-skelter at places) scherzo is followed by a lofty finale. D.

Wallingford Riegger. *Piano Quintet* Op.47 1951 (AMP) 68pp., parts. 25 min. Allegro: octotonic, alternating hands, wide melodic skips, thin textures, large span required. Untitled second movement: 3 with 2, sustained with repeated chords, dramatic gestures. Untitled third movement: chordal punctuation; octotonic, repeated octaves; boisterous honky-tonk conclusion is unusual, even for Riegger. All three movements show an imaginative adventurousness, spiced with rugged and percussive use of the piano. Free twelve-tone treatment in angular style with strong contrast of mood and materials. D.

Miklós Rózsa. *Quintet* Op.2 f 1928 (Br&H No.1940a/f) 64pp., parts. 28 min. Allegro non troppo, ma appassionato; Molto adagio; Allegro capriccioso; Vivace. Freely tonal with strong pianistic gestures, sequences, large skips. Generally successful ensemble writing throughout. D.

Edmund Rubbra. *Lyric Movement* Op.24 (Lengnick 1947) 18pp., parts. Opens with undulating thirds and octaves over widely spread triadic harmony in the left hand. Quartal and quintal harmony add a mildly contemporary flavor in parallel chordal passages. Flowing melodies, hand-crossings, rich sonorities through most of the work. A mid-section Allegro provides contrast. Big Romantic climax is reached, then subsides to a Lento *ppp* chordal close. M-D.

Anton Rubinstein. *Quintette* Op.99 g (Hamelle) 95pp., parts. Molto lento–con molto moderato; Moderato; Moderato; Moderato. Overflowing with nineteenth–century pianistic clichés and idioms. The piano has the most interest, and at places the strings seem almost superfluous. M-D to D.

Camille Saint-Saëns. *Quintet* Op.14 a 1855 (Leuckart; Hamelle 63pp., parts; UE). Allegro moderato e maestoso: opening theme is impatient; form is clearly crafted; tremolo; fluent triplet figuration. Andante: a broad liturgical motif opens the movement; light arpeggi in the piano; a hint of the coming Presto is heard near the end of the movement. Presto: strings engage in fugal acrobatics. Allegro assai, ma tranquillo: versatile pianistic patterns; brilliant scales in octaves round off work. Light textures with the balance between severity and heavier textures carefully observed. D.

Franz Schmidt. *Quintet* G 1926 (Weinberger JW3761a 1954) 76pp., parts. Lebhaft, doch nicht schnell, Sehr ruhig; Sehr lebhaft. The piano part is written for the left hand alone, for Paul Wittgenstein, but the work is also published in a version for two hands: made by Friedrich Wührer (Wein-berger). Conservative and chromatic writing. M-D.

Florent Schmitt. *Quintette* Op.51 (Mathot 1910) 135pp., parts. Lent et grave–Animé; Lent; Animé. Tremolo chords, long lines accompanied by shorter chromatic figures, syncopated chords, large skips, brilliant passage work, chromatic octave runs, alternating hand figuration, long arpeggi. Requires four staves to notate piano part in some places. This work is a catalogue of pianistic techniques that were in general use at the time it was composed. Difficult and involved writing with some moments of great beauty. D.

Arnold Schoenberg. *Weihnachtsmusik* 1921 (Belmont 1020). For 2 violins, cello, harmonium, and piano. Score, parts. A tonal setting of the well-known Christmas tunes "Lo, How a Rose" and "Silent Night." This fantasy shows that the composer knew how to relax his contrapuntal craft when required. M-D.
See: Arnold Whittall, *Schoenberg Chamber Music*, BBC Music Guide 21 (Seattle: University of Washington, 1972), 64pp. Includes analyses of Schoenberg's chamber music, with the exception of the *Fantasia* for violin and piano.

Franz Schubert. *Piano Quintet* (The Trout) Op.114 A 1819 (CFP 51pp., parts; Br&H; Mercury; K; IMC; EPS rev. ed. 118, 86pp.; Dover, in the *Complete Chamber Music for Pianoforte and Strings*). For violin, viola, cello, double bass, and piano. Allegro vivace; Andante; Scherzo—Presto; Tema—Andantino (and 6 variations); Finale—Allegro giusto. There is no happier or more playful music in all of Schubert than this work. The unusual combination of instruments was used by Hummel before Schubert in his *Quintet* Op.87. The piano part lies high because of the presence of the two low stringed instruments, and tends to double its fluent passages in octaves. The fourth movement uses the song "The Trout," which gave the quintet its popular name. The pastoral finale adds the exotic sound of a Hungarian or Bohemian dance. D.

Robert Schumann. *Quintet* Op.44 E♭ 1843 (Br&H 57pp., parts; UE; Litolff; GS L1648; Augener; IMC) 30 min. Allegro brillante: mainly a piano solo in which the strings double the piano part or fill in with isolated phrases. In modo d'una Marcia—Un Poco largamente: combines different rhythms and is highly effective. Scherzo: resorts to much doubling but the piano accompaniment provides a delightful substructure for melodic ideas provided by the strings. Finale: opens with a unison melody in the piano supported by repeated chords in the strings; a brilliant coda lets the pianist present the first subject from the opening movement in the right hand while the left hand and the second violin bring out the first subject of the Finale; all instruments agree on a joyous conclusion. D.

Cyril Scott. *Quintet* (St&B 3048 1925) 85pp., parts. Andante con esaltazione; Allegro grazioso ma non troppo; Adagio con gran espressione; Finale. Traditional writing for all instruments, chromatic, chordal, with fluent figuration. M-D.

Giovanni Sgambati. *Quintuor I* Op.4 f (Schott 22575) 76pp., parts. Adagio–Allegro ma non troppo; Vivacissimo; Andante sostenuto; Allegro moderato (theme and four contrasting variations). Full-blooded Romantic writing littered with octaves, broken-chord passages, and numerous other nineteenth-century pianistic clichés. D.

Arthur Shepherd. *Quintet* 1940 (copy at LC) 53pp., parts. Andante: Andante con fermezza; Allegro spiritoso. Freely tonal, centers around f♯–F♯. Post-Romantic vocabulary, well-integrated writing, clear forms. D.

Dmitri Shostakovich. *Piano Quintet* Op.57 g 1940 (USSR 1941; CFP; MCA; IMC 2063 60pp., parts) 30 min. Prelude; Fugue; Scherzo; Intermezzo; Finale. A spacious calm and strange desolation is found in much of this lyrical piece. Compelling dramatic moments are contrasted with an austere repose. Limpid in texture, direct in appeal, and free from much of the bombast that mars numerous Soviet scores (including some of Shostakovich's). The Fugue is based on a traditional Russian song, while the Scherzo is one of the composer's happiest and most boisterous inventions. The Intermezzo has much diatonic serenity about it. The terse Finale is a blend of physical and spiritual energies, of lyricism and fleeting drama. The piano has some pure athletic lines that verge on the virtuosic. D.

Kaikhosru Sorabji. *Quintet* 1920 (London & Continental Music Publishing Co.). 64pp., parts. One movement, Modéré: beats are indexed underneath the score (20/8); three staves necessary to notate the piano part. Highly chromatic with sweeping lines and fast-changing chords. Changing meters, harmonic fourths in flowing figuration, tremolo. Enormous climax suddenly drops to *pp* and *ppp* with indication "Enigmatique equivoque." Complex and D.

Václav Stépan. *Les Premiers Printemps* Op.5 (Lerolle 1921) 73pp., parts. Joie et Jeu: light staccato chords; broken octaves; freely chromatic; arpeggi left hand; melody in thirds in right hand; opening mood closes movement. Douleur et désir: lugubrious sustained chords; fast harmonic rhythm;

agitato mid-section with alternating hand passages; triplets; Molto lento climax; *ppp* closing. Lutte et joie: march tempo; quick, repeated chords; curling chromatic figuration; intensity builds; tempi changes; thoroughly colorful writing with a brilliant conclusion; polyphonic. D.

Josef Suk. *Quintet* Op.8 g 1893–1915 (Supraphon 1973) 88pp., parts. Rev. by Vlastimil Musil. Allegro energico; Adagio (Religioso) Scherzo; Finale. This tonal but freely chromatic work utilizes a late nineteenth-century pianistic, harmonic, and melodic vocabulary. D.

George Szell. *Quintet* Op.2 E 1911 (UE 3694) 61pp., parts. Bewegt: E; SA; sweeping post-Romantic lines; chromatic; 2 with 3; hemiola; alternating hands. Scherzo: C; octotonic; strings frequently play alone; piano also frequently plays alone. Mässig langsam: A♭; Brahmsian pianism; syncopated closing in G leads directly to Finale: E; rondo; bright and cheerful; rhythmic sixteenth-note figuration; contrasted chordal episodes; hand-crossings; strong gestures in coda. Lyrical Romantic writing throughout. D.

Serge I. Tanieff. *Quintuor* Op.30 (Editions Russe du Musique) 101pp., parts. Introduzione–Adagio maestoso–Allegro Patetico; Scherzo; Largo; Finale—Allegro vivace. Utilizes strong nineteenth-century virtuoso techniques and idioms. D.

Alexander Tcherepnin. *Quintette* Op.44 (UE 1927) 15 min. Allegro (SA); Allegretto (ABA); Allegro (Rondo). Written in a complex polyphonic style with a slightly Russian flavor. The Allegretto employs the composer's "interpoint" technique, in which vertical and horizontal elements are equal. The final Allegro is based on one theme that is treated contrapuntally. Highly chromatic. This piece is perhaps the culmination of Tcherepnin's chamber music. D.

Georg Philipp Telemann. *Suite* B♭ Telemann Werke Verzeichnis 55: B8 (A. Hoffman—Möseler 1975) 28pp., parts. 2 violins, viola, cello, basso continuo. Preface in French, English, and German. Ouverture; Scaramousches; Harlequinade; Columbine; Pierrot; Menuet I,II; Mezzetin en turc. Fine realizations. M-D.

Ernst Toch. *Piano Quintet* Op.64 1938 (Delkas) 75pp., parts. The Lyrical Part: bold lines. The Whimsical Part: ABA, antiphonal, muted strings. The Contemplative Part: ABA; strings alone in part A, piano alone in B; strings return; coda brings all together. The Dramatic Part: more writing for all five instruments, contrapuntal. Programmatic titles, Romantic tendencies in an overall neoclassic style. Lines and textures are generally clear and operate within freely tonal bounds. Strings are combined as one voice, the piano as another. D.

Joaquín Turina. *Quintette* 1907 (Rouart Lerolle) 58pp., parts. Fugue lente: piano embellishes fugue with full but *pp* sonorities; fugue is treated freely; broken-chord figuration; subject heard at end of movement. Animé: march-like, strong rhythmic emphasis, fast harmonic rhythm. Andante Scherzo: flowing; chromatic, undulating dolcissimo and cantabile; short figures evolve into longer ones; octotonic; moves through various keys. Final: recitative opening, sustained syncopated chords, Lento coda and *fff* ending. Does not sound like the later Turina that pianists know; a transitional work. M-D to D.

John Verrall. *Quintet* (CFE).

Louis Vierne. *Quintette* Op.42 (Senart 1924) 63pp., parts. Poco lento–Moderato; Larghetto sostenuto; Maestoso. Chromatic, many octaves, many triplets, arpeggi figuration. This work looks more impressive on the page than it sounds, although there are some lovely spots. M-D.

John Vincent. *Consort* (Belwin-Mills 1962) 95pp., parts. 26 min. Allegro con brio; Andante; Allegro vivo. Bitonal, secco bass, shifting rhythms, scalar passages, driving rhythms, flowing melody in Andante, repeated octaves in alternating hands, dancelike rhythms. Attractive, mildly contemporary. M-D.

Anton Webern. *Quintet* 1907, rev. ed. 1974 (Boelke-Bomart) 30pp., parts. 12 min. Composed immediately before Op.1 and not included by Webern in his own catalogue of works. A one-movement form in SA design. Strong early Schönberg influence. Principal groups in C with subordinate group around the dominant! Themes include most of the twelve tones; series-like. The harmony is mainly triadic. Piano style is Brahmsian with octave doublings, thick chords, and subtle rhythmic shifts, but a few spots of thin textures and widely spread skips suggest future Webernesque techniques. A lyric work that would work well for groups not yet prepared to undertake later Webern. M-D.
See: Dika Newlin, "Webern's Quintet for String Quartet and Piano," *Notes*, 10/4 (September 1953): 674–75.

Moisei Weinberg. *Quintet* Op.18 1944 (USSR 1964) 87pp., parts. Moderato con moto: SA, Slavic theme for main idea, second theme animated and whimsical; develops naturally and effortlessly; closes with first theme diminuendo. Allegretto: in the nature of an intermezzo; piano has cadenza; *ppp* closing. Presto: scherzo with an irresistible drive. Largo: stirringly lyric and profoundly meditative; piano performs solo. Allegro agitato: fleeting and dynamic; based on the alternation of an austere ostinato theme and a gentle, lyrical one; at the climax (figure 142) the opening theme of the first movement is heard and serves to unify the cyclic work into an integrated whole; the progress of the finale resumes, but the music seems calmer, less impetuous, and the ostinato gradually melts away. Post-Romantic Russian style, mildly contemporary, chromatic, and tonal. M-D to D.

Charles Marie Widor. *Quintette* Op.7 (Hamelle) 65pp., parts. Allegro; Andante; Molto Vivace; Allegro con moto.

_____ *Quintette* Op.68 (Schott 25731) 65pp., parts. Moderato; Andante; Allegro con fuoco; Moderato.

Malcolm Williamson. *Quintet* 1968 (Weinberger) 68pp., parts. 16 min. Adagio: chordal for piano, individual lines in other parts. Allegro molto: pointillistic, trills, extreme ranges exploited, large span required. Adagio: similar to opening Adagio but more developed. Dissonant, large formal blocks of organized material, harmonics, clusters, fluent and pianistic style. Writing is easy to follow with the ear. D.

Wawrzyniec Zulawski. *Kwintet Fortepianowy* 1966 (PWM) 102pp., parts. 20 min. Andante: quiet chromatic opening leads to a short piano cadenza, which leads to an Agitato; these tempi are juxtaposed against each other throughout the movement. Allegro vivace: a scherzo, chromatic chords and figuration, octotonic. Andante molto tranquillo: added-note chords, large climax à la Szymanowski, Lento *pp* close. Allegro moderato: tremolo, fast harmonic rhythm, broken left-hand figuration under right-hand octave melody, Allegretto episodes, *pp* closing, freely tonal around C. M-D to D.

Quintets for Piano(s), Strings, and Winds

William Albright. *Danse Macabre* 1971 (Bowdoin College Music Press) 31pp., parts. 14½ min. For flute, clarinet, violin, cello, and piano. Completed April 6, 1971, the day Igor Stravinsky died. Percussion required: 1 pair maracas, 2 pair antique cymbals, 1 pair claves, 2 wood blocks, 1 large and 1 small triangle, bass drum, hi hat, large tam tam. Pianist also needs a brush, nail file, coin, glass ashtray, soft mallet. Piano part includes irregular tremolo on tritone, plucked strings, nail file on string, sudden tempo changes, glissandi, pointillistic treatment, low-sounding pitches to be played ugly and dry, improvisation on certain pitches, rambling with pitches ad lib, spoken words, tongue clicks, knuckles on lid and crossbeams, tempo di Valse section, soft irregular improvisation on insides of piano, Tarantella fantastica section. Piano must improvise and give the impression of "smothered virtuosity." Directions in Maniacal section to play crass, ugly, hammered, forearm clusters; all performers clap together at conclusion. Contains some awesome and startling sonorities. Avant-garde. D.

Milton Babbitt. *Arie da Capo* (CFP 66584) 14 min. For flute, clarinet, violin, cello, and piano. In one movement.

Johann Christian Bach. *Quintet* Op.11/1 C (Steglich—Br; Musica Rara 26pp., parts). For flute, oboe, violin, viola, and basso continuo. Allegretto; Andantino; Menuetto con variatione. M-D.
_____ *Quintet* Op.11/2 G (Steglich—Br; Musica Rara). For flute, oboe, violin, viola, and basso continuo.
_____ *Quintet* Op.11/3 F (Steglich—Br; Musica Rara 19pp., parts). For flute, oboe, violin, viola, and basso continuo. Andante; Rondo. M-D.
_____ *Quintet* Op.11/4 E♭ (Nag). For 3 violins, (or flute, oboe, and violin), viola, and basso continuo; cello ad lib.
_____ *Quintet* Op.11/5 A (Steglich—Br; Musica Rara). For flute or violin, oboe or violin, violin, viola, cello, and basso continuo.

_____ *Quintet* Op.11/6 D (Nag). For 3 violins (or flute, oboe, and violin), viola, and basso continuo; cello ad lib.

_____ *Quintet* Op.22/1 D (R. Ermler—HM 42) 27pp., parts. 16½ min. For flute, oboe, violin, cello, and continuo; realization by Walter Kraft. A charming work. Probably one of the first compositions of Bach's time to use an obbligato keyboard for chamber music with larger instrumentation. M-D.

_____ *Quintet* Op.22/2 F (Erhardt—Schott 4167). For oboe, violin, viola, cello, and piano.

Johann Christoph Friedrich Bach. *Sonate* D (Ruf—Br). For flute, violin, viola, cello, and piano. M-D.

Harrison Birtwistle. *3 Lessons in a Frame* (UE) 12½ min. For flute, clarinet, violin, cello, and piano.

Joseph Bodin de Boismortier. *Concerto* e (Ruf—Ric) 23pp., parts. For flute, oboe, bassoon, violin, and basso continuo. Figured bass part is well realized. M-D.

William Bolcom. *Duets for Quintet, A Farce for Fun* (Bowdoin College Music Press 1971) 21pp., parts. For flute, clarinet, violin, cello, and piano (and stage manager for lights). Includes instructions for performance. ''This is a 'theater-piece' but the 'theater' resides almost totally in the music . . . .Each instrument has a sort of musical role, and a very *definite personality*, in his utterances. For the player, the object is to find his own 'profile' from (1) listening to his own part; (2) listening to the other parts, particularly the one he is 'in dialogue' with at the moment. The controlling idea is that of a duet-texture. 'Dialogues' are carried on between pairs of instruments; at some time a third instrument may interrupt'' (from notes in the score). Serial influence, pointillistic treatment, dynamic extremes, clusters, varied tempi. This is a fun piece but it requires thorough musicianship to bring it off. Avant-garde. D.

_____ *Whisper Moon (Dream Music Number Three)* 1971 (Bowdoin College Music Press 1973) 22pp., parts. For alto flute, clarinet, violin, cello, and piano. Includes extensive instructions for performance. Requires improvisation, plucked and stopped strings. Pointillistic broken octaves and improvisation in this style, jazz rhythms, popular-music context with fragments of ''Blue Moon'' and ''Louise'' mixed in, sweeping glissandi inside piano, free time, skittery, half-pedals, clusters, harmonics. Violin and cello whisper words almost to themselves while playing ad lib; ''everybody stops wherever he is when flute gives the little whoop signal.'' Delightful mixture of pop writing with avant-garde. D.

Roque Cordero. *Quinteto* 1949 (PIC 1967) 95pp., parts. For flute, clarinet, violin, cello, and piano. Vivace e con spirito: serial, piano lends strong rhythmic punctuation. varied tempi. Lento assai: chromatic figuration, strong octave gestures, octotonic. Allegro molto: requires a fine octave technique. Largo–Allegro molto: mixture of fugal and serial textures. Generally vigorous and robust writing. D.

David Diamond. *Quintet* 1937 (PIC) 52pp., parts. 13 min. For flute, violin, viola, cello, and piano. Allegro deciso e molto ritmico: SA; clear diatonic lines; strong rhythmic thrust; preference for seconds, sevenths, and octaves in the piano part; white-key glissando in piano ends movement. Romanza: flowing melodies, more dissonant harmony; piano has sustained chords and some melodic emphasis. Allegro veloce: jig with folklike melody; piano has some polytonal treatment; upward white-key glissandi, strong propulsive rhythms. An economical and tightly constructed work with an overall brilliant effect. D.

Theodore Dubois. *Quintette* F (Heugel 1905) 58pp., parts. For oboe (or second violin or clarinet), violin, viola, cello, and piano. Allegro; Canzonetta; Adagio non troppo; Allegro con fuoco. Not of great musical worth but effectively scored for the instruments. Traditional turn-of-the century idioms and techniques. M-D.

William Duckworth. *Seven Shades of Blue* (Bowdoin College Music Press 1974) 10pp., parts. For flute, clarinet, violin, cello, and piano. Sections should be played without pause. Patterns are given that are to be repeated in specific ways (legato, rhythmically, diminuendo, etc.) for the indicated length of time. Piano part involves chords, single lines, arpeggi figuration, trills, long pedals, pointillistic treatment, sudden dynamic changes. Avant-garde. Requires a large span. M-D.

Donald Erb. *Quintet* 1976 (MS available from composer, % Cleveland Institute of Music, 11021 East Blvd., Cleveland, OH 44106. For flute, clarinet, violin, cello, and electric piano. A one-movement work with four internal sections, based on motivic structure—according to the score, intervallic: the perfect fifth and minor third. Unusual sonoric effects; mildly avant-garde. D.

Morton Feldman. *Projection II* 1962 (CFP 6940) 10pp. For flute, violin, cello, trumpet, and piano. Graphic notation. Reproduced from holograph. Includes instructions for performance. Avant-garde. M-D.

Zdeněk Fibich. *Quintet* Op.42 (Supraphon 1973) 62pp., parts. For violin, clarinet, horn, cello, and piano. Preface and critical notes in Czech, Russian, German, and English. M-D to D.

Gerardo Gandini. *Música Nocturna* 1964 (PAU) 11pp., 5 scores required for performance. For piano, flute, violin, viola, and cello. Pointillistic, string glissandi, long pedals, experimental, avant-garde. M-D.

Walter Gieseking. *Quintett* B♭ 1919 (Adolf Fürstner) 54pp., parts. For oboe, clarinet, horn, bassoon, and piano. Allegro moderato: opens with flowing legato dolcissimo lines; broken octaves; arpeggiated chords; heroic quality in development; opening mood returns to close movement; large span required. Andante: syncopated accompaniment in piano to melody in other instruments; duplet and triplet figures prominent; interesting harmonic relationships; many added notes in chords; *pppp* closing. Vivace molto scherzando: scampering figuration, strong rhythmic emphasis in alternating hands, subito dynamics, dancelike, contrasting episodes. French sonorities; mildly contemporary. M-D.

Donald Harris. *Ludus II* 1973 (Jobert) 20pp., 10½ min. For flute, clarinet, violin, cello, and piano. 5 scores necessary for performance. Performance instructions in French and English. One movement. Freely chromatic, serial influence, extensive use of multiphonics for woodwinds. Taut organization, rhythmically complex, wide leaps, fast notes. Shows a strong craft. Requires virtuoso players with ensemble experience. D.

Franz Joseph Haydn. *Sonata* Op.4 E♭ (CFP MV1208). For 2 horns, violin, cello, and piano.
———— *Sinfonie Concertante* Op.84 (F. Sitt—Br&H; Sitt—IMC 986 40pp., parts). For oboe, bassoon, violin, cello, and piano. Allegro; Andante; Allegro con spirito. Writing that endears itself to both performers and listeners. M-D.

Johann David Heinichen. *Concerto* G (H. Fischer—Vieweg 2152) 11pp., parts. For flute, 2 violins, cello, and piano. M-D.
———— *Sonata a 3* 1726 (Hofmeister) 22pp., parts. For 2 oboes, bassoon, cello, and keyboard. The bassoon is treated as a concertante instrument. M-D.

Paul Hindemith. *Drei Stücke* 1925 (Schott 3312). For clarinet, trumpet in C, violin, double bass, and piano. 1. Scherzando: bouncy rhythms; chromatic; grace notes add to gaiety. 2. Langsamer achtel: small intervals expand; rustling mood created in upper register for mid-section; effective syncopation. 3. Lebhafte halbe: martial quality; patterns prevalent; long chromatic lines provide contrast; dies away to *pp*. M-D.

Ignaz Holzbauer. *Quintet* G (F. Schroeder—Br&H 2111) 19pp., parts. For flute, violin, viola, cello, and piano. Andante spiritoso; Menuetto grazioso–(5)Variations–Menuetto (Allegro). Classic style; refined and tasteful writing. The variations on the Menuetto and its return are unusually interesting. M-D.

Charles Ives. *Adagio Sostenuto*, before 1912 (PIC 1969) 1p. (13 measures); parts. For English horn (flute), 3 violins (3rd violin ad lib or viola), cello ad lib, and piano or harp. Chromatic chords, extreme registers, quiet. Large span required. M-D.

———— *Scherzo—All The Way Around and Back* (PIC) 2pp., parts. For clarinet (flute), violin, trumpet, horn, and piano. Can be played by one or two pianists. Complex rhythms, chromatic, dynamic extremes, large span required if performed by one pianist. D. For fuller description see quintets for piano(s), percussion and/or tape, and other instruments.

Friedrich Kalkbrenner. *Grand Quintet* Op.81 1826 (Br&H). For piano, clarinet, horn, cello, and double bass. Sounds like Schubert. Attractive melodies, lively rhythmic foundation. Somewhat like a chamber concerto; piano has by far the finest part. M-D.

Karl Kohn. *Capriccios* 1962 (CF) 12 min. For flute, clarinet, cello, harp, and piano. Three movements. Masterly manipulation of sounds; macro and micro structures well shaped by a polyphonic discipline. Sustained cries of the final movement, which gradually climax in an instrumental dirge, are especially arresting. M-D to D.

Konradin Kreutzer. *Quintet* A (Musica Rara). For flute, clarinet, viola, cello, and piano. The piano dominates but the themes are fairly distributed. Attractive material, especially the martial first movement and the engaging polonaise finale. Piano has much activity in the taxing florid lines of the finale. M-D to D.

István Láng. *Rhymes for Chamber Ensemble* (EMB 1972) 14pp., 5 copies necessary for performance. For flute, clarinet, viola, cello, and piano.

Elisabeth Lutyens. *Concertante for Five Players* Op.22 1950 (Belwin-Mills 1970) 24pp., parts. 10 min. For flute (piccolo), clarinet (bass clarinet), violin (viola), cello, and piano. Sectionalized; constantly changing sounds in a fascinating and always logically ordered serial manner. Subtle and convincing. M-D.

Gian Francesco Malipiero. *Sonata a Cinque* 1934 (Ric) 28pp., parts. 16 min. For flute (violin), violin, viola, cello, and piano. One large movement, varied tempi, chromatic coloration, large arpeggiated chords, open-fifth sonorities, four octaves apart, glissandi. M-D.

Tomás Marco. *Albor* (Noli tangere meos circulos) (Editorial de Música Española Contemporánea 1972) 19pp. For flute, clarinet, violin, cello, and piano.

Thea Musgrave. *Chamber Concerto II* (JWC 1966) 59pp., parts. 15 min. Subtitled "In Homage to Charles Ives." One movement divided into sections. Metrical freedom for players. Incorporates popular tunes, as "The Keel-Row," "Swanee River," and "All Things Bright and Beautiful," which are placed in a dissonant environment. Highly dramatic and chromatic. D.

Pauline Oliveros. *Aeolian Partitions* 1970 (Bowdoin College Music Press) 5pp., 2pp. general directions, 2pp. directions for each performer. For flute (alto flute, piccolo), violin (viola), cello, clarinet (bass clarinet), and piano. "Composed for a proscenium stage with wings. Performers must be able to enter and exit from stage right and left during the performance and to get on to the stage from the house. A total house and stage blackout is necessary. If these directions cannot be met, abandon the performance entirely" (from the score). Prop list includes broom, newspaper, flashlight, transistor radio to be used by extra, page turner, megaphone, large gong, bow, suction cup arrows and quiver, stage crew, 7 six-volt flasher lights, slide projector, slide of Star of David, 2 extras, preferably familiar to the audience, e.g., dean of the college, department chairman, mayor of the town, etc., who walk across performance on cue. Extensive directions help make this one of the funniest "theater pieces" this writer has seen. Climax of work arrives when audience is (may be) invited to join in the telepathic improvisation (with detailed instructions). Great fun for all! Avant-garde. M-D.

Robert Palmer. *Quintet* 1952, 1963 (PIC) 67pp., parts. 26 min. For piano, clarinet, violin, viola, and cello. Poco lento ma con moto: the most impressive movement in this large and ambitious work; modified SA design; develops two main melodic ideas over a broad time period; climax breaks off into a number of short cadenzas, followed by a recapitulation of the opening material. Allegro molto: a lively Scherzo. Andante grazioso: contrapuntally conceived; each instrument unwinds its lyrical melodic lines. Allegro vivo: a frivolous finale; busy figuration and a frequently repeated Hindemithian melodic figure conclude the work. The piano and clarinet essentially frame the ensemble. D.

Juan Carlos Paz. *Dédalus* 1950 (Ediciones Culturales Argentinas—Impreso por Ricordi Americana 1964) 62pp., parts. For piano, flute, clarinet, violin, and cello. Expositio: serial, changing meters, pointillistic. Choral: sustained and chorale-like. Ostinato: row is run through all the instruments. Variacion I: cantus firmus. II: staccato chords contrast with sustained chords. III: light, fleeting. IV: ostinato and choral together. V: Fugato; canon a 4 voices; Reexpositio. VI: choral and ostinato varied together. VII: similar techniques to Var. II; piano Recitativo. VIII: cantus firmus and Recitativo together. IX: Fugato; Improvisatio; Reexposito. X: Praeludium; canon perpetum; coda-cancrizans. This work is a catalogue of serial and contrapuntal techniques. D.

John Christopher Pepusch. *Quintet* F (T. Dart—Schott 10688) 10pp., parts. For 2 recorders, 2 violins, and keyboard; cello ad lib. Largo; Allegro; Adagio; Presto. Delightful writing, excellent keyboard realization. M-D.
——— *Four Concerti* Op.8/1, 4, 5, 6 (D. Lasocki—Musica Rara 1974). For 2 treble recorders, 2 flutes or 2 oboes or 2 violins, and basso continuo. Score and parts available separately for each concerto. M-D.

Raoul Pleskow. *Three Movements for Quintet* (Of a November Morning 1970) 1971 (Bowdoin College Music Press) 25pp., parts. Reproduced from composer's MS. For flute, clarinet, violin, cello, and piano. Untitled movements, serial influence, pointillistic, chromatic, plucked strings, sudden dynamic changes, expressionistic, proportional rhythmic relationships, cluster-like sonorities. Complex writing. D.

Henri Pousseur. *Quintette a la memoire d'Anton Webern* 1955 (SZ 5428) 63pp., miniature score, 14 min. For violin, cello, clarinet, bass clarinet, and piano. Highly organized, complex rhythmic ratios, pointillistic, intense, expressionistic, short pauses set off sections. Only for the most venturesome and experienced ensemble players. D.

Alan Rawsthorne. *Quintet* 1970 (OUP) 22pp., parts. 9 min. For clarinet, horn, violin, cello, and piano. One movement, divided into five sections (Andante; Allegro; Andante; Allegro; Andante); uses mirror form for the various sections. Austere writing, mildly dissonant with tonal and serial techniques. Piano part is the most difficult, with mainly chordal and chromatic scalar sections plus some martellato octaves in alternating hands. M-D to D.

Constantin Regamey. *Quintet* 1944 (PWM). For clarinet, bassoon, violin, cello, and piano.

Daniel Ruyneman. *Reflexions III* 1960–1 (Donemus 1973) 20pp., parts. For flute, violin, viola, cello, and piano (or harpsichord).

Johann Heinrich Schmelzer. *Sonata* G "La Carioletta" (Musica Rara 1974) 12pp., parts. For cornetto (trumpet), violin, trombone, bassoon, and basso continuo.

Arnold Schoenberg. *Chamber Symphony* Op.9 (Webern—UE 12505) 97pp., parts. 22min. Originally for 15 instruments. Arranged for flute (or 2 violins), clarinet, violin, cello, and piano. Constantly unfolds with varying tempi, dynamics, and mood. The piano part moves in a non-pointillistic manner and serves as a binding influence on the other instruments. Thematic variation takes place simultaneously rather than in succession. D.
See: CCSCM, II, pp.346–47 for a thorough analysis of the formal structure of this composition.

Robert Schumann. *Andante and Variations* Op.46 1843 (W. Wollenweber UWKR 11 1972) 33pp., parts. For 2 pianos, 2 cellos, and horn. Usually heard performed by only the two pianos, but the work is more effective in this, the original version. Filled with much dialogue between the instruments, this beautiful Romantic piece is pleasurable for performers and audience. One variation is more difficult than the others. M-D.

Seymour Shifrin. *In Eius Memoriam* (CFP 66479a 1976) 17pp., parts. 6 min. For piano, flute, clarinet, violin, and cello.
———— *Serenade* 1954 (Litolff 5853) 38pp., parts. For oboe, clarinet, horn, viola, and piano. Allegro molto, energico; Largo assai; Presto molto. Neo-classic orientation with clear structures, mildly pointillistic, freely tonal, fast harmonic motion, fragmentary lines, strongly contrasted ideas superimposed on each other produce dramatic tension. Flexible meters, especially in the last movement. Large span required. D.

Halsey Stevens. *Quintet* 1956 (Helios) 55pp., parts. 21 min. For flute, violin, viola, cello, and piano. Pastorale—Andante non troppo: harmonic fourths and fifths prevalent in the piano part; flowing; piano treated harmonically and melodically. Scherzo—Vivo e ritmico: 5/8; some changing meters; rhythmically driving; Poco meno mosso section is more lyrical; Tempo primo returns. Threnody—Lento: piano supplies rich chords that bind other melodically fragmented instruments together. Fugue—Lieto: thoroughly worked out; elegant contrapuntal technique displayed. Epilogue—Riflessivo: sums up work by echoing ideas from other movements; *ppp* ending. Clear counterpoint and tonalities mixed with infrequent dissonance. Displays extraordinary refinement in texture and melodious expressiveness. Contains no unnecessary notes. M-D.

Gottfried Heinrich Stölzel. *Sonata* F (G. Hausswald—Br&H No.1980) 5pp., parts. For oboe, horn, violin, cello, and piano. M-D.

Bruce J. Taub. *Quintet I* 1972 (ACA) 29pp., parts. For flute/piccolo, clarinet, violin, cello, and piano. Also printed in ASUC Journal of Music Scores. Sectional, stopped strings, freely tonal, sudden extreme dynamic changes, sequences, triplet figure important, secco style, chordal punctuation, thin textures, individual style. D.

Georg Philipp Telemann. *Quartet* D (Seiffert—Br&H) *Tafelmusik II*. For bassoon, 2 flutes, cello, and keyboard. M-D.

Anatol Vieru. *Crible d'Eratosthène* 1969 (Sal) 32pp., parts. Variable duration. For clarinet, violin, viola, cello, and piano. Performance directions in French. Improvisation mixed with traditional, avant-garde, and proportional notation. Fragments of the Beethoven "Moonlight" Sonata and a Rossini piece are interspersed with laughing and other sounds the performers are asked to make. This is a partially controlled "happening" and theoretically falls in the multimedia category. It could be very funny or a complete bore! Performers need a sense of humor. M-D.

Antonio Vivaldi. *Concerto* C, F.XII/30; P.81 (Musica Rara) 15pp., parts. For soprano recorder, oboe, 2 violins, and basso continuo. Adagio–Allegro; Largo; Allegro assai. M-D.

——— *Concerto* C, P.82 (Musica Rara). For flute, oboe, violin, bassoon, and basso continuo.

——— *Concerto* D, F.XII/9 P.155 (Musica Rara 1217) 22pp., parts. For flute, oboe, bassoon, violin, and basso continuo. (Allegro); Largo; Allegro. Valuable preface and critical commentary by the editor, David Lasocki. M-D.

——— *Concerto* g, F.XII/5; P.342 (Lasocki—Musica Rara 1185) 13pp., parts. For flute (violin), 2 violins, bassoon, and basso continuo. La Notte; Fantasmi; Il Sonno; Allegro. Helpful preface. M-D.

——— *Concerto* g, F.XII/6; P.360 (S. Sadie—Musica Rara 1148) 18pp., parts. For flute, oboe, bassoon, violin, and basso continuo. Allegro; Presto. M-D.

"P." stands for Marc Pincherle, *Antonio Vivaldi et la musique instrumentale*, 2 vols, Vol.II: *Inventaire thématique* (Paris, 1948).

——— *Concerto* g (Ghedini—IMC). For flute, oboe, violin, bassoon, and keyboard.

Matthias Weckman. *Sonata a 4* d (A. Lumsden—Musica Rara) 8pp., parts. For oboe, violin, trombone, bassoon, and basso continuo. One continuous movement: Moderato–Adagio–Allegro. M-D.

Lawrence Widdoes. *From a Time of Snow* 1970 (Bowdoin College Music Press) 21pp. For flute, clarinet, violin, cello, and piano. One movement, complex textures, fast-shifting pitches, cross-rhythms, many grace notes, random pizzicatos performed by pianist. M-D.

Quintets for Piano and Winds

Josef Alexander. *Festivities* (PIC 1972) 52pp., parts. For trumpet, horn, trombone, tuba, and piano or organ. Separate parts are written for piano and organ. Piano part is well integrated with the brass ensemble. Moderato maestoso is the basic tempo and mood but short contrasting sections are heard from time to time. Compositional language is mildly contemporary and comes off remarkably well in this combination. M-D.

Henry Barraud. *Concertino* (Marbot 1955) 58pp., parts. For piano, flute, clarinet, horn, and bassoon. Vif et décidé; Dans un sentiment nostalgique; Avec entrain. Full of Gallic wit and glitter. Somewhat reminiscent of the Jean Françaix *Concertino,* but the Barraud work requires more piano technique and a larger span (tenth). Thoroughly enjoyable for performers and audience. The piano part gets the most attention. M-D to D.

Ludwig van Beethoven. *Quintet* Op.16 E♭ (CFP; Br&H; Boonin: Musica Rara; K; IMC 42pp., parts). For piano, oboe, clarinet, bassoon, and horn. Grave–Allegro ma non troppo; Andante cantabile; Rondo. Beethoven issued a quartet version of this work for piano, violin, viola, and cello at the same time that the wind version appeared, (1796) with the same opus number (16). The style of this work is more like a piano solo with wind accompaniment, as the themes are usually stated by the piano and answered by the concerted winds. The Andante movement integrates all instruments more thoroughly. M-D.

Franz Danzi. *Quintet* Op.41 d (CFP; Musica Rara 48pp., parts; GS; B&VP). For oboe, clarinet, bassoon, horn, and piano. Larghetto–Allegro; Andante sostenuto; Allegretto. "Danzi introduces in the piano part brilliant passages typical of late Beethoven, although always preserving the purity of classical form. The present Op.41 Quintet is fully worthy to stand by the side of the famous works of Beethoven (Op.16) and Mozart (K.452) for the same combination" (from the Musica Rara preface). M-D.

———— *Quintet* Op.53 (Musica Rara). For flute, oboe, clarinet, bassoon, and piano.

———— *Quintet* Op.54 (Musica Rara). For flute, oboe, clarinet, bassoon, and piano.

———— *Sinfonia Concertante* (Musica Rara). For flute, oboe, clarinet, bassoon, and piano.

Heinrich von Herzogenberg. *Quintet* Op.43 E♭ (CFP 2191, 72pp., parts; Musica Rara). For oboe, clarinet, bassoon, horn, and piano. Allegro; Adagio; Allegretto; Allegro giocoso. Effective and convincing late nineteenth-century style. This composer's works are worth reviving. M-D.

Léon Jongen. *Quintuor* 1958 (CeBeDeM) 72pp., parts. 22 min. For flute, clarinet, bassoon, horn, and piano. Moderato; Calme et Doux; Rondino. Written in a basically Impressionistic style. Sectional tempo changes in all movements. M-D to D.

Noël Lee. *Quintet* 1952 (American Music Center) 20 min. For flute, oboe, clarinet, bassoon, and piano.

Nicholas Maw. *Chamber Music* (JWC 1962) 74pp., parts. 26 min. For oboe, clarinet, horn, bassoon, and piano. Introduction; Sonata; Complaint; Scherzo and Trio; Phrase; Dialogue and Lied; Variations (8)–Promenade; Invention; Berceuse; Recitativo espansivo; Pastorale; Canone all'quarto; Arietta; Perpetuum mobile. "All or any of movements 2, 4 and 5 may be omitted if so desired. Furthermore, the order of these three movements may be changed, but they should always be placed before and/or after the Scherzo" (from the score). Much thematic interplay between players and melodies. Romantic inspiration shows in fullness and opulence of harmonic texture. D.

Wolfgang Amadeus Mozart. *Sinfonia Concertante* K.297B, E♭ (Musica Rara). For oboe, clarinet, bassoon, horn, and piano. M-D.

———— *Quintet* K.452 E♭ (H. Federhofer—Br 43pp., parts; Leech—Hin; Musica Rara 31pp., parts; ST; IMC). For oboe, clarinet, horn, bassoon, and piano. Largo–Allegro moderato; Larghetto; Rondo—Allegretto. Each part becomes or may at any time become an equal partner in its own right. One of the greatest examples in this category. Excellent preface in Br edition. D.

Jean Papineau-Couture. *Suite pour Flute, Clarinette, Basson, Cor et Piano* (CMC 1947) 26pp., parts. 15 min. Prélude: displays elaborate contrast between two subjects, one rhythmical and one lyrical. Sérénade: bitonal;

for horn and piano alone. Canon: in strict form, for clarinet and flute. Scherzo: all five instruments used; piano plays an important role; Trio features winds alone. Neoclassic. M-D.

John Christopher Pepusch. *Four Concerti* Op.8/1, 4, 5, 6 (D. Lasocki—Musica Rara 1974). For 2 treble recorders, 2 flutes or 2 oboes or 2 violins, and basso continuo. Score and parts available separately for each concerto. M-D.

Ignaz J. Pleyel. *Quintet* C (W. Genuit—Musica Rara 1969) 20pp., parts. For oboe, clarinet, bassoon, horn, and piano. Allegro; Adagio; Allegro. An exemplary work showing early classical character. A fine addition to the otherwise scanty eighteenth-century literature of works for wind instruments and piano. M-D.
—————*Sinfonia Concertante* (Musica Rara; EMT). For flute, oboe, bassoon, horn, and piano.

Alan Rawsthorne. *Quintet* 1963 (OUP) 51pp., parts. 20½ min. For clarinet, oboe, bassoon, horn, and piano. Poco lento, languido–Allegro non assai: serial devices used but freely tonal; piano has a short cadenza-like passage that begins *ppp* and works up to *ff* before the final two-line Meno Mosso closes out the movement with *ff* marcatissimo octaves in the piano. Adagio: piano part unwinds chromatically to the affrettando, where cluster-like chords set off a new Più mosso section, in which the piano has some biting dissonances that soon subside to Tempo I and the opening quiet mood. Allegro non troppo, poco misterioso: the most serial of all the movements. Lento, poco tragico: dramatic octave gestures; chromatic runs lead to the Allegro risoluto: opens with a row; chromatic parallel chords soften this blow only to be followed by diverse figuration for the rest of the movement, with serial techniques permeating some of the writing. A highly effective piece in a personal style, thoroughly contemporary, with terse and concise formal structures always present. The concept of preparation–tension–relaxation infuses this entire work. M-D.

Vittorio Rieti. *Sonata a Cinque* 1966 (Gen) 33pp., parts. For flute, oboe, clarinet, bassoon, and piano. Allegretto: open harmonies, strong rhythms, freely tonal. Allegro scherzando: dance character, flexible meters, moving chromatic lines over broken octaves, repeated chords. Andante alla croma: frequent modulations, key changes, fugal textures. Allegro: strong lyric lines with dancelike rhythms, sectional, perpetual motion figuration, neoclassic. Delightful to play and hear. M-D.

Nikolai Rimsky-Korsakov. *Quintet* B♭ 1876 (USSR 88pp., parts; Bo&H;

Belaieff; IMC). For piano, flute, clarinet, horn, and bassoon. Allegro con brio; Andante; Rondo. M-D to D.

Anton Rubinstein. *Quatuor* Op.55, published as a quintet (Schuberth). For piano, flute, clarinet, horn, and bassoon. See detailed entry under quartets for piano and strings.

Giuseppe Sinopoli. *Numquid* (SZ). For oboe, English horn, oboe d'amore, heckelphone, and keyboards (piano, harpsichord, celesta). Only one keyboard player is required. Vivid writing, fragmentary, metrically notated. Oboes are treated melismatically. Keyboard parts bind the whole piece together. M-D.

Louis Spohr. *Quintet* Op.52 c 1820 (E. Schmitz—Br 2304, 79pp., parts; Musica Rara; A. Broude; CFP) 26½ min. For piano, flute, clarinet, horn, and bassoon. Allegro moderato; Larghetto con moto (contains a surprising anticipation of *Tristan);* Menuetto; Finale. A lovely piece of scoring for this combination; some striking modulations. The piano has most of the dialogue, with the winds adding coloristic effects in the sombre c-minor hue. Facile and taxing if sometimes rambling writing, but this is first-rate Spohr. Running thirds and octave passages have echoes of Clementi. M-D to D.

Quintets for Piano(s), Percussion and/or Tape, and Other Instruments

David Amram. *Discussion* 1960 (CFP) 20pp., parts. 10 min. For flute, cello, piano, and 2 percussionists. This work is a theme and four variations with the last variation extended to include a brilliant coda. The piano part completely shares the activity, and Amram's interest in jazz gives the rhythms a strong sense of vitality. Written in a generally contemporary idiom with longer lines than many post-Webern composers. The variations are effectively contrasted. M-D.

William Bolcom. *Session 3* (Merion 1975) 27pp., 5 scores required. For E♭ clarinet, violin, cello, piano, and percussion. Percussion required: 4 tenor drums or tom toms, 3 cymbals, glass chimes, glockenspiel. Contains a glossary, performance notes, and explanation of ideographic squiggles. Piano part includes clusters, plucked strings, pointillistic treatment, flutter pedal, wide dynamic range, harmonics, tremolo chords, improvisation. Avant-garde. Large span required. D.

David Burge. *Aeolian Music* 1968 (Bowdoin College Music Press) 16pp., parts. For flute, clarinet, violin, cello, piano, and tape. The performers are to make their own tape in order that a more homogenous performance can result. Pointillistic, serial influence, long pedals, sudden dynamic extremes, changing meters, chromatic clusters, string glissandi, muted strings, crossbeams struck with knuckles, soundboard struck, fifth-partial harmonics, tremolo by rubbing fingernails across strings, clusters on bass strings. Free uncoordinated section (aleatoric), some spoken text by performers. Avant-garde. Large span required. D.

Richard Felciano. *Vineyards Music* (ESC 1970) 27pp., parts. 15½ min. For 2 violins, viola, cello, piano, and tape. Contains extensive performance directions. Clusters; fingernails and percussion mallet used on strings; strings damped with fingers. Aleatoric, pointillistic, varied notation, slow glissandi, up-and-down head movements, mechanical doll gestures, unusual sonorities, avant-garde. D.

Morton Feldman. *De Kooning* (CFP 1963) 7pp.For horn, percussion, piano, violin, and cello.

Marius H. Flothuis. *Adagio* Op.74 (Donemus 1975) 43pp., parts. Photostat of MS. For 2 timpanists, percussion, and piano four-hands. Explanations in English.

Arsenio Giron. *Vias* 1966 (CF 1972) 51pp., parts. Facsimile edition. For flute, clarinet, cello, piano, and percussion. Percussion required: glockenspiel, xylophone, vibraphone, tenor drums, suspended cymbals, 5 temple blocks. Serial, pointillistic, flexible meters, expressionistic. Interesting sonorities. D.

Peggy Glanville-Hicks. *Sonata for Piano and Percussion* 1951 (AMP) 10 min. Requires 4 percussionists. Allegro (based on an African folk melody); Lento sombreroso; Presto. Percussion required: xylophone, cymbals, tam tam, tom tom, timpani, and bass drum. Works well if the piano is loud and the xylophonist is first-rate. The style is somewhat like that of Hovhaness. M-D.

Lou Harrison. *Concerto in Slendro* (CFP 6610) 11 min. For violin solo, celesta, 2 tackpianos, and percussion. The title refers to Indonesian modes. This work has many extraordinary appealing and luxurious sounds. The Far East has inspired Harrison to write some of his finest music. M-D.

Charles Ives. *Scherzo—All the Way Around and Back* ca.1906 (PIC 1971) 5pp., parts. For clarinet (flute), violin, bugle (trumpet), middle bells (horn), piano I or right hand, and piano II or left hand. One of Ives's experimental works "in part made to strengthen the ear muscles, the mind muscles, and perhaps the soul muscles too . . .it had a reasonable plan to build on, from a technical standpoint" (Ralph Kirkpatrick, *Charles E. Ives Memos* [New York: W. W. Norton Co., 1972], p.63). Left hand (or piano II) has ostinato-like figures while right hand (or piano I) increases number of notes from one per measure to eleven per measure. Ends *ff*. Large span required. M-D for two pianists, D for one.

Dennis Kam. *Re-actions* (MS available from composer: 1204 W. Stroughton, Apt. 22, Urbana, IL 61801). For piano, three trombones, and timpani. Piano notation includes heavy density chord (4-5 tones but not "clustered"; chord with some intervals larger than semitones) within the range indicated by the two outer notes, and low density chord (2-3 tones; close harmony—no more than a perfect fourth in spread). Vertical lines indicate that the previous range or note holds. Adjacent chords should differ from each other (at least one note different). Enclosed events may be repeated once or twice. Sectionalized, avant-garde. D.

Jouko Linjama. *Fünf Metamorphosen für fünf Instrumente über fünf Canons von Anton Webern Op. 5*, Op.16 1963 (Finnish Music Information Centre) 7 min. For piano, harpsichord, guitar, celesta, and vibraphone. Serial canonic technique. Linjama said of this work: "It led to a tonal and total vacuum, where the rediscovery of the triad as the basis for a multi-directional pluristic tonality opened a road forward: backward."

Vincent F. Luti. *Mixed Quintet* 1967 (Bowdoin College Music Press) 19pp. 5 scores required. For flute/alto flute, clarinet/bass clarinet, violin/viola, cello, piano, and tape (optional). I. Invention, Toccata, Prelude, Fugue. II. Theme and Cadenzas. III. Chorale: Lass, O Herr, dein Ohr sich neigen: built on chorale tune with the pitches sustained and overlapped with each other to form the harmonies. IV. Variation and Cadenzas. Inspired by Baroque forms and practices. "There is an option to play the second movement. It may be performed or omitted. However, it must be taped prior to performance and must then be played back during the performance of the fourth movement. Cues are notated in the score to get an approximate (closer the better) alignment of the two movements. Improvisational pitches should not be played in the order notated" (from the score). Piano part requires tack hammer, marimba stick, and long glass bottle. It utilizes harmonics, non-standard notation, pointillistic treatment, fingernail tremolo on strings, and other effects with the glass bottle. Avant-garde. D.

Vaclav Nelhybel. *Quintetto Concertante* 1967 (Gen) 27pp., parts. For piano, violin, trumpet, trombone, and xylophone. Allegro marcato: samba rhythms with syncopated chords; alternating hands; changing meters; cross-accents; quartal harmony; imitation; highly interesting rhythmically; large span required. Slow: octotonic; harmonic fourths in alternating hands; Agitato section provides punctuated chords and an accented melody. Vivo: sweeping arpeggi; hammered repeated notes; extension of rhythm found in first movement with even more off-accents; octotonic; coda adds chords in the right hand for the pianist over the left-hand shifting rhythms; arrives at an exciting climax. The whole piece is a "rhythmic showcase." M-D.

Fred Noak. *Three Chicks and a Worm* (IU 1951) 12pp., parts. Humoresque for piano, 3 percussionists, and bass clarinet. 1½ pp. narration. A clever story with instrumental writing that underlines every part of the action.

Percussion required: temple blocks, 4 timpani, marimba, vibraphone. Contemporary harmonic, melodic, and rhythmic treatment; staccato chords; chromatic; clever ending. M-D.

Marta Ptaszynska. *Suite Variée* (Leduc 1973) 8pp., parts. For piano and 4 percussionists. Percussion required: suspended cymbal, triangle, maracas, wood block, tambourin, small and large timpani, xylophone, glockenspiel. Prélude; Dance chinoise; Polka. Piano provides melody, harmony, and some rhythmic interest. Traditional harmonic usage. M-D.

William Sydeman. *Quintet* 1960 (Seesaw) 6 min. For clarinet, horn (trombone), double bass, piano, and percussion.

Elias Tanenbaum. *Chamber Piece I* 1956 (ACA) 71pp., parts. For flute/piccolo, clarinet, cello, piano, and percussion. Percussion required: 2 timpani, snare drum, suspended cymbal, crash cymbal, wood block, large triangle, xylophone, 4 temple blocks. Andante: chromatic chords, arpeggi figures, octotonic, rhythmic interest in Allegro molto section; large span required. Moderato: flexible meters; sustained cluster-like chords; leads to an Allegro molto dancelike section that is interrupted by a brief Andante before the Allegro molto leads to a stunning conclusion. Thin textures, neoclassic. M-D.

Music for Six Instruments

Sextets for Piano and Strings

Tomaso Albinoni. *Sonata* a 5 Op.2/6 g (F. Giegling—Nag 189) 22pp., parts. For 2 violins, 2 violas, cello, and keyboard. Adagio; Allegro; Grave; Allegro. The final Allegro (12/8) is especially delightful and flowing. M-D.

Johann Christian Bach. *Sechs Quintette* Op.11 (R. Steglich—Das Erbe Deutscher Musik Vol.3 1953) 96pp. 1 C: Allegretto; Andantino; Menuetto con Variatione. 2 G: Allegro; Allegro assai. 3 F: Andante; Allegretto. 4 E♭: Andante; Menuetto; Allegro. 5 A: Allegretto; Tempo di Menuetto. 6 D: Allegro; Andantino; Allegro assai. All are M-D.
Available separately: Op.11/1 (S. Sadie—Musica Rara 1071 1962) 26pp., parts. Op.11/3 (S. Sadie—Musica Rara 1075 1962) 19pp., parts. Op.11/4 (Nag 123), for 3 violins or 3 flutes or 3 oboes, viola, cello, and keyboard. Op.11/6 (Nag 124; HM 42), for 3 violins or 3 flutes or 3 oboes, viola, cello, and keyboard.

Leslie Bassett. *Sextet* 1972 (CFP 1975) 30pp., parts. 19 min. For 2 violins, 2 violas, cello, and piano. In four movements. The strings of the piano are to be touched, plucked, or stopped. Stopped notes are muffled yet sonorous. "Stopping" directions are given. Most of the piano range is exploited; flat five-finger tremolo on lowest 8–10 strings (inside piano); harmonics; long pedals in third movement. Serial-like but not always strict. Some sections are free and unbarred. Highly sophisticated writing that is well-crafted throughout; effects called for inside the piano seem to be appropriate. Only for the most experienced performers. D.

William Sterndale Bennett. *Sextet* Op.8 f♯ 1846 (K&S1466; Augener 9240) 35pp., parts. For 2 violins, viola, cello, double bass, and piano. Allegro moderato; Scherzo; Andante grazioso; Finale. Much emphasis is placed on the piano writing with Romantic idioms and gestures and cantabile lines. The Andante grazioso, the outstanding movement, has an unusual subject of varied note values; however, the finale, although lively, seems to amble along in a very conventional way. M-D.

Ernest Chausson. *Concerto* Op.21 D 1891 (R. Lerolle 85pp., parts; IMC) for piano, violin, and string quartet. Décidé: 2/2, 4/4; sweeping scalar and arpeggi gestures with interwoven melody; trills; alternating hands; broken-chordal passages; chromatic; 3 with 4; fleet thirds divided between hands; syncopation; large span required. Sicilienne: 6/8; added-note chords; piano chordal sonorities provide binding effects; left-hand arpeggi include embedded chords; melodic line in piano often requires poetic interpretation; alternating hands in contiguous five-note patterns; charming; Fauré characteristics. Grave: 3/4; light chromatic lines with widely spread arpeggiated chords worked into the sonority; chromatic broken-octave triplets; fluid lines between hands; opening mood closes movement; wistful; melancholy. Très animé: 6/8; opens with clever rhythmic figuration one octave apart; alternating chords and octaves between hands; syncopated melodic line; effective metrical division of 3/2 into 3/4; octaves forcefully employed; similar idioms from previous movements used; somewhat in the nature of variation form with highly successful rhythmic transformation. D.

David Holden. *Music for Piano and Strings* 1937 (SPAM) 52pp., parts. For 2 violins, viola, cello, double bass, and piano. The double bass is optional. With virile accent; Veiled; Boisterously; Rota. Mildly contemporary style. Third movement uses "Sumer is icumen in." Pleasant writing with Romantic and Impressionist influences. M-D.

Serge Liapounow. *Sextet* Op.63 (Zimmermann) 36pp., parts. Allegro maestoso; Scherzo; Nocturne; Finale. Traditional late-Romantic writing. The Nocturne is especially lovely, and the outer movements show the influence of Brahms. More elegant and polished than original. M-D to D.

Felix Mendelssohn. *Sextet* Op.110 D 1824 (Nov; Litolff 54pp., parts) 22 min. For piano, violin, 2 violas, cello, and double bass. Allegro vivace: bubbly writing, dazzling technical display. Adagio: muted strings. Minuet: notated in 6/8 for some strange reason. Allegro vivace: its merry frolic is interrupted with a statement of the minor minuet just before the conclusion. Flowing Mendelssohnian style that is ever so pianistic. D.

Knudåge Riisager. *Concertino* Op.28a 1933 (WH 24278) 16pp., parts. 8 min. For piano and 5 violins. Allegro: octotonic, changing meters, short motifs, chromatic. Lento: imitative, descending line. Allegro: scalar, chords, large span required. Neoclassic orientation. M-D.

Joaquin Turina. *Scène Andalouse* Op.7 (Sal 1913) 19pp., parts. 10½ min. For viola solo, 2 violins, viola, cello, and piano. Crépuscule du Soir (Twilight): long preamble for the piano, evocative, song and dance elements in the Serenata and Habañera. À la Fenêtre (By the Window): strong Spanish expression; Impressionist influences permeated with ingenious variations on native rhythms. M-D.

Felix Weingartner. *Sextett* Op.33 e (Br&H 810/813 1903, 1917) 67pp., parts. For piano, 2 violins, viola, cello, and double bass. Allegro appassionato: undulating first subject catches attention immediately; contrasted with more delicate second idea. Allegretto scherzoso: two contrasted trios, one sentimental and the other more melancholy. Adagio ma non troppo: improvisatory; uses a canon and a waltz. Danza funèbre: interesting rhythmic treatment. This piece sounds well and is distinguished in a number of ways, but it is not a great work. Post-Brahms writing. D.

Sextets for Piano(s) and Miscellaneous Instruments

William Albright. *Danse Macabre* 1971 (Bowdoin College Music Press). For flute, clarinet/bass clarinet, violin, cello, piano, and percussion.

Johann Christian Bach. *Sextet* C (Musica Rara). For oboe, violin, 2 horns, cello, and basso continuo.
———— *Quintet* Op.11/4 (Nag 123). For 3 violins or 3 flutes or 3 oboes, viola, cello, and keyboard.
———— *Quintet* Op.11/6 (Nag 124; HM 42). For 3 violins or 3 flutes or 3 oboes, viola, cello, and keyboard.

Heinrich Ignaz Franz von Biber. *Sonata à 6* (GS). For trumpet, 2 violins, viola, cello, and keyboard. M-D.

André Boucourechliev. *Anarchipel V* (Leduc 1972). For amplified harp, amplified harpsichord, electronic organ, piano, and 2 percussionists. Consists of 5 large sheets of notation laid out like maps, one for each instrument (both percussionists use the same page), which can be played simultaneously, depending on the performers' choice. Diverse materials. Piano part contains passages of single pitches and chords, clusters, trills, tremolos. Everything can be played at various dynamic levels, diagrams are patterns to be pursued and freely developed in the same character as long as one wishes. The score is not too helpful but the reproduction of the autograph is original and fascinating! Avant-garde. D.

Raynor Brown. *Variations* (WIN 1973) 56pp., parts. For 2 trumpets, horn, trombone, tuba, and piano. Chromatic subject is heard octotonically in the piano to open the work. Followed by eleven variations, with the last one the most extensive. The piano is mainly treated to thin textures; unusual instrumental combination. Large span required. M-D.

Robert Casadesus. *Sextuor* Op.58 (Durand 1961) 91pp., parts. For flute, oboe, clarinet, horn, bassoon, and piano. Allegro con brio: 4/4; syncopated chordal opening; scales in octaves and tenths; arpeggi; octotonic; more sustained Grazioso second idea; repeated marcato chords; Molto quieto closing. Scherzo vivace: 3/8; fleet movement over keyboard; dry staccato style; thin, widely spread textures; Trio en musette uses octotonic melodic writing. Andante: 3/4; sustained long phrases use open fourths and fifths; alternating and crossing hands. Molto vivo: 3/4; sweeping gestures in eighth notes and triplets up and down keyboard; parallel chords; double notes; sustained passages contrast with fast-moving, staccato, chromatic lines; staccato style; grace notes add humor; effective broken-octave melodic writing at Tranquillo. Neoclassic style. D.

Niccolo Castiglioni. *Tropi* 1959 (SZ) 21pp., parts. $7\frac{1}{2}$ min. For flute, clarinet, violin, cello, percussion (1 player), and piano. Serial: piano part separates sections and is heard by itself as well as in combination with the other instruments. Dynamic extremes, dramatic pauses, long pedals, spatial relationships, harmonics, pointillistic. Avant-garde. M-D.

Aaron Copland. *Sextet* (Bo&H 1948) 45pp., parts. 15 min. This is a 1937 arrangement of the 1932 *Short Symphony*. For piano, clarinet, 2 violins, viola, and cello. Allegro vivace: bold rhythmic style throughout; asymmetrical Hispano-American rhythms; 3/4 juxtaposed with 6/8. Lento: modal, has characteristics of Latin American chants; solemnly eloquent. Finale—precise and rhythmic: rhythmic treatment similar to the Afro-Cuban danzon; piano part has jazz patterns. Written in an athletic style, full of irregular, stylized, and primitive rhythms and wide-skipping melodies; cast in a clarity and an economy of development. The harmonic idiom and textures owe a good deal to the Stravinsky of *Symphonies d'Instruments à vent*. D.

Damiano Cozzella. *Discontinuo* (PAU 1964) 15pp., parts. For piano, 2 violins, viola, cello, and double bass. Performance directions; separate directions for the piano. The five tempo signs are more an indication of density of sound per beat. A good example of sound-mass; individual pitches are not important or perceptible. Aleatoric. Avant-garde. D.

Johann Baptist Cramer. *Sextuor* Op.85 E♭ (Br&H 6057) 33pp., parts. For piano, 2 violins, viola, cello, and double bass. Allegro vivace; Andante quasi Allegretto (Marche funèbre 29 Juillet); Presto (Menuet); Finale. Facile writing. M-D.

Paul Creston. *Concertino* Op.99 (E. C. Kerby). For piano and wind quintet.

Arthur Custer. *Sextet* 1961 (Joshua) 15 min. For flute, oboe, clarinet, horn, bassoon, and piano. Sinfonia; Cantilena; Finale. Ebullient; delightful and debonair writing with ironic tinges. M-D.

Peter Maxwell Davies. *Ave Maris Stella* (Bo&H 1975). For flute, clarinet, marimba, viola, cello, and piano. One of the composer's most poetic scores, yet it is full of sharp corners and sudden turns. A strange work of formidable exploration. M-D to D.
See: Stephen Pruslin, "The Triangular Space: Peter Maxwell Davies's 'Ave Maris Stella,'" *Tempo*, 120 (March 1977):16–22. This excellent article throws much light on this complex work.

Emma Lou Diemer. *Sextet* 1962 (Seesaw) 73pp., parts. 20 min. For piano, flute, oboe, clarinet, horn, and bassoon. With energy: seventh chords with quartal harmony, octotonic, driving rhythmic figures, staccato chords in alternating hands, strong bitonal implications. Slow: sustained, trills, longer lines, chromatic figuration, parallel chords, dramatic pianistic gestures in climax, incisive skips. Moderately fast: cadenza-like opening by solo piano moves to a 7/8 faster fughetta section; thin textures interlaced with thicker chords in alternating hands; contrasting expressive section follows. Freely tonal, strong contemporary writing. D.

Ernst von Dohnanyi. *Sextet* Op.37 C 1933 (Lengnick) 106pp., parts. For clarinet, horn, violin, viola, cello, and piano. Allergro appassionato: 4/4; sustained chords; parallel sonorities; rotating broken octaves; chromatic patterns in runs; arpeggio figuration; octotonic; 3 with 4; strong full chords. Intermezzo: 12/8; full chords in various inversions; Alla marcia section with broken chords that evolve over the keyboard. Allegro con sentimento: 2/4; tranquil chromatic legato chordal movement; octotonic runs; chordal punctuation; parallel broken chordal accompaniment; alternating hands; chromatic arpeggi; opening idea returns in 6/4 to close out movement and goes immediately to Finale: a marked cheerful figure opens the movement; chromatic double notes; other idioms from previous movements used; thin textures contrasted with thicker ones. Long, demanding writing. D.

Richard Donovan. *Music for Six* (CFP 6666). For oboe, clarinet, trumpet, viola, cello, and piano.

Anton Eberl. *Sextet* Op.47 E♭ 1800 (W. Genuit, D. Klocker—Musica Rara 1969) 24pp., parts. For clarinet, horn, violin, viola, cello, and piano. Adagio–Allegro vivace; Andante molto; Menuetto; Rondo. Influence of Mozart is unmistakable. Delightful and highly interesting writing. Preface by the editors. M-D.

Donald Erb. *Three Pieces* (TP). For 2 trumpets, horn, trombone, tuba, and piano. Includes tapping or rattling the bell, muttering, hissing or yelling into instrument, kissing instrument, etc. Visual interest is greater than the musical interest. Avant-garde. M-D.

Blair Fairchild. *Concerto de Chambre* Op.26 (Augener 1912) 57pp., parts. For violin, piano, 2 violins, viola, and cello; double bass ad lib. Allegro; Andante; Allegro. Strongly chordal, chromatic lines, alternating chords, mildly Impressionistic. M-D.

Morton Feldman. *Durations V* (CFP 6905 1962) 8pp., parts. For violin, cello, horn, vibraphone, harp, and piano/celesta. "The first sound with all instruments simultaneously. The duration of each sound is chosen by the performer. All beats are slow. All sounds should be played with a minimum of attack. . . . Numbers between sounds indicate silent beats. Dynamics are very low" (from notes in the score). Avant-garde, interesting sonorities. Performers must be super "counters"! Unbarred throughout. M-D.
———— *The Viola in My Life* (I) 1970 (UE 15395) 10pp., parts. $9\frac{1}{2}$ min. For flute, violin, viola (solo), cello, piano, and percussion. Changing meters, cluster-like chords. Not a dynamic mark in entire score, only crescendo signs. Passing suggestions of tonality. A sonority study that uses the full range of the keyboard. Large span required. M-D.
There are four pieces by Feldman with this same title, all separate and independent works, not single movements.

Géza Frid. *Sextet* Op.70 1965 (Donemus). For flute, oboe, clarinet, horn, bassoon, and piano.

Roberto Gerhard. *Libra* 1968 (OUP) 122pp., parts. 15 min. For flute/piccolo, clarinet, violin, piano, guitar, and percussion. Percussion required: glockenspiel, wood block, large and medium cymbals, large Korean block, vibraphone, timpani, castenets. Highly organized, sectionalized. Clusters, pointillistic, shifting meters, toccata-like martellato passages, ringing and unusual sonorities, dynamic extremes, fades away to nothing. Requires large span. D.

Roger Goeb. *Concertant IVB* (CFE). For clarinet, 2 violins, viola, cello, and piano.

Lionel Greenberg. *Sextet* 1963 (CMC) $14\frac{1}{2}$ min. For flute, oboe, clarinet, bassoon, horn, and piano. Allegro; Andante; Lento; Moderato: Largo. "The basic structural unit in this piece is the interval of the third. In a sense the entire piece is variations on that interval. The form of the first move-

ment is free; second movement—canons, choral canons; third movement—free; fourth movement—giocoso—free; fifth movement is twelve-
tone and is composed of two simultaneous three-part canons and their
retrogrades over an isorhythmic bass'' (composer).

Alexei Haieff. *Dance Suite—The Princess Zondilda and her Entourage*
(Belaieff 1965) 8pp., parts. For flute, bassoon, trumpet, violin, cello, and
piano. Allegro; Andante; Allegro. Octotonic, chordal punctuation, widely
spread textures, ostinati, mildly contemporary. Octaves in alternating
hands; large span required. M-D.

Talib Rasul Hakim. *Placements* 1970 (Bo&Bo 1975) 6pp. 6 copies necessary for performance. For 5 percussion and piano. Explanations in English.

Iain Hamilton. *Sextet* 1962 (Schott) 11 min. For flute, 2 clarinets, violin,
cello, and piano.

Roy Harris. *Concerto* Op.2 1926 (AMP 1932) 58pp., parts. For clarinet,
piano, and string quartet. Fantasia: solid formal construction, much poetic
beauty, interval of the augmented fourth important. Second Fantasia: effective scherzo, ABA with B equalling one measure of very slow 12/2 time.
Third Fantasia: beautifully contrasted Adagio, quiet and contemplative.
Fourth Fantasia: free fugal form, impetuous and wild. Contrapuntal techniques are very important in this work. D.

Karel Husa. *Sérénade* 1963 (Leduc) 44pp., parts. 15 min. For piano, flute,
oboe, clarinet, horn, and bassoon. Also exists in another version for wind
quintet with string orchestra, xylophone, and harp or piano. La Montagne:
trills, some melodic function for piano although mainly rhythmic. La Nuit:
some agitated forte chords for the piano, glissando, imitation, coda without
the piano. La Danse: staccato rhythmic octaves and chords, repeated notes,
tremolo chords in upper register, glissando at end. M-D.
_____ *Concerto* 1965 (Leduc) 63pp., parts. 24½ min. For piano, 2 trumpets
in C, horn, trombone, and tuba. Quasi fanfara: much tremolo in piano, bold
gestures, widely spaced chords. Misterioso: harmonic sevenths and ninths
used frequently; complex rhythms; spread-out octaves used in contrary
motion; dissonance colorfully exploited. Adagio: Impressionistic *ppp* full
chords; tremolos; staccatissimo rhythmic seconds; trills; opposite dynamics
between hands; bombastic conclusion. Requires experienced ensemble
player with complete pianistic equipment. D.

Charles Ives. *Allegretto Sombreoso* ca.1908 (When The Moon Is on the
Wave) (PIC 1958) 6pp., parts. For flute, English horn, 3 violins, and

piano. Trumpet or basset horn may be substituted for the English horn. Long arpeggiated lines in 13/16, a few chords in 11/8, and a final arpeggiation in 18/16. Words (by Lord Byron) are included for the English horn part. M-D.

Robert Sherlaw Johnson. *Triptych* 1973 (OUP) 22pp. for small complete score. For flute, clarinet, violin, cello, piano, and percussion (one player). Percussion required: vibraphone, marimba, Chinese blocks, cymbals, tam tam. Catenary 1: serial; pointillistic; piano has a quasi-cadenza; clusters. Catenary 2: *pppp* trills; certain small sections are played out of time; quasi-tremolo; large span required. Procession: clusters, pedal instructions, unusual sonorities. Avant-garde. D.

Werner Josten. *Concerto Sacro I & II* (H. Elkan) 19pp., parts. For piano, 2 violins, viola, cello, and double bass. I. Annunciation; The Miracle. II. Lament; Sepulchre and Resurrection. Many short sections with titles that tell the story. Chromatic and picturesque writing. M-D.

Piet Kingma. *Sextet* 1973 (Donemus) 26pp., photostat of MS. For flute, oboe, violin, viola, cello, and piano.

Karl Kohn. *Serenade* 1961 (CF 1972) 19pp., parts. Facsimile edition. For flute/piccolo, oboe, clarinet, horn, bassoon, and piano. Moderato; Lento; Andante grazioso; Quasi adagio–in tempo rubato; Allegro non troppo. Serial, pointillistic. Small notes are to be played as fast as possible, chromatic clusters silently depressed. In those bars that lack precise conventional measurement, the notes are to be distributed in approximation of their graphic position between the bar lines. Strong expressionistic style with traditional and avant-garde idioms combined. D.

Hans Kox. *Sextet II* 1957 (Donemus) 23pp., parts. Reproduced from holograph. For piano, harpsichord, 2 violins, viola, and cello. Allegro: added notes, chromatic, syncopation, rhythmic shifting figuration, piano cadenza. Largo: piano is silent. Allegretto: running and chordal gestures. M-D.
_____ *Sextet III* 1959 (Donemus). For woodwind quintet and piano.
_____ *Sextet IV* 1960 (Donemus). For woodwind quintet and piano.

Yehoshua Lakner. *Sextet* 1951 (IMI 62) 24pp. Study score. For woodwinds, horn, and piano.

Jean Yves Daniel Lesur. *Sextuor* (Amphion 1961) 36pp., parts. For piano, flute, oboe, violin, viola, and cello. Transcription by the composer of the

Suite from *Trio a cordes et piano*. Nocturne; Ricercare; Berceuse; Tarentelle. Mildly contemporary with Impressionistic techniques. M-D.

Sergei Liapunov. *Sextet* Op.63 (USSR 1967) 100pp., parts. For piano, 2 violins, viola, cello, and double bass. Allegro maestoso; Scherzo; Nocturne; Finale. Traditional late-Romantic writing that displays a fine craft. The outer movements follow Brahms's lead. M-D to D.

Donald Martino. *Notturno* 1973 (Ione 659) 54pp., parts. For flute, clarinet, violin, cello, percussion, and piano. Percussion required: glockenspiel, vibraphone, xylophone, marimba, 6 temple blocks, 3 tam tams. Two large sections with smaller sectionalized portions. Colorful directions such as "Hyperdramatic; in an intensely anguished whisper." Strings plucked, damped, and struck with a bass drum beater. Expressionistic, serial, dramatically imaginative. Requires fine pacing. D. Winner of 1974 Pulitzer Prize.

Bohuslav Martinů. *Musique de Chambre I* (ESC 7280 1966) 65pp., parts. 18 min. For violin, viola, cello, clarinet, harp, and piano. Allegro moderato: octaves in low register; harmonic seconds and ninths prevalent; alternating hands; chromatic; triplets both chordal and single notes; added-note sonorities; ostinati. Andante moderato: cluster-like chords; tremolo; chromatic figuration; arpeggiated octaves; short piano cadenza. Poco allegro: low-register chords; melodic clusters; fugal textures; piano provides much incisive rhythmic impetus. M-D.
———— *Sextet* 1929 (Br). For flute, oboe, clarinet, 2 bassoons, and piano. Displays Martinů's classical style interlaced with jazz elements. M-D.

Shin-Ichi Matsushita. *Gestalt* 17 1969–70 (UE 15894) 14pp., parts. Reproduced from holograph. For 3 trombones, percussion, piano, and harp. Percussion required: vibraphone, xylophone, electric organ, 4 timpani, 12 campane tubolare, 3 tamburi piccoli, 2 tam tam, 2 tom tom, 3 piatti, 2 bongos, 2 congos, blocco di legno. Clusters, pointillistic, serial, dynamic extremes, expressionistic, avant-garde. D.

Francisco Mignone. *Sexteto* 1937 (Escola Nacional de Musica da Universidade do Brazil, Rio de Janeiro; Copy at LC) 61pp., parts. For flute, oboe, clarinet, horn, bassoon, and piano. Sostenuto–Moderato: dramatic chords; sweeping scales and octaves; long pedals; large span required. Lento: chordal, ostinati, builds to grand climax; moves directly into Allegro: chromatic figuration, varied tempi, driving rhythms to the end. Virtuoso writing. D.

George Onslow. *Sextuor* Op.30 E♭ ca.1830 (Br&H) 35pp., parts. For piano, flute, clarinet, horn, bassoon, double bass. Largo–Allegro vivace assai; Menuetto; Andante con Variazioni (5 variations and a finale). Flowing, sometimes elegant and even clever writing from the pen of a second-rank composer. M-D.

———— *Grand Sextuor* Op.77 a 1851 (Kistner No.1782) 33pp., parts. For piano, flute, clarinet, bassoon, horn, and double bass. Allegro spiritoso; Minuetto; Tema con Variazioni (6 variations and a finale). M-D.

Juan Orrego-Salas. *Sextet* Op.38 1954 (PIC 1967) 84pp., parts. For clarinet, 2 violins, viola, cello, and piano. Sonata: accented and punctuated chords; rhythmic subject of four sixteenths and four eighths; freely tonal; melodic and contrapuntal lines; alternating hands; octotonic chromatic scales. Differencias: full chords for chorale subject; seven variations and closing; this movement is the "heart" of the work and is a catalogue of variation techniques for all the instruments. Scherzo: variable meters; toccata-like in its drive; Meno mosso trio is expressive and cantabile; opening mood and slightly altered figuration return. Recitativo, Contrappunto e Coda: Lento clarinet opening; Tempo..giusto section displays contrapuntal elements including single lines that evolve into four-voiced textures for a climax; piano participates in chordal, two-voice structures and finally in *pp* octaves in the lower register as the movement evaporates. Firm handling of formal structure and neoclassic style throughout. M-D.

Hans Pfitzner. *Sextet* Op.55 g 1945 (Oertel) 48pp., parts. 25 min. For clarinet, violin, cello, viola, double bass, and piano. Allegro con passione, quasi minuetto; Rondoletto; Semplice, misterioso; Comodo. It is amazing that this work, composed in 1945, could be conceived in a Brahms–Reger style, but it is straight out of that tradition. M-D.

Willem Pijper. *Sextet* 1923 (Donemus) 35pp., parts. 15 min. For flute, oboe, clarinet, bassoon, horn, and piano. Lento; Andantino, quasi Allegretto; Comodo, alla ticinese; Vivo, con agrezza. Clear form and texture. Shows influence of Mahler, French predilections, and Dutch folk music. Beautifully contrasted movements. M-D.

Raoul Pleskow. *Sextet* 1963 (Seesaw). For flute, oboe, clarinet, violin, cello, and piano.

Francis Poulenc. *Sextet* 1932–9 (WH) 68pp., parts. For piano, flute, oboe, clarinet, horn, and bassoon. Three movements of verve and wit. The outer movements are free in form and employ varied melodic and rhythmic gestures. The breezy middle movement, Divertissement, is in ABA design with a quicker mid-section that alludes to the opening idea in Mozart's *Sonata* C, K.545. A frivolous and delightful romp that blends the best of Chopin and the music hall! M-D.

Henri Pousseur. *Madrigal III* 1962 (UE 13804) 29pp., parts. For piano, clarinet, violin, cello, and 2 percussionists. Percussion required: vibraphone, 3 cow bells, cymbal, tam tam, marimba, 2 bongos, 3 tom toms. Directions in French, German, and English. Unusual notation, partly graphic. Piano has punctuated tremolo and pointillistic chords, long trills, dynamic extremes, half pedals. Unusual sonorities, avant-garde. M-D.

Almeida Prado. *Portrait de Lili Boulanger* 1972 (Tonos 10306). For flute, piano, and string quartet.

Claudio Prieto. *Al-gamara, para conjunto de camara* (Editorial de Música Española Contemporánea 1973) 67pp., parts. 14 min. For piano, electric guitar, marimba, and wind, string, and percussion instruments. Avant-garde.

Serge Prokofiev. *Sextet* Op.34 g "Overture on Jewish Themes" 1919 (Bo&H 23pp., parts; USSR 1944; K; IMC) 8½ min. For clarinet, 2 violins, viola, cello, and piano. Prokofiev's only work based on folk material. Grotesque and lyric elements are worked out with brilliant craft. Alternating hands, secco style, tenuto chords, rapid finger passages, open fifths and sixths, dancelike quality, broken-chord figuration, syncopated soprano and bass melodic usage (at No.17, cantando), scalar passages, accented chords at conclusion. An unusual piece of writing. Large span required. M-D to D.

Bernard Rands. *Tableau* 1970 (UE 15416) 12pp., parts, 6pp. performance instructions. For flute/alto flute, clarinet/bass clarinet, viola, cello, piano/celesta, and percussion. Percussion required: 3 triangles, 2 cymbals, glockenspiel, vibraphone, 5 temple blocks, xylophone, bongos, 2 tom toms, hard and soft sticks, brushes. Chance composition, duration variable from 10 to 20 min. Contains five sections: Monotone; Labyrinth; Epiphanies; Tutto è sciolto; Monologue intérieur. In any performance each section should be played at least twice, but not immediately follow itself. Written in proportional notation—absolute duration and rhythmic values are not indicated but are suggested by relative tone proportions. Numerous other directions for each section. Piano has thick chords, is treated pointillistically. Dynamics are attached to most notes. Aleatoric, avant-garde. D.

——*Déjà* 1972 (UE 16006) 10pp., parts. For flute/alto flute, clarinet/bass clarinet, viola, cello, piano, and percussion. Percussion required: 3 temple blocks, 1 pair bongos, 2 tom toms, 2 triangles, 2 cymbals, 2 gongs, tam tam, vibraphone. Extensive performance directions, including a diagram for arranging instruments. Several sections provide fine ideas to the performers. Choice of instrumentation and combination. Aleatoric. The piano part looks rather simple but demands the maximum of invention within the prescribed limits. M-D.

H. Owen Reed. *Symphonic Dance* (Belwin-Mills 1963) 19pp., parts. For flute, oboe, clarinet, horn, bassoon, and piano. Allegro giusto: chromatic; contrary figuration; chords used for rhythmic punctuation; chorale-like mid-section; opening ideas return; freely tonal; closing in C. M-D.

Hermann Regner. *Klangspiele* 1971 (Schott WKS5) 23pp., parts. For piano duet (four hands) and four percussion players. Schnell; Langsam; Schnell. 12 types of percussion instruments used (timpani, xylophone, metalophone, drums, 4 cymbals, wood blocks, 2 rattles, 2 bongos, triangle, tambourine). In style of Hindemith. Short. M-D.

Verne Reynolds. *Concertare III* 1969 (CF) 27pp., parts. $17\frac{1}{2}$ min. Facsimile edition. For flute, oboe, clarinet, horn, bassoon, and piano. Slow: serial influence, pointillistic, dramatic gestures, fast figuration. Fast: atonal fugues; syncopated chords; sudden dramatic extremes; closing section utilizes improvisation; long pedals; large span required. Very Fast: contrapuntal fast lines move to a long stopping position by holding one low key. Slow: brief reference to opening. Strong dissonances. D.

Wallingford Riegger. *Concerto for Piano and Woodwind Quintet* Op.53 1953 (AMP) 44pp., parts. For flute, oboe, clarinet, horn, bassoon, and piano. Allegro: octotonic, neoclassic, triplets in alternating hands, quartal and quintal harmonies. Andante: rhythmic figure in lower register, chromatic fifths, trills, staccato sixteenths in octotonic treatment. Allegro molto: triplets in alternating hands, changing meters, tritone exploited, octaves in lower register as well as chromatic octaves, large skips, *p* smorzando closing. D.

Albert Roussel. *Divertissement* Op.6 1905 (Sal) 17pp., parts. For flute, oboe, clarinet, bassoon, horn, and piano. Animé: lively use of seventh chords, vigorous rhythmic treatment, broken-chord triplets, arpeggio figuration. Lent: sustained chords in left hand under broken seventh-chord figuration in right hand. En animant en peu: rhythmic emphasis in chromatic figures, octotonic scales. Lent: same ideas as in other Lent section. Animé: like opening. Fun for all; imaginative and racy writing. M-D.

Karl Schiske. *Sextet* 1937 (UE 11209) 47pp., parts. For clarinet, 2 violins, viola, cello, and piano. Schreitend; Schnell und lustig; Langsam; Sehr bewegt. Strongly chromatic, big chords, sweeping lines, post-Romantic characteristics. M-D to D.

William Schmidt. *Concertino* (WIM 1969). For piano, 2 trumpets, horn, trombone, and bass tuba or tuba. Allegro con brio; Largo; Allegro con spirito. A combination of classic form with post-Impressionistic harmonies and rhythms peculiar to American jazz. M-D.

Morton Subotnick. *Serenade I* 1959–60 (McGinnis & Marx) 30pp., parts. For flute, clarinet, cello, vibraphone, mandoline, and piano. Three untitled movements. Serial influence, changing meters, pointillistic, sectional, some sections marked "Freely," expressionistic, broad chromatic arpeggi gestures, Webernesque. Piano has some solos. D.

———— *Play I* 1964 (MCA) 19pp., parts. For flute, oboe, clarinet, bassoon, horn, piano, tape, and film. Film by Anthony Martin available on rental. Includes performance directions. Graphic and traditional notation. Clusters; glissandi; pianist must clap, stamp, "wine," "spent," and "freeze" to end of tape. Aleatoric. A fun piece. M-D.

Georg Philipp Telemann. *Concerto à 6* F (I. Hechler—Pegasus 6009) 24pp., parts. For alto recorder, bassoon or gamba or cello, 2 violins, viola or 3rd violin, and basso continuo. Largo; Allegro; Grave; Allegro. Displays Telemann's well-known preference for unusual instrumental combinations and tone colors. M-D.

———— *Concerto* G (K. Flattschacher—Müller 97) 20pp., parts. For 2 violas (concertata), 2 violins, viola, and basso continuo. Avec Douceur; Gay; Largo; Vivement. The editor warns against too rapid a tempo. This work stresses most ingeniously the peculiarity of the viola continuo realization by G. Frotscher. M-D.

———— *Konzert* F (M. Ruetz—HM 130) 16pp., parts. For alto recorder, 2 violins, viola, cello, and basso continuo. Affettuoso; Allegro; Adagio (violins 1 and 2 and viola tacet); Menuett 1 and 2. Excellent realizations. The Adagio, for solo recorder and keyboard, is very beautiful. M-D.

———— *Suite* F TWV 55:F9 (A. Hoffmann—Möseler 1975) 24pp., parts. For 2 oboes, 2 horns, bassoon, and basso continuo. Preface in German, French, and English. M-D.

Michael Tippett. *Prelude. Summer*, from *Crown of the Year* (Schott). For 2 recorders or flutes, trumpet or cornet, violin, drum, and piano.

Volker Wangenheim. *Klangspiel II* (Litolff 1973) 45pp., parts. 14 min. For flute, clarinet, cello, piano, percussion, and unspecified melodic instrument. Each performer also plays a number of percussion instruments. The character of the work calls for atonal improvisation. Diagrammatic notation in part. M-D to D.

David Ward-Steinman. *Putney Three* (EBM). For flute, oboe, clarinet, bassoon, horn, piano, and tape.

Adolph Weiss. *Sextet* 1947 (ACA) 76pp., parts. 18 min. For flute, oboe, bass clarinet, horn, bassoon, and piano. Adagio: chordal; sustained, spread-out sonorities; requires large span; moves to Allegro Moderato: rhythmic punctuation in upper register; contrary chromatic patterns; syncopated (almost jazzy) melodies; alternating hands with triplets and chords; legato, flowing, uneven rhythmic patterns (5 in the space of 4, etc.); wide-spread chromatic arpeggi; complex rhythmic conclusion. Andante: flowing, atonal lines; pointillistic chords. Allegro: chromatic triplets accompany atonal melody that evolves into a more rhythmic guise; one section uses five eighths in the space of six; corky conclusion. D.

Stefan Wolpe. *Piece in Two Parts for Six Players* 1961–2 (British & Continental Music Agencies) 79pp., parts. 9 min. For violin, clarinet, trumpet, cello, harp, and piano. Part One: quarter note = 72; changing meters; pointillistic; serial; some long pedals. Part Two: quarter note = 120; similar characteristics to Part I; perhaps a little more sustained; builds to exciting climax. Highly organized, complex. D.

Russell Woollen. *Sextet* (CFE). For clarinet, 2 violins, viola, cello, and piano.

Charles Wuorinen. *Speculum Speculi* (CFP) 39pp., parts. Reproduced from holograph. $14\frac{1}{2}$ min. For flute, oboe, bass clarinet, double bass, percussion, and piano.

Iannis Xenakis. *Eonta* 1964 (Bo&H) 78pp., parts. For piano, 2 trumpets, and 3 trombones. "Eonta (=``being''—the present participle of the Greek verb "to be") is so entitled in homage to Parmenides . . . .The work makes use of stochastic music (based on the theory of probabilities) and of symbolic music (based on logistics). Some of the instrumental parts, notably the piano solo at the opening, were calculated on an IBM 7090 Computer at the Plâce Vendôme, Paris. The Greek characters in the full score have nothing to do with performance; they indicate choice of particular pitches and of logical operations, and serve as an *aide-mémoire* to analysis'' (from notes in the score). The solo piano opens the first 30 bars with a static, complex, twelve-chord arrangement all over the keyboard. Brass are stereophonically disposed by moving about the piano in three different positions. Increasing rhythmic involvement for brass while the piano retains its basic rhythmic structure. Enormously D.

Music for Seven Instruments

Septets for Piano(s) and Miscellaneous Instruments

Manuel Angulo. *Siglas: ocho piezas para conjunto de camara* (Editorial Alpuerto 1973) 11pp., parts. For flute, English horn, clarinet, harp, piano, percussion, and cello.

Theodore Antoniou. *Events III* 1969 (Br) 20pp., parts. 12 min. For flute, oboe, clarinet, bassoon, piano, 2 percussionists, tape, and slides. Contains extensive performance directions. "Events, musical and otherwise, determine the technique, form, and general function of all elements of the piece. At some level musical and extra-musical ideas are integrated. The way the material is combined (relation, antithesis, chance, etc.) determines the character of each movement. I. Analoga: homogeneous, analogous, relatives (from Preface), glissandi on strings, harmonics, clusters, spatial and graphic notation. II. Paraloga: of different meaning, of abstract relation, of actual events. Sound events with a cadenza character are developed in various ways, at the same time as others (in strict tempo; tapes or synchronized passages), controlled within the general tempo and the maximum possibilities which the ensemble can achieve. The continuous change between 'free' and synchronized situations gives the impression of two different ensembles" (from the preface). A catalogue of avant-garde techniques. D.

Larry Austin. *A Broken Consort* 1962 (MJQ) 33pp., parts. For flute, clarinet, trumpet, horn, percussion, piano, and double bass. Intrada: random improvisation using suggested pitch and rhythmic motifs; varying dynamic levels; piano treated percussively. Fancy: tremolo chords, complex rhythms, pointillistic. Funke: piano has a motif to repeat several times, growing faster and softer; piano cues others for re-entry; involved rhythmic structure. Blue: sustaining piano pedal is held down throughout for strings to vibrate sympathetically. Dumpe: in a hard, swinging, jazz tempo; movement is concluded with improvisation; directions given. Coda:

Amarissimo, strong emphatic gestures in all instruments. An interesting "third-stream" work. D.

Carl Philipp Emanuel Bach. *Sonatina* C (Dameck—Bo&Bo). For piano, 2 flutes, 2 violins, viola, and cello.

———— *Sonatine* d 1764 (F. Oberdörffer—Br 2006). For 2 flutes, 2 violins, viola, cello, and keyboard.

———— *Sonatine* E♭ 1766 (F. Oberdörffer—Br 2007) 20pp., parts. For 2 flutes, 2 violins, viola, cello, and keyboard. Largo; Allegro di molto; Tempo di Minuetto. A good deal of ornamentation. Tasteful realizations. M-D.

Johann Christoph Friedrich Bach. *Septet* C (Schünemann—K&S). For oboe, 2 horns, violin, viola, cello, and piano.

Johann Sebastian Bach. *Musikalisches Opfer* S.1079 (K. H. Pillney—Br&H 3863) 93pp., parts. For flute, 2 violins, viola, 2 cellos, and piano. Based on a theme by Frederick the Great. Includes realizations of the canons in modern clefs for various instrumentations, and of the figured bass for the keyboard. D.

Arthur Berger. *Septet* 1966 (CFP) 12 min. For flute, clarinet, bassoon, violin, viola, cello, and piano.

William Bergsma. *Changes for Seven* (Galaxy 1975) 20pp., parts. 9 min. For flute, oboe, clarinet, bassoon, horn, percussion, and piano. One continuous movement with five different sections, numerous other tempi changes, flexible meters, a few clusters, many octaves for the pianist, interpretive directions, dramatic writing. D.

Wallace Berry. *Divertimento* 1964 (EV) 36pp., parts. For flute, oboe, clarinet, bassoon, horn, piano, and percussion. Preludio: serial; unwinding figuration; pointillistic; strong percussive use of piano; large span required. Moto costante: 32nd-note figuration; broken ninths; chordal punctuation; flowing lines; *fff* conclusion. Improvisazione: free opening; ostinato-like figures expand over keyboard; dynamic extremes; sonorous and rubato but quiet ending. Sensitive sonorities. M-D to D.

Konrad Boehmer. *Zeitläufte* 1962 (Tonos 7217 1968) 31pp., parts. 15 min. For 2 pianos, English horn, clarinet, bass clarinet, horn, and trombone. Highly organized, serial, pointillistic, extreme registers exploited, dynamics attached to most notes, flexible meters and tempi, piano parts are of equal difficulty. Somewhat in the style of the Boulez *Structures* for 2 pianos. D.

Anne Boyd. *As It Leaves the Bell* (Faber). For piano, 2 harps, and 4 percussionists. Loose sheets. For rent.

Jolyon Smith Brettingham. *O Rise* Op.6 1973 (Bo&Bo) 18pp., parts. For flute, trombone, 2 percussionists, harpsichord, piano, and cello. Explanations in German and English.

Matthew Camidge. *Sonatina* (C. Bowen—SP 1974) 12pp., parts. 3 min. For piano, 3 violins (or 2 violins and viola), viola, cello, and double bass. From *Ten Easy Sonatas for the Pianoforte or Harpsichord*.

Roque Cordero. *Permutaciones 7* (PIC 1967) 36pp., parts. For clarinet, trumpet, timpani, piano, violin, viola, and double bass. Sectional, highly organized, serial, piano part treated pointillistically, numerous dynamic markings, frequent meter changes. Requires experienced chamber music performers. D.

Richard Felciano. *Crasis* (ECS) 39pp., parts. $8\frac{1}{2}$ min. For flute, clarinet, violin, cello, harp, percussion, piano, and tape. Written after Felciano had seen a performance of a Noh drama by a troupe from Japan. The sound substance of *Crasis* is related to the Noh. "The notation, which includes miniature mobiles, is both traditional and proportional. As the work progresses, the relation of the live instruments to the electronic sounds proceeds from complement to fusion, hence the title (crasis: the joining of two vowels into one)" (from the preface). Clusters, pointillistic, aleatoric, avant-garde. D.

Morton Feldman. *The Straits of Magellan* (CFP 1962) 9pp. For flute, horn, trumpet, amplified guitar, harp, piano, and double bass. Box notation. "Each box is equal to MM 88. Numbers indicate the amount of sounds to be played within the duration of each box. Arabic numerals indicate single sounds for all the instruments except the piano, which interprets the numbers given as simultaneous sounds." Contains other detailed directions. Avant-garde. M-D.

———— *False Relationships and the Extended Ending* 1968 (CFP) 15pp. For 3 pianos, cello, violin, trombone, and chimes. Durations for simultaneous and single sounds are extremely slow. All sounds are connected without pause unless otherwise notated. Dynamic level is extremely low, but audible. Specific metronome marks are listed for many measures. Avant-garde. M-D.

_____ *The Viola in My Life* (II) 1970 (UE 15400) 14pp., parts. 12 min. For piano, flute, clarinet, violin, viola (solo), cello, and percussion. Only a celesta part is notated for keyboard. The entire piece is to be played extremely quietly, all attacks at a minimum with no feeling of a beat. Only crescendo and decrescendo signs are used for dynamics. Celesta has only a chord, an octave, or a single note. Flexible meters. Sonority study. M-D. There are four separate and independent pieces by Feldman with the title *The Viola in My Life*.

Mikhail Glinka. *Serenade on themes from Anna Bolena by Donizetti* (USSR Vol.4 [Supp.] of Complete Works) 17pp., parts. For piano, harp, horn, bassoon, viola, cello, and double bass. Introduzione; Cantabile; Moderato; Variations 1 and 2; Larghetto; Presto; Andante cantabile; Finale. Sectionalized, combination of melodious and glittering writing. Elegant salon style. M-D.

Jean Guillou. *Cantilia* 1968 (Leduc) 40pp., parts. 15 min. For piano, 4 cellos, harp, and timbales. One movement. Chromatic marcato figuration spread in upper register, octotonic, sevgnth chords, syncopated chromatic chords, quartal harmony, many added-note chords, fast harmonic rhythm. A long climax is shattered by a subito Lento e molto espressivo: low chromatic chords in the piano add color, *pp* ending. The style is reminiscent of Messiaen but a unique and individual voice is speaking. Colorful sonorities. Large span required. M-D.

Johann Nepomuk Hummel. *Septet* Op.74 d 1818 (CFP 1304) 75pp., parts. For flute, oboe, horn, viola, cello, double bass, and piano. Allegro con spirito: emphatic chords, florid chromatic and scalar figuration, tremolo, broken octaves, turns, triplets with melodic significance, sweeping arpeggi, some unusual harmonic usage. Menuetto scherzo: capricious triplets in right hand versus dotted eighths and sixteenths in left hand; written-out turns; large skips; clever grace note usage in Alternativo, where piano takes on more importance. Andante con variazioni: folklike sentimental theme; varied pianistic figurations, including fast repeated notes, are used in the variations. Finale: fugal textures, fast octaves, idioms similar to those in other movements, tempestuous climax. Facile virtuoso writing. D.
_____ *Military Septett* Op.114 (Musica Rara; Lienau). For flute, clarinet, trumpet, violin, cello, double bass, and piano. 24 min. Attractive, imaginative writing with a brilliant piano part. The title reflects the fact that the trumpet, not normally used in chamber music at that time, is featured. Three contrasting movements. D.

Andrew Imbrie. *Dandelion Wine* (SP 1970) 4pp., parts. For piano, oboe, clarinet, 2 violins, viola, and cello. *"Dandelion Wine* is the title of a novel by Ray Bradbury concerning memories of a boyhood spent in a small town. It described the bottling of dandelion wine, with each bottle dated. These became symbols of memory, since each date recalls a particular summer day and its activities. My piece attempts to implant and then, at the end, recall certain musical ideas in new context to give, if possible, the effect of poignant reminiscences, all 'bottled' in a very brief container. It was written in Princeton, at a time and place quite conducive to a mood similar to that invoked in the novel" (from notes in the score). Freely tonal, a few pointillistic gestures, thoroughly contemporary idiom. M-D.

Leoš Janáček. *Concertino* 1925 (Artia; IMC 35pp., parts) 19 min. For piano, 2 violins, viola, clarinet, horn, and bassoon. Moderato: dialogue between piano and horn, chromatic motifs, alternating hands, trills, widely imitated intervals, whimsical. Più mosso: dialogue between piano and clarinet, repeated chords, skipping staccato left hand, trills over chromatic lines, chromatic chords. Con moto: full ensemble utilized; seconds and sevenths become part of the chromatic fabric; arpeggi; moving chromatic chords; piano cadenza. Allegro: sweeping chromatic patterns, energetic octave melodic line, highly chromatic, forceful octaves in recitative passages, 5 versus 4, hammered conclusion. D.

Harrison Kerr. *Dance Suite* (ACA). For 2 pianos and 5 percussionists.

Willem Kersters. *Septet* Op.37 "De drie Tamboers" 1966 (CeBeDeM) 48pp., parts. 14 min. For four clarinets, percussion, kettledrum, and piano. Allegro spiritoso: octotonic melody, chromatic runs and figuration, large marcato chords, glissandi. Andante con moto quasi allegretto: sustained, triplet and quick chromatic figures, shifting meters, rhythmic punctuation. Tempo di marcia: rhythmic chords; chromatic runs and octaves; "De drie Tamboers" tune is heard in the piano, accompanied by percussion; chromatic runs and chords return to finish the movement in a *p* closing. M-D.

Wilhelm Killmayer. *Schumann in Endenich.* Kammermusik No.2 1972 (Schott 6431) 11pp. 6 copies necessary for performance. 8 min. For piano, organ, and 5 percussionists. Percussion required: glockenspiel, bass drum, timpani, vibraphone, marimba, gongs, tam tam, bongos. Long pedal passages for piano, upper register exploited, percussive triplets in left hand with hammered-out punctuated octaves in right hand, clusters, unusual sonorities. M-D.

Karl Korte. *Matrix* 1967 (ECS) 47pp., parts. For flute, oboe, clarinet, horn, bassoon (alto sax is optional), piano, and percussion. Percussion required:

medium-sized suspended cymbal, small tam tam, 2 bongos (high-pitched), snare drum, one side drum pitched lower than the snare, thunder sheet, marimba, vibraphone. Pairs of hard, soft, and medium rubber beaters. Snare sticks and soft timpani sticks. "Due to variations in frame construction not all pianos are capable of producing all effects as notated. In this case, pianist is to rearrange pitches as needed in order to come as close as possible to the effect as notated" (note from the score). Piano part: pointillistic; serial; requires harmonics; clusters with palms; stopped strings; metal-tipped pencil to be moved across strings; sudden dynamic changes; black- and white-key contrary motion glissandi at same time. Interesting and subtle sonorities. Avant-garde. D.

Jos Kunst. *No Time, XXI:4* 1974 (Donemus) 28pp., parts. Photostat of MS. For 3 clarinets, bass clarinet, piano, and 2 percussionists. Explanations in English.

Edward Laufer. *Variations for Seven Instruments* (New Valley Press 1967) 24pp., For flute, clarinet, bassoon, trumpet, violin, cello, and piano. Score is a reproduction of the MS. Parts are supplied for transposing instruments only; others use full score. Includes 2 leaves of isolated measures to be pasted into scores to facilitate page turns. Originally an orchestral work. Serially derived mainly from nine pitches. Long exposition followed by six complex variations that develop ideas, followed by a short conclusion. Imaginative writing that requires a first-rate group with ensemble experience. D.

Daniel Lesur. *Sextuor* (Amphion 1961) 33pp., parts. Transcribed for 6 clarinets and piano by Armand Birbaum. Nocturne; Ricercare; Berceuse; Tarentelle. Effective transcription, mildly contemporary with Impressionistic characteristics, generally thin textures, unusual sonorities. M-D.

Peter Tod Lewis. *Septet* (TP 1967) 27pp., parts. For flute, clarinet, bassoon, violin, viola, cello, and piano. First movement untitled: serial; sudden dynamic changes; pointillistic; broken minor ninths used as accompaniment; chordal punctuation; quotes from the Berg *Sonata*, Op.1; large span required. Lullaby: sustained, wide dynamic range with *pppp* closing. M–D.

Teo Macero. *One-Three Quarters* (CFP 66178 1970) 11pp., parts. 8 min. For 2 pianos, piccolo/flute, violin, cello, trombone, and tuba. One piano is to be tuned down a quarter tone; strings play up or down a quarter tone at specific indication. Tremolando, octotonic, dramatic arpeggiated gestures, syncopation, chromatic chords. Extreme registers exploited; short sections are repeated. Colorful sonorities. M-D.

Giacomo Manzoni. *Musica Notturna* 1966 (SZ 6562) 22pp., parts. 9 min. For flute, clarinet, bass clarinet, horn, bassoon, piano, and percussion. Picturesque, quiet dynamics, chromatic, pointillistic, tremolo, atonal. Study in quiet and quieter sonorities. Large span required. M-D.

Bohuslav Martinů. *Rondi* 1930 (Artia 1954) 24pp., parts. For oboe, clarinet, bassoon, trumpet, 2 violins, and piano. Six pieces. Poco Allegro: major seventh chords, accented ninth chords, octotonic in upper register, octaves. Poco Andantino: ostinato-like, chromatic chords, repeated harmonic fifths. Allegro: broken octaves, expanding chromatic intervals, cluster-like chords, alternating hands, tremolo, glissandi. Tempi di Valse: parallel chords, left-hand melody under right-hand chromatic chords. Andantino: rotational figures such as broken thirds and fifths, syncopated chords. Allegro vivo: staccato and legato arpeggi, alternating chromatic octaves. Most of the pieces are strongly rhythmic. An attractive set. M-D.

———— *Fantaisie pour Ondes Martenot* 1944 (ESC) 15 min. For Ondes Martenot, oboe, 2 violins, viola, cello, and piano.

Ignaz Moscheles. *Septet* Op.88 D ca.1840 (Musica Rara) 39pp., parts. For piano, clarinet, horn, violin, viola, cello, and double bass. Allegro con spirito; Scherzo; Adagio con moto; Finale. Orchestral conception with the piano predominant. M-D to D.

Luigi Nono. *Polifonica–Monodica–Ritmica* 1951 (Schott) miniature study score 20pp. For flute, clarinet, bass clarinet, alto sax, horn, piano, and percussion. 12 min. Percussion required: gran cassa, cassa chiara, 3 tamburi, 4 piatti, tom tom, xylophone. Polifonica–Adagio–Allegro: ideas unraveled between instruments with fragments tossed back and forth. Monodica–Largo: slower fragmented ideas; repeated notes lead directly to Ritmica–Allegro moderato: triplet figures play important role; piano has stopped strings and percussive chords; *pppp* closing. M-D.

George Onslow. *Septuor* Op.79 B♭ 1851 (Kistner No.1831) 41pp., parts. For piano, flute, oboe, clarinet, horn, bassoon, and double bass. Allegro moderato; Scherzo; Andante; Finale. Chromatic, many early Romantic traits. M-D.

Willem Pijper. *Septet* 1920 (Donemus 1949). For flute/piccolo, oboe/English horn, clarinet, bassoon, horn, double bass, and piano. Largo: parallel chords, widely spread arpeggiated chords over keyboard. Pastorale: duple and some triple meter, rocking motion, hemiola, broken parallel chords. Pantomine: alternating hands in bitonal patterns, humorous quasi Valse, glissando lands on a chord à la Debussy. Passacaille: freely tonal subject; low martellato octaves; sustained sonorities in middle register while upper octaves move in triplets in top register; large chords. Peripetie: alternating hands, left-hand octaves with contrary right-hand chords, syncopation, *pp* closing. Strong Impressionist influences. M-D.

Raoul Pleskow. *Music for Seven Players* (Seesaw). For flute, cello, violin, clarinet, harp, piano, and percussion. Characteristic of this well- proportioned piece is a continual crossing and recrossing of chromatic space, which produces a mercurial sequence of flashing figuration, lit here and there from within by such stabilizing factors as a discreetly held harmony. It throbs with restlessness, and constantly changes direction and intention with stimulating poetry. M-D to D.

Francis Poulenc. *Rhapsodie Nègre* 1917 (JWC) 27pp., parts. For flute, clarinet, 2 violins, viola, cello, and piano; voice ad lib. Prélude: right-hand parallel chords over left-hand moving ninvh chords, octotonic melodic treatment. Ronde: staccato left hand, right hand syncopated melody, bitonal, stringendo whole-tone run. Honoloulou: voice used here but piano can play this solo; all seventh chords (lent et monotone) except for whole-tone usage at end of movement. Pastorale: rocking harmonic fifths in left hand with melody in right hand; luscious chords at end. Final: octotonic scales, glissandi on white and black keys. A fun work. M-D.

Camille Saint-Saëns. *Septet* Op.65 (Durand 49pp., parts; IMC 35pp., parts). For piano, trumpet, 2 violins, viola, cello, and double bass. Allegro moderato; Menuet; Intermède; Gavotte et Final. Displays enormously facile writing for the piano. Chords, scales, broken-arpeggiated figuration, octaves in alternating hands, all completely pianistic. M-D.

Peter Schat. *Septet* (Donemus 1958) 12pp., parts. For flute, oboe, bass clarinet, horn, cello, piano, and percussion. Variaties: various sections with the following titles—Pianissimo; Scherzino; Con fuoco; Presto; Adagio— uses such devices as long pedals, clusters, tremolo, sudden dynamic changes, large arpeggiated chords. Allegro: conventional notation throughout; chromatic; extremes in registers exploited; works to large climax then ends subito *pp*; large span required. Mildly contemporary. M-D.

Arnold Schönberg. *Suite* Op.29 (UE 1927) 111pp., parts. 32 min. For 3 clarinets and piano quartet. Overture: a sonata that is overly long for the material employed. Tanzschritte (Dance Steps): ideas are transformed and embroidered, rhythms exploited. Thema mit Variationen: mastery of this form, high degree of inspiration felt. Gigue: scintillating charm, free sonata style. Transparent scoring throughout, twelve-tone. The three types of instruments (strings, clarinets, and piano) provide great contrast possibilities. Broken chords in piano part are effectively used. A work of trenchant complexity that unravels itself only after thorough study. D.

Ludwig Spohr. *Septet* Op.145 a (Musica Rara 1145) 94pp., parts. For violin, cello, flute, clarinet, bassoon, horn, piano. Allegro vivace; Pastorale; Scherzo; Finale. M-D.

Igor Stravinsky. *Septet* 1953 (Bo&H) 29pp., parts. 12 min. For clarinet, horn, bassoon, piano, violin, viola, and cello. First movement: SA seething with contrapuntal treatment. Passacaglia: built on a sixteenth-note subject developed serially. Gigue: same subject as the Passacaglia worked out in various fugues and rhythmic transformations. Serial techniques prominent but this piece is basically neoclassically and tonally (A) oriented. D.
See: H. Schatz, "Igor Stravinsky: Septett," *Melos*, 25/2 (February 1958); E. Stein, "Strawinsky's Septet (1953)," *Tempo*, 31 (Spring 1954).

Zsigmond Szathmary. *Alpha* 1968 (Moeck 5055) 16pp., parts. 8 min. For flute/piccolo, clarinet/bass clarinet, trumpet, violin, viola, cello, and piano/celesta. Harmonics, serial, clusters, pointillistic, dynamic extremes, tremolo, expressionistic, complex ensemble problems. M-D to D.

Georg Philipp Telemann. *Concerto* a (I. Hechler—Schott 4968) 18pp., parts. For 6 melody instruments and basso continuo. Preface in French, German, and English. Adagio; Allegro; Affettuoso; Allegro. Realization is only a suggestion but it is a good one. M-D.
_____ *Concerto* B♭ (H. Töttcher—Sikorski 494) 27pp., parts. For 3 oboes, 3 violins, and basso continuo. Allegro; Largo; Allegro. Graceful and dance-like. M-D.
_____ *Concerto* D (Kölbel—Heinrichshofen). For 2 flutes, 2 oboes, 2 violins, and basso continuo.
_____ *Concerto à 7* F (F. Brüggen, W. Bergmann—Schott RMS 1262) 19pp., parts. For 2 treble recorders, 2 oboes, 2 violins, and basso continuo. Grave; Vivace; Adagio–Allegro. M-D.
_____ *Ouverture à 7* C (G. Kehr—Schott 5916) 46pp., parts. For 3 oboes, 2 violins, viola, and basso continuo. Grave–Allegro; Harlequinade; Espagniol; Bourrée en Trompette; Sommeille; Rondeau; Menuette I,II; Gigue. M-D.

Ivan Vandor. *Musica per Sette Esecutori* (SZ 1967) 50pp., parts. 10 min. For harp, celesta, piano, 2 percussionists, violin, and cello. *Ffff* arm clusters, percussive single notes, chordal, long pedals. A study in loud and rhythmic sonorities. Large span required. M-D.

Renier van der Velden. *Concertino* 1965 (CeBeDeM) 44pp., parts. 12 min. For 2 pianos, 2 trumpets, horn, trombone, and tuba. One movement with varied moods and tempi. Serial, octotonic, chordal, scalar, atonal, trills. Pulls freely towards b. Both piano parts are of equal interest. Effective combination. M-D.

Ben Weber. *Concerto* Op.32 (ACA). For piano solo, cello, flute, oboe, clarinet, bassoon, and horn.

Malcolm Williamson. *Concerto* (Weinberger). For 2 pianos, flute, oboe, clarinet, bassoon, and horn.

Stefan Wolpe. *Piece for Two Instrumental Units* 1962 (McGinnis & Marx) 56pp., parts. For flute/piccolo, cello, piano, oboe, violin, double bass, and percussion. Percussion required: vibraphone, glockenspiel, bongos, xylophone. One unit consists of flute, cello, and piano; the second consists of the other instrumentation. Chordal, motivic material carefully transformed, cluster-like sonorities, dynamic extremes, pointillistic, proportional rhythmic relationships, lines interchanged between instruments, stopped strings, cumulative form, traces of Beethoven's *9th Symphony* appear, extremely complex ensemble problems. Requires large span. D.

Charles Wuorinen. *Tiento Sobre Cabezón* 1961 (ACA) 36pp., parts. 4 min. For flute, oboe, harpsichord, piano, violin, viola, and cello. Based on the "Tiento del Primer Tono" from the *Obras de Musica para Tecla, Arpa, y Vihuela* (1578). Piano part is varied, some parts sustained, others staccato; flexible rhythmic usage; some alternating hand octaves. Mainly diatonic style; wide dynamic range. Instrumental combinations provide some unusual sonorities. M-D.

Yehudi Wyner. *Serenade* 1958 (CFE) 40pp., parts. For flute, horn, trumpet, trombone, viola, cello, and piano. Nocturne; Toccata; Capriccio–Aria; Nocturne II. Piano has a quasi-cadenza at end of the first Nocturne with broken chords in alternating hands. Toccata has ostinato-like figures and dance rhythms, spread-out figuration. Capriccio: serial-like, pointillistic. Piano is melodically treated in opening half of the Aria and more rhythmically projected in the second half. Nocturne II: repeated broken figuration, quiet, lines in other instruments. M-D.

Vasily Zagorsky. *Rhapsody* 1968 (USSR) 55pp., parts. For 2 pianos, violin, and 4 percussionists. Percussion includes: timpani, small drum, legni, bells, triangle, tom tom, campane, piatti, cassa, tam tam, crotali, gong. One large colorful movement, in the style of Khachaturian. M-D.

Music for Eight Instruments

Octets for Piano(s) and Miscellaneous Instruments

William Albright. *Caroms* 1966 (Jobert) 34pp., parts. 7 min. For flute/alto flute, bass clarinet, trumpet, double bass, piano, celesta, and 2 percussionists. Percussion required: vibraphone, marimba, glockenspiel, large triangle, 2 suspended cymbals (high and low), bass drum, gong, large tam tam. Vertical lines spaced throughout the first part of the score represent seconds and should be used only as an indication of the approximate spacing of events. Notes are to be played according to their placement on the page and their spatial relationships to each other. Contains other performance directions. Pointillistic, many major seventh chords, dynamic extremes, tremolando, clusters. Pianist must whistle. Avant-garde, sonority oriented. D.

Joseph Alexander. *Three Pieces for Eight* (Gen) 109pp., parts. For flute/piccolo, clarinet, trumpet, violin, cello, double bass, piano, and percussion. Percussion required: timpani, snare drum, maracas, triangle, tenor drum, xylophone, cymbal, small bass drum, wood block. Facsimile of the MS. Allegro brillante: bitonal syncopated chords, octotonic, strong rhythms. Presto gaio: vigorous, driving rhythms, contrary chromatic scales and arpeggi, parallel broken-chord figures, grazioso contrasting section. Moderato: mixed bravura and lyric writing, poco meno mosso section, strong marcato ending. More technical than interpretive problems. D.

Milton Babbitt. *All Set* 1957 (AMP) 50pp., parts. 8 min. For alto sax, tenor sax, trumpet, double bass, trombone, percussion, vibes, and piano. A sophisticated and brilliant serial work that uses cool, glossy jazz techniques. Breathless rhythmic vivacity and a good deal of intellectual stimulus are both brought out with the jazz-band instrumentation. M-D to D.

Mily Balakirev. *Octet* Op.3 c (Musica Rara; I. Jordan—USSR 1959, 65pp., parts). For piano, flute, oboe, horn, violin, viola, cello, and double bass. In the USSR edition editor's notes and comments are in Russian and English. Editorial additions are given in square brackets. Only the first movement was completed by Balakirev. Allegro molto: SA, heroic theme, arpeggiation, chromatic scales, chords and octaves in alternating hands, tremolando; second tonal area introduced in e but quickly moves to f. M-D.

Erik Bergman. *Concertino da Camera* Op.53 1961 (Fazer) 11 min. For flute, clarinet, bass clarinet, percussion, piano, violin, viola, and cello.

Lennox Berkeley. *Octet* (JWC, available through GS). For oboe, clarinet, bassoon, horn, violin, viola, cello, and piano.

Earle Brown. *Twenty Five Pages* 1953 (UE 15587 1975). For 1 to 25 pianos. "The *Twenty Five Pages* may be played in any sequence; each page may be performed either side up; events within each two-line system may be read as either treble or bass clef; the total time duration of the piece is between eight minutes and 25 minutes, based on 5 seconds and 15 seconds per two-line system as probable but not compulsary time extremities. After the 'Folio' experiments of 1952-3, this is the first extended work using what I call 'time notation' (durations extended in space relative to time, rather than expressed in metric symbols as in traditional notation) and which has since been called proportional notation" (from the score). Aleatoric, clusters, dynamic extremes, ten different attacks, performance directions, avant-garde. D.

Fernando Cerqueira. *Quanta: para conjunto de Câmara* 1972 (Tonos) 21pp., parts. 9½ min. For piccolo/flute, oboe/English horn, clarinet, violin/ viola, cello, piano, harpsichord, and percussion.

Wen-Chung Chou. *Yün* 1969 (CFP) 37pp., parts. For flute, clarinet, bassoon, horn, trumpet, trombone, piano, and percussion. Reproduced from holograph. "Yün, from the expression 'ch'i yün,' foremost principle in Chinese art and poetry, means 'reverberations in nature'" (from the score). Large percussion battery, one page of symbol explanations. Piano participation is minimal but integral. The pianist is required to stop and pluck strings. Some pointillistic treatment, sensitive and usually thin textures throughout, fascinating sonorities. M-D.

Aldo Clementi. *Concerto* (SZ 1975) 16pp., parts. 8 min. For piano (2 or 4 hands), 3 violas, horn, bcssoon, trumpet, and electric harmonium. The harmonium sustains a given tone cluster throughout the work by means of a wooden board held down by a weight. Instructions for performance in Italian and English. Avant-garde.

Paul Creston. *Ceremonial* Op.103 (GS 1973) 32pp., parts. 4½ min. For piano and 7 percussion players. Explanation of tone cluster symbols is given. A twelve-bar introduction is followed by Allegro for the rest of the work. The piano part provides low chordal sonorities during much of the piece although the upper register is shown off a few times. Effective ensemble writing for this unusual combination. M-D.

Paul Dessau. *Quattrodramma* 1965 (Bo&Bo) 31pp., parts. For 2 pianos, 4 cellos, and 2 percussionists. Serial, harmonics, pointillistic, subdivided rhythms, long trills, double glissandi, atonal, *ppp* closing. Three quotations from Sean O'Casey are given near the end. M-D to D.

Jacques Dupont. *Octuor* Op.4 1930 (Hamelle) 51pp., parts. For clarinet, bassoon, horn, 2 violins, viola, cello, and piano. One movement, ABA plus coda; chordal introduction (Très large); Allegro con fuoco has a syncopated rhythmic subject. Chromatic chords and figures, Impressionistic, tremolando, *ppp* broken chord conclusion. M-D.

Morton Feldman. *Between Categories* 1969 (CFP 6971) 9pp., parts. Photostat of MS. For 2 pianos, 2 chimes, 2 violins, and 2 cellos. "Durations of simultaneous and single sounds are extremely slow. All sounds are connected without pauses unless otherwise notated. The dynamic level is extremely low, but audible" (from the score). Changing meters, unusual subtle chordal sonorities throughout, avant-garde. Requires large span. M-D.

Roberto Gerhard. *Concert for Eight* 1962 (OUP) 91pp., parts. 10½ min. For flute, clarinet, guitar, percussion, double bass, piano, mandolin, and accordion. "My intention was to write a piece of chamber music in the nature of a Divertimento, almost in the spirit of the *commedia dell' arte*. The eight instruments are introduced somewhat in the manner of *dramatis personae,* but the play itself consists of purely musical events, and must not be taken as evoking or illustrating any extra-musical parallels whatever. From the conventions of the *commedia* two have been adopted: that of extempore invention and, sometimes, that of disguise or masking—by which I mean unusual ways of playing the instruments. The piece falls into eight sections, which are played without a break" (from the composer's note). Changing meters, extreme registers exploited, pointillistic, repeated notes, long pedals, unusual sonorities. M-D.

Ray Green. *Three Pieces for a Concert* (EBM 1958). For flute, 2 clarinets, 2 trumpets, trombone, percussion, and piano. Percussion required: snare and bass drums, cymbals, triangle. 11pp., parts. March; Quiet Song; Piece to End. Contrasting, mildly contemporary, attractive, M-D.

Tibor Harsanyi. *L'Histoire du Petit Tailleur* 1939 (ESC 1950) 76pp., parts. 25 min.; with recitation, 30 min. For flute, clarinet, bassoon, trumpet, piano, violin, cello, and percussion. Thirteen short movements to go with Grimms' *Fairytales*. Requires a rather large percussion battery. Mildly contemporary, chromatic style, attractive. Similar to Poulenc's *L'Histoire de Babar*. M-D.

Hans W. Henze. *Concerto per il Marigny* 1956 (Schott) 5 min. For piano, clarinet, bass clarinet, horn, trumpet, trombone, viola, and cello.

Joaquin Homs. *Music for Eight* 1964 (Seesaw) 38pp., parts. For flute, clarinet, violin, viona, cello, trumpet, piano, and percussion. Passacaglia: serial; row evolves through various guises. Derivaciones: pointillistic, repeated notes, octotonic, octaves, syncopated chords. Poorly reproduced copy of MS. D.

Leoš Janáček. *Capriccio for Solo Piano (Left Hand) and Seven Instruments* 1926 (Artia 1953) 18½ min. For piano, flute/piccolo, 2 trumpets, 3 trombones, and tenor tuba. Four movements. Treatment of the parts causes this work to straddle the field of chamber and solo–accompaniment music. Virtuosity is avoided, thereby making the work more like a sonata for concerted instruments. Originally called *Defiance*, moments of solemn disapproval are contrasted with intimate and quiet moods. "According to the correspondence and some authentic statements, *Capriccio* expresses a revolt against the cruel destiny" (from a note in the score). Melodic treatment simulating speech and cryptic motifs stand out in bold relief. Tense emotional writing. D.

Paul Juon. *Octet* Op.27a B♭ (Lienau 1905) 80pp., parts. For oboe, clarinet, bassoon, horn, violin, viola, cello, and piano. Allegro non troppo: SA, sequences, chromatic, octotonic, fast harmonic rhythm, scalar; large span required. Andante elegiaco: melodic and chordal. Allegro non troppo quasi moderato: triplets, staccato octotonic writing, sweeping chords. Moderato: chordal, octaves, in Brahms–Dohnányi tradition. M-D.·

Tristan Keuris. *Concertante Muziek* (Donemus 1973) 34pp., parts. For clarinet, horn, bassoon, piano, and string quartet.

Hans J. Koellreuter. *Constructio ad Synesin* 1962 (Edition Modern). For piccolo, English horn, bass clarinet, bassoon, violin, harp, piano, and percussion.

Karl Kohn. *Introduction and Parodies* 1967 (CF 1972) 23pp., parts. 23 min. Facsimile edition. For clarinet, horn, bassoon, string quartet, and piano. Largo: pointillistic; chromatic clusters silently depressed and struck with stiff, flat hand, crisp and staccato; coda for solo piano starts with instruments entering at specific points and then treats materials in aleatoric fashion; directions for performing Coda I are given; Coda II follows and quickly concludes the movement. Allegro con brio: piano not used until near the end of the movement; "Fragments and Cadenza" section also includes extensive notes describing entrances, etc. Aleatoric. Pianist must give many signals. For the adventurous who are especially looking for unusual sonorities. D.

Gail Kubik. *Divertimento II* 1958 (MCA) 44pp., parts. $10\frac{1}{2}$ min. For flute/ piccolo, oboe, clarinet, bassoon, trumpet, trombone, viola, and piano. Overture and Pastorale; bright; thin textures; cheerful tunes; slightly frantic; joined without break to the first of 2 Pastorales, both of which are leisurely, flowing, and meditative in character. Sound Pastorale. Scherzino—The Puppet Show: fast and furious opening sets the scene; woodwinds have much dialogue suggesting Punch and Judy. Dialogue: a short, intimate conversation between oboe and viola. Dance Toccata: bright sounds and abrupt rhythmical changes; returns the divertimento to its happy and gay mood. Mildly contemporary. M-D.

Jacques Lenot. *Solacium* 1974 (Amphion 339) 50pp., parts. For piano, flute/ alto flute, oboe/English horn, clarinet/bass clarinet, harp, violin, viola, and cello. Highly organized (pitch, rhythm, dynamics) work, complex rhythms, pointillistic, strong dissonance. Only for the most adventurous and experienced group. Avant-garde. D.

Shin'ichi Matsushita. *Composizione da Camera* (TP). For lute, clarinet, trumpet, trombone, violin, cello, piano, and percussion.

Francis Miroglio. *Phases* (UE 14691 1968) 15pp., parts. MS reproduced, easy to read. For flute, piano, violin, viola, cello, and 3 percussionists. May be played in the following four forms: 1. flute and piano; 2. flute, piano, and string trio; 3. flute, piano, and 3 percussion; 4. flute, piano, string trio, and 3 percussion. The order of sections A, B, C, D, and E may be varied. In version 4 it is left to the flutist to decide whether he will move about the stage in accordance with the included diagram. Colored spotlights point up the changes of location and illuminate the accompanying groups. Numerous notational directions. Harmonics, tremolo, pointillistic, avant-garde. D.

Bo Nilsson. *Scene I* (UE). For 2 flutes, 2 trumpets, vibraphone, harp, piano, and percussion.

Ferdinand Ries. *Octet* Op.128 A♭ (Musica Rara) 25pp., parts in the original Probst edition (Leipzig). For clarinet, bassoon, horn, violin, viola, cello, double bass, and piano. Allegro; Andante; Rondo. Straightforward writing with brief Romantic intrusions; uses the traditional pianistic idioms of the day. Thematic material is frequently given to the piano in this attractive and unpretentious work. M-D.

Anton Rubinstein. *Octet* Op.9 D (CFP). For piano, violin, viola, cello, flute, clarinet, horn, and double bass. Beethoven influence noted. Each instrument has a share in the total work, but the conception of the piece is somewhat shallow and a lack of integration is obvious. M-D to D.

Alfred Schnitke. *Dialog per Violoncello solo e 7 Esecutori* (UE 1972) 19pp., parts. For cello, flute, oboe, clarinet, trumpet, horn, piano, and percussion.

Elliott Schwartz. *Octet 1971* (ASUC Journal Vol. I, performance material available from the composer: % Bowdoin College, Music Department, Brunswick, ME 04011) 16pp., no separate parts. For flute, oboe, clarinet, violin, cello, percussion, and 2 keyboard players (piano, celesta, harpsichord, music boxes, and drumsticks). Performance directions included. A performance consists of two movements separated by the Interlude. Contains directions for aleatory sections. Each notational section equals fifteen seconds. Free entrances are selected by performers within duration of brackets. Uses clusters, loud whispers, string sweeping. Pianist must slap under the keyboard and strike strings with mallettes, slam keyboard cover, snap and clap, finger trill on case. Avant-garde. D.

Felix Weingartner. *Octuor* Op.73 G (Birnbach 1925) 112pp., parts. For clarinet, horn, bassoon, 2 violins, viola, cello, and piano. Allegro; Andante; Tempo di Menuetto; Allegro moderato. Clear forms, sufficient originality to make for some interest, composite style. M-D.

Charles Wuorinen. *Octet* 1962 (McGinnis & Marx) 111pp., parts. For piano, oboe, clarinet, horn, trombone, violin, cello, and double bass. Pointillistic, hand and forearm clusters, wide dynamic range, highly chromatic, glissandi, expressionistic, extreme ranges exploited, flexible meters, octotonic. Wide span required. D.

Annotated Bibliography

This section is an extension of the suggested readings that appear after individual composers or single compositions. It concentrates on English-language books, periodicals, and, particularly, dissertations. These sources are most helpful when used in conjunction with the musical scores. University Microfilms (Ann Arbor, MI 48103) can supply the dissertations in microfilm as well as in xerographically printed form. UM numbers are listed for those that are readily available; dissertations and theses without UM numbers are usually available on inter-library loan from the library of the listed institution.

Yvett Bader. "The Chamber Music of Charles Ives." MR, 33 (November 1972): 292–99.

Stephen Banfield. "British Chamber Music at the Turn of the Century." MT, 115 (March 1974) 211–13. Mainly a discussion of the chamberworks of Parry, Stanford, and Mackenzie.

BBC Music Library Catalogues: Chamber Music. London: British Broadcasting Corp., 1965.

William Charles Bedford. "Elizabeth Sprague Coolidge—the Education of a Patron of Chamber Music; the Early Years." Diss., University of Missouri, 1964. 350pp.

Helmut Braunlich. "Violin Sonatas and the Standard Repertoire." AMT, 25 (April–May 1976): 19–21.

A. Peter Brown, in collaboration with C. V. Brown. "Joseph Haydn in Literature: A Survey." *Notes*, 31 (1975): 530–47. A fine introduction to any facet of Haydn research.

———. "Critical Years for Haydn's Instrumental Music: 1787–90." MQ, 62 (July 1976): 374–94.

M.-D. Calvocoressi. "Charles Koechlin's Instrumental Works." ML, 5 (October 1924).

Canadian Chamber Music Catalogue. Toronto, Canada: Canadian Music Centre, 1967. 288pp. A listing of the chamber music available on loan from the library of the Canadian Music Centre.

Chamber Music by Living British Composers. London: British Music Information Centre, 1969. 42pp. A listing of the chamber music holdings, both published and unpublished, of twentieth-century British composers.

Joan Chissell. "Style in Bloch's Chamber Music." ML, 24 (January 1943).

John Clapham. "Martinů's Instrumental Style." MR, 24 (1963).

Walter W. Cobbett. *Cobbett's Cyclopedic Survey of Chamber Music*, with supplementary material edited by Colin Mason, 2d. ed., 3 vols. London: Oxford University Press, 1963.

Henry Cope Colles. *The Chamber Music of Brahms*. New York: AMS Press, 1976. Reprint, London: Oxford University Press, 1933.

Composium Directory of New Music. Los Angeles, California: Crystal Record Co., 1971 (59pp.), 1972 (64pp.), 1973 (48pp.), 1974 (70pp.). This annual index of contemporary compositions is a list of works by living composers, composed or published in the two previous years. Includes both published and unpublished compositions indexed by instrumentation. Also includes brief biographical sketches of each composer.

Archibald T. Davison and Willi Apel, eds. *Historical Anthology of Music*. 2 vols. Cambridge: Harvard University Press, 1947, 1950.

Angelo Eagon. *Catalog of Published Concert Music by American Composers*. Metuchen, N.J.: The Scarecrow Press, 1969. 348pp. Also Supplement to the Second Edition, 1971 (150pp.) and Second Supplement to the Second Edition, 1974 (148pp.)

Edwin Evans, Sr. *Handbook to the Works of Brahms*. 4 vols. London: W. Reeves, 1933–35. Vol.II, *Chamber Works*.

David Edward Fenske. "Texture in the Chamber Music of Brahms." Ph.D. diss., University of Wisconsin, 1973. 540pp. A statistical study of each of the movements of Brahms's eighteen chamber works.

Donald N. Ferguson. *Image and Structure in Chamber Music*. Minneapolis: University of Minnesota Press, 1964. 339pp.

Robert Fink and Robert Ricci. *The Language of Twentieth Century Music*. New York: Schirmer Books, 1975. 125pp. A dictionary of terms.

H. Foss. "The Instrumental Music of Frederick Delius." *Tempo* 26 (Winter 1952–3).

Robert Eugene Frank. "Quincy Porter: A Survey of the Mature Style and a Study of the Second Sonata for Violin and Piano." D.M.A. diss., Cornell University, 1973. 303pp.

Floyd Donald Funk. "The Trio Sonatas of Georg Philip Telemann (1681–1767)." Diss. George Peabody College for Teachers, 1954. On 64 of the trio sonatas.

Eugene Gratovich. "The Sonatas for Violin and Piano by Charles E. Ives: A Critical Commentary and Concordance of the Printed Editions and the Autographs and Manuscripts of the Yale Ives Collection." D.M.A. diss., Boston University School of Fine and Applied Arts, 1968. 242pp..

Elizabeth Remsberg Harkins. "The Chamber Music of Camille Saint-Saëns." Diss., New York University, 1976. 216pp.

George Hart. *The Violin and Its Music*. Boston: Milford House, 1973. Reprint of the 1885 edition (London: Dulau).

Anthony Hoboken. *Joseph Haydn, thematisch-bibliographisches Werkverzeichnis*. Mainz: Schott, 1957—. Vol.I. *Instrumental Works*.

John Horton. *The Chamber Music of Mendelssohn*. London: Oxford University Press, 1946. 65pp. The Musical Pilgrim series.

Charles Williams Hughes. "Chamber Music in American Schools." Ed.D. diss., Columbia University, 1933. 62pp.

A. J. B. Hutchings. "The Chamber Music of Delius." MT, 76 (1935): 17–20, 214–16, 310–11, 401–403.

Milan R. Kaderavek. "Stylistic Aspects of the Late Chamber Music of Leoš Janáček: An Analytic Study." Diss., University of Illinois, 1970. "A critical study of Janáček's mature style, based on the chamber works of his last five years. Provides an analysis of the stylistic aspects of these works and demonstrates the influence of his native folk song on the instrumental compositions. A summary of his stylistic traits is based on a systematic examination of each work. Melodic design is given special attention, since it was perhaps most influenced by folk music and by Janáček's concept of what he called *napevky mluvy* (generally translated as 'speech melody'). Janáček's harmonic procedures, also folk-influenced, are illustrated by graphs using a modified form of the linear reduction technique developed by Heinrich Schenker. The unique and original aspects of Janáček's music are described" (author).

Ivor Keys. *Brahms Chamber Music*. London: 1974; Seattle: University of Washington Press, 1974. 68pp., BBC Music Guides series.

Ronald R. Kidd. "The Emergence of Chamber Music with Obbligato Keyboard in England." AM, 44 (July 1972): 122–44. "The sonata for obbligato keyboard and accompanying instruments in England acquired characteristics which distinguished it from the Parisian varieties. Especially notable in English works is the borrowing from the Italian concerto. Beginning with Giardini's Op.3, thematic material is often presented in a concertante exchange between instruments, comparable to the tutti/solo opening of a concerto. The English practice of printing accompanied sonatas in score led to greater independence in the added parts but did not eliminate the option of a solo keyboard performance. In the 1760's a number of Italians, Germans, and Englishmen produced sonatas that vacillated between optional and obbligato scoring. Towards the end of the decade, superfluous accompaniments became the more frequent owing to influence exerted by the imported works of Schobert. Examples of sonatas with concertante treatment remained isolated until the end of the century when that style became predominant" (author).

A. Hyatt King. *Chamber Music*. New York: Chanticleer Press, 1948. 72pp. An overall survey, particularly notable for its outstanding illustrations.

Bjarne Kortsen. *Contemporary Norwegian Chamber Music*. Fyllingsdalen, Norway: Edition Norvegica, 1971. 235pp.

Jerome Leonard Landsman. "An Annotated Catclog of American Violin Sonatas, Suites, and Works of Similar Character; 1947–1961, with a Survey of Traditional and Contemporary Technique." D.M.A. diss., University of Southern California, 1966. 488pp.

Marlene Joan Langosch, "The Instrumental Chamber Music of Bernhard Heiden." Ph.D. diss., Indiana University, 1974.

Abram Loft. *Violin and Keyboard: The Duo Repertoire*. New York: Grossman Publishers, 1973. Vol.I: *From the Seventeenth Century to Mozart*. 360pp. Vol.II: *From Beethoven to the Present*. 417pp.

Jean Marie Londeix. *125 Years of Music for Saxophone*. Paris: Leduc, 1971. 398pp. A general listing of over 700 pieces and educational literature for the saxophone. Includes biographical notes on composers in French.

Colin Mason. "The Chamber Music of Milhaud." MQ, 43 (July 1957): 326–41.

_____. "Some Aspects of Hindemith's Chamber Music." ML, 41 (April 1960): 150–55.

_____. "Webern's Late Chamber Music." ML, 38 (July 1957): 232–37.

Daniel Gregory Mason. *The Chamber Music of Brahms*. New York: Macmillan Co., 1933.

Samuel Midgley. *Handbook to Beethoven's Sonatas for Violin and Pianoforte*. London: Breitkopf & Härtel, 1911.

William S. Newman. *The Sonata in the Baroque Era*. Chapel Hill: University of North Carolina Press, 1959; rev. ed. 1966. 3d ed., New York: W. W. Norton, 1972.

_____. *The Sonata in the Classic Era*. Chapel Hill: University of North Carolina Press, 1963. 2d ed., New York: W. W. Norton, 1972. 897pp.

_____. *The Sonata Since Beethoven*. Chapel Hill: University of North Carolina Press, 1969. 2d ed., New York: W. W. Norton, 1972. 854pp.

Juan A. Orrego-Salas, ed. *Music from Latin America*. Bloomington: LAMC, Indiana University, 1971. 412pp. A listing of scores, tapes, and records available at the LAMC of Indiana University.

Thomas Montgomery Osborn. "Sixty Years of Clarinet Chamber Music: A Survey of Music Employing Clarinet with Stringed Instruments Composed 1900–1960 for Two to Five Performers." Diss., University of Southern California, 1964. 388pp. UM 64-13, 504. Chapter 2, "Traditional Instrumental Combinations," includes a discussion of works for clarinet, strings, and piano as well as for clarinet, strings, winds, and piano. Chapter 3, "Novel Instrumental Combinations," is devoted to works for clarinet, strings, and piano as well as for clarinet, strings, other winds, and piano. A number of appendixes give more detailed information on each work.

Roger Paul Phelps. "The History and Practice of Chamber Music in the United States from Earliest Times up to 1875." Ph.D. diss., University of Iowa, 1951. 2 vols., 991pp.

Alec Robertson, ed. *Chamber Music*. Baltimore: Penguin Books, 1957. 423pp.

Ruth Halle Rowen. *Early Chamber Music*. New York: King's Crown Press, 1949. Offers interesting information concerning pre-Haydn chamber music.

Harold Duane Rutan. "An Annotated Bibliography of Written Material Pertinent to the Performance of Brass and Percussion Chamber Music." Ph.D. Diss., University of Illinois, 1960. 368pp.

Stanley J. Sadie. "British Chamber Music, 1720–1790." 3 vols. Diss., Cambridge University, 1957.

Edith A. Sagul. "Development of Chamber Music Performance in the United States." Diss., Columbia University, 1952. 221pp.

Harold C. Schonberg. *Chamber and Solo Instrument Music*. New York: Knopf, 1955, 280pp. A discussion of recordings of the previous ygar in these categories.

Otto Schumann. *Handbuch der Kammermusik*. Wilhelmshaven, Germany: Heinrichshofen's Verlag, 1956. 557pp.

D. A. Shand. "The Sonata for Violin and Piano from Schumann to Debussy." Diss., Boston University, 1948.

Robert Virgil Sibbing. "An Analytical Study of the Published Sonatas for Saxophone by American Composers." Ed.D. diss., University of Illinois, 1969. 179pp.

Otakar Šourek. *The Chamber Music of Antonín Dvořák*. Prague: Artia, 1969? 177pp. English version by Roberta Finlayson Samsour.

James Gwynn Staples III. ''Six Lesser-Known Piano Quintets of the Twentieth Century.'' D.M.A. diss., University of Rochester, Eastman School of Music, 1972. 295pp. UM 73–984. Investigates the use of the piano quintet medium by each of six twentieth-century composers chosen to represent a wide diversity of countries and dates of composition as well as of compositional style and idiomatic treatment. Discusses quintets by Edward Elgar, Ross Lee Finney, Martinů, Medtner, Vierne, and Webern.

Giuseppe Tartini. ''Treatise on the Ornaments of Music.'' Translated and edited by Sol Babitz. *Journal of Research in Music Education,* 4 (Fall 1956): 75–102.

Telemann Werke Verzeichnis. Kassel-Wilhelmshöhe: Bärenreiter, 1950-. A complete catalogue prepared in conjunction with the Telemann *Musikalische Werke.*

Donald Francis Tovey. *Essays in Musical Analysis; Chamber Music.* London: Oxford University Press, 1944.

Bruce Clarence Trible. ''The Chamber Music of Henry Cowell.'' Diss., Indiana University, 1952. 116pp. Includes a chapter on general stylistic analysis. Chapter 3 is devoted to Cowell's compositions for solo instrument and piano. Includes a discussion of *Suite* (violin and piano), *6 Casual Developments* (clarinet and piano), *3 Ostinati with Chorales* (oboe and piano), *How Old is Song* (violin and piano), *Hymn and Fuguing Tune No. 7* (viola and piano), and *Fuguing Tune* (cello and piano). Also contains chapters on compositions for stringed instruments, wind instruments, and miscellaneous combinations.

Burnet C. Tuthill. ''Sonatas for Clarinet and Piano: Annotated Listings.'' *Journal of Research in Music Education,* 20 (Fall 1972): 308–28.

Homer Ulrich. *Chamber Music.* New York: Columbia University Press. 2d ed., 1966. 401pp.

Frans Vester. *Flute Repertoire Catalogue.* London: Musica Rara. Over 373pp.

John Vinton, ed. *Dictionary of Contemporary Music.* New York: E.P. Dutton, 1974. 834pp.

Himie Voxman and Lyle Merriman. *Woodwind Ensemble Music Guide.* Evanston, Ill.: The Instrumentalist Co., 1973. 280pp.

J. A. Westrup. *Schubert Chamber Music.* Seattle: University of Washington Press, 1969. 63pp. BBC Music Guides series.

G. Larry Whatley. ''Donald Francis Tovey: A Survey of His Life and Works.'' AMT, 25 (April–May 1976): 9–12.

Arnold Whittall. *Schoenberg Chamber Music.* Seattle: University of Washington Press, 1972. 64pp., BBC Music Guides series.

David Wilkins. ''Recitalectics No. 2: The Role of the Pianist.'' AMT, 25 (January 1976): 24, 26. Discusses the role of the pianist in a chamber ensemble.

Wayne Wilkins. *The Index of Flute Music Including the Index of Baroque Trio Sonatas.* Magnolia, Ark.: Music Register, 1974. 131pp.

––––––. *Index of Violin Music (Strings).* Magnolia, Ark.: Music Register, 1973. 246pp.

––––––. *1974 Supplement to Index of Violin Music.* Magnolia, Ark.: Music Register, 42pp.

Index of Works for Two or More Pianos and Other Instruments

Index of Works for Piano, Tape, and Other Instruments

Index of Composers

DORDT COLLEGE LIBRARY
Sioux Center, Iowa 51250